THE BOOK OF
SCOTTISH POETRY

BEING AN ANTHOLOGY OF THE
BEST SCOTTISH VERSE FROM THE
EARLIEST TIMES TO THE PRESENT

CHOSEN AND EDITED BY
SIR GEORGE DOUGLAS, BART.

T. FISHER UNWIN
LONDON: ADELPHI TERRACE
LEIPSIC: INSELSTRASSE 20
1911

INTRODUCTORY NOTE

IN compiling the following Anthology, care has been taken to adopt the best critical texts of the older Scottish Poets. Thus the selections from "Sir Tristrem," from "The King's Quair," from Blind Harry, from Henryson, Dunbar, Alexander Montgomerie, Alexander Scott, and Alexander Hume, have been made from the Scottish Text Society's Editions of those poets, edited respectively by Mr. George P. McNeill, LL.B., by the Rev. Walter W. Skeat, M.A., and by Messrs. James Moir, M.A., G. Gregory Smith, John Small, M.A., F.S.A. Scot., James Cranstoun, LL.D., and Alexander Lawson, B.D. As presenting fewer difficulties to the average reader, the specimen of Huchown has, however, been taken from David Laing's Select Remains of Ancient Popular and Romance Poetry of Scotland, the edition of John Small. The selections from "The Brus" are from C. Innes's Spalding Club Edition; whilst that from Androw of Wyntoun is from David Laing's Edition, and those from Gavin Douglas from Small's three-volume edition of 1874.

For the ballads, the editor has drawn, wherever possible, upon Sir Walter Scott's Minstrelsy of the Scottish Border, a version of those priceless old writings, which, though certainly not the most scientifically accurate, he ventures notwithstanding to consider beyond comparison the best. For the acknowledged liberties taken with the text are the liberties of a man of genius, and of a genius, too, who was marvellously akin to, or in sympathy with, the original authors of the poems.

In dealing with Scott's own writings, the original edition of "Marmion"[1] has been followed, as in the case

[1] Published 1808.

of Hogg has that of "The Queen's Wake"[1]; it being thought probable that, where reprints from later editions are common and easy of access, greater interest might attach to the poems in the form in which they first appeared. The specimens of Robert Burns are from Scott Douglas's standard edition. As being outside the sphere of this collection, as well by its Gaelic origin as by its non-metrical form, Macpherson's Ossian has been omitted. And, finally, among the specimens of recent and living poets, there has been included a certain limited amount of work which is probationary, or still upon its trial. But from this saving clause the editor desires to except by name the work of " Hugh Haliburton," which in Scotland, as the work of a Scottish poet, has already taken rank as a classic.

He does not apologise for the introduction of a few pieces of his own ; for he holds that to have practised an art, though humbly and imperfectly, ensures a certain insight into the conditions of that art not easily to be obtained by external study only. He desires to acknowledge his indebtedness to such existing bulkier anthologies as, for example, the admirable Abbotsford Poets of Mr. George Eyre-Todd, Sibbald's Chronicle of Scottish Poetry, Grant Wilson's Poets and Poetry of Scotland, Rogers's Modern Scottish Minstrel, and others ; and he would likewise thank authors and publishers who have allowed specimens of copyright work to appear in his book, and among these, in particular, Messrs Chatto and Windus for leave to reprint the " Requiem " of R. L. Stevenson, Messrs. Longmans for leave to print three poems by Dr. Andrew Lang, and Messrs. Bertram Dobell and John Lane respectively for leave to print specimens of the late James Thomson, (" B. V."), and of the late John Davidson.

[1] Published 1813.

INDEX OF AUTHORS

The Book of Scottish Poetry

ANONYMOUS

1 *On the Death of King Alexander the Third* [1]

A.D. 1286

QUHEN Alysandyr oure King was dede,
    That Scotland led in luwe and lé,[2]
Away wes sons[3] off ale and brede,
Off wyne and wax, off gamyn[4] and glé :

Oure gold wes changyd in to lede.
    Cryst, borne in to Vyrgynyté,
Succoure Scotland and remede,
    That stad[5] [is in] perplexyté.

---

[1] Quoted in Androw of Wyntoun's "Orygynale Cronykil of Scotland," Book VII., but generally ascribed to the period immediately following the event referred to.
[2] law. [3] abundance. [4] sport. [5] placed.

11

THOMAS OF ERCELDOUNE, CALLED "THE RHYMER"

(ATTRIBUTED TO)

Circ. 1225–*circ.* 1300

2   *The Drinking of the Love-Potion*

(From "Sir Tristrem")

TRISTREM swore that thing ;
     Thai seyd it schuld stand
That he schuld Ysonde bring
—Thai token [1] it vnder hand—
To Mark, the riche king,
Olive yif thai him fand,
And make hir with his ring
Queen of Ingeland,
To say ;
The forward [2] fast thai band [3]
Er thai parted oway.

     *   *   *   *

     No asked he lond no lithe [4],
Bot that maiden bright ;
He busked [5] him al so swithe [6]
Bothe squier and knight.
Her moder about was blithe
And tok a drink of might,
That love wald kithe [7],

---

[1] took.   [2] compact.   [3] bound.   [4] people.   [5] prepared.
[6] swiftly.   [7] beget.

And tok it Brengwain the bright.
To think :
" At er spousing anight
Yif Mark and hir to drink."
   Ysonde bright of hewe
Is fer out in the se.
A winde oyain hem blewe
That sail no might ther be.
So rewe [1] the knightes trewe,
Tristrem so rewe he,
Euer as thai com newe—
He on oyain hem thre [2]—
Gret swink [3].
Swete Ysonde the fre [4]
Asked Bringwain a drink.

   The coupe was richeli wrought,
Of gold it was, the pin [5] ;
In al the warld nas nought
Swiche drink as ther was in.
Brengwain was wrong [6] bi thought
To that drink sche gan win
And swete Ysonde it bi taught [7] ;
She bad Tristrem bigin,
To say.
Her [8] loue might no man tvin [9]
Til her endingday.

   An hounde her was beside,
That was y cleped Hodain ;
The coupe he licked that tide
Tho doun it sett Bringwain ;
Thai loued al in lide [10]
And ther of were thai fain ;

[1] rowed. [2] *I.e.*, Tristram rowed without being relieved as the others were. [3] toil. [4] noble. [5] a pin was used in ancient times to measure draughts. [6] distracted. [7] gave. [8] their. [9] divide. [10] the month of March (Halliwell's Dictionary).

To gider thai gun abide
In ioie and ek in pain
For thought :
In iuel time, to sain [1],
The drink was y wrought.
  Tristrem in schip lay
With Ysonde ich night,
Play miri he may,
With that worthli [2] wight
In boure night and day.
Al blithe was the knight,
He might with hir play ;
That wist Brengwain the bright
As tho ;
Thai loued with al her might,
And Hodain dede al so.
  Tvai wikes [3] in the strand
No seyl thai no drewe ;
Into Inglond
A winde to wille hem blewe.
The king on hunting thai fand ;
A knaue that he knewe,
He made him knight with hand
For his tidinges newe,
Gan bring.
Ysonde bright of hewe
Her spoused Mark the king.

    [1] forsooth. [2] fair. [3] two weeks.

"HUCHEON OF THE AWLE RYALE [1]" [2]

Died circ. 1381

3   *Description of a Garden*

(From "The Pystyl [3] of Swete Susan")

I

IN the seson of somere, with Sibell and Jone,
  Heo [4] grethed hire [5] til hire gardin, that growed
    so grene,
Ther lyndes [6] and lorers were lent vpon lone [7],
The sauyne [8] and sypres, selcouth to sene [9],
The palme, and the poplere, the pirie, the plone,
The iuniper ientel, jonyng bi-twene,
The rose ragged on rys [10], richest on rone [11]
I-theuwed [12] with the thorn thrivand [13] to sene
    So tiht [14];
    Ther weore popeiayes prest [15],
    Nightyngales uppon nest,
    Blithest briddes o the best,
    In blossoms so briht.

[1] Royal Hall.
[2] As to the identity of Hucheon with Sir Hew of Eglintoun, see "Huchown of the Awle Ryale, the Alliterative Poet : a Historical Criticism, of Fourteenth Century Poems ascribed to Sir Hew of Eglintoun," by George Neilson (Maclehose, Glasgow, 1902).
[3] epistle. [4] she (A.S.). [5] prepared herself. [6] lime-trees. [7] an avenue. [8] sabine-tree. [9] wondrous to behold. [10] on its notched stem. [11] shrub. [12] close-surrounded. [13] thriving. [14] arranged. [15] sprightly parrots.

II

The briddes in blossoms thei beeren [1] wel loude
On olyues, and amylliers [2], and al kynde of trees,
The popeiayes perken and pruynen for proude [3],
On peren and pyn-appel thei ioyken [4] in pees ;
On croppes of canel [5] keneliche [6] thei croude,
On grapes the goldfinch thei gladen and glees [7] ;
Thus schene [8] briddes in schawe [9] schewen heore
    schronde [10],
On figges and fygers thei fongen heore sees,[11]
      In fay ;
    Ther weore growyng so grene
    The date, with the damesene,
    Turtils troned on trene,
      By sixti, I saygh.

III

The fyge and the filbert were fodemed [12] so fayre,
The chirie and the chestein, that chosen [13] is of hewe,
Apples and almaundes that honest are of ayre [14],
Grapes and garnettes [15] gayliche thei grewe,
The costardes comeliche in cuththes thei cayre [16],
The britouns [17], the blaunderers [17], [the] braunches the
    bewe [18],
Fele [19] floures and fruit, frelich of flayre [20],
With wardons winlich [21] and walshe notes [22] newe,

[1] clamour. [2] almond-trees. [3] pose and preen themselves for
pride. [4] perch. [5] cinnamon. [6] eagerly. [7] delight and enjoy
themselves. [8] bright. [9] grove. [10] show their plumage. [11] on
figs and fig-trees they took their seats. [12] produced. [13] chestnut
that choice. [14] appearance. [15] pomegranates. [16] grew comely in
the lands. [17] different kinds of apples. [18] bowed down the
branches. [19] many. [20] of fine scent. [21] handsome pears.
[22] walnuts.

They wald
Ouer heor hedes gon hyng,
The wince and the wederlyng [1],
Spyces speden to spryng,
    In erbers [2] enhaled.

IV

The chyue [3], and the chollet [4], the chibolle, the cheue [5],
The chouwet [6], the cheuerol [7], that shaggen on niht [8],
The parsel, the passenep, poretes to preue [9],
The pyon [10], the peere, wel proudliche i-piht [11];
The lilye, the louache [12], launsyng with leue [13],
The sauge, the sorsecle [14], so semeliche to siht;
Columbyne and charawe [15], clottes thei creve [16],
With ruwe and rubarbe, ragged ariht,
        No lees;
    Daysye, and ditoyne,
    Ysope, and aueroyne [17],
    Peletre, and plaentoyne,
        Proudest in pres [18].

V

Als this schaply thing yede in hire yerde [19],
That was hir hosbondes and hire, that holden with
    hende [20];
Now folk be faren [21] from us, thar us not be ferde [22]
Aftur myn oynement, warliche ye wende [23].
Espieth now specialy, the yates ben sperde [24]
For we wol wassche us I-wis bi this welle strende.

[1] quince and codling.　　[2] gardens.　　[3] onion.　　[4] cabbage (?)
[5] two other varieties of onion.　　　　[6] an unknown vegetable.
[7] chervil.　　[8] shake by night.　　[9] young leeks to taste.　　[10] peony.
[11] planted.　　[12] lovage.　　[13] shooting forth with leaf.　　[14] marigold.
[15] caraway.　　[16] burst through the clods (?).　　[17] southernwood.
[18] in the throng.　　[19] went in her garden.　　[20] graciously.　　[21] gone.
[22] thereof be we not afraid.　　[23] go cautiously.　　[24] barred.

For-thi [1] the wyf werp of hir wedes vnwerde [2],
Under a lorere ful lowe that ladi gan lende [3],
     So sone :
   By a wynliche [4] well,
   Susan caste of hir kelle [5],
   Bote feole ferlys [6] hire bi-felle,
     Bi midday or none.

---

  [1] thereupon.   [2] threw off her garments alone.   [3] did tarry.
[4] pleasant. [5] covering. [6] many wonders.

JOHN BARBOUR

Circ. 1316–*probably* 1395

4 *Bruce's Adventure with the Three Brothers*
Makyndrosser

(*From* "*The Brus*")

QUHEN that the lord of Lorne saw
    His men stand of him ane sic aw
    That tha durst nocht folow the chas,
Richt angry in his hart he was,
And for wondir that he suld sa
Stot [1] tham him ane but ma [2]
He said, " Methink, Marthokis sone,
Richt as Golmakmorn was wone [3]
To haf fra Fingal his menyhe [4],
Richt sa all his fra us has he."
He set ensampill thus midlik [5],
The quhethir he micht mar manerlik
Liknit him to Gaudifer de Larys,
Quhen that the michty duk Betys
Assalyheit in Gaderis the forayouris,
And, quhen the king tham mad rescours [6],
Duk Betys tuk on him the flicht
That wald na mar abid to ficht.
Bot gud Gaudifer the worthy
Abandonit him sa hardely
For to reskew all the flearis

[1] stop. [2] without more. able. [4] attendants. [5] moderately.
[6] rescue.

19

And for to stonay [1] the chasaris,
That Alexander to erd [2] he bar,
And alsua [3] did he Tholimar,
And gud Coneus alsua,
Dauklyne alsua, and othir ma :
Bot at the last thar slane he wes,
In that falyheit the liklynes,
For the king full chevelrously
Defendit all his cumpany,
And was set in full gret danger,
And yhet eschapit hale and fer [4].
For twa brethir war in that land
That war the hardyast of hand
That war intill all that cuntre,
And tha had sworn, gif tha micht se
The Brus quhar tha micht him ourta [5],
That tha suld de or than him sla.
Thar surnam was Makyndrosser,
That is all sa mekill to say her
As the Durwarth sonnis perfay :
Of thar covyn [6] the thrid had tha
That was richt stout, ill, and feloun.
Quhen tha the King of gud renoun
Saw sa behind his menyhe rid,
And saw him turn sa mony tid,
Tha abad [7] quhill that he was
Enterit in ane narow plas
Betuix ane lochside and ane bra [8]
That was sa strat [9], I undirta,
That he micht nocht wele turn his sted.
Than with ane will till him tha yhed [10],
And ane him be the bridill hynt [11],
Bot he raucht till him sic ane dint [12]

---

[1] astonish.   [2] earth.   [3] also.   [4] well.   [5] overtake.   [6] breed
[7] waited.   [8] a lake-side and a slope.   [9] narrow.   [10] went.
[11] grasped.   [12] reached him such a blow.

That arm and schuldir flaw him fra.
With that ane othir can him ta [1]
Be the leg, and his hand can schut [2]
Betuix the sterap and his fut.
And, quhen the king feld thar his hand,
In this sterapis stithly [3] can he stand,
And strak with spuris the sted in hy,
And he lansit furth deliverly [4],
Sa that the tothir falyheit fet [5],
And nocht forthi [6] his hand was yhet
Undir the sterap magre his [7].
The thrid with full gret hy [8] with this
Richt to the bra-sid [9] he yhed,
And stert behind him on his sted.
The king was than in full gret pres [10]:
The quhethir he thocht, as he that wes
In all his dedis avise [11],
To do ane outrageous bounte [12].
He hynt [13] him that behind him was,
And magre his him can he ras
Fra behind him, thouch he had sworn,
And laid him evin him beforn,
Syn with the suerd sic dint him gaf
That he the hed to the harnis [14] claf [15].
He ruschit doun of blud all red
As he that stound feld of ded [16],
And than the king in full gret hy
Strak at the tothir vigorously
That he eftir his sterap drew,
That at the first strak he him slew.
On this wis him deliverit he
Of all tha feloun fais thre.

[1] did him take. [2] thrust. [3] stoutly. [4] promptly. [5] lost his footing. [6] none the less. [7] in spite of him. [8] haste. [9] hill-side. [10] jeopardy. [11] prudent. [12] extraordinary act of valour. [13] reached. [14] brains. [15] clove. [16] felt the pang of death.

5   *Bruce, challenged to battle by Sir Aymer de*
    Valence, beholds the pomp and splendour
    of the English host, and addresses his
    troops

(*From* "*The Brus*")

SCHIR AMER on the tothir party
  Gaderit sa gret chevelry
That he micht be thre thousand ner
Armit and dicht [1] on gud maner,
And than as man of gret noblay [2]
He held toward the tryst his way.
Quhen the set day cummin was,
He sped him fast toward the plas
That he had nemmit for to ficht:
The sone was risin schynand bricht
That blenknit [3] on the scheldis brad.
In twa eschelis [4] ordanit he had
The folk that he had in leding:
The king wele sone in the morning
Saw first cumand thar first eschele
Arait sarraly [5] and wele,
And at thar bak sumdele ner hand
He saw the tothir folowand.
Thar basnetis burnisit all bricht
Agane the sone glemit of licht:
Thar speris, pennounis, and thar scheldis
Of licht enlumynit all the feldis:
Thar best [6] and browdyn [7] bricht baneris,
And hors hewit on ser maneris [8],
And cot-armouris of ser colour,
And hawbrekis [9] that war quhit as flour,

---

[1] appointed.   [2] nobility.   [3] gleamed.   [4] divisions.   [5] artfully.
fluttering (?) *Jamieson*.   [7] broidered.   [8] horses of divers colours.
hauberk, coat of mail.

Mad tham gletirand as tha war lik
Till angelis he [1] of hevinis rik [2].
The king said, " Lordingis, now yhe se
How yhon men throu thar gret pouste [3]
Wald, and tha micht fulfill thar will,
Sla us, and makis sembland [4] thartill :
And, sen we knaw thar felony,
Gar we and met tham sa hardely
That the stoutast of thar menyhe [5]
Of our meting abasit be,
For, gif the formast egirly
Be met, yhe sall se sudanly
The henmast [6] sall abasit be :
And, thouch that tha be ma than we,
That suld abas us litill thing,
For, quhen we cum to the fichting,
Thar may met us na ma than we.
Tharfor, lordingis, ilkane [7] suld be
Of worschip and of gret valour
For till mantem [8] her our honour.
Thinkis quhat gladschip [9] us abidis
Gif that we may, as us betidis,
Haf victor of our fais her,
For thar is nane her, fer na ner,
In all this land that us thar [10] dout [11]."
Than said tha all that stud about,
" Schir, gif God will, we sall sa do
That na repruf sall ly tharto."
" Than ga we furth now," said the king,
" And he that mad of nocht all thing
Led us and saf us for his micht
And help us for till hald our richt."

[1] high. [2] kingdom. [3] prowess. [4] assembly, or show. [5] company. [6] hindmost. [7] every man. [8] uphold. [9] gladness. [10] it behoves. [11] fear.

With that tha held thar way in hy [1]
Wele sex hundreth in cumpany,
Stalward and stout, worthy and wicht [2] :
Bot tha war all to few I hicht [3]
Agane sa fele [4] to stand in stour [5],
Ne war thar outrageous valour [6].

6 *The Battle of Loudoun*

NOW gais the nobill king his way
    Richt stoutly and in gud aray,
And to the formast dik is gane,
And in the slop [7] the feld has tane.
The carriage-men and the pouerale [8]
That was nocht worth in the battale,
Behind levit he tham all still
Standand all sammyn [9] on the hill.
Schir Amer the king has sene
With his men that stout war and kene
Cum to the plane doun fra the hill,
As him thocht into full gud will
For to defend or till assale,
Gif ony wald bid him battale.
Tharfor his men confortit he,
And bad tham wicht [10] and worthy be,
For, gif that tha micht win the king
And victor haf of the fichting,
Tho suld richt wele rewardit be
And greatly ek [11] thar renoune.
With that tha war wele ner the king,
And he left his amonisting [12]
And gert trump [13] till the assemblé,

---

[1] haste.   [2] valiant.   [3] suspect.   [4] many.   [5] battle.   [6] but for
their extreme valour.   [7] gap.   [8] camp-followers.   [9] together.
[10] valiant.   [11] increase.   [12] admonishing.   [13] caused sound.

And the formast of his menyhe [1],
Enbrasit with the scheldis brad,
And richt sarray [2] togidder raid,
With hedis stoupand and speris straucht
Richt to the king thar way tha raucht [3].
That met tham with sa gret vigour
That the best and of mast valour
War laid at erd [4] at thar meting :
Quhar men micht her sic ane breking
Of speris that to-fruschit [5] war,
And of woundit sa cry and rar [6]
That it anoyus [7] was to her,
For tha that first assemblit wer
Funyheit [8] and faucht full sturdely :
The noys begouth than and the cry.
A! michty God, quha thar had bene
And had the kingis worschip sene,
And his brothir that was him by,
That contenit tham [9] sa hardely
That thar gud ded and thar bounte
Confort monyfald [10] thar menyhe,
And how Douglas sa manfully
Confortit tham that war him by,
He suld wele say that tha had will
To win honour and cum thartill.
The kingis men that worthy war,
With thar speris that scharply schar [11]
Tha stekit [12] men and stedis bath
Quhill red blud ran of woundis rath [13].
The hors that woundit war can fling [14]
And ruschit the folk in thar flinging,

---

[1] company.　[2] artfully.　[3] reached.　[4] on the ground.
[5] splintered.　[6] roar.　[7] grievous.　[8] struck out, or thrust.
[9] demeaned themselves.　[10] encouraged many times.　[11] shore,
cut.　[12] pierced.　[13] fresh.　[14] began to kick.

Sa that tha that than formast war
War scalit in soppis[1] her and thar.
The king that saw tham ruschit sa,
And saw tham reland to and fra,
Ran apon tham sa egirly
And dang[2] on tham sa hardely
He gert fele[3] of his fais fall :
The feld was wele ner coverit all
Bath with slane hors and with men,
For the gud king tham folowit then
With wele fif hundreth that wapnis bar[4]
That wald thar fais nathing spar.
Tha dang on tham sa hardely
That in schort tym men micht se ly
At erd ane hundreth wele and mar :
The remanand sa fleyit[5] war
That tha begouth tham to withdraw,
And, quhen tha of the rerward saw
Thar avaward[6] be discumfit,
Tha fled withouten mar respit.
And, quhen Schir Amer has sene
His men fleand haly beden[7],
Wit yhe wele he was full wa[8],
Bot he micht nocht amonist sa
That ony for him wald turn agane :
And, quhen he saw he tynt his pane[9],
He turnit his bridill and to ga,
For the gud king tham pressit sa
That sum war ded, and sum war tane,
The remanand thar gat ar gane[10].

---

[1] dispersed in small numbers.　[2] struck.　[3] many.　[4] bore weapons.　[5] terrified.　[6] front.　[7] all at once.　[8] sorrowful.　[9] lost his labour.　[10] gone their way.

7   *The Capture of Roxburg Castle*

THIS tym that the gud erl Thomas
  Assegit, as the lettir sais,
Edinburgh, James of Douglas
Set all his wit for till purchas[1]
How Roxburgh throu subtilite
Or ony craft micht wonnin be,
Quhill he gert Sym of the Ledous,
That was ane man richt craftyous,
Of hempin rapis ledderis ma
With treyn[2] steppis bundin sa
That wald brek apon nakyn wis[3].
Ane cruk tha mad at thar devis
Of irn that was stith[4] and squar,
That fra it in ane kyrnell[5] war,
And the leddir tharfra stratly
Strekit[6], it suld stand sekirly[7].
This lord of Douglas than, alsone[8]
As this devisit was and done,
Gaderit gud men in prevate,
Thre scor I trow that tha micht be,
And on the Fastryn-evin[9] full richt
In the beginning of the nicht
To the castell tha tuk the way.
With blak froggis[10] all helit[11] tha
The armouris that tha on tham had,
Tha com nerby thar but abad[12],
And send haly thar hors tham fra,
And on range[13] in ane rout can ga
On handis and fet, quhen tha war ner,

---

[1] contrive. [2] wooden. [3] in no sort of way. [4] strong.
[5] crenelation. [6] stretched. [7] firmly. [8] as soon. [9] eve of Shrove
Tuesday. [10] surcoats. [11] hid. [12] without halting. [13] as an
advanced guard.

Richt as tha ky [1] or oxen wer
That war unbandonit left tharout.
It was richt mirk withouten dout :
The quhethir [2] ane on the wall that lay
Besid him till his fer [3] can say,
" This man thinkis to mak gud cher,"
And nemmit ane husband [4] tharby ner,
" That has left all his oxin out."
The tothir said, " That is na dout
He sall mak mery this nicht, thouch tha
Be with the Douglas led away."
Tha wend [5] the Douglas and his men
Had bene oxin, for tha yhed [6] then
On handis and fet ay ane and ane.
The Douglas richt gud tent [7] has tane
Till all thar spek [8] : bot all sone tha
Held carpand [9] inward on thar way.
The Douglas men tharof war blith,
And to the wall tha sped tham swith [10],
And sone has up thar leddir set
That mad ane clap [11] quhen the cleket [12]
Was festnit fast in the kyrnele.
That herd ane of the wachis wele,
And buskit [13] thiddirward but bad,
Bot Ledous that the leddir mad
Sped him to clym first to the wall,
Bot, or he was up gottin all,
He that that ward had in keping
Met him richt at the upcuming,
And, for he thocht to ding him doun,
He mad na noys, na cry, na soun,
Bot schot till him deliverly [14],

[1] cows. [2] however. [3] comrade. [4] husbandman. [5] supposed.
[6] went. [7] heed. [8] speech. [9] speaking. [10] swift. [11] sound.
[12] hook. [13] turned. [14] struck at him nimbly.

And he that was in juperdy
To de, ane lans[1] till him he mad,
And gat him be the nek but bad,
And stekit[2] him upward with ane knif
Quhill in his hand he lost the lif.
And, quhen he ded sa saw him ly,
Apon the wall he went in hy[3],
And doun the body kest tham till,
And said, "All gangis as we will :
Sped yhou upward deliverly."
And tha did sa in full gret hy :
Bot, or tha wan up, thar com ane
And saw Ledous stand him alane,
And knew he was nocht of thar men.
In hy he ruschit till him then,
And him assalit sturdely,
But he him slew deliverly,
For he was armit and was wicht,
The tothir nakit[4] was I hicht,
And had nocht for to stint na strak[5].
Sic melle[6] tharup can he mak
Quhill Douglas and his menyhe all
War wonnin up apon the wall :
Than in the tour tha went in hy.
The folk that tym was halely
Intill the hall at thar dansing,
Singing, and othirwais playing,
As apon Fastryn-evin it is
The custum to mak joy and blis
To folk that ar in savite[7].
Sa trowit tha that tym to be :
Bot, or tha wist, richt in the hall
Douglas and his men cumin war all,

[1] spring.   [2] pierced.   [3] haste.   [4] unarmed.   [5] break a blow.
[6] fight.   [7] safety.

And cryit on hicht " Douglas ! Douglas ! "
And tha, that ma[1] war then he was
Herd " Douglas " cryit richt hidwisly,
Tha war abasit[2] for the cry,
And schup richt na defens to ma[3],
And tha but pite[4] can tham sla
Quhill tha had gottin the ovirhand :
The tothir fled to sek warand[5]
That outour mesur ded can dred.
The wardane sae how that it yhed
That callit was Gilmyn de Fynis :
In the gret tour he gottin is
And othir of his company,
And sparit the entre[6] hastely :
The laf that levit war without
War tane or slane forouten dout,
Bot gif[7] that ony lap the wall.
The Douglas held that nicht the hall,
Althouch his fais tharof war wa :
His men war gangand to and fra
Throuout the castell all that nicht
Quhill on the morn that day was licht.

8   *The Capture Completed*

THE wardane that was in the tour,
    That was ane man of gret valour,
Gilmyn de Fynis, quhen he saw
The castell tynt bath he and law[8],
He set his micht for till defend
The tour : bot tha without him send

---

[1] more.   [2] confounded.   [3] took no proper measures of defence.
[4] without remorse.   [5] a place of defence.   [6] secured the entry.
[7] unless.   [8] high and low.

Arowis in sa gret quantite
That anoyit tharof was he.
Bot quhill the tothir day [1] nocht forthi [2]
He held the tour full sturdely,
And than at ane assalt he was
Woundit sa felly in the fas
That he was dredand of his lif :
Tharfor he tretit [3] tham belif [4],
And yhald the tour on sic maner
That he and all that with him wer
Suld safly pas intill Ingland.

Douglas held tham gud cunand [5],
And convoyit tham to thar cuntre :
Bot thar full schort tym livit he,
For throu the wound intill his fas
He deit sone and beryit was.

Douglas the castell sesit all
That than was closit with stalward wall,
And send this Ledous till the king
That mad him full gret rewarding,
And his brothir in full gret hy,
Schir Eduard that was sa douchty,
He send thiddir to tummill doun
Bath tour and castell and dongeoun,
And he com with gret cumpany,
And gret travale sa besaly
That tour and wall richt to the ground
Was tumlit in ane litill stound [6],
And duelt still thar quhill Tevydale
Com to the kingis pes all hale,
Outane Jedworth and othir that ner
The Inglismenis boundis wer.

---

[1] next day. [2] none the less. [3] entreated. [4] presently.
[5] covenant. [6] while.

9   *The Siege of Edinburgh Castle*

QUHEN Roxburgh won was on this wis,
      The erl Thomas, that he empris [1]
      Set ay apon soverane bounte [2],
At Edinburgh with his menyhe
Was lyand at the sege, as I
Tald yhou befor, all opinly.
Bot, fra he herd how Roxburgh was
Tane with ane trane [3], all his purchas
And wit and besynes, I hicht [4],
He set for to purchas sum slicht [5]
How he micht help him throu body [6]
Mellit [7] with full he chevelry
To win the wall of the castele
Throu sumkyn slicht, for he wist wele
That na strinth micht it planly get
Quhill tha within had men and met.
Tharfor prevely sperit he [8]
Gif ony man micht fundin be
That couth ony gud juperdy [9]
To clym the wallis prevely,
And he suld haf his warisoun [10],
For it was his entencioun
To put him in all aventur
Or that that sege on him misfur [11].
Than was thar ane Wilyham Fransas,
Wicht and apert [12], wis and curtas,
That intill his youthed had bene
In the castell. Quhen he has sene
The erl sa enkirly [13] him set

[1] high endeavour or performance.   [2] roused ever to the highest pitch of valour.   [3] stratagem.   [4] I assure you.   [5] contrive some device.   [6] strength.   [7] mingled.   [8] sought he out.   [9] could conceive any likely stratagem.   [10] reward.   [11] should prove too much for him.   [12] bold.   [13] ardently.

Sum sutelte or wile to get
Quharthrou the castell haf micht he,
He com till him in prevate,
And said, "Methink yhe wald blithly
That men fand yhou sum juperdy
How yhe micht our the wallis win :
And certis, gif yhe will begin
For till assay on sic awis,
I undirtak for my servis
To ken yhou to clym the wall,
And I sall formast be of all,
Quhar with ane schort leddir may we,
I trow of tuelf fut it may be,
Clym to the wall up all quytly.
And, gif that yhe will wit how I
Wat this, I sall yhou lichtly say.
Quhen I was yhoung this hendir day [1],
My fadir was kepar of yhon hous,
And I was sumdele volageous [2],
And lufit ane wench her [3] in the toun,
And, for I but [4] suspicioun
Micht repar till her prevely,
Of rapis ane leddir to me mad I,
And with that our the wall I slad :
Ane strat rod that spyit I had
Intill the crag syn doun I went,
And oftsis [5] com to myn entent,
And, quhen it ner drew to the day,
I held agane that ilke way
And ay com in but persaving [6].
I usit lang that travaling,
Sa that I can that rod ga richt,
Thouch men se nevir, sa mirk the nicht :

[1] in past times. [2] lively. [3] here. [4] without. [5] often. [6] without being seen.

And, gif yhou thinkis yhe will assay
To pas up eftir me that way,
Up to the wall I sall yhou bring
Gif God us kepis fra persaving
Of tham that wachis on the wall :
And, gif that us sa far may fall [1]
That we our leddir up may set,
Gif a man on the wall may get,
He sall defend, gif it be ned,
Quhill the remanand up them sped."
The erl was blith of his carping [2],
And hicht him full far rewarding,
And undirtuk that gat to ga,
And bad him sone his leddir ma
And hald him preve [3] quhill tha micht
Set for thar purpos on ane nicht.

10   *The Scaling of the Castle Rock*

SONE eftir was the leddir mad,
And than the erl but mar abad [4]
Purvait him [5] a nicht prevely
With thretty men wicht and hardy,
And in ane nicht held thar way
That put tham in full hard assay
And in gret perill. Sekirly
I trow, micht tha haf sene clerly [6],
That gat had nocht bene undirtane
Thouch tha to let tham had nocht ane,
For the crag was he and hidous,
And the clyming richt peralous,
For, hapnit ony to slid or fall,

---

[1] so fairly may befall.   [2] discourse.   [3] bound him to secrecy.
[4] without further delay.   [5] provided himself.   [6] could they have
seen clearly.

He suld be sone to-fruschit [1] all.
The nicht was mirk, as I herd say,
And to the fut sone cumin ar tha
Of the crag that was he and schor [2] :
Than Wilyham Fransas tham befor
Clam in the crykis [3] forouth [4] ay,
And at the bak him folowit tha :
With mekill pane, quhile to, quhile fra,
Tha clam intill the crykis sa
Quhill half the crag tha clummin had,
And thar ane plas tha fand sa brad
That tha micht sit on anerly [5],
And tha war ayndles [6] and wery,
And thar abad thar aynd to ta.
And, richt as tha war sitand sa,
Abovin tham apon the wall
The chak wachis [7] assemblit all :
Now help tham God that all thing may,
For in full gret perill ar tha,
For, micht tha se tham, thar suld nane
Eschap out of that plas unslane,
To ded with stanis tha suld tham ding [8]
That tha micht help thamself nathing.
Bot wondir mirk was all the nicht
Sa that tha had of tham na sicht,
And nocht forthi [9] yhet was thar ane
Of tham that swappit [10] doun ane stane,
And said, "Away ! I se yhou wele,"
The quhethir [11] he saw tham nocht adele [12].
Outour [13] thar hedis flaw the stane,
And tha sat still lurkand ilkane [14].
The wachis, quhen tha herd nocht ster,

---

[1] dashed to pieces. [2] sheer. [3] crevices. [4] in advance. [5] singly.
[6] breathless. [7] check watches, visiting rounds. [8] strike. [9] none
the less. [10] flung. [11] notwithstanding that. [12] at all. [13] over.
[14] each one.

Fra that ward passit all sammyn[1] wer,
And carpand[2] held fer by thar way.
Erl Thomas than alsone, and tha
That on the crag thar sat him by,
Toward the wall clam hastely,
And thiddir com with mekill mane,
And nocht but[3] gret perill and pane,
For fra thine[4] up was grevouser
To clym up na beneth be fer.
Bot, quhatkyn pane that evir tha had[5]
Richt to the wall tha com but bad
That had wele ner tuelf fut on hicht,
And forout persaving or sicht
Tha set thar leddir to the wall,
And syn Fransas befor tham all
Clam up, and syn Schir Andro Gray,
And syn the erl himself perfay[6]
Was the thrid man the wall can ta[7].
Quhen tha thar doun thar lord sa
Saw clym up agane the wall,
As wod[8] men tha clam eftir all :
Bot, or up cumin all war tha,
Tha that war wachis till assay
Herd bath stering and ek speking,
And alsua fraying of arming[9],
And on tham schot[10] full sturdely,
And tha met tham richt hardely,
And slew of tham dispitwisly.
Than throu the castell ras the cry :
"Tresoun ! tresoun !" tha cryit fast :
Than sum of tham war sa agast
That tha fled and lap our the wall,

together. [2] chatting. [3] not without. [4] thence. [5] whatever
their difficulties might be. [6] indeed. [7] began to take (surmount).
[8] wild. [9] clank of arms. [10] pressed.

Bot, to say suth, tha fled nocht all.
For the constabill that was hardy
All armit schot furth to the cry,
And with him fele hardy and stout.
Yhet was the erl with his rout
Fichtand with tham apon the wall,
Bot sone he tham discumfit all.
Be that his men war cumin ilkane
Up to the wall, and he has tane
His way doun to the castell sone :
In gret perill he has him done,
For thar war fer ma [1] men tharin,
And tha had bene of gud covyn [2],
Then he : bot tha affrait war,
And nocht forthi with wapnis bar
The constabill and his cumpany
Met him and his richt hardely.
Thar men micht se gret bargane [3] ris,
For with wapnis on mony wis
Tha dang on othir at thar micht,
Quhill suerdis that war far and bricht
War till the hiltis all bludy :
Than hidwisly begouth [4] the cry,
For tha that fellit or stekit [5] war
With gret noys can cry and rar.
The gud erl and his cumpany
Faucht in that ficht sa sturdely
That all thar fais ruschit war :
The constabill was slane richt thar,
And, fra he fell the remanand
Fled quhar tha best micht to warand [6] :
Tha durst nocht bid to mak debat.
The erl was handlit thar sa hat
That, had it nocht hapnit throu cas

[1] far more. [2] avail. [3] contention. [4] began. [5] pierced. [6] safety.

That the constabill thar slane was,
He had bene in gret perill thar.
Bot than tha fled : there was na mar
Bot ilk man for to saf his lif
And furth his dais for to drif,
And sum slad doun outour the wall :
The erl has tane the castell all,
For than was nane durst him withstand.
I herd nevir quhar in ane land
Was castell tane sa hardely,
Outakin Tyre allanerly,
Quhen Alexander the conquerour
That conquerit Babilonis tour
Lap fra ane berfrois[1] on the wall,
Quhar he emang his fais all
Defendit him ful douchtely
Quhill that his nobill chevelry
With ledderis our the wallis yhed[2]
That nouthir left for ded na dred,
For, fra tha wist wele that the king
Was in the toun, thar was nathing
Intill that tym that stint tham mocht,
For all perill tha set at nocht.
Tha clam the wallis, and Areste
Com first to the gud king, quhar he
Defendit him with all his micht,
That than was set[3] sa hard, I hicht,
That he was fellit on a kne :
He till his bak had set ane tre
For dred tha suld behind assale.
Areste than to the battale
Sped him in all hy sturdely,
And dang on tham sa douchtely
That the king wele reskewit was,

[1] belfry.   [2] went.   [3] beset.

For his men into sindry plas
Clam our the wall, and socht the king,
And him reskewit with hard fichting,
And wan the toun deliverly.
Outane [1] this taking anerly [2]
I herd nevir in na tym gane
Castell that was sa stoutly tane.
And of this taking that I mene
Sanct Mergaret the gud haly quene
Wist in hir tym throu reveling
Of him that knawis and wat all thing :
Tharfor insted of prophesy
Scho left ane takning [3] richt joly,
That is, that scho in hir chapell
Gert wele be portrait ane castell,
Ane leddir up to the wall standand,
And ane man tharapon clymand,
And wrat owth [4] him, as ald men sais,
In Franch, GARDYS VOUS DE FRANSAIS.
And for this word scho gert writ sa
Men wend the Franchman suld it ta :
Bot, for Fransas hattin [5] was he
That sa clam up in prevate,
Scho wrat that as in prophesy,
And it fell eftirward suthly
Richt as scho said, for tane it was,
And Fransas led them up that plas.

11   *The Combat of Bruce and De Boune*

NOW Douglas furth his way he tais,
      And in that self tym fell throu cas [6]
That the king of Ingland, quhen he
Was cumin with his gret menyhe

[1] except.   [2] only.   [3] warning.   [4] above.   [5] named.   [6] chance.

Ner to the plas, as I said ar [1],
Quhar Scottis men arait war,
He gert arest [2] all his battale
At othir als to tak consale,
Quhethir tha wald tham herbry [3] that nicht
Or than but mar [4] ga till the ficht.
The vaward, that wist nakyn thing [5]
Of this arest na thar duelling,
Rad to the Park all straucht thar way
Forout stinting [6] in gud aray.
And, quhen the king wist that tha wer
In hale battale cumand sa ner,
His battale gert he wele aray.
He rad apon ane gay palfray
Litill and joly, arayand
His battale, with ane ax in hand :
And on his basnet he [7] he bar
Ane hat of quyrbolle [8] ay quhar [9],
And tharapon intill takning [10]
Ane he croun that he was ane king.
And, quhen Glousister and Herfurd wer
With thar battale approchand ner,
Befor tham all thar com ridand
With helm on hed and sper in hand
Schir Henry of Boune the worthy,
That was ane gud knicht and ane hardy
And to the erl of Herfurd cosyn,
Armit in armis gud and fyn
Com on ane sted ane bowschot ner
Befor all othir that thar wer,
And knew the king for that he saw
Him sa aray his men on raw [11],

---

[1] before.　[2] caused to delay.　[3] shelter.　[4] forthwith.　[5] nothing.
[6] without pause.　[7] high.　[8] hardened leather.　[9] habitually.
[10] in token.　[11] in line.

And by the croun that was set
Abouin his hed on the basnet,
And toward him he went in hy.
And, quhen the king sa apertly
Saw him cum forouth [1] all his feris,
In hy till him the hors he steris.
And, quhen Schir Henry saw the king
Cum on forouten [2] abasing,
Till him he rad in full gret hy :
He thocht that he suld wele lichtly [3]
Win him and haf him at his will,
Sen he him horsit saw sa ill.
Than sprent tha sammyn intill ane ling [4] ;
Schir Henry missit the nobill king,
And he, that in his sterapis stud,
With the ax that was hard and gud
With sa gret mane [5] raucht him ane dint [6],
That nouthir hat na helm micht stint [7]
The hevy dusch [8] that he him gaf,
That he the hed till harnis claf [9].
The handax schaft fruschit [10] in twa,
And he doun till the erd can ga
All flatlingis, for him falyheit micht [11].
This was the first strak of the ficht
That was pèrfornist douchtely :
And, quhen the kingis men sa stoutly
Saw him richt at the first meting
Forouten dout or abasing
Haf slane ane knicht sa at a strak,
Sic hardyment [12] than can tha tak
That tha com on richt hardely.

---

[1] before. [2] without. [3] quite easily. [4] then sprang these together forward. [5] might. [6] reached him a crushing blow. [7] withstand. [8] stroke. [9] cleft to the brain. [10] splintered. [11] his strength failed him. [12] courage.

Quhen Inglismen saw tham stoutly
Cum on, tha had gret abasing,
And specially for that the king
Sa smertly that gud knicht had slane,
That tha withdrew tham evirilkane [1]
And durst nocht than abid to ficht,
Sa dred tha for the kingis micht.
And, quhen the kingis men tham saw
Sa in hale battale tham withdraw,
Ane gret schot [2] till tham can tha mak,
And tha in hy tuk all the bak,
And tha that followit tham has slane
Sum of tham that tha haf ourtane :
Bot tha war few, for, suth to say,
Thar hors fet [3] had ner all away.
Bot, howsa quhene [4] deit thar,
Rebutit [5] foulely tha war,
And rad thar gat [6] with wele mar scham
Be full fer than tha com fra ham.

12   *The Eve of Battle: Bruce's Address to his Army*

QUHEN the king herd tham sa manly
   Spek to the ficht, and hardely,
    In hart gret gladschip can he ta,
And said, " Lordingis, sen yhe will sa,
Schap we us [7] tharfor in the morning,
Sa that we be the sone rising [8]
Haf herd mes, and he buskit [9] wele
Ilk man intill his awn eschele [10],

---

[1] every one.   [2] advance.   [3] fetched.   [4] however few.   [5] repulsed.
[6] rode their way.   [7] let us arrange.   [8] by sunrise.   [9] got ready.
[10] division.

Without the palyheounis [1] wele arait
In battale with baneris displait.
And luk yhe na wis [2] brek aray,
And, as yhe luf me, I yhou pray
That ilk man for his awn honour
Purvay him ane gud baneour [3],
And, quhen it cumis till the ficht,
Ilk man set his hart, will, and micht,
To stint our fais mekill of prid.
On hors tha will arait rid,
And cum on yhou in full gret hy [4] :
Met tham with speris hardely,
And wrek on tham the mekill ill
That tha and tharis has done us till
And ar in will yhet for to do,
Gif tha haf micht to cum tharto.
And certis methink wele that we
Forout [5] abasing aucht to be
Worthy and of gret vassalagis [6],
For we haf thre gret avantagis.
The first is, that we haf the richt,
And for the richt ay God will ficht.
The tothir is, tha ar cumin her
For lipning in [7] thar gret power
To sek us in our awn land,
And has brocht her richt till our hand
Riches intill sa gret plente
That the pouerast of yhou sall be
Bath rich and michty tharwithall,
Gif that we win, as wele may fall.
The thrid is, that we for our lifis,
And for our childir, and for our wifis,
And for the fredom of our land,

[1] tents.   [2] on no wise.   [3] standard-bearer.   [4] speed.   [5] without.
valour.   [7] relying on.

Ar strenyeit[1] in battale for to stand ;
And tha for thar micht anerly[2],
And for tha let[3] of us lichtly,
And for tha wald distroy us all,
Mais tham to ficht. Bot yhet may fall
That tha sall rew thar barganing :
And certis I warn yhou of a thing,
That, hapin tham, as God forbed,
To find faltis intill our ded
Sa that tha win us opinly,
Tha sall haf of us na mersy.
And, sen we knaw thar feloun will,
Methink it suld accord to skill
To set stoutnes agane felony
And mak sagat[4] ane juperdy[5].
Quharfor I yhou requer and pray,
That with all micht that evir yhe may
Yhe pres yhou at the beginning
But[6] cowardis or abasing
To met tham that first sall assemmill
Sa stoutly that the henmast trimmill[7],
And menis on[8] yhour gret manhed,
Yhour worschip, and yhour douchty ded,
And on the joy that we abid
Gif that us fall, as wele may tid,
Hap to vencus[9] the gret battale.
Intill yhour handis forouten fale[10]
Yhe ber honour, pris, and riches,
Fredom, welth, and gret blithnes,
Gif yhe contene yhou manfully :
And the contrar all halely
Sall fall, gif yhe lat cowardis

---

[1] constrained. [2] alone. [3] account. [4] in this wise. [5] a warlike
enterprise. [6] without. [7] hindmost tremble. [8] reflect on.
[9] vanquish. [10] without fail.

And wikkitnes yhour hartis suppris.
Yhe micht haf livit into thrildom,
Bot, for yhe yharnit till haf fredom,
Yhe ar assemblit her with me :
Tharfor is nedfull that yhe be
Worthy and wicht[1] but abasing.
I warn yhou wele yhet of a thing,
That mar mischef may fall us nane
Than in thar handis to be tane,
For tha suld sla us, I wat wele,
Richt as tha did my brothir Nele.
Bot, quhen I mene on yhour stoutnes,
And on the mony gret prowes
That yhe haf done sa worthely,
I trast and trowis sekirly
Till haf plane victor[2] in this ficht :
For, thouch our fais haf mekill micht,
Tha haf the wrang ; and succudry[3]
And covatis of senyhory[4]
Amovis tham forouten mor ;
Na us thar[5] dred tham bot befor,
For strinth of this plas, as yhe se,
Sall let us environit to be[6].
And I pray yhou als[7] specialy
Bath mar and les all comonly,
That nane of yhou for gredynes
Haf e[8] to tak of thar riches,
Na presoneris yhet for to ta,
Quhill yhe se tham cummerit sa[9]
That the feld planly ouris be,
And than at yhour liking may yhe
Tak all the riches that thar is.

[1] strong. [2] absolute victory. [3] arrogance. [4] desire of lordship.
[5] need we. [6] prevent our being surrounded. [7] also. [8] have an
eye to. [9] in such strait.

Gif yhe will wirk apon this wis,
Yhe sall haf victor sekirly[1] :
I wat nocht quhat mar say sall I :
Yhe wat wele all quhat honour is :
Contene yhou tharfor on sic wis
That yhour honour ay savit be :
And I hicht[2] her in my lawte[3],
Gif ony deis in this battale,
His ar[4], but ward, relef, or tale,
On the first day his land sall weld,
All be he nevir sa yhoung of eld.
Now mak yhou redy till the ficht :
God help us that is mast of micht !
I red[5] armit all nicht yhe be,
Purvait in battale, sa that we
To met our fais be redy boun."
Than ansuerd tha all with a soun,
"As yhe devis, sa sall be done."
Than till thar innis[6] went tha sone
And ordanit tham for the fichting,
Syn assemblit in the evinning,
And sagat all the nicht bad tha
Quhill on the morn that it was day.

I3   *Before the Battle*

THE Scottismen, quhen it was day,
   Thar mes[7] devoutly herd tha say,
Syn tuk ane sop and mad tham yhar[8] :
And, quhen tha all assemblit war
And in thar battalis[9] all purvait[10]
With thar brad baneris all displait,

---

[1] certainly. [2] undertake. [3] by mine honour. [4] heir. [5] counsel.
[6] quarters. [7] mass. [8] ready. [9] order of battle. [10] disposed.

Tha mad knichtis as it efferis [1]
To men that usis tha misteris [2].
The king mad Walter Steward knicht,
And James of Douglas that was wicht,
And othir als of gret bounte
He mad ilkane [3] in thar degre.
Quhen this was done that I yhou say,
Tha went all furth in gud aray
And tuk the plane full apertly.
Mony gud man wicht and hardy
That war fulfillit of gret bounte
Intill tha routis men micht se.
The Inglismen on other party,
That richt as angelis schane brichtly,
War nocht arait on sic maner,
For all thar battalis [4] sammyn [5] wer
In a schiltrum [6]. Bot, quhethir it was
Throu the gret stratnes of the plas
That tha war in to bid fichting,
Or that it was for abasing,
I wat nocht, bot in a schiltrum
It semit tha war all and sum
Outane the vaward anerly [7]
That with ane richt gret cumpany
Be thamselvin arait war
And till the battale mad tham yhar.
That folk ourtuk [8] ane mekill [9] feld
On bred [10], quhar mony ane schynand scheld,
And mony ane burnist bricht armour,
And mony ane man of gret valour,
And mony ane baner bricht and schene [11],
Micht in that gret schiltrum be sene.

---

[1] beseems. [2] rights. [3] each one. [4] battalions. [5] together.
[6] a host ranged in a circle. [7] except only the vanguard. [8] overspread. [9] wide. [10] in breadth. [11] shining.

And, quhen the king of Ingland ·
Saw Scottismen sa tak on hand
To tak the hard feld sa planly
And apon fut, he had ferly [1]
And said, " Quhat ! will yhon Scottis ficht ? "
" Yha sekirly, schir," said ane knicht.
Schir Ingeram Umphravill hat he [2],
And said, " Forsuth, schir, now I se
All the mast ferlyfull sicht
That evir I saw, quhen for to ficht
The Scottismen has tane on hand
Agane the gret micht of Ingland
In plane hard feld to gif battale :
Bot, and yhe will trow my consale,
Yhe sall discumfit tham lichtly.
Withdrawis yhou hine [3] sudanly
With battalis, baneris, and pennounis,
Quhill that we pas our palyheounis [4],
And yhe sall se alsone [5] that tha
Magre [6] thar lordis sall brek aray
And scale tham our harnas to ta [7] :
And, quhen we se tham scalit sa,
Prik we than on tham hardely,
And we sall haf tham wele lichtly,
For than sall nane be knit to ficht
That may withstand our mekill micht."
" I will nocht," said the king, " perfay
Do sa, for thar sall na man say
That I suld eschew the battale
Na withdraw me for sic rangale [8]."
Quhen this was said that er said I,
The Scottismen all full devotly
Tha knelit doun to God to pray,

---

[1] marvelled.   [2] was he called.   [3] hence.   [4] tents.   [5] as soon
[6] despite.   [7] disperse to capture our equipment.   [8] rabble.

And ane schort prayer thar mad tha
To God till help tham in that ficht.
And, quhen the Inglis king had sicht
Of tham kneland, he said in hy,
"Yhon folk knelis till ask mersy."
Schir Ingeram said, "Yhe say suth now ;
Tha ask mersy, but nocht at yhou ;
For thar trespas to God tha cry.
I tell yhou a thing sekirly,
That yhon men will win all or de,
For dout of ded [1] tha sall nocht fle."
"Now be it sa," than said the king,
"We sall it se." But delaying
He gert trump till the assemble [2].
On athir sid than men micht se
Full mony wicht man and worthy
All redy till do chevelry.

14

The Battle of Bannockburn

THUS war tha boun [3] on athir sid ;
   And Inglismen with mekill prid,
That war intill thar avaward [4],
Till the battale that Schir Eduard
Governit and led held straucht thar way.
The hors with spuris hardnit tha
And prikit apon tham sturdely,
And tha met tham richt hardely,
Sa that at the assemble thar
Sic ane frusching [5] of speris war
That fer away men micht it her.
At thar meting forouten wer [6]
War stedis stekit [7] mony ane,

[1] fear of death.   [2] caused sound the assembly.   [3] got ready.
[4] vanguard.   [5] breakage.   [6] without or besides worse things.
[7] pierced.

Mony gud man born doun and slane,
And mony ane hardyment[1] douchtely
Was thar eschevit : full hardely
Tha dang[2] on othir with wapnis ser :
Sum of the hors that stekit wer
Ruschit and relit richt rudly.
Bot the remanand nocht forthi[3]
That micht cum till the assembling
For that let mad richt na stinting[4],
Bot assemblit full hardely,
And tha met tham full sturdely
With speris that war scharp to scher
And axis that wele grundin wer,
Quharwith was raucht mony ane rout.
The ficht was thar sa fell and stout
That mony worthy man and wicht
Throu fors was fellit in that ficht
That had na micht to rise agane.
The Scottismen fast can tham pane[5]
Thar fais mekill micht to rus[6] :
I trow tha sall na pane refus
Na perill quhill that fais be
Set intill hard perplexite.

And, quhen the erl of Murref sa
Thar avaward saw stoutly ga
The way to Schir Eduard all straucht,
That met tham with full mekill maucht,
He held his way with his baner
To the gret rout quhar sammyn[7] wer
The nyn battalis that war sa brad,
That sa fele[8] baneris with tham had
And of men sa gret quantite

---

[1] deed of valour. [2] struck. [3] none the less. [4] abated nothing
for that hindrance. [5] bestirred themselves. [6] overthrow. [7] together. [8] many.

That it war wondir for to se.
The gud erl thiddir tuk the way
With his battale in gud aray,
And assemblit sa hardely
Quhill men micht her that had bene by
Ane gret frusch[1] of the speris that brast[2],
For thar fais assalyheit fast
That on stedis with mekill prid
Com prikand as tha wald ourrid
The erl and all his cumpany.
Bot tha met tham sa sturdely
That mony of tham till erd[3] tha bar,
And mony ane sted was stekit thar,
And mony gud man fellit undir fet
That had na power to ris up yhet.
Thar men micht se ane hard battale,
And sum defend, and sum assale,
And mony ane riall rimmill rid
Be raucht thar apon athir sid,
Quhill throu the birneis[4] brast[5] the blud
That till the erd doun stremand yhud[6].
The erl of Murref and his men
Sa stoutly tham contenit then
That tha wan plas ay mar and mar
On thar fais, the quhethir[7] tha war
Ay ten for ane, or ma perfay,
Sa that it semit wele that tha
War tynt[8] emang sa great menyhe
As tha war plungit in the se.
And, quhen the Inglismen has sene
The erl and all his men bedene[9]
Ficht sa stoutly but affraying
Richt as tha had nane abasing,

---

[1] crash.   [2] broke.   [3] earth.   [4] corslets.   [5] burst.   [6] went.
[7] although.   [8] lost.   [9] at once.

Tha pressit tham with all thar micht ;
And tha with speris and suerdis bricht
And axis that richt scharply schar,
In mid the visage met tham thar.
Thar men micht se ane stalward stour [1],
And mony men of gret valour
With speris, masis, and with knifis,
And othir wapnis wissill [2] lifis,
Sa that mony fell doun all ded :
The gyrs [3] wox with the blud all red.
The erl that wicht was and worthy
And his men faucht sa manfully,
That, quhasa had sene tham that day,
I trow forsuth that tha suld say
That tha suld do thar devour [4] wele
Sa that thar fais suld it fele.

Quhen that thir twa first battalis wer
Assemblit, as I said yhou er,
The Steward Walter that than was
And the gud lord als of Douglas
In a battale, quhen that tha saw
The erl forouten dred or aw
Assemmill with his cumpany
On all that folk sa sturdely,
For till help him tha held thar way
With thar battale in gud aray,
And assemblit sa hardely
Besid the erl ane litill by,
That thar fais feld thar cuming wele,
For with wapnis stalward of stele
Tha dang [5] on tham with all thar micht.
Thar fais resavit tham wele, I hicht [6],
With suerdis, speris, and with mas ;
The battale thar sa feloun was,

---

[1] fight. [2] exchange. [3] grass. [4] duty. [5] struck. [6] promise.

And sa richt gret spilling of blud,
That on the erd the flussis [1] stud ;
The Scottismen sa wele tham bar,
And sa gret slauchtir mad tha thar,
And fra sa fele the lifis revit,
That all the feld was bludy levit.
That tym thir thre battalis wer
All sid be sid fichtand wele ner,
Thar micht men her richt mony dint
And wapnis apon armour stint [2],
And se tummill knichtis and stedis,
With mony rich and riall wedis
Defoulit rudly undir fet ;
Sum held on loft, sum tynt the suet [3].
Ane lang quhile thus fichtand tha wer
That men na noys na cry micht her ;
Men herd nocht els bot granis, and dintis [4]
That slew [5] fyr as men dois on flintis ;
Sa faucht tha ilkane egirly
That tha mad nouthir noys na cry,
Bot dang on othir at thar micht
With wapnis that war burnist bricht.
The arowis als [6] sa thik tha flaw,
That tha micht se wele that tham saw
That tha ane hidwis schour can ma,
For quhar tha fell, I undirta,
Tha left eftir tham takinning [7]
That sall ned, as I trow, leching [8].
The Inglis archaris schot sa fast
That, micht thar schot haf ony last [9],
It had bene hard to Scottismen :
Bot King Robert, that wele can ken
That the archaris war peralous,

---

[1] pools.   [2] stop.   [3] life.   [4] blows.   [5] struck.   [6] also   [7] token.
[8] a doctor's work.   [9] endurance.

And thar schot hard and richt grevous
Ordanit forouth [1] the assemble
His marschall with ane gret menyhe,
Fif hundreth armit wele in stele
That on licht hors war horsit wele,
For to prik emang the archeris,
And sa assalyhe tham with speris
That tha na laser haf to schut.
This marschall that I of mut [2],
That Schir Robert of Keth was cald
As I befor haf till yhou tald,
Quhen that he saw the battalis sa
Assemmill and togidder ga,
And saw the archaris schut stoutly,
With all tham of his cumpany
In hy apon tham can he rid,
And ourtuk tham at a sid [3],
And ruschit emang tham sa rudly,
Strikand tham sa dispitfully,
And in sic fusoun [4] berand doun
And slayand tham without ransoun,
That tha tham scalit evirilkane [5],
And fra that tym furth thar was nane
That assemblit sic schot to ma.
Quhen Scottis archaris saw it was sa
Tha war rebutit, tha wox hardy,
With all thar micht schot egirly
Emang the horsmen that thar rad,
And woundis wid to tham tha mad,
And slew of tham ane full gret dele.
Tha bar tham hardely and wele,
For, fra tha fais archaris war
Scalit as I haf said yhou ar,

---

[1] out of.   [2] treat of.   [3] in flank.   [4] number or strength.   [5] took
to flight each one.

That ma then tha war be gret thing,
Sa that tha dred nocht thar schuting,
Tha wox sa hardy that tham thocht
Tha suld set all thar fais at nocht.
　　The marschall and his cumpany
Was yhet, as till yhou er said I,
Emang tha archaris, quhar tha mad
With speris roum quhar that tha rad,
And slew all that tha micht ourta:
And tha wele lichtly [1] micht do sa,
For tha had nocht ane strak to stint [2]
Na for to hald agane ane dint [3],
And agane armit men to ficht.
May nakit men haf litill micht.
Tha scalit tham on sic maner
That sum to thar gret battale wer
Withdrawin tham in full gret hy,
And sum war fled all utrely.
Bot the folk that behind tham was,
That for thar awn folk had na spas
Yhet to cum till the assembling,
In agane smertly can tha ding [4]
The archaris that tha met fleand,
That than war mad sa recreand
That thar hartis war tynt [5] clenly:
I trow tha sall nocht scath gretly
The Scottismen with schot that day.
And the gud king Robert, that ay
Was fillit full of gret bounte,
Saw how that his battalis thre
Sa hardely assemblit thar,
And sa wele in the ficht tham bar,
And sa fast on thar fais can ding,
That him thocht nane had abasing,

[1] very easily.　[2] parry.　[3] blow.　[4] drive.　[5] lost.

And how the archaris war scalit then,
He was all blith, and till his men
He said, " Lordingis, now luk that yhe
Worthy and of gud covyn [1] be
At this assemble, and hardy,
And assemmill sa sturdely
That nathing may befor yhou stand.
Our men sa freschly ar fichtand
That tha thar fais has cummerit sa [2]
That, be tha pressit, I undirta,
Ane litill fastar, yhe sall se
That tha discumfit sone sall be. "
Quhen this was said, tha held thar way,
And on a sid assemblit tha
Sa stoutly that at thar cuming
Thar fais war ruschit ane gret thing.
Thar men micht se men freschly ficht,
And men that worthy war and wicht
Do mony worthy vassalage [3].
Tha faucht as tha war in ane rage :
For, quhen the Scottis enkirly [4]
Saw thar fais se sturdely
Stand into battale tham agane [5],
With all thar micht and all thar mane
Tha laid on as men out of wit,
And, quhar tha with full strak micht hit,
Thar micht na arming stint thar strak :
Tha to-fruschit [6] tham tha micht ourtak,
And with axis sic duschis [7] gaf
That tha helmis and hedis claf :
And thar fais richt hardely
Met tham and dang on douchtely
With wapnis that war stith [8] of stele

[1] courage.   [2] put to such straits.   [3] deed of valour.   [4] ardently.
[5] against him.   [6] crushed.   [7] strokes.   [8] strong.

Thar was the battale strikin wele:
Sa gret dinning[1] thar was of dintis,
As wapnis apon armour stintis,
And of speris sa gret bristing,
And sic thrawing, and sic thristing[2],
Sic girning[3], graning, and sa gret
Ane noys, as tha can othir bet[4]
And cryit ensenyheis[5] on ilka sid,
Gifand and takand woundis wid,
That it was hidwis for till her
All four the battalis wicht that wer
Fichtand in a front halely.
Almichty God ! full douchtely
Schir Eduard the Brus and his men
Emang thar fais contenit tham then,
Fichtand intill sa gud covyn,
Sa hardy, worthy, and sa fyn,
That thar avaward ruschit was,
And magre tharis[6] left the plas,
And till thar gret rout till warand[7]
Tha went, that than had apon hand
Sa gret noy that tha war affrait,
For Scottismen tham hard assait
That than war in ane schiltrum all.
Quha hapnit in that ficht to fall,
I trow agane he sall nocht ris :
Thar men micht se on mony wis
Hardymentis eschevit douchtely,
And mony that wicht war and hardy
Doun undir fet lyand all ded,
Quhar all the feld of blud was red :
Armouris and quentis[8] that tha bar

[1] resounding. [2] thrusting. [3] crying aloud. [4] as one began to overcome the other. [5] war-cries. [6] in spite of them. [7] for protection. [8] devices, heraldic.

With blud war sa defoulit thar
That tha micht nocht discrivit be.
A! michty God, quha than micht se
The Steward Walter and his rout,
And the gud Douglas that was stout,
Fichtand intill that stalward stour,
He suld say that till all honour
Tha war worthy that in that ficht
Sa fast pressit thar fais micht
That tha tham ruschit quhar tha yhed [1]:
Thar micht men se mony ane sted
Fleand on stray that lord had nane.
A! Lord, quha than gud tent had tane
Till the gud erl of Murref
And his, that sa gret routis gef [2],
And faucht sa fast in that battale,
Tholand [3] sic panis and travale,
That tha and tharis mad sic debat
That quhar tha com tha mad tham gat [4]:
Than micht men her ensenyheis cry,
And Scottismen cry hardely,
"On tham! on tham! on tham! they fale."
With that sa hard tha can assale,
And slew all that tha micht ourta,
And the Scottis archaris alsua
Schot emang tham sa sturdely,
Engrevand tham sa gretumly [5],
That, quhat for [6] tham that with tham faucht
And sa gret routis till tham raucht,
And pressit tham full egirly,
And quhat for arowis that felly
Mony gret woundis can tham ma
And slew fast of thar hors alsua,

---

[1] went.   [2] blows gave.   [3] enduring.   [4] a way.   [5] annoying them so sorely.   [6] what with.

That tha wandist [1] ane litill we.
Tha dred sa gretly than to de
That thar covyn was wer [2] then er,
For tha that with tham fichtand wer
Set hardyment and strinth and will,
And hart and curage als thartill,
And all thar mane and all thar micht,
And put tham fouly to the flicht.

[1] became demoralised. [2] morale was worse.

ANDROW OF WYNTOUN

Circ. 1350–*circ.* 1420

15   *Magnanimity of Malcolm Canmore*

(*From "The Orygynale Cronykil of Scotland"*)

A THOWSAND sex and fyfty yhere
    Efftyre the byrth off oure Lord dere,
Makbeth-Fynlayk and Lulawch-Fule
Oure-drevyn had all thare dayis in dule,
The Kyng Malcolme Dunkannys sowne
Come wyth ane honest court to Skowne ;
Thare wyth gret solemnyté
Hys Coronatyowne than tuk he,
And Scotland in herytage
Till hym fra thine [1] and hys lynage,
And wyth athe off thaire fewté [2]
All thare homage than tuk he,
That awcht [3] homage to the Crowne.
Swa [4] entryd he in possessyowne,
And joysyd [5] sevyn and thretty yhere
That state wyth honowre and powere.
In the Crystyndome, I trow, than
Wes noucht in deid a bettyr man,
Na lyvand [6] a bettyr knycht
Na mare manly, stowt and wycht [7].
    Amang all othir famows dedis
Mony men thus off hym redis [8] ;

---

[1] thenceforward.   [2] fealty.   [3] owed.   [4] so.   [5] enjoyed.   [6] living.
powerful.   [8] relate.

That in his court thare wes a Knycht,
A lord off powere and off mycht,
That set hym till hawe slayne the Kyng,
Hys purpos gyve¹ he till end mycht bryng.
In to the Kyngys court than
Thare wes duelland a lele man,
That tald the Kyngys awyne persowne,
That that lord set hym be tresowne
To sla the Kyng, gyve that he
Mycht wyt hys oportunyté.
This lord that tyme wes noucht present
In to the court, bot wes absent,
Bot swne agayne he come, wyth ma²
Than he wes wont, the Kyng to sla.
Wyth curtasy yhit nevyretheles
Than, as befor, ressayvyd he wes.
The Kyng than warnyd hys menyhé³
Wyth hym at hwntyng for to be :
And to that knycht he sayd alsua,
That wyth hym-selff he wald hym ta⁴
By hym to syt at that huntyng :
The knycht consentyd to the Kyng.
Than on the morne wytht-owtyn let⁵,
The setys and the stable sete⁶,
The Kyng and that lord alsua
Togydder rad, and nane bot tha,
Fere in the wode, and thare thay fand
A fayre brade land and a plesand,
A lytill hill off nobill ayre,
All wode abowt bathe thyk and fayre.
    Than thus the Kyng sayd to the knycht,
"On fwte at lykyng thow may lycht,
Or on hors gyve thow will be,

¹ if.   ² more.   ³ retinue.   ⁴ take.   ⁵ without hindrance.
⁶ snares and the positions of the hunters being adjusted.

As thé thynk best, now ches thow thé [1].
·Horsyd and armyd als welle
. As I am, thow art ilke dele [2].
Thi wapnys [3] ar scharpe, and mare redy
Than ony in to this sted [4] hawe I,
Dergat [5], spere, knyff, and swerd,
Betwene ws dele we now the werd [6];
Here is best now to begyn
Thi purpos, gyve thow will honowre wyn ;
Here is nane, that may ws se,
Na help may owthir me, or thé :
For-thi fande [7] now wyth all thi mycht
To do thi purpos, as a knycht.
Set thow hawe fadyt thi lawté [8],
Do this dede yhit wyth honesté,
Gyve othir thow may or dare, or wille.
Fenyhé thé nowcht [9] to fulfille
Thi heycht [10], thi purpos, and thine athe :
Do fourth thi dedys, and be noucht lathe.
Gyve thow thynkys to sla me,
Quhat tyme na [11] nowe may bettyr be
Wytht fredome, or wyth mare manhed ?
Or gyve thow wald put me to dede,
Wyth venowne, or wytht scharpe poysowne,
That is a wyffis condytyown [12].
Or gyve thow wald in to my bede
Prevaly put me to dede,
That war as in adultery
Murthrysyd to be wnhonestly [13].
Or a knyff gyve thow wald hyd
Prewëly, and thi tyme abyd,

---

[1] choose thou.   [2] every whit.   [3] weapons.   [4] in this place.
[5] shield.   [6] let us now take each our parts of destiny.   [7] therefore
strive.   [8] tho' thou have failed in loyalty.   [9] fail not.   [10] promise.
[11] than.   [12] a woman's method.   [13] to be dishonourably murdered.

Quhill thow mycht at ese me sla
A murtherere mycht do na war than sua[1].
For-thi do, as suld a knycht.
Ga we togyddyr, God dele the rycht !
Wyth oure foure handys, and no ma :
Thare-on mot all the gamyn ga[2]."

    Wyth this the Knycht all changyd hewe
Lyk hys purpos all to rewe ;
And hys wysage worthyd[3] wan,
As he had bene rycht a mad man.
Thare fell he downe, and asked mercy,
For all hys purpos wes foly ;
And sayd, hys Lord mycht, wyth the lawe,
Hym, as he wald, bathe hang and drawe.
And swa he yhald[4] hym till hys will
On hym hys lust all to fulfill,
Bwt ony kyn condytyowne[5].

    The Kyng than all his actyowne
Forgawe the Knycht thare qwytly,
And tuk hym all till his mercy :
And thare he become his man
Mare lele, than he wes befor than.
And the Kyng, that wes hys lord,
Let na man wyt[6] off thare discord,
Quhill[7] the Knycht hym-selff this cas
Tald, in all as hapnyd was.

---

[1] worse than that.   [2] let that alone decide the play.   [3] became.
[4] yielded.   [5] without condition of any kind.   [6] know.   [7] until.

KING JAMES THE FIRST OF SCOTLAND

1394–1436

16 *From " The Kingis Quair "*

IN vere[1], that full of vertu is and gude,
  Quhen nature first begynneth hir enprise,
That quhilum was be cruell frost and flude
  And schouris scharp opprest In many wyse,
  And Synthius[2] (be)gynneth to aryse
Heigh in the est, a morow[3] soft and suete,
Vpward his course to driue In ariete[4]:

Passit mydday bot fourë greis evin[5],
  Off lenth and brede his angel wingis bryght
He spred vpon the ground doun fro the hevin ;
  That, for gladnesse and confort of the sight,
  And with the tiklyng of his hete and light,
The tender flouris opnyt thame and sprad ;
And, in thaire nature, thankit him for glad.

Noght fer passit the state of Innocence,
  Bot nere about the nowmer of yeris thre,
Were It causit throu hevinly Influence
  Off goddis will, or othir casualtee,
  Can I noght say ; bot out of my contree,
By thaire avise that had of me the cure,
Be see to pas, tuke I myn auenture.

[1] Spring.   [2] Cynthius (the Sun).   [3] in the morning.   [4] in the
sign of Aries.   [5] just four degrees.

Puruait [1] of all that was vs necessarye,
  With wynd at will, vp airly by the morowe,
Streight vnto schip, no longere wold we tarye,
  The way we tuke, the tyme I tald to-forowe [2],
  With mony "fare wele" and "sanct Iohne to
    borowe [3]"
Off falowe and frende ; and thus with one assent
We pullit vp saile, and furth oure wayis went.

Vpon the wawis weltering to and fro,
  So infortunate was vs that fremyt [4] day ;
That maugre, playnly, quhethir we wold or no,
  With strong hand, (as) by forse, schortly to say,
  Off Inymyis takin and led away
We weren all, and broght in thaire contree ;
Fortune It schupe [5], non othir wayis to be.

Quhare as In strayte ward and in strong prisoun,
  So fer-forth [6], of my lyf the heuy lyne,
Without confort, in sorowe abandoun,
  The secund sistere [7] lukit [8] hath to twyne,
  Nere by the space of yeris twise nyne ;
Till Iupiter his merci list aduert,
And send confort in relesche of my smert.

Quhare as In ward full oft I wold bewaille
  My dedely lyf, full of peyne and penance,
Saing ryght thus, quhat haue I gilt [9] to faille
  My fredome in this warld and my plesance ?
  Sen euery wight has thereof suffisance,
That I behold, and I a creature
Put from all this—hard Is myn auenture !

[1] provided.   [2] at the time I told before.   [3] St. John be your protection.   [4] unlucky.   [5] shaped.   [6] far forward.   [7] the second of the Three Fates.   [8] given heed.   [9] in what have I offended ?

The bird, the beste, the fisch eke In the see,
   They lyve in fredome euerich In his kynd ;
And I a man, and lakkith libertee ;
   Quhat schall I seyne, quhat resoun may I fynd,
   That fortune suld do so ? thus In my mynd
My folk I wold argewe [1], bot all for noght ;
Was non that myght, that on my peynes rought [2].

Than wold I say, "gif god me had deuisit
   To lyve my lyf in thraldom thus and pyne,
Quhat was the cause that he (me) more comprisit
   Than othir folk to lyve in suich ruyne ?
   I suffer allone amang the figuris nyne [3],
Ane wofull wrecche that to no wight may spede,
And yit of euery lyvis help hath nede."

The long(ë) dayes and the nyghtis eke
   I wold bewaille my fortune in this wise,
For quhich, agane distresse confort to seke,
   My custum was on mornis for to ryse
   Airly as day ; o happy excercise !
By the come I to Ioye out of turment,
Bot now to purpose of my first entent :—

Bewailing In my chamber thus allone,
   Despeired of all Ioye and remedye.
For-tirit of my thoght, and wo begone,
   Unto the wyndow gan I walk In hye [4],
   To se the warld and folk that went forby ;
As for the tyme, though I of mirthis fude
Myght haue no more, to luke It did me gude.

---

[1] I would argue with my attendants.   [2] took heed of.   [3] the speaker is comparing himself to a cypher in arithmetic.   [4] haste.

Now was there maid fast by the touris wall
  A gardyn faire, and in the corneris set
Ane herbere [1] grene, with wandis long and small
  Railit about ; and so with treis set
  Was all the place, and hawthorn hegis knet,
That lyf [2] was non walking there forby [3],
That myght within scarse ony wight aspye.

So thik the bewis and the leues grene
  Beschadit all the aleyes that there were,
And myddis euery herbere myght be sene
  The scharp(ë) grenë suetë Ienepere [4],
  Growing so faire with branchis here and there,
That, as It semyt to a lyf without,
The bewis spred the herbere all about ;

And on the small(ë) grenë twistis sat
  The lytill suetë nyghtingale, and song
So loud and clere, the ympnis [5] consecrat
  Off lufis vse, now soft, now lowd among,
  That all the gardyng and the wallis rong
Ryght of thaire song, and on the copill next
Off thaire suete armony [6], and lo the text :

CANTUS

" Worschippë, ye that loueris bene, this may,
  For of your blisse the kalendis are begonne,
And sing with vs, away, winter, away !

---

[1] this word seems to be used here in the sense of shrubbery and
in the next verse in that of flower-bed.   [2] person.   [3] past.
[4] Juniper. [5] hymns. [6] " and with the verse next following, containing their sweet harmony."

Cum, somer, cum, the suete sesoun and sonne !
Awake for schame ! that haue your hevynnis
wonne,
And amorously lift vp your hedis all,
Thank lufe that list you to his merci call."

Quhen thai this song had song a lytill thrawe [1],
Thai stent [2] a quhile, and therewith vnaffraid,
As I beheld and kest myn eyne a-lawe,
From beugh to beugh thay hippit and thai
plaid,
And freschly in thaire birdis kynd arraid
Thaire fetheris new, and fret [3] thame In the sonne,
And thankit lufe, that had thaire makis wonne.

This was the planë ditee of thaire note,
And there-with-all vnto my-self I thoght,
" Quhat lyf [4] is this, that makis birdis dote ?
Quhat may this be, how cummyth It of ought ?
Quhat nedith It to be so dere ybought ?
It is nothing, trowe I, bot feynit chere [5],
And that men list to counterfeten chere."

Eft [6] wald I think ; " o lord, quhat may this be ?
That lufe is of so noble myght and kynde,
Lufing his folk, and suich prosperitee
Is It of him, as we in bukis fynd ?
May he oure hertes setten and vnbynd ?
Hath he vpon oure hertis suich maistrye ?
Or all this is bot feynyt fantasye !

[1] while.   [2] ceased.   [3] adorned.   [4] mode of life.   [5] cheerfulness.
[6] again.

For gif he be of so grete excellence,
   That he of euery wight hath cure and charge,
Quhat haue I gilt to him or doon offense
   That I am thrall, and birdis gone at large,
   Sen him to serue he might set my corage [1]?
And gif he be noght so, than may I seyne,
Quhat makis folk to Iangill [2] of him In veyne?

Can I noght elles fynd, bot gif that he
   Be lord, and as a god may lyue and regne,
To bynd and louse, and maken thrallis free,
   Than wold I pray his blisfull grace benigne,
   To hable [3] me vnto his seruice digne;
And euermore for to be one of tho [4]
Him trewly for to serue In wele and wo.

And there-with kest I doun myn eye ageyne,
   Quhare as I sawe, walking vnder the toure,
Full secretly new cummyn hir to pleyne [5],
   The fairest or the freschest yong(ë) floure
   That euer I sawe, me thoght, before that houre,
For quhich sodayn abate [6], anon astert [7]
The blude of all my body to my hert.

And though I stude abaisit tho a lyte [8],
   No wonder was; for for-quhy my wittis all
Were so ouercom with plesance and delyte,
   Onely throu latting of myn eyën fall,
   That sudaynly my hert became hir thrall,
For euer, of free wyll; for of manace
There was no takyn [9] In hir suetë face.

---

[1] heart.   [2] talk.   [3] enable.   [4] those.   [5] play.   [6] surprise.
[7] started.   [8] then a little while.   [9] token.

And In my hede I drewe ryght hastily,
  And eft-sonës I lent It forth ageyne,
And sawe hir walk, that verray womanly,
  With no wight mo, bot onely wommen tueyne.
  Than gan I studye in my-self and seyne,
" A ! suete, ar ye a warldly creature,
Or hevinly thing in likenesse of nature ?

Or ar ye god Cupidis owin princesse,
  And cummyn are to louse me out of band [1] ?
Or ar ye verray nature the goddesse,
  That haue depaynted with your hevinly hand
  This gardyn full of flouris, as they stand ?
Quhat sall I think, allace ! quhat reuerence
Sall I min(i)ster to your excellence ?

Gif ye a goddesse be, and that ye like
  To do me payne, I may It noght astert [2] ;
Gif ye be warldly wight, that dooth me sike [3],
  Quhy lest [4] god mak you so, my derrest hert,
  To do a sely prisoner thus smert,
That lufis yow all, and wote of noght bot wo ?
And therefor, merci, suete ! sen It is so."

Quhen I a lytill thrawe had maid my moon,
  Bewailling myn infortune and my chance,
Vnknawin how or quhat was best to doon,
  So ferre I-fallyng [5] Into lufis dance,
  That sodeynly my wit, my contenance,
My hert, my will, my nature, and my mynd,
Was changit clene ryght In an̄-othir kynd.

[1] bond. [2] escape. [3] causes me sigh. [4] did it please. [5] fallen.

Off hir array the form gif I sall write,
   Toward hir goldin haire and rich atyre
In fret-wise couchit (was) with perllis ¹ quhite
   And gretë balas ² lemyng³ as the fyre,
    With mony ane emeraut and faire saphire ;
And on hir hede a chaplet fresch of hue,
Off plumys partit rede, and quhite, and blewe ;

Full of quaking spangis ⁴ bryght as gold,
   Forgit of schap like to the amorettis ⁵,
So new, so fresch, so plesant to behold,
   The plumys eke like to the floure-Ionettis ⁶,
    And othir of schap like to the (round crokettis) ⁷,
And, aboue all this, there was, wele I wote,
Beautee eneuch to mak a world to dote.

About hir nek, quhite as the fyre amaille ⁸,
   A gudely cheyne of smale orfeuerye ⁹,
Quhareby there hang a ruby, without faille ¹⁰,
   Lyke to ane hert(ë) schapin verily,
    That, as a sperk of lowe ¹¹, so wantonly
Semyt birnyng vpon hir quhytë throte ;
Now gif there was gud partye ¹², god It wote !

And forto walk that fresche mayes morowe,
   And huke ¹³ sche had vpon hir tissew quhite,
That gudeliare had noght bene seen toforowe,
   As I suppose ; and gert sche was a lyte ¹⁴ ;
    Thus halflyng ¹⁵ louse for haste, to suich delyte ¹⁶
It was to see hir youth In gudelihede,
That for rudenes to spek thereof I drede.

---

¹ was arranged with a fretwork of pearls.   ² rubies.   ³ flaming.
⁴ spangles.   ⁵ love-devices.   ⁶ flowers of the St. John's wort.
⁷ curls.   ⁸ fire enamel.   ⁹ goldsmith's work.   ¹⁰ doubt.   ¹¹ flame.
¹² an eligible match.   ¹³ frock.   ¹⁴ she was loosely girt.   ¹⁵ partly.
¹⁶ so delightful.

In hir was youth, beautee, with humble aport[1],
 Bountee, richesse, and wommanly facture,
God better wote than my pen can report :
 Wisedome, largesse, estate, and connyng[2] sure
 In euery poynt so guydit hir mesure,
In word, in dede, in schap, in contenance,
That nature myght no more hir childe auance.

Throw quhich anon I knew and vnderstude
 Wele, that sche was a warldly creature ;
On quhom to rest myn eyë, so mich gude
 It did my wofull hert, I yow assure,
 That It was to me Ioye without mesure ;
And, at the last, my luke vnto the hevin
I threwe furthwith, and said thir versis sevin :

" O venus clere ! of goddis stellifyit[3] !
 To quhom I yelde homage and sacrifise,
Fro this day forth your grace be magnifyit,
 Thet me ressauit haue in suich (a) wise,
 To lyve vnder your law and do seruise ;
Now help me furth, and for your merci lede
My hert to rest, that deis nere for drede."

[1] deportment. [2] skill. [3] made into a star by the gods.

ROBERT HENRYSON

Before 1425–before 1506

The Testament of Cresseid [1]

ANE doolie sessoun to ane cairfull dyte [2]
   Suld correspond, and be equiualent.
Richt sa it wes quhen I began to wryte
This tragedie ; the wedder richt feruent [3],
Quhen Aries, in middis of the Lent,
Schouris of Haill can fra the North discend,
That scantlie fra the cauld I micht defend.

Yit, neuertheles, within myne Oratur
I stude, quhen Titan had his bemis bricht
Withdrawin doun, and sylit vnder cure [4],
And fair Venus, the bewtis of the nicht,
Uprais, and set vnto the west full richt
Hir golden face, in oppositioun
Of God Phebus, direct discending doun.

Throw out the glas hir bemis brast [5] sa fair
That I micht se on euerie syde me by
The Northern wind had purifyit the Air,
And sched the mistie cloudis fra the sky ;
The froist freisit, the blastis bitterly
Fra Pole Artick come quhisling loud and schill,
And causit me remufe aganis my will.

---

[1] Written as a sequel to Chaucer's "Troilus and Cresseide."
[2] doleful season to a tale of woe.   [3] severe.   [4] concealed under
cover.   [5] burst.

For I traistit that Venus, luifis Quene,
To quhome sum tyme I hecht [1] obedience,
My faidit hart of lufe scho walde mak grene ;
And therupon, with humbill reuerence,
I thocht to pray hir hie Magnificence ;
Bot for greit cald as than I lattit [2] was,
And in my Chalmer to the fyre can pas.

Thocht lufe be hait [3], yit in ane man of age
It kendillis nocht sa sone as in youtheid,
Of quhome the blude is flowing in ane rage,
And in the auld the curage doif and deid [4],
Of quhilk the fire outward is best remeid :
To help be Phisike quhair that nature faillit,
I am expert—for baith I haue assailit [5].

I mend the fyre, and beikit me [6] about,
Than tuik ane drink my spreitis to comfort,
And armit me weill fra the cauld thairout :
To cut the winter nicht, and mak it schort,
I tuik ane Quair [7], and left all vther sport,
Written be worthie Chaucer glorious,
Of fair Creisseid and worthie Troylus.

And thair I fand, efter that Diomeid
Ressauit had that Lady bricht of hew,
How Troilus neir out of wit abraid [8],
And weipit soir, with visage paill of hew ;
For quhilk wanhope [9], his teiris can renew,
Quhill Esperus reioisit him agane :
Thus quhyle in Ioy he leuit, quhile in pane.

---

[1] promised.   [2] hindered.   [3] hot.   [4] dull and dead.   [5] tried.
[6] warmed myself.   [7] book.   [8] almost went out of his mind.
[9] wanhap, misfortune.

Of hir behest he had greit comforting,
Traisting to Troy that scho suld mak retour,
Quhilk he desyrit maist of eirdly thing,
For quhy scho was his only Paramour ;
Bot quhen he saw passit baith day and hour
Of hir ganecome[1], than sorrow can oppres
His wofull hart in cair and heuines.

Of his distres me neidis nocht reheirs,
For worthie Chauceir, in the samin buik,
In gudelie termis, and in Ioly veirs,
Compylit hes his cairis, quha will luik,
To brek my sleip ane vther quair I tuik,
In quhilk I fand the fatall destenie
Of fair Cresseid, that endit wretchitlie.

Quha wait[2] gif all that Chaucer wrait was trew ?
Nor I wait nocht gif this narratioun
Be authoreist, or fenyeit of the new[3],
Be sum Poeit, throw his Inuentioun
Maid to report the Lamentation
And wofull end of this lustie[4] Creisseid,
And quhat distres scho thoillit[5], and quhat deid[6].

Quhen Diomed had all his appetyte,
And mair, fulfillit of this fair Ladie,
Upon ane vther he set his haill delyte,
And send to hir ane Lybell of repudie[7],
And hir excludit fra his companie.
Than desolait scho walkit vp and doun,
And, sum men sayis, into the Court commoun.

---

[1] return.　[2] knows.　[3] newly imagined.　[4] pleasing.　[5] endured.
[6] death.　[7] notice of dismissal.

O, fair Creisseid ! the flour and A per se [1]
Of Troy and Grece, how was thow fortunait [2] !
To change in filth all thy feminitie,
And be with fleschelie lust sa maculait,
And go amang the Greikis air and lait,
So giglotlike [3], takand thy foull plesance !
I haue pietie thow suld fall sic mischance.

Yit, neuertheles, quhat euer men deme or say
In scornefull langage of thy brukkilnes [4],
I sall excuse, als far furth as I may,
Thy womanheid, thy wisdome, and fairnes :
The quhilk Fortoun hes put to sic distres
As hir pleisit, and nathing throw [5] the gilt
Of the, throw wickit langage to be spilt.

This fair Lady, in this wyse destitute
Of all comfort and consolatioun
Richt priuelie, but fellowschip, on fute
Disagysit passit far out of the toun
Ane myle or twa, vnto ane Mansioun,
Beildit full gay, quhair hir Father Calchas
Quhilk than amang the Greikis dwelland was.

Quhen he hir saw, the caus he can Inquyre
Of hir cumming ; scho said, siching full soir,
"Fra Diomeid had gottin his desyre
He wox werie, and wald of me no moir."
Quod Calchas, "douchter, weip thow not thairfoir ;
Perauenture all cummis for the best :
Welcum to me, thow art full deir ane Gest [6]."

---

[1] paragon. [2] what a destiny was thine. [3] like a light creature.
[4] frailty. [5] thraw, cast up, reproach. [6] guest.

This auld Calchas, efter the Law was tho [1],
Wes keiper of the Tempill, as ane Preist,
In quhilk Venus and hir Sone Cupido
War honourit, and his Chalmer was thame neist,
To quhilk Cresseid with baill [2] aneuch in breist
Usit to pas, hir prayeris for to say;
Quhill at the last, vpon ane Solempne day,

As custome was, the pepill far and neir,
Befoir the none, vnto the Tempill went
With Sacrifice, deuoit in thair maneir.
Bot still Cresseid, heuie in hir Intent,
Into the Kirk wald not hir self present,
For giuing of the pepill ony deming
Of hir expuls fra Diomeid the King;

Bot past into ane secreit Orature
Quhair scho micht weip hir wofull desteny.
Behind hir bak scho cloisit fast the dure,
And on hir kneis bair fell down in hy [3];
Upon Uenus and Cupide angerly
Scho cryit out, and said on this same wyse:
"Allace! that euer I maid you Sacrifice.

"Ye gaue me anis deuine responsaill [4]
That I suld be the flour of luif in Troy;
Now am I maid ane vnworthie outwaill [5],
And all in cair translatit is my Ioy.
Quha sall me gyde? quha sall me now conuoy,
Sen I fra Diomeid, and Nobill Troylus,
Am clene excludit, as abiect odious?

[1] as the law then was.   [2] sorrow.   [3] haste.   [4] assurance.
[5] outcast.

"O fals Cupide, is nane to wyte [1] bot thow,
And thy Mother, of lufe the blind Goddes !
Ye causit me alwayis vnderstand and trow
The seid of lufe was sawin in my face,
And ay grew grene throw your supplie and grace.
But now, allace, that seid with froist is slane,
And I fra luifferis left, and all forlane."

Quhen this was said, doun in ane extasie,
Rauischit in spreit, intill ane dreame scho fell,
And be appearance hard, quhair scho did ly,
Cupide the King ringand ane siluer bell,
Quhilk men micht heir fra heuin vnto hell ;
At quhais sound befoir Cupide appeiris,
The seuin Planetis, discending fra thair Spheiris,

Quhilk hes power of all thing generabill
To reull and steir be their greit Influence,
Wedder and wind, and coursis variabill.
And first of all, Saturne gaue his sentence,
Quhilk gaue to Cupide litill reuerence,
But, as ane busteous [2] Churle on his maneir,
Come crabitlie, with auster luik and cheir.

His face frosnit [3], his lyre [4] was like the Leid ;
His teith chatterit and cheuerit with the Chin ;
His Ene drowpit, how sonkin in his heid ;
Out of his Nois the Meldrop [5] fast can rin ;
With lippis bla [6], and cheikis leine and thin ;
The Ice-schoklis that fra his hair doun hang
Was wonder greit, and as ane speir als lang.

[1] none is to blame.   [2] rude.   [3] frosted.   [4] skin.   [5] pendent
drop.   [6] livid.

Atouir [1] his belt his lyart [2] lokkis lay
Felterit [3] vnfair, ouirfret [4] with Froistis hoir ;
His garmound and his gyis full gay of gray ;
His widderit weid fra him the wind out woir ;
Ane busteous bow within his hand he boir ;
Under his girdill ane flasche of felloun flanis [5],
Fedderit with Ice, and heidit with hailstanis.

Than Iuppiter richt fair and amiabill,
God of the Starnis in the Firmament,
And Nureis of all thing generabill,
Fra his Father Saturne far different,
With burelie [6] face, and browis bricht and brent [7],
Upon his heid ane Garland, wonder gay,
Of flouris fair, as it had bene in May.

His voice was cleir ; as Cristall wer his Ene ;
As goldin wyre as glitterand was his hair ;
His garmound and his gyis full gay of grene,
With golden listis [8] gilt on euerie gair [9] ;
Ane burelie brand about his middill bair ;
In his right hand he had ane groundin speir,
Of his Father the wraith fra vs to weir [10].

Nixt efter him came Mars, the God of Ire,
Of strife, debait, and all dissensioun,
To chide and fecht, als feirs as ony fyre ;
In hard Harnes, hewmound, and Habirgeoun [11] ;
And on his hanche ane roustie fell Fachioun ;
And in his hand he had ane roustie sword ;
Wrything his face with mony angrie word.

[1] over.   [2] grey.   [3] tangled.   [4] decked over.   [5] sheaf of cruel
arrows.   [6] majestic.   [7] smooth.   [8] borders.   [9] indentation at the
bottom of a robe.   [10] ward off.   [11] helmet and breast-plate.

Schaikand his sword, befoir Cupide he come
With reid visage and grislie glowrand ene[1];
And at his mouth ane bullar[2] stude of fome,
Lyke to ane Bair quhetting his Tuskis kene,
Rich Tuitlyeour lyke, but temperance in tene[3];
Ane horne he blew with mony bosteous brag,
Quhilk all this warld with weir hes maid to wag.

Than fair Phebus, Lanterne and Lamp of licht
Of man and beist, baith frute and flourisching,
Tender Nureis, and banischer of nicht,
And of the warld causing be his mouing
And Influence lyfe in all eirdlie thing,
Without comfort of quhome, of force[4] to nocht
Must all ga die that in this warld is wrocht.

As King Royall he raid vpon his Chair,
The quhilk Phaeton gydit sum tyme vpricht;
The brichtness of his face, quhen it was bair,
Nane micht behald for peirsing of his sicht:
This goldin Cart with fyrie bemis bricht
Four yokkit steidis full different of hew,
But bait or tyring[5], throw the Spheiris drew.

The first was soyr[6], with Mane als reid as Rois,
Callit Eoye[7] into the Orient;
The secund steid to Name hecht Ethios.
Quhitlie and paill, and sum deill[8] ascendent;
The thrid Peros, richt hait and richt feruent;
The feird was blak, (and) callit Phlegonie,
Quhilk rollis Phebus down into the sey.

---

[1] awful glaring eyes.   [2] bubble.   [3] right brawler-like, without bounds in anger.   [4] by necessity.   [5] without pause or fatigue.   [6] sorrel.   [7] Eous.   [8] somewhat.

Venus was thair present, that Goddes (gay),
Hir Sonnis querrel for to defend, and mak
Hir awin complaint, cled in ane nyce array,
The ane half grene, the vther half Sabill black ;
Quhyte hair as gold, kemmit and sched abak ;
Bot in hir face semit greit variance,
Quhyles perfyte treuth, and quhyles Inconstance.

Under smyling scho was dissimulait,
Prouocative with blenkis [1] amorous,
And suddanely changit and alterait,
Angrie as ony Serpent vennemous,
Richt pungitiue with wordis odious :
Thus variant scho was, quha list tak keip [2],
With ane Eye lauch, and with the uther weip.

In taikning [3] that all fleschelie Paramour
Quhilk Venus hes in reull and gouernance,
Is sum tyme sweit, sum tyme bitter and sour,
Richt vnstabill, and full of variance,
Mingit [4] with cairfull Ioy and fals plesance,
Now hait, now cauld, now blyith, now full of wo.
Now grene as leif, now widderit and ago [5].

With buik in hand than come Mercurius,
Richt Eloquent and full of Rethorie,
With polite termis and delicious,
With pen and Ink to report all reddie,
Setting sangis and singand merilie ;
His Hude was reid, heklit atouir [6] his Croun,
Lyke to ane Poeit of the auld fassoun.

[1] glances.   [2] let who will heed.   [3] token.   [4] mingled.   [5] fading.
[6] hooked above.

6

Boxis he bair with fine Electuairis,
And sugerit Syropis for digestioun,
Spycis belangand to the Pothecairis,
With mony hailsum sweit Confectioun,
Doctour in Phisick cled in ane Skarlot goun,
And furrit weill, as sic ane aucht to be,
Honest and gude, and not one word culd lie.

Nixt efter him come Lady Cynthia,
The last of all, and swiftest in hir Spheir,
Of colour blak, buskit [1] with hornis twa,
And in the nicht scho listis best appeir ;
Haw as the Leid [2], of colour nathing cleir ;
For all hir licht scho borrowis at hir brother
Titan, for of hir self scho hes nane vther.

Hir gyse was gray, and full of spottis blak ;
And on hir breist ane Churle paintit full euin,
Beirand ane bunche of Thornis on his bak,
Quhilk for his thift micht clim na nar the heuin.
Thus quhen thay gadderit war thir Goddes seuin,
Mercurius thay cheisit with ane assent
To be foirspeikar in the Parliament.

Quha had bene thair, and liken for to heir
His facound toung and termis exquisite,
Of Rhetorick the prettick he micht leir [3],
In breif Sermone ane pregnant sentence wryte :
Befoir Cupide veiling his Cap alyte [4],
Speiris [he] the caus of that vocatioun.
And he anone schew his Intentioun.

[1] adorned.   [2] as pale as lead.   [3] might learn the practice.
[4] a little.

" Lo (quod Cupide) quha will blaspheme the name
Of his awin God, outher in word or deid,
To all Goddis he dois baith lak [1] and schame,
And suld haue bitter panis to his meid :
I say this by yone wretchit Cresseid,
The quhilk throw me was sum tyme flour of lufe,
Me and my Mother starklie can reprufe ;

" Saying of hir greit Infelicitie
I was the caus, and my Mother Venus,
Ane blind Goddes hir cald, that micht not se,
With sclander and defame Iniurious :
Thus hir leuing vnclene and Lecherous
Scno wald returne on me and my Mother,
To quhome I schew [2] my grace abone all vther.

" And sen ye ar all seuin deificait,
Participant of deuyne sapience,
This greit Iniurie done to our hie estait
Me think with pane we suld mak recompence ;
Was neuer to Goddes done sic violence.
As weill for you, as for myself I say ;
Thairfoir ga help to reuenge I you pray."

Mercurius to Cupide gaue answeir
And said, " Schir King, my counsall is that ye
Refer yow to the hiest Planeit heir,
And tak to him the lawest of degre,
The pane of Cresseid for to modifie [3] :
As God Saturne, with him tak Cynthia."
" I am content (quod he) to tak thay twa."

[1] reproach.   [2] showed.   [3] determine the manner of.

Than thus proceidit Saturne and the Mone,
Quhen thay the mater rypelie had degest,
For the dispyte to Cupide scho had done,
And to Uenus oppin and manifest,
In all hir lyfe with pane to be opprest,
And torment sair, with seiknes Incurabill,
And to all louers be abhominabill.

This duleful sentence Saturne tuik on hand,
And passit doun quhair cairfull Cresseid lay,
And on hir heid he laid ane frostie wand ;
Than lawfullie on this wyse can he say :
"Thy greit fairness, and all thy bewtie gay,
Thy wantoun blude, and eik thy goldin hair,
Heir I exclude fra the for euermair.

" I change thy mirth into melancholy,
Quhilk is the mother of all pensiuenes ;
Thy Moisture and thy heit in cald and dry ;
Thyne Insolence, thy play and wantones
To greit diseis ; thy Pomp and thy riches
In mortall neid ; and greit penuritie
Thow suffer sall ; and as ane beggar die."

O cruell Saturne ! fraward and angrie,
Hard is thy dome, and to malitious :
On fair Cresseid quhy hes thow na mercie,
Quhilk was sa sweit, gentill, and amorous ?
Withdraw thy sentence and be gracious
As thow was neuer ; so schawis thow thy deid,
Ane wraikfull [1] sentence geuin on fair Cresseid.

---

[1] vindictive.

Than Cynthia, quhen Saturne past away.
Out of hir sait discendit down belyue [1],
And red ane bill on Cresseid quhair scho lay,
Contening this sentence diffinityue ;
" Fra heit of bodie I the now depryue,
And to thy seiknes sal be na recure,
Bot in dolour thy dayis to Indure.

" Thy Cristall Ene minglit with blude I mak ;
Thy voice sa cleir, vnpleasand, hoir, and hace [2] ;
Thy lustie lyre [3] ouirspred with spottis blak,
And lumpis haw [4] appeirand in thy face ;
Quhair thow cummis, Ilk man sall fle the place ;
This sall thow go begging fra hous to hous,
With Cop and Clapper lyke ane Lazarous."

This doolie dreame, this vglye visioun
Brocht to ane end, Cresseid fra it awoik.
And all that Court and conuocatioun
Uanischit away ; than rais scho vp and tuik
Ane poleist glas, and hir schaddow culd luik ;
And quhen scho saw hir face sa deformait,
Gif scho in hart was wa aneuch, God wait !

Weiping full sair, " lo, quhat it is (quod sche)
With fraward langage for to mufe and steir
Our craibit Goddis, and sa is sene on me !
My blaspheming now haue I bocht full deir ;
All eirdlie Ioy and mirth I set areir. [5]
Allace, this day ! allace, this wofull tyde !
Quhen I began with my Goddis for to chyde."

---

[1] at once.   [2] worn and hoarse.   [3] beauteous skin.   [4] livid
[5] behind me, in the past.

Be this was said, ane Chyld come fra the hall,
To warne Cresseid the Supper was reddy;
First knokkit at the dure, and syne culd call,
"Madame, your Father biddis you cum in hy,
He hes merwell sa lang on grouf [1] ye ly,
And sayis, your prayers bene to lang sum deill,
The Goddis wait all your Intent full weill."

Quod scho, "fair Chylde, ga to my Father deir
And pray him cum to speik with me anone."
And sa he did, and said, "douchter, quhat cheir?"
"Allace (quod scho), Father, my mirth is gone."
"How sa!" (quod he) and scho can all expone,
As I haue tauld, the vengeance and the wraik,
For hir trepas, Cupide on hir culd tak.

He luikit on hir vglye Lipper [2] face,
The quhilk befor was quhite as Lillie flour;
Wringand his handis, oftymes he said, allace,
That he had leuit to se that wofull hour;
For he knew weill that thir was na succour
To hir seiknes, and that dowblit his pane;
Thus was thair cair aneuch betuix thame twane.

Quhen thay togidder murnit had full lang,
Quod Cresseid, "Father, I wauld not be kend;
Thairfor in secreit wyse ye let me gang
Wnto yone Hospitall at the tounis end;
And thidder sum meit for Cheritie me send,
To leif vpon; for all mirth in this eird
Is fra me gane—sic is my wickit weird."

---

[1] face downward.   [2] leprous.

Than in ane Mantill and ane bawer [1] Hat,
With Cop and Clapper, wonder priuely
He opnit ane secreit yet, [2] and out thair at
Conuoyit hir, that na man suld espy,
Wnto ane uillage half ane myle thairby ;
Delyuerit hir in at the Spittaill hous,
And daylie sent hir part of his Almous [3].

Sum knew hir weill, and sum had na knawledge
Of hir, becaus scho was sa deformait
With bylis blak ouirspred in hir visage,
And hir fair colour faidit and alterait.
Yit thay presumit, for hir hie regrait,
And still murning, scho was of Nobill Kin :
With better will thairfoir thay tulk hir in.

The day passit, and Phebus went to rest,
The Cloudis blak ouirquhelmit all the sky :
God wait gif Cresseid was ane sorrowfull Gest,
Seeing that vncouth fair and Harbery [4] !
But meit or drink scho dressit hir to ly
In ane dark Corner of the Hous allone ;
And on this wyse, weiping, scho maid her mone.

The Complaint of Cresseid

" O SOP of sorrow, sonken into cair !
O Catiue Creisseid ! for now and euer mair
Gane is thy Ioy, and all thy mirth in Eird ;
Of all blyithnes now art thou blaiknit bair [5];
Thair is na Salue may saif the of thy sair.

---

[1] beaver.   [2] gate.   [3] alms.   [4] board and lodging.   [5] blackened
bare (in allusion to her ailment).

Fell is thy Fortoun, wickit is thy weird :
Thy blys is baneist, and thy baill on breird [1];
Under the Eirth God gif I grauin wer,
Quhair nane of Grece nor yit of Troy micht heird.

"Quhair is thy Chalmer wantounlie besene [2],
With burely [3] bed and bankouris browderit bene [4],
Spycis and Wyne to thy Collatioun,
The Cowpis all of gold and siluer schene,
The sweit Meitis, seruit in plattis clene,
With Saipheron sals of ane gud sessoun [5],
Thy gay garmentis with mony gudely Goun,
Thy plesand Lawn pinnit with goldin prene [6] ?
All is areir, thy greit Royall Renoun.

"Quhair is thy garding with thir greissis gay,
And fresche Flowris, quhilk the Quene Floray
Had paintit plesandly in euerie pane [7],
Quhair thou was wont full merilye in May
To walk and tak the dew be it was day,
And heir the Merle and Mawis mony ane,
With Ladyis fair in Carrolling to gane [8],
And se the Royall Rinkis [9] in their array,
In garmentis gay, garnischit on euerie grane ?

"Thy greit triumphand fame and hie honour,
Quhair thou was callit of Eirdlye wichtis Flour—
All is decayit, thy weird is welterit so,
Thy hie estait is turnit in darknes dour.
This Lipper Ludge tak for thy burelie Bour,

---

[1] on the increase.   [2] fitted out.   [3] stately.   [4] well-broidered
tapestries.   [5] saffron sauce of a good seasoning.   [6] pin.   [7] piece.
[8] go.   [9] champions.

And for thy Bed tak now ane bunche of stro ;
For waillit [1] Wyne and Meitis thou had tho [2],
Tak mowlit [3] Breid, Peirrie, and Ceder sour :
Bot Cop and Clapper, now is all ago.

" My cleir voice and courtlie carrolling,
Quhair I was wont with Ladyis for to sing,
Is rawk as Ruik [4], full hiddeous, hoir, and hace ;
My plesand port, all vtheris precelling—
Of lustines I was hald maist conding [5]—
Now is deformit the Figour of my face—
To luik on it na Leid [6] now lyking hes :
Sowpit in syte [7], I say with sair siching,
Ludgeit amang the Lipper Leid, allace !

" O Ladyis fair of Troy and Grece attend
My miserie, quhilk nane may comprehend,
My friuoll [8] Fortoun, my Infelicitie,
My greit mischief, quhilk na man can amend ;
Be war in tyme, approchis neir the end,
And in your mynd ane mirrour mak of me ;
As I am now, peraduenture that ye,
For all your micht, may cum to that same end,
Or ellis war [9], gif ony war may be.

" Nocht is your fairnes bot ane faiding Flour,
Nocht is your famous laud and hie honour
Bot wind inflat in vther mennis eiris !
Your roising reid [10] to rotting sall retour.
Exempill mak of me in your Memour,

---

[1] choice.   [2] then.   [3] mouldy.   [4] raucous as a rook.   [5] agreeable.   [6] person.   [7] steeped in grief.   [8] fickle.   [9] worse.   [10] rosy
red.

Quhilk of sic thingis wofull witnes beiris,
All Welth in Eird away as Wind it weiris ;
Be war, thairfoir, approchis neir the hour :
Fortoun is fikkil, quhen scho beginnis and steiris [1]."

Thus chydand with her drerie destenye,
Weiping, scho woik the nicht fra end to end ;
Bot all in vane ; hir dule, hir cairfull cry,
Micht not remeid, nor yit hir murning mend.
Ane Lipper Lady rais, and till hir wend,
And said, " quhy spurnis thow aganis the Wall,
To sla thyself, and mend nathing at all ?

" Sen thy weiping dowbillis bot thy wo,
I counsall the mak vertew of ane neid
To leir to clap thy Clapper to and fro,
And leir efter the Law of Lipper Leid [2]."
Thair was na buit [3], bot furth with thame scho yeid [4],
Fra place to place, quhill cauld and hounger sair
Compellit hir to be ane rank beggair.

That samin tyme of Troy the Garnisoun,
Quhilk had to Chiftane Worthie Troylus.
Throw Ieopardie of Weir had strikken down
Knichtis of Grece in number maruellous :
With greit tryumphe and Laude victorious
Agane to Troy richt Royallie they raid,
The way quhair Cresseid with the Lipper baid [5].

Seing that companie, thai come all with ane steuin [6];
Thay gaif ane cry, ond schuik coppis gude speid ;
Said, " worthie Lordis, for goddis lufe of Heuin,

[1] begins to shift.   [2] leper folk.   [3] help.   [4] went.   [5] abode.
[6] noise.

To vs Lipper part of your Almous deid."
Than to thair cry Nobill Troylus tuik heid,
Hauing pietie, neir by the place can pas
Quhair Cresseid sat, not witting quhat scho was.

Than vpon him scho kest vp baith her Ene,
And with ane blenk [1] it come into his thocht
That he sumtime hir face befoir had sene ;
Bot scho was in sic plye [2] he knew hir nocht ;
Yit than hir luik into his mynd it brocht
The sweit visage and amorous blenking
Of fair Cresseid, sumtyme his awin darling.

Na wonder was, suppois in mynd that he
Tuik her figure sa sone, and lo ! now quhy ?
The Idole of ane thing in cace may be
Sa deip Imprentit in the fantasy,
That it deludis the wittis outwardly
And sa appeiris in forme and lyke estait
Within the mynd as it was figurait.

Ane spark of lufe than till his hart culd spring,
And kendlit all his bodie in ane Fyre,
With hait fewir ane sweit and trimbling
Him tuik, quhill he was reddie to expyre !
To beir his Scheild his Breist began to tyre ;
Within ane quhyle he changit mony hew,
And, neuertheles, not ane ane vther knew.

For knichtlie pietie and memoriall
Of fair Cresseid, ane Gyrdill can he tak,
Ane Purs of gold, and mony gay Iowall [3],

---

[1] glance.   [2] plight.   [3] This line is repeated in the original.

And in the Skirt of Cresseid doun can swak [1] ;
Than raid away, and not ane word (he) spak,
Pensiwe in hart, quhill he come to the Toun,
And for greit cair oft syis [2] almost fell doun.

The Lipper folk to Cresseid than can draw,
To se the equall distribution
Of the Almous ; bot quhen the gold thay saw,
Ilk ane to vther prewelie can roun [3],
And said, "yone Lord hes mair affectioun,
How euer it be, vnto yone Lazarous
Than to vs all ; we knaw be his Almous."

"Quhat Lord is yone (quod scho), haue ye na feill [4]
Hes done to vs so greit humanitie?"
"Yes (quod a Lipper man), I knaw him weill ;
Schir Troylus it is, gentill and fre."
Quhen Cresseid vnderstude that it was he,
Stiffer than steill thair stert ane bitter stound [5]
Throwout hir hart, and fell doun to the ground.

Quhen scho, ouircome with siching sair and sad,
With mony cairfull cry and cald "ochane !
Now is my breist with stormie stoundis stad [6],
Wrappit in wo, ane wretch full will of wane [7] :"
Than swounit scho oft or scho culd refrane,
And euer in hir swouning cryit scho thus :
"O, fals Cresseid ! and trew Knicht Troylus !

"Thy lufe, thy lawtie [8], and thy gentilnes,
I countit small in my prosperitie,
Sa eleuait I was in wantones,

---

[1] to cast with force, *i.e.*, haste.   [2] often.   [3] whisper.   [4] knowledge.   [5] pang.   [6] beset.   [7] a homeless wretch indeed.   [8] loyalty.

And clam vpon the fickill quheill[1] sa hie ;
All Faith and Lufe, I promissit to the,
Was in the self[2] fickill and friuolous :
O, fals Cresseid ! and trew knicht Troilus !

" For lufe of me thow keipt gude continence,
Honest and chaist in conuersatioun,
Of all Wemen protectour and defence
Thou was, and helpit thair opinioun[3] :
My mynd in fleschelie foull affectioun
Was Inclynit to Lustis Lecherous :
Fy, fals Cresseid ! O, trew Knicht Troylus !

" Louers, be war, and tak gude heid about
Quhome that ye lufe, for quhome ye suffer paine ;
I lat you wit[4], thair is richt few thairout
Quhome ye may traist to haue trew lufe agane ;
Preif[5] quhen ye will, your labour is in vaine ;
Thairfoir, I reid ye tak thame as ye find,
For thay ar sad[6] as Widdercock in Wind,

" Becaus I knaw the greit vnstabilnes,
Brukkill[7] as glas, into my self I say,
Traisting in vther als greit vnfaithfulnes,
Als vnconstant, and als vntrew of fay ;
Thocht sum be trew, I wait richt few are thay ;
Quha findis treuth, lat him his Lady ruse[8] ;
Nane but my self, as now, I will accuse."

Quhen this was said, with Paper scho sat doun,
And on this maneir maid hir Testament :
" Heir I beteiche[9] my Corps and Carioun

[1] clomb upon the fickle wheel (of Fortune). [2] same. [3] espoused
their cause. [4] I tell you, [5] prove. [6] firm. [7] brittle. [8] praise.
[9] bequeath.

With Wormis and with Taidis to be rent ;
My Cop and Clapper, and myne Ornament,
And all my gold, the Lipper folk sall haue,
Quhen I am deid, to burie me in graue.

" This Royall Ring, set with this Rubie reid,
Quhilk Troylus in drowrie [1] to me send,
To him agane I leif it quhen I am deid,
To mak my cairfull deid wnto him kend [2] :
Thus I conclude schortlie, and mak ane end ;
My Spreit I leif to Diane, quhair scho dwellis,
To walk with hir in waist Woddis and Wellis [3].

" O Diomeid ! thou hes baith Broche and Belt,
Quhilk Troylus gaue me in takning
Of his trew lufe "—and with that word scho swelt [4] ;
And sone ane Lipper man tuik of the Ring,
Syne buryit hir withouttin tarying :
To Troylus furthwith the Ring he bair,
And of Cresseid the deith he can declair.

Quhen he had hard hir greit infirmitie,
Hir Legacie and Lamentatioun,
And how scho endit in sic pouertie,
He swelt [5] for wo, and fell doun in ane swoun ;
For greit sorrow his hart to brist was boun [6] :
Siching full sadlie, said, " I can no moir ;
Scho was untrew, and wo is me thairfoir ! "

Sum said he maid ane Tomb of Merbell gray,
And wrait hir name and superscriptioun,
And laid it on hir graue, quhair that scho lay,

[1] love-token.   [2] to make my sad death known to him.   [3] fields.
[4] expired.   [5] choked.   [6] ready to burst.

In golden Letteris, conteining this ressoun [1]:
" Lo, fair Ladyis, Cresseid of Troyis toun,
Sumtyme countit the flour of Womanheid,
Under this stane, lait Lipper, lyis deid."

Now worthie Wemen, in this Ballet schort,
Made for your worschip and Instructioun,
Of Cheritie I monische and exhort,
Ming [2] not your lufe with fals deceptioun ;
Beir in your mynd this schort conclusion
Of fair Cresseid, as I haue said befoir :
Sen scho is deid, I speik of hir no moir.

18   *Robene and Makyne*

ROBENE sat on gud grene hill,
        Kepand a flok of fe [3] :
mirry makyne said him till,
" Robene, thow rew [4] on me ;
I haif the luvit lowd and still,
Thir yeiris two or thre ;
my dule in dern [5] bot gif thow dill [6],
Dowtless but dreid [7] I de."

Robene anfsuerit, " be the rude [8],
nathing of lufe I knaw,
Bot keipis my scheip vndir yone wid,
Lo quhair thay raik on raw [9] :
quhat hes marrit the in thy mude,
makyne, to me thow schaw ;
Or quhat is lufe, or to be lude [10] ?
Fane wald I leir [11] that law."

[1] legend.   [2] mix.   [3] sheep.   [4] have pity.   [5] in secret.
[6] assuage.   [7] without fail.   [8] cross.   [9] range in a row.   [10] love or
to be loved.   [11] learn.

"At luvis lair gife thow will leir,
Tak thair ane a b c :
be heynd[1], courtass, and fair of feir[2],
 Wyse, hardy, and fre ;
So that no denger do the deir[3],
quhat dule in dern thow dre[4] ;
preiss the[5] with pane at all poweir,
be patient and previe."

Robene anssuerit hir agane,
"I wait nocht quhat is luve ;
Bot I haif mervell incertane
Quhat makis the this wanrufe[6] :
The weddir is fair, and I am fane,
my scheip gois haill aboif[7] ;
And[8] we wald play ws in this plane,
Thay wald ws bayth reproif."

"Robene, tak tent[9] vnto my taill,
And wirk all as I reid[10],
And thow sall haif my hairt all haill,
Eik and my madinheid.
Sen god sendis bute for baill,[11]
And for mvrnyng remeid,
I dern[12] with the, bot gif I daill,[13]
Dowtles I am bot deid."

"Makyne, to morne this ilk a tyde[14],
And ye will meit me heir,
Perauenture my scheip ma gang besyd,
quhill we haif liggit[15] full neir ;

[1] gentle.   [2] mien.   [3] daunt.   [4] endure.   [5] press forward.
[6] thus joyless.   [7] healthy on the high ground.   [8] if.   [9] heed.
[10] counsel.   [11] help for distress.   [12] perceive.   [13] deal.   [14] at this
time to-morrow.   [15] lain.

Bot mawgre haif I and I byd,
Fra thay begin to steir [1];
quhat lyis on hairt I will nocht hyd;
makyn, than mak gud cheir."

" Robene, thow reivis me roif [2] and rest;
I luve bot the allone."
" Makyne, adew, the sone gois west,
The day is neir hand gone."
" Robene, in dule I am so drest,
That lufe wilbe my bone [3]."
" Ga lufe, makyne, quhair evir thow list,
For lemman I lue none."

" Robene, I stand in sic a styll [4];
I sicht [5], and that full sair."
" makyne, I haif bene heir this quhyle;
at hame god gif I wair [6]."
" my huny, robene, talk ane quhill,
gif thow will do na mair."
" makyne, sum uthir man begyle,
For hamewart I will fair."

Robene on his wayis went,
als licht as leif of tre;
mawkin mvrnit in hir intent,
and trowd him nevir to se.
Robene brayd [7] attour the bent [8];
Than mawkyne cryit on hie,
" Now ma thow sing, for I am schent [9]!
quhat alis lufe at me [10]?"

[1] I am uneasy if I stay behind when they begin to move.
[2] peace.   [3] bane.   [4] state.   [5] sighed.   [6] God grant I were.
[7] made off.   [8] across the moor.   [9] disgraced.   [10] what spite has love against me?

Mawkyne went hame withowttin faill,
Full wery eftir cowth weip [1] :
Than robene in a ful fair daill
Assemblit all his scheip.
Be that [2] sum pairte of mawkynis aill
Outthrow his hairt cowd creip ;
he fallowit hir fast thair till assaill,
and till hir tuke gude keip [3].

"Abyd, abyd, thow fair makyne,
a word for ony thing ;
For all my luve it salbe thyne,
Withowttin depairting [4].
all haill, thy harte for till haif myne [5]
Is all my cuvating ;
my scheip to morne quhill houris nyne
Will neid of no keping."

"Robene, thow hes hard soung and say,
In gestis and storeis auld,
The man that will nocht quhen he may
sall haif nocht quhen he wald.
I pray to Jesu every day
mot eik thair cairis [6] cauld,
that first preissis [7] with thee to play,
be firth, forrest, or fawld."

"Makyne, the nicht is soft and dry,
The wedder is warme and fair,
And the grene woid rycht neir ws by
To walk attour all quhair ;

---

[1] ready to cry.   [2] by that time.   [3] and paid good regard to her.
[4] division.   [5] to have your heart entirely mine.   [6] may he increase
their cares.   [7] essays.

Thair ma na Ianglour [1] ws espy,
That is to lufe contrair ;
Thairin, makyne, bath ye and I
Vnsene we ma repair."

" Robene, that warld is all away
and quyt brocht till ane end,
and nevir agane thairto perfay [2]
Sall it be as thow wend [3] ;
For of my pane thow maid it play,
and all in vane I spend ;
as thow hew done, sa sall I say,
mvrne on, I think to mend."

" Mawkyne, the howp of all my heill [4],
my hairt on the is sett,
and evirmair to the be leill [5],
quhilt I may leif but lett [6] ;
nevir to faill, as vtheris feill,
quhat grace that evir I gett."
" Robene, with the I will nocht deill ;
Adew, for thus we mett."

Malkyne went hame blyth annewche [7],
Attour the holttis hair [8] ;
Robene mvrnit, and Malkyne lewche [9] ;
Scho sang, he sichit sair ;
and so left him, bayth wo and wrewche [10],
In dolour and in cair,
Kepand his hird vnder a huche [11],
amangis the holtis hair.

[1] tell-tale.   [2] in faith.   [3] deem.   [4] welfare.   [5] loyal.
[6] without ceasing.   [7] enough.   [8] over the cold hills.   [9] laughed.
[10] woeful and sorely grieved.   [11] crag.

HENRY THE MINSTREL (BLIND HARRY)

Fl. circ. 1450–1492

(*From "The Actis and Deidis of the Illustere and Vailyeant Campioun Schir William Wallace, Knicht of Ellerslie"*)

19   *Lament for Wallace*

ALLACE, Scotland, to quhom sall thow compleyn!
    Allace, fra payn quha sall the now restreyn!
Allace, thi help is fastlie [1] brocht to ground,
Thi best chyftane in braith [2] bandis is bound;
Allace, thow has now lost thi gyd off lycht!
Allace, quha sall defend the in thi rycht?
Allace, thi payn approchis wondyr ner,
With sorow sone thow mon bene [3] set in feyr!
Thi gracious gyd, thi grettast gouernour,
Allace, our neir is cumyn his fatell hour!
Allace, quha sall the beit now off thi baill [4]?
Allace, quhen sall off harmys thow be haill?
Quha sall the defend? quha sall the now mak fre?
Allace, in wer quha sall thi helpar be?
Quha sall the help? quha sall the now radem?
Allace, quha sall the Saxons fra the flem [5]?
I can no mar, bot besek God off grace
The to restor in haist to rychtwysnace;
Sen gud Wallace may succour the no mar.
The loss off him encressit mekill cair.

---

[1] for, falsely.　　[2] violent.　　[3] must be.　　[4] cure thee of thy woe.
[5] drive off.

20 *The Death of Wallace*

ON Wednysday the fals Sotheroun furth brocht,
  Till martyr him as thai before had wrocht.
Rycht suth it is, a martyr was Wallace,
Als Osauold, Edmunt, Eduuard, and Thomas
Off men in armes led him a full gret rout.
With a bauld spreit gud Wallace blent [1] about :
A preyst he askyt, for God at [2] deit on tre.
King Eduuard than cummandyt his clerge,
And said ; " I charge, apayn [3] off loss off lywe,
Nane be sa bauld yon tyrand for to schrywe.
He has rong [4] lang in contrar my hienace."
A blyst [5] byschop sone, present in that place,
Off Canterbery he than was rychtwys [6] lord,
Agayn the king he maid this rycht record [7] ;
And said ; " My selff sall her his confessioun,
Gyff I haiff mycht, in contrar off thi croun.
And [8] thou throu force will stop me off this thing,
I wow to God, quhilk is my rychtwys king,
That all Ingland I sall her enterdyt [9],
And mak it knawin thou art ane herretyk.
The sacrement off kyrk I sall him geiff ;
Syn tak thi chos, to sterwe [10] or lat him leiff.
It war mar waill [11], in worschip off thi croun,
To kepe sic ane in lyff in thi bandoun [12],
Than all the land and gud at thow has refyd [13].
Bot cowatice [14] the ay fra honour drefyd [15].
Thow has thi lyff rongyn [16] in wrangwis deid ;
That sall be seyn on the, or on thi seid."
The king gert [17] charge thai suld the byschop ta [18];
Bot sad [19] lordys consellyt to lat him ga.

---

[1] glanced.   [2] that.   [3] under pain.   [4] reigned.   [5] blessed.
[6] righteous.   [7] reply.   [8] if.   [9] excommunicate.   [10] put to death.
[11] profit.   [12] at thy mercy.   [13] robbed.   [14] covetousness.   [15] drove.
[16] reigned.   [17] caused.   [18] commit.   [19] wise.

All Inglismen said, at [1] his desyr was rycht;
To Wallace than he rakyt [2] in thar sicht,
And sadly hard his confessioun till ane end
Humbly to God his spreyt he thar comend
Lawly him serwyt with hartlye [3] deuocioun
Apon his kneis, and said ane orysoun.
His leyff he tuk, and to West monastyr [4] raid.
The lokmen [5] than thai bur Wallace but baid [6]
On till a place, his martyrdom to tak;
For till his ded [7] he wald no forthyr mak.
Fra the fyrst nycht he was tane in Scotland,
Thai kepyt him in to that sammyn band [8].
Na thing he had at suld haiff doyn him gud;
Bot Inglismen him seruit off carnaill [9] fud.
Hys warldly lyff desyrd the sustenance,
Thocht he it gat in contrar off plesance.
Thai xxxty dayis his band thai durst nocht slaik,
Quhill he was bundyn on a skamyll off ayk [10],
With irn chenyeis that was bath stark and keyn [11].
A clerk thai set to her quhat he wald meyn [12].
" Thow Scot," he said, " that gret wrangis has don,
Thi fatell hour, thow seis, approchis son.
Thow suld in mynd remembyr thi mysdeid,
At clerkis may, quhen thai thair psalmis reid
For Crystyn saullis, that makis thaim to pray,
In thair nowmyr [13] thow may be ane off thai;
For now thow seis on fors [14] thou mon decess."
Than Wallace said; " For all thi roid rahress [15],
Thow has na charge, suppos at I did myss [16];
Yon blyst byschop has hecht [17] I sall haiff blis;
And I trew weill, at God sall it admyt:

---

[1] that.   [2] passed.   [3] hearty.   [4] Westminster.   [5] executioners.
[6] without stay.   [7] death.   [8] same chain.   [9] flesh.   [10] oaken bench.
[11] strong and sharp.   [12] how he would bemoan himself.   [13] number.
[14] of force.   [15] severe speech.   [16] went astray.   [17] promised.

Thi febyll wordis sall nocht my conscience smyt.
Conford[1] I haiff off way that I suld gang,
Maist payn I feill at I bid her our lang."
Than said the clerk ; " Our king oft send the till ;
Thow mycht haiff had all Scotland at thi will,
To hald off him, and cessyt off thi stryff ;
So as a lord rongyn furth all thi lyff."
Than Wallace said ; " The spekis off mychty thing.
Had I lestyt[2], and gottyn my rychtwys king,
Fra worthi Bruce had rasauit his croun,
I thocht haiff maid Ingland at his bandoun.
So wttraly it suld beyn at his will,
Quhat plessyt him, to sauff thi king or spill[3]."
" Weill," said this clerk, " than thow repentis nocht :
Off wykkydness thow has a felloun thocht.
Is nayn in warld at has sa mony slane ;
Tharfor till ask, me think thow suld be bane[4],
Grace off our king, and syn at his barnage[5]."
Than Wallace smyld a litill at his langage.
" I grant," he said, " part Inglismen I slew
In my quarrel, me thocht nocht halff enew.
I mowyt na wer[6] bot for to win our awin ;
To God and man the rycht full weill is knawin.
Thi frustyr[7] wordis dois nocht bot taris me,
I the commaund, on Goddis halff[8] lat me be."
A schyrray[9] gart this clerk son fra him pass ;
Rycht as thai durst, thai grant quhat he wald as[10].
A Psaltyr buk Wallace had on him euir ;
Fra his childeid fra it wald nocht deseuir.
Bettyr he trowit in wiage[11] for to speid.
Bot than he was dispalyeid off his weid.
This grace he ast at lord Clyffurd that knycht,

---

[1] comfort.   [2] continued.   [3] destroy.   [4] ready.   [5] baronage.
[6] went not to war.   [7] futile.   [8] in God's name.   [9] sheriff.   [10] ask.
[11] journey.

To lat him haiff his Psaltyr buk in sycht.
He gert a preyst it oppyn befor him hauld,
Quhill thai till him had done all at thai wauld.
Stedfast he red, for ocht thai did him thar :
Feyll[1] Sotheroun said, as Wallace feld na sayr[2].
Gud deuocioun sa was his begynnyng,
Conteynd[3] tharwith, and fair was his endyng ;
Quhill spech and spreyt at anys all can fayr[4]
To lestand blyss, we trow, for euirmayr.

[1] many. [2] felt no pain. [3] continued. [4] did depart.

WILLIAM DUNBAR

Circ. 1460–1520(?)

21   *The Dance of the Sevin Deidly Synnis.*

OFF Februar the fyiftene nycht,
    Full lang befoir the dayis lycht,
I lay in till a trance;
And then I saw baith hevin and hell:
Me thocht, amangis the feyndis fell,
Mahoun [1] gart cry ane dance [2]
Off schrewis that wer nevir schrevin,
Aganiss the feist of Fasternis evin [3],
To mak thair observance;
He bad gallandis ga graith a gyiss [4],
And kast vp gamountis [5] in the skyiss,
That last came out of France.

"Lat se," quod he, "Now quha begynnis;"
With that the fowll Sevin Deidly Synnis
Begowth [6] to leip at anis.
PRYD. And first of all in dance wes Pryd,
With hair wyld [7] bak and bonet on syd,
Lyk to mak vaistie wanis [8];
And round abowt him, as a quheill,
Hang all in rumpillis to the heill

---

[1] Satan.   [2] caused a dance to be called for.   [3] Shrove Tuesday.
[4] fit out a masquerade.   [5] capers.   [6] began.   [7] combed.   [8] as if to
make wide wings.

His kethat for the nanis[1] :
Mony prowd trumpour[2] with him trippit
Throw skaldand fyre, ay as thay skippit
Thay gyrnd[3] with hiddouss granis.

Heilie[4] harlottis on hawtane[5] wyiss
Come in with mony sindrie gyiss,
Bot yit luche nevir Mahoun ;
Quhill preistis come in with bair schevin
nekkis,
Than all the feyndis lewche, and maid gekkis[6],
Blak Belly and Bawsy Brown.

YRE.   Than Yre come in with sturt[7] and stryfe ;
His hand wes ay vpoun his knyfe,
He brandeist lyk a beir :
Bostaris, braggaris, and barganeris,
Eftir him passit in to pairis,
All bodin[8] in feir of weir ;

In iakkis, and stryppis and bonettis of steill,
Thair leggis wer chenyeit to the heill,
Ffrawart wes thair affeir[9] :
Sum vpoun vdir with brandis beft[10],
Sum jaggit vthiris to the heft,
With knyvis that scherp cowd scheir.

INVY. Nixt in the dance followit Invy,
Fild full of feid and fellony,
Hid malyce and dispyte ;

---

[1] cassock for the occasion.   [2] deceiver.   [3] grinned.   [4] disdainful.
[5] haughty.   [6] laughed and made mows.   [7] violence.   [8] accoutred.
[9] insolent was their demeanour.   [10] beat.

Ffor pryvie hatrent[1] that tratour trymlit.
Him followit mony freik dissymlit[2],
With fenyeit wirdis quhyte[3];

And flattereris in to menis facis;
And bakbyttaris of sindry racis,
To ley that had delyte;
And rownaris[4] of fals lesingis[5];
Allace! that courtis of noble kingis
Of thame can nevir be quyte.

AUARYCE. Nixt him in dans come Cuvatyce,
Rute of all evill and grund of vyce,
That nevir cowd be content;
Catyvis, wrechis and okkeraris[6],
Hud-pykis[7], hurdaris and gadderaris,
All with that warlo[8] went:

Out of thair throttis thay schot on vdder
Hett moltin gold, me thocht a fudder[9],
As fyreflawcht[10] maist fervent;
Ay as thay tomit[11] thame of schot,
Ffeyndis fild thame new vp to the thrott
With gold of allkin prent[12]

SUEIRNES. Syne Sweirnes[13], at the secound bidding,
Come lyk a sow out of a midding[14],
Full slepy wes his grunyie[15]:
Mony sweir bumbard belly huddroun[16],
Mony slute daw[17] and slepy duddroun[18],
Him serwit ay with sounyie[19];

[1] hatred.   [2] a masked man.   [3] show of blameless words.
[4] whisperers.   [5] calumnies.   [6] extortionate persons.   [7] misers.
[8] sorcerer.   [9] mass.   [10] lightning.   [11] discharged.   [12] of every
mintage.   [13] sloth.   [14] dung-hill.   [15] aspect.   [16] lazy tun-bellied
sloven.   [17] slothful trull.   [18] drab.   [19] grudgingly.

He drew thame furth in till a chenyie,
And Belliall, with a brydill renyie,
Evir lascht thame on the lunyie [1] :
In dance thay war so slaw of feit,
Thay gaif thame in the fyre a heit,
And maid thame quicker of counyie [2].

LICHERY. Than Lichery, that lathly corss,
Berand lyk a bagit horss [3],
And Ydilness did him leid ;
Thair wes with him ane vgly sort,
And mony stynkand fowll tramort [4],
That had in syn bene deid.

Quhen that wer entrit in the dance,
Thay wer full strenge of countenance,
Lyk turkass [5] birnand reid ;
All led thay vthir by the tersis,
Suppoiss thay fycket [6] with thair ersis,
It mycht be na remeid.

GLUTTONY. Than the fowll monstir Glutteny,
Off wame vnsasiable and gredy,
To dance he did him dress :
Him followit mony fowll drunckart,
With can and collep [7], cop and quart,
In surffet and excess ;

Full mony a waistless wallydrag [8],
With wamiss vnweildable [9], did furth wag,
In creische [10] that did incress ;

[1] loin.   [2] apprehension.   [3] neighing like a stallion.   [4] corpse.
[5] pincers.   [6] fidgeted.   [7] drinking-cup.   [8] ill-grown person.
[9] unwieldy bellies.   [10] grease.

Drynk ! ay thay cryit, with mony a gaip,
The feyndis gaif thame hait leid to laip,
Thair lovery [1] wes na less.

Na menstrallis playit to thame but dowt [2],
Ffor glemen thair wer haldin owt.
Be day, and eik by nycht ;
Except a menstrall that slew a man,
Swa till his heretage he wan,
And entirt be breif of richt.

Than cryd Mahoun for a Heleand padyane [3] ;
Syne ran a feynd to feche Makfadyane,
Ffar northwart in a nuke ;
Be he the correnoch [4] had done schout,
Erschemen so gadderit him abowt,
In Hell grit rowme thay tuke.

Thae tarmegantis, with tag and tatter,
Ffull lowd in Ersche begowth to clatter,
And rowp lyk revin and ruke [5] :
The Devill sa devit [6] wes with thair yell,
That in the depest pot of hell
He smorit [7] thame with smvke.

22   *[To a Ladye]*

SWEIT roiss of vertew and of gentilnes,
    Delytsum lillie of everie lustynes [8],
Richest in bontie, and in bewtie cleir,
And everie vertew that is held most deir,
Except onlie that ye ar mercyless.

---

[1] bounty or desert.   [2] without doubt.   [3] pageant.   [4] war-cry.
[5] croak like raven and rook.   [6] deafened.   [7] smothered.
[8] pleasantness.

In to your garthe[1] this day I did persew,
Thair saw I flowris that fresche wer of hew ;
Baithe quhyte and reid moist lusty[2] wer to seyne,
And halsum herbis vpone stalkis grene ;
Yit leif nor flour fynd could I name of rew.

I dout that Merche, with his cauld blastis keyne,
Hes slane this gentill herbe, that I of mene ;
Quhois petewous deithe dois to my hart sic pane
That I wald mak to plant his rute agane,
So confortand his levis vnto me bene.

23   *Lament for the Makaris, quhen he wes Seik*

I THAT in heill wes and glaidnes,
    Am trublit now with gret seiknes,
And feblit with infirmitie ;
    Timor Mortis conturbat me.

Our plesance heir is all vane glory,
This fals warld is bot transitory,
The flesche is brukle[3], the Fend is sle[4] ;
    Timor Mortis conturbat me.

The stait of man dois change et vary,
Now sound, now seik, now blyth, now sary,
Now dansand mirry, now like to dee ;
    Timor Mortis conturbat me.

No stait in erd heir standis sickir[5] ;
As with the wynd wavis the wicker[6],
So wavis this warldis vanite ;
    Timor Mortis conturbat me.

---

[1] garden enclosure.   [2] pleasant.   [3] fragile.   [4] Fiend is cunning.
[5] secure.   [6] twig.

Onto the ded gois all Estatis,
Princis, Prelotis, and Potestatis,
Baith riche et pur of all degre ;
  Timor Mortis conturbat me.

He takis the knychtis in to feild,
Anarmit [1] vnder helme et scheild ;
Wictour he is at all melle ;
  Timor Mortis conturbat me.

That strang vnmercifull tyrand
Takis on the moderis breist sowkand
The bab, full of benignite ;
  Timor Mortis conturbat me.

He takis the campion in the stour [2],
The capitane closit in the tour,
The lady in bour full of bewte ;
  Timor Mortis conturbat me.

He spairis no lord for his piscence [3],
Na clerk for his intelligence ;
His awfull strak may no man fle ;
  Timor Mortis conturbat me.

Art, magicianis, and astrologgis,
Rethoris, logicianis, et theologgis,
Thame helpis no conclusionis sle ;
  Timor Mortis conturbat me.

---

[1] armed.   [2] champion in the fight.   [3] power.

In medicyne the most practicianis,
Lechis, surrigianis, et phisicianis,
Thame self fra ded may not supple ;
    Timor Mortis conturbat me.

I see that markaris [1] amang the laif [2]
Playis heir ther pageant, syne gois to graif ;
Sparit is nocht ther faculte ;
    Timor Mortis conturbat me.

He hes done petuously devour [3],
The noble Chaucer, of makaris flouir,
The Monk of Bery, and Gower, all thre ;
    Timor Mortis conturbat me.

The gude Syr Hew of Eglintoun,
Et eik, Heryot, et Wyntoun,
He hes tane out of this cuntre ;
    Timor Mortis conturbat me.

That scorpioun fell has done infek [4]
Maister Iohne Clerke, and James Afflek,
Fra balat making et trigide ;
    Timor Mortis conturbat me.

Holland et Barbour he has berevit ;
Allace ! that he nought with ws lewit
Schir Mungo Lokert of the Le ;
    Timor Mortis conturbat me.

---

[1] poets.   [2] rest.   [3] swallowed up, alas.   [4] Mr. Eyre Todd
suggests 'inhibited.'

Clerk of Tranent eik he has tane,
That maid the anteris [1] of Gawane ;
Schir Gilbert Hay endit has he ;
    Timor Mortis conturbat me.

He has Blind Hary, et Sandy Traill
Slaine with his schour of mortall haill,
Quhilk Patrik Iohnestoun mycht nought fle ;
    Timor Mortis conturbat me.

He hes reft Merseir his endite [2],
That did in luf so lifly [3] write,
So schort, so quyk, of sentence hie ;
    Timor Mortis conturbat me.

He hes tane Roull of Aberdene,
And gentill Roull of Corstorphine ;
Two bettir fallowis did no man se ;
    Timor Mortis conturbat me.

In Dumfermelyne he has done rovne
With Maister Robert Henrisoun ;
Schir Iohne the Ros enbrast [4] hes he ;
    Timor Mortis conturbat me.

And he has now tane, last of aw,
Gud gentill Stobo et Quintyne Schaw,
Of quham all wichtis hes pete [5] :
    Timor Mortis conturbat me.

[1] adventures.   [2] writings.   [3] in so lively a style.   [4] embraced.
[5] men have pity.

Gud Maister Walter Kennedy,
In poynt of dede lyis veraly,
Gret reuth it wer that so suld be ;
    Timor Mortis conturbat me.

Sen he has all my brether tane,
He will naught lat me lif alane,
On forse I man[1] his nyxt pray be ;
    Timor Mortis conturbat me.

Sen for the deid remeid is non,
Best is that we for dede dispone[2]
Eftir our deid that lif may we ;
    Timor Mortis conturbat me.

24   *The Thistle and the Rose*[3]

QUHEN Merche wes with variand windis past
    And Appryll had, with hir siluer schouris,
    Tane leif at nature with ane orient blast ;
And lusty May, that mvddir is of flouris,
Had maid the birdis to begyn thair houris[4]
Amang the tendir odouris reid and quhyt,
Quhois armony to heir it wes delyt ;

In bed at morrow, sleiping as I lay,
Me thocht Aurora, with hir cristall ene,
In at the window lukit by the day,
And halsit[5] me, with visage paill and grene ;
On quhois hand a lark sang fro the splene[6],
Awalk, luvaris, out of your slomering,
Se how the lusty morrow dois vp spring.

---

[1] of force I must.   [2] so act.
[3] written to celebrate the marriage of James IV. of Scotland
with Margaret, daughter of Henry VII. of England.
[4] matins.   [5] saluted.   [6] from its heart.

Me thocht fresche May befoir my bed vpstude,
In weid depaynt [1] of mony diuerss hew,
Sobir, benyng, and full of mansuetude [2],
In brycht atteir of flouris forgit new,
Hevinly of color, quhyt, reid, broun and blew,
Balmit [3] in dew, and gilt with Phebus bemys,
Quhill all the houss illumynit of hir lemys [4].

" Slugird," scho said, "awalk annone for schame,
And in my honour sum thing thow go wryt ;
The lork hes done the mirry day proclame [5],
To raiss vp luvaris with confort and delyt,
Yit nocht incressis thy curage to indyt,
Quhois hairt sum tyme hes glaid and blisfull bene,
Sangis to mak vndir the levis grene."

" Quhairto," quod I, sall I vpryss at morrow,
For in this May few birdis herd I sing ?
Thai haif moir causs to weip and plane thair sorrow
Thy air it is nocht holsum nor benyng ;
Lord Eolus dois in thy sessone ring [6] ;
So busteous [7] ar the blastis of his horne,
Amang thy bewis to walk I haif forborne."

With that this lady sobirly did smyll,
And said, " Vpryss, and do thy observance ;
Thou did promyt [8], in Mayis lusty quhyle,
For to discryve the Ross of most plesance.
Go se the birdis how thay sing and dance,
Illumynit our [9] with orient skyis brycht,
Annamyllit richely with new asur lycht."

[1] robe coloured.   [2] meekness.   [3] embalmed.   [4] shining.   [5] The
lark has proclaimed cheerful day.   [6] reign.   [7] boisterous.
[8] promise.   [9] over.

Quhen this wes said, depairtit scho, this quene,
And enterit in a lusty gairding gent [1];
And than, me thocht, full hestely besene [2],
In serk and mantill efter hir I went
In to this garth, most dulce and redolent
Off herb and flour, and tendir plantis sueit,
And grene levis doing of dew doun fleit [3].

The purpour sone, with tendir bemys reid,
In orient bricht as angell did appeir,
Throw goldin skyis putting vp his heid,
Quhois gilt tressis schone so wondir cleir,
That all the world tuke confort, fer and neir,
To luke vpone his fresche and blisfull face,
Doing all sable fro the hevynnis chace [4].

And as the blisfull sonne of cherarchy [5]
The fowlis song throw confort of the licht ;
The birdis did with oppin vocis cry,
O, luvaris fo, away thow dully nycht,
And welcum day that confortis every wicht ;
Haill May, Haill Flora, haill Aurora schene,
Haill princes Natur, haill Venus luvis quene.

Dame Nature gaif ane inhibitioun thair
To ferss Neptunus, and Eolus the bawld,
Nocht to perturb the wattir nor the air,
And that no schouris, nor blastis cawld,
Effray suld flouris nor fowlis on the fold [6];
Scho bad eik Juno, goddes of the sky,
That scho the hevin suld keip amene and dry.

---

[1] fair and pleasant garden.   [2] equipped.   [3] dropping dew.
[4] chasing all sable.   [5] sound of the heavenly host.   [6] ground.

Scho ordand eik that every bird and beist,
Befoir hir hienes suld annone compeir [1],
And every flour of vertew, most and leist,
And every herb be feild fer and neir,
As thay had wont in May, fro yeir to yeir,
To hir thair makar to mak obediens,
Full law inclynnand with all dew reuerens.

With that annone scho send the swyft Ro
To bring in beistis of all conditioun ;
The restles Suallow commandit scho also
To feche all fowll of small and greit renown ;
And to gar flouris compeir of all fassoun,
Full craftely conjurit scho the Yarrow [2],
Quhilk did furth swirk [3] als swift as ony arrow.

All present wer in twynkling of ane e,
Baith beist, and bird and flour, befoir the quene,
And first the Lyone, gretast of degre,
Was callit thair, and he, most fair to sene,
With a full hardy contenance and kene,
Befoir dame Natur come, and did inclyne,
With visage bawld, and curage leonyne.

This awfull beist full terrible wes of cheir [4],
Persing of luke, and stout of countenance,
Rycht strong of corpis, of fassoun fair, but feir [5],
Lusty of schaip, lycht of deliuerance [6],
Reid of his cullour, as is the ruby glance ;
On feild of gold he stude full mychtely,
With flour delycis sirculit [7] lustely.

---

[1] make its appearance.   [2] herb milfoil, reputed a witches' steed.
[3] dart.   [4] aspect.   [5] without mate.   [6] movement.   [7] encircled by
fleurs-de-lys.   The passage presents a picture of the royal arms of
Scotland.

This lady liftit vp his cluvis¹ cleir,
And leit him listly² lene vpon hir kne,
And crownit him with dyademe full deir,
Off radyous stonis, most ryall for to se ;
Saying, "The King of Beistis mak I the,
And the cheif protector in woddis and schawis³ ;
Onto thi leigis go furth, and keip the lawis.

Exerce justice with mercy and conscience,
And lat no small beist suffir skaith, na skornis
Of greit beistis that bene of moir piscence⁴ ;
Do law elyk⁵ to aipis and vnicornis,
And lat no bowgle⁶, with his busteous hornis,
The meik pluch ox⁷ oppress, for all his pryd,
Bot in the yok go peciable him besyd."

Quhen this was said, with noyis and soun of joy,
All kynd of beistis in to thair degre,
At onis cryit lawd, "Viue le Roy !"
And till his feit fell with humilite,
And all thay maid him homege and fewte⁸ ;
And he did thame ressaif with princely laitis⁹,
Quhois noble yre is proceir prostratis¹⁰.

Syne crownit scho the Egle King of Fowlis,
And as steill dertis scherpit scho his pennis¹¹,
And bawd him be als just to awppis¹² and owlis,
As vnto pacokkis, papingais¹³, or crennis,
And mak a law for wycht fowlis and for wrennis ;
And lat no fowll of ravyne do efferay¹⁴,
Nor devoir birdis bot his awin pray.

---

¹ claws.   ² as he chose.   ³ thickets.   ⁴ puissance.   ⁵ alike.
⁶ wild bull.   ⁷ plough ox.   ⁸ fealty.   ⁹ manners.   ¹⁰ whose anger
is noble and spares the prostrate.   ¹¹ quills.   ¹² whaups, *i.e.*, cur-
lews.   ¹³ the parrot kind.   ¹⁴ no bird of prey affray.

Than callit scho all flouris that grew on feild,
Discirnyng all thair fassionis and effeiris [1] ;
Vpone the awfull Thrissill scho beheld,
And saw him kepit with a busche of speiris ;
Concedring him so able for the weiris,
A radius [2] croun of rubeis scho him gaif,
And said, " In feild go furth, and fend the laif [3] ;

And, sen thow art a king, thow be discreit ;
Herb without vertew thow hald nocht of sic pryce
As herb of vertew and of odor sueit ;
And lat no nettill vyle, and full of vyce,
Hir fallow [4] to the gudly flour delyce ;
Nor latt no wyld weid, full of churlicheness,
Compair hir till the lilleis nobilness.

Nor hald non vdir flour in sic denty [5]
As the fresche Ross, of cullour reid and quhyt [6] ;
For gife [7] thow dois, hurt is thyne honesty,
Conciddering that no flour is so perfyt,
So full of vertew, plesans and delyt,
So full of blisfull angeilik bewty,
Imperiall birth, honour and dignite."

Than to the Ross scho turnyt hir visage,
And said, "O lusty dochtir most benyng,
Aboif the lilly, illustare of lynnage,
Fro the stok ryell rysing fresche and ying,
But ony spot or macull doing spring [8] ;
Cum blowme of joy with jemis to be cround,
For our the laif [9] thy bewty is renownd."

[1] makes and properties.   [2] radiant.   [3] protect others.   [4] liken
herself.   [5] regard.
[6] An allusion to the union of the Houses of York and Lancaster
in the persons of Henry VII. and his Queen.
[7] if.   [8] springing without spot or stain.   [9] above others.

A coistly croun, with clarefeid[1] stonis brycht,
This cumly quene did on hir heid incloiss,
Quhill all the land illumynit[2] of the licht ;
Quhairfoir me thocht all flouris did reioss,
Crying attonis[3], " Haill, be thow richest Ross !
Haill, hairbis empryce[4], haill, freschest quene of
    flouris,
To the be glory and honour at all houris."

Thane all the birdis song with voce on hicht,
Quhois mirthfull soun wes mervelus to heir ;
The mavyss[5] song, Haill, Roiss most riche and richt,
That dois vp flureiss vndir Phebus speir[6] ;
Haill, plant of yowth, haill, princes dochtir deir,
Haill, blosome breking out of the blud royall,
Quhois pretius vertew is imperiall."

The merle scho sang, " Haill, Roiss of most delyt,
Haill, of all flouris quene and souerane ; "
The lark scho song, " Haill, Roiss, both reid and
    quhyt,
Most plesand flour, of michty cullouris twane ; "
The nychtingaill song, " Haill, naturis suffragene[7],
In bewty, nurtour and every nobilness,
In riche array, renown and gentilness."

The common voce vpraiss of birdis small,
Apone this wyss, " O blissit be the hour
That thow wes chosin to be our principall ;
Welcome to be our princes of honour,
Our perle, our plesans[8] and our paramour,
Our peax[9], our play, our plane felicite,
Chryst the conserf frome all aduersite."

<hr>

[1] polished.   [2] shone brightly.   [3] together.   [4] empress of herbs.
[5] thrush.   [6] sphere.   [7] suffragan.   [8] delight.   [9] peace.

Than all the birdis song with sic a schout,
That I annone awoilk quhair that I lay,
And with a braid¹ I turnyt me about
To se this court ; bot all wer went away :
Than vp I lenyt, halflingis in affrey²,
And thuss I wret, as ye haif hard to forrow³,
Off lusty May vpone the nynt morrow.

25   *The Goldyn Targe*

RYGHT as the stern of day begouth to schyne,
   Quhen gone to bed war Vesper and Lucyne⁴,
      I raise, and by a rosere⁵ did me rest ;
Wp sprang the goldyn candill matutyne,
With clere depurit⁶ bemes cristallyne,
   Glading the mery foulis in thair nest ;
   Or Phebus was in purpur cape revest
Wp raise the lark, the hevyns menstrale fyne
   In May, in till a morow myrthfullest.

Full angellike thir birdis sang thair houris⁷
Within thair courtyns grene, in to thair bouris,
   Apparalit quhite and red, wyth blomes suete ;
Anamalit was the felde wyth all colouris,
The perly droppis schake in silvir schouris,
   Quhill all in balme did branch and levis flete⁸ ;
   To part fra Phebus, did Aurora grete⁹,
Hir cristall teris I saw hyng on the flouris,
   Quhilk he for lufe all drank vp with his hete.

---

¹ start.   ² half afraid.   ³ heretofore.   ⁴ the moon.   ⁵ rosegarden.   ⁶ purged.   ⁷ matins.   ⁸ float.   ⁹ weep.

For mirth of May, wyth skippis and wyth hoppis,
The birdis sang vpon the tender croppis [1],
   With curiouse note, as Venus chapell clerkis :
The rosis yong, new spreding of thair knoppis [2],
War powderit brycht with hevinly beriall [3] droppis,
   Throu bemes rede, birnyng as ruby sperkis ;
   The skyes rang for schoutyng of the larkis,
The purpur hevyn our scailit [4] in silvir sloppis [5]
   Ourgilt the treis, branchis, lefis and barkis.

Doun throu the ryce [6] a ryuir ran wyth stremys,
So lustily agayn thai lykand lemys [7],
   That all the lake as lamp did leme of licht,
Quhilk schadovit all about wyth twynkling glemis [8] ;
That bewis [9] bathit war in secund bemys
   Throu the reflex of Phebus visage brycht ;
   On every side the hegies raise on hicht,
The bank was grene, the bruke vas full of bremys [10],
   The stanneris [11] clere as stern in frosty nycht.

The cristall air, the sapher firmament,
The ruby skyes of the orient,
   Kest beriall bemes on emerant bewis grene ;
The Rosy garth depaynt [12] and redolent,
With purpur, asure, gold, and goulis gent [13]
   Arayed was, by dame Fflora the quene,
   So nobily, that ioy was for to sene [14] ;
The roch agayn the rywir resplendent
   As low illumynit all the leues schene [15].

---

[1] shoots. [2] buds. [3] beryl. [4] overspread. [5] patches. [6] undergrowth. [7] towards those pleasant beams. [8] reflected twinkling gleams on all around. [9] in such manner that boughs. [10] bream. [11] pebbles. [12] coloured. [13] pleasing red. [14] it was pleasure to behold. [15] the rock resplendent over against the river lit up the shining leaves like a flame.

Quhat throu the mery foulys armony,
And throu the ryueris sounn rycht ran me by,
  On Fflorais mantill I slepit as I lay,
Quhare șone in to my dremes fantasy
I saw approach agayn the orient sky,
  A saill, als quhite as blossum vpon spray,
  Wyth merse [1] of gold, brycht as the stern of day ;
Quhilk tendit to the land full lustily,
  As falcounn swift desyrouse of hir pray.

And hard on burd [2] vnto the blomyt medis,
Amang the grene rispis [3] and the redis,
  Arrivit sche, quhar fro anonn thare landis
Ane hundreth ladyes, lusty in to wedis,
Als fresch as flouris that in May vp spredis,
  In kirtillis grene, withoutyn kell or bandis [4] :
  Thair brycht hairis hang gletering on the strandis
In tressis clere, wyppit [5] with goldyn thredis,
  With pappis quhite, and mydlis small as wandis.

Discriue I wald, bot quho coud wele endyte
How all the feldis wyth thai lilies quhite
  Depaynt war brycht, quhilk to the hevyn did glete [6] :
Noucht thou, Homer, als fair as thou coud wryte,
For all thine ornate stilis so perfyte ;
  Nor yit thou, Tullius, quhois lippis suete
  Off rethorike did in to termes flete :
Your aureate tongis both bene all to lyte [7],
  For to compile that paradise complete.

---

[1] the round top of a ship's mast. [2] close inshore. [3] grasses.
[4] cap or neckerchief. [5] confined. [6] gleam. [7] little, weak.

Thare saw I Nature, and als [1] dame Venus quene,
The fresch Aurora, and lady Flora schene,
  Iuno, Appollo, and Proserpyna,
Dyane the goddesse chaste of woddis grene,
My lady Cleo, that help of Makaris [2] bene,
  Thetes, Pallas, and prudent Minerua,
  Fair feynit [3] Fortune, and lemand [4] Lucina,
Thir mychti quenis in crounis mycht be sene,
  Wyth bemys blith, bricht as Lucifera.

There saw I May, of myrthfull monethis quene,
Betuix Aprile, and June, and sister schene,
  Within the gardyng walking vp and doun,
Quham of the foulis gladdith al bedene [5] ;
Scho was full tender in hir yeris grene.
  Thare saw I Nature present hir a gounn
  Rich to behald, and nobil of renounn,
Off ewiry hew under the hevin that bene
  Depaynt, and broud [6] be gude proporcioun.

Full lustily thir ladyes all in fere [7]
Enterit within this park of most plesere,
  Quhare that I lay our helit with leuis ronk [8] ;
The mery foulis, blisfullest of chere,
Salust [9] Nature, me thoucht, on thair manere,
  And ewiry blome on branch, and eke on bonk [10],
  Opnyt and spred thair balmy leuis donk [11],
Full low enclynyng to thair Quene so clere,
  Quham of thair nobill norising thay thonk.

---

  [1] also. [2] poets. [3] falsely fair. [4] shining. [5] instantly rejoice.
[6] embroidered.   [7] company.   [8] covered with decaying leaves.
[9] saluted. [10] bank. [11] moist.

Syne to dame Flora, on the samyn wyse,
Thay saluse, and thay thank a thousand syse [1] ;
  And to dame Wenus, lufis mychti quene,
They sang ballettis in lufe, as was the gyse [2],
With amourouse notis lusty to devise [3],
  As thay that had lufe in thair hertis grene ;
  Thair hony throtis, opnyt fro the splene,
With werblis suete did perse the hevinly skyes,
  Quhill loud resownyt the firmament serene.

Ane othir court thare saw I consequent,
Cupide the king, wyth bow in hand ybent,
  And dredefull arowis grundyn scharp and square :
Thare saw I Mars, the god armypotent,
Aufull and sterne, strong and corpolent ;
  Thare saw I crabbit Saturn ald and haire [4],
  His luke was lyke for to perturb the aire ;
Thare was Mercurius, wise and eloquent,
  Of rethorike that fand the flouris faire ;

Thare was the god of gardingis, Priapus ;
Thare was the god of wildernes, Phanus ;
  And Ianus, god of entree delytable ;
Thare was the god of fludis, Neptunus ;
Thare was the god of wyndis, Eolus,
  With variand luke, rycht lyke a lord vnstable ;
  Thare was Bacus the gladder of the table ;
Thare was Pluto, the elrich [5] incubus,
  In cloke of grene, his court usit no sable.

---

[1] times.   [2] way.   [3] pleasing to utter.   [4] hoary.   [5] fearsome.

And ewiry one of thir, in grene arayit,
On harp or lute full merily thai playit,
    And sang ballettis with michty notis clere :
Ladyes to dance full sobirly assayit,
Endlang [1] the lusty rywir so thai mayit :
    Thair obseruance rycht hevynly was to here ;
    Than crap I throu the leuis, and drew nere,
Quhare that I was richt sudaynly affrayit,
    All throu a luke, quhilk I haue boucht full dere.

And schortly for to speke, be lufis quene
I was aspyit, scho bad hir archearis kene
    Go me arrest ; and thay no time delayit ;
Than ladyes fair lete fall thair mantillis grene,
With bowis big in tressit hairis schene,
    All sudaynly thay had a fielde arayit ;
    And yit rycht gretly was I noucht affrayit,
The party was so pleasand for to sene,
    A wonder lusty bikkir [2] me assayit.

And first of all, with bow in hand ybent,
Come dame Beautee, rycht as scho wald me schent [3] ;
    Syne followit all hir dameselis yfere [4],
With mony diuerse aufull instrument,
Wnto the pres, Fair Having [5] wyth hir went,
    Fyne Portature [6], Pleasnce [7], and lusty Chere [8].
    Than come Resoun, with schelde of gold so clere,
In plate and maille, as Mars armypotent,
    Defendit me that nobil cheuallere.

----

[1] along.   [2] a strangely pleasing contest.   [3] destroy.   [4] together.
[5] good manners.   [6] noble bearing.   [7] amiability.   [8] good countenance.

Syne tender Youth come wyth hir virgyns ying[1],
Grene Innocence, and schamefull [2] Abaising,
   And quaking Drede, wyth humble Obedience ;
The Goldyn Targe [3] harmyt thay no thing ;
Curage in thame was noucht begonne to spring ;
   Full sore thay dred to done a violence :
   Suete Womanhede I saw cum in presence,
Of artilye [4] a warld sche did in bring,
   Seruit wyth ladyes full of reuerence.

Scho led wyth hir Nurture and Lawlynes,
Contenance, Pacience, Gude Fame and Stedfastnes,
   Discretioun, Gentrise, and Considerance [5],
Leuefull [6] Company, and Honest Besynes,
Benigne Luke, Mylde Chere, and Sobirnes :
   All thir bure ganyeis [7] to do me greuance ;
   But Resonn bure the Targe wyth sik constance,
Thair scharp assayes mycht do no dures [8]
   To me, for all their aufull ordynance.

Wnto the pres persewit Hie Degree,
Hir Folowit ay Estate and Dignitee,
   Comparisoun [9], Honour, and Noble Array,
Will, Wantonnes, Renoun, and Libertee,
Richesse, Fredomm, and eke Nobilitee :
   Wit ye thay did thair baner hye display ;
   A cloud of arowis as hayle schour lousit thay,
And schot, quhill wastit was thair artilye,
   Syne went abak reboytit [10] of thair pray.

   [1] young.   [2] modest.   [3] shield, defence.   [4] artillery.   [5] gentility
and consideration.   [6] friendly.   [7] weapons.   [8] injury.   [9] supe-
riority.   [10] repulsed.

Quhen Venus had persauit this rebute,
Dissymilance [1] scho bad go mak persute,
  At all powere to perse the Goldyn Targe ;
And scho that was of doubilnes the rute,
Askit hir choise of archeris in refute [2].
  Wenus the best bad hir go wale [3] at large ;
  Scho tuke Presence plicht ankers [4] of the barge,
And Fair Callyng [5] that wele a flayn [6] coud schute,
  And Cherising for to complete hir charge.

Dame Hamelynes [7] scho tuke in company,
That hardy was, and hende [8] in archery,
  And broucht dame Beautee to the felde agayn ;
With all the choise of Venus cheualry
Thay come, and bikkerit vnabaisitly [9] ;
  The schour of arowis rappit on as rayne ;
  Perilouse Presence, that mony syre has slayne,
The bataill broucht on bordour hard vs by,
  The salt was all the sarar suth to sayn [10].

Thik was the schote of grundyn dartis kene ;
Bot Resoun with the Scheld of Gold so schene,
  Warly [11] defendit quho so ewir assayit ;
The aufull stoure he manly did sustene,
Quhill Presence kest a pulder [12] in his ene,
  And than as drunkyn man he all forvayit : [13]
Quhen he was blynd the fule wyth hym thay
  playit.
And banyst hym amang the bewis grene ;
  That sory sicht me sudaynly affrayit.

[1] dissembling. [2] in aid. [3] choose. [4] sheet anchor. [5] fair speech. [6] arrow. [7] intimacy. [8] skilled. [9] undaunted attack. [10] the assault was all the sorer truth to tell. [11] in war-like sort. [12] powder. [13] went astray.

Than was I woundit to the deth wele nere,
And yoldyn [1] as a wofull prisonnere
  To lady Beautee, in a moment space ;
Me thoucht scho semyt lustiar of chere [2],
Efter that Resoun tynt [3] had his eyne clere,
  Than of before, and lufliare of face :
  Quhy was thou blyndit, Resoun ? quhi, allace !
And gert [4] ane hell my paradise appere,
  And mercy seme, quhare that I fand no grace.

Dissymulance was besy me to sile [5],
And Fair Calling did oft apon me smyle,
  And Cherising me fed wyth wordis fair ;
New Acquyntance enbracit me a quhile,
And fauouryt me, quhill men mycht go a myle,
  Syne tuk hir leve, I saw hir nevir mare :
  Than saw I Dangere toward me repair,
I could eschew hir presence be no wyle,
  On syde scho lukit wyth ane fremyt fare [6].

And at the last departing coud hir dresse [7],
And me delyuerit vnto Hevynesse
  For to remayne, and scho in cure [8] me tuke ;
Be this the Lord of Wyndis, wyth wodenes [9],
God Eolus, his bugill blew I gesse ;
  That with the blast the leuis all to-schuke,
  And sudaynly, in the space of a luke,
All was hyne went [10], thare was bot wilderness,
  There was no more bot birdis, bank, and bruke.

---

[1] yielded.　[2] more pleasing of countenance.　[3] lost.　[4] caused.
[5] blindfold.　[6] adverse expression.　[7] began her preparations.
[8] charge.　[9] fury.　[10] gone hence.

9

In twynkling of ane eye to schip thai went,
And swyth [1] vp saile vnto the top thai stent [2],
   And with swift course atour the flude thay frak [3] ;
Thay fyrit gunnis wyth powder violent,
Till that the reke [4] raise to the firmament,
   The rochis all resownyt wyth the rak [5],
   For reird [6] it semyt that the raynbow brak ;
Wyth spirit affrayde apon my fete I sprent [7]
   Amang the clewis [8], so carefull was the crak [9].

And as I did awake of my sueving [10],
The ioyfull birdis merily did syng
   For myrth of Phebus tendir bemes schene ;
Suete war the vapouris, soft the morowing,
Halesum the vale, depaynt wyth flouris ying ;
   The air attemperit, sobir, and amene [11] ;
   In quhite and rede was all the felde besene [12],
Throu Naturis nobil fresch anamalyng,
   In mirthfull May, of ewiry moneth Quene.

O reuerend Chaucere rose of rethoris [13] all,
As in oure tong ane flour imperiall,
   That raise in Britane ewir, quho redis rycht [14],
Thou beris of makaris the tryumph riall ;
Thy fresch anamalit termes celicall [15]
   This mater coud illumynit haue full brycht ;
   Was thou noucht ot oure Inglisch all the lycht,
Surmounting ewiry tong terrestriall,
   Alls fer as Mayes morow dois mydnycht ?

---

[1] swiftly.   stretched.   [3] sped.   [4] smoke.   [5] crash.   [6] tumult.
[7] sprang.   [8] cliffs.   [9] terrifying was the sound.   [10] dreaming.
[11] pleasant.   [12] arrayed.   [13] rhetoricians.   [14] speaks aright.
[15] celestial.

O morall Gower, and Ludgate laureate,
Your sugurit lippis and tongis aureate,
  Bene to oure eris cause of grete delyte ;
Your angel mouthis most mellifluate
Our rude langage has clere illumynate,
  And faire our-gilt oure speche, that imperfyte
  Stude, or your goldyn pennis schupe [1] to wryte ;
This Ile before was bare, and desolate
  Off rethorike, or lusty fresch endyte.

Thou lytill Quair, be ewir obedient,
Humble, subiect, and symple of entent,
  Before the face of ewiry connyng wicht :
I knaw quhat thou of rethorike hes spent ;
Off all hir lusty rosis redolent
  Is nonn in to thy gerland sett on hicht [2] ;
  Eschame [3] thar of, and draw the out of sicht.
Rude is thy wede, disteynit, bare, and rent,
  Wele aucht thou be afiret of [4] the licht.

[1] got ready.   [2] on high.   [3] be ashamed.   [4] well may you shun.

GAVIN DOUGLAS

1475 (?)–1522

26 *The Proloug of the Sevynt Buik of Eneados* [1]

A DESCRIPTION OF WINTER

AS brycht Phebus, schene [2] souerane, hevynnis E,
 The opposit held of his chymmis [3] hie,
Cleir schynand bemys, and goldin symmeris hew,
In lattoun [4] colour altering haill of new [5];
Kithing no syng of heyt [6] be his visage,
So neir approchit he his wynter staige;
Redy he was to entir the thrid morne
In cloudy skyis vndir Capricorne.
All thocht [7] he be the hart and lamp of hevin,
Forfeblit wolx his lemand giltly lewyne [8],
Throw the declyning of his large round speir.
The frosty regioun ringis [9] of the yeir,
The tyme and sessoune bitter cald and paill,
Thai schort days that clerkis clepe brumaill [10];
Quhen brym [11] blastis of the northyne art [12]
Ourquhelmit had Neptunus in his cart,
And all to schaik the levis of the treis,
The rageand storm outwalterand wally seis [13];

---

[1] That is, to the Seventh Book of the author's translation of the Aeneid.
[2] shining.   [3] mansions.   [4] a mixed metal.   [5] entirely different.
[6] showing no sign of heat.   [7] although.   [8] enfeebled grew his flaming gilded lightning.   [9] reigns.   [10] name brumal, *i.e.*, wintry, Lat. *brumalis*.   [11] fierce.   [12] direction.   [13] o'er-riding the sea-waves.

Reveris ran reid on spait[1] with watteir broune,
And burnis hurlis all thair bankis downe,
And landbrist rumland[2] rudely wyth sic beir[3],
So loud ne rummist wyld lioun or beir[4].
Fludis monstreis, sic as meirswyne or quhailis[5],
For the tempest law in the deip devallyis[6].
Mars occident[7], retrograide in his speir,
Provocand stryff, regnit as lord that yeir ;
Rany Orioune wyth his stormy face
Bewalit of the schipman by his rays ;
Frawart Saturne, chill of complexioune,
Throw quhais aspect derth and infectioune
Bene causit oft, and mortale pestilens,
Went progressiue the greis of his ascens[8] ;
And lusty Hebe, Junois douchtir gay,
Stud spulyeit[9] of hir office and array.
The soill ysowpit[10] into wattir wak,
The firmament ourkest with rokis blak[11],
The ground fadyt, and fauch wolx[12] all the feildis,
Montayne toppis sleikit wyth snaw ourheildis[13],
On raggit rolkis of hard harsk quhyne stane[14],
With frosyne frontis cauld clynty clewis schane[15] ;
Bewtie wes lost, and barrand[16] schew the landis,
With frostis haire ourfret[17] the feildis standis.
Soure bittir bubbis[18], and the schowris snell[19],
Semyt on the sward ane similitude of hell,
Reducyng to our mynd, in every steid,
Goustly schaddois of eild and grisly deid[20],
Thik drumly scuggis[21] dirknit so the hevyne.

[1] flood. [2] landslip rumbling. [3] noise. [4] that savage lion or bear bellow not so loud. [5] dolphins or whales. [6] descend. [7] declining. [8] degrees of his ascent. [9] despoiled. [10] soaked. [11] overcast with black fogs. [12] reddish grew. [13] spread smooth with snow. [14] whinstone. [15] stony cliffs shone. [16] barren. [17] embroidered with hoar-frost. [18] blasts. [19] keen. [20] old age and fearful death. [21] turbid shades.

Dym skyis oft furth warpit [1] feirfull levyne,
Flaggis [2] of fyir, and mony felloun flawe [3],
Scharp soppis [4] of sleit, and of the snypand [5] snawe.
The dowy [6] dichis war all donk and wait,
The law vaille flodderit all wyth spait,
The plane stretis [7] and every hie way
Full of fluschis, doubbis [8], myre and clay.
Laggerit leys wallowit farnys schewe [9],
Broune muris kithit thair wysnit [10] mossy hewe,
Bank, bra, and boddum [11] blanschit wolx and bair ;
For gurll weddir growyt bestis [12] haire ;
The wynd maid wayfe [13] the reid weyd on the dyk,
Bedovin in donkis [14] deyp was every syk [15] ;
Our [16] craggis, and the front of rochis seyre [17],
Hang gret isch-schoklis lang as ony spere ;
The grund stude barrand, widderit, dosk and gray,
Herbis, flouris, and gersis wallowit [18] away ;
Woddis, forestis, wyth nakyt bewis blout [19],
Stud strypyt of thair weyd in every hout [20].
So bustuysly [21] Boreas his bugill blew,
The deyr full dern [22] dovne in the dalis drew ;
Smal byrdis, flokand throw thik ronnis [23] thrang,
In chyrmyng and with cheping [24] changit thair sang,
Sekand hidlis and hirnys [25] thaim to hyde
Fra feirfull thudis of the tempestuus tyde.
The wattir lynnis routtis [26], and every lynde [27]
Quhyslyt and brayt of the swouchand [28] wynde.
Puire laboraris and byssy husband men

---

[1] discharged.   [2] flashes.   [3] blast.   [4] showers.   [5] nipping.
[6] dreary.   [7] level streets.   [8] overflows, pools.   [9] miry leas displayed withered ferns.   [10] brown moors revealed their faded.
[11] slope and bottom.   [12] stormy weather made the hair of animals to grow.   [13] waved.   [14] stained with damp.   [15] channel.   [16] over.
[17] many.   [18] grasses faded.   [19] bare.   [20] wood.   [21] rudely.
[22] secretly.   [23] brambles.   [24] twittering and chirping.   [25] hiding-places and corners.   [26] waterfalls roar.   [27] lime-tree.   [28] sighing.

Went wayt[1] and wery draglyt in the fen ;
The silly scheip and thair lytill hyrd gromis
Lurkis vndir le of bankis, wodys, and bromys ;
And wthir dantit gretar bestial,
Within thair stabillis sesyt[2] into stall,
Sic as mulis, horsis, oxin and ky,
Fed tuskit baris, and fat swyne in sty,
Sustenit war by mannis gouernance
On hervist and on symmeris purviance.
Widequhair[3] with fors so Eolus schouttis schyll[4]
In this congelyt sessioune scharp and chyll,
The callour[5] air, penetrative and puire,
Dasyng[6] the bluide in every creature,
Maid seik warm stovis, and beyne[7] fyris hoyt,
In double garmont cled and wyly coyt[8],
Wyth mychty drink, and meytis confortive,
Agayne the storme wyntre for to strive.
  Repaterit weill[9], and by the chymnay beykyt[10],
At evin be tyme dovne a bed I me streikit[11],
Warpit[12] my heid, kest on claythis thrinfauld,
For till expell the perrellus peirsand cauld.
I crocit me, syne bownit[13] for to sleip,
Quhair, lemand throw the glas, I did tak keip[14]
Latonia, the lang irksum nycht,
Hir subtell blenkis sched and wattry lycht,
Full hie wp quhyrlyt in hir regioune,
Till Phebus rycht in oppositioune,
Into the Crab hir propir mansioune draw,
Haldand the hycht allthocht the son went law.
Hornit Hebawde, quhilk clepe we the nycht owle,
Within hir caverne hard I schout and yowle ;

---

[1] wet.   [2] secured.   [3] wheresoever.   [4] shrill   [5] fresh.
[6] dulling.   [7] comfortable.   [8] underjacket.   [9] well fed.
[10] warmed.   [11] stretched.   [12] wrapped.   [13] then prepared.
[14] observe.

Laithlie of forme, wyth crukit camschow [1] beik,
Vgsum [2] to heir was hir wyld elriche [3] screik:
The wyld geis claking eik by nychtis tyde
Attoure [4] the citie fleand hard I glyde.

On slummyr I slaid full sad, and slepit sownd
Quhill the oriyont wpwart gan rebound.
Phebus crownit byrd, the nychtis orloger [5],
Clappand his wyngis thryse had crawin cleir.
Approching neir the greiking [6] of the day,
Wythin my bed I waikynnit quhair I lay,
So fast declinis Synthea the mone,
And kais keklis [7] on the ruiff abone.
Palamedes byrdis [8] crouping [9] in the sky,
Fleand on randoune [10] schapin lik ane Y,
And as ane trumpat rang thair vocis soun,
Quhais cryis bene pronosticatioun
Off wyndy blastis and ventositeis.
Fast by my chalmir, in heych wysnit [11] treis,
The soir gled [12] quhislis loud wyth mony ane pew,
Quhairby the day was dawin weil I knew;
Bid beit [13] the fyire, and the candill alycht,
Syne blissit me, and, in my wedis dycht
Ane schot wyndo vnschet a lytill on char [14],
Persawit the mornying bla [15], wan, and har [16],
Wyth cloudy gum and rak [17] ourquhelmyt the air,
The soulye stythlie hasart, rowch and hair [18],
Branchis brattlyng [19], and blayknit schew the brays [20],
With hyrstis harsk [21] of waggand wyndilstrays;
The dew droppis congelyt on stibyll and rynd [22],

---

[1] distorted. [2] fearful. [3] eerie. [4] above. [5] clock. [6] lightening.
[7] jackdaws cackle. [8] wild geese. [9] crying. [10] on their course.
[11] leafless. [12] kestrel. [13] mend. [14] set a projecting window
a little ajar. [15] livid. [16] grey. [17] mist and fog. [18] the ground
hard frozen, rough and hoar. [19] clattering. [20] bleached appeared
the slopes. [21] bare places rough. [22] hide.

And scharp hailstanis, mortfundit [1] of kynd,
Hoppand on the thak and on the causay by.
The schot I clossit and drew inwart in hy [2],
Chiverand for cauld, the sessoun was so snell ;
Schup [3] wyth hait flambe to fleme [4] the fresyng fell.

And, as I bownit me [5] to the fyre me by,
Bayth wp and downe the hous I did aspy ;
And seand Virgill on ane lettrune [6] stand,
To writ anone I hynt [7] ane pen in hand,
For tyll performe the poet grave and sad,
Quham sa fer furth, or than [8], begun I had ;
And wolx ennoyit sum deyll [9] in my hart,
Thair restit vncompleittit so gret ane part.
And til myself I said : In guid effect,
Thow man [10] draw furth, the yok lyis on thi nek.
Wythin my mynd compasing thocht I so,
Na thing is dome quhill ocht remains to do.
For byssines, quhilk occurrit on cace [11],
Ourvoluit [12] I this volume lay ane space ;
And, thocht I wery was, me lyst nocht [13] tyre,
Full laith to leve our werk, swa in the myre,
Or yit to stynt [14] for byttir storme or rane :
Heyr I assayit to yok our pleuch agane :
And, as I culd, with afauld [15] diligence,
This nixt buike following of profund sentence
Has thus begoune in the chyll wyntir cauld,
Quhen frostis days ourfret bayth fyrth [16] and fauld.

[1] cold as death.   [2] haste.   [3] endeavoured.   [4] drive away.
[5] turned me.   [6] reading-desk.   [7] grasped.   [8] ere then.   [9] grew
somewhat concerned.   [10] must.   [11] by accident.   [12] laid aside.
[13] I would not.   [14] stop.   [15] single-minded.   [16] outlying field.

SIR DAVID LYNDSAY OF THE MOUNT

1490–1555

27   *Prolog to The Dreme*

IN-TO the Calendis of Januarie,
    Quhen fresche Phebus, he movyng circulair,
Frome Capricorne was enterit in Aquarie,
    With blastis that the branchis maid full bair,
    The snaw and sleit perturbit all the air,
And flemit [1] Flora frome every bank and bus,
Throuch supporte of the austeir Eolus.

Efter that I the lang wynteris nycht
    Had lyne walking [2] in-to my bed, allone,
Throuch hevy thocht, that no way sleip I mycht,
    Rememberyng of divers thyngis gone :
    So up I rose, and clethit me anone.
Be this, fair Tytane, with his lemis [3] lycht,
Ouer all the land had spred his baner brycht.

With cloak and hude I dressit me belyve [4],
    With dowbyll schone, and myttanis on my handis ;
Howbeit the air was rycht penetratyve,
    Yit fure I furth, lansing ouirthorte [5] the landis
    Toward the see, to schorte [6] me on the sandis,
Because unblomit was baith bank and braye [7],
And so, as I was passing be the waye,

---

[1] banished.   [2] lain waking.   [3] beams.   [4] quickly.   [5] Yet fared
I forth, speeding athwart.   [6] divert.   [7] hillside.

I met dame Flora, in dule weid dissagysit [1],
  Quhilk in-to May wes dulce and delectabyll ;
With stalwart [2] stormis hir sweitnes wes supprisit [3] ;
  Hir hevynlie hewis war turnit in-to sabyll,
  Quhilkis umquhile [4] war to luffaris amiabyll.
Fled frome the froste, the tender flouris I saw
Under dame Naturis mantyll lurking law.

The small fowl in flokkis saw I flee,
  To Nature makand greit lamentatioun.
Thay lychtit doun besyde me on ane tree,
  Of thair complaynt I had compassioun ;
  And with ane pieteous exclamatioun
Thay said, " Blyssit be Somer, with his flouris ;
And waryit [5] be thow, Wynter, with thy schouris ! "

" Allace ! Aurora," the syllie [6] Larke can crye,
  " Quhare hes thou left thy balmy liquour sweit
That us rejosit, we mounting in the skye ?
  Thy sylver droppis ar turnit in-to sleit.
  O fair Phebus ! quhare is thy hoilsum heit ?
Quhy tholis [7] thow thy hevinlie plesand face
With mystie vapouris to be obscurit, allace !

" Quhar art thow May, with June thy syster schene [8],
  Weill bordourit with dasyis of delyte ?
And gentyll Julie, with thy mantyll grene,
  Enamilit with rosis red and quhyte ?
  Now auld and cauld Januar, in dispyte,
Reiffis [9] frome us all pastyme and plesour.
Allace ! quhat gentyll hart may this indure ?

   [1] disguised in sad attire.   [2] violent.   [3] oppressed.   [4] formerly.
[5] cursed.   [6] frail.   [7] sufferest.   [8] fair.   [9] robs.

" Ouersylit [1] ar with cloudis odious
　The goldin skyis of the Orient,
Changeyng in sorrow our sang melodious,
　Quhilk we had wount to sing with gude intent,
　Resoundand to the hevinnis firmament :
Bot now our daye is changeit in-to nycht."
With that thay rais, and flew furth of my sycht.

Pensyve in hart, passing full soberlie
　Unto the see, fordward I fure anone.
The see was furth, the sand wes smooth and drye ;
　Then up and doun I musit myne allone [2],
　Till that I spyit ane lyttill cave of stone
Heych [3] in ane craig : upwart I did approche
But tarying [4], and clam up in the roche :

And purposit, for passing of the tyme,
　Me to defend from ociositie [5],
With pen and paper to register in ryme
　Sum mery mater of antiquitie ;
　Bot Idelnes, ground of iniquitie,
Scho maid so dull my spreitis, me within,
That I wyste nocht at quhat end to begin,

But satt styll in that cove, quhare I mycht see
　The wolteryng of the wallis [6], up and doun,
And this fals warldis instabilytie
　Unto that see makkand comparisoun,
　And of this warldis wracheit variatioun
To thame that fixis all thair hole intent,
Consideryng quho most had suld most repent.

---

[1] obscured.　[2] by myself.　[3] high.　[4] without delay.　[5] idleness.
[6] waves.

So, with my hude my hede I happit warme,
 And in my cloke I fauldit boith my feit ;
I thocht my corps with cauld suld tak no harme,
 My mittanis held my handis weill in heit ;
 The skowland [1] craig me coverit frome the sleit.
Thare styll I satt, my bonis for to rest,
Tyll Morpheus with sleip my spreit opprest.

So, throw the bousteous [2] blastis of Eolus,
 And throw my walkyng on the nycht before,
And throw the seyis movyng marvellous,
 Be Neptunus, with mony route [3] and rore,
 Constrainit I was to sleip, withouttin more :
And quhat I dremit, in conclusioun
I sall you tell, ane marvellous Visioun.

28   *Kitteis Confessioun*

            The Curate, and Kittie

THE Curate Kittie culd [4] confesse,
 And scho tald on baith mair and lesse.
 Quhen scho was telland as scho wist,
The Curate Kittie wald have kist ;
Bot yit ane countenance he bure
Degeist [5], devote, daine [6], and demure ;
And syne began hir to exempne [7].
He wes best at the efter game.
Quod he, " Have ye na wrangous geir ? "
Quod scho, " I staw [8] ane pek of beir [9]."
Quod he, " That suld restorit be,
Tharefor delyver it to me.

---

[1] scowling.   [2] boisterous.   [3] bellow.   [4] did.   [5] sedate.
[6] worthy. [7] examine. [8] stole. [9] barley.

Tibbie and Peter bad me speir [1];
Be my conscience, thay sall it heir."
Quod he, "Leve ye in lecherie?"
Quod scho, "Will Leno mowit [2] me."
Quod he, "His wyfe that sall I tell,
To mak hir acquentance with my-sell."
Quod he, "Ken ye na heresie?"
"I wait [3] nocht quhat that is," quod sche.
Quod he, "Hard ye na Inglis bukis?"
Quod scho, "My maister on thame lukis."
Quod he, "The bischop that sall knaw,
For I am sworne that for to schaw."
Quod he, "What said he of the King?"
Quod scho, "Of gude he spak na-thing."
Quod he, "His Grace of that sall wit [3],
And he sall lose his lyfe for it."
   Quhen scho in mynd did mair revolve,
Quod he, "I can nocht you absolve,
Bot to my chalmer cum at even
Absolvit for to be and schrevin."
Quod scho, "I wyll pas tyll ane-uther.
And I met with Schir Andro, my brother,
And he full clenely did me schryve.
Bot he wes sumthing talkatyve;
He speirit money strange case,
How that my lufe did me inbrace,
Quhat day, how oft, quhat sort, and quhare?
Quod he, 'I wald I had bene thare.'
He me absolvit for ane plak [4],
Thocht [5] he na pryce with me wald mak;
and mekil [6] Latyne he did mummill,
I hard na-thing bot hummill bummill.
He schew me nocht of Goddis word,

---

[1] enquire.   [2] jested with.   [3] know.   [4] the third of a penny.
[5] though.   [6] much.

Quhilk scharper is than ony sword,
And deip intill our hart dois prent
Our syn, quharethrow we do repent.
He pat me na-thing into feir,
Quharethrow I suld my syn forbeir;
He schew me nocht the maledictioun
Of God for syn, nor the afflictioun
And in this lyfe the greit mischeif
Ordanit to punische hure and theif;
Nor schew he me of hellis pane,
That I mycht feir, and vice refraine;
He counsalit me nocht till abstene,
And leid ane holy lyfe, and clene.
Of Christis blude na-thing he knew,
Nor of His promisses full trew,
That saifis all that wyll beleve,
That Sathan sall us never greve.
He teichit me nocht for till traist
The confort of the Haly Ghaist.
He bad me nocht to Christ be kynd [1],
To keip His law with hart and mynd,
And lufe and thank His greit mercie,
Fra syn and hell that savit me;
And lufe my nichtbour as my-sell.
Of this na-thing he culd me tell,
Bot gave me pennance, ilk ane [2] day
Ane *Ave Marie* for to say,
And Fridayis fyve na fische to eit,
(Bot butter and eggis ar better meit),
And with ane plak to buy ane messe
Fra drounkin Schir Jhone Latynelesse.
Quod he, 'Ane plak I wyll gar [3] Sandie
Give thee agane, with handie bandie."
Syne [4] into pilgrimage to pas—

[1] kindred.　[2] every.　[3] cause.　[4] afterwards.

The verray way to wantounes.
Of all his pennance I was glaid,
I had them all perqueir [1], I said.
To mow and steill I ken the pryce,
I sall it set on cincq and syce [2].
Bot he my counsale culd nocht keip ;
He maid him be the fyre to sleip,
Syne cryit, " Colleris [3], beif and coillis [4],
Hois, and schone with dowbill soillis,
Caikis and candill, creische [5] and salt,
Curnis [6] of meill, and luiffillis [7] of malt,
Wollin and linning, werp and woft—
Dame ! keip the keis of your woll loft ! "
Throw drink and sleip maid him to raif ;
And swa with us thay play the knaif."

  Freiris sweiris be thair professioun
Nane can be saif but [8] this Confessioun,
And garris all men understand
That it is Goddis awin [9] command.
Yit it is nocht but mennis drame [10].
The pepill to confound and schame.
It is nocht ellis but mennis law,
Maid mennis mindis for to knaw,
Quharethrow thay syle [11] thame as thay will,
And makis thair law conforme tharetill,
Sittand in mennis conscience
Abone Goddis magnificence ;
And dois the pepill teche and tyste [12]
To serve the Pape the Antechriste.

  To the greit God Omnipotent
Confess thy syn, and sore repent ;
And traist in Christ, as wrytis Paule,

---

[1] by heart.   [2] "five and six," terms in dice play.   [3] collars.
[4] coals.   [5] fat.   [6] grains.   [7] handfuls.   [8] without.   [9] own.
[10] dream.   [11] abuse.   [12] entice.

Quhilk sched his blude to saif thy saule ;
For nane can thee absolve bot He,
Nor tak away thy syn frome thee.

Gif of gude counsall thow hes neid,
Or hes nocht leirnit weill thy Creid,
Or wickit vicis regne in thee,
The quhilk thow can nocht mortifie,
Or be in desperatioun,
And wald have consolatioun,
Than till ane preichour trew thow pas,
And schaw thy syn and thy trespas.
Thow neidis nocht to schaw him all,
Nor tell thy syn baith greit and small,
Quhilk is unpossible to be ;
Bot schaw the vice that troubillis thee,
And he sall of thy saule have reuth,
And thee instruct in-to the treuth,
And with the Word of Veritie
Sall confort and sall counsall thee,
The sacramentis schow thee at lenth,
Thy lytle faith to stark and strenth [1],
And how thow suld thame richtlie use,
And all hypocrisie refuse.

Confessioun first wes ordanit fre
In this sort in the Kirk to be.
Swa to confes as I descryve [2].
Wes in the gude Kirk primityve ;
Swa wes confessioun ordanit first,
Thocht Codrus [3] kyte [4] suld cleve and birst.

[1] to confirm and strengthen.   [2] describe.
[3] As to this allusion commentators are at variance.   [4] belly.

29   *The Historie of ane Nobil and Valyeand Squyer William Meldrum*

HARY the Aucht, King of Ingland,
    That tyme at Caleis wes lyand [1],
With his triumphand ordinance,
Makand weir [2] on the realme of France.
The King of France his greit armie
Lay neir hand by in Picardie,
Quhair aither uther did assaill.
Howbeit thair was na sic battaill,
Bot thair wes daylie skirmishing,
Quhare men of armis brak monie sting [3].
Quhen to the Squyer Meldrum
Wer tauld thir novellis [4] all and sum,
He thocht he wald vesie [5] the weiris ;
And waillit furth [6] ane hundred speiris,
And futemen quhilk wer bauld and stout,
The maist worthie of all his rout.

Quhen he come to the King of France
He wes sone put in ordinance :
Richt so was all his companie
That on him waitit continuallie.

    Thair was into the Inglis oist [7]
Ane campioun [8] that blew greit boist.
He was ane stout man and ane strang,
Quhilk oist wald with his conduct gang
Outthrow the greit armie of France
His valiantnes for to avance ;
And Maister Talbart was his name,
Of Scottis and Frenche quhilk spak disdane,
And on his bonnet usit to beir,

---

[1] in July, 1513.   [2] making war.   [3] pikes.   [4] this news.   [5] view.
[6] made choice of.   [7] host.   [8] champion.

Of silver fine, takinnis of weir [1];
And proclamatiounis he gart mak
That he wald, for his ladies saik,
With any gentilman of France
To fecht with him with speir or lance :
Bot no Frencheman in all that land
With him durst battell hand for hand.
Than lyke ane weriour vailyeand [2]
He enterit in the Scottis band :
And quhen the Squyer Meldrum
Hard tell this campioun wes cum,
Richt haistelie he past him till,
Demanding him quhat was his will.
" Forsuith I can find none," quod he,
" On hors nor fute dar fecht with me.'
Than said he, " It wer greit schame
Without battell ye suld pass hame ;
Thairfoir to God I mak ane vow,
The morne [3] my-self sall fecht with yow
Outher on horsback or on fute.
Your crakkis I count thame not ane cute [4].
I sall be fund into the feild
Armit on hors with speir and schield."
Maister Talbart said, " My gude chyld,
It wer maist lyk that thow wer wyld.
Thow art too young, and hes no micht
To fecht with me that is so wicht [5].
To speik to me thow suld have feir,
For I have sik practik in weir
That I wald not effeirit [6] be
To mak debait aganis sic three ;
For I have stand in monie stour [7],
And ay defendit my honour.

---

[1] tokens of war. [2] a valiant warrior. [3] to-morrow. [4] your boasts I value not a straw. [5] powerful. [6] fearful. [7] fight.

Thairfoir, my barne, I counsell thee
Sic interprysis to let be."
　　Than said this Squyer to the Knicht,
" I grant ye ar baith greit and wicht.
Young David was far les than I
Quhen with Golias manfullie,
Withouttin outher speir or scheild,
He faucht, and slew him in the feild.
I traist that God sal be my gyde,
And give me grace to stanche thy pryde.
Thocht thow be greit like Gowmakmorne,[1]
Traist weill I sall yow meit the morne.
Beside Montruill[2] upon the grene
Befoir ten houris I sal be sene.
And gif ye wyn me in the feild
Baith hors and geir I sall yow yeild,
Sa that siclyke[3] ye do to me."
" That I sall do, be God ! " quod he,
" And thairto I give thee my hand."
And swa betwene thame maid ane band[4]
That thay suld meit upon the morne.
Bot Talbart maid at him bot scorne,
Lychtlyand[5] him with wordis of pryde,
Syne hamewart to his oist culd ryde,
And shew the brethren of his land
How ane young Scot had tane on hand,
To fecht with him beside Montruill ;
" Bot I traist he sall prufe the fuill."
Quod thay, " The morne that sall we ken ;
The Scottis are haldin hardie men."
Quod he, " I compt thame not ane cute.
He sall returne upon his fute,
And leif with me his armour bricht ;

---

[1] one of Ossian's heroes.　　[2] in Picardy.　[3] on such wise.
[4] bond.　[5] slighting.

For weill I wait [1] he has no micht,
On hors nor fute, to fecht with me,"
Quod thay, " The morne that sall we se."
  Quhan to Monsieour De Obenie [2]
Reportit was the veritie,
How that the Squyer had tane on hand
To fecht with Talbart hand for hand,
His greit courage he did commend,
Syne haistelie did for him send.
And quhen he come befoir the lord
The veritie he did record,
How for the honour of Scotland
That battell he had tane on hand ;
" And sen [3] it givis me in my hart,
Get I ane hors to tak my part,
My traist is sa, in Goddis grace,
To leif hym lyand in the place.
Howbeit he stalwart be and stout,
My lord, of him I have no dout."
  Than send the Lord out throw the land,
And gat ane hundreth hors fra hand :
To his presence he brocht in haist,
And bad the Squyer cheis [4] him the best.
Of that the Squyer was rejoisit,
And cheisit the best as he suppoisit,
And lap on hym delyverlie [5].
Was never hors ran mair plesantlie
With speir and sword at his command,
And was the best of all the land.
  He tuik his leif and went to rest,
Syne airlie in the morne him drest
Wantonlie in his weirlyke weid [6],
All weill enarmit, saif the heid.

[1] wot.   [2] Robert Stewart, Lord of Aubigny.   [3] since.   [4] choose
[5] nimbly.   [6] warlike garb.

He lap upon his cursour wicht,
And straucht him [1] in his stirroppis richt.
His speir and scheild and helme wes borne
With squyeris that raid him beforne.
Ane velvot cap on heid he bair,
Ane quaif of gold to heild his hair [2].

This Lord of him tuik so greit joy
That he himself wald hym convoy,
With him ane hundreth men of armes,
That thair suld no man do hym harmes.
The Squyer buir into his scheild
Ane otter in ane silver feild.
His hors was bairdit [3] full richelie,
Coverit with satyne cramesie [4].
Than fordward raid this campioun
With sound of trumpet and clarioun,
And spedilie spurrit ouir the bent [5],
Lyke Mars the God armipotent.

Thus leif we rydand our Squyar,
And speik of Maister Talbart mair :
Quhilk gat airlie in the morrow [6],
And no manner of geir to borrow,
Hors, harnes, speir, nor scheild,
Bot was ay reddie for the feild ;
And had sic practik into weir,
Of our Squyer he tuik na feir,
And said unto his companyeoun,
Or he come furth of his pavilyeoun,
" This nicht I saw into my dreame,
Quhilk to reheirs I think greit schame,
Me-thocht I saw cum fra the see
Ane greit otter rydand to me,
The quhilk was blak, with ane lang taill,

---

[1] straightened himself.   [2] coif of gold to contain his hair.
[3] caparisoned.   [4] crimson.   [5] herbage.   [6] morning.

And cruellie did me assail,
And bait [1] me till he gart [2] me bleid,
And drew me backwart fra my steid.
Quhat this suld mene I cannot say,
Bot I was never in sic ane fray [3]."
His fellow said, " Think ye not schame
For to gif credence till ane dreame ?
Ye knaw it is aganis our faith,
Thairfoir go dres yow in your graith [4],
And think weill throw your hie courage
This day ye sall wyn vassalage."

Then drest he him into his geir
Wantounlie like ane man of weir
Quhilk had baith hardines and fors,
And lichtlie lap upon his hors.
His hors was bairdit full bravelie,
And coverit was richt courtfullie
With browderit [5] wark and velvot grene.
Sanct George's croce thare micht be sene
On hors, harnes, and all his geir.
Than raid he furth withouttin weir [6],
Convoyit with his capitane
And with monie ane Inglisman
Arrayit all with armes bricht ;
Micht no man see ane fairer sicht.

Than clariounis and trumpettis blew ;
And weriouris monie hither drew.
On everie side come monie man
To behald quha the battell wan.
The feild wes in the medow grene,
Quhair everie man micht weill be sene.
The heraldis put thame sa in ordour
That no man passit within the bordour :

---

[1] beat.   [2] made.   [3] such a fright.   [4] armour.   [5] embroidered
[6] delay.

Nor preisit to come within the grene
Bot heraldis and the campiounis kene.
The ordour and the circumstance
Wer lang to put in remembrance.
Quhen thir twa nobilmen of weir
Wer weill accowterit in their geir
And in their handis strang burdounis [1],
Than trumpettis blew and clariounis,
And heraldis cryit hie on hicht,
" Now let tham go ! God shaw the richt ! "
   Than spedilie thay spurrit thair hors,
And ran to uther with sic fors
That baith thair speiris in sindrie [2] flaw.
Than said thay all that stude on raw,
Ane better cours than they twa ran
Wes not sene sen the warld began.
   Than baith the parties were rejoisit.
The campiounis ane quhyle repoisit ;
Till they had gotten speiris new.
Than with triumph the trumpettis blew,
And they with all the force thay can
Wounder [3] rudelie at aither ran,
And straik at uther with sa greit ire
That fra thair harnes flew the fyre.
Thair speiris wer sa teuch [4] and strang
That aither uther to eirth doun dang [5].
Baith hors and man, with speir and scheild,
Than flatlingis [6] lay into the feild.
Than Maister Talbart was eschamit.
" Forsuith for ever I am defamit ! "
And said this, " I had rather die
Without that I revengit be."
   Our young Squyer, sic was his hap,

---

[1] spears. [2] in pieces. [3] wondrous. [4] tough. [5] that each the other to earth down threw. [6] prostrate.

Was first on fute ; and on he lap
Upon his hors, without support.
Of that the Scottis tuke gude comfort,
Quhen thay saw him sa feirelie [1]
Loup on his hors sa galyeardlie [2].
The Squyer liftit his visair
Ane lytill space to take the air.
Thay bad [3] hym wyne, and he it drank,
And humillie he did thame thank.
Be that Talbart on hors wes mountit,
And of our Squyer lytill countit.
And cryit gif he durst undertak
To run anis [4] for his ladies saik ?
The Squyer answerit hie on hicht,
" That sall I do, be Marie bricht !
I am content all day to ryn,
Tyll ane of us the honour wyn."
Of that Talbart was weill content,
And ane greit speir in hand he hent [5].
The Squyer in his hand he thrang [6]
His speir, quhilk was baith greit and lang,
With ane sharp heid of grundin steill,
Of quhilk he was appleisit weill [7].
That plesand feild was lang and braid,
Quhair gay ordour and rowme was ma'd,
And everie man micht have gude sicht,
And their was mony weirlyke knicht.
Sum man of everie natioun
Was in that congregatioun.
   Than trumpettis blew triumphantlie,
And thai [8] twa campiounis egeirlie
Thai spurrit thair hors, with speir on breist,

---

[1] nimbly.   [2] gallantly.   [3] offered.   [4] once.   [5] laid hold of.
[6] tossed.   [7] well pleased.   [8] these.

Pertlie to preif thair pith thay preist [1].
That round, rink roume wes at utterance [2] ;
Bot Talbartis hors with ane mischance,
He outterit [3], and to ryn was laith ;
Quhairof Talbart was wonder wraith.
The Squyer furth his rink [4] he ran,
Commendit weill with everie man ;
And him dischargeit of his speir
Honestlie lyke ane man of weir.
Becaus that rink thay ran in vane
Than Talbart wald not ryn agane
Till he had gottin ane better steid ;
Quhilk was brocht to him with gude speid.
Quhairon he lap, and tuik his speir,
As brym [5] as he had bene ane beir.
And bowtit [6] fordward with ane bend [7],
And ran on to the rinkis end,
And saw his hors was at command.
Than wes he blyith, I understand,
Traistand na mair to ryn in vane.
Than all the trumpettis blew agane.
Be that with all the force thay can
Thay rycht rudelie at uther ran.
Of that meiting ilk [8] man thocht wounder,
Quhilk soundit lyke ane crak of thunder.
And nane of thame thair marrow [9] mist :
Sir Talbartis speir in sunder brist,
Bot the Squyer with his burdoun [10]
Sir Talbart to the eirth dang doun.
That straik was with sic micht and fors
That on the ground lay man and hors ;
And throw the brydell-hand him bair,

---

[1] boldly to prove their strength they pressed.　　[2] coursing room
was from the extremity.　　[3] ran out of the course.　　[4] course.
[5] fierce.　　[6] bolted.　　[7] bound.　　[8] each.　　[9] match.　　[10] spear.

And in the breist ane span and mair,
Throw curras [1] and throw gluifis of plait,
That Talbart micht mak na debait,
The trencheour [2] of the Squyeris speir
Stak still into Sir Talbartis geir.

    Than everie man into that steid [3]
Did all beleve that he was deid.
The Squyer lap rycht haistelie
From his cursour deliverlie,
And to Sir Talbart maid support,
And humillie did him comfort.
Quhen Talbart saw into his scheild
Ane otter in ane silver feild,
" This race," said he, " I may sair rew,
For I see weill my dreme wes trew.
Me-thocht yone otter gart me bleid,
And buir me backwart from my steid.
Bot heir I vow to God soverane
That I sall never just [4] agane."
And sweitlie to the Squyer said,
" Thow knawis the cunning [5] that we maid,
 Quhilk of us twa suld tyne [6] the feild
He suld baith hors and armour yield
Till him that wan : quhairfoir I will
My hors and harnes geve thee till."

    Then said the Squyer courteouslie,
" Brother, I thank yow hartfullie.
Of yow forsuith nathing I crave,
For I have gottin that I wald have."
With everie man he was commendit,
Sa vailyeandlie he him defendit.
The Capitane of the Inglis band
Tuke the young Squyer be the hand,

---

[1] cuirasse. [2] point. [3] place. [4] joust. [5] compact. [6] lose.

And led him to the pailyeoun [1],
And gart him mak collatioun.
Quhen Talbartis woundis wes bund up fast
The Inglis capitane to him past,
And prudentlie did him comfort,
Syne said, " Brother, I yow exhort
To tak the Squyer be the hand."
And sa he did at his command ;
And said, " This bene but chance of armes."
With that he braisit [2] him in his armes,
Sayand, " Hartlie I yow forgeve."
And then the Squyer tuik his leve,
Commendit weill with everie man.
Than wichtlie [3] on his hors he wan,
With monie ane nobyll man convoyit.

Leve we thair Talbart sair annoyit.
Some sayis of that discomfitour
He thocht sic schame and dishonour
That he departit of that land,
And never wes sene into Ingland.

[1] pavilion   [2] pressed.   [3] gallantly.

SIR RICHARD MAITLAND

1496–1586

30

Auld Kyndnes Foryett [1]

THIS warld is all bot fenyeit [2] fair,
    And als unstable as the wind,
Gud faith is flemit [3], I wat nocht quhair,
Trest [4] fallowship is evil to find ;
Gud conscience is all maid blind,
    And cheritie is nane to gett,
Leill [5] loif, and lawté lyis behind,
    And auld kyndnes is quyt foryett.

Quhill I had ony thing to spend,
    And stuffit weill with warldis wrak [6],
Amang my freinds I wes weill kend :
Quhen I wes proud, and had a pak,
They wald me be the oxtar [7] tak,
    And at the hé [8] buird I wes set ;
Bot now thay latt me stand abak,
    Sen auld kyndnes is quyt foryett.

Now I find bot freindis few,
    Sen I wes prysit [9] to be pure ;
They hald me now bot for a schrew [10],
    To me thay tak bot littill cure ;

---

[1] A note in Sibbald's "Chronicle of Scottish Poetry," vol. iii. p. 319, says that this poem "seems partly altered from a similar ballad by Sir R[ichard] Maitland."
[2] seeming.   [3] fled.   [4] trusty.   [5] faithful.   [6] goods.   [7] arm.
[8] high.   [9] esteemed.   [10] worthless person.

All that I do is bot injure :
Thocht I am bair I am nocht bett [1],
Thay latt me stand bot on the flure,
Sen auld kyndnes is quyt foryett.

Suppois I mene, I am nocht mendit,
Sen I held pairt with poverté,
Away sen that my pak wes spendit,
Adew all liberalité.
The proverb now is trew, I sé,
"Quha may nocht gife, will littill gett ; "
Thairfoir to say the varité,
Now auld kyndnes is quyt foryett.

Thay wald me hals [2] with hude and hatt,
Quhyle I wes riche and had anewch [3],
About me freindis anew [3] I gatt,
Rycht blythlie on me thay lewch [4] ;
Bot now they mak it wondir tewch [5],
And lattis me stand befoir the yett [6] :
Thairfoir this warld is verry frewch [7],
And auld kyndnes is quyt foryett.

Als lang as my cop stud evin,
I yeid bot seindill [8] myne allane ;
I squyrit wes with sex or sevin,
Ay quhyle I gaif thame twa for ane ;
Bot suddanly fra that wes gane,
Thay passit by with handis plett [9],
With purtye [10] fra I wes ourtane,
Than auld kyndnes was quyt foryett.

---

[1] bettered.   [2] embrace.   [3] enough.   [4] laughed.   [5] tedious.
[6] gate.   [7] frail.   [8] went but seldom by myself.   [9] plaited.
[10] poverty.

Into this warld suld na man trow ;
Thow may weill sé the ressoun quhy ;
For evir bot gif thy hand be fow,
Thow art bot littill settin by [1].
Thow art nocht tane in cumpany,
Bot thair be sum fisch in thy nett ;
Thairfoir this fals warld I defy,
Sen auld kyndnes is quyt foryett.

[1] esteemed.

ANONYMOUS

31

The Murning Maidin

(*Reign of James the Fourth ?*)

STILL under the levis grene,
  This hinder day, I went alone :
I hard ane may[1] sair murne, and meyne[2] ;
To the king of love scho maid hir mone.
Scho sychit sely soir[3] ;
Said "Lord, I luif thi lore ;
"Mair wo dreit[4] never woman one.
"O langsum[5] lyfe, and thow war gone,
"Than suld I murne no moir !"

As rid gold-wyir schynit hir hair ;
And all in grene the may scho glaid[6].
Ane bent bow in hir hand scho bair ;
Undir hir belt war arrowis braid.
I followit on that fre[7],
That semelie wes to se.
Withe still murning hir mone scho maid.
That bird[8] under a bank scho baid,
And lenit to ane tre.

---

[1] maiden.   [2] moan.   [3] she sighed most heavily.   [4] endured.
[5] weary.   [6] glided along.   [7] woman.   [8] damsel.

"Wanweird [1]!" scho said, "Quhat have I wrocht,
"That on me kytht [2] hes all this cair ?
"Trew lufe so deir I have thé bocht !
"Certis so sall I do na mair.
"Sen [3] that I go begyld
"With ane that faythe has fyld [4].
"That gars me oft-syis [5] sich full sair ;
"And walk amang the holtis hair [6],
"Within the woddis wyld.

"This grit disese for luif I dre
"Thair is no toung can tell the wo !
"I lufe the luif, that lufes not me ;
"I may not mend—but murning mo [7],
"Quhill God send sum remeid,
"Throw destany, or deid.
"I am his freind—and he my fo.
"My sueit, alace ! quhy dois he so ?
"I wrocht him never. na feid [8] !

"Withoutin feyn I wes his freynd,
"In word, and wark. Grit God it wait [9] !
"Quhair he wes placit, thair list I leynd [10],
"Doand him service ayr [11] and late,
"He kepand eftir syne
"Till his honour and myne.
"Bot now he gais ane uther gait ;
"And hes no e to my estait ;
"Quhilk dois me all this pyne [12].

[1] hard fate ! [2] caused. [3] since. [4] tarnish. [5] ofttimes. [6] cold
heights. [7] except by mourning on. [8] offence. [9] knows.
[10] gladly I abode. [11] early. [12] grief.

"It dois me pyne that I may prufe,
"That makis me thus murning mo.
"My luif he lufes ane uther lufe—
"Alas, sweithart! Quhy does he so?
"Quhy sould he me forsaik—
"Have mercie on his maik [1] !—
"Thairfoir my hart will birst in two.
"And thus, walking with da and ro [2],
"My leif now heir I taik."

Than wepit scho, lustie in weyd [3] ;
And on hir wayis can scho went.
In hy [4] eftir that heynd [5] I yeyd [6],
And in my armis culd hir hent [7].
And said, " Fayr lady at this tyde,
"With leif ye man abyde.
"And tell me quho yow hidder sent?
"Or quhy ye beir your bow so bent
"To sla our deir of pryde?

"In waithman weid [8] sen I yow find
"In this wod walkand your alone,
"Your mylk-quhyte handis we sall bind
"Quhill that the blude birst fra the bone,
"Chairgeand yow to preisoun,
"To the king's deip dungeoun.
"Thai may ken be your fedderit flane [9]
"Ye have bene mony beistis bane,
"Upon thir bentis broun [10]."

---

[1] mate.   [2] doe and roe.   [3] beautiful in attire.   [4] haste.
[5] maid.   [6] went.   [7] did her seize.   [8] hunter's garb.   [9] feathered
arrow.   [10] on these brown bents.

That fre answered with fayr afeir [1],
And said, "Schir, mercie for your mycht!
"Thus man [2] I bow and arrowis beir,
"Becaus I am ane baneist wycht.
"So will I be full lang.
"For God's luif lat me gang;
"And heir to yow my treuth I plycht,
"That I sall, nowder [3] day nor nycht,
"No wyld beist wait [4] with wrang.

"Thoch I walk in this forest fre,
"With bow, and eik with fedderit flane,
"It is weill mair than dayis thre,
"And meit or drink yit saw I nane.
"Thoch I had never sic neid
"My selfe to wyn my breid,
"Your deir may walk, schir, thair alane;
"Yet wes I nevir na beistis bane.
"I may not se thame bleid.

"Sen that I never did yow ill,
"It wer no skill ye did me skayth.
"Your deir may walk quhairevir thai will:
"I wyn my meit with na sic waithe [5].
"I do bot litil wrang,
"Bot gif I flouris fang [6].
"Gif that ye trow not in my aythe,
"Tak heir my bow and arrowis baythe,
"And lat my awin self gang."

---

[1] manner.   [2] must.   [3] neither.   [4] persecute.   [5] hunting.
[6] gather flowers.

" I say your bow and arrowis bricht !—
" I bid [1] not have thame, be Sanct Bryd ;
" Bot ye man rest with me all nycht,
" All nakit sleipand be my syd."
" I will not do that syn !
" Leif yow [2] this warld to wyn ! "—
" Ye ar so haill [3], of hew and hyd,
" Luif hes me fangit [4] in this tyd.
" I may not fra you twyn [5]."

Than lukit scho to me, and leuch [6] ;—
And said, " Sic luf I rid yow layne [7],
" Albeid ye mak it never sa teuch [8] ;
" To me your labour is in vane.
" Wer I out of your sycht,
" The space of halfe a nycht,
" Suppois ye saw me never agane—
" Luif hes yow streinyeit [9] with little paine ;
" Thairto my treuth I plycht."

I said, "My sueit, forsuythe I sall
" For ever luif yow, and no mo [10].
" Thoch uthers luif, and leif [11], with all ;
" Maist certanlie I do not so.
" I do yow trew luif hecht,
" Be all thy bewty bricht !
" Ye are so fair be not my fo !
" Ye sall have syn and ye me slo [12]
" Thus throw ane suddan sycht."

---

[1] may.   [2] believe.   [3] lovely, lit. healthy.   [4] seized.   [5] part.
[6] laughed.   [7] hide.   [8] altho' you do it never so reluctantly.
[9] constrained.   [10] other.   [11] leave.   [12] slay.

" That I yow sla, that God forscheild !
" Quhat have I done, or said, yow till ?
" I wes not wont wapyns to weild—
" Bot am ane woman—gif ye will ;
" That suirlie feiris yow [1],
" And ye not me, I trow.
" Thairfor, gude schir, tak in none ill ;
" Sall never berne gar breif the bill
" At bidding me to bow [2].

" Into this wode ay walk I sall,
" Ledand my lyf as woful wycht ;
" Heir I forsaik bayth bour and hall,
" And all thir bygings [3] that are brycht !
" My bed is maid full cauld,
" With beistis bryme [4] and bauld.—
" That gars me say, bayth day and nycht,
" Alace that ever the toung sould hecht [5]
" That hart thocht not to hauld ! "

Thir words out throw my heart so went
That neir I wepit for hir wo.
But thairto wald I not consent ;
And said that it sould not be so.
Into my armis swythe [6]
Embrasit I that blythe [7],
Sayand, " Sweit hart, of harmis ho [8] !
" Found [9] sall I never this forest fro,
" Quhill ye me comfort kyth [10]."

---

[1] surely fears you.   [2] none shall ever be at the trouble of drawing up a writ to make *me* conform.   [3] buildings.   [4] fierce.
[5] promise.   [6] quickly.   [7] gladdener of my eyes.   [8] no more.
[9] depart.   [10] show.

Than knelit I befoir that cleir ;
And meiklie could [1] hir mercie craif.
That semelie than, with sobir cheir,
Me of hir gudlines forgaif.
It wes no neid, I wys,
To bid us uther kys ;
Thair mycht no hairts mair joy resaif,
Nor [2] ather culd of uther haif.
Thus brocht wer we to blys.

[1] did.   [2] than.

KING JAMES THE FIFTH

(ATTRIBUTED TO)

1512–1542

32

Peblis to the Play

AT Beltane,[1] quhen ilk bodie bownis[2]
   To Peblis to the play,
To heir the singin' and the soundis,
   The solace, suth to say ;
Be firth[3] and forrest furth they found[4],
   Thay graythit[5] tham full gay ;
God wait that wald thay do that stound[6],
   For it was thair feist day,
        Thay said,
Of Peblis to the play.

All the wenchis of the west
   War up or the cok crew ;
For reiling[7] thair micht na man rest,
   For garray and for glew[8].
Ane said " My curches[9] ar nocht prest ! "
   Than answerit Meg full blew[10],
"To get an hude I hald it best."
   " Be Goddis saull that is true ! "
        Quod scho,
Of Peblis to the play.

---

[1] May 1st, Old Style.   [2] when each person sets forth.   [3] by outland.   [4] went.   [5] clad.   [6] time.   [7] turmoil.   [8] for preparation and sport.   [9] kerchiefs for head-wear.   [10] disconcerted.

She tuik the tippet be the end ;
　To lat it hing scho leit not [1].
Quod he, " Thy bak sall beir ane bend [2] ; "
　" In faith," quod she, " we meit not ! "
Scho was so guckit and so gend [3]
　That day ane byt scho eit nocht.
Than spak hir fallowis that hir kend,
　" Be still, my joy, and greit not,
　　　　Now,
Of Peblis to the play ! "

" Evir, allace ! " then said scho,
　" Am I nocht cleirlie tynt [4] ?
I dar nocht cum yon mercat [5] to,
　I am so evvil sone-brint [6].
Amang yon merchands my dudds [7] do,
　Marie ; I sall anis mynt [8],
Stand of far and keik [9] thaim to,
　As I at hame was wont,"
　　　　Quod scho,
Of Peblis to the play.

Hop, calye, and cardronow [10]
　Gaderit out thik-fald [11] ;
With " hey and how rohumbelow "
　The young folk were full bald.
The bagpipe blew, and thai out-threw [12]
　Out of the townis untald [13].
Lord, sic ane schout was thame amang
　Quhen thai were ower the wald [14],
　　　　Thair west,
Of Peblis to the play !

[1] permitted not.　[2] band.　[3] so foolish and skittish.　[4] lost.
[5] market.　[6] sunburnt.　[7] rags.　[8] shall once venture.　[9] peep.
[10] man, woman, and prentice-lad.　[11] gathered thick.　[12] thronged
out.　[13] farms unnumbered.　[14] over the plain.

Thocht all hir kin had sworn hir deid [1]
  Scho wald haif bot sweit Willie
        Allone,
At Chrystis kirk of the grene.

Scho skornit Jok and skraipit [2] at him,
  And mvrionit him with mokkis [3] ;
He wald haif luvit, scho wald nocht lat him,
  For all his yallow loikkis :
He chereist hir, scho bad ga chat him [4],
  Scho compt [5] him nocht twa clokkis [6] ;
So schamefully his schort goun set him,
  His lymmis wes lyk twa rokkis [7],
        Scho said,
At Chrystis kirk of the grene.

Thome Lular wes thair menstrall meit ;
  O Lord ! as he cowd lanss [8] ;
He playit so schill [9], and sang so sweit
  Quhill Towsy tuke a transs [10].
Auld Lychtfute thair he did forleit [11],
  And counterfutit Franss ;
He vse [12] him-self as man discreit
  And vp tuke moreiss danss,
        Full lowd,
At Chrystis kirk of the grene.

Than Stevin come stoppand in with stendis [13] ;
  No rynk [14] mycht him arreist.
Platfute [15] he bobbit vp with bendis [16] ;
  For Mald he maid requeist.

[1] death.   [2] girded.   [3] mocked him by making mouths.   [4] go hang himself.   [5] valued.   [6] particles of chaff.   [7] distaffs.   [8] how he could draw the fiddle-bow.   [9] shrill.   [10] an ancient dance.   [11] forsake.   [12] behaved.   [13] stepping in with long strides.   [14] ring.   [15] flat-footed.   [16] bounds.

He lap quhill he lay on his lendis [1] ;
    Bot rysand he was preist [2]
Quhill that he oistit [3] at bath the endis
    For honour of the feist,
                That day,
At Chrystis kirk of the grene.

Syne Robene Roy begowth [4] to revell,
    And Downy till him druggit [5] ;
"Lat be," quo Jok ; and cawd him javell [6]
    And be the taill him tuggit.
The kensy cleikit to the cavell [7],
    Bot Lord ! than gif thay luggit [8],
Thay pairtit hir manly with a nevell [9],
    God wait gif hair wes ruggit [10]
                Betuix thame,
At Chrystis kirk of the grene.

Ane bent a bow, sic sturt cowd steir him [11] ;
    Grit skayth wesd to haif skard [12] him ;
He chesit a flane [13] as did affeir [14] him,
    The toder [15] said " Dirdum Dardum [16]."
Throwch baith the cheikis he thocht to cheir [17]
        him,
    Or throw the —— haif chard [18] him ;
Bot be ane akerbraid [19] it come nocht neir him,
    I can nocht tell quhat mard him,
                Thair,
At Chrystis kirk of the grene.

---

[1] he leaped till he lay on his buttocks.   [2] praised.   [3] coughed.
[4] began.   [5] dragged.   [6] drove him sidewise.   [7] the angry man
clutched the stave.   [8] tugged.   [9] blow of the fist.   [10] pulled.
[11] such wrath did move him.   [12] great hurt was it to have
frightened.   [13] chose an arrow.   [14] become.   [15] other.   [16] an
expression of contempt.   [17] pierce.   [18] pierced.   [19] acre's breadth.

With that a freynd of his cryd " Fy !"
   And vp ane arrow drew ;
He forgit[1] so fowriously
   The bow in flenders[2] flew ;
Sa wes the will of God, trow I,
   For had the tre[3] bene trew
Men said that kend his archery
   That he had slane anew[4],
              That day,
At Chrystis kirk on the grene.

Ane hasty hensure[5] callit Hary,
   Quha wes ane archer heynd[6],
Tilt[7] vp a taikle withowttin tary[8],
   That torment so him teynd[9].
I wait nocht quhidder his hand cowd wary[10],
   Or the man wes his freynd,
For he eschaipit[11] throw michtis of Mary
   As man that no ill meynd[12],
             Bot gud,
At Chrystis kirk of the grene.

Than Lowry as ane lyon lap,
   And sone a flane cowd fedder[13] ;
He hecht[14] to perss him at the pap,
   Thair-on to wed a weddir[15].
He hit him on the wame a wap[16],
   It buft[17] lyk ony bledder ;
Bot swa his fortoun wes and hap
   His dowblet wes maid of ledder,
            And saift him,
At Chrystis kirk of the grene.

[1] let fly.   [2] splinters.   [3] wood.   [4] enough.   [5] giddy fellow.
[6] skilful.   [7] snatched.   [8] delay.   [9] enraged.   [10] did shift.
[11] escaped.   [12] designed.   [13] arrow did feather.   [14] offered.   [15] to
stake a wether.   [16] on the belly a knock.   [17] sounded.

A yaip [1] yung man that stude him neist
    Lowsd [2] of a schot with yre ;
He ettlit the bern [3] in at the breist,
    The bolt flew our the byre [4].
Ane cryit Fy ! he had slane a preist
    A myll beyond ane myre ;
Than bow and bag [5] fra him he keist
    And fled as ferss as fyre
            Of flynt,
At Chrystis kirk of the grene.

With forkis and flailis thay lait [6] grit slappis,
    And flang [7] togiddir lyk friggis [8] :
With bowgaris [9] of barnis thay beft [10] blew kappis
    Quhill thay of bernis maid briggis [11].
The reird [12] raiss rudly with the rappis,
    Quhen rungis [13] wes layd on riggis [14] ;
The wyffis come furth with cryis and clappis,
    " Lo quhair my lyking liggis [15] ! "
            Quo thay
At Chryst kirk of the grene.

Thay girnit and lait gird with granis [16]
    Ilk gossep vder grevit [17] ;
Sum straik with stingis [18], sum gadderit stanis,
    Sum fled and evill mischevit ;
The menstrall wan within twa wanis [19],
    That day full weill he previt [20],

---

[1] eager. [2] loosed. [3] aimed at the man. [4] cowhouse. [5] quiver.
[6] let (drive).   [7] kicked.   [8] stout fellows.   [9] roof beams.
[10] buffeted. [11] till they of men made bridges. [12] uproar. [13] spars.
[14] backs. [15] my love lies. [16] snarled and let drive with groans.
[17] vexed the other. [18] pikes. [19] waggons. [20] proved.

For he come hame with vnbirsed banis [1]
  Quhair fechtaris wer mischevit
      For evir,
At Chrystis kirk of the grene.

Heich [2] Hucheoun, with a hissill ryss [3],
  To red [4] can throw thame rummill [5];
He mudlet [6] thame doun lyk ony myss [7],
  He wes no barty-bummill. [8]
Thocht he wes wicht [9] he wes nocht wyss
  With sic jangleris to jummill [10],
For fra his thowme thay dang a sklyss [11],
  Quhill he cryd " Barla-fummyll [12]!
      I am slane,"
At Chrystis kirk of the grene.

Quhen that he saw his blude so reid,
  To fle micht no man lat [13] him;
He wend [14] it bene for auld done feid [15],
  The far sarar it set [16] him.
He gart his feit defend his heid,
  He thocht ane cryd 'haif at him,'
Quhill he wes past out of all pleid [17]
  He suld bene swift that gat him
      Throw speid,
At Chrystis kirk of the grene.

The toun sowtar [18] in greif wes bowdin [19],
  His wyfe hang in his waist;
His body wes with blud all browdin [20],
  He granit lyk ony gaist.

[1] unbruised bones. [2] tall. [3] a hazel twig. [4] separate. [5] rage.
[6] mowed. [7] mice. [8] inactive fellow. [9] stout. [10] with such
wranglers to meddle. [11] struck a slice. [12] "a truce." [13] prevent.
[14] deemed. [15] feud. [16] distressed. [17] debate. [18] shoemaker
[19] swollen with rage. [20] besmeared.

Hir glitterand hair that wes full goldin
    So hard in lufe him lest[1]
That for hir saik he wes nocht yoldin[2],
    Sevin myll quhill he wes chest[3],
                And mair,
At Chrystis kirk of the grene.

The miller wes of manly mak ;
    To meit him wes na mowis[4] ;
Thair durst nocht ten cum him to tak,
    So nowit he thair nowis[5].
The buschment haill[6] about him brak
    And bikkerit[7] him with bowis[8],
Syne tratourly behind his bak
    Thay hewit him on the howiss[9]
                Behind,
At Chrystis kirk of the grene.

Twa that wes heidmen of the heird
    Ran vpoun vtheris lyk rammis :
Than followit feymen[10] rycht on affeird[11],
    Bet on with barrow trammis.
Bot quhair thair gobbis wes vngeird[12]
    Thay gat vpoun the gammis[13],
Quhill bludy berkit[14] wes thair beird ;
    As thay had wirreit[15] lammis,
                Maist lyk,
At Chryst kirk of the grene

The wyvis kest vp ane hiddouss yell
    Quhen all thir yunkeris yokkit[16] ;

[1] delayed.   [2] did not yield.   [3] chased.   [4] jest.   [5] hammered he their crowns.   [6] the whole ambush.   [7] battered.   [8] ox-collars. [9] hams.   [10] crofters.   [11] right unafraid.   [12] their mouths were unguarded.   [13] gums.   [14] barked.   [15] worried.   [16] youngsters engaged.

Als ferss as ony fyr-flaught [1] fell
    Freikis [2] to the feild thay flokkit :
Tha cairlis [3] with clubbis cowd vder quell [4],
    Quhill blud at breistis out bokkit [5].
So rudly rang the commoun bell,
    Quhill all the stepill rokkit
              For reird [6],
At Chrystis kirk of the grene.

Quhen thay had berit [7] lyk baitit bulis,
    And branewod brynt in bailis [8],
Thay wer als meik as ony mvlis
    That mangit wer with mailis [9].
For fantness tha forfochin fulis [10]
    Fell doun lyk flawchtir-failis [11],
And freschmen come in and held thair dulis [12],
    And dang [13] thame doun in dailis [14]
              Be-dene [15],
At Chryst kirk on the grene.

Quhen all wes done, Dik with ane aix
    Come furth to fell a fidder [16].
Quod he, " Quhair ar yone hangit smaix [17]
    Rycht now wald slane my bruder ? "
His wyfe bade him ga hame gub-glaikis [18],
    And sa did Meg his muder.
He turnd and gaif thaim bayth thair paikis [19],
    For he durst ding nane vdir [20],
              For feir,
At Chryst kirk of the grene that day.

---

[1] lightning.   [2] stout fellows.   [3] men.   [4] did each other quell.
[5] belched.   [6] noise.   [7] bellowed.   [8] firewood burnt in flames.
[9] overpowered were with burdens.   [10] these fatigued fools.   [11] turfs
cut for burning.   [12] stations.   [13] struck.   [14] numbers.   [15] forthwith.   [16] waggon-load.   [17] mean fellows.   [18] folly-mouth.
[19] drubbing.   [20] strike no other.

34 *The Gaberlunzieman* [1]

THE pauky [2] auld carle came ovir the lee,
  Wi' mony good-e'ens and days to mee,
Saying, "Goodwife, for zour courtesie,
  Will ze lodge a silly [3] poor man?"
The night was cauld, the carle was wat,
And down azont [4] the ingle he sat;
My dochter's shoulders he gan to clap,
  And cadgily [5] ranted and sang.

"O wow!" quo he, "wer I as free
As first when I saw this countrie,
How blyth and merry wad I bee!
  And I wad nevir think lang [6]."
He grew canty [7] and she grew fain,
But little did her auld minny [8] ken
What thir slee twa togither were sayn
  When wooing they were sa thrang [9].

"And O!" quo he, "ann [10] ze were as black
As evir the crown o' your dadye's hat
'Tis I wad lay thee by my back,
  And awa wi' me thou sould gang!"
"And O!" quoth she, "ann I were as whyte
As evir the snaw lay on the dike [11]
Ild clead me braw [12] and lady-like,
  And awa wi' thee Ild gang!"

---

[1] man with the wallet. Throughout this poem, it will be observed, the consonant sound of "y" is represented by the letter "z." [2] artful. [3] weakly. [4] beyond. [5] cheerfully. [6] grow weary. [7] lively. [8] mother. [9] busy. [10] if. [11] wall. [12] clothe myself gaily.

Between the twa was made a plot,
They raise a wee before the cock,
And wyliely they shot the lock,
   And fast to the bent[1] are they gane.
Up the morn the auld wife raise,
And at her leisure put on her claiths,
Syne to the servants' bed she gaes
   To speir[2] for the silly poor man.

She gaed to the bed whair the beggar lay ;
The strae was cauld, he was away ;
Scho clapt her hands, cry'd " Dulefu' day !
   For some of our geir[3] will be gane."
Some ran to coffer and some to kist[4],
But nought was stown[5] that could be mist.
She danced her lane[6], cry'd, " Praise be blest !
   I have lodg'd a leal[7] poor man.

" Since naithings awa, as we can learn,
The kirn's to kirn[8], and milk to earn ;
Gae butt the house[9], lass, and waken my bairn,
   And bid her come quickly ben[10]."
The servant gaed where the dochter lay—
The sheets was cauld, she was away ;
And fast to her goodwife can say[11],
   " She's aff with the gaberlunzieman."

" O fy gar ride[12], and fy gar rin,
And haste ze, find these traiters agen !
For shee's be burnt, and hee's be slein,
   The wearifou[13] gaberlunzieman ! "

---

[1] moorland.   [2] seek.   [3] property.   [4] chest.   [5] stolen.   [6] alone.
[7] faithful.   [8] churn.   [9] to the other room.   [10] to this room.
[11] did say.   [12] haste, bid ride.   [13] vexatious.

Some rade upo' horse, some ran a-fit [1] ;
The wife was wood [2], and out o' her wit ;
She could na gang, not yet could she sit
    But ay did curse and did ban.

Mean-time far hind, out owre [3] the lee,
Fu' snug in a glen where nane could see,
The twa, with kindlie sport and glee,
    Cut frae a new cheese a whang [4].
The prieving [5] was gude, it pleas'd them baith ;
To lo'e her for ay he gae her his aith.
Quo she, " To leave thee I will be laith,
    My winsome gaberlunzieman.

" O kend my minny I were wi' zou,
Ill-fardly [6] wald she crook her mou'.
Sic a poor man sheld nevir trow [7]
    Aftir the gaberlunzieman."
" My dear," quo he, " zee're zet owre zonge,
And hae na learnt the beggar's tonge,
To follow me frae toun to toun,
    And carrie the gaberlunzie on :

" Wi' kauk and keel [8] I'll win zour bread,
And spindles and whorles [9] for them wha need—
Whilk is a gentil trade indeed,
    The gaberlunzie to carrie O !
I'll bow [10] my leg and crook my knee,
And draw a black clout [11] owre my e'e ;
A criple or blind they will cau me,
    While we sall sing and be merry O ! "

[1] afoot. [2] furious. [3] far off, across. [4] slice. [5] sampling. [6] in
an ugly manner. [7] she'd never trust. [8] chalk and reddle.
[9] perforated stones used in spinning. [10] bend. [11] cloth.

35   *The Jolly Beggar*

THERE was a jolly beggar, and a-begging he
      was boun,
And he took up his quarters in-to a land'art town, [1]
      And we'll gang nae mair a roving
      Sae late in-to the night ;
      And we'll gang nae mair a roving, boys,
      Let the moon shine ne'er so bright.

He wad neither ly in barn, nor yet wad he in byre ;
But in ahint the ha' door, or else afore the fire.

The beggar's bed was made at e'en wi' good clean
      straw and hay,
And in ahint the ha' door, and there the beggar lay.

Up raise the goodman's dochter and for to bar the
      door,
And there she saw the beggar standin' i' the floor.

He took the lassie in his arms, and to the bed he
      ran,
O hooly [2], hooly wi' me, sir, ye'll waken our goodman.

The beggar was a cunnin' loon, and ne'er a word
      he spake
Until he got his turn done, syne he began to crack [3].

" Is there ony dogs into this toun ? maiden, tell me
      true."
" And what wad ye do wi' them, my hinny and my
      dow [4] ? "

      [1] outlying farm.   [2] gently.   [3] chat.   [4] sweetheart.

" They'll rive a' my meal pocks, and do me meikle
    wrang."
" O dool¹ for the doing o't! are ye the poor man?"

Then she took up the meal pocks, and flang them
    o'er the wa';
" The deil gae wi' the meal pocks, my maidenhead,
    and a'!"

" I took ye for some gentleman, at least the laird
    of Brodie;
O dool for the doing o't! are ye the poor bodie?"

He took the lassie in his arms, and gae her kisses
    three,
And four and twenty hunder merk² to pay the
    nurice-fee³.

He took a horn frae his side, and blew baith loud
    and shrill,
And four and twenty belted knights came skipping
    o'er the hill.

And he took out his little knife, loot a' his duddies⁴
    fa';
And he was the brawest gentleman that was amang
    them a'.

The beggar was a cliver loon, and he lap shoulder
    height:
" O, ay for sicken⁵ quarters as I gat yesternight!"
        And we'll gang nae mair, &c.

---

¹ woe.   ² a silver coin.   ³ nurse's charge.   ⁴ rags.   ⁵ such.

ALEXANDER MONTGOMERIE

1540 (?)–1610 (?)

37   *The Night is Neir Gone*

HAY! nou the day dauis [1];
     The jolie Cok crauis;
Nou shroudis the shauis [2],
     Throu Natur anone.
The thissell-cok [3] cryis
On louers vha lyis,
Nou skaillis [4] the skyis:
     The nicht is neir gone.

The feildis ouerflouis
With gouans [5] that grouis,
Quhair lilies lyk lou [6] is,
     Als rid as the rone [7].
The turtill that treu is,
With nots that reneuis,
Hir pairtie perseuis,
     The night is neir gone.

Nou Hairtis with Hyndis,
Conforme to thair kyndis,
Hie tursis thair tyndis [8],
     On grund vhair they grone.

---

[1] dawns.   [2] the woods clothe themselves.   [3] common bunting, *emberiza miliaria*.   [4] scatter.   [5] daisies.   [6] flame.   [7] red as the rowan (mountain-ash).   [8] toss high their antlers.

Nou Hurchonis[1], with Hairis,
Ay passis in pairis;
Quhilk deuly declaris
      The night is neir gone.

The sesone excellis
Thrugh sueetnes that smellis;
Nou Cupid compellis
      Our hairtis echone[2]
On Venus vha vaikis[3],
To muse on our maikis[4],
Syn sing, for thair saikis :—
      The night is neir gone.

All curageous knichtis
Aganis the day dichtis[5]
The breist plate that bright is,
      To feght with thair fone[6].
The stoned steed[7] stampis
Throu curage and crampis[8],
Syn on the land lampis[9] :
      The night is neir gone.

The freikis[10] on feildis
That wight[11] wapins weildis
With shyning bright shieldis
      As Titan in trone[12] :
Stiff speiris in reistis,
Ouer cursoris cristis,
Ar brok on thair breistis :
      The night is neir gone.

---

[1] hedgehogs.   [2] each one.   [3] is thrall to.   [4] matches.   [5] make
ready.   [6] foes.   [7] stallion.   [8] paws the air, lit., climbs.   [9] gallops.
[10] stout fellows.   [11] strong.   [12] throne.

So hard are thair hittis,
Some sueyis, some sittis,
And some perforce flittis [1]
   On grund vhill they grone.
Syn groomis that gay is,
On blonkis that brayis [2],
With suordis assayis :
   The night is neir gone.

37   *The Cherrie and the Slae* [3]

ABOUT ane bank, quhair birdis on bewis [4]
   Ten thousand tymis thair notis renewis
Ilke houre into the day,
The merle and maueis [5] micht be sene,
The Progne and the Phelomene, [6]
   Quhilk caussit me to stay.
I lay and leynit me to ane bus [7]
   To heir the birdis beir [8] ;
Thair mirth was sa melodius
   Throw nature of the yeir :
     Sum singing, sum springing
      With wingis into the sky ;
     So trimlie and nimlie
      Thir birdis they flew me by.

I saw the hurcheoun [9] and the hair,
Quha fed amangis the flowris fair,
   Wer happing to and fro :
I saw the cunning [10] and the cat,
Quhais downis with the dew was wat,
   With mony beistis mo.

---

[1] shift.   [2] white steeds that neigh.   [3] sloe, wild plum.   [4] boughs.
[5] thrush. [6] swallow and nightingale.   [7] bush. [8] song. [9] hedge-hog. [10] coney.

The hart, the hynd, the dae, the rae,
  The fowmart [1], and the foxe
War skowping [2] all fra brae to brae,
  Amang the water broxe [3];
    Sum feiding, sum dreiding
      In cais of suddain snairis;
    With skipping and tripping
      They hantit all in pairis.

The air was sa attemperate,
  But [4] ony myst immaculate,
    Bot purefeit and cleir;
The flouris fair wer flurischit,
As Nature had them nurischit,
    Baith delicate and deir:
And euery blome on branche and bewch
    So prettily were spred,
And hang their heidis out ouir the hewch [5]
    In Mayis colour cled;
      Sum knopping [6], sum dropping
        Of balmie liquor sweit,
      Distelling and smelling
        Throw Phœbus hailsum heit.

The cukkow and the cuschet [7] cryde,
The turtle, on the vther syde,
    Na plesure had to play;
So schil [8] in sorrow was her sang,
That, throw her voice, the roches rang;
    For Eccho answerit ay,
Lamenting sair Narcissus cace,
    Quha staruit [9] at the well;

---

[1] polecat. [2] skipping. [3] badgers. [4] without. [5] cliff, scaur.
[6] budding. [7] wood-pigeon. [8] shrill. [9] perished.

Quha with the shaddow of his face
  For lufe did slay himsell :
    Quhylis weiping and creiping
      About the well he baid ;
    Quhylis lying, quhylis crying,
      Bot it na answere maid.

The dew as diamondis did hing,
Vpon the tender twistis [1] and ying,
  Ouir-twinkling all the treis :
And ay quhair flowris flourischit faire,
Thair suddainly I saw repaire,
  In swarmes, the sownding beis.
Sum sweitly hes the hony socht,
  Quhil they war cloggit soir ;
Sum willingly the waxe hes wrocht,
  To heip it vp in stoir :
    So heiping, with keiping,
      Into thair hyuis they hyde it,
    Precyselie and wyseli
      For winter they prouyde it.

To pen the pleasures of that park,
How euery blossome, branch, and bark,
  Agaynst the sun did schyne,
I leif to poetis to compyle
In staitlie verse and lofty style :
  It passis my ingyne. [2]
Bot, as I mussit myne allane [3],
  I saw an river rin
Out ouir ane craggie rok of stane,
  Syne lichtit in ane lin [4],

_____
[1] twigs.   [2] understanding.   [3] by myself.   [4] the pool below a
waterfall, sometimes the waterfall itself.

With tumbling and rumbling
   Amang the rochis round,
Dewalling[1] and falling
   Into that pit profound.

To heir thae startling stremis cleir,
Me thocht it musique to the eir
   Quhair deskant[2] did abound ;
With trible sweit, and tenor iust,
And ay the echo repercust
   Hir diapason sound,
Set with the Ci-sol-fa-uth cleife,
   Thairby to knaw the note :
Thair soundt a michtie semibreif
   Out of the Elphis[3] throte ;
     Discreitlie, mair sweitlie,
       Nor craftie Amphion,
     Or Musis that vsis[4]
       At fountaine Helicon.

Quha wald haue tyrit to heir that tune,
Quhilk birdis corroborate ay abune[5],
   Throw schowting of the larkis !
Sum flies sa high into the skyis,
Quhill Cupid walkinnes[6] with the cryis
   Of Natures chappell clarkis ;
Quha, leving all the hevins aboue,
   Alighted in the eird[7].
Loe ! how that little God of Loue
   Befoir me thair appeird !
     So myld-lyke, and chyld-lyke,
       With bow thrie quarteris scant ;
     So moylie[8] and coylie,
     . He lukit like ane sant.

---

[1] descending. [2] several musical parts. [3] *i.e.*, echo. [4] haunt.
[5] above. [6] wakens. [7] earth. [8] mildly.

Ane cleinlie crispe [1] hang ouir his eyis ;
His quauer by his naked thyis
　　Hang in ane siluer lace :
Of gold, betwix his schoulders, grew
Twa pretty wingis quhairwith he flew ;
　　On his left arme, ane brace [2] :
This god aff all his geir he schuik,
　　And laid it on the grund :
I ran als busie for to luik
　　Quhair ferleis [3] might be fund :
　　　　Amasit I gasit
　　　　　　To see that geir sa gay :
　　　　Persawing my hawing [4],
　　　　　　He countit me his pray.

His youth and stature made me stout ;
Of doubleness I had nae doubt,
　　Bot bourded [5] with my boy :
Quod I, " How call they thee, my chyld ? "
" Cupido, Sir," quod he, and smyld,
　　" Please you me to imploy ;
For I can serve you in your suite,
　　If you please to impyre [6],
With wings to flie, and schafts to schute,
　　Or flamis to set on fyre.
　　　　Mak choice then of those then,
　　　　　　Or of a thousand things ;
　　　　Bot craue them, and haue them " :
　　　　　　With that I wowd [7] his wings.

" Quhat wald thou giue, my friend," quod he,
" To haf thae prettie wingis to flie,
　　To sport thee for a quhyle ?

---

[1] veil of cobweb lawn.　[2] sleeve.　[3] wonders.　[4] perceiving my
conduct.　[5] jested.　[6] command.　[7] sued for.

Or quhat, gif I suld len thee heir
My bow and all my shuting geir,
  Sum bodie to begyle ? "
"That geir," quod I, "can not be bocht,
  Yit I wald haif it faine."
"Quhat gif," quod he, "it cost thee nocht
  Bot randring it againe ? "
    His wingis than he bringis than,
      And band them on my back :
    "Go flie now," quod he now,
      "And so my leif I tak."

I sprang vp on Cupidoes wingis,
Quha bow and quauir baith resingis [1],
  To lend me for ane day :
As Icarus with borrowit flicht
I mountit hichar nor I micht ;
  Ouir [2] perrelous ane play.
Than furth I drew that deadlie dairt
  Quhilk sumtyme schot his mother,
Quhair with I hurt my wanton heart,
  In hope to hurt ane vther ;
    It hurt me, it burt [3] me,
      The ofter I it handill :
    Cum se now, in me now,
      The butter-flie and candill.

As scho delytis into the low [4],
Sa was I browdin in [5] my bow,
  Als ignorant as scho :
And as scho flies quhill sche be fyrit,
Sa, with the dart that I desyrit,
  My hand hes hurt me to.

---

[1] resigns.   [2] too.   [3] burned.   [4] flame.   [5] fond of.

As fulisch Phaëton, be sute [1],
  His fatheris cart obteind,
I langt [2] in Luiffis bow to shute,
  Bot weist not what it meind ;
    Mair wilfull than skilfull,
      To flie I was so fond,
    Desyring, impyring,
      And sa was sene vpond [3].

To late I knaw, quha hewis [4] to hie,
The spail [5] sall fall into his eie :
  To late I went to scuillis :
To late I heard the swallow preiche [6] :
To late Experience dois teiche—
  The skuill-maister of fuillis :
To late to fynde the nest I seik,
  Quhen all the birdis are flowin ;
To late the stabill dore I steik [7],
  Quhen all the steids are stowin [8].
    To lait ay their stait ay
      All fulische folk espye :
    Behynd so, they fynd so
      Remeid, an so do I.

38   *Echo*

TO the, echo, and thou to me agane,
  In the deserts among the wods and wells,
Quhair destinie hes bund the to remane,
But [9] company within the firths and fells,
Let vs complein, with wofull youts and yells,
On shaft and shooter that our hairts hes slane :
To the, Echo, and thou to me agane.

---

[1] by suit.   [2] longed.   [3] upon it.   [4] hews.   [5] chip.   [6] an
allusion to one of Æsop's fables, versified by Henryson.   [7] fasten.
[8] stolen. [9] without.

Thy pairt to mine may justlie be compaird
In mony poynts, vhilk both we may repent,
Thou hes no hope, and I am clene dispaird ;
Thou tholis [1] but caus, I suffer innocent ;
Thou does bewaill, and I do still lament ;
Thou murns for nocht, I shed my teirs in vane :
To the, Echo, and thou to me agane.

Thou pleins [2] Narcissus, I my love also ;
He did the hurt, bot I am kild by myne ;
He fled from the, myne is my mortall fo,
Without offence, and crueller nor thyne.
The Weirds [3] vs baith predestinat to pyne,
Continually to others to complane :
To the, Echo, and thou to me agane.

Thou hyds thyslf ; I list not to be sene ;
Thou banisht art, and I am in exyle—
By Juno thou, and I by Venus Quene.
Thy love wes fals, and myn did me begyle ;
Thou hoped once, so was I glaid a vhyle ;
Yit lost our tyme in love, I will not lane [4] ;
To the, Echo, and thou to me agane.

Thy elrish skirlis [5] do penetrat the roks ;
The roches rings, and rendirs me my cryis.
Our saikles [6] plaints to pitie tham provoks,
Quhill they compell our sounds to pierce the skyis.
All thing bot love to plesur vs applyis,
Quhais end, alace ! I say is bot disdane :
To the, Echo, and thou to me agane.

[1] endurest.   [2] bewailest.   [3] fates.   [4] lie.   [5] unearthly shrieks.
[6] luckless.

Som thing, Echo, thou hes for to rejose,
Suppose Narcissus some tyme the forsook.
First he is dead, syne changed in a rose,
Quhom thou nor nane hes pouer for to brook [1].
Bot, be the contrair, evirie day I look
To sie my love attraptit in a trane [2]
From me, Echo, and nevir come agane.

Nou welcome, Echo, patience perforce.
Anes eviry day, with murning, let vs meet.
Thy love nor myne in mynds haif no remorse ;
We taist the sour that nevir felt the sueet.
As I demand, then ansueir and repeit.
Let teirs aboundant ouir our visage rane :
To the, Echo, and thou to me agane.

Quhat lovers, Echo, maks sik querimony [3] ?   Mony.
Quhat kynd of fyre doth kindle thair curage ?   Rage.
Quhat medicine, (O Echo ! knouis thou ony ?)   Ony.
Is best to stay this love of his passage ?   Age.
Quhat merit thay that culd our sigh assuage.   Wage.
Quhat wer we first in this our love profane ?   Fane.
Quhair is our joy ? O Echo ! tell agane.   Gane.

[1] enjoy.   [2] caught in a snare.   [3] complaint.

ALEXANDER SCOTT

Floruit 1547–1584

39   *Of May*

M AY is the moneth maist amene [1],
     For thame in Venus seruice bene,
To recreat thair havy hartis ;
May caussis curage from the splene
     And every thing in May revartis [2].

In May the plesant spray vpspringis ;
In May the myrthfull maveiss singis ;
     And now in May to madynnis fawis [3]
With tymmer wechtis [4] to trip in ringis,
     And to play upcoill [5] with the bawis.

In May gois [6] gallandis bring in symmer,
And trymly occupyis thair tymmer [7]
     With " Hunts vp," every morning plaid ;
In May gois gentill wemen gymmer [8],
     In gardynnis grene thair grumis to glaid.

In May quhen men yeid everich one,
With Robene Hoid and Littill Johne,
     To bring in bowis and birkin bobbynis [9] ;
Now all sic game is fastlingis [10] gone
     Bot gif it be amangis clovin Robbynis.

---

[1] pleasant.   [2] revives.   [3] appertains.   [4] tambourines.   [5] toss up.   [6] go.   [7] tabor.   [8] more gaily dressed.   [9] branches and seed-pods of the birch.   [10] all but.

Abbotis by [1] rewll, and Lordis but [2] ressone,
Sic senyeoris [3] tymis ourweill [4] this sessone ;
Upoun thair vyce war lang to waik [5],
Quhais falsatt, fibilnes, and tressone,
Hes rung [6] thryis oure this zodiak.

In May begynnis the golk to gaill [7] ;
In May drawis deir to doun and daill ;
In May men mellis [8] with famyny,
And ladeis meitis thair luvaris laill [9],
Quhen Phebus is in Gemyny.

Butter, new cheis, and beir in May,
Condamis [10], cokkillis, curds and quhay,
Lapstaris, lempettis, mussillis in schellis,
Grene leikis and all sic, men may say [11],
Suppois sum of thame sourly smellis.

In May grit men within thair boundis
Sum halks the walteris [12], sum with houndis
The hairis owtthrowch the forrestis cachis ;
Syne efter thame thair ladeis founds [13],
To sent [14] the rynnyng of the rachis [15].

In May frank archeris will affix
In place to meit, syne marrowis [16] mix,
To schute at buttis, at bankis and brais ;
Sum at the reveris [17], sum at the prikkis [17],
Sum laich [18] and to beneth the clais.

[1] against.   [2] without (in allusion to the pre-Reformation May-
time revels). [3] lords. [4] exceed. [5] wait. [6] prevailed. [7] cuckoo
to call. [8] meddles with. [9] leal. [10] possibly " connanis," rabbits.
[11] try, taste.   [12] spend the time fishing.   [13] go.   [14] scent.
[15] hounds.   [16] equals.   [17] casual and fixed marks for shooting at.
[18] low.

In May gois dammosalis and dammis
In gardyngis grene to play lyk lammis ;
   Sum at the bairis [1] they brace lyk billeis [2] ;
Sum rynis at barlabreikis [3] lyk rammis,
   Sum round abowt the standand pilleis [4].

In May gois madynis till Lareit [5],
And hes thair mynyonis [6] on the streit
   To horss thame quhair the gait is ruch [7] :
Sum at the Inchebukling bray [8] thay meit,
   Sum in the midds of Mussilburch. [8]
         [Two verses omitted.]

40   *A Rondel of Love*

L O ! quhat it is to lufe,
   Lerne ye, that list to prufe,
Be me, I say, that no wayis may
   The grund of greif remvfe,
Bot still decay, both nycht and day :
   Lo ! what it is to lufe.

Lufe is ane fervent fyre,
   Kendillit without desyre :
Schort plesour, lang displesour ;
   Repentence is the hyre [9] ;
Ane pure tressour without mesour [10] :
   Lufe is ane fervent fyre.

To lufe and to be wyiss,
   To rege [11] with gud adwyiss,

[1] the game of Prisoners' Bars.   [2] clasp each other like brothers.
[3] a catching game.   [4] stakes.   [5] Loretto.   [6] lovers.   [7] way is
rough.   [8] Musselburgh and Edgebucklin Brae, a few miles from
Edinburgh.   [9] wage, price.   [10] a treasure poor beyond measure.
[11] to rage in accordance with reason.

Now thus, now than, so gois the game,
  Incertane is the dyiss :
Thair is no man, I say, that can
  Both lufe and to be wyiss.

Fle alwayis frome the snair ;
  Lerne at me to be ware ;
It is ane pane and dowbill trane [1]
  Of endles wo and cair ;
For to refrane [2] that denger plane,
  Fle alwayis frome the snair.

41   *Only to yow in Erd that I lufe best*

ONLY to yow in erd that I lufe best
   I me commend ane hundreth thowsand syiss [3] ,
Exorting yow with pensyfe hairt opprest,
  As ye ar scho quhom in my confort lyiss,
  Gif I misvse my pen, or done dispyss [4]
Ocht at this tyme, will God, I sall amend,
Protesting [5] that this ballat ye attend.

Sum luvaris thame delytis till indyte
  Fair facound speich, blandit [6] with eloquence ;
And vthir sum dois sett thair wit perfyte
  To pleiss thair ladeis with all thair diligens ;
  Sum luffaris wantis throw thair negligens,
For falt of speich, the lufe of his maistres,
Without hir witting he was in distress.

---

[1] deceitful lure. [2] escape. [3] times. [4] give offence. [5] stipulating. [6] adorned.

As to my parte, my lusty lady schene[1],
   Throw laik of speich I thoill[2] ryght grit distress,
Bayth nyght and day, hard persit to the splene
   With deidly dert, and can find no redress :
   Thus me behuffis[3] my panis to express,
Or than ye knaw ryght weill, but wirds moir[4],
That crewell dert onthrow my hart wald boir.

Rathir nor smart, I mon my harme reweill,
   To yow, my hairt, quha ma my baills beit[5] ;
For, and ye start[6], adew all warldly weill ;
   Will ye rewart, my cairis ar compleit[7] ;
   Tuiching your parte, I prey you be discreit ;
For eftirwart, gif ye vpoun me rew,
Quill deid departe my lyfe, I salbe trew.

Secreit alswa, in every maner sort[8],
   For weill nor wa sall ony knaw our mynd ;
Than be not thra[9] your scherwand to confort ;
   Sum answswer ma[10], as ye ar gud and kynd,
   That may me fra my languor appeill that is pynd,
And to sla me throw your negligence[11] :
This I yow pra, for your he excellens.

Adew, ryght trew, adew, my deirest hairt,
   Fairest of hew, for this tyme haif gud nyght ;
Remord[12] and rew, and pondir weill my parte,
   Sen I persew nathing of yow bot ryght ;
   Quhilk gif ye knew my mynd as it is plicht[13],
Ye wald subdew your inwart thought and mynd,
And me reskew, quhilk for your lufe is pynd.

---

[1] lovely lady bright. [2] endure. [3] it behoves me. [4] without more words. [5] my woes mitigate. [6] if you leave me. [7] at an end. [8] in all ways. [9] reluctant. [10] make. [11] these lines are corrupt, but their sense seems to be "that may free me from my painful languor, and do not slay me with neglect."—S.T.S. Ed. [12] relent. [13] plighted.

42   *Lament of the Master of Erskine* [1]

DEPARTE, departe, departe,
    Allace ! I most departe
Frome hir that hes my hart,
    With hairt full soir,
Aganis my will in deid,
And can find no remeid :
I wait [2] the pains of deid [3]
    Can do no moir.

Now most I go, allace !
Ffrome sicht of hir sueit face,
The ground of all my grace,
    And souerane ;
Quhat chanss that may fall me [4],
Sall I nevir mirry be,
Unto the tyme I se
    My sweit agane.

I go, and wait not quhair,
I wandir heir and thair,
I weip and sichis rycht sair
    With panis smart ;
Now must I pass away, away,
In wildirness and wilsum [5] way,
Allace ! this wofull day
    We suld departe.

My spreit, dois quake for dreid,
My thirlit [6] hairt dois bleid,
My panis dois exceid—
    Quhat suld I say ?

[1] Lover of the Queen-Dowager, Mary of Lorraine, was slain at the battle of Pinkiecleuch, 1547.   [2] know, ween.   [3] death.
[4] whate'er befall me. [5] lonesome. [6] pierced.

I wofull wycht, allone,
And mak ane petouss mone,
Allace ! my hairt is gone
  For evir and ay.

Throw langour [1] of my sueit
So thirlit is my spreit,
My dayis ar most compleit [2]
  Throw hir absence :
Chryst ! sen scho knew my smert
Ingrawit in my hairt,
Becaus I most depairte
  Ffrome hir presens.

Adew, my awin sueit thing,
My joy and comforting,
My mirth and sollesing
  Of erdly gloir :
Fair weill, my lady bricht,
And my remembrance rycht;
Fair weill and haif gud nycht :
  I say no moir.

[1] longing for.   [2] almost ended.

ANONYMOUS

Sir Patrick Spens

THE king sits in Dunfermline town,
   Drinking the blude-red wine ;
" O whare will I get a skeely [1] skipper,
   To sail this new ship of mine ? "

O up and spake an eldern knight,
   Sat at the king's right knee,
" Sir Patrick Spens is the best sailor,
   That ever sail'd the sea."

Our king has written a braid letter,
   And seal'd it with his hand,
And sent it to sir Patrick Spens,
   Was walking on the strand.

" To Noroway, to Noroway,
   To Noroway o'er the faem ;
The king's daughter of Noroway,
   'Tis thou maun bring her hame,"

The first word that sir Patrick read,
   Sae loud loud laughed he ;
The neist word that sir Patrick read,
   The tear blinded his e'e.

[1] skilful.

" O wha is this has done this deed,
    And tauld the king o' me,
To send us out, at this time of the year,
    To sail upon the sea?

" Be it wind, be it weet, be it hail, be it sleet,
    Our ship must sail the faem;
The king's daughter of Noroway,
    'Tis we must fetch her hame."

They hoysed their sails on Monenday morn,
    Wi' a' the speed they may;
They hae landed in Noroway,
    Upon a Wodensday.

They hadna been a week, a week,
    In Noroway, but twae,
When that the lords o' Noroway
    Began aloud to say,

" Ye Scottishmen spend a' our king's goud,
    And a' our queenis fee!"
" Ye lie, ye lie, ye liars loud!
    Fu' loud I hear ye lie.

" For I brought as much white monie,
    As gane [1] my men and me,
And I brought a half-fou [2] o' gude red goud,
    Out o'er the sea wi' me.

" Make ready, make ready, my merrymen a'!
    Our gude ship sails the morn."
" Now, ever alake, my master dear,
    I fear a deadly storm!

[1] supplies.   [2] the eighth of a peck.

" I saw the new moon, late yestreen,
　　Wi' the auld moon in her arm ;
And if we gang to sea, master,
　　I fear we'll come to harm."

They hadna sailed a league, a league,
　　A league but barely three,
When the lift grew dark, and the wind blew loud,
　　And gurly [1] grew the sea.

The ankers brak, and the topmasts lap [2],
　　It was sick a deadly storm ;
And the waves came o'er the broken ship,
　　Till a' her sides were torn.

" O where will I get a gude sailor,
　　To take my helm in hand,
Till I get up to the tall top-mast,
　　To see if I can spy land ? "

" O here am I, a sailor gude,
　　To take the helm in hand,
Till you go up to the tall top-mast,
　　But I fear you'll ne'er spy land."

He hadna' gane a step, a step,
　　A step, but barely ane,
When a bout [3] flew out of our goodly ship,
　　And the salt sea it came in.

" Gae fetch a web o' the silken claith,
　　Another o' the twine,
And wap [4] them into our ship's side,
　　And let na the sea come in."

---

[1] raging.　[2] sprung.　[3] bolt.　[4] wrap.

They fetched a web o' the silken claith,
  Another of the twine,
And they wapped them round that gude ship's
    side,
  But still the sea came in.

O laith, laith, were our gude Scots lords
  To weet their cork-heel'd shoon !
But lang or a' the play was play'd,
  They wat their hats aboon.

And mony was the feather-bed,
  That flattered [1] on the faem ;
And mony was the gude lord's son,
  That never mair cam hame.

The ladyes wrang their fingers white,
  The maidens tore their hair,
A' for the sake of their true loves ;
  For them they'll see na mair.

O lang, lang, may the ladyes sit,
  Wi' their fans into their hand,
Before they see sir Patrick Spens,
  Come sailing to the strand !

And lang, lang, may the maidens sit,
  Wi' their goud kaims in their hair,
A' waiting for their ain dear loves !
  For them they'll see na mair.

O forty miles off Aberdeen,
  'Tis fifty fathom deep,
And there lies gude sir Patrick Spens,
  Wi' the Scots lords at his feet.

[1] rocked.

44 *The Dowie Dens of Yarrow*

LATE at e'en, drinking the wine,
  And ere they paid the lawing,
They set a combat them between,
  To fight it in the dawing[1].

"O stay at hame, my noble lord!
  O stay at hame, my marrow[2]!
My cruel brother will you betray,
  On the dowie[3] houms[4] of Yarrow."

"O fare ye weel, my ladye gaye!
  O fare ye weel, my Sarah!
For I maun gae, though I ne'er return,
  Frae the dowie banks o' Yarrow.

She kissed his cheek, she kaimed his hair,
  As oft she had done before O;
She belted him with his noble brand,
  And he's awa' to Yarrow.

As he gaed up the Tennies bank,
  I wot he gaed wi' sorrow,
Till, down in a den, he spied nine arm'd men
  On the dowie houms of Yarrow.

"O come ye here to part your land,
  The bonnie forest thorough?
Or come ye here to wield your brand,
  On the dowie houms of Yarrow?"

[1] dawning. [2] mate. [3] dreary. [4] shores.

"I come not here to part my land,
  And neither to beg nor borrow;
I come to wield my noble brand,
  On the bonny banks of Yarrow.

"If I see all, ye're nine to ane;
  And that's an unequal marrow [1]:
Yet will I fight, while lasts my brand,
  On the bonny banks of Yarrow."

Four has he hurt, and five has slain,
  On the bloody braes of Yarrow,
Till that stubborn knight came him behind,
  And ran his bodie thorough.

"Gae hame, gae hame, good-brother [2] John,
  And tell your sister Sarah,
To come and lift her leafu' [3] lord!
  He's sleepin sound on Yarrow."

"Yestreen I dream'd a dolefu' dream;
  I fear there will be sorrow!
I dream'd, I pu'd the heather green,
  Wi' my true love, on Yarrow.

"O gentle wind, that bloweth south,
  From where my love repaireth,
Convey a kiss from his dear mouth,
  And tell me how he fareth!

"But in the glen strive armed men;
  They've wrought me dole and sorrow;
They've slain—the comeliest knight they've slain—
  He bleeding lies on Yarrow."

[1] match. [2] brother-in-law. [3] lonely.

As she sped down yon high high hill,
  She gaed wi' dole and sorrow,
And in the den spyed ten slain men,
    On the dowie banks of Yarrow.

She kiss'd his cheek, she kaim'd his hair,
  She search'd his wounds all thorough ;
She kiss'd them till her lips grew red,
    On the dowie houms of Yarrow.

"Now, haud your tongue, my daughter dear !
  For a' this breeds but sorrow ;
I'll wed ye to a better lord,
    Than him ye lost on Yarrow."

"O haud your tongue, my father dear !
  Ye mind me but of sorrow ;
A fairer rose did never bloom
    Than now lies cropp'd on Yarrow."

45   *The Lament of the Border Widow*

MY love he built me a bonny bower
    And clad it a' wi' lilye flour ;
A brawer bower ye ne'er did see,
Than my true love he built for me.

There came a man, by middle day,
He spied his sport, and went away ;
And brought the king, that very night,
Who brake my bower, and slew my knight.

He slew my knight, to me sae dear;
He slew my knight, and poin'd[1] his gear;
My servants all for life did flee,
And left me in extremitie.

I sew'd his sheet, making my mane;
I watched the corpse, myself alane;
I watched his body, night and day;
No living creature came that way.

I took his body on my back,
And whiles I gaed, and whiles I sate;
I digg'd a grave, and laid him in,
And happ'd[2] him with the sod sae green.

But think na ye my heart was sair,
When I laid the moul' on his yellow hair?
O think na ye my heart was wae,
When I turn'd about, away to gae?

Nae living man I'll love again,
Since that my lovely knight is slain;
Wi' ae lock of his yellow hair,
I'll chain my heart for evermair.

46   *The Twa Corbies*[3]

A S I was walking all alane,
      I heard twa corbies making a mane,
The tane unto the t'other say,
"Where sall we gang and dine to-day?"

---

[1] confiscated.   [2] covered.   [3] ravens.

" In behint yon auld fail dyke [1],
I wot there lies a new slain knight ;
And nae body kens that he lies there,
But his hawk, his hound, and lady fair.

" His hound is to the hunting gane,
His hawk to fetch the wild-fowl hame,
His lady's ta'en another mate,
So we may mak our dinner sweet.

" Ye'll sit on his white hause bane [2],
And I'll pike out his bonny blue e'en :
Wi' ae lock o' his gowden hair,
We'll theek [3] our nest when it grows bare.

" Mony a one for him makes mane,
But nane sall ken whare he is gane :
O'er his white banes, when they are bare,
The wind sall blaw for evermair."

47   *The Douglas Tragedy*

" RISE up, rise up, now, lord Douglas," she says,
     "And put on your armour so bright,
Let it never be said, that a daughter of thine
   Was married to a lord under night.

" Rise up, rise up, my seven bold sons,
   And put on your armour so bright,
And take better care of your youngest sister,
   For your eldest's awa the last night."

[1] turf fence.   [2] breast-bone.   [3] thatch.

He's mounted her on a milk-white steed,
  And himself on a dapple grey,
With a bugelet horn hung down by his side,
  And lightly they rode away.

Lord William lookit o'er his left shoulder,
  To see what he could see,
And there he spy'd her seven brethren bold
  Come riding over the lee.

" Light down, light down, lady Marg'ret," he said,
  " And hold my steed in your hand,
Until that against your seven brethren bold,
  And your father I mak a stand."

She held his steed in her milk-white hand,
  And never shed one tear,
Until that she saw her seven brethren fa',
    And her father hard fighting, who lov'd her so
      dear.

" O hold your hand, lord William!" she said,
  " For your strokes they are wond'rous sair ;
True lovers I can get many a ane,
  But a father I can never get mair."

O she's ta'en out her handkerchief,
  It was o' the holland sae fine,
And ay she dighted her father's bloody wounds,
  That ware redder than the wine.

" O chuse, O chuse, lady Marg'ret," he said,
  " O whether will ye gang or bide ? "
" I'll gang, I'll gang, lord William," she said,
  " For ye have left me no other guide."

He's lifted her on a milk-white steed,
　And himself on a dapple grey,
With a bugelet horn hung down by his side,
　And slowly they baith rade away.

O they rade on, and on they rade,
　And a' by the light of the moon,
Until they came to yon wan water,
　And there they lighted down.

They lighted down to tak a drink,
　Of the spring that ran sae clear ;
And down the stream ran his gude heart's blood,
　And sair she gan to fear.

" Hold up, hold up, lord William," she says,
　" For I fear that you are slain ! "
" 'Tis naething but the shadow of my scarlet cloak,
　That shines in the water sae plain."

O they rade on, and on they rade,
　And a' by the light of the moon,
Until they cam to his mother's ha' door,
　And there they lighted down.

"Get up, get up, lady mother," he says,
　" Get up, and let me in !—
" Get up, get up, lady mother," he says,
　" For this night my fair lady I've win.

"O mak my bed, lady mother," he says,
　"O mak it braid and deep !
And lay lady Marg'ret close at my back,
　And the sounder I will sleep."

Lord William was dead long ere midnight,
  Lady Margaret lang ere day—
And all true lovers that go thegither,
  May they have mair luck than they!

Lord William was buried in St. Marie's kirk,
  Lady Margaret in Mary's quire,
Out o' the lady's grave grew a bonny red rose,
  And out o' the knight's a briar.

And they twa met, and they twa plat,
  And fain they wad be near;
And a' the warld might ken right weel,
  They were twa lovers dear.

But bye and rade the Black Douglas,
  And wow but he was rough!
For he pull'd up the bonny brier,
  And flang'd in St. Mary's loch.

48   *Lord Randal*

"O WHERE hae ye been, lord Randal, my son?
    O where hae ye been, my handsome young
      man?"
"I hae been to the wild wood; mother, make my
    bed soon,
For I'm weary wi' hunting, and fain wald lie
    down."

"Where gat ye your dinner, lord Randal, my son?
Where gat ye your dinner, my handsome young
    man?"

" I din'd wi' my true-love ; mother, make my bed
 soon,
For I'm weary wi' hunting, and fain wald lie
 down."

"What gat ye to your dinner, lord Randal, my son,
What gat ye to your dinner, my handsome young
 man ? "
" I gat eels boil'd in broo' [1] ; mother, make my bed
 soon,
For I'm weary wi' hunting, and fain wald lie
 down."

" What became of your bloodhounds, lord Randal,
 my son ?
What became of your bloodhounds, my handsome
 young man ? "
" O they swell'd and they died—mother, make my
 bed soon,
For I'm weary wi' hunting, and fain wald lie
 down."

" O I fear ye are poison'd, lord Randal, my son !
O I fear ye are poison'd, my handsome young
 man ! "
" O yes ! I am poison'd—mother, make my bed
 soon,
For I'm sick at the heart, and I fain wald lie
 down."

[1] broth.

49 *The Broom of Cowdenknows*

O THE broom, and the bonny bonny broom,
 And the broom of the Cowdenknows !
And aye sae sweet as the lassie sang,
 I' the bought [1], milking the ewes.

The hills were high on ilka [2] side,
 An' the bought i' the lirk [3] o' the hill ;
And aye, as she sang, her voice it rang,
 Out o'er the head o' yon hill.

There was a troop o' gentlemen,
 Came riding merrilie by,
And one o' them has rode out o' the way,
 To the bought to the bonny may [4].

" Weel may ye save an' see, bonny lass,
 An' weel may ye save an' see."
" An' sae wi' you, ye weel-bred knight,
 And what's your will wi' me ? "

" The night is misty and mirk, fair may,
 And I have ridden astray,
And will ye be so kind, fair may,
 As come out and point my way ? "

" Ride out, ride out, ye ramp [5] rider !
 Your steed's baith stout and strang ;
For out of the bought I dare na come,
 For fear 'at ye do me wrang."

[1] sheep-pen. [2] each. [3] hollow, or slack. [4] maiden. [5] bold.

" O winna ye pity me, bonny lass,
  O winna ye pity me ?
An' winna ye pity my poor steed,
  Stands trembling at yon tree ? "

" I wadna pity your poor steed,
  Tho' it were tied to a thorn ;
For if ye wad gain my love the night,
  Ye wad slight me ere the morn.

" For I ken you by your weel-busked [1] hat,
  And your merrie twinkling e'e ;
That ye're the laird o' the Oakland hills,
  An ye may weel seem for to be."

" But I am not the laird o' the Oakland hills,
  Ye're far mista'en o' me ;
But I'm ane o' the men about his house,
  An' right aft in his companie."

He's ta'en her by the middle jimp [2],
  And by the grass-green sleeve ;
He's lifted her over the fauld [3] dyke,
  And speer'd at [4] her sma' leave.

O he's ta'en out a purse o' gowd,
  And streek'd [5] her yellow hair,
" Now, take ye that, my bonnie may,
  Of me till you hear mair."

O he's leapt on his berry-brown steed,
  An' soon he's o'erta'en his men ;
And ane and a' cried out to him,
  " O master, ye've tarry'd lang ! "

---

[1] modish.   [2] slim.   [3] turf.   [4] asked of.   [5] stroked.

"O I hae been east, and I hae been west,
　An' I hae been far o'er the know,
But the bonniest lass that ever I saw,
　Is i' the bought milkin the ewes."

She set the cog [1] upon her head,
　An' she's gane singing hame—
"O where hae ye been, my ae daughter?
　Ye hae na been your lane [2]."

"O nae body was wi' me, father,
　O nae body has been wi' me :
The night is misty and mirk, father,
　Ye may gang to the door and see.

"But wae be to your ewe-herd, father,
　And an ill deed [3] may he die ;
He bug [4] the bought at the back o' the know [5],
　And a tod [6] has frighted me.

"There came a tod to the bought door,
　The like I never saw ;
And ere he had taken the lamb he did,
　I had lourd [7] he had ta'en them a'."

O whan fifteen weeks was come and gane,
　Fifteen weeks and three,
That lassie began to look thin and pale,
　An' to long for his merry twinkling e'e.

It fell on a day, on a het simmer day,
　She was ca'ing [8] out her father's kye,
By came a troop o' gentlemen,
　A' merrilie riding bye.

---

[1] milking-pail.　[2] by yourself.　[3] death.　[4] built.　[5] hillock.
[6] fox.　[7] rather.　[8] driving.

" Weel may ye save an' see, bonny may,
  Weel may ye save and see !
Weel I wat, ye be a very bonny may,
  But whae's aught that babe ye are wi'."

Never a word could that lassie say,
  For never a ane could she blame,
An' never a word could the lassie say,
  But " I have a good man at hame."

" Ye lied, ye lied, my very bonny may,
  Sae loud as I hear you lie ;
For dinna ye mind that misty night,
  I was i' the bought wi' thee ?

" I ken you by your middle sae jimp,
  An' your merry twinkling e'e,
That ye're the bonny lass i' the Cowdenknow,
  An' ye may weel seem for to be."

Than he's leap'd off his berry-brown steed,
  An' he's set that fair may on—
" Caw out your kye, gude father [1], yoursel,
  For she's never caw them out again."

" I am the laird of the Oakland hills,
  I hae thirty plows and three ;
An' I hae gotten the bonniest lass,
  That's in a' the south country."

----

[1] father-in-law.

50   *Edom of Gordon*

IT fell about the Martinmas,
    Quhen the wind blew shril and cauld,
Said Edom of Gordon to his men,
    " We maun draw till a hauld.

" And quhat a hauld sall we draw till,
    My mirry men and me ?
We wul gae to the house o' the Rodes,
    To see that fair ladie. "

The lady stude on hir castle wa',
    Beheld baith dale and down :
There she was ware of a host of men
    Cum ryding towards the toun.

" O see ye nat, my mirry men a' ?
    O see ye nat quhat I see ?
Methinks I see a host of men :
    I marveil quha they be. "

She weend it had been hir luvely lord,
    As he cam ryding hame ;
It was the traitor Edom o' Gordon,
    Quha reckt nae sin nor shame.

She had nae sooner buskit [1] hirsel,
    And putfen on hir goun,
But Edom o' Gordon and his men
    Were round about the toun.

----

[1] attired.

They had nae sooner supper sett,
   Nae sooner said the grace,
But Edom o' Gordon and his men
   Were light about the place.

The lady ran up to hir towir head,
   So fast as she could hie,
To see if by hir fair speeches
   She could wi' him agree.

But quhan he see this lady saif,
   And hir yates all locked fast,
He fell into a rage of wrath,
   And his look was all aghast.

"Cum doun to me, ye lady gay,
   Cum doun, cum doun to me :
This night sall ye lig within mine armes,
   To-morrow my bride sall be."

"I winnae cum doun, ye fals Gordon,
   I winnae cum doun to thee ;
I winnae forsake my ain dear lord,
   That is sae far frae me."

"Give owre your house, ye lady fair,
   Give owre your house to me,
Or I sall brenn yoursel therein,
   Bot and your babies three."

"I winnae give owre, ye fals Gordon,
   To nae sik traitor as yee ;
And if ye brenn my ain dear babes,
   My lord sall make ye drie.

"But reach my pistoll, Glaud, my man,
   And charge ye weil my gun :
For, but an I pierce that bluidy butcher,
   My babes, we been undone."

She stude upon hir castle wa',
   And let twa bullets flee :
She mist that bluidy butcher's hart,
   And only raz'd his knee.

"Set fire to the house," quo' fals Gordon,
   All wood [1] wi' dule and ire :
"Fals lady, ye sall rue this deid,
   As ye bren in the fire."

"Wae worth [2], wae worth ye, Jock, my man,
   I paid ye weil your fee ;
Quhy pu' ye out the ground-wa' stane,
   Lets in the reek to me ?

"And ein wae worth ye, Jock, my man,
   I paid ye weil your hire ;
Quhy pu' ye out the ground-wa' stane,
   To me lets in the fire ?"

"Ye paid me weil my hire, lady ;
   Ye paid me weil my fee :
But now I'm Edom o' Gordon's man,
   Maun either doe or die."

O than bespaik hir little son,
   Sate on the nurse's knee :
Sayes, "Mither deare, gi' owre this house,
   For the reek it smithers me."

[1] wild.   [2] woe betide.

" I wad gie a' my gowd, my childe,
  Sa wald I a' my fee,
For ane blast o' the western wind
  To blaw the reek frae thee."

O than bespaik hir dochter dear,
  She was baith jimp [1] and sma :
"O row [2] me in a pair o' sheits,
  And tow me ower the wa."

They rowd hir in a pair o' sheits,
  And towd hir ower the wa :
But on the point o' Gordon's spear
  She gat a deadly fa.

O bonnie bonnie was hir mouth,
  And cherry were her cheiks,
And clear clear was hir yellow hair,
  Whereon the reid bluid dreips.

Then wi' his spear he turned hir owre,
  O gin hir face was wan !
He sayd, " Ye are the first that eir
  I wisht alive again."

He turned hir owre and owre againe,
  O gin hir skin was whyte !
"I might ha spared that bonnie face,
  To hae been sum man's delyte.

" Busk and boun [3], my merry men a',
  For ill dooms I doe guess ;
I cannae luik in that bonnie face,
  As it lyes on the grass."

---

[1] slim.   [2] roll.   [3] make ready.

" Thame, luiks to freits [1], my master deir,
   Then freits wil follow thame :
Let it neir be said brave Edom o' Gordon
   Was daunted by a dame."

But quhen the ladye see the fire
   Cum flaming owre hir head,
She wept, and kist her children twain,
   Sayd, " Bairns, we been but dead."

The Gordon then his bougill blew,
   And said, " Awa', awa' ;
This house o' the Rodes is a' in flame,
   I hauld it time to ga'."

O then bespyed hir ain dear lord,
   As hee cam owr the lee ;
He seid his castle all in blaze
   Sa far as he could see.

Then sair, O sair his mind misgave,
   And all his hart was wae ;
" Put on, put on, my wighty [2] men,
   So fast as ye can gae.

" Put on, put on, my wighty men,
   Sa fast as ye can drie ;
For he that is hindmost of the thrang
   Sall neir get guid o' me."

Than sum they rade, and sum they rin,
   Fou fast out owr the bent ;
But eir the foremost could get up,
   Baith lady and babes were brent.

[1] omens.   [2] stalwart.

He wrang his hands, he rent his hair,
  And wept in teenefu' muid [1] :
" O traitors, for this cruel deid
  Ye sall weep teirs o' bluid."

And after the Gordon he is gane,
  Sa fast as he might drie ;
And soon i' the Gordon's foul hartis bluid
  He's wroken [2] his dear Ladie.

51   *The Battle of Otterbourne*

IT fell about the Lammas tide,
  When the muir-men win their hay,
The doughty Douglas bound him to ride
  Into England, to drive a prey.

He chose the Gordons and the Græmes,
  With them the Lindesays, light and gay,
But the Jardines wald not with him ride,
  And they rue it to this day.

And he has burn'd the dales of Tyne,
  And part of Bambrough shire ;
And three good towers on Reidswire fells,
  He left them all on fire.

And he march'd up to Newcastle,
  And rode it round about ;
" O wha's the lord of this castle,
  Or wha's the lady o't ? "—

____

[1] sorrowful mood.   [2] revenged.

But up spake proud lord Percy, then,
    And O but he spake hie!
"I am the lord of this castle,
    My wife's the lady gay."—

"If thou'rt the lord of this castle,
    Sae weel it pleases me!
For, ere I cross the Border fells,
    The tane of us shall dee."—

He took a lang spear in his hand,
    Shod with the metal free,
And for to meet the Douglas there,
    He rode right furiouslie.

But O how pale his lady look'd,
    Frae aff the castle wa',
When down before the Scottish spear,
    She saw proud Percy fa'.

"Had we twa been upon the green,
    And never an eye to see,
I wad hae had you, flesh and fell [1];
    But your sword sall gae wi' me."—

"But gae ye up to Otterbourne,
    And wait there dayis three;
And, if I come not ere three dayis end,
    A fause knight ca' ye me."—

"The Otterbourne's a bonnie burn;
    'Tis pleasant there to be;
But there is nought at Otterbourne,
    To feed my men and me.

[1] Fell—Hide. Douglas insinuates, that Percy was rescued by his soldiers.

" The deer rins wild on hill and dale,
   The birds fly wild from tree to tree ;
But there is neither bread nor kale,
   To fend [1] my men and me.

"Yet I will stay at Otterbourne,
   Where you shall welcome be ;
And, if you come not at three dayis end,—
   A fause lord I'll ca' thee."—

" Thither will I come," proud Percy said,
   By the might of Our Ladye ! "—
" There will I bide thee," said the Douglas,
   My troth I plight to thee."—

They lighted high on Otterbourne,
   Upon the bent sae brown ;
They lighted high on Otterbourne,
   And threw their pallions down.

And he that had a bonnie boy,
   Sent out his horse to grass ;
And he that had not a bonnie boy,
   His ain servant he was.

But up then spake a little page,
   Before the peep of dawn—
" O waken ye, waken ye, my good lord,
   For Percy's hard at hand."—

" Ye lie, ye lie, ye liar loud !
   Sae loud I hear ye lie :
For Percy had not men yestreen
   To dight my men and me.

[1] support.

"But I have dreamed a dreary dream,
  Beyond the Isle of Skye;
I saw a dead man win a fight,
  And I think that man was I."

He belted on his guid braid sword,
  And to the field he ran;
But he forgot the helmet good,
  That should have kept his brain.

When Percy with the Douglas met,
  I wat he was fu' fain!
They swakked [1] their swords, till sair they swat,
  And the blood ran down like rain.

But Percy, with his good broad sword,
  That could so sharply wound,
Has wounded Douglas on the brow,
  Till he fell to the ground.

Then he called on his little foot-page,
  And said—"Run speedilie,
And fetch my ain dear sister's son,
  Sir Hugh Montgomery.

"My nephew good," the Douglas said,
  "What recks the death of ane!
Last night I dream'd a dreary dream,
  And I ken the day's thy ain.

"My wound is deep; I fain would sleep;
  Take thou the vanguard of the three,
And hide me by the braken bush,
  That grows on yonder lilye lee.

[1] clashed.

"O bury me by the braken bush,
  Beneath the blooming brier,
Let never living mortal ken,
  That ere a kindly Scot lies here."

He lifted up that noble lord,
  Wi' the saut tears in his eee;
He hid him in the braken bush,
  That his merrie-men might not see.

The moon was clear, the day drew near,
  The spears in flinders flew,
But mony a gallant Englishman
  Ere day the Scotsmen slew.

The Gordons good, in English blood,
  They steep'd their hose and shoon;
The Lindsays flew like fire about,
  Till all the fray was done.

The Percy and Montgomery met,
  That either of other were fain;
They swapped swords, and they twa swat,
  And aye the blood ran down between.

"Now yield thee, yield thee, Percy," he said,
  "Or else I vow I'll lay thee low!"—
"To whom must I yield," quoth earl Percy,
  "Now that I see it must be so?"—

"Thou shalt not yield to lord nor loun,
  Nor yet shalt thou yield to me;
But yield ye to the braken bush,
  That grows upon yon lilye lee!"—

" I will not yield to a braken bush,
   Nor yet will I yield to a brier ;
But I would yield to earl Douglas,
   Or sir Hugh the Montgomery, if he were here."

As soon as he knew it was Montgomery,
   He struck his sword's point in the gronde ;
The Montgomery was a courteous knight,
   And quickly took him by the honde.

This deed was done at Otterbourne
   About the breaking of the day ;
Earl Douglas was buried at the braken bush,
   And the Percy led captive away.

52   *Johnie Armstrang*

SUM speikis of lords, sum speikis of lairds,
   And sic lyke men of hie degrie ;
Of a gentleman I sing a sang,
   Sum tyme called Laird of Gilnockie.

The King he wrytes a luving letter,
   With his ain hand sae tenderly,
And he hath sent it to Johnie Armstrang,
   To cum and speik with him speedily.

The Elliots and Armstrangs did convene ;
   They were a gallant cumpanie—
" We'll ride and meit our lawful king,
   And bring him safe to Gilnockie.

" Make kinnen [1] and capon ready, then,
  And venison in great plentie ;
We'll wellcum here our royal king ;
  I hope he'll dine at Gilnockie ! "—

They ran their horse on the Langholme howm [2],
  And brak their spears wi' mickle main ;
The ladies lukit frae their loft windows—
  " God bring our men weel hame agen ! "

When Johnie cam before the king,
  Wi' a' his men sae brave to see,
The king he movit his bonnet to him ;
  He ween'd he was a king as weel as he.

" May I find grace, my sovereign liege,
  Grace for my loyal men and me?
For my name it is Johnie Armstrang,
  And a subject of yours, my liege," said he.

" Away, away, thou traitor strang !
  Out o' my sight soon mayst thou be !
I grantit never a traitor's life,
  And now I'll not begin wi' thee."—

" Grant me my life, my liege, my king !
  And a bonny gift I'll gie to thee—
Full four-and-twenty milk-white steids,
  Were a' foal'd in ae yeir to me.

" I'll gie thee a' these milk-white steids,
  That prance and nicher [3] at a speir ;
And as mickle gude Inglish gilt [4],
  As four o' their braid backs dow [5] bear."—

[1] rabbits. [2] riverside meadow. [3] neigh. [4] gold. [5] are able to.

"Away, away, thou traitor strang!
　Out o' my sight soon mayst thou be!
I grantit never a traitor's life,
　And now I'll not begin wi' thee!"

"Grant me my life, my liege, my king!
　And a bonny gift I'll gie to thee—
Gude four-and-twenty ganging mills,
　That gang thro' a' the yeir to me.

"These four-and-twenty mills complete
　Sall gang for thee thro' a' the yeir;
And as mickle of gude reid wheit,
　As a' thair happers dow to bear."—

"Away, away, thou traitor strang!
　Out o' my sight soon mayst thou be!
I grantit never a traitor's life,
　And now I'll not begin wi' thee."—

"Grant me my life, my liege, my king!
　And a great great gift I'll gie to thee—
Bauld four-and-twenty sisters' sons
　Sall for thee fecht, tho' a' should flee!"

"Away, away, thou traitor strang!
　Out o' my sight soon mayst thou be!
I grantit never a traitor's life,
　And now I'll not begin wi' thee."—

"Grant me my life, my liege, my king!
　And a brave gift I'll gie to thee—
All betweeen heir and Newcastle town [1]
　Sall pay their yeirly rent to thee."—

[1] Newcastleton.

"Away, away, thou traitor strang !
  Out o' my sight soon mayst thou be !
I grantit never a traitor's life,
  And now I'll not begin wi' thee."—

"Ye lied, ye lied, now, king," he says,
  "Altho' a king and prince ye be !
For I've luved naething in my life,
  I weel dare say it, but honesty—

"Save a fat horse, and a fair woman,
  Twa bonny dogs to kill a deir ;
But England suld have found me meal and
      mault
    Gif I had lived this hundred yeir !

"She suld have found me meal and mault,
  And beef and mutton in a' plentie ;
But never a Scots wyfe could have said,
  That e'er I skaith'd her a puir flee.

"To seik het water beneith cauld ice,
  Surely it is a greit follie—
I have asked grace at a graceless face,
  But there is nane for my men and me !

"But had I kenn'd ere I cam frae hame,
  How thou unkind wadst been to me !
I wad have keepit the border side,
  In spite of all thy force and thee.

"Wist England's king that I was ta'en,
  O gin a blythe man he wad be !
For anes I slew his sister's son,
  And on his breist bane brak a trie."—

John wore a girdle about his middle,
   Imbroider'd ower wi' burning gold,
Bespangled wi' the same metal,
   Maist beautiful was to behold.

There hang nine targats[1] at Johnie's hat,
   And ilk ane worth three hundred pound—
" What wants that knave that a king suld have,
   But the sword of honour and the crown ?

" O where got thee these targats, Johnie,
   That blink sae brawly[2] abune thy brie ? "
" I gat them in the field fechting,
   Where, cruel king, thou durst not be.

" Had I my horse, and harness gude,
   And riding as I wont to be,
It suld have been tauld this hundred yeir,
   The meeting of my king and me !

" God be with thee, Kirsty[3], my brother,
   Lang live thou laird of Mangertoun !
Lang mayst thou live on the Border syde,
   Ere thou see thy brother ride up and down !

" And God be with thee, Kirsty, my son,
   Where thou sits on thy nurse's knee !
But an thou live this hundred yeir,
   Thy father's better thou'lt never be.

" Farewell ! my bonny Gilnock-hall,
   Where on Esk side thou standest stout !
Gif I had lived but seven yeirs mair,
   I wad hae gilt thee round about."

[1] tassels. [2] Glance so bravely. [3] Christopher.

John murdered was at Carlinrigg,
  And all his gallant companie ;
But Scotland's heart was ne'er sae wae,
  To see sae mony brave men die—

Because they saved their country deir
  Frae Englishmen ! Nane were sa bauld,
Whyle Johnie lived on the Border syde,
  Nane of them durst cum neir his hauld.

53   *The Wife of Usher's Well*

A FRAGMENT

THERE lived a wife at Usher's Well,
  And a wealthy wife was she ;
She had three stout and stalwart sons,
  And sent them o'er the sea.

They hadna been a week from her,
  A week but barely ane,
Whan word came to the carline wife [1],
  That her three sons were gane.

They hadna been a week from her
  A week but barely three,
Whan word came to the carlin wife,
  That her sons she'd never see.

---

[1] aged woman ; the word carline sometimes carries the meaning
of witch.

"I wish the wind may never cease,
    Nor fishes in the flood,
Till my three sons come hame to me,
    In earthly flesh and blood."—

It fell about the Martinmass,
    When nights are lang and mirk,
The carlin wife's three sons came hame,
    And their hats were o' the birk.

It neither grew in syke [1] nor ditch,
    Nor yet in ony sheugh [2];
But at the gates o' paradise,
    That birk grew fair eneugh.

   *   *   *   *   *

"Blow up the fire, my maidens;
    Bring water from the well:
For a' my house shall feast this night,
    Since my three sons are well."—

And she has made to them a bed,
    She's made it large and wide;
And she's ta'en her mantle her about,
    Sat down at the bed-side.

   *   *   *   *   *

Up then crew the red red cock,
    And up and crew the gray;
The eldest to the youngest said,
    "'Tis time we were away."—

The cock he hadna craw'd but once,
    And clapp'd his wings at a',
When the youngest to the eldest said,
    "Brother, we must awa:

---

[1] marshy ground. [2] furrow.

"The cock doth craw, the day doth daw,
  The channerin'[1] worm doth chide ;
Gin we be mist out o' our place,
  A sair pain we maun bide.

"Fare ye well, my mother dear !
  Fareweel to barn and byre !
And fare ye well, the bonny lass,
  That kindles my mother's fire."

* * * *

54   *Fair Helen*

Part I

O! SWEETEST sweet, and fairest fair,
  Of birth and worth beyond compare,
Thou art the causer of my care,
  Since first I lovèd thee.

Yet God hath given to me a mind,
The which to thee shall prove as kind,
As any one that thou shalt find,
  Of high or low degree.

The shallowest water makes maist din,
The deadest pool the deepest linn[2],
The richest man least truth within,
  Tho' he preferrèd be.

Yet nevertheless I am content,
And never a whit my love repent,
But think the time was a' well spent,
  Tho' I disdainèd be.

[1] fretting. [2] fall.

16

O ! Helen sweet, and maist compleat,
My captive spirit's at thy feet,
Thinks thou still fit thus for to treat
    Thy captive cruelly.

O ! Helen brave, but this I crave,
Of thy poor slave some pity have,
And do him save that's near his grave,
    And dies for love of thee.

Part II

I wish I were where Helen lies,
Night and day on me she cries,
O that I were where Helen lies,
    On fair Kirconnell Lee !

Curst be the heart that thought the thought
And curst the hand that fired the shot,
When in my arms burd[1] Helen dropt,
    And died to succour me.

O think na ye my heart was sair,
When my love dropt down and spak nae mair,
There did she swoon wi' meikle care,
    On fair Kirconnell Lee.

As I went down the water side,
None but my foe to be my guide,
None but my foe to be my guide,
    On fair Kirconnell Lee.

---

[1] maid.

I lighted down, my sword did draw,
I hackèd him in pieces sma,
I hackèd him in pieces sma,
   For her sake that died for me.

O Helen Fair, beyond compare,
I'll make a garland of thy hair,
Shall bind my heart for evermair,
   Untill the day I die.

O that I were where Helen lies,
Night and day on me she cries,
Out of my bed she bids me rise,
   Says, " Haste, and come to me ! "

O Helen fair ! O Helen chaste !
If I were with thee I were blest,
Where thou lies low, and takes thy rest
   On fair Kirconnell Lee.

I wish my grave were growing green,
A winding sheet drawn ower my e'en,
And I in Helen's arms lying
   On fair Kirconnell Lee.

I wish I were where Helen lies,
Night and day on me she cries,
And I am weary of the skies,
   For her sake that died for me.

55   *Armstrong's Goodnight*

THIS night is my departing night,
   For here nae langer must I stay ;
There's neither friend nor foe o' mine
   But wishes me away.

What I have done thro' lack of wit,
   I never, never, can recall ;
I hope ye're a' my friends as yet,
   Goodnight, and joy be with you all !

56   *The Young Tamlane*

" O I forbid ye, maidens a',
     That wear gowd on your hair,
To come or gae by Carterhaugh ;
   For young Tamlane is there.

" There's nane, that gaes by Carterhaugh,
   But maun leave him a wad [1] ;
Either goud rings, or green mantles,
   Or else their maidenheid."

But up then spake her, fair Janet,
   The fairest o' a' her kin ;
" I'll come and gang to Carterhaugh,
   And ask nae leave o' him."—

Janet has kilted her green kirtle [2],
   A little aboon her knee ;
And she has braided her yellow hair,
   A little aboon her bree.

And she's away to Carterhaugh,
   And gaed beside the wood ;
And there was sleeping young Tamlane,
   And his steed beside him stood.

[1] pledge.   [2] petticoat.

She pu'd the broom flower frae the bush,
  And strewed it on's white hause-bane [1];
And that was to be a witter [2] true,
  That maiden she had gane.

"O where was ye, my milk-white steed,
  That I did love sae dear,
That wadna watch, and waken me,
  When there was maiden here?"—

"I stamped wi' my foot, master,
  I gar'd [3] my bridle ring;
But no kin' thing would waken ye,
  Till she was past and gane."—

"And wae betide ye, my gray goshawk,
  That I did love sae well;
That wadna watch, and waken me,
  When my love was here hersell!"—

"I clapped wi' my wings, master,
  And ay my bells I rang;
And ay cried, 'Waken, waken, master,
  Afore your true love gang.'"—

"But haste, and haste, my good white steed,
  To come the maiden till;
Or a' the birds, in good green wood,
  O' your flesh shall hae their fill."—

"Ye needna burst your good white steed,
  By running o'er the howm [4];
Nae hare runs swifter o'er the lea,
  Nor your love ran thro' the broom."—

[1] breast-bone. [2] token. [3] caused. [4] holm.

Fair Janet, in her green cleiding,
   Returned upon the morn ;
And she met her father's ae brother,
   The laird of Abercorn.

" I'll wager, I'll wager, I'll wager wi' you
   Five hunder merk and ten,
I'll maiden gang to Carterhaugh,
   And maiden come again."—

She princked hersell, and prin'd hersell [1],
   By the ae [2] light of the moon ;
And she's away to Carterhaugh,
   As fast as she could win.

And whan she cam to Carterhaugh,
   She gaed beside the wall ;
And there she fand his steed standing,
   But away was himsell.

She hadna pu'd a red red rose,
   A rose but barely three,
Till up and starts a wee wee man,
   At Lady Janet's knee.

Says—" Why pu' ye the rose, Janet ?
   What gars ye break the tree ?
Or why come ye to Carterhaugh,
   Withoutten leave o' me ! "—

Says—" Carterhaugh it is mine ain ;
   My daddie gave it me ;
I'll come and gang to Carterhaugh,
   And ask nae leave o' thee."—

[1] decked and preened herself. [2] sole.

He's ta'en her by the milk-white hand,
  And by the grass-green sleeve ;
He's led her to the Fairy ground,
  And spier'd at her nae leave.

When she came to her father's ha',
  She looked pale and wan ;
They thought she'd dried[1] some sair sickness,
  Or been wi' some leman.

She didna comb her yellow hair,
  Nor make meikle o' her heid ;
And ilka thing, that lady took,
  Was like to be her deid.

Its four and twenty ladies fair
  Were in her father's ha' ;
Whan in there came the fair Janet,
  The flower amang the   a'.

Four and twenty ladies fair
  Were playing at the chess ;
And out there came the fair Janet,
  As green as any grass.

Out and spake an auld gray-headed knight,
  Lay o'er the castle wa'—
" And ever alas ! for thee, Janet,
  But we'll be blamed a'."—

" Now had your tongue, ye auld gray knight ;
  And an ill deid may ye die !
Father my bairn on whom I will,
  I'll father nane on thee."—

---

[1] dreed, undergone.

Out then spake her father dear,
    And he spoke meek and mild—
" And ever alas ! my sweet Janet,
    I fear ye gae with child."—

"And if I be with child, father,
    Mysell maun bear the blame ;
There's ne'er a knight, about your ha',
    Shall hae the bairnie's name.

" If my love were an earthly knight,
    As he's an elfin grey,
I wadna gie my ain true love
    For nae lord that ye hae."—

" Is it to a man o' might, Janet,
    Or is it to a man o' mean ?
Or is it unto young Tamlane,
    That's wi' the Fairies gane ?"—

" 'Twas down by Carterhaugh, father,
    I walked beside the wa ;
And there I saw a wee wee man,
    The least that e'er I saw.

" His legs were skant a shathmont lang [1],
    Yet umber was his thie ;
Between his brows there was ae span,
    And between his shoulders, thrie.

" He's ta'en and flung a meikle stane,
    As far as I could see ;
I could na, had I been Wallace wight,
    Hae lifted it to my knee.

[1] The length of the hand clenched with the thumb extended.

" 'O wee wee man, but ye be strang !
    Where may thy dwelling be ? '—
' It's down beside yon bonny bower ;
    Fair lady, come and see.'—

" On we lap, and away we rade,
    Down to a bonny green ;
We lighted down to bait our steed,
    And we saw the Fairy Queen.

" With four and twenty at her back,
    Of ladies clad in green ;
Tho' the King of Scotland had been there,
    The worst might hae been his Queen.

" On we lap, and away we rade,
    Down to a bonny ha' ;
The roof was o' the beaten goud,
    The floor was of chrystal a'.

" And there were dancing on the floor,
    Fair ladies jimp [1] and sma' ;
But, in the twinkling o' an eye,
    They sainted [2] clean awa'.

" And, in the twinkling of an eye,
    The wee wee man was gane ;
And he says, gin he binna won by me,
    He'll ne'er be won by nane."—

Janet's put on her green cleiding,
    Whan near nine months were gane ;
And she's awa to Carterhaugh,
    To speak wi' young Tamlane.

[1] slim.   [2] vanished.

And when she came to Carterhaugh,
  She gaed beside the wall ;
And there she saw the steed standing,
  But away was himsell.

She hadna pu'd a double rose,
  A rose but only twae,
When up and started young Tamlane,
  Says—" Lady, thou pu's nae mae !

" Why pu' ye the rose, Janet,
  Within this garden green ?
And a' to kill the bonnie babe,
  That we got us between."—

" The truth ye'll tell to me, Tamlane ;
  A word ye mauna lie ;
Gin e'er ye was in haly chapel,
  Or sained [1] in Christentie."—

" The truth I'll tell to thee, Janet ;
  A word I winna lie ;
A knight me got, and a lady me bore,
  As well as they did thee.

" Roxburgh was my grandfather ;
  Took me with him to bide ;
And, as we frae the hunting came,
  This harm did me betide.

" Roxburgh was a hunting knight,
  And loved hunting well ;
And, on a cauld and frosty day,
  Down frae my horse I fell.

[1] blessed.

" The Queen o' Fairies keppit[1] me,
  In yon green hill to dwell ;
And I'm a fairy, lyth and limb ;
  Fair lady, view me well.

" And pleasant is the fairy land ;
  But, an eiry tale to tell !
Ay, at the end o' seven years,
  We pay the teind[2] to hell ;
And I'm sae fair and fu' o' flesh,
  I'm fear'd it be mysell.

"This night is Hallowe'en, Janet ;
  The morn is Hallowday ;
And, gin ye dare your true love win,
  Ye have nae time to stay.

" The night it is good Hallowe'en,
  When fairy folk will ride ;
And they, that wad their true love win,
  At Miles Cross they maun bide."—

" But how shall I thee ken, Tamlane ?
  Or how shall I thee knaw ?
Amang so many unearthly knights,
  The like I never saw ? "—

" The first company that passes by,
  Say na, and let them gae ;
The next company that passes by,
  Say na, and do right sae ;
The third company that passes by,
  Then I'll be ane o' thae.

[1] caught.   [2] tythe.

" First let pass the black, Janet,
   And syn let pass the brown ;
But grip ye to the milk-white steed,
   And pu' the rider down.

" For I ride on the milk-white steed,
   And ay nearest the town ;
Because I was a christened knight,
   They gave me that renown.

" My right hand will be gloved, Janet,
   My left hand will be bare ;
And thae's the tokens I gie thee,
   Nae doubt I will be there.

" They'll turn me in your arms, Janet,
   An adder and a snake ;
But had me fast, let me not pass,
   Gin ye wad be my maik [1]

" They'll turn me in your arms, Janet,
   An adder and an ask [2] ;
They'll turn me in your arms, Janet,
   A bale [3] that burns fast.

" They'll turn me in your arms, Janet,
   A red-hot gad [4] o' iron ;
But had me fast, let me not pass,
   For I'll do you no harm.

" First, dip me in a stand o' milk,
   And then in a stand o' water ;
But had me fast, let me not pass,
   I'll be your bairn's father.

[1] mate.   [2] newt.   [3] faggot.   [4] rod.

"And next they'll shape me in your arms,
　A toad, but and an eel ;
But had me fast, nor let me gang,
　As you do love me weel.

"They'll shape me in your arms, Janet,
　A dove, but and a swan ;
And last they'll shape me in your arms,
　A mother-naked man :
Cast your green mantle over me—
　I'll be mysell again."—

Gloomy, gloomy, was the night,
　And eiry was the way,
As fair Janet, in her green mantle,
　To Miles Cross she did gae.

About the dead hour o' the night,
　She heard the bridles ring ;
And Janet was as glad o' that,
　As any earthly thing !

And first gaed by the black black steed,
　And then gaed by the brown ;
But fast she gript the milk-white steed,
　And pu'd the rider down.

She pu'd him frae the milk-white steed,
　And loot the bridle fa' ;
And up there raise an erlish [1] cry—
　"He's won amang us a' !"—

　　　　　　　[1] ghostly.

They shaped him in fair Janet's arms,
  An esk, but and an adder ;
She held him fast in every shape,
  To be her bairn's father.

They shaped him in her arms at last,
  A mother-naked man ;
She wrapt him in her green mantle,
  And sae her true love wan.

Up then spake the Queen o' Fairies,
  Out o' a bush o' broom—
" She that has borrowed young Tamlane,
  Has gotten a stately groom."

Up then spake the Queen o' Fairies,
  Out o' a bush of rye—
" She's ta'en awa the bonniest knight,
  In a' my companie.

" But, had I kenn'd, Tamlane," she says,
  " A lady wad borrowed thee—
I wad ta'en out thy twae gray een,
  Put in twae een o' tree.

" Had I but kenn'd, Tamlane," she says,
  " Before ye came frae hame—
I wad ta'en out your heart o' flesh,
  Put in a heart o' stane.

" Had I had but the wit yestreen,
  That I hae coft [1] the day—
I'd paid my kane [2] seven times to hell,
  Ere you'd been won away ! "—

[1] bought. [2] tribute.

57   *The Cruel Sister*

THERE were two sisters sat in a bour ;
    Binnorie, O Binnorie ;
There came a knight to be their wooer ;
    By the bonny milldams of Binnorie.

He courted the eldest with glove and ring ;
    Binnorie, O Binnorie ;
But he lo'ed the youngest aboon a' thing ;
    By the bonny milldams of Binnorie.

He courted the eldest with broach and knife ;
    Binnorie, O Binnorie ;
But he lo'ed the youngest aboon his life ;
    By the bonny milldams of Binnorie.

The eldest she was vexèd sair ;
    Binnorie, O Binnorie ;
And sore envied her sister fair ;
    By the bonny milldams of Binnorie.

The eldest said to the youngest ane,
    Binnorie, O Binnorie ;
"Will ye go and see our father's ships come in ?"—
    By the bonny milldams of Binnorie.

She's tae'n her by the lilly hand,
    Binnorie, O Binnorie ;
And led her down to the river strand ;
    By the bonny milldams of Binnorie.

The youngest stude upon a stane,
    Binnorie, O Binnorie ;
The eldest came and pushed her in ;
    By the bonny milldams of Binnorie.

She took her by the middle sma',
    Binnorie, O Binnorie ;
And dashed her bonnie back to the jaw [1],
    By the bonny milldams of Binnorie.

" O sister, sister, reach your hand,
    Binnorie, O Binnorie ;
And ye shall be heir of half my land."—
    By the bonny milldams of Binnorie.

" O sister, I'll not reach my hand,
    Binnorie, O Binnorie ;
And I'll be heir to all your land :
    By the bonny milldams of Binnorie.

" Shame fa' the hand that I should take,
    Binnorie, O Binnorie ;
It's twin'd [2] me and my world's make [3]."
    By the bonny milldams of Binnorie.

" O sister, reach me but your glove,
    Binnorie, O Binnorie ;
And sweet William shall be your love."—
    By the bonny milldams of Binnorie.

" Sink on, nor hope for hand or glove,
    Binnorie, O Binnorie ;
And sweet William shall better be my love."—
    By the bonny milldams of Binnorie.

    [1] flood.   [2] separated.   [3] mate.

"Your cherry cheeks and your yellow hair,
    Binnorie, O Binnorie ;
Garr'd me gang maiden evermair."—
    By the bonny milldams of Binnorie.

Sometimes she sunk, and sometimes she swam,
    Binnorie, O Binnorie ;
Untill she came to the miller's dam,
    By the bonny milldams of Binnorie.

"O father, father, draw your dam !
    Binnorie, O Binnorie ;
There's either a mermaid or a milk-white swan."—
    By the bonny milldams of Binnorie.

The miller hasted and drew his dam,
    Binnorie, O Binnorie ;
And there he found a drowned woman,
    By the bonny milldams of Binnorie.

You could not see her yellow hair,
    Binnorie, O Binnorie ;
For gowd and pearls that were sae rare,
    By the bonny milldams of Binnorie.

You could na see her middle sma',
    Binnorie, O Binnorie ;
Her gowden girdle was sae bra' ;
    By the bonny milldams of Binnorie.

A famous harper passing by
    Binnorie, O Binnorie ;
The sweet pale face he chanced to spy ;
    By the bonny milldams of Binnorie.

17

And when he looked that ladye on,
    Binnorie, O Binnorie ;
He sighed and made a heavy moan ;
    By the bonny milldams of Binnorie.

He made a harp of her breast bone,
    Binnorie, O Binnorie ;
Whose sounds would melt a heart of stone ;
    By the bonny milldams of Binnorie.

The strings he framed of her yellow hair,
    Binnorie, O Binnorie ;
Whose notes made sad the listening ear ;
    By the bonny milldams of Binnorie.

He brought it to her father's hall ;
    Binnorie, O Binnorie ;
And there was the court assembled all ;
    By the bonny milldams of Binnorie.

He laid his harp upon a stone,
    Binnorie, O Binnorie ;
And straight it began to play alone ;
    By the bonny milldams of Binnorie.

" O yonder sits my father, the king,
    Binnorie, O Binnorie ;
And yonder sits my mother, the queen ;
    By the bonny milldams of Binnorie.

" And yonder stands my brother Hugh,
    Binnorie, O Binnorie ;
And by him my William sweet and true."—
    By the bonny milldams of Binnorie.

But the last tune that the harp play'd then,
    Binnorie, O Binnorie ;
Was " Woe to my sister, false Helen ! "—
    By the bonny milldams of Binnorie.

58   *Lament of the Queen's Marie*

" O YE mariners, mariners, mariners,
        That sail upon the sea,
Let not my father nor mother to wit,
    The death that I maun die ! "—

When she cam to the Netherbow port,
    She laughed loud laughters three ;
But when she cam to the gallows foot,
    The tear blinded her e'e.

" Yestreen the queen had four Maries,
    The night she'll hae but three ;
There was Marie Seton, and Marie Beatoun,
And Marie Carmichael, and me."—

59   *Brown Adam*

O WHA wad wish the wind to blaw,
        Or the green leaves fa' therewith ?
Or wha' wad wish a lealer love
    Than Brown Adam the Smith ?

But they hae banished him, Brown Adam,
    Frae father and frae mother ;
And they hae banished him, Brown Adam,
    Frae sister and frae brother.

And they hae banished him, Brown Adam,
   The flow'r o' a' his kin ;
And he's bigged [1] a bour in gude green wood
   Atween his ladye and him.

It fell upon a summer's day,
   Brown Adam he thought lang ;
And for to hunt some venison,
   To green wood he wald gang.

He has ta'en his bow his arm o'er,
   His bolts and arrows lang ;
And he is to the gude green wood,
   As fast as he could gang.

O he's shot up, and he's shot down,
   The bird upon the brier :
And he's sent it hame to his ladye,
   Bade her be of gude cheir

O he's shot up, and he's shot down,
   The bird upon the thorn ;
And sent it hame to his ladye,
   Said he'd be hame the morn.

When he cam to his ladye's bour door,
   He stude a little forebye [2] ;
And there he heard a fou' fause knight
   Tempting his gaye ladye.

For he has ta'en out a gay goud ring,
   Had cost him mony a poun'—
" O grant me love for love, ladye,
   And this sall be thy own."—

             [1] builded. [2] apart.

"I lo'e Brown Adam weel," she said ;
  "I trew sae does he me :
I wadna gie Brown Adam's love
  For nae fause knight I see."—

Out has he ta'en a purse o' gowd,
  Was a' fou to the string—
"O grant me love for love, ladye,
  And a' this sall be thine."—

"I loe Brown Adam weel," she says ;
  "I wot sae does he me :
I wadna be your light lemman,
  For mair than ye could gie."

Then out he drew his lang bright brand,
  And flashed it in her een—
"Now grant me love for love, ladye,
  Or thro' ye this sall gang ! "—
Then, sighing, says that ladye fair—
  "Brown Adam tarries lang ! "—

Then in and starts him Brown Adam,
  Says—"I'm just at your hand."—
He's gar'd him leave his bonny bow,
  He's gar'd him leave his brand,
He's gar'd him leave a dearer pledge—
  Four fingers o' his right hand.

60 *Clerk Saunders*

CLERK SAUNDERS and May Margaret
　　Walked ower yon garden green ;
And sad and heavy was the love
　　That fell thir twa between.

"A bed, a bed," Clerk Saunders said,
　　" A bed for you and me."—
" Fye na, fye na," said May Margaret,
　　" Till anes we married be.

" For in may come my seven bauld brothers,
　　Wi' torches burning bright ;
They'll say—' We hae but ae sister,
　　And behold she's wi' a knight !'"—

" Then take the sword frae my scabbard,
　　And slowly lift the pin ;
And you may swear, and safe your aith,
　　Ye never let Clerk Saunders in.

" And take a napkin in your hand,
　　And tie up baith your bonny een ;
And you may swear, and safe your aith,
　　Ye saw me na since late yestreen."—

It was about the midnight hour,
　　When they asleep were laid ;
When in and came her seven brothers,
　　Wi' torches burning red.

When in and came her seven brothers,
  Wi' torches shining bright ;
They said " We hae but ae sister,
  And behold her lying with a knight ! "—

Then out and spake the first o' them,—
  " I bear the sword shall gar him die."—
And out and spake the second o' them,—
  " His father has nae mair than he ! "—

And out and spake the third o' them,—
  " I wot that they are lovers dear."—
And out and spake the fourth o' them,—
  " They hae been in love this mony a year."—

Then out and spake the fifth o' them,—
  " It were great sin true love to twain."—
And out and spake the sixth o' them,—
  " It were shame to slay a sleeping man ! "—

Then up and gat the seventh o' them,
  And never a word spake he ;
But he has striped [1] his bright brown brand
  Out thro' Clerk Saunders' fair bodye.

Clerk Saunders he started, and Margaret she turned
  Into his arms as asleep she lay ;
And sad and silent was the night
  That was atween thir twae.

And they lay still and sleeped sound,
  Until the day began to daw [2] ;
And kindly to him she did say,
  " It is time, true love, you were awa."—

[1] thrust. [2] dawn.

But he lay still, and sleeped sound,
    Albeit the sun began to sheen ;
She looked atween her and the wa,'
    And dull and drowsie were his een.

Then in and came her father dear,
    Said—" Let a' your mourning be :
I'll carry the dead corpse to the clay,
    And I'll come back and comfort thee."—

" Comfort weel your seven sons ;
    For comforted will I never be :
I ween 'twas neither knave nor lown
    Was in the bower last night wi' me."—

The clinking bell gaed thro' the town,
    To carry the dead corse to the clay ;
And Clerk Saunders stood at May Margaret's
        window,
    I wot, an hour before the day.

" Are ye sleeping, Margaret ? " he says,
    " Or are ye waking presentlie ?
Gie me my faith and troth again,
    I wot, true love, I gied to thee."—

" Your faith and troth ye sall never get,
    Nor our true love sall never twin ¹,
Until ye come within my bower,
    And kiss me cheik and chin."—

" My mouth it is full cold, Margaret,
    It has the smell, now, of the ground ;
And, if I kiss thy comely mouth,
    Thy days of life will not be lang.

¹ divide.

"O cocks are crowing a merry mid night,
  I wot the wild fowls are boding day;
Give me my faith and troth again,
  And let me fare me on my way."—

"Thy faith and troth thou sall na get,
  And our true love sall never twin,
Untill ye tell what comes of women,
  I wot, who die in strong traivelling?"—

"Their beds are made in the heavens high,
  Down at the foot of our good Lord's knee,
Weel set about wi' gillyflowers:
  I wot sweet company for to see.

"O cocks are crowing a merry mid night,
  I wot the wild fowl are boding day;
The psalms of heaven will soon be sung,
  And I ere now will be missed away."—

Then she has ta'en a chrystal wand,
  And she has stroken her troth thereon;
She has given it him out at the shot window,
  Wi' mony a sad sigh, and heavy groan.

"I thank ye, Marg'ret; I thank ye, Marg'ret
  And aye I thank ye heartilie;
Gin ever the dead come for the quick,
  Be sure, Marg'ret, I'll come for thee."

It's hosen and shoon, and gown alone,
  She climbed the wall and followed him,
Untill she came to the green forest;
  And there she lost the sight o' him.

" Is there ony room at your head, Saunders,
   Is there ony room at your feet ?
Or ony room at your side, Saunders,
   Where fain, fain, I wad sleep."—

"There's nae room at my head, Marg'ret,
   There's nae room at my feet ;
My bed it is full lowly now :
   Amang the hungry worms I sleep.

" Cauld mould is my covering now,
   But and my winding sheet ;
The dew it falls nae sooner down,
   Than my resting place is weet."—

          *   *   *   *   *

61   *Edward, Edward*

" QUHY dois your brand sae drop wi' bluid,
         Edward, Edward ?
         Quhy dois your brand sae drop wi' bluid,
         And why sae sad gang yee, O ?"
"O, I hae killed my hauke sae guid,
         Mither, mither :
O, I hae killed my hauke sae guid :
         And I had nae mair bot hee, O."

" Your haukis bluid was nevir sae reid,
         Edward, Edward.
Your haukis bluid was nevir sae reid,
         My deir son I tell thee, O."
"O, I hae killed my reid-roan steid,
         Mither, mither :
O, I hae killed my reid-roan steid,
         That erst was sae fair and free, O."

"Your steid was auld, and ye hae gat mair,
       Edward, Edward :
Your steid was auld, and ye hae gat mair,
       Sum other dule ye drie [1], O."
"O, I hae killed my fadir deir,
       Mither, mither :
O, I hae killed my fadir deir,
       Alas ! and wae is me, O !"

"And quhatten penance wul ye drie for that,
       Edward, Edward ?
And quhatten penance wul ye drie for that ?
       My deir son, now tell me, O."
"Ile set my feit in yonder boat,
       Mither, mither :
Ile set my feit in yonder boat,
       And Ile fare ovir the sea, O."

"And quhat wul ye doe wi' your towris and your ha',
       Edward, Edward ?
And quhat wul ye doe wi' your towris and your ha',
       That were sae fair to see, O ?"
"Ile let thame stand til they doun fa',
       Mither, mither :
Ile let thame stand til they doun fa',
       For here nevir mair maun I bee, O."

"And quhat wul ye leive to your bairns and your wife,
       Edward, Edward ?
And quhat wul ye leive to your bairns and your wife,
       Quhan ye gang ovir the sea, O ?"

[1] sorrow you suffer.

"The warldis room, let thame beg throw life,
    Mither, mither :
The warldis room, let thame beg throw life,
    For thame nevir mair wul I see, O."

"And quhat wul ye leive to your ain mither deir,
    Edward, Edward ?
And quhat wul ye leive to your ain mither deir ?
    My deir son, now tell me, O."
"The curse of hell frae me sall ye beir,
    Mither, mither :
The curse of hell frae me sall ye beir,
    Sic counseils ye gave to me, O."

ALEXANDER HUME

1557 (?)–1609

Of the Day Estivall

O PERFITE light, quhilk schaid away[1]
   The darkenes from the light,
And set a ruler our the day,
   Ane-other our the night!

Thy glorie when the day foorth flies
   Mair viuely[2] dois appeare
Nor at midday vnto our eyes
   The shining sun is cleare.

The shaddow of the earth anon
   Remooues and drawes by,
Sine[3] in the east, when it is gon,
   Appeares a clearer sky.

Quhilk sun perceaues the little larks,
   The lapwing and the snyp,
And tunes their sangs like Nature's clarks
   Our midow, mure, and stryp[4].

Bot euerie bais'd[5] nocturnall beast
   Na langer may abide:
They hy[6] away, baith maist and least,
   Themselues in houis to hide.

[1] separated. [2] in more lively fashion. [3] then. [4] rill. [5] abased.
haste.

They dread the day fra they it see,
    And from the sight of men
To saits and couars [1] fast they flee,
    As lyons to their den.

Oure hemisphere is poleist clein,
    And lightened more and more,
While euerie thing be clearely sein
    Quhilk seemed dim before.

Except the glistering astres [2] bright
    Which all the night were cleere,
Offusked [3] with a greater light,
    Na langer dois appeare.

The golden globe incontinent
    Sets vp his shining head,
And our the earth and firmament
    Displayes his beims abread.

For ioy the birds with boulden [4] throts
    Agains his visage shein [5]
Takes vp their kindelie musicke nots
    In woods and gardens grein.

Up braids [6] the carefull husbandman,
    His cornes and vines to see,
And euerie tymous [7] artizan
    In buith [8] worke busilie.

The pastor quits the slouthfull sleepe,
    And passis forth with speede,
His little camow-nosed [9] sheepe
    And rowtting kie [10] to feede.

---

[1] seats and coverts. [2] stars. [3] darkened. [4] swelling. [5] bright.
[6] forth goes. [7] early-risen. [8] booth. [9] flat-nosed. [10] bellowing
cattle.

The passenger from perrels sure
　　Gangs gladly foorth the way ;
Breife, euerie liuing creature
　　Takes comfort of the day.

The subtile mottie [1] rayons light,
　　At rifts thay are in wonne [2] ;
The glansing thains [3] and vitre [4] bright
　　Resplends against the sunne.

The dew vpon the tender crops,
　　Lyke pearles white and round,
Or like to melted silver drops,
　　Refreshes all the ground.

The mystic rocke [5], the clouds of rain,
　　From tops of mountaines skails [6] ;
Cleare are the highest hils and plaine,
　　The vapors takes the vails.

Begaried [7] is the saphire pend [8]
　　With spraings [9] of skarlet hew,
And preciously from end till end
　　Damasked white and blew.

The ample heauen of fabrik sure
　　In cleannes dois surpas
The chrystall and the siluer pure,
　　Or clearest poleist glas.

The time so tranquill is and still
　　That na where sall ye find,
Saife on ane high and barren hill
　　Ane aire of peeping [10] wind.

[1] full of motes.　　　[2] have penetrated chinks.　　　[3] gossamer ?
[4] glass.　[5] vapour.　[6] disperse.　[7] variegated.　[8] vault.　[9] streaks.
[10] softly piping.

All trees and simples great and small
  That balmie leife do beir
Nor thay were painted on a wall
  Na mair they moue nor steir.

Calme is the deepe and purpoure [1] se,
  Yee smuther nor the sand,
The wals [2] that woltring wont to be
  Are stable like the land.

Sa silent is the cessile [3] air
  That euery cry and call,
The hils and dails and forrest fair
  Againe repeates them all.

The riuers fresh, the callor [4] streames,
  Our [5] rockes can [6] softlie rin ;
The water cleare like chrystall seames,
  And makes a pleasant din.

The fields and earthlie superfice [7]
  With verdure greene is spread,
And naturallie, but [8] artifice,
  In partie coulors cled.

The flurishes [9] and fragrant flowers,
  Throw Phœbus fostring heit,
Refresht with dew and silver showres,
  Casts vp ane odor sweit.

The clogged busie humming beis,
  That neuer thinks to drowne,
On flowres and flourishes of treis
  Collects their liquor browne.

[1] purple   [2] waves.   [3] yielding.   [4] fresh   [5] o'er.   [6] do.
[7] surface.   [8] without.   [9] blossoms.

The sunne, maist like a speedie post,
  With ardent course ascends :
The beautie of the heavenlie host
  Up to our zenith tends.

Nocht guided be na Phaeton,
  Nor trained in a chyre [1],
Bot be the high and haly On
  Quhilk dois all where impire [2].

The burning beims downe from his face
  Sa fervently can beat,
That man and beast now seekes a place
  To saue them fra the heat.

The brethles flocks draws to the shade
  And frechure of thair fald ;
The startling nolt as they were made
  Runnes to the rivers cald.

The heardes beneath some leaffie trie
  Amids the flowers they lie ;
The stabill ships vpon the sey
  Tends vp [3] their sails to drie.

The hart, the hynd, and fallow deare
  Are tapisht [4] at their rest,
The foules and birdes that made the beare [5]
  Prepares their prettie nest.

The rayons dures [6] descending downe
  All kindles in a gleid [7],
In citie nor in borroughstowne
  May name set foorth their heid.

[1] drawn in a chariot. [2] rule. [3] stretch. [4] squatted. [5] sound.
[6] strong rays. [7] flame.

18

Back from the blew paymented whun [1]
   And from ilk plaister wall,
The hote reflexing of the sun
   Inflams the aire and all.

The labowrers that timelie raise,
   All wearie, faint, and weake,
For heat downe to their houses gais,
   Noone-meate and sleepe to take.

The callowr wine in caue is sought,
   Men's brothing [2] breists to cule ;
The water cald and cleare is brought
   And sallets steeped in vle [3].

Sume plucks the honie plowm and peare,
   The cherrie and the pesche ;
Sume likes the reamand London beare,
   The bodie to refresh.

Forth of their skepps [5] come raging bees,
   Lyes out and will not cast [6],
Some vther swarmes hyves on the trees
   In knots togidder fast.

The corbeis and the kekling kais [7]
   May scarce the heate abide,
Halks prunyeis [8] on the sunnie brais
   And wedders back and side.

With gilted eyes and open wings
   The cock his courage shawes,
With claps of ioy his breast he dings [9],
   And twentie times he crawes.

[1] blue trap or igneous rock from which pavement was made.
[2] sweating. [3] oil. [4] foaming. [5] hives. [6] swarm. [7] ravens and cackling jackdaws. [8] preen them. [9] smites.

The dow [1] with whisling wings sa blew,
  The winds can fast collect;
Her pourpour pennes turnes mony hew
  Against the sunne direct.

Now noone is went, gaine is midday,
  The heat dois slake at last;
The sunne descends downe west away
  Fra three of clock be past.

A little cule of braithing wind
  Now softly can arise,
The warks throw heate that lay behind
  Now men may enterprise.

Furth fairis the flocks to seeke their fude
  On euerie hill and plaine,
Ilk labourer as he thinks gude
  Steppis to his turne agaime.

The rayons of the sunne we see
  Diminish in their strength;
The schad of euerie towre and tree
  Extended is in length.

Great is the calme, for euerie-quhair
  The wind is sitten downe;
The reik [2] thrawes right vp in the air
  From euerie towre and towne.

Their firdoning [3] the bony birds
  In banks they do begin;
With pipes of reides the iolie hirds
  Halds vp the mirrie din.

[1] pigeon. [2] smoke. [3] chanting.

The maveis and the philomen,
　　The stirling whissiles lowd;
The cuschetts [1] on the branches green
　　Full quietly they crowd [2].

The gloming comes, the day is spent,
　　The sun goes out of sight,
And painted is the occident
　　With pourpour sanguine bright.

The skarlet nor the golden threid,
　　Who would their beautie trie,
Are nathing like the colour reid
　　And beautie of the sky.

Our west horizon circuler,
　　Fra time the sunne be set,
Is all with rubies (as it wer),
　　Or rosis reid ourfret [3].

What pleasour were to walke and see,
　　Endlang a riuer cleare,
The perfit forme of euerie tree
　　Within the deepe appeare!

The salmon out of cruifs [4] and creils
　　Up hailed into skowts [5];
The bels [6] and circles on the weills [7]
　　Throw lowpping of the trouts.

O! then it were a seemely thing,
　　While all is still and calme,
The praise of God to play and sing
　　With cornet and with shalme [8].

[1] wood-pigeons.　[2] coo.　[3] besprent.　[4] osier traps and baskets.
[5] boats.　[6] bubbles.　[7] pools.　[8] shawm.

Bot now the hirds with mony schout
    Cals vther be their name ;
Ga, Billie, turne our gude about,
    Now time is to go hame.

With bellie fow the beastes belive [1]
    Are turned fra the corne,
Quhilk soberly they hameward driue
    With pipe and lilting horne.

Throw all the land great is the gild [2]
    Of rustik folks that crie,
Of bleiting sheepe fra they be fild
    Of calues and rowting ky.

All labourers drawes hame at even,
    And can till vther say,
Thankes to the gracious God of heauen
    Quhilk send this summer day !

            [1] at once.   [2] clamour.

ALEXANDER HUME

Het now the birds with many a shout
Call other their that tane;
For Rhibes teine one gisle about
Now time is to go home.

Whise now the ... ... contentive
Are musant ... ...ne;
Quhilk chearly they hamewart dring
With …

SIR ROBERT AYTOUN

1570–1638

63   *To a Careless Mistress*

D EAR, why do you say you love,
    When indeed you careless prove?
Reason better can digest
Ernest hate, than love in rest.

Wherefore do your smiling eyes
Help your tongue to make sweet lies?
Leave to statesman tricks of state;
Love doth politicians hate.

You perchance presume to find
Love of some chameleon kind;
But be not deceived, my fair,
Love will not be fed on air.

Love's a glutton of his food;
Surfeits make his stomach good:
Love whose diet grows precise
Sick from some consumption dies.

Then, dear love, let me obtain
That which may true love maintain;
Or, if kind you cannot prove,
Prove true—say you cannot love.

278

64   *On Love*

THERE is no worldly pleasure here below
  Which by experience doth not folly prove ;
But, among all the follies that I know,
  The sweetest folly in the world is love.

But not that passion which, by fools' consent,
  Above the reason bears imperious sway,
Making their lifetime a perpetual Lent,
  As if a man were born to fast and pray.

No ! that is not the humour I approve,
  As either yielding pleasure or promotion ;
I like a mild and lukewarm zeal in love,
  Altho' I do not like it in devotion.

For it hath no coherence with my creed
  To think that lovers die as they pretend ;
If all that say they die had died indeed,
  Sure long ere now the world had had an end.

Besides, we need not love but if we please ;
  No destiny can force man's disposition ;
And how can any die of that disease
  Whereof himself may be his own physician ?

But some seem so distracted of their wits
  That I would think it but a venial sin
To take one of those innocents that sits
  In Bedlam out, and put some lover in.

Yet some men, rather than incur the slander
  Of true apostates, will false martyrs prove ;
But I am neither Iphis nor Leander,
  I'll neither drown nor hang myself for love.

Methinks a wise man's actions should be such
　　As always yield to reason's best advice.
Now, for to love too little or too much
　　Are both extremes, and all extremes are vice.

Yet have I been a lover by report,
　　Yea, I have died for love, as others do ;
But, praised be God, it was in such a sort
　　That I revived within an hour or two.

Thus have I lived, thus have I loved till now,
　　And found no reason to repent me yet ;
And whosoever otherwise will do
　　His courage is as little as his wit.

65　　　　　*To a Haughty Mistress*

SONG

WHAT means this niceness now of late ?
　　Since time doth truth approve,
This distance may consist with state,
　　It cannot stand with love.

'Tis either cunning or distrust
　　That doth such ways avow.
The first is base, the last's unjust ;
　　Let neither blemish you.

If you intend to draw me on,
　　You over-act your part,
And if you mind to send me gone,
　　You need not half this art.

Speak but the word, or do but cast
    A look which seems to frown,
I'll give you all the love that's past ;
    The rest shall be my own.

And such a fair and eafauld way
    On both sides, none can blame,
Since every one is bound to play
    The fairest of his game.

66   *To a Variable Mistress*

WHY did I wrong my judgement so
        As to affect where I did know
There was no hold for to be taken ?
That which her heart thirsts after most,
If once of it her hope can boast,
    Straight by her folly is forsaken.

Thus, while I still pursue in vain,
Methinks I turn a child again,
    And of my shadow am a-chasing :
For all her favours are to me
Like apparitions which I see,
    Yet ne'er come near th' embracing.

Oft have I wished that there had been
Some almanac whereby to've seen
    When love with her had been in season.
But I perceive there is no art
Can find the epact of the heart,
    That loves by chance, and not by reason.

Yet will I not for this despair ;
For time her humour may prepare
　　To love him who is now neglected :
For what unto my constancy
Is now denied, one day may be
　　From her inconstancy expected.

67　　　　*To an Inconstant Mistress*

I LOVED thee once, I'll love no more,
　　Thine be the grief, as is the blame ;
Thou art not what thou wast before,
　　What reason should I be the same ?
　　　He that can love unloved again
　　　Hath better store of love than brain ;
　　　God send me love my debts to pay,
　　　While unthrifts fool their love away !

Nothing could have my love o'erthrown
　　If thou hadst still continued mine ;
Nay, if thou hadst remained thine own
　　I might perchance have yet been thine.
　　　But thou thy freedom did recall
　　　That it thou might elsewhere enthrall,
　　　And then how could I but disdain
　　　A captive's captive to remain ?

When new desires had conquered thee,
　　And changed the object of thy will,
It had been lethargy in me,
　　Not constancy, to love thee still :
　　　Yea, it had been a sin to go
　　　And prostitute affection so,
　　　Since we are taught no prayers to say
　　　To such as must to others pray.

Yet do thou glory in thy choice,
   Thy choice of his good fortune boast;
I'll neither grieve nor yet rejoice
   To see him gain what I have lost.
      The height of my disdain shall be
      To laugh at him, to blush for thee;
      To love thee still, but go no more
      A-begging at a beggar's door.

68   *The Author's Answer*

      (*Written at the King's Command*)

THOU that loved once, now lov'st no more,
      For fear to show more love than brain;
With heresy unhatched before,
   Apostasy thou dost maintain.
      Can he have either brain or love
      That doth inconstancy approve?
      A choice well made no change admits,
      And changes argue after-wits.

Say that she had not been the same,
   Shouldst thou therefore another be?
What thou in her as vice did blame,
   Can that take virtue's name in thee?
      No, thou in this her captive was,
      And made thee ready by her glass;
      Example led revenge astray,
      When true love should have kept the way.

True love hath no reflected end ;
  The object good sets all at rest ;
And noble breasts will freely lend
  Without expecting interest.
    'Tis merchant love, 'tis trade for gain,
    To barter love for love again ;
    'Tis usury, nay, worse than this,
    For self-idolatry it is.

Then let her choice be what it will,
  Let constancy be thy revenge ;
If thou retribute good for ill,
  Both grief and shame shall check her change.
    Thus mayst thou laugh, when thou shalt see
    Remorse reclaim her home to thee ;
    And where thou beg'st of her before,
    She now sits begging at thy door.

69   *Inconstancy Reproved*

(ATTRIBUTED TO AYTOUN)

I DO confess thou'rt smooth and fair,
  And I might have gone near to love thee,
Had I not found the slightest prayer
That lips could speak had power to move thee.
  But I can let thee now alone
  As worthy to be loved by none.

I do confess thou'rt sweet, yet find
  Thee such an unthrift of thy sweets,
Thy favours are but like the wind
  Which kisseth everything it meets ;
    And since thou canst love more than one
    Thou'rt worthy to be loved by none.

The morning rose that untouched stands,
　　Armed with her briers, how sweet she smells !
But pluck'd, and strain'd through ruder hands,
　　Her sweet no longer with her dwells ;
　　　　But scent and beauty both are gone,
　　　　And leaves fall from her one by one.

Such fate, ere long, will thee betide,
　　When thou hast handled been awhile,
Like fair flowers to be thrown aside,
　　And thou shalt sigh when I shall smile
　　　　To see thy love to every one
　　　　Hath brought thee to be loved by none.

70   *Sonnet*

                (*Left in a Lady's Mirror*)

TO view thy beauty well, if thou be wise,
　　Come not to gaze upon this glass of thine ;
　But come and look upon these eyes of mine,
Where thou shalt see thy true resemblance twice.
Or, if thou think'st that thou profan'st thine eyes,
　　When on my wretched eyes they deign to shine,
　　Look on my heart, wherein, as in a shrine,
The lovely picture of thy beauty lies.
Or, if thy harmless modesty think shame
　　To gaze upon the horrors of my heart,
Come read these lines, and, reading, see in them
　　The trophies of thy beauty, and my smart.
Or, if to none of these thou'lt deign to come,
Weep eyes, break heart, and then my verse be dumb.

71   *On a Lady that was Painted*

PAMPHILIA hath a number of good arts,
    Which commendation to her worth imparts ;
But, above all, in one she doth excel—
That she can paint incomparably well.
And yet so modest that, if praised for this,
She'll swear she does not know what painting is,
But straight will blush with such a portrait grace
That one would think vermilion dyed her face.
One of her pictures I have ofttimes seen,
And would have sworn that it herself had been ;
And when I bade her it on me bestow,
I swear I heard the picture's self say No.
What ! think you this a prodigy ?   'Tis none—
The painter and the picture both were one.

72   *On Tobacco*

FORSAKEN of all comforts but these two,
    My faggot and my pipe, I sit and muse
On all my crosses, and almost accuse
The Heavens for dealing with me as they do.
Then Hope steps in, and with a smiling brow
    Such cheerful expectations doth infuse
    As make me think erelong I cannot choose
But be some grandee, whatsoe'er I'm now.

But having spent my pipe, I then perceive
That hopes and dreams are cousins—both deceive.
    Then make I this conclusion in my mind,
'Tis all one thing—both tend into one scope—
To live upon tobacco and on hope :
    The one's but smoke, the other is but wind.

SIR WILLIAM ALEXANDER, EARL OF STIRLING

1580–1640

73   *From Aurora*

THE thoughts of those I cannot but disprove
   Who, basely lost, their thraldom must bemoan ;
I scorn to yield myself to such a one
Whose birth and virtue is not worth my love.
No, since it is my fortune to be thrall,
   I must be fettered with a golden band ;
   And if I die, I'll die by Hector's hand,
So may the victor's fame excuse my fall ;
And if by any means I must be blind,
   Then it shall be by gazing on the sun.
   Oft by those means the greatest have been won,
Who must like best of such a generous mind.
At least by this I have allowed of fame
Much honour if I win, if lose, no shame.

74

WHEN as the sun doth drink up all the streams,
    And with a fervent heat the flowers doth kill,
The shadow of a wood or of a hill
Doth serve us for a targe against his beams.

But ah, those eyes that burn me with desire,
   And seek to parch the substance of my soul,
   The ardour of their rays for to control
I wot not where myself for to retire.
'Twixt them and me, to have procured some ease,
   I interposed the seas, woods, hills, and rivers,
   And yet am of those never-emptied quivers
The object still, and burn, be where I please.
But of the cause I need not for to doubt—
Within my breast I bear the fire about.

75

OFT have I heard, which now I must deny,
   That nought can last if that it be extreme;
   Times daily change, and we likewise in them;
Things out of sight do straight forgotten die.
There is nothing more vehement than love,
   And yet I burn, and burn still with one flame;
   Times oft have changed, yet I remain the same;
Nought from my mind her image can remove.
The greatness of my love aspires to ruth;
   Time vows to crown my constancy in th' end,
   And absence doth my fancies but extend.
Thus I perceive the poet spake the truth,
That who to see strange countries were inclined
Might change the air, but never change the mind.

76

AH, thou, my love, wilt lose thyself at last,
   Who can to match thyself with none agree.
Thou ow'st thy father nephews [1], and to me
A recompence for all my passions past.

            [1] *i.e.*, grand-children.

Ah, why shouldst thou thy beauty's treasure waste,
  Which will begin for to decay, I see?
    Erst, Daphne did become a barren tree
Because she was not half so wise as chaste;
And all the fairest things do soonest fade,
  Which O, I fear, thou with repentance try;
    The roses blasted are, the lilies die,
And all do languish in the summer's shade.
Yet will I grieve to see those flowers fall down
Which for my temples should have framed a crown.

77

AWAKE, my Muse, and leave to dream of loves!
    Shake off soft fancy's chains! I must be free.
  I'll perch no more upon the myrtle tree,
Nor glide through th' air with beauty's sacred doves;
But with love's stately bird I'll leave my nest,
  And try my sight against Apollo's rays;
    Then, if that aught my venturous course dismays,
Upon the olive's boughs I'll light and rest.
I'll tune my accents to a trumpet now,
  And seek the laurel in another field.
    Thus I that once, as beauty means did yield,
Did divers garments on my thoughts bestow,
Like Icarus, I fear, unwisely bold,
Am purposed other's passions now t' unfold.

WILLIAM DRUMMOND OF HAWTHORNDEN

1585–1649

78

I KNOW that all beneath the moon decays,
  And what by mortals in this world is brought
In Time's great periods shall return to nought;
That fairest states have fatal nights and days;
I know how all the Muse's heavenly lays,
With toil of spright which are so dearly bought,
As idle sounds, of few or none are sought,
And that nought lighter is than airy praise;
I know frail beauty's like the purple flower,
To which one morn oft birth and death affords;
That love a jarring is of minds' accords,
Where sense and will invassal reason's power:
  Know what I list, this all can not me move,
  But that, O me! I both must write and love.

79

FAIR is my yoke, though grievous be my pains,
  Sweet are my wounds, although they deeply smart,
My bit is gold, though shortened by the reins,
My bondage brave, though I may not depart:
Although I burn the fire which doth impart
Those flames so sweet reviving force contains,
That, like Arabia's bird, my wasted heart,
Made quick by death, more lively still remains.
I joy though oft my waking eyes spend tears,
I never want delight even when I groan,
Best companied when most I am alone;
A heaven of hopes I have midst hells of fears.
  Thus every way contentment strange I find,
  But most in her rare beauty, my rare mind.

80

NOW while the night her sable veil hath spread,
    And silently her resty coach doth roll,
Rousing with her from Tethys' azure bed
Those starry nymphs which dance about the pole ;
While Cynthia, in purest cypress clad,
The Latmian shepherd in a trance descries,
And whiles looks pale from height of all the skies,
Whiles dyes her beauties in a bashful red ;
While sleep, in triumph, closèd hath all eyes,
And birds and beasts a silence sweet do keep,
And Proteus' monstrous people in the deep,
The winds and waves, husht up, to rest entice ;
    I wake, muse, weep, and who my heart hath slain
    See still before me to augment my pain.

81

AH ! burning thoughts, now let me take some rest,
    And your tumultuous broils a while appease ;
Is't not enough, stars, fortune, love molest
Me all at once, but ye must too displease ?
Let hope, though false, yet lodge within my breast,
My high attempt, though dangerous, yet praise.
What though I trace not right heaven's steepy ways ?
It doth suffice, my fall shall make me blest.
I do not doat on days, nor fear not death,
So that my life be brave, what though not long ?
Let me renown'd live from the vulgar throng,
And when ye list, Heavens ! take this borrowed
    breath.
    Men but like visions are, time all doth claim ;
    He lives who dies to win a lasting name.

82

TO hear my plaints, fair river crystalline,
    Thou in a silent slumber seems to stay;
Delicious flow'rs, lily and columbine,
Ye bow your heads when I my woes display;
Forests, in you the myrtle, palm, and bay,
Have had compassion list'ning to my groans;
The winds with sighs have solemniz'd my moans
'Mong leaves, which whispered what they could not
        say;
The caves, the rocks, the hills, the Sylvans' thrones,
(As if even pity did in them appear,)
Have at my sorrows rent their ruthless stones;
Each thing I find hath sense except my dear,
    Who doth not think I love, or will not know
    My grief, perchance delighting in my woe.

83

WHEN Nature now had wonderfully wrought
    All Auristella's parts, except her eyes,
To make those twins two lamps in beauty's skies
She counsel of her starry senate sought.
Mars and Apollo first did her advise
In colour black to wrap those comets bright,
That Love him so might soberly disguise,
And, unperceived, wound at every sight.
Chaste Phœbe spake for purest azure dyes,
But Jove and Venus green about the light
To frame thought best, as bringing most delight,
That to pin'd hearts hope might for aye arise:
    Nature, all said, a paradise of green
    There plac'd to make all love which have them
        seen.

84

IN vain I haunt the cold and silver springs,
    To quench the fever burning in my veins ;
In vain, love's pilgrim, mountains, dales, and plains,
I overrun ; vain help long absence brings :
In vain, my friends, your counsel me constrains
To fly, and place my thoughts on other things.
Ah ! like the bird that fired hath her wings,
The more I move, the greater are my pains.
Desire, alas ! Desire, a Zeuxis new,
From Indies borrowing gold, from western skies
Most bright cynoper, sets before mine eyes
In every place, her hair, sweet look, and hue ;
    That fly, run, rest I, all doth prove but vain,
    My life lies in those looks which have me slain.

85

NYMPHS, sister nymphs, which haunt this crystal
        brook,
And, happy, in these floating bowers abide,
Where trembling roofs of trees from sun you hide,
Which make ideal woods in every crook ;
Whether ye garlands for your locks provide,
Or pearly letters seek in sandy book,
Or count your loves when Thetis was a bride,
Lift up your golden heads and on me look.
Read in mine eyes mine agonizing cares,
And what ye read recount to her again :
Fair nymphs, say, all these streams are but my tears,
And if she ask you how they sweet remain,
    Tell, that the bitterest tears which eyes can pour,
    When shed for her do cease more to be sour.

86   *Madrigal*

LIKE the Idalian queen,
    Her hair about her eyne,
With neck and breast's ripe apples to be seen,
At first glance of the morn,
In Cyprus' gardens gathering those fair flow'rs
Which of her blood were born,
I saw, but fainting saw, my paramours.
The Graces naked danc'd about the place,
The winds and trees amaz'd
With silence on her gaz'd;
The flow'rs did smile, like those upon her face,
And as their aspen stalks those fingers band,
That she might read my case,
A hyacinth I wish'd me in her hand.

87

IN mind's pure glass when I myself behold,
    And vively see how my best days are spent,
What clouds of care above my head are roll'd,
What coming harms which I can not prevent!
My begun course I, wearied, do repent,
And would embrace what reason oft hath told;
But scarce thus think I, when love hath controll'd
All the best reasons reason could invent,
Though sure I know my labour's end is grief,
The more I strive that I the more shall pine,
That only death can be my last relief:
Yet when I think upon that face divine,
    Like one with arrow shot in laughter's place,
    Malgré my heart, I joy in my disgrace.

88

DEAR quirister, who from those shadows sends,
  Ere that the blushing dawn dare show her light,
Such sad lamenting strains, that night attends
(Become all ear), stars stay to hear thy plight ;
If one whose grief even reach of thought transcends,
Who ne'er (not in a dream) did taste delight,
May thee importune who like case pretends,
And seems to joy in woe, in woe's despite ;
Tell me (so may thou fortune milder try,
And long, long sing) for what thou thus complains,
Sith, winter gone, the sun in dappled sky
Now smiles on meadows, mountains, woods, and plains?
  The bird, as if my questions did her move,
    With trembling wings sobb'd forth, I love, I love!

89

TRUST not, sweet soul, those curlèd waves of gold,
  With gentle tides which on your temples flow,
Nor temples spread with flakes of virgin snow,
Nor snow of cheeks with Tyrian grain enroll'd ;
Trust not those shining lights which wrought my woe,
When first I did their burning rays behold,
Nor voice, whose sounds more strange effects do show
Than of the Thracian harper have been told.
Look to this dying lily, fading rose,
Dark hyacinth, of late whose blushing beams
Made all the neighbouring herbs and grass rejoice,
And think how little is 'twixt life's extremes :
  The cruel tyrant that did kill those flowers,
    Shall once, ay me ! not spare that spring of yours.

90

SOUND hoarse, sad lute, true witness of my woe,
    And strive no more to ease self-chosen pain
With soul-enchanting sounds ; your accents strain
Unto these tears incessantly which flow.
Shrill treble, weep ; and you, dull basses, show
Your master's sorrow in a deadly vein ;
Let never joyful hand upon you go,
Nor consort keep but when you do complain,
Fly Phœbus' rays, nay, hate the irksome light ;
Woods, solitary shades, for thee are best,
Or the black horrors of the blackest night,
When all the world, save thou and I doth rest :
    Then sound, sad lute, and bear a mourning part,
    Thou hell mayst move, though not a woman's
        heart.

91

DEAR eye, which deign'st on this sad monument
    The sable scroll of my mishaps to view,
Though with the mourning Muses' tears besprent,
And darkly drawn, which is not feign'd, but true ;
If thou not dazzled with a heavenly hue,
And comely feature, didst not yet lament,
But happy liv'st unto thyself content,
O let not Love thee to his laws subdue.
Look on the woful shipwreck of my youth,
And let my ruins for a Phare thee serve,
To shun this rock Capharean of untruth,
And serve no god who doth his church-men starve ;
    His kingdom is but plaints, his guerdon tears,
    What he gives more are jealousies and fears.

92

I F crost with all mishaps be my poor life,
    If one short day I never spent in mirth,
If my spright with itself holds lasting strife,
If sorrow's death is but new sorrow's birth ;
If this vain world be but a sable stage
Where slave-born man plays to the scoffing stars ;
If youth be toss'd with love, with weakness age,
If knowledge serve to hold our thoughts in wars ;
If time can close the hundred mouths of fame,
And make what long since past like that to be ;
If virtue only be an idle name,
If I, when I was born, was born to die ;
    Why seek I to prolong these loathsome days ?
    The fairest rose in shortest time decays.

93

O CRUEL beauty, meekness inhumane,
    That night and day contend with my desire,
And seek my hope to kill, not quench my fire,
By death, not balm, to ease my pleasant pain ;
Though ye my thoughts tread down which would
    aspire,
And bound my bliss, do not, alas ! disdain
That I your matchless worth and grace admire,
And for their cause these torments sharp sustain.
Let great Empedocles vaunt of his death,
Found in the midst of those Sicilian flames,
And Phaëton, that heaven him reft of breath,
And Daedal's son, who nam'd the Samian streams :
    Their haps I envy not ; my praise shall be,
    The fairest she that liv'd gave death to me.

94

THE Hyperborean hills, Ceraunus' snow,
    Or Arimaspus cruel, first thee bred ;
The Caspian tigers with their milk thee fed,
And Fauns did human blood on thee bestow ;
Fierce Orithyia's lover in thy bed
Thee lull'd asleep, where he enrag'd doth blow ;
Thou didst not drink the floods which here do flow,
But tears, or those by icy Tanais' head.
Sith thou disdains my love, neglects my grief,
Laughs at my groans, and still affects my death,
Of thee, nor heaven, I'll seek no more relief,
Nor longer entertain this loathsome breath,
    But yield unto my star, that thou mayst prove
    What loss thou hadst in losing such a love.

95

PHŒBUS, arise,
    And paint the sable skies
With azure, white, and red ;
Rouse Memnon's mother from her Tython's bed,
That she thy carrier may with roses spread ;
The nightingales thy coming each where sing ;
Make an eternal spring,
Give life to this dark world which lieth dead ;
Spread forth thy golden hair
In larger locks than thou wast wont before,
And emperor-like, decore
With diadem of pearl thy temples fair :
Chase hence the ugly night,
Which serves but to make dear thy glorious light.

This is that happy morn,
That day, long-wishèd day,
Of all my life so dark
(If cruel stars have not my ruin sworn,
And fates not hope betray),
Which, only white, deserves
A diamond for ever should it mark:
This is the morn should bring unto this grove
My love, to hear and recompense my love.
Fair king, who all preserves,
But show thy blushing beams,
And thou two sweeter eyes
Shalt see than those which by Peneus' streams
Did once thy heart surprise;
Nay, suns, which shine as clear
As thou when two thou did to Rome appear.
Now, Flora, deck thyself in fairest guise;
If that ye, winds, would hear
A voice surpassing far Amphion's lyre,
Your stormy chiding stay;
Let zephyr only breathe,
And with her tresses play,
Kissing sometimes these purple ports of death.
The winds all silent are,
And Phœbus in his chair,
Ensaffroning sea and air,
Makes vanish every star:
Night like a drunkard reels
Beyond the hills to shun his flaming wheels;
The fields with flow'rs are deck'd in every hue,
The clouds bespangle with bright gold their blue:
Here is the pleasant place,
And ev'ry thing, save her, who all should grace.

96

WHO hath not seen into her saffron bed
    The morning's goddess mildly her repose;
Or her, of whose pure blood first sprang the rose,
Lull'd in a slumber by a myrtle shade,—
Who hath not seen that sleeping white and red
Makes Phœbe look so pale, which she did close
In that Ionian hill to ease her woes,
Which only lives by nectar kisses fed,—
Come but and see my lady sweetly sleep,
The sighing rubies of those heavenly lips,
The Cupids which breast's golden apples keep,
Those eyes which shine in midst of their eclipse :
    And he them all shall see, perhaps, and prove
    She waking but persuades, now forceth love.

97

OF Cytherea's birds, that milk-white pair,
    On yonder leafy myrtle-tree which groan,
And waken, with their kisses in the air,
Enamour'd zephyrs murmuring one by one,
If thou but sense hadst like Pygmalion's stone,
Or hadst not seen Medusa's snaky hair,
Love's lessons thou might'st learn ; and learn, sweet
    fair,
To summer's heat ere that thy spring be grown.
And if those kissing lovers seem but cold,
Look how that elm this ivy doth embrace,
And binds, and clasps with many a wanton fold,
And courting sleep o'ershadows all the place ;
    Nay, seems to say, dear tree, we shall not part,
    In sign whereof, lo ! in each leaf a heart.

98

THE sun is fair when he with crimson crown,
  And flaming rubies, leaves his eastern bed;
Fair is Thaumantias in her crystal gown,
When clouds engemm'd hang azure, green, and red:
To western worlds when wearied day goes down,
And from Heaven's windows each star shows her
    head,
Earth's silent daughter, night, is fair, though brown;
Fair is the moon, though in love's livery clad;
Fair Chloris is when she doth paint April;
Fair are the meads, the woods, the floods are fair;
Fair looketh Ceres with her yellow hair,
And apples' queen when rose-cheek'd she doth smile.
    That heaven, and earth, and seas are fair is true,
    Yet true that all not please so much as you.

99   *Madrigal*

SWEET rose, whence is this hue
  Which doth all hues excel?
Whence this most fragrant smell,
And whence this form and gracing grace in you?
In flow'ry Pæstum's field perhaps ye grew,
Or Hybla's hills you bred,
Or odoriferous Enna's plains you fed,
Or Tmolus, or where boar young Adon slew;
Or hath the queen of love you dy'd of new
In that dear blood, which makes you look so red?
    No, none of those, but cause more high you blest:
    My lady's breast you bare, and lips you kiss'd.

100 *Madrigal*

ON this cold world of ours,
    Flower of the seasons, season of the flow'rs,
Son of the sun, sweet Spring,
Such hot and burning days why dost thou bring?
Is this for that those high eternal pow'rs
Flash down that fire this all environing?
Or that now Phœbus keeps his sister's sphere?
Or doth some Phaëton
Inflame the sea and air?
Or rather is it, usher of the year,
For that, last day, amongst thy flow'rs alone,
Unmask'd thou saw'st my fair?
    And whilst thou on her gaz'd she did thee burn,
    And in thy brother Summer doth thee turn?

101

DEAR wood, and you, sweet solitary place,
    Where from the vulgar I estranged live,
Contented more with what your shades me give,
Than if I had what Thetis doth embrace;
What snaky eye, grown jealous of my peace,
Now from your silent horrors would me drive,
When sun, progressing in his glorious race
Beyond the Twins, doth near our pole arrive?
What sweet delight a quiet life affords,
And what is it to be of bondage free,
Far from the madding worldling's hoarse discords,
Sweet flow'ry place I first did learn of thee:
    Ah! if I were mine own, your dear resorts
    I would not change with princes' stately courts.

102   *Madrigal*

UNHAPPY light,
  Do not approach to bring the woful day,
When I must bid for aye
Farewell to her, and live in endless plight.
Fair moon, with gentle beams
The sight who never mars,
Long clear heaven's sable vault ; and you, bright
      stars,
Your golden locks long glass in earth's pure streams ;
Let Phœbus never rise
To dim your watchful eyes :
    Prolong, alas ! prolong my short delight,
    And, if ye can, make an eternal night.

103

WITH grief in heart, and tears in swooning
        eyes,
When I to her had giv'n a sad farewell,
Close sealèd with a kiss, and dew which fell
On my else-moisten'd face from beauty's skies,
So strange amazement did my mind surprise,
That at each pace I fainting turn'd again,
Like one whom a torpedo stupefies,
Not feeling honour's bit, nor reason's rein.
But when fierce stars to part me did constrain,
With back-cast looks I envied both and bless'd
The happy walls and place did her contain,
Till that sight's shafts their flying object miss'd.
  So wailing parted Ganymede the fair,
    When eagles' talons bare him through the air.

104

I FEAR not henceforth death,
   Sith after this departure yet I breathe;
Let rocks, and seas, and wind,
Their highest treasons show;
Let sky and earth combin'd
Strive, if they can, to end my life and woe;
Sith grief can not, me nothing can o'erthrow:
   Or if that aught can cause my fatal lot,
   It will be when I hear I am forgot.

105

HOW many times night's silent queen her face
    Hath hid, how oft with stars in silver mask
In Heaven's great hall she hath begun her task,
And cheer'd the waking eye in lower place!
How oft the sun hath made by Heaven's swift
   race
The happy lover to forsake the breast
Of his dear lady, wishing in the west
His golden coach to run had larger space!
I ever count, and number, since, alas!
I bade farewell to my heart's dearest guest,
The miles I compass, and in mind I chase
The floods and mountains hold me from my
   rest:
   But, woe is me! long count and count may I,
   Ere I see her whose absence makes me die.

106

O FATE! conspir'd to pour your worst on me,
    O rigorous rigour, which doth all confound!
With cruel hands ye have cut down the tree,
And fruit and flower dispersèd on the ground.
A little space of earth my love doth bound;
That beauty which did raise it to the sky,
Turn'd in neglected dust, now low doth lie,
Deaf to my plaints, and senseless of my wound.
Ah! did I live for this? Ah! did I love?
For this and was it she did so excel,
That ere she well life's sweet-sour joys did prove,
She should, too dear a guest, with horror dwell?
    Weak influence of Heaven! what fair ye frame
    Falls in the prime, and passeth like a dream.

107

SWEET soul, which in the April of thy years
    So to enrich the Heaven mad'st poor this round,
And now with golden rays of glory crown'd
Most blest abid'st above the sphere of spheres;
If Heavenly laws, alas! have not thee bound
From looking to this globe that all upbears,
If ruth and pity there above be found,
O deign to lend a look unto those tears.
Do not disdain, dear ghost, this sacrifice,
And though I raise not pillars to thy praise,
Mine offerings take; let this for me suffice,
My heart a living pyramid I raise;
    And whilst kings' tombs with laurels flourish green,
    Thine shall with myrtles and these flow'rs be seen.

20

108 *Song*

(*Damon bewails his love*)

SAD Damon being come
    To that for ever lamentable tomb,
Which those eternal powers that all control
Unto his living soul
A melancholy prison had prescriv'd ;
Of hue, of heat, of motion quite depriv'd,
In arms weak, trembling, cold,
A marble, he the marble did infold ;
And having made it warm with many a show'r,
Which dimmèd eyes did pour,
When grief had given him leave, and sighs them
    stay'd,
Thus with a sad alas at last he said :
    Who would have thought to me
The place where thou didst lie could grievous be ?
And that, dear body, long thee having sought,
O me ! who would have thought
Thee once to find it should my soul confound,
And give my heart than death a deeper wound ?
Thou didst disdain my tears,
But grieve not that this ruthful stone them bears ;
Mine eyes serve only now for thee to weep,
And let their course them keep ;
Although thou never wouldst them comfort show,
Do not repine, they have part of thy woe.
    Ah, wretch ! too late I find,
How virtue's glorious titles prove but wind ;
For if she any could release from death,
Thou yet enjoy'd hadst breath ;
For if she e'er appear'd to mortal eyne,
If was in thy fair shape that she was seen.

But, O ! if I was made
For thee, with thee why too am I not dead ?
Why do outrageous fates, which dimm'd thy
      sight,
Let me see hateful light ?
They without me made death thee to surprise,
Tyrants, perhaps, that they might kill me twice.
    O grief ! and could one day
Have force such excellence to take away ?
Could a swift-flying moment, ah ! deface
Those matchless gifts, that grace
Which art and nature had in thee combin'd,
To make thy body paragon thy mind ?
Have all past like a cloud,
And doth eternal silence now them shroud ?
Is what so much admir'd was nought but dust,
Of which a stone hath trust ?
O change ! O cruel change ! thou to our sight
Shows destine's rigour equal doth their might.
    When thou from earth didst pass,
Sweet nymph, perfection's mirror broken was,
And this of late so glorious world of ours,
Like meadow without flow'rs,
Or ring of a rich gem made blind, appear'd,
Or night, by star nor Cynthia neither clear'd,
Love, when he saw thee die,
Entomb'd him in the lid of either eye,
And left his torch within thy sacred urn,
There for a lamp to burn :
Worth, honour, pleasure, with thy life expir'd,
Death since, grown sweet, begins to be desir'd.
    Whilst thou to us wast given,
The earth her Venus had as well as heaven,
Nay, and her sun, which burnt as many hearts
As he doth eastern parts ;

Bright sun, which, forc'd to leave these hemispheres,
Benighted set into a sea of tears.
Ah, Death, who shall thee fly,
Sith the most worthy be o'erthrown by thee?
Thou spar'st the ravens, and nightingales dost kill,
And triumphs at thy will;
But give thou canst not such another blow,
Because like her earth can none other show.
  O bitter sweets of love!
How better is't at all you not to prove,
Than when we do your pleasure most possess,
To find them then made less!
Oh! that the cause which doth consume our joy,
Remembrance of it too, would too destroy!
What doth this life bestow
But flowers on thorns which grow,
Which though they sometime blandishing delight,
Yet afterwards us smite?
And if the rising sun them fair doth see,
That planet, setting, too beholds them die.
This world is made a hell,
Depriv'd of all that in it did excel.
O Pan, Pan, winter is fallen in our May,
Turn'd is in night our day;
Forsake thy pipe, a sceptre take to thee,
Thy locks dis-garland, thou black Jove shalt be.
Thy flocks do leave the meads,
And, loathing three-leav'd grass, hold up their heads;
The streams not glide now with a gentle roar,
Nor birds sing as before;
Hills stand with clouds, like mourners, veil'd in
      black,
And owls on cabin roofs foretel our wrack.
  That zephyr every year
So soon was heard to sigh in forests here,

It was for her : that wrapt in gowns of green
Meads were so early seen,
That in the saddest months oft sung the merles,
It was for her ; for her trees dropt forth pearls.
That proud and stately courts
Did envy those our shades, and calm resorts,
It was for her ; and she is gone, O woe !
Woods cut again do grow,
Bud doth the rose and daisy, winter done,
But we, once dead, no more do see the sun.
   Whose name shall now make ring
The echoes? of whom shall the nymphets sing ?
Whose heavenly voice, whose soul-invading strains,
Shall fill with joy the plains ?
What hair, what eyes, can make the morn in east
Weep, that a fairer riseth in the west ?
Fair sun, post still away,
No music here is found thy course to stay.
Sweet Hybla swarms, with wormwood fill your
     bowers,
Gone is the flower of flowers ;
Blush no more, rose, nor, lily, pale remain,
Dead is that beauty which yours late did stain.
   Ay me ! to wail my plight
Why have not I as many eyes as night,
Or as that shepherd which Jove's love did keep,
That I still still may weep ?
But though I had, my tears unto my cross
Were yet not equal, nor grief to my loss:
Yet of your briny showers,
Which I here pour, may spring as many flowers
As came of those which fell from Helen's eyes ;
And when ye do arise,
May every leaf in sable letters bear
The doleful cause for which ye spring up here.

109

DEAR night, the ease of care,
　　Untroubled seat of peace,
Time's eldest child, which oft the blind do see,
On this our hemisphere,
What makes thee now so sadly dark to be?
Com'st thou in funeral pomp her grave to grace?
Or do those stars which should thy horror clear,
In Jove's high hall advise,
In what part of the skies,
With them, or Cynthia, she shall appear?
Or, ah, alas! because those matchless eyes
　　Which shone so fair, below thou dost not find,
　　Striv'st thou to make all other eyes look blind?

110

MY lute, be as thou wast when thou didst grow
　　With thy green mother in some shady grove,
When immelodious winds but made thee move,
And birds on thee their ramage did bestow.
Sith that dear voice which did thy sounds approve,
Which us'd in such harmonious strains to flow,
Is reft from earth to tune those spheres above,
What art thou but a harbinger of woe?
Thy pleasing notes be pleasing notes no more,
But orphan wailings to the fainting ear,
Each stop a sigh, each sound draws forth a tear:
Be therefore silent as in woods before,
　　Or if that any hand to touch thee deign,
　　Like widow'd turtle, still her loss complain.

111

SITH it hath pleas'd that First and only Fair
    To take that beauty to himself again,
Which in this world of sense not to remain,
But to amaze, was sent, and home repair;
The love which to that beauty I did bear
(Made pure of mortal spots which did it stain,
And endless, which even death cannot impair),
I place on Him who will it not disdain.
No shining eyes, no locks of curling gold,
No blushing roses on a virgin face,
No outward show, no, nor no inward grace,
Shall force hereafter have my thoughts to hold :
    Love here on earth huge storms of care do toss,
    But placed above, exempted is from loss.

112   *Song*

IT autumn was, and on our hemisphere
    Fair Ericyne began bright to appear;
Night westward did her gemmy world decline,
And hide her lights, that greater light might shine;
The crested bird had given alarum twice
To lazy mortals, to unlock their eyes;
The owl had left to plain, and from each thorn
The wing'd musicians did salute the morn,
Who, while she glass'd her locks in Ganges' streams,
Set open wide the crystal port of dreams;
When I, whose eyes no drowsy night could close,
In sleep's soft arms did quietly repose,
And, for that heavens to die me did deny,
Death's image kissèd, and as dead did lie.
I lay as dead, but scarce charmed were my cares,

And slakèd scarce my sighs, scarce dried my tears,
Sleep scarce the ugly figures of the day
Had with his sable pencil put away,
And left me in a still and calmy mood,
When by my bed methought a virgin stood,
A virgin in the blooming of her prime,
If such rare beauty measur'd be by time.
Her head a garland wore of opals bright,
About her flow'd a gown as pure as light,
Dear amber locks gave umbrage to her face,
Where modesty high majesty did grace ;
Her eyes such beams sent forth that but with pain
Here weaker sights their sparkling could sustain.
No deity feign'd which haunts the silent woods
Is like to her, nor syren of the floods :
Such is the golden planet of the year,
When blushing in the east he doth appear.
Her grace did beauty, voice yet grace did pass,
Which thus through pearls and rubies broken was.

How long wilt thou, said she, estrang'd from joy,
Paint shadows to thyself of false annoy ?
How long thy mind with horrid shapes affright,
And in imaginary evils delight ;
Esteem that loss which, well when view'd, is gain,
Or if a loss, yet not a loss to plain ?
O leave thy tired soul more to molest,
And think that woe when shortest then is best.
If she for whom thou deaf'nest thus the sky
Be dead, what then ? was she not born to die ?
Was she not mortal born ? If thou dost grieve
That times should be in which she should not live,
Ere e'er she was weep that day's wheel was roll'd,
Weep that she liv'd not in the age of gold ;
For that she was not then, thou may'st deplore
As duly as that now she is no more.

If only *she* had died, thou sure hadst cause
To blame the destinies, and heaven's iron laws;
But look how many millions her advance,
What numbers with her enter in this dance,
With those which are to come : shall heavens them
    stay,
And all fair order break, thee to obey?
Even at thy birth, death, which doth thee appal,
A piece is of the life of this great all.
Strong cities die, die do high palmy reigns,
And, weakling, thou thus to be handled plains.
  If she be dead, then she of loathsome days
Hast past the line, whose length but loss bewrays;
Then she hath left this filthy stage of care,
Where pleasure seldom, woe doth still repair.
For all the pleasures which it doth contain
Not countervail the smallest minute's pain.
And tell me, thou who dost so much admire
This little vapour, smoke, this spark, or fire,
Which life is call'd, what doth it thee bequeath
But some few years which birth draws out to death ?
Which if thou paragon with lustres run,
And them whose carrier is but now begun,
In day's great vast they shall far less appear
Than with the sea when matchèd is a tear.
But why wouldst thou here longer wish to be ?
One year doth serve all nature's pomp to see,
Nay, even one day and night : this moon, that sun,
Those lesser fires about this round which run,
Be but the same which, under Saturn's reign,
Did the serpenting seasons interchain.
How oft doth life grow less by living long ?
And what excelleth but what dieth young?
For age, which all abhor yet would embrace,
Whiles makes the mind as wrinkled as the face;

And when that destinies conspire with worth,
That years not glory wrong, life soon goes forth.
Leave then laments, and think thou didst not live
Laws to that first eternal cause to give,
But to obey those laws which he hath given,
And bow unto the just decrees of Heaven,
Which cannot err, whatever foggy mists
Do blind men in these sublunary lists.
  But what if she for whom thou spend'st those
        groans,
And wastest life's dear torch in ruthful moans,
She for whose sake thou hat'st the joyful light,
Court'st solitary shades, and irksome night,
Doth live ? O ! if thou canst, through tears, a space
Lift thy dimm'd lights, and look upon this face,
Look if those eyes which, fool, thou didst adore,
Shine not more bright than they were wont before ;
Look if those roses death could aught impair,
Those roses to thee once which seem'd so fair ;
And if those locks have lost aught of that gold,
Which erst they had when thou them didst behold.
I live, and happy live, but thou art dead,
And still shalt be, till thou be like me made.
Alas ! while we are wrapt in gowns of earth,
And, blind, here suck the air of woe beneath,
Each thing in sense's balances we weigh,
And but with toil and pain the truth descry.
  Above this vast and admirable frame,
This temple visible, which world we name,
Within whose walls so many lamps do burn,
So many arches opposite do turn,
Where elemental brethren nurse their strife,
And by intestine wars maintain their life,
There is a world, a world of perfect bliss,
Pure, immaterial, bright, more far from this

Than that high circle which the rest enspheres
Is from this dull ignoble vale of tears ;
A world where all is found that here is found,
But further discrepant than heaven and ground.
It hath an earth, as hath this world of yours,
With creatures peopled, stor'd with trees and flow'rs ;
It hath a sea, like sapphire girdle cast,
Which decketh of harmonious shores the waste ;
It hath pure fire, it hath delicious air,
Moon, sun, and stars, heavens wonderfully fair :
But there flow'rs do not fade, trees grow not old,
The creatures do not die through heat nor cold ;
Sea there nor tossèd is, nor air made black,
Fire doth not nurse itself on others' wrack ;
There heavens be not constrain'd about to range,
For this world hath no need of any change ;
The minutes grow not hours, hours rise not days,
Days make no months but ever-blooming Mays.
　　Here I remain, but hitherward do tend
All who their span of days in virtue spend :
Whatever pleasure this low place contains,
It is a glance but of what high remains.
Those who, perchance, think there can nothing be
Without this wide expansion which they see,
And that nought else mounts stars' circumference,
For that nought else is subject to their sense,
Feel such a case as one whom some abysm
Of the deep ocean kept had all his time ;
Who, born and nourish'd there, can scarcely dream
That aught can live without that briny stream ;
Cannot believe that there be temples, towers,
That go beyond his caves and dampish bowers,
Or there be other peoples, manners, laws,
Than them he finds within the roaring waves ;
That sweeter flow'rs do spring than grow on rocks,

Or beasts be which excel the scaly flocks ;
That other elements be to be found
Than is the water, and this ball of ground.
But think that man from those abysms were brought,
And saw what curious nature here hath wrought,
Did see the meads, the tall and shady woods,
The hills did see, the clear and ambling floods ;
The diverse shapes of beasts which kinds forth bring,
The feathered troops that fly and sweetly sing ;
Did see the palaces, the cities fair,
The form of human life, the fire, the air,
The brightness of the sun that dims his sight,
The moon, the ghastly splendours of the night :
What uncouth rapture would his mind surprise !
How would he his late-dear resort despise !
How would he muse how foolish he had been
To think nought be, but what he there had seen !
Why did we get this high and vast desire
Unto immortal things still to aspire ?
Why doth our mind extend it beyond time,
And to that highest happiness even climb,
If we be nought but what to sense we seem,
And dust, as most of worldlings us esteem ?
We be made for earth, though here we come,
More than the embryon for the mother's womb ;
It weeps to be made free, and we complain
To leave this loathsome jail of care and pain.

But thou, who vulgar footsteps dost not trace,
Learn to raise up thy mind unto this place,
And what earth-creeping mortals most affect,
If not at all to scorn, yet to neglect :
O chase not shadows vain, which, when obtain'd,
Were better lost than with such travail gain'd.
Think *that* on earth, which humans greatness call,
Is but a glorious title to live thrall ;

That sceptres, diadems, and chairs of state,
Not in themselves, but to small minds are great ;
How those who loftiest mount do hardest light,
And deepest falls be from the highest height ;
How fame an echo is, how all renown,
Like to a blasted rose, ere night falls down ;
And though it something were, think how this round
Is but a little point, which doth it bound.
O leave that love which reacheth but to dust,
And in that love eternal only trust,
And beauty, which, when once it is possest,
Can only fill the soul, and make it blest.
Pale envy, jealous emulations, fears,
Sighs, plaints, remorse, here have no place, nor tears,
False joys, vain hopes, here be not hate nor wrath ;
What ends all love, here most augments it, death.
If such force had the dim glance of an eye,
Which some few days thereafter was to die,
That it could make thee leave all other things,
And like the taper-fly there burn thy wings ;
And if a voice, of late which could but wail,
Such pow'r had as through ears thy soul to steal ;
If once thou on that only fair couldst gaze,
What flames of love would he within thee raise ?
In what a mazing maze would it thee bring,
To hear but once that quire celestial sing ?
The fairest shapes on which thy love did seize,
Which erst did breed delight, then would displease ;
Then discords hoarse were earth's enticing sounds,
All music but a noise which sense confounds.
This great and burning glass that clears all eyes,
And musters with such glory in the skies ;
That silver star which with its sober light
Makes day oft envy the eye-pleasing night ;
Those golden letters which so brightly shine

In heaven's great volume gorgeously divine ;
The wonders all in sea, in earth, in air,
Be but dark pictures of that sovereign Fair ;
Be tongues, which still thus cry unto your ear,
(Could ye amidst worlds' cataracts them hear,)
From fading things, fond wights, lift your desire,
And in our beauty, his, us made, admire :
If we seem fair, O think how fair is he
Of whose fair fairness shadows, steps, we be.
No shadow can compare it with the face,
No step with that dear foot that did it trace ;
Your souls immortal are, then place them hence,
And do not drown them in the must of sense :
Do not, O do not, by false pleasures' might
Deprive them of that true and sole delight.
That happiness ye seek is not below ;
Earth's sweetest joy is but disguisèd woe.
    Here did she pause, and with a mild aspect
Did towards me those lamping twins direct ;
The wonted rays I knew, and thrice essay'd
To answer make, thrice falt'ring tongue it stay'd ;
And while upon that face I fed my sight,
Methought she vanish'd up in Titan's light,
Who gilding with his rays each hill and plain,
Seem'd to have brought the goldsmith's world again.

113   *Of Phillis*

IN petticoat of green,
    Her hair about her eyne,
Phillis beneath an oak
Sat milking her fair flock :
Among that strainèd moisture, rare delight !
Her hand seem'd milk in milk, it was so white.

114   *Kisses Desired*

THOUGH I with strange desire
      To kiss those rosy lips am set on fire,
Yet will I cease to crave
Sweet touches in such store
As he, who, long before,
From Lesbia them in thousands did receive.
Heart mine, but once me kiss,
And I by that sweet bliss
Even swear to cease you to importune more :
Poor one no number is ;
Another word of me ye shall not hear
After one kiss, but still one kiss, my dear.

115   *Of Amintas*

OVER a crystal source
      Amintas laid his face,
Of popling[1] streams to see the restless course.
But scarce he had o'ershadowèd the place,
When (spying in the ground a child arise,
Like to himself in stature, face and eyes),
He rose, o'erjoy'd, and cried,
Dear mates, approach, see whom I have descried ;
The boy of whom strange stories shepherds tell,
Oft-callèd Hylas, dwelleth in this well.

[1] Bubbling.

116　　*Upon a Glass*

IF thou wouldst see threads purer than the gold,
　Where love his wealth doth show,
But take this glass, and thy fair hair behold:
If whiteness thou wouldst see more white than snow,
And read on wonder's book,
Take but this glass, and on thy forehead look.
Wouldst thou in winter see a crimson rose,
Whose thorns do hurt each heart,
Look but in glass how thy sweet lips do close:
Wouldst thou see planets which all good impart,
Or meteors divine,
But take this glass, and gaze upon thine eyne.
No, planets, rose, snow, gold, cannot compare
With you, dear eyes, lips, brows, and amber hair!

SIR DAVID MURRAY

Fl. 1610–1630

117 *A Question*

AND is it true, dear, that you are unkind?
 Shall I believe, sweet saint, that you are so?
I fear you are; but stay, O stay, my mind!
 Too soon to credit that that breeds my woe.
 Yet whither shall my resolutions go?
To think you are, or not, unkind, I must.
 Th' effect says Aye, and yet my fancy No,
Being loth such undeserved harm to trust.
My passions thus such operations breed
 In my divided soul, that I cannot
Conceive you are that which you are indeed,
 Imperious love doth so control my thought.
Unhappy I that did such love embrace!
Unconstant you that hates such love, alas!

118 *Adieu!*

ADIEU, sweet Cœlia! for I must depart
 And leave thy sight, and with thy sight all joy,
 Convoyed with care, attended with annoy,
A vagabonding wretch from part to part.
 Only, dear Cœlia, grant me so much grace
 As to vouchsafe this heart befraught with sorrow
 T' attend upon thy shadow even and morrow,
Whose wonted pleasure was to view thy face.

And if sometimes thou solitar remain,
    And for thy dearest dear a sigh lets slide,
    This poor attender, sitting by thy side,
Shall be thy echo, to reply't again.
Then farewell, Cœlia! for I must away,
And to attend thee my poor heart shall stay.

119   *Love's Idea*

DAYS, hours, and nights thy presence may detain,
    But neither day nor hour nor night shall not
Bar thy sweet beauty from mine eyes unseen,
    Since so divinely printed in my thought.
    That skilful Greek that Love's idea wrought,
And limned it so exactly to the eye,
    When beauty's rarest patterns he had sought—
With this thy portrait could not matchèd be.
Though on a table he—most skilful he—
    In rarest colour rarest parts presented,
So on a heart, if one may match a tree,
    Though skill-less, I thy rarer shape have painted.
Not by Love's self Love's beauty formed he;
But by thyself thyself art formed in me.

JAMES GRAHAME, MARQUIS OF MONTROSE

1612–1650

120   *An excellent new Ballad to the tune of "I'll never love thee more"*

M Y dear and only love, I pray
    That little world of thee
Be governed by no other sway
    Than purest monarchy ;
For if confusion have a part,
    Which virtuous souls abhor,
And hold a synod in thine heart,
    I'll never love thee more.

As Alexander I will reign,
    And I will reign alone ;
My thoughts did evermore disdain
    A rival on my throne.
He either fears his fate too much,
    Or his deserts are small,
That dares not put it to the touch,
    To gain or lose it all.

But I will reign and govern still,
    And always give the law,
And have each subject at my will,
    And all to stand in awe ;

But 'gainst my batteries if I find
　　Thou kick, or vex me sore,
As that thou set me up a blind,
　　I'll never love thee more.

And in the empire of thine heart,
　　Where I should solely be,
If others do pretend a part,
　　Or dare to vie with me,
Or if committees thou erect,
　　And go on such a score,
I'll laugh and sing at thy neglect,
　　And never love thee more.

But if thou wilt prove faithful, then,
　　And constant of thy word,
I'll make thee glorious by my pen,
　　And famous by my sword ;
I'll serve thee in such noble ways
　　Was never heard before ;
I'll crown and deck thee all with bays,
　　And love thee more and more.

121　　　　　*" Unhappy is the Man "*

UNHAPPY is the man
　　In whose breast is confined
The sorrows and distresses all
　　Of an afflicted mind.

The extremity is great :
　　He dies if he conceal,—
The world's so void of secret friends,
　　Betrayed if he reveal.

Then break, afflicted heart !
   And live not in these days,
When all prove merchants of their faith,—
   None trusts what other says.

For when the sun doth shine,
   Then shadows do appear ;
But when the sun doth hide his face
   They with the sun retire.

Some friends as shadows are,
   And fortune as the sun ;
They never proffer any help
   Till fortune hath begun ;

But if, in any case,
   Fortune shall first decay,
Then they, as shadows of the sun,
   With fortune run away.

FRANCIS SEMPLE, OF BELTREES

Circ. 1616–1682

Maggie Lauder

WHA wadna be in love
    Wi' bonnie Maggie Lauder?
A piper met her gaun to Fife
    And spiered what was't they ca'd her;
Richt scornfully she answered him,
    " Begone, you hallan-shaker [1] !
Jog on your gate, you bladderskate [2] !
    My name is Maggie Lauder."

" Maggie ! " quoth he, " and, by my bags,
    I'm fidgin' fain to see thee :
Sit down by me, my bonnie bird ;
    In troth I winna steer [3] thee,
For I'm a piper to my trade,
    My name is Rob the Ranter ;
The lassies loup as they were daft
    When I blaw up my chanter."

" Piper," quo' Meg, " hae ye your bags,
    Or is your drone in order?
If ye be Rob, I've heard o' you ;
    Live you upo' the Border?

---

[1] sturdy beggar.   [2] idle prater.   [3] disturb.

The lasses a' baith far and near
  Have heard o' Rob the Ranter,
I'll shake my foot wi' richt gude will
  Gif ye'll blaw up your chanter."

Then to his bags he flew wi' speed ;
  About the drone he twisted ;
Meg up and walloped ower the green,
  For brawly could she frisk it.
" Weel done !" quo' he. " Play up !" quo' she.
  " Weel bobbed !" quo' Rob the Ranter,
" It's worth my while to play, indeed,
  When I hae sic a dancer !"

" Weel hae you played your part," quo' Meg ;
  " Your cheeks are like the crimson :
There's nane in Scotland plays sae weel
  Sin' we lost Habbie Simson.
I've lived in Fife, baith maid and wife,
  This ten years and a quarter ;
Gin ye should come to Anster Fair [1],
  Speir ye for Maggie Lauder."

123   *Old Longsyne* [2]

MY soul is ravished with delight
  When you I think upon ;
All griefs and sorrows take the flight
  And hastily are gone.
The fair resemblance of your face
  So fills this breast of mine,
No fate nor force can it displace,
  For old longsyne.

---

[1] A famous fair, held at Anstruther, in Fife.   [2] This song is claimed for Sir Robert Aytoun by Charles Roger, editor of his poems.

Since thoughts of you do banish grief
   When I'm from you removed,
And if in them I find relief
   When with sad cares I'm moved,
How doth your presence me affect
   With ecstasy divine,
Especially when I reflect
   On old longsyne !

Since thou hast robbed me of my heart
   By those resistless powers
Which Madam Nature doth impart
   To those fair eyes of yours,
With honour it doth not consist
   To hold a slave in pine ;
Pray let your vigour then desist,
   For old longsyne.

'Tis not my freedom I do crave
   By deprecating pains ;
Sure liberty he would not have
   Who glories in his chains ;
But this—I wish the gods would move
   That noble soul of thine
To pity, since thou cannot love,
   For old longsyne.

LORD YESTER

1646–1713

Tweedside

WHEN Maggie and I were acquaint
　　I carried my noddle fu' hie ;
Nae lintwhite on a' the green plain,
　　Nae gowdspink [1] sae happy as me.
But I saw her sae fair, and I lo'ed,
　　I wooed, but I cam' nae great speed ;
So now I maun wander abroad,
　　And lay my banes far frae the Tweed.

To Maggie my love I did tell,
　　Saut tears did my passion express ;
Alas ! for I lo'ed her o'erweel,
　　And the women lo'e sic a man less.
Her heart it was frozen and cauld,
　　Her pride had my ruin decreed ;
Therefore I will wander abroad,
　　And lay my banes far frae the Tweed.

[1] goldfinch.

LADY GRISELL BAILLIE

1665–1746

125   *Werena my heart licht I wad dee*

THERE ance was a may[1], and she loo'd na men ;
　　She biggit[2] her bonnie bower doun in yon glen ;
But now she cries, Dool[3] ! and well-a-day !
Come doun the green gait[4] and come here away !

When bonnie young Johnnie cam' ower the sea,
He said he saw naething sae lovely as me ;
He hecht[5] me baith rings and mony braw things,—
And werena my heart licht I wad dee.

He had a wee titty[6] that loo'd na me,
Because I was twice as bonnie as she ;
She raised such a pother 'twixt him and his mother
That werena my heart licht I wad dee.

The day it was set, and the bridal to be :
The wife took a dwam[7] and lay doun to dee ;
She maned and she graned out o' dolour and pain,
Till he vow'd he never wad see me again.

His kin was for ane of a higher degree,
Said, What had he to do wi' the like of me ?
Albeit I was bonnie, I wasna for Johnnie,—
And werena my heart licht I wad dee.

---

[1] maid.　[2] builded.　[3] Sorrow !　[4] way.　[5] promised.　[6] sister.
[7] faintness.

LADY GRISELL BAILLIE

They said I had neither cow nor calf,
Nor dribbles o' drink rins through the draff [1];
Nor pickles o' meal rins through the mill-e'e [2];
And werena my heart licht I wad dee.

His titty she was baith wylie and slee [3]:
She spied me as I cam' ower the lea;
And then she ran in and made a loud din,—
Believe your ain een an' ye trow na me.

His bonnet stood aye fu' round on his brow,—
His auld ane look'd aye as weel as some's new;
But now he lets 't wear ony gait it will hing,
And casts himself dowie upon the corn-bing.[4]

And now he gaes daund'ring [5] about the dykes [6],
And a' he dow [7] do is to hund the tykes [8]:
The live-lang nicht he ne'er steeks his e'e [9];
And werena my heart licht I wad dee.

Were I but young for thee, as I hae been,
We should hae been gallopin' doun on yon green,
And linkin' it [10] on the lily-white lea,—
And wow! gin I were but young for thee!

[1] grain (the allusion is to brewing). [2] opening in the frame of a mill. [3] sly. [4] heap. [5] rambling. [6] fences. [7] is equal to.
[8] hound on the dogs. [9] closes an eye. [10] walking arm in arm.

SIR JOHN CLERK

1680–1755

The Miller

MERRY may the maid be
   That marries the miller ;
For, foul day and fair day,
   He's aye bringing till her,—
Has aye a penny in his purse
   For dinner and for supper ;
And, gin ¹ she please, a good fat cheese
   And lumps of yellow butter.

When Jamie first did woo me,
   I speir'd ² what was his calling :
" Fair maid," says he, " O come and see—
   Ye're welcome to my dwalling."
Though I was shy, yet I could spy
   The truth of what he told me,
And that his house was warm and couth ³,
   And room in it to hold me.

Behind the door a bag of meal ;
   And in the kist ⁴ was plenty
Of good hard cakes his mither bakes,
   And bannocks werena scanty :

¹ if. ² asked. ³ comfortable. ⁴ chest.

A good fat sow ; a sleeky cow
　　Was standin' in the byre [1];
While lazy puss, with mealy mou',
　　Was playing at the fire.

Good signs are these, my mither says,
　　And bids me tak' the miller ;
For, foul day and fair day,
　　He's aye bringing till her :
For meal and malt she doesna want,
　　Nor anything that's dainty,—
And noo and then a keckling hen
　　To lay her eggs in plenty.

In winter when the wind and rain
　　Blaws o'er the house and byre,
He sits beside a clean hearth-stane
　　Before a rousing fire :
With nut-brown ale he tells his tale,
　　Which rows [2] him o'er fu' nappy [3] :
Who'd be a king—a petty thing,
　　When a miller lives so happy ?

　　　[1] cattle-shed.　[2] rolls.　[3] tipsy.

ALLAN RAMSAY

1686–1758

127   *The Gentle Shepherd*

ACT FIRST

SCENE I

PROLOGUE

BENEATH the south side of a craigy beild [1],
    Where crystal springs their halesome waters
       yield,
Twa youthfu' Shepherds on the gowans lay,
Tenting their flocks ae bonny morn of May.
Poor Roger granes, till hollow echoes ring;
But blyther Patie likes to laugh an' sing.

PATIE AND ROGER

SANG

PATIE

My Peggy is a young thing,
    Just enter'd in her teens,
Fair as the day, and sweet as May,
Fair as the day, and always gay.
    My Peggy is a young thing,
    And I'm nae very auld,
Yet weel I like to meet her at
    The wauking o' the fauld [2].

[1] rocky shelter. [2] watching of the sheepfold.

334

My Peggy speaks sae sweetly,
   Whene'er we meet alane,
I wish nae mair to lay my care,
I wish nae mair o' a' that's rare.
My Peggy speaks sae sweetly,
   To a' the lave I'm cauld,
But she gars a' my spirits glow,
   At wauking o' the fauld.

My Peggy smiles sae kindly,
   Whene'er I whisper love,
That I look down on a' the town,
That I look down upon a crown.
My Peggy smiles sae kindly,
   It maks me blythe and bauld,
And naething gies me sic delyte
   As wauking o' the fauld.

My Peggy sings sae saftly,
   When on my pipe I play;
By a' the rest it is confest,
By a' the rest that she sings best.
My Peggy sings sae saftly,
   And in her sangs are tauld,
Wi' innocence, the wale o' sense [1],
   At wauking o' the fauld.

PATIE. This sunny morning, Roger, cheers my
    blood,
And puts all nature in a jovial mood,
How heartsome it's to see the rising plants!
To hear the birds chirm [2] o'er their pleasing rants!

---

[1] soul of sense.   [2] hum.

How halesome it's to snuff the cauler [1] air,
And a' the sweets it bears, when void o' care !
What ails ye, Roger, then ? what gars ye grane ?
Tell me the cause o' thy ill-season'd pain.

ROGER. I'm born, O Patie, to a thrawart [2] fate,
I'm born to strive wi' hardships sad and great.
Tempests may cease to jaw [3] the rowin' flood,
Corbies an' tods to grien [4] for lambkins' blood ;
But I, opprest wi' never-ending grief,
Maun aye despair o' lighting on relief.

PATIE. The bees shall loathe the flow'r, and quit
the hive,
The saughs [5] on boggy ground shall cease to thrive,
Ere scornfu' queans, or loss o' warldly gear,
Shall spoil my rest, or ever force a tear.

ROGER. Sae might I say ; but it's no easy dune
By ane whase saul's sae sadly out o' tune.
Ye hae sae saft a voice, an' slid [6] a tongue,
Ye are the darling o' baith auld and young.
If I but ettle [7] at a sang, or speak,
They dit their lugs, syne up their leglens cleek [8],
And jeer me hameward frae the loan or bught [9],
While I'm confus'd wi' mony a vexing thought.
Yet I am tall, and as weel built as thee,
Nor mair unlikely to a lass's eye,
For ilka sheep ye hae, I'll number ten,
An' should, as ane may think, come farer ben. [10]

[1] bracing.   [2] contrary.   [3] stir.   [4] ravens and foxes to hunger
for.   [5] sallows.   [6] cajoling.   [7] aim.   [8] milk-pails catch.
[9] cattle-path or fold.   [10] further forward.

PATIE. But aiblins, neibour, ye have not a heart,
And downa eithly wi' your cunzie part[1].
If that be true, what signifies your gear ?
A mind that's scrimpit never wants some care.

ROGER. My byre tumbl'd, nine braw nowt were
    smoored[2],
Three elf-shot were ; yet I these ills endur'd :
In winter last my cares were very sma',
Tho' scores o' wathers perish'd in the snaw.

PATIE. Were your bein[3] rooms as thinly stock'd
    as mine,
Less ye wad lose, and less ye wad repine.
He that has just enough can soundly sleep ;
The o'ercome only fashes fouk to keep.

ROGER. May plenty flow upon thee for a cross,
That thou may'st thole the pangs of mony a loss !
O may'st thou doat on some fair paughty[4] wench,
That ne'er will lout[5] thy lowin' drouth to quench,
Till, bris'd beneath the burden, thou cry dool[6],
And awn that ane may fret that is nae fool !

PATIE. Sax good fat lambs, I sald them ilka clute
At the West-port, and bought a winsome flute
O' plum-tree made, with ivory virles[7] round ;
A dainty whistle, with a pleasant sound ;
I'll be mair canty[8] wi't, and ne'er cry dool,
Than you, wi' a' your cash, ye dowie fool !

ROGER. Na, Patie, na ! I'm nae sic churlish beast ;
Some other thing lies heavier at my breast ;
I dream'd a dreary dream this hinder night,
That gars my flesh a' creep yet wi' the fright.

[1] don't "part" easily.   [2] overwhelmed.   [3] cosy.   [4] petulant.
[5] stoop. [6] woe. [7] rings. [8] cheery.

PATIE. Now, to a friend, how silly's this pretence,
To ane wha you and a' your secrets kens ;
Daft[1] are your dreams, as daftly wad ye hide
Your weel-seen love, and dorty[2] Jenny's pride ;
Tak courage, Roger, me your sorrows tell,
And safely think nane kens them but yoursel.

ROGER. Indeed, now, Patie, ye hae guess'd owre
         true,
And there is naething I'll keep up frae you.
Me dorty Jenny looks upon asquint,
To speak but till her I daur hardly mint[3] :
In ilka place she jeers me air[4] and late,
And gars me look bombaz'd, and unco blate[5].
But yesterday I met her yont a knowe[6],
She fled, as frae a shelly-coated cow[7] :
She Bauldy loes, Bauldy that drives the car,
But gecks[8] at me, and says I smell o' tar.

PATIE. But Bauldy loes not her, right weel I wat,
He sighs for Neps—sae that may stand for that.

ROGER. I wish I cou'dna loe her—but, in vain,
I still maun doat, and thole[9] her proud disdain.
My Bawty is a cur I dearly like,
Even while he fawn'd, she strak the poor dumb
         tyke[10] ;
If I had fill'd a nook within her breast,
She wad hae shawn mair kindness to my beast.
When I begin to tune my stock and horn[11],
Wi' a' her face she shaws a cauldrife[12] scorn.
Last night I play'd, (ye never heard sic spite !)

---

[1] disordered. [2] saucy. [3] attempt. [4] early. [5] confused and
very bashful. [6] behind a hill. [7] the water-cow of Scottish fable.
[8] mocks. [9] endure. [10] dog. [11] sheep and cattle (a song in praise
of). [12] chilling.

"O'er Bogie" was the spring, and her delyte ;
Yet, tauntingly, she at her cousin speer'd,
Gif she cou'd tell what tune I play'd, and sneer'd.
Flocks, wander where ye like, I dinna care,
I'll break my reed, and never whistle mair !

PATIE.   E'en do sae, Roger, wha can help mis-
        luck,
Saebeins she be sic a thrawn-gebbit chuck ¹ ?
Yonder's a craig, sin' ye hae tint ² a' houp,
Gae till't your ways, and tak the lover's loup.
ROGER.   I needna mak sic speed my blood to spill,
I'll warrant death come soon eneugh a-will.

PATIE.   Daft gowk ³ ! leave aff that silly whinging ⁴
        way ;
Seem careless, there's my hand ye'll win the day.
Hear how I serv'd my lass I lo'e as weel
As ye do Jenny, and wi' heart as leal.
Last morning I was gay and early out,
Upon a dyke I lean'd, glowring ⁵ about ;
I saw my Meg come linking ⁶ o'er the lea ;
I saw my Meg, but Meggy saw nae me ;
For yet the sun was wading thro' the mist,
And she was close upon me ere she wist ;
Her coats were kiltit, an' did sweetly shaw
Her straught bare legs, that whiter were than snaw.
Her cockernony snooded ⁷ up fu' sleek,
Her haffet-locks ⁸ hung waving on her cheek ;
Her cheeks sae ruddy, and her e'en sae clear ;
And, oh ! her mouth's like ony hinny pear.
Neat, neat she was, in bustine ⁹ waistcoat clean,
As she cam skiffing o'er the dewy green :

¹ perversely-spoken jade.   ² lost.   ³ fool.   ⁴ peevish.   ⁵ staring.
⁶ tripping.   ⁷ *chignon* gathered in a fillet.   ⁸ side-locks.   ⁹ fustian.

Blythesome, I cry'd, "My bonny Meg, come here,
I ferly [1] wherefore ye're sae soon asteer ;
But I can guess, ye're gawn to gather dew :"
She scour'd awa, an' said, 'What's that to you ?'
'Then fare ye weel, Meg Dorts, and e'en's ye like,'"
I careless cry'd, and lap in o'er the dyke ;
I trow, when that she saw, within a crack,
She cam with a right thieveless [2] errand back ;
Misca'd me first, then bade me hound my dog,
To wear up three waff [3] ewes stray'd on the bog.
I leugh, and sae did she ; then with great haste
I clasp'd my arms about her neck and waist ;
About her yielding waist, an' took a fouth [4]
O' sweetest kisses frae her glowing mouth.
While hard an' fast I held her in my grips,
My very saul came louping to my lips.
Sair, sair she flet [5] wi' me 'tween ilka smack,
But weel I kend she meant nae as she spak.
Dear Roger, when your joe puts on her gloom,
Do ye sae too, and never fash your thumb [6],
Seem to forsake her, soon she'll change her mood :
Gae woo anither, and she'll gang clean wud [7].

SANG

Dear Roger, if your Jenny geck,
    And answer kindness with a slight,
Seem unconcerned at her neglect ;
    For women in a man delight ;
But them despise wha're soon defeat,
    And with a simple face gie way
To a repulse—then be not blate,
    Push bauldly on, and win the day.

---

[1] marvel. [2] unlikely. [3] strayed, waif. [4] abundance. [5] argued,
protested. [6] trouble yourself. [7] wild.

When maidens, innocently young,
    Say aften what they never mean,
Ne'er mind the pretty lying tongue ;
    But tent[1] the language o' their een :
If these agree, and she persist
    To answer all your love with hate,
Seek elsewhere to be better blest,
    And let her sigh when 'tis too late.

ROGER.   Kind Patie, now fair fa'[2] your honest
      heart,
Ye're ay sae cadgy[3], and hae sic an art
To hearten ane : For now, as clean's a leek,
Ye've cherish'd me since ye began to speak.
Sae for your pains, I'll make you a propine[4],
(My mother, rest her saul ! she made it fine ;)
A tartan plaid, spun of good haslock woo[5],
Scarlet an' green the sets, the borders blue ;
Wi' springs[6] like gowd an' siller, cross'd wi' black ;
I never had it yet upon my back.
Weel are ye wordy o't, wha hae sae kind
Redd[7] up my ravel'd doubts, and clear'd my mind.

PATIE.   Weel, haud ye there—and since ye've frankly
      made
To me a present o' your braw new plaid,
My flute's be yours, and she too that's sae nice
Shall come a-will, gif ye'll tak my advice.

ROGER.   As ye advise, I'll promise to observ't ;
But ye maun keep the flute, ye best deserv't.

---

[1] heed.   [2] befall.   [3] kindly.   [4] present.   [5] wool from the
sheep's neck, esteemed the finest.   [6] stripes.   [7] cleared.

Now tak it out, and gie's a bonny spring ;
For I'm in tift[1] to hear you play and sing.

PATIE.   But first we'll tak a turn up to the height,
And see gif a' our flocks be feeding right :
By that time bannocks, and a shave o' cheese,
Will mak a breakfast that a laird might please ;
Might please the daintiest gabs, were they sae wise
To season meat wi' health instead o' spice :
When we hae tane the grace-drink at this well,
I'll whistle fine, and sing t'ye like mysel.   [*Exeunt.*

128   *The Lass o' Patie's Mill*

THE lass o' Patie's Mill,
    Sae bonnie, blythe, and gay,
In spite of a' my skill,
    She stole my heart away.
When teddin' out the hay,
    Bareheaded on the green,
Love mid her locks did play,
    And wanton'd in her een.

Without the help of art,
    Like flowers that grace the wild,
She did her sweets impart,
    Whene'er she spak' or smiled :
Her looks they were so mild,
    Free from affected pride,
She me to love beguiled ;
    I wish'd her for my bride.

[1] in the right mood.

Oh ! had I a' the wealth
   Hopetoun's high mountains fill,
Insured lang life and health,
   And pleasure at my will ;
I'd promise, and fulfil,
   That nane but bonnie she,
The lass o' Patie's Mill,
   Should share the same wi' me.

ROBERT CRAWFORD

1695 (?)–1733 (?)

Doun the Burn, Davie

WHEN trees did bud, and fields were green,
　　And broom bloom'd fair to see ;
When Mary was complete fifteen,
　　And love laugh'd in her e'e ;
Blythe Davie's blinks her heart did move
　　To speak her mind thus free :
Gang doun the burn, Davie, love,
　　And I will follow thee !

Now Davie did each lad surpass
　　That dwelt on this burnside ;
And Mary was the bonniest lass,
　　Just meet to be a bride :
Her cheeks were rosy-red and white,
　　Her e'en were bonny blue,
Her looks were like Aurora bright,
　　Her lips like dropping dew.

*　　　*　　　*　　　*　　　*

What pass'd, I guess, was harmless play,
　　And naething sure unmeet ;
For, ganging hame, I heard them say
　　They liked a walk sae sweet,
And that they aften should return
　　Sic pleasure to renew.
Quoth Mary, Love, I like the burn,
　　And aye shall follow you !

130   *The Broom of the Cowdenknowes*

WHEN summer comes, the swains on Tweed
    Sing their successful loves,—
Around the ewes and lambkins feed,
    And music fills the groves.

But my loved song is then the broom
    So fair on Cowdenknowes ;
For sure so sweet, so soft, a bloom
    Elsewhere there never grows.

There Colin tuned his oaten reed,
    And won my yielding heart ;—
No shepherd e'er that dwelt on Tweed
    Could play with half such art.

He sang of Tay, of Forth, and Clyde,
    The hills and dales all round,
Of Leader-haughs and Leader-side,—
    Oh ! how I bless'd the sound.

Yet more delightful is the broom
    So fair on Cowdenknowes ;
For sure so fresh, so bright, a bloom
    Elsewhere there never grows.

Not Teviot braes so green and gay
    May with this broom compare,—
Not Yarrow banks in flowery May,
    Nor the bush aboon [1] Traquair.

[1] above.

More pleasing far are Cowdenknowes,
   My peaceful, happy home,—
Where I was wont to milk my ewes
   At e'en among the broom.

Ye powers that haunt the woods and plains
   Where Tweed with Teviot flows,
Convey me to the best of swains
   And my loved Cowdenknowes!

131   *The Bush Aboon Traquair*

HEAR me, ye nymphs and every swain,—
   I'll tell how Peggy grieves me!
Tho' thus I languish, thus complain,
   Alas! she ne'er believes me.
My vows and sighs, like silent air
   Unheeded, never move her:
At the bonny bush aboon Traquair,
   'Twas there I first did love her!

That day she smiled and made me glad—
   No maid seem'd ever kinder:
I thought myself the luckiest lad,
   So sweetly there to find her.
I tried to soothe my am'rous flame
   In words that I thought tender:
If more there pass'd, I'm not to blame—
   I meant not to offend her.

Yet now she scornful flees the plain,
   The fields we then frequented:
If e'er we meet she shows disdain,—
   She looks as ne'er acquainted.

The bonny bush bloom'd fair in May,—
  It's sweets I'll aye remember ;
But, now her frowns make it decay,
  It fades as in December.

Ye rural powers who hear my strains,
  Why thus should Peggy grieve me ?
Oh ! make her partner in my pains ;
  Then let her smiles relieve me.
If not, my love will turn despair,—
  My passion no more tender,
I'll leave the bush aboon Traquair—
  To lonely wilds I'll wander.

The bonny lass blooms fair in May—
It's sweet I'll aye remember:
But now far frae my native dear,
It fades as in December.

Ye cruel fates, and ill-starr'd skies,
Why thus sae cruelly grieve me?
Oh! make her mistress of my paines,
Then let her love relieve me.

My passions all—

ALEXANDER ROSS

1699–1784

132   *Woo'd and Married and A'*

THE bride cam' out o' the byre[1],
    An' O! as she dighted[2] her cheeks,
"Sirs, I'm to be married the night,
    And hae neither blankets nor sheets—
Hae neither blankets nor sheets,
    Nor scarce a coverlet too:
The bride that has a' thing to borrow
    Has e'en right muckle ado!"
       Woo'd and married and a',
       Married and woo'd and a'!
       And was she na very weel aff
       That was woo'd and married and a'?

Out spake the bride's father,
    As he cam' in frae the pleugh:
"O haud your tongue, my dochter,
    And ye'se get gear eneugh:
The stirk[3] stands i' the tether,
    And our braw bawsint yade[4]
Will carry ye hame your corn:—
    What wad ye be at, ye jade?"

[1] cow-house.   dried.   [3] ox.   [4] an old mare with a white patch on her face.

Out spake the bride's mither :
    " What, deil, needs a' this pride ?
I hadna a plack in my pouch [1]
    That night I was a bride :
My gown was linsy-woolsy,
    And ne'er a sark [2] ava ;
And ye hae ribbons and buskin's [3]
    Mae [4] than ane or twa ! "

Out spake the bride's brither,
    As he cam' in wi' the kye :
" Poor Willie wad ne'er hae ta'en ye,
    Had he kent ye as weel as I ;
For ye're baith proud and saucy,
    Ane no for a poor man's wife :
Gin I canna get a better,
    I'se ne'er tak' ane i' my life ! "

Out spake the bride's sister,
    As she cam' in frae the byre :
" O, gin I were but married,
    It's a' that I desire !
But we poor fouk maun live single,
    And do the best we can :
I dinna ken what I should want
    If I could get but a man ! "

133   *Song from " Helenore "*

OF a' the lads that be
    On Flavinia's braes,
My Colin bears the gree [5],
    And that a thousand ways.

[1] small coin in my pocket.   [2] chemise.   [3] ornaments.   [4] more.
[5] carries off the prize.

Best on the pipe he plays,
  Is merry, blyth and gay,
And " Jenny fair," he says,
  " Has stown my heart away :

Had I ten thousand pounds,
  I'd a' to Jenny gi'e ;
And thole[1] a thousand wounds,
  To keep my Jenny free.
For Jenny is to me,
  O' a' the maidens fair,
My jo[2], and ay sall be ;
  Wi' her I'll only pair.

O' roses I will weave
  To her a flow'ry crown ;
A' ither cares I'll leave,
  And busk her haffets[3] roun'.
I'll buy her a new gown,
  Wi' strips o' red and blue,
And never mair look brown,
  For Jane will ay be new."

My Jenny made reply,
  " Since ye have chosen me,
Then a' my wits I'll try,
  A loving wife to be.
If I my Colin see,
  I'll lang for naething mair,
Wi' him I do agree
  In weal and woe to share."

---

  [1] endure.   [2] sweetheart.   [3] temples.

134   *Bydby and the Fairies*

(*From "Helenore, or The Fortunate Shepherdess"*)

THUS making at her main, and lewdring [1] on,
    Thro' scrubs and craigs, wi' mony a heavy groan,
Wi' bleeding legs and sair massacr'd shoon,
Wi' Lindy's coat aye feltring [2] her aboon ;
Till on a high brae head she lands at last,
That down to a how [3] burnie pathlins [4] past.
Clear was the burnie, and the bushes green,
But rough and steep the brae that lay between ;
Her burning drowth inclin'd her to be there,
But want of maughts [5] and distance eek'd her care.
Now by this time the ev'ning's falling down,
Hill-heads were red, and hows were eery grown.
Yet wi' what pith she had, she taks the gate [6],
And wan the burn, but it's now growing late.
The birds about were making merry cheer,
She thinks their music sang, " Ye're welcome here,"
With the cauld stream she quench'd her lowan [7] drouth,
Syne of the Etnagh [8]-berries ate a fouth [9],
That black and ripe upon the busses grew,
And were new water'd wi' the evening dew.
Then sat she down aneth a birken shade,
That spread aboon her, and hang o'er her head,
Cowthy [10] and warm, and gowany [11] the green,
Had it, instead o' night, the day time been.
But grim and gousty [12] and pit mark [13], wi' fright
A' thing appear'd upon the dead o' night.
For fear she cowr'd like maukin [14] in the seat,
And dunt for dunt [15] her heart began to beat.

---

[1] moving heavily.   [2] entangling.   [3] hollow.   [4] by a steep path.
[5] might.   [6] road.   [7] burning.   [8] juniper.   [9] good supply.
[10] pleasant.   [11] with daisies pied.   [12] desolate.   [13] pitch dark.
[14] a hare.   [15] stroke.

Amidst this horror, sleep began to steal,
And for a wee her flightring [1] breast to heal,
As she half sleeping and half waking lay,
An unco din she hears of fouk [2] and play.
The sough [3] they made gar'd her lift up her eyn,
And O, the gathering that was on the green !
Of little foukies, clad in green and blue,
Kneefer [4] and trigger [5] never trod the dew :
In mony a reel they scamper'd here and there,
Whiles on the yird [6] and whiles up in the air ;
The pipers play'd like ony touting horn,
Sic sight she never saw since she was born.
As she's behading a' this mirthful glee,
Or e'er she wist they're dancing in the tree
Aboon her head, as nimble as the bees
That swarm, in search of honey, round the trees.
Fear's like to fell her, reed [7] that they sud fa'
And smore [8] her dead, afore she wan awa' ;
Syne in a clap [9], as thick's the motty sin [10],
They hamphis'd [11] her wi' unco fyke [12] and din.
Some cry'd " Tak ye the head, I'se tak a foot.
We'll lear [13] her upon this tree-head to sit,
And spy about her." Others said, " Out fy,
Lat be, she'll keep the king of Elfin's ky [14]."
Anither said, " O gin she had but milk,
Then sud she gae frae head to foot in silk,
Wi' castings [15] rare, and a gueed nooriss-fee [16],
To nurse the king of Elfin's heir Fizzee."
Syne ere she wist, like house aboon her head,
Great candles burning, and braw table spread ;
Braw dishes reeking [17], and just at her hand,

---

[1] fluttering. [2] folk. [3] rustling. [4] more active. [5] smarter.
[6] ground. [7] lest. [8] smother. [9] moment. [10] as motes in the sun.
[11] surrounded. [12] fuss. [13] teach. [14] cattle. [15] cast clothes.
[16] good nurse's fee. [17] smoking.

Trig green coats sairing [1], a' upon command.
To cut they fa', and she amang the lave [2];
The sight was bonny, and her mou' did crave.
The mair she ate, the mair her hunger grew,
Eat fat [3] she like, and she could ne'er be fu';
The knible [4] elves about her ate ding dang [5],
Syne to the play they up, and danc'd and flang [6]:
Drink in braw cups was ca'd [7] about gelore,
Some fell asleep, and loud began to snore.
Syne in a clap, the fairies a' sat down,
And fell to crack [8] about the table roun'.
Ane at another speer'd [9], "Fat tricks play'd ye,
Whan in a riddle ye sail'd o'er the sea?"
Quoth it, "I steal'd the king of Sweden's knife,
Just at his dinner, sitting by his wife,
Whan frae his hand he newlins [10] laid it down;
He blam'd the steward, said he had been the lown [11].
The sakeless [12] man deny'd, syne yeed [13] to look,
And lifting aff the table-claith, the nook
I gae a tit [14], and tumbled o'er the bree [15];
Tam got the wyte [16], and I gae the tehee [17];
I think I never saw a better sport,
But dool [18] fell'd Tam, for sadly he paid for't."
But quoth another, "I play'd a better prank:
I gar'd a witch fa' headlines [19] in a stank [20]
As she was riding on the windle-strae;
The carling gloff'd [21], and cry'd out will awae [22]."
Another said, "I coupet [23] Mungo's ale
Clean heels o'er head, fan it was ripe and stale,
Just whan the tapster the first chapin [24] drew;

[1] serving.   [2] rest.   [3] what.   [4] nimble.   [5] pell-mell.   [6] flung up their legs.   [7] pushed.   [8] gossip.   [9] one of another asked.   [10] newly.   [11] traitor.   [12] luckless.   [13] went.   [14] twitched the corner.   [15] drink.   [16] blame.   [17] guffaw.   [18] sorrow.   [19] fall headlong.   [20] pond.   [21] shuddered.   [22] well-a-day.   [23] overturned.   [24] measure.

Then bade her lick the pail, and aff I flew :
Had ye but seen how blate[1] the lassie looked,
Whan she was blam'd, how she the drink miscooked[2]."
Says a gnib[3] elf, " As an auld carl was sitting
Amang his bags, and loosing ilka knitting,
To air his rousty coin, I loot a claught[4],
And took a hundred dollars at a fraught[5].
Whan wi' the sight the carle had pleas'd himsel,
Then he began the glancing heap to tell.
As soon's he miss'd it, he rampag'd red-wood[6],
And lap[7] and danc'd, and was in unco[8] mood :
Ran out and in, and up and down ; at last
His reeling eyn upon a raip he cast,
Knit till a bauk[9], that had hung up a cow :
He taks the hint, and there hings he I trow."

135   *Courtship against the Grain*
(Dialogue of Aunt and Nephew)

(*From " Helenore, or The Fortunate Shepherdess "*)

*   *   *   *   *

" BY now I think ye need na hae great fear,
    That ye maun tak the lass wi' mikle gear ;
He was to blame, my brother as he was,
Against your will to bid you tak the lass."
" Ay, aunty, gin ye kent the bonny aught[10] ;
'Tis true, she had of warld's gear a fraught[11],
But what was that to peace and saught[12] at hame,
And, whilk is warse, to kirk and market shame ;
For had my father sought the warld round,

---

[1] abashed.   [2] mismanaged.   [3] sprightly.   [4] made a snatch.
[5] freight.   [6] mad with rage.   [7] leapt.   [8] extraordinary.   [9] rafter.
[10] a term of disparagement.   [11] freight.   [12] ease.

Till he the very dightings [1] o't had found,
An odder hag could not come in his way,
Than for my truncher [2] what he had laid by.
An ugly hulgie-backed [3] canker'd wasp,
And like to die for breath at ilka gasp.
Her teeth, betweesh a yellow and a black,
Some out, some in, and a' of a different mak ;
Black hairy warts about an inch between,
O'er ran her atry [4] phyz beneath her eyn ;
Her head lay back, and a lang gap [5] sat out,
Wi' the addition of a sniviling snout ;
And tak her a' together, rough and right,
She wad na been by far four foot of height ;
And for her temper, maik [6] she could hae nane,
She'd gar twa paps cast out on ae breast-bane ;
And yet, say what I lik'd, nought would do,
But I maun gang, that bonny chap [7] to woo.
My father he yeed [8] with me at the first,
But a' the time, my heart was like to birst ;
To think to lead my life wi' sic an ape,
I'd rather mak my tesment in a raip [9].
But ugly as she was, there was nae cure,
But I maun kiss her 'cause I was the wooer ;
My father briskly loot me see the gate [10],
But I assure you, I look'd wondrous blate [11] ;
And very thrawart like [12] I yeed in by.
' A young man look sae blate ! ' says he, ' O fy ! '
Nor was it fairly, for her stinking breath
Was just enough to sconfice [13] ane to death ;
But frae my father mony a smack she gat ;
And I, just like to spue [14], like blunty [15] sat ;

[1] refuse. [2] trencher. [3] hump-backed. [4] grim. [5] gab, mouth.
[6] match. [7] a term of contempt. [8] went. [9] go to the gallows.
[10] way. [11] shame-faced. [12] reluctantly. [13] stifle. [14] puke.
[15] an oaf.

I canna say, but she was wondrous kind,
And for her dresses, wow[1] but they were fine ;
And mony a bonny thing was in our sight,
And a' thing that was there was snug and tight ;
Nae little wealth, I 'sure you, there we saw,
And ilka thing was rich, and fine, and braw ;
But for it a' I did not care a straw,
And wad hae geen my neck to be awa'.
At last and lang, as we were riding hame,
My father says, ' Yon is a wealthy dame ;
What think ye, Mundy, winna ye be braw,
When ye yon bonny things your ain can ca' ?
Does not your heart ly to the bargain now,
And hae ye not encouragement to woo ? '
' A's well,' I says, ' except what sud be best,
And when that's wrang, what worth is a' the rest ? '
' I grant,' he says, ' she's nae a beauty spot,
But he that wad refuse her is a sot ;
Though ye look'd shy, she wad get ten for ane,
And I'll engage, she'll no be lang her lane[2] :
Her riggs[3] 'll gar the wooers come ding dang[4],
And she'll strike up wi' ane ere it be lang ;
Sae strike the iron, laddie, when it's het,
And a' the land, and wealth, and baggage get :
Ye see her riggs run just unto our ain,
'Twill mak a swinging lairdship a' in ane ;
And Mundy, she's for you aboon[5] them a',
Sae, when 'tis at your foot, man, strike the ba'.
And mind you, billy[6], though ye looked dry,
Ye'll change your fashions, and gae sharp in by,
And daut[7] her o'er and o'er, I'll wad[8] my head,
At the neist courting bout but ye'll come speed.
But wha wad hae you, when ye sit sae dumb,

---

[1] (ejaculation.) [2] alone. [3] ridges, as opposed to furrows : hence
land. [4] pell-mell. [5] above. [6] "my boy." [7] fondle. [8] stake.

And never open mou', to say a mum [1] ?
Ye maun mak o' her, kiss her o'er and o'er,
Say ye're in love, and but [2] her cannot cowr [3] :
But, for her sake, maun view the lands o' leal [4],
Except she pity, and your ailment heal.
But out of jest, and in gueed earnest, lad,
Ye maun gae forward and the bargain had [5],
Or else ye's tyne [6] whate'er ye had of me ;
There is nae other boot, but it maun be.'
Syne in a little I maun gang again,
And which was worst of a', maun gang my lane [7],
Am bidden court and daut, and see the lass,
O aunt, but I was at an unco pass !
But I resolv'd upon't to put a face,
And see gin I had can [8] to turn the chace."
    " Well, how behav'd ye ? did ye gie'r the mou',"
Says aunty, " neest, wi' mony a scrape and bow,
Syne laid your arm athwart her ugly back,
And now and then to steal a quiet smack ?"
    " Na by my sooth I ; I came fierclins [9] in,
And wi' my trantlims [10] made a clattering din ;
And hailst [11] her roughly, and began to say,
I'd got a lump of my ain death this day,
Wi' weet and wind sae tyte [12] into my teeth,
That it was like to cut my very breath :
Gin this be courting, well I wat 'tis clear,
I gat na sic a teezle [13] this seven year :
And ye maun gee your answer just perqueer [14],
I maun na ilka day be coming here,
To get sic snifters [15] ; courting's nae a jest,
Another day like this'll be my priest [16]."
" Well," quoth she, " nephew, that was wanton sports,

[1] mutter. [2] without. [3] recover. [4] Heaven. [5] hold. [6] lose.
[7] alone. [8] ability. [9] blusteringly. [10] accoutrements.
[11] embraced. [12] straight. [13] mauling. [14] exactly, right away.
[15] repulses. [16] "do for me."

I hope ye gar'd the lady tak the dorts[1] ;
For sic rough courting I hae never seen,
Sin I was born, a lad and lass between."
" Na, aunty," says he, " she was not sae skeegh[2] ;
Nor wi' her answer very blate or dreegh[3] ;
But says, ' I'm wae ye've got so foul a day,
But makesna[4], till't grow better ye may stay,
Tho't 'were this month, ye're very welcome here ;
Of what I hae, yese get the best of cheer.'"
   " I think," quoth she, " ye're fairly nicked[5] now."
" Nae hauf sa far," he says, "as ye wad trow ;
I tauld her that was kind, but then that I
Nae for a night out of my bed could ly :
Or if I did, it would be seen ere day
There wad be mair than cause to rue my stay ;
That I the reason did na care to tell,
It was enough I kent the cause mysel."
Quoth she, " I wiss I could your wanrest[6] ken,
'Tis maybe cause ye canna ly your lane :
Gin that be it, yese be provided here,
Though maybe nae so gueed, but wi' as near."
I now began to think she meant hersel,
But how my stomach raise, I sanna tell.
"Na, na," quoth I, " 'tis wi' kend fouk I ly,
I never liked yet to gang astray :
This night I maun be hame afore I sleep,
Gin ganging winna do't, though I sud creep."
" Well, gin ye be sae positive," she says,
" I sanna argue, come back whene'er you please,
Afore you aye your welcome ye sall find,
And blame yoursel, in case ye come behind."
"I'se see to that," I says, and aff I scours,
Blessing my lucky stars, and hame I tours.

    [1] "the pet."   [2] shy.   [3] slow.   [4] no matter.   [5] caught.   [6] cause
of disquiet.

Whan I came hame, the auld boy says to me,
" How hae ye sped ? Is Ketty frank and free ? "
" As frank," I says, " as heart of man could wiss,
I hae nae fear that I my market miss.
" Well, Mundy, that's a man," my father says,
" We's hae you coupl'd then afore lang days ;
Gin [1] this day fortnight we's be cut and dry,
There may be danger in't gin we delay."
Thus wi' my lad I play'd at fast and loose,
And he begins to think, that now I'm douse [2].
" Content," says I, " but I maun gang and see
My honest aunt, afore I married be."
And ye may mind, I tauld you crap and root [3],
Fan I came here ; and that I ne'er wad do't.

[1] against.   [2] soft, compliant.   [3] the whole story.

DAVID MALLET

About 1700–1765

136 *William and Margaret*

'TWAS at the silent, solemn hour
    When night and morning meet;
In glided Margaret's grimly ghost,
    And stood at William's feet.

Her face was like an April morn
    Clad in a wintry cloud;
And clay-cold was her lily hand,
    That held her sable shroud.

So shall the fairest face appear
    When youth and years are flown:
Such is the robe that kings must wear,
    When death has reft their crown.

Her bloom was like the springing flower,
    That sips the silver dew;
The rose was budded in her cheek—
    Just opening to the view.

But love had, like the canker-worm,
    Consumed her early prime:
The rose grew pale, and left her cheek—
    She died before her time.

"Awake!" she cried, "thy true love calls—
  Come from her midnight grave:
Now let thy pity hear the maid
  Thy love refused to save.

"This is the dumb and dreary hour
  When injured ghosts complain;—
When yawning graves give up their dead
  To haunt the faithless swain.

" Bethink thee, William, of thy fault,
  Thy pledge and broken oath!
And give me back my maiden-vow,
  And give me back my troth.

"Why did you promise love to me,
  And not that promise keep?
Why did you swear my eyes were bright—
  Yet leave those eyes to weep?

"How could you say my face was fair,
  And yet that face forsake?
How could you win my virgin heart,
  Yet leave that heart to break?

"Why did you say my lip was sweet,
  And made the scarlet pale?
And why did I, young witless maid!
  Believe the flattering tale?

"That face, alas! no more is fair,
  Those lips no longer red:
Dark are my eyes, now closed in death,
  And every charm is fled.

" The hungry worm my sister is ;
  This winding sheet I wear :
And cold and weary lasts our night,
  Till that last morn appear.

" But hark ! the cock has warned me hence—
  A long and last adieu !
Come see, false man, how low she lies,
  Who died for love of you."

The lark sang loud ; the morning smiled,
  With beams of rosy red :
Pale William quaked in every limb,
  And raving left his bed.

He hied him to the fatal place
  Where Margaret's body lay ;
And stretch'd him on the green-grass turf
  That wrapt her breathless clay.

And thrice he called on Margaret's name,
  And thrice he wept full sore ;
Then laid his cheek to her cold grave,
  And word spake never more !

JAMES THOMSON

1700–1748

From the Seasons

AUTUMN

BUT see the fading many-coloured woods,
  Shade deepening over shade, the country round
Imbrown ; a crowded umbrage, dusk and dun,
Of every hue from wan declining green
To sooty dark. These now the lonesome muse,
Low-whispering, lead into their leaf-strown walks,
And give the season in its latest view.
  Meantime, light shadowing all, a sober calm
Fleeces unbounded ether ; whose least wave
Stands tremulous, uncertain where to turn
The gentle current ; while, illumined wide,
The dewy-skirted clouds imbibe the sun,
And through their lucid veil his softened force
Shed o'er the peaceful world.
  Then is the time
For those whom wisdom and whom nature charm
To steal themselves from the degenerate crowd,
And soar above this little scene of things—
To tread low-thoughted vice beneath their feet,
To soothe the throbbing passions into peace,
And woo lone Quiet in her silent walks.
  Thus solitary, and in pensive guise,
Oft let me wander o'er the russet mead,

And through the saddened grove, where scarce is
　　heard
One dying strain to cheer the woodman's toil.
Haply some widowed songster pours his plaint
Far in faint warblings through the tawny copse ;
While congregated thrushes, linnets, larks,
And each wild throat whose artless strains so late
Swelled all the music of the swarming shades,
Robbed of their tuneful souls, now shivering sit
On the dead tree, a dull despondent flock,
With not a brightness waving o'er their plumes,
And naught save chattering discord in their note.
Oh, let not, aimed from some inhuman eye,
The gun the music of the coming year
Destroy, and harmless, unsuspecting harm,
Lay the weak tribes, a miserable prey !
In mingled murder fluttering on the ground !
　　The pale descending year, yet pleasing still,
A gentler mood inspires ; for now the leaf
Incessant rustles from the mournful grove,
Oft startling such as studious walk below,
And slowly circles through the waving air.
But, should a quicker breeze amid the boughs
Sob, o'er the sky the leafy deluge streams ;
Till, choked and matted with the dreary shower,
The forest-walks, at every rising gale,
Roll wide the wither'd waste, and whistle bleak.
Fled is the blasted verdure of the fields ;
And, shrunk into their beds, the flowery race
Their sunny robes resign. Even what remained
Of bolder fruits falls from the naked tree ;
And—woods, fields, gardens, orchards, all around—
The desolated prospect thrills the soul.
　　He comes ! he comes ! in every breeze the Power
Of Philosophic Melancholy comes !

His near approach the sudden-starting tear,
The glowing cheek, the mild dejected air,
The softened feature, and the beating heart,
Pierced deep with many a virtuous pang, declare.
O'er all the soul his sacred influence breathes ;
Inflames imagination ; through the breast
Infuses every tenderness ; and far
Beyond dim earth exalts the swelling thought.
Ten thousand thousand fleet ideas, such
As never mingled with the vulgar dream,
Crowd fast into the mind's creative eye.
As fast the correspondent passions rise,
As varied, and as high—devotion raised
To rapture, and divine astonishment ;
The love of nature unconfined, and, chief,
Of human race ; the large ambitious wish
To make them blest ; the sigh for suffering worth
Lost in obscurity ; the noble scorn
Of tyrant pride ; the fearless great resolve ;
The wonder which the dying patriot draws,
Inspiring glory through remotest time ;
The awakened throb for virtue and for fame ;
The sympathies of love and friendship dear,
With all the social offspring of the heart.
Oh ! bear me then to vast embowering shades,
To twilight groves, and visionary vales,
To weeping grottoes, and prophetic glooms ;
Where angel forms athwart the solemn dusk,
Tremendous, sweep, or seem to sweep along ;
And voices more than human, through the void
Deep-sounding, seize the enthusiastic ear.
  Or is this gloom too much ? Then lead, ye Powers
That o'er the garden and the rural seat
Preside, which, shining through the cheerful land
In countless numbers, blest Britannia sees—

Oh! lead me to the wide extended walks,
The fair majestic paradise of Stowe!
Not Persian Cyrus on Ionia's shore
E'er saw such sylvan scenes, such various art
By genius fired, such ardent genius tamed
By cool judicious art, that in the strife
All-beauteous Nature fears to be outdone.
And there, O Pitt; thy country's early boast,
There let me sit beneath the sheltered slopes,
Or in that Temple where, in future times,
Thou well shalt merit a distinguished name,
And, with thy converse blest, catch the last smiles
Of Autumn beaming o'er the yellow woods.
While there with thee the enchanted round I walk,
The regulated wild, gay fancy then
Will tread in thought the groves of Attic land;
Will from thy standard taste refine her own,
Correct her pencil to the purest truth
Of nature, or, the unimpassioned shades
Forsaking, raise it to the human mind.
Oh, if hereafter she with juster hand
Shall draw the tragic scene, instruct her thou
To mark the varied movements of the heart,
What every decent character requires,
And every passion speaks! Oh, through her strain
Breathe thy pathetic eloquence, that moulds
The attentive senate, charms, persuades, exalts,
Of honest zeal the indignant lightning throws,
And shakes Corruption on her venal throne!

*   *   *   *   *

The western sun withdraws the shortened day;
And humid evening, gliding o'er the sky,
In her chill progress, to the ground condensed
The vapours throws. Where creeping waters ooze,
Where marshes stagnate, and where rivers wind,

Cluster the rolling fogs, and swim along
The dusky-mantled lawn. Meanwhile the moon,
Full-orbed and breaking through the scattered clouds,
Shows her broad visage in the crimsoned east.
Turned to the sun direct, her spotted disk
(Where mountains rise, umbrageous dales descend,
And caverns deep, as optic tube descries)
A smaller earth, gives all his blaze again,
Void of its flame, and sheds a softer day.
Now through the passing cloud she seems to stoop,
Now up the pure cerulean rides sublime.
Wide the pale deluge floats, and streaming mild
O'er the skied mountain to the shadowy vale,
While rocks and floods reflect the quivering gleam,
The whole air whitens with a boundless tide
Of silver radiance trembling round the world.
  But when, half blotted from the sky, her light,
Fainting, permits the starry fires to burn
With keener lustre through the depth of heaven ;
Or quite extinct her deadened orb appears,
And scarce appears, of sickly beamless white ;
Oft in this season, silent from the north
A blaze of meteors shoots—ensweeping first
The lower skies, they all at once converge
High to the crown of heaven, and, all at once
Relapsing quick, as quickly re-ascend,
And mix and thwart, extinguish and renew,
All ether coursing in a maze of light.
  From look to look, contagious through the crowd,
The panic runs, and into wondrous shapes
The appearance throws—armies in meet array,
Thronged with aerial spears and steeds of fire ;
Till, the long lines of full-extended war
In bleeding fight commixed, the sanguine flood
Rolls a broad slaughter o'er the plains of heaven.

As thus they scan the visionary scene,
On all sides swells the superstitious din,
Incontinent ; and busy frenzy talks
Of blood and battles ; cities overturned,
And late at night in swallowing earthquake sunk,
Or hideous wrapt in fierce ascending flame ;
Of sallow famine, inundation, storm ;
Of pestilence, and every great distress ;
Empires subversed, when ruling fate has struck
The unalterable hour : even nature's self
Is deemed to totter on the brink of time.
Not so the man of philosophic eye
And inspect sage : the waving brightness he
Curious surveys, inquisitive to know
The causes and materials, yet unfixed,
Of this appearance beautiful and new.

138   *A Hymn on the Seasons*

THESE, as they change, Almighty Father ! these
    Are but the varied God. The rolling year
Is full of thee. Forth in the pleasing Spring
Thy beauty walks, thy tenderness and love.
Wide flush the fields ; the softening air is balm ;
Echo the mountains round ; the forest smiles ;
And every sense, and every heart, is joy.
Then comes thy glory in the Summer-months,
With light and heat refulgent. Then thy sun
Shoots full perfection through the swelling year :
And oft thy voice in dreadful thunder speaks,
And oft, at dawn, deep noon, or falling eve,
By brooks and groves, in hollow-whispering gales.
Thy bounty shines in Autumn unconfined,
And spreads a common feast for all that lives.
In Winter awful thou ! with clouds and storms

Around thee thrown, tempest o'er tempest rolled,
Majestic darkness ! On the whirlwind's wing
Riding sublime, thou bidst the world adore,
And humblest nature with thy northern blast.

Mysterious round ! what skill, what force divine,
Deep-felt in these appear ! a simple train,
Yet so delightful mixed, with such kind art,
Such beauty and beneficence combined,
Shade unperceived so softening into shade,
And all so forming an harmonious whole
That, as they still succeed, they ravish still.
But, wandering oft with brute unconscious gaze,
Man marks not thee, marks not the mighty hand
That, ever busy, wheels the silent spheres,
Works in the secret deep, shoots steaming thence
The fair profusion that o'erspreads the Spring,
Flings from the sun direct the flaming day,
Feeds every creature, hurls the tempest forth,
And, as on earth this grateful change revolves,
With transport touches all the springs of life.

Nature, attend ! join, every living soul
Beneath the spacious temple of the sky,
In adoration join ; and ardent raise
One general song ! To him, ye vocal gales,
Breathe soft, whose spirit in your freshness breathes :
Oh ! talk of him in solitary glooms,
Where, o'er the rock, the scarcely-waving pine
Fills the brown shade with a religious awe.
And ye, whose bolder note is heard afar,
Who shake the astonished world, lift high to Heaven
The impetuous song, and say from whom you rage.
His praise, ye brooks, attune, ye trembling rills ;
And let me catch it as I muse along.

24

Ye headlong torrents, rapid and profound ;
Ye softer floods, that lead the humid maze
Along the vale ; and thou, majestic main,
A secret world of wonders in thyself,
Sound his stupendous praise, whose greater voice
Or bids you roar or bids your roarings fall.
Soft roll your incense, herbs and fruits, and flowers,
In mingled clouds to him, whose sun exalts,
Whose breath perfumes you, and whose pencil paints.
Ye forests, bend ; ye harvests, wave to him—
Breathe your still song into the reaper's heart
As home he goes beneath the joyous moon.
Ye that keep watch in heaven, as earth asleep
Unconscious lies, effuse your mildest beams,
Ye constellations ! while your angels strike
Amid the spangled sky the silver lyre.
Great source of day ! best image here below
Of thy Creator, ever pouring wide
From world to world the vital ocean round !
On nature write with every beam his praise.
The thunder rolls : be hushed the prostrate world,
While cloud to cloud returns the solemn hymn.
Bleat out afresh, ye hills ; ye mossy rocks,
Retain the sound ; the broad responsive low,
Ye valleys, raise ; for the Great Shepherd reigns,
And his unsuffering kingdom yet will come.
Ye woodlands all, awake : a boundless song
Burst from the groves ; and, when the restless day,
Expiring, lays the warbling world asleep,
Sweetest of birds, sweet Philomela ! charm
The listening shades, and teach the night his praise !
Ye, chief, for whom the whole creation smiles,
At once the head, the heart, the tongue of all,
Crown the great hymn ! In swarming cities vast,
Assembled men, to the deep organ join

The long-resounding voice, oft breaking clear
At solemn pauses through the swelling bass ;
And, as each mingling flame increases each,
In one united ardour rise to heaven.
Or, if you rather choose the rural shade,
And find a fane in every sacred grove,
There let the shepherd's flute, the virgin's lay,
The prompting seraph, and the poet's lyre
Still sing the God of Seasons as they roll.
For me, when I forget the darling theme,
Whether the blossom blows, the summer-ray
Russets the plain, inspiring autumn gleams,
Or winter rises in the blackening east,
Be my tongue mute, may fancy paint no more,
And, dead to joy, forget my heart to beat !

Should fate command me to the farthest verge
Of the green earth, to distant barbarous climes,
Rivers unknown to song, where first the sun
Gilds Indian mountains, or his setting beam
Flames on the Atlantic isles, 'tis nought to me ;
Since God is ever present, ever felt,
In the void waste as in the city full,
And where he vital spreads there must be joy.
When even at last the solemn hour shall come,
And wing my mystic flight to future worlds,
I cheerful will obey ; there, with new powers,
Will rising wonders sing : I cannot go
Where universal love not smiles around,
Sustaining all yon orbs and all their sons :
From seeming evil still educing good,
And better thence again, and better still,
In infinite progression. But I lose
Myself in him, in light ineffable !
Come then, expressive Silence, muse his praise.

WILLIAM HAMILTON, OF BANGOUR

1704–1754

139   *The Braes of Yarrow*

A. " BUSK[1] ye, busk ye, my bonny bonny bride,
     Busk ye, busk ye, my winsome marrow[2] !
Busk ye, busk ye, my bonny bonny bride,
     And think nae mair on the braes of Yarrow."

B. "Where got ye that bonny bonny bride,
     Where got ye that winsome marrow?"
A. "I got her where I durst not well be seen—
     Pu'ing the birks[3] on the braes of Yarrow.

Weep not, weep not, my bonny bonny bride,
     Weep not, weep not, my winsome marrow ;
Nor let thy heart lament to leave
     Pu'ing the birks on the braes of Yarrow !"

B. "Why does she weep, thy bonny bonny bride ?
     Why does she weep, thy winsome marrow?
And why dare ye nae mair weel be seen
     Pu'ing the birks on the braes of Yarrow ?"

A. "Lang maun she weep, lang maun she, maun she weep,
     Lang maun she weep with dule and sorrow ;
Aud lang maun I nae mair weel be seen
     Pu'ing the birks on the braes of Yarrow :

[1] attire, adorn.   [2] mate.   [3] birch.

For she has tint[1] her lover, lover dear—
　Her lover dear, the cause of sorrow ;
And I have slain the comeliest swain
　That e'er pu'd birks on the braes of Yarrow !

Why runs thy stream, O Yarrow, Yarrow, reid ?
　Why on thy braes heard the voice of sorrow ?
And why yon melancholious weeds,
　Hung on the bonny birks of Yarrow ?

What's yonder floats on the rueful, rueful flood ?
　What's yonder floats ? O dule and sorrow !
'Tis he, the comely swain I slew
　Upon the duleful braes of Yarrow

Wash, O wash his wounds, his wounds in tears,
　His wounds in tears of dule and sorrow ;
And wrap his limbs in mourning weeds,
　And lay him on the braes of Yarrow.

Then build, then build, ye sisters, sisters sad,
　Ye sisters sad, his tomb with sorrow ;
And weep around, in woeful wise,
　His hapless fate on the braes of Yarrow.

Curse ye, curse ye his useless, useless shield,
　My arm that wrought the deed of sorrow,
The fatal spear that pierced his breast—
　His comely breast on the braes of Yarrow !

Did I not warn thee not to, not to love
　And warn from fight ? but, to my sorrow,
Too rashly bold, a stronger arm
　Thou met'st—and fell on the braes of Yarrow !"

[1] lost.

C. "Sweet smells the birk, green grows, green grows
      the grass,
   Yellow on Yarrow's braes the gowan[1];
Fair hangs the apple frae the rock,
   Sweet the wave of Yarrow flowan."

A. "Flows Yarrow sweet? as sweet, as sweet flows
      Tweed,
   As green its grass, its gowan as yellow;
As sweet smells on its braes the birk,
   The apple from its rocks as mellow.

Fair was thy love, fair, fair indeed thy love;
   In flowery bands thou didst him fetter:
Tho' he was fair, and well beloved again,
   Than me he never loved thee better.

Busk ye then, busk, my bonny bonny bride,
   Busk ye, busk ye, my winsome marrow;
Busk ye and lo'e on the banks of Tweed,
   And think nae mair on the braes of Yarrow."

C. "How can I busk, a bonny bonny bride,
   How can I busk, a winsome marrow;
How lo'e him on the banks of Tweed
   That slew my love on the braes of Yarrow?

O Yarrow fields, may never, never rain,
   Nor dew thy tender blossoms cover;
For there was basely slain my love—
   My love as he had not been a lover!

The boy put on his robes, his robes of green,
   His purple vest—'twas my ain sewing:
Ah, wretched me! I little, little knew
   He was in these to meet his ruin.

[1] daisy.

The boy took out his milk-white, milk-white steed,
  Unheedful of my dule and sorrow ;
But ere the to-fall of the night
  He lay a corpse on the braes of Yarrow.

Much I rejoiced that woeful, woeful day :
  I sang—my voice the woods returning ;—
But lang ere night the spear was flown
  That slew my love and left me mourning.

What can my barbarous, barbarous father do
  But with his cruel rage pursue me ?
My lover's blood is on thy spear ;
  How canst thou, barbarous man, then woo me ?

My happy sisters may be, may be proud ;
  With cruel and ungentle scoffin',
May bid me seek on Yarrow's braes
  My lover nailèd in his coffin :

My brother Douglas may upbraid,
  And strive with threatening words to move me :—
My lover's blood is on thy spear,
  How canst thou ever bid me love thee ?

Yes, yes, prepare the bed, the bed of love ;
  With bridal sheets my body cover ;
Unbar, ye bridal maids, the door,
  Let in the expected husband lover.

But who the expected husband, husband is ?
  His hands, methinks, are bathed in slaughter.
Ah me ! what ghastly spectre's yon,
  Comes, in his pale shroud, bleeding after ?

Pale as he is, here lay him, lay him down ;
  O lay his cold head on my pillow :
Take aff, take aff these bridal weeds,
  And crown my careful head with willow.

Pale tho' thou art, yet best, yet best beloved,
  O, could my warmth to life restore thee,
Ye'd lie all night between my breasts,—
  No youth lay ever there before thee !

Pale, pale indeed ! O lovely, lovely youth,
  Forgive, forgive so foul a slaughter ;
And lie all night between my breasts,—
  No youth shall ever lie there after."

" Return, return, O mournful, mournful bride ;
  Return and dry thy useless sorrow :
Thy lover heeds naught of thy sighs,—
  He lies a corpse on the braes of Yarrow."

JOHN ARMSTRONG, M.D.

1709–1779

(From " The Art of Preserving Health ")

140 *Exercise*

BY health the peasant's toil
  Is well repaid ; if exercise were pain
Indeed, and temperance pain. By arts like these
Laconia nurs'd of old her hardy sons ;
And Rome's unconquered legions urged their way,
Unhurt, thro' every toil in every clime.

Toil, and be strong. By toil the flaccid nerves
Grow firm, and gain a more compacted tone ;
The greener juices are by toil subdu'd,
Mellow'd and subtiliz'd ; the vapid old
Expell'd, and all the rancour of the blood.
Come, my companions, ye who feel the charms
Of nature and the year ; come let us stray
Where chance or fancy leads our roving walk :
Come, while the soft voluptuous breezes fan
The fleecy heavens, enwrap the limbs in balm,
And shed a charming langour o'er the soul.
Nor when bright Winter sows with prickly frost
The vigorous ether, in unmanly warmth
Indulge at home ; nor even when Eurus' blasts
This way and that convolve the lab'ring woods.

My liberal walks, save when the skies in rain
Or fogs relent, no season should confine
Or to the cloister'd gallery or arcade.
Go, climb the mountain ; from th' ethereal source
Imbibe the recent gale. The cheerful morn
Beams o'er the hills ; go, mount th' exulting steed.
Already, see, the deep-mouth'd beagles catch
The tainted mazes ; and, on eager sport
Intent, with emulous impatience try
Each doubtful trace. Or, if a nobler prey
Delight you more, go chase the desperate deer ;
And thro' its deepest solitudes awake
The vocal forest with the jovial horn.

But if the breathless chase o'er hill and dale
Exceed your strength ; a sport of less fatigue,
Not less delightful, the prolific stream
Affords. The crystal rivulet, that o'er
A stony channel rolls its rapid maze,
Swarms with the silver fry. Such, thro' the bounds
Of pastoral Stafford, runs the brawling Trent ;
Such Eden, sprung from Cumbrian mountains ; such
The Esk, o'erhung with woods ; and such the
    stream
On whose Arcadian banks I first drew air,
Liddal ; till now, except in Doric lays
Tun'd to her murmurs by her love-sick swains,
Unknown in song : Tho' not a purer stream,
Thro' meads more flowery or more romantic groves,
Rolls toward the western main. Hail, sacred flood !
May still thy hospitable swains be blest
In rural innocence ; thy mountains still
Teem with the fleecy race ; thy tuneful woods
For ever flourish ; and thy vales look gay
With painted meadows, and the golden grain !

Oft, with thy blooming sons, when life was new,
Sportive and petulant, and charm'd with toys,
In thy transparent eddies have I lav'd :
Oft trac'd with patient steps thy fairy banks,
With the well imitated fly to hook
The eager trout, and with the slender line
And yielding rod solicite to the shore
The struggling, panting prey ; while vernal clouds
And tepid gales obscur'd the ruffled pool,
And from the deeps call'd forth the wanton swarms.

141   *The Passions*

THE choice of Aliment, the choice of Air,
    The use of Toil and all external things,
Already sung ; it now remains to trace
What good, what evil from ourselves proceeds :
And how the subtle Principle within
Inspires with health, or mines with strange decay
The passive Body. Ye poetic Shades,
Who know the secrets of the world unseen,
Assist my song ! For, in a doubtful theme
Engag'd, I wander thro' mysterious ways.

There is, they say, (and I believe there is)
A spark within us of th' immortal fire,
That animates and moulds the grosser frame ;
And when the body sinks escapes to heaven,
Its native seat, and mixes with the Gods.
Meanwhile this heavenly particle pervades
The mortal elements ; in every nerve
It thrills with pleasure, or grows mad with pain.
And in its secret conclave, as it feels
The body's woes and joys, this ruling power
Wields at its will the dull material world,
And is the body's health or malady.

By its own toil the gross corporeal frame
Fatigues, extenuates, or destroys itself.
Nor less the labours of the mind corrode
The solid fabric ; for by subtle parts
And viewless atoms, secret Nature moves
The mighty wheels of this stupendous world.
By subtle fluids pour'd thro' subtle tubes
The natural, vital, functions are perform'd.
By these the stubborn aliments are tam'd ;
The toiling heart distributes life and strength ;
These the still-crumbling frame rebuild ; and these
Are lost in thinking, and dissolve in air.

But 'tis not Thought (for still the soul's employ'd)
'Tis painful thinking that corrodes our clay.
All day the vacant eye without fatigue
Strays o'er the heaven and earth ; but long intent
On microscopic arts its vigour fails.
Just so the mind, with various thoughts amus'd,
Nor akes itself, nor gives the body pain.
But anxious Study, Discontent, and Care,
Love without Hope, and Hate without revenge,
And Fear, and Jealousy, fatigue the soul,
Engross the subtle ministers of life,
And spoil the lab'ring functions of their share.
Hence the lean gloom that Melancholy wears ;
The Lover's paleness ; and the sallow hue
Of Envy, Jealousy ; the meagre stare
Of sore Revenge : the canker'd body hence
Betrays each fretful motion of the mind.

The strong-built pedant ; who both night and day
Feeds on the coarsest fare the schools bestow,
And crudely fattens at gross Burman's stall ;

O'erwhelm'd with phlegm lies in a dropsy drown'd,
Or sinks in lethargy before his time.
With useful studies you, and arts that please
Employ your mind, amuse but not fatigue.
Peace to each drowsy metaphysic sage !
And ever may all heavy systems rest !
Yet some there are, even of elastic parts,
Whom strong and obstinate ambition leads
Thro' all the rugged roads of barren lore,
And gives to relish what their generous taste
Would else refuse. But may not thirst of fame,
Nor love of knowledge, urge you to fatigue
With constant drudgery the liberal soul.
Toy with your books : and, as the various fits
Of humour seize you, from Philosophy
To Fable shift : from serious Antonine
To Rabelais' ravings, and from prose to song.

While reading pleases, but no longer, read ;
And read aloud resounding Homer's strain,
And wield the thunder of Demosthenes.
The chest so exercised improves its strength ;
And quick vibrations thro' the bowels drive
The restless blood, which in unactive days
Would loiter else thro' unelastic tubes.
Deem it not trifling while I recommend
What posture suits : To stand and sit by turns,
As nature prompts, is best. But o'er your leaves
To lean for ever, cramps the vital parts,
And robs the fine machinery of its play.

'Tis the great art of life to manage well
The restless mind. For ever on pursuit
Of knowledge bent, it starves the grosser powers ;
Quite unemployed, against its own repose

It turns its fatal edge, and sharper pangs
Than what the body knows embitter life.
Chiefly where Solitude, sad nurse of Care,
To sickly musing gives the pensive mind,
There Madness enters : and the dim-ey'd Fiend,
Sour Melancholy, night and day provokes
Her own eternal wound. The sun grows pale ;
A mournful visionary light o'erspreads
The cheerful face of nature : earth becomes
A dreary desert, and heaven frowns above.
Then various shapes of curs'd illusion rise :
Whate'er the wretched fears, creating Fear
Forms out of nothing ; and with monsters teems
Unknown in hell. The prostrate soul beneath
A load of huge imagination heaves ;
And all the horrors that the murderer feels
With anxious flutterings wake the guiltless breast.

Such phantoms Pride in solitary scenes,
Or Fear, on delicate Self-love creates.
From other cares absolv'd, the busy mind
Finds in yourself a theme to pore upon ;
It finds you miserable, or makes you so.
For while yourself you anxiously explore,
Timorous Self-love, with sickning Fancy's aid,
Presents the danger that you dread the most,
And ever galls you in your tender part.
Hence some for love and some for jealousy,
For grim religion some, and some for pride,
Have lost their reason ; some for fear of want
Want all their lives ; and others every day
For fear of dying suffer worse than death.
Ah ! from your bosoms banish, if you can,
Those fatal guests ; and first the Dæmon Fear ;
That trembles at impossible events,

Lest aged Atlas should resign his load,
And heaven's eternal battlements rush down.
Is there an evil worse than Fear itself?
And what avails it, that indulgent heaven
From mortal eyes has wrapt the woes to come,
If we, ingenious to torment ourselves,
Grow pale at hideous fictions of our own?
Enjoy the present; nor with needless cares,
Of what may spring from blind misfortune's
    womb,
Appal the surest hour that life bestows.
Serene, and master of yourself, prepare
For what may come; and leave the rest to
    Heaven.

ALISON RUTHERFORD

1712–1794

The Flowers of the Forest

I'VE seen the smiling of Fortune beguiling,
   I've tasted her favours, and felt her decay :
Sweet is her blessing, and kind her caressing ;
   But soon it is fled—it is fled far away.

I've seen the Forest adornèd the foremost
   With flowers of the fairest—most pleasant and
      gay :
Full sweet was their blooming—their scent the air
      perfuming :
   But now they are wither'd and a' wede away.

I've seen the morning with gold the hills adorning,
   And the red tempest storming before parting day :
I've seen Tweed's silver streams, glittering in the
      sunny beams,
   Grow drumly and dark as they roll'd on their way.

O fickle Fortune ! why this cruel sporting ?
   Why thus perplex us poor sons of a day ?
Thy frowns cannot fear me, thy smiles cannot cheer
      me—
   Since the Flowers of the Forest are a' wede away.

GEORGE HALKET
(ATTRIBUTED TO)

Died 1756

Logie o' Buchan

O LOGIE o' Buchan, O Logie the laird,
   They hae ta'en awa' Jamie, that delved in the
      yaird [1] ;
Wha play'd on the pipe, and the viol sae sma',—
They hae ta'en awa' Jamie, the flower o' them a' !

He said, Thinkna lang, lassie, tho' I gang awa' ;
He said, Thinkna lang, lassie, tho' I gang awa' ;
For simmer is coming—cauld winter's awa',
And I'll come and see thee in spite o' them a'.

Tho' Sandy has owsen [2], has gear, and has kye [3],
A house and a hadden [4], and siller [5] forbye [6] ;
Yet I'd tak' my ain lad, wi' his staff in his hand,
Before I'd hae him, wi' the houses and land.

My daddie looks sulky, my minnie [7] looks sour ;
They frown upon Jamie because he is poor :
Tho' I lo'e them as weel as a daughter should do,
They're nae hauf sae dear to me, Jamie, as you.

I sit on my creepie [8], I spin at my wheel,
And think on the laddie that lo'ed me sae weel ?
He had but ae saxpence—he brak it in twa,
And gied me the hauf o't when he gaed awa'.

   [1] garden. [2] oxen. [3] cows. [4] holding. [5] money. [5] besides.
[7] mammy. [8] stool.

Then haste ye back, Jamie, and bide na awa';
Then haste ye back Jamie, and bide na awa';
The simmer is coming—cauld winter's awa',
And ye'll come and see me in spite o' them a'!

REV. JOHN SKINNER

1721–1807

144

The Ewie wi' the Crookit Horn

I

WERE I but able to rehearse
　　My Ewie's praise in proper verse,
I'd sound it forth as loud and fierce
　　As ever piper's drone could blaw ;
The Ewie wi' the crookit horn,
Wha had kent her might hae sworn
Sic a Ewe was never born,
　　Hereabout nor far awa',
Sic a Ewe was never born,
　　Hereabout nor far awa'.

II

I never needed tar nor keil [1]
To mark her upo' hip or heel,
Her crookit horn did as weel
　　To ken her by amo' them a' ;
She never threaten'd scab nor rot,
But keepit ay her ain jog-trot,
Baith to the fauld and to the cot,
　　Was never sweir [2] to lead nor caw [3].

III

Cauld nor hunger never dang [4] her,
Wind nor wet could never wrang her,
Anes she lay an ouk [5] and langer
　　Furth aneath a wreath o' snaw :

[1] reddle.　[2] stubborn.　[3] drive.　[4] o'ercame.　[5] week.

Whan ither Ewies lap the dyke,
And eat the kail [1] for a' the tyke [2],
My Ewie never play'd the like,
　　But tyc'd [3] about the barn wa'.

IV

A better or a thriftier beast,
Nae honest man could weel hae wist,
For silly thing she never mist,
　　To hae ilk' year a lamb or twa';
The first she had I gae to Jock,
To be to him a kind o' stock,
And now the laddie has a flock
　　O' mair nor thirty head ava'.

V

I lookit aye at even' for her,
Lest mischanter [4] shou'd come o'er her,
Or the fowmart [5], might devoor her.
　　Gin the beastie bade awa;
My Ewie wi' the crookit horn,
Well deserv'd baith girse and corn,
Sic a Ewe was never born,
　　Here-about nor far awa.

VI

Yet last ouk, for a' my keeping,
(Wha can speak it without *greeting?*)
A villain cam when I was sleeping,
　　Sta' [6] my Ewie, horn and a';
I sought her sair upo' the morn,
And down aneath a buss o' thorn
I got my Ewie's crookit horn,
　　But my Ewie was awa'.

[1] cabbage.　　[2] dog.　　[3] moved in a staid manner.　　[4] mishap.
[5] polecat.　　[6] stole.

VII

O ! gin I had the loun¹ that did it,
Sworn I have as well as said it,
Tho' a' the warld should forbid it,
  I wad gie his neck a thra'² :
I never met wi' sic a turn,
As this sin ever I was born,
My Ewie wi' the crookit horn,
  Silly Ewie stown awa'.

VIII

O ! had she died o' crook³ or cauld,
As Ewies do when they grow auld,
It wad na been, by mony fauld,
  Sae sair a heart to nane o's a' :
For a' the claith that we hae worn,
Fra her and her's sae aften shorn,
The loss o' her we cou'd hae born,
  Had fair strae-death ta'en her awa'⁴.

IX

But thus, poor thing, to lose her life,
Aneath a bleedy villain's knife,
I'm really fley't⁵ that our guidwife
  Will never win aboon't ava⁶ :
Oh ! a' ye bards benorth Kinghorn,
Call your muses up and mourn,
Our Ewie wi' the crookit horn,
  Stown frae's, and fellt and a' !

¹ rascal.   ² twist.   ³ halt, foot-rot.   ⁴ had she died in her bed.
⁵ afraid.   ⁶ get over it at all.

JOHN HOME

1722–1808

145 *From Douglas : A Tragedy*

ACT IV.

Flourish of Trumpets.

Enter LORD RANDOLPH *attended.*

LORD RANDOLPH.   Summon an hundred horse,
    by break of day ;
To wait our pleasure at the castle gate.

Enter LADY RANDOLPH.

LADY RANDOLPH.   Alas ! my Lord ! I've heard un-
    welcome news ;
The Danes are landed.

LORD RANDOLPH.   Ay, no inroad this
Of the Northumbrian bent to take a spoil :
No sportive war, no tournament essay,
Of some young knight resolv'd to break a spear,
And stain with hostile blood his maiden arms.
The Danes are landed : we must beat them back,
Or live the slaves of Denmark.

LADY RANDOLPH.   Dreadful times !

LORD RANDOLPH.   The fenceless villages are all
    forsaken ;
The trembling mothers, and their children lodg'd
In wall-girt towers and castles ; whilst the men
Retire indignant.   Yet, like broken waves,
They but retire more awful to return.

LADY RANDOLPH. Immense, as fame reports, the
  Danish host——
LORD RANDOLPH. Were it as numerous as loud
  fame reports,
An army knit like ours wou'd pierce it thro' :
Brothers, that shrink not from each other's side,
And fond companions, fill our warlike files :
For his dear offspring, and the wife he loves,
The husband, and the fearless father arm.
In vulgar breasts heroic ardor burns,
And the poor peasant mates his daring lord.
  LADY RANDOLPH. Men's minds are tempered, like
    their swords, for war ;
Lovers of danger, on destruction's brink
They joy to rear erect their daring forms.
Hence, early graves ; hence, the lone widow's life ;
And the sad mother's grief-embitter'd age.
Where is our gallant guest ?
  LORD RANDOLPH.   Down in the vale
I left him, managing a fiery steed,
Whose stubbornness had foil'd the strength and skill
Of every rider. But behold he comes,
In earnest conversation with GLENALVON.

Enter NORVAL *and* GLENALVON.

GLENALVON ! with the lark arise ; go forth
And lead my troops that lie in yonder vale :
Private I travel to the royal camp :
NORVAL, thou goest with me. But say, young man ;
Where didst thou learn so to discourse of war,
And in such terms as I o'erheard to-day ?
War is no village science, nor its phrase
A language taught amongst the shepherd swains.
  NORVAL. Small is the skill my lord delights to
    praise

In him he favours.——Hear from whence it came.
Beneath a mountain's brow, the most remote
And inaccessible by shepherds trod,
In a deep cave, dug by no mortal hand,
A hermit liv'd ; a melancholy man,
Who was the wonder of our wand'ring swains.
Austere and lonely, cruel to himself,
Did they report him : the cold earth his bed,
Water his drink, his food the shepherd's alms.
I went to see him, and my heart was touch'd
With rev'rence and with pity. Mild he spake,
And, entring on discourse, such stories told
As made me oft revisit his sad cell.
For he had been a soldier in his youth ;
And fought in famous battles, when the Peers
Of Europe, by the bold GODFREDO led,
Against th' usurping Infidel display'd
The cross of Christ, and won the Holy Land.
Pleas'd with my admiration, and the fire
His speech struck from me, the old man wou'd shake
His years away, and act his young encounters :
Then, having shew'd his wounds, he'd sit him down,
And all the live-long day discourse of war.
To help my fancy, in the smooth green turf
He cut the figures of the marshall'd hosts ;
Describ'd the motions, and explain'd the use
Of the deep column, and the lengthen'd line,
The square, the crescent, and the phalanx firm.
For all that Saracen or Christian knew
Of war's vast art was to this hermit known.

    LORD RANDOLPH. Why did this soldier in a desart
        hide
Those qualities that should have graced a camp ?

    NORVAL. That too at last I learn'd. Unhappy
        man !

Returning homewards by Messina's port,
Loaded with wealth and honours bravely won,
A rude and boist'rous captain of the sea
Fasten'd a quarrel on him. Fierce they fought:
The stranger fell, and with his dying breath
Declar'd his name and lineage! Mighty God!
The soldier cried, my brother! Oh! my brother!

LADY RANDOLPH. His brother!

NORVAL.   Yes; of the same parents born;
His only brother. They exchanged forgiveness:
And happy, in my mind, was he that died:
For many deaths has the survivor suffer'd.
In the wild desart on a rock he sits,
Or on some nameless stream's untrodden banks,
And ruminates all day his dreadful fate.
At times, alas! not in his perfect mind!
Holds dialogues with his loved brother's ghost;
And oft each night forsakes his sullen couch,
To make sad orisons for him he slew.

LADY RANDOLPH. To what mysterious woes are
    mortals born!
In this dire tragedy were there no more
Unhappy persons? did the parents live?

NORVAL. No; they were dead: kind heav'n had
    clos'd their eyes
Before their son had shed his brother's blood.

LORD RANDOLPH. Hard is his fate; for he was
    not to blame!
There is a destiny in this strange world,
Which oft decrees an undeservèd doom:
Let schoolmen tell us why.—From whence these
    sounds?

                        [Trumpets at a distance.

Enter an OFFICER.

OFFICER.   My Lord, the trumpets of the troops of
    Lorn :

The valiant leader hails the noble RANDOLPH.

    LORD RANDOLPH.   Mine antient guest ! does he the
    warriors lead ?

Has Denmark rous'd the brave old knight to arms ?

    OFFICER.   No ; worn with warfare, he resigns the
    sword.

His eldest hope, the valiant JOHN of LORN,

Now leads his kindred bands.

    LORD RANDOLPH.   GLENALVON, go.

With hospitality's most strong request

Intreat the chief.   [*Exit* GLENALVON.

    OFFICER.   My Lord, requests are vain.

He urges on, impatient of delay,

Stung with the tidings of the foe's approach.

    LORD RANDOLPH.   May victory sit on the warrior's
    plume !

Bravest of men ! his flocks and herds are safe ;

Remote from war's alarms his pastures lie,

By mountains inaccessible secur'd :

Yet foremost he into the plain descends,

Eager to bleed in battles not his own.

Such were the heroes of the ancient world :

Contemners they of indolence and gain ;

But still for love of glory, and of arms,

Prone to encounter peril, and to lift

Against each strong antagonist the spear.

I'll go and press the hero to my breast.

                             [*Exit* RANDOLPH.

Manent LADY RANDOLPH *and* NORVAL.

    LADY RANDOLPH.   The soldier's loftiness, the pride
    and pomp

Investing awful war, NORVAL, I see,
Transport thy youthful mind.

NORVAL.   Ah ! should they not ?
Bless'd be the hour I left my father's house !
I might have been a shepherd all my days,
And stole obscurely to a peasant's grave.
Now, if I live, with mighty chiefs I stand ;
And, if I fall, with noble dust I lie.

LADY RANDOLPH. There is a gen'rous spirit in thy
     breast,
That could have well sustain'd a prouder fortune.
This way with me ; under yon spreading beech,
Unseen, unheard, by human eye or ear,
I will amaze thee with a wond'rous tale.

NORVAL. Let there be danger, Lady, with the
     secret,
That I may hug it to my grateful heart,
And prove my faith. Command my sword, my life :
These are the sole possessions of poor NORVAL.

LADY RANDOLPH. Know'st thou these gems ?

NORVAL.   Durst I believe mine eyes
I'd say I knew them, and they were my father's.

LADY RANDOLPH. Thy father's, say'st thou ! ah !
     they were thy father's !

NORVAL. I saw them once, and curiously inquir'd
Of both my parents, whence such splendour came ?
But I was check'd, and more could never learn.

LADY RANDOLPH. Then learn of me, thou art not
     NORVAL's son.

NORVAL.   Not NORVAL's son ?

LADY RANDOLPH. Nor of a shepherd sprung.

NORVAL. Lady, who am I then ?

LADY RANDOLPH.   Noble thou art ;
For noble was thy Sire !

NORVAL.   I will believe—

O ! tell me farther ! Say who was my father ?

LADY RANDOLPH. DOUGLAS !

NORVAL. LORD DOUGLAS, whom to-day I saw ?

LADY RANDOLPH. His younger brother.

NORVAL. And in yonder camp ?

LADY RANDOLPH. Alas !

NORVAL. You make me tremble——Sighs and tears !
Lives my brave father ?

LADY RANDOLPH. Ah ! too brave indeed !
He fell in battle ere thyself was born.

NORVAL. Ah me unhappy ! ere I saw the light ?
But does my mother live ? I may conclude,
From my own fate, her portion has been sorrow.

LADY RANDOLPH. She lives ; but wastes her life in
    constant woe,
Weeping her husband slain, her infant lost.

NORVAL. You that are skilled so well in the sad
    story
Of my unhappy parents, and with tears
Bewail their destiny, now have compassion
Upon the offspring of the friends you lov'd !
O ! tell me who, and where my mother is !
Oppress'd by a base world, perhaps she bends
Beneath the weight of other ills than grief ;
And desolate, implores of heav'n the aid
Her son should give. It is, it must be so——
Your countenance confesses that she's wretched.
O ! tell me her condition ! Can the sword——
Who shall resist me in a parent's cause ?

LADY RANDOLPH. Thy virtue ends her woe.——My
    son, my son !
I am thy mother, and the wife of DOUGLAS !

                        [*Falls upon his neck.*

NORVAL. O heav'n and earth, how wondrous is my
    fate !

Art *thou* my mother ? Ever let me kneel !

    LADY RANDOLPH. Image of DOUGLAS ! Fruit of
      fatal love !
All that I owe thy Sire, I pay to thee.

    NORVAL. Respect and admiration still possess me,
Checking the love and fondness of a son.
Yet I was filial to my humble parents.
But did my Sire surpass the rest of men,
As thou excellest all of womankind ?

    LADY RANDOLPH. Arise, my son ! In me thou dost
      behold
The poor remains of beauty once admir'd :
The autumn of my days is come already ;
For sorrow made my summer haste away.
Yet in my prime I equall'd not thy father :
His eyes were like the eagle's, yet sometimes
Liker the dove's ; and, as he pleas'd, he won
All hearts with softness, or with spirit aw'd.

    NORVAL. How did he fall ? Sure 'twas a bloody
      field
When DOUGLAS died. O I have much to ask !

    LADY RANDOLPH. Hereafter thou shalt hear the
      lengthen'd tale
Of all thy father's and thy mother's woes.
At present this : thou art the rightful heir
Of yonder castle, and the wide domains
Which now LORD RANDOLPH, as my husband, holds.
But thou shalt not be wrong'd ; I have the power
To right thee still : before the King I'll kneel,
And call LORD DOUGLAS to protect his blood.

    NORVAL. The blood of DOUGLAS will protect
      itself.

    LADY RANDOLPH. But we shall need both friends
      and favour, boy,
To wrest thy lands and lordship from the gripe

Of RANDOLPH and his kinsman. Yet I think
My tale will move each gentle heart to pity,
My life incline the virtuous to believe.

 NORVAL. To be the son of DOUGLAS is to me
Inheritance enough. Declare my birth,
And in the field I'll seek for fame and fortune.

 LADY RANDOLPH. Thou dost not know what perils
   and injustice
Await the poor man's valour. O! my son!
The noblest blood in all the land's abash'd,
Having no lacquey but pale poverty.
Too long hast thou been thus attended, DOUGLAS!
Too long hast thou been deem'd a peasant's child.
The wanton heir of some inglorious chief
Perhaps has scorn'd thee, in the youthful sports;
Whilst thy indignant spirit swelled in vain!
Such contumely thou no more shalt bear:
But how I purpose to redress thy wrongs
Must be hereafter told. Prudence directs
That we should part before yon chiefs return.
Retire, and from thy rustic follower's hand
Receive a billet, which thy mother's care,
Anxious to see thee, dictated before
This casual opportunity arose
Of private conference. Its purport mark;
For as I there appoint we meet again.
Leave me, my son! and frame thy manners still
To NORVAL's, not to noble DOUGLAS' state.

 NORVAL. I will remember. Where is NORVAL
   now?
That good old man.

 LADY RANDOLPH. At hand conceal'd he lies,
An useful witness. But beware, my son,
Of yon GLENALVON; in his guilty breast
Resides a villain's shrewdness, ever prone

To false conjecture. He hath griev'd my heart.

NORVAL. Has he indeed? Then let yon false
GLENALVON
Beware of me. [*Exit* DOUGLAS.

Manet LADY RANDOLPH.

There burst the smother'd flame!
O! thou all righteous and eternal King!
Who father of the fatherless art call'd,
Protect my son!——Thy inspiration, Lord!
Hath fill'd his bosom with that sacred fire,
Which in the breasts of his forefathers burn'd:
Set him on high like them, that he may shine
The star and glory of his native land!
Then let the minister of death descend,
And bear my willing spirit to its place.
Yonder they come. How do bad women find
Unchanging aspects to conceal their guilt?
When I, by reason, and by justice urg'd,
Full hardly can dissemble with these men
In nature's pious cause.

Enter LORD RANDOLPH *and* GLENALVON.

LORD RANDOLPH. Yon gallant chief,
Of arms enamour'd, all repose disclaims,

LADY RANDOLPH. Be not, my Lord, by his
example sway'd:
Arrange the business of to-morrow now,
And, when you enter, speak of war no more.
[*Exit* LADY RANDOLPH.

Manent LORD RANDOLPH *and* GLENALVON.

LORD RANDOLPH. 'Tis so, by heav'n! her mien,
her voice, her eye,
And her impatience to be gone, confirm it.

GLENALVON. He parted from her now : behind the mount,
Amongst the trees, I saw him glide along.

LORD RANDOLPH. For sad, sequester'd virtue she's renown'd !

GLENALVON. Most true, my Lord.

LORD RANDOLPH. Yet this distinguish'd Dame
Invites a youth, the acquaintance of a day,
Alone to meet her at the midnight hour.
This assignation, [*shews a letter*] the assassin freed,
Her manifest affection for the youth,
Might breed suspicion in a husband's brain,
Whose gentle consort all for love had wedded ;
Much more in mine. MATILDA never lov'd me.
Let no man, after me, a woman wed,
Whose heart he knows he has not ; tho' she brings
A mine of gold, a kingdom for her dowry,
For let her seem, like the night's shadowy queen,
Cold and contemplative ;—He cannot trust her :
She may, she will, bring shame and sorrow on him ;
The worst of sorrows, and the worst of shames !

GLENALVON. Yield not, my Lord, to such afflicting thoughts ;
But let the spirit of an husband sleep,
Till your own senses make a sure conclusion.
This billet must to blooming NORVAL go :
At the next turn awaits my trusty spy ;
I'll give it him refitted for his master.
In the close thicket take your secret stand ;
The moon shines bright, and your own eyes may judge
Of their behaviour.

LORD RANDOLPH. Thou dost counsel well.

GLENALVON. Permit me now to make one slight essay.
Of all the trophies which vain mortals boast,

By wit, by valour, or by wisdom won,
The first and fairest, in a young man's eye,
Is woman's captive heart. Successful love
With glorious fumes intoxicates the mind ;
And the proud conqueror in triumph moves
Air-born, exalted above vulgar men.

LORD RANDOLPH. And what avails this maxim?
GLENALVON.   Much, my Lord !
Withdraw a little : I'll accost young NORVAL,
And with ironical derisive counsel
Explore his spirit. If he is no more
Than humble NORVAL, by thy favour rais'd,
Brave as he is, he'll shrink astonish'd from me :
But if he be the fav'rite of the fair,
Lov'd by the first of Caledonia's dames,
He'll turn upon me, as the lion turns
Upon the hunter's spear.

LORD RANDOLPH.   'Tis shrewdly thought.
GLENALVON. When we grow loud, draw near.
        But let my Lord
His rising wrath restrain.   [*Exit* RANDOLPH.

                Manet GLENALVON.

                        'Tis strange, by heav'n !
That she should run full tilt her fond career,
To one so little known. She too that seem'd
Pure as the winter stream, when ice emboss'd
Whitens its course. Even I did think her chaste,
Whose charity exceeds not. Precious sex !
Whose deeds lascivious pass GLENALVON's thoughts !
                        [NORVAL *appears*.
His port I love ; he's in a proper mood
To chide the thunder, if at him it roar'd.
Has NORVAL seen the troops ?

NORVAL.   The setting sun

26

With yellow radiance lighten'd all the vale,
And as the warriors mov'd, each polish'd helm,
Corslet, or spear, glanc'd back his gilded beams.
The hill they climb'd, and halting at its top,
Of more than mortal size, tow'ring, they seem'd,
An host angelic, clad in burning arms.

    GLENALVON. Thou talk'st it well ; no leader of our
        host,
In sounds more lofty, speaks of glorious war.

    NORVAL. If I shall e'er acquire a leader's name,
My speech will be less ardent. Novelty
Now prompts my tongue, and youthful admiration
Vents itself freely ; since no part is mine
Of praise pertaining to the great in arms.

    GLENALVON. You wrong yourself, brave Sir ; your
        martial deeds
Have rank'd you with the great : but mark me, NORVAL ;
LORD RANDOLPH's favour now exalts your youth
Above his veterans of famous service.
Let me, who know these soldiers, counsel you.
Give them all honour ; seem not to command :
Else they will scarcely brook your late sprung power,
Which nor alliance props, nor birth adorns.

    NORVAL. Sir, I have been accustom'd all my days
To hear and speak the plain and simple truth :
And tho' I have been told, that there are men
Who borrow friendship's tongue to speak their scorn,
Yet in such language I am little skill'd.
Therefore I thank GLENALVON for his counsel,
Altho' it sounded harshly. Why remind
Me of my birth obscure ? Why slur my power
With such contemptuous terms ?

    GLENALVON.   I did not mean
To gall your pride, which now I see is great.

    NORVAL. My pride !

GLENALVON. Suppress it as you wish to prosper.
Your pride's excessive. Yet for RANDOLPH's sake
I will not leave you to its rash direction.
If thus you swell, and frown at high-born men,
Will high-born men endure a shepherd's scorn?

NORVAL. A shepherd's scorn!

GLENALVON.   Yes, if you presume
To bend on soldiers these disdainful eyes,
As if you took the measure of their minds,
And said in secret, You're no match for me:
What will become of you?

NORVAL.   If this were told—— [*Aside.*
Hast thou no fears for thy presumptuous self?

GLENALVON. Ha! Dost thou threaten me?

NORVAL.   Didst thou not hear?

GLENALVON. Unwillingly I did; a nobler foe
Had not been question'd thus. But such as thee——

NORVAL. Whom dost thou think me?

GLENALVON.   *Norval.*

NORVAL.   So I am——
And who is NORVAL in GLENALVON's eyes?

GLENALVON. A peasant's son, a wand'ring beggar-
boy;
At best no more, even if he speaks the truth.

NORVAL. False as thou art, dost thou suspect my
truth?

GLENALVON. Thy truth! thou'rt all a lie; and
false as hell
Is the vain-glorious tale thou told'st to RANDOLPH.

NORVAL. If I were chain'd, unarm'd, and bedrid
old,
Perhaps I should revile: But as I am
I have no tongue to rail. The humble NORVAL
Is of a race who strive not but with deeds.
Did I not fear to freeze thy shallow valour,

And make thee sink too soon beneath my sword,
I'd tell thee—what thou art. I know thee well.

GLENALVON. Dost thou not know GLENALVON, born
to command
Ten thousand slaves like thee?

NORVAL.   Villain, no more:
Draw and defend thy life. I did design
To have defy'd thee in another cause:
But heaven accelerates its vengeance on thee.
Now for my own and LADY RANDOLPH's wrongs.

Enter LORD RANDOLPH.

LORD RANDOLPH. Hold, I command you both.
The man that stirs
Makes me his foe.

NORVAL.   Another voice than thine
That threat had vainly sounded, noble RANDOLPH.

GLENALVON. Hear him, my Lord; he's wondrous
condescending!
Mark the humility of shepherd NORVAL!

NORVAL. Now you may scoff in safety.

[*Sheaths his sword.*

LORD RANDOLPH.   Speak not thus,
Taunting each other; but unfold to me
The cause of quarrel, then I judge betwixt you.

NORVAL. Nay, my good Lord, tho' I revere you
much,
My cause I plead not, nor demand your judgment.
I blush to speak; I will not, cannot speak
Th' opprobrious words that I from him have borne.
To the liege-lord of my dear native land
I owe a subject's homage; but even him
And his high arbitration I'd reject.
Within my bosom reigns another lord;
Honour, sole judge and umpire of itself.

If my free speech offend you, noble RANDOLPH,
Revoke your favours, and let NORVAL go
Hence as he came, alone, but not dishonour'd.

LORD RANDOLPH.   Thus far I'll mediate with impartial voice :
The antient foe of Caledonia's land
Now waves his banners o'er her frighted fields.
Suspend your purpose, till your country's arms
Repel the bold invader ; then decide
The private quarrel.

GLENALVON.   I agree to this.

NORVAL. And I.

Enter SERVANT.

SERVANT.   The banquet waits.

LORD RANDOLPH.'   We come.

[*Exit* RANDOLPH.

GLENALVON.   Norval,
Let not our variance mar the social hour,
Nor wrong the hospitality of RANDOLPH.
Nor frowning anger, nor yet wrinkl'd hate,
Shall stain my countenance. Smooth thou thy brow ;
Nor let our strife disturb the gentle Dame.

NORVAL.   Think not so lightly, Sir, of my resentment ;
When we contend again, our strife is mortal.

JANE ELLIOT

1727–1805

146   *The Flowers of the Forest*

I 'VE heard them lilting at our ewe-milking—
   Lasses a' lilting before dawn of day ;
But now they are moaning on ilka green loaning[1]—
   The Flowers of the Forest are a' wede[2] away.

At buchts[3], in the morning, nae blythe lads are
     scorning ;
   Lasses are lonely and dowie and wae[4] ;
Nae daffin', nae gabbin'[5]—but sighing and sabbing
   Ilk ane lifts her leglin[6] and hies her away.

In hair'st, at the shearing, nae youths now are
     jeering—
   Bandsters are runkled and lyart or grey :
At fair or at preaching, nae wooing, nae fleeching—
   The Flowers of the Forest are a' wede away.

At e'en, in the gloaming, nae younkers are roaming,
   'Bout stacks with the lasses at bogle[7] to play ;
But ilk maid sits drearie, lamenting her dearie—
   The Flowers of the Forest are weded away.

---

[1] rural pathway.   [2] withered.   [3] sheep-folds.   [4] down-hearted and sorrowful.   [5] No frolic, no banter.   [6] milking-stool.   [7] hide and seek.

Dool and wae [1] for the order sent our lads to the
   Border !
The English, for ance, by guile wan the day ;—
The Flowers of the Forest, that foucht aye the
   foremost—
The prime of our land—are cauld in the clay.

We'll hear nae mair lilting at the ewe-milking ;
   Women and bairns are heartless and wae,
Sighing and moaning on ilka green loaning—
   The Flowers of the Forest are a' wede away.

[1] sorrow and ill-luck.

WILLIAM JULIUS MICKLE

1734–1788

The Sailor's Wife

AND are ye sure the news is true?
    And are ye sure he's weel?
Is this a time to think o' wark?
    Ye jauds, fling bye your wheel!
Is this the time to spin a thread,
    When Colin's at the door?
Rax¹ down my cloak—I'll to the quay,
    And see him come ashore.
        For there's nae luck aboot the house,
           There's nae luck ava;
        There's little pleasure in the house
           When our gudeman's awa'.

And gie to me my bigonet²,
    My bishop's satin gown;
For I maun tell the bailie's wife
    That Colin's in the town.
My Turkey slippers maun gae on,
    My hose o' pearly blue,—
It's a' to pleasure our gudeman,
    For he's baith leal and true.

Rise up and mak' a clean fireside,
    Put on the muckle pot;
Gie little Kate her button gown,
    And Jock his Sunday coat;

¹ reach.   ² coif.

And mak' their shoon as black as slaes,
  Their stockin's white as snaw—
It's a' to please my ain gudeman—
  He likes to see them braw.

There's twa fat hens upon the bauk[1],
  Hae fed this month and mair ;
Mak' haste and thraw[2] their necks about,
  That Colin weel may fare ;
And spread the table neat and clean—
  Gar ilka[3] thing look braw ;
For wha can tell how Colin fared
  When he was far awa' ?

Sae true his heart, sae smooth his speech,
  His breath like caller air ;
His very foot has music in't
  As he comes up the stair.
And will I see his face again ?
  And will I hear him speak ?
I'm downright dizzy wi' the thought,—
  In troth I'm like to greet[4] !

If Colin's weel, and weel content,
  I hae nae mair to crave ;
And gin I live to keep him sae,
  I'm blest aboon the lave[5].
And will I see his face again,
  And will I hear him speak ?—
I'm downright dizzy wi' the thought,—
  In troth I'm like to greet !
      For there's nae luck aboot the house,
        There's nae luck ava ;
      There's little pleasure in the house
        When our gudeman's awa'.

[1] cross-beam, roost. [2] twist. [3] every. [4] weep. [5] the rest, others.

JAMES BEATTIE

1735–1803

148 *Retirement: An Ode*

WHEN in the crimson cloud of Even
    The lingering light decays,
And Hesper on the front of heaven
    His glittering gem displays ;
Deep in the silent vale unseen,
    Beside a lulling stream,
A pensive Youth, of placid mien,
    Indulged this tender theme.

"Ye cliffs, in hoary grandeur piled
    High o'er the glimmering dale ;
Ye woods, along whose windings wild
    Murmurs the solemn gale :—
Where Melancholy strays forlorn,
    And Woe retires to weep,
What time the wan moon's yellow horn
    Gleams on the western deep !

"To you, ye wastes—whose artless charms
    Ne'er drew Ambition's eye—
'Scaped a tumultuous world's alarms,
    To your retreats I fly :
Deep in your most sequester'd bower
    Let me at last recline,
Where Solitude, mild, modest power,
    Leans on her ivied shrine.

410

" How shall I woo thee, matchless fair ?
  Thy heavenly smile how win ?—
Thy smile that smooths the brow of Care,
  And stills the storm within.
O wilt thou to thy favourite grove
  Thine ardent votary bring ;
And bless his hours, and bid them move
  Serene, on silent wing ?

" Oft let Remembrance soothe his mind
  With dreams of former days,
When, in the lap of Peace reclined,
  He framed his infant lays ;—
When Fancy roved at large, nor Care,
  Nor cold Distrust alarm'd ;
Nor Envy, with malignant glare,
  This simple youth had harm'd.

" 'Twas then, O Solitude ! to thee
  His early vows were paid,
From heart sincere, and warm, and free,
  Devoted to the shade.
Ah, why did Fate his steps decoy
  In stormy paths to roam,
Remote from all congenial joy ?—
  O take the Wanderer home !

" Thy shades, thy silence, now be mine,
  Thy charms my only theme ;
My haunt the hollow cliff, whose pine
  Waves o'er the gloomy stream,—
Whence the scared owl on pinions grey
  Breaks from the rustling boughs,
And down the lone vale sails away
  To more profound repose.

"O ! while to thee the woodland pours
    Its wildly warbling song,
And balmy from the banks of flowers
    The zephyr breathes along,—
Let no rude sound invade from far,
    No vagrant foot be nigh,
No ray from Grandeur's gilded car
    Flash on the startled eye.

"But, if some pilgrim through the glade
    Thy hallow'd bowers explore,
O guard from harm his hoary head,
    And listen to his lore ;
For he of joys divine shall tell,
    That wean from earthly woe,
And triumph o'er the mighty spell
    That chains this heart below.

"For me no more the path invites
    Ambition loves to tread ;
No more I climb those toilsome heights,
    By guileful Hope misled ;
Leaps my fond fluttering heart no more
    To Mirth's enlivening strain ;
For present pleasure soon is o'er,
    And all the past is vain."

JOHN EWEN

1741–1821

149

The Boatie Rows

O WEEL may the boatie row,
  And better may she speed !
And leesome [1] may the boatie row,
  That wins the bairns's bread !
The boatie rows, the boatie rows,
  The boatie rows indeed !
And happy be the lot of a'
  That wishes her to speed !

I cuist [2] my line in Largo Bay,
  And fishes I caught nine :
There's three to boil, and three to fry,
  And three to bait the line.
The boatie rows, the boatie rows,
  The boatie rows indeed !
And weel may the boatie row
  That wins my bairns's bread !

O weel may the boatie row
  That fills a heavy creel [3],
And cleads [4] us a' frae head to feet,
  And buys our parritch meal !
The boatie rows, the boatie rows,
  The boatie rows indeed !
And happy be the lot of a'
  That wish the boatie speed.

[1] happily. [2] cast. [3] fish-basket. [4] clothes.

When Jamie vow'd he would be mine,
 And wan frae me my heart,
O muckle lighter grew my creel!
 He swore we'd never part.
The boatie rows, the boatie rows,
 The boatie rows fu' weel!
And muckle lighter is the lade
 When love bears up the creel.

My kurtch[1] I put upon my head,
 And dress'd mysel' fu' braw[2]:
I trow my heart was dowf[3] and wae
 When Jamie gaed awa!
But weel may the boatie row,
 And lucky be her part!
And lightsome be the lassie's care
 That yields an honest heart!

When Sawnie, Jock, and Janetie,
 Are up and gotten lear[4],
They'll help to gar the boatie row,
 And lighten a' our care.
The boatie rows, the boatie rows
 The boatie rows fu' weel!
And lightsome be her heart that bears
 The murlain[5] and the creel!

And when wi' age we are worn doun,
 And hirpling[6] round the door,
They'll row to keep us hale and warm,
 As we did them before:
Then, weel may the boatie row
 That wins the bairns's bread!
And happy be the lot of a'
 That wish the boat to speed!

[1] kerchief. [2] bravely. [3] dull and sad. [4] learning. [5] fish-basket of another form. [6] limping.

ISOBEL PAGAN

1741–1821

150

Ca' the Yowes to the Knowes

CA' the yowes to the knowes [1],
   Ca' them where the heather grows,
Ca' them where the burnie rows [2],
   My bonnie dearie.

As I gaed down the water side,
There I met my shepherd lad;
He row'd me sweetly in his plaid,
   As he ca'd [3] me his dearie.

"Will ye gang down the water side,
And see the waves sae sweetly glide
Beneath the hazels spreading wide?
   The moon it shines fu' clearly.

"Ye shall get gowns and ribbons meet,
Cauf-leather shoon upon your feet,
And in my arms ye'se lie and sleep,
   And ye shall be my dearie."

"I was bred up at nae sic school,
My shepherd lad, to play the fool,
And a' the day to sit in dool,
   And naebody to see me.

[1] drive the ewes to the grassy hillocks. [2] rolls. [3] called.

"If ye'll but stand to what ye've said,
I'se gang wi' you, my shepherd lad ;
And ye may row me in your plaid,
    And I shall be your dearie."

"While waters wimple [1] to the sea,
While day blinks in the lift [2] sae hie,
Till clay-cauld death shall blin' my e'e,
    Ye aye shall be my dearie ! "

[1] flow gently.   [2] firmament.

MICHAEL BRUCE

1746–1767

151

From the Elegy to Spring

NOW Spring returns : but not to me returns
　　The vernal joy my better years have known ;
Dim in my breast life's dying taper burns,
　　And all the joys of life with health are flown.

Starting and shivering in th' inconstant wind,
　　Meagre and pale—the ghost of what I was,
Beneath some blasted tree I lie reclined,
　　And count the silent moments as they pass—

The wingèd moments, whose unstaying speed
　　No art can stop, or in their course arrest :—
Whose flight shall shortly count me with the dead,
　　And lay me down in peace with them that rest.

Oft morning dreams presage approaching fate ;—
　　And morning dreams, as poets tell, are true :
Led by pale ghosts, I enter Death's dark gate,
　　And bid the realms of light and life adieu.

I hear the helpless wail, the shriek of woe ;
　　I see the muddy wave, the dreary shore,
The sluggish streams that slowly creep below,
　　Which mortals visit—and return no more.

Farewell, ye blooming fields ! ye cheerful plains !
   Enough for me the churchyard's lonely mound,
Where Melancholy with still Silence reigns,
   And the rank grass waves o'er the cheerless ground.

There let me wander at the shut of eve,
   When Sleep sits dewy on the labourer's eyes,—
The world and a its busy follies leave,
   And talk with Wisdom where my Daphnis lies.

There let me sleep forgotten in the clay,
   When Death shall shut these weary aching eyes,—
Rest in the hopes of an eternal day,
   Till the long night is gone, and the last morn arise

152   *Ode to the Cuckoo*[1]

HAIL, beauteous stranger of the grove !
   Thou messenger of Spring !
Now Heaven repairs thy rural seat,
   And woods thy welcome sing.

What time the daisy decks the green,
   Thy certain voice we hear :
Hast thou a star to guide thy path,
   Or mark the rolling year ?

Delightful visitant, with thee
   I hail the time of flowers ;
And hear the sound of music sweet
   From birds among the bowers.

[1] The authorship of this poem was claimed also by John Logan.

The schoolboy, wandering through the wood,
  To pull the primrose gay,
Starts the new voice of Spring to hear,
  And imitates thy lay.

What time the pea puts on the bloom,
  Thou fliest thy vocal vale—
An annual guest, in other lands,
  Another Spring to hail.

Sweet bird! thy bower is ever green,
  Thy sky is ever clear;
Thou hast no sorrow in thy song,
  No winter in thy year!

O could I fly, I'd fly with thee!
  We'd make, with joyful wing,
Our annual visit o'er the globe—
  Companions of the Spring.

JOHN LOGAN
1748–1788

The Braes of Yarrow

THY braes[1] were bonny, Yarrow stream,
  When first on them I met my lover;
Thy braes how dreary, Yarrow stream,
When now thy waves his body cover!
For ever now, O Yarrow stream!
Thou art to me a stream of sorrow;
For never on thy banks shall I
Behold my love, the flower of Yarrow.

He promised me a milk-white steed,
To bear me to his father's bowers;
He promised me a little page,
To squire me to his father's towers;
He promised me a wedding-ring,—
The wedding-day was fix'd to-morrow:
Now he is wedded to his grave,
Alas! his watery grave in Yarrow.

Sweet were his words when last we met;
My passion I as freely told him:
Clasp'd in his arms, I little thought
That I should never more behold him!

[1] hill-sides, slopes.

Scarce was he gone I saw his ghost ;
It vanish'd with a shriek of sorrow :
Thrice did the water-wraith ascend,
And gave a doleful groan thro' Yarrow.

His mother from the window look'd,
With all the longing of a mother ;
His little sister weeping walk'd
The greenwood path to meet her brother :
They sought him east, they sought him west,
They sought him all the Forest through ;
They only saw the cloud of night,
They only heard the roar of Yarrow.

No longer from thy window look—
Thou hast no son, thou tender mother !
No longer walk, thou little maid ;
Alas ! thou hast no more a brother.
No longer seek him east or west,
And search no more the Forest thorough ;
For, wandering in the night so dark,
He fell a lifeless corpse in Yarrow.

The tear shall never leave my cheek,
No other youth shall be my marrow [1]—
I'll seek thy body in the stream,
And then with thee I'll sleep in Yarrow.
—The tear did never leave her cheek,
No other youth became her marrow ;
She found his body in the stream,
And now with him she sleeps in Yarrow.

[1] mate.

HECTOR MACNEILL

1746–1818

154 *My Boy Tammy*

" WHAR hae ye been a' day,
  My boy Tammy ?
Whar hae ye been a' day,
  My boy Tammy ? "
" I've been by burn and flow'ry brae,
Meadow green and mountain grey,
Courting o' this young thing
  Just come frae her mammy."

 " And whar got ye that young thing,
  My boy Tammy ? "
" I gat her down in yonder howe [1],
Smiling, on a broomy knowe [2],
Herding a wee lamb and ewe
  For her poor mammy."

 " What said ye to the bonny bairn,
  My boy Tammy ? "
" I praised her een sae lovely blue,
Her dimpled cheek and cherry mou',—
I pree'd [3] it aft, as ye may trow :
  She said she'd tell her mammy.

[1] hollow. [2] knoll. [3] taste, try.

422

"I held her to my beating heart,
　　My young, my smiling lammie :
'I hae a house—it cost me dear ;
I've wealth o' plenishin'[1] and gear[2]—
Ye'se get it a' were't ten times mair,
　　Gin ye will leave your mammy.'

"The smile gaed aff her bonny face :
　　'I maunna leave my mammy !
She's gi'en me meat, she's gi'en me claise ;
She's been my comfort a' my days ;—
My father's death brought mony waes :
　　I canna leave my mammy.'

"'We'll tak her hame and mak her fain[3],
　　My ain kind-hearted lammie.
We'll gie her meat, we'll gie her claise ;
We'll be her comfort a' her days.'
The wee thing gies her hand and says :
　　'There ! gang and ask my mammy.'"

"Has she been to the kirk wi' thee,
　　My boy Tammy ?"
"She has been to the kirk wi' me,
And the tear was in her e'e ;
For, oh ! she's but a young thing
　　Just come frae her mammy."

155   *Come under my Plaidie*

"COME under my plaidie,—the night's gaun to
　　fa' ;
Come in frae the cauld blast, the drift, and the snaw :
Come under my plaidie, and sit down beside me,—
There's room in't, dear lassie, believe me, for twa.

---

[1] furniture.　[2] movable property.　[3] glad.

Come under my plaidie and sit down beside me,—
I'll hap ye frae every cauld blast that can blaw :
Oh, come under my plaidie and sit down beside me !
There's room in't, dear lassie, believe me, for twa."

" Gae 'wa wi' your plaidie, auld Donald, gae 'wa !
I fearna the cauld blast, the drift, nor the snaw :
Gae 'wa wi' your plaidie ; I'll no sit beside ye,—
Ye may be my gutcher [1] ;—auld Donald, gae 'wa.
I'm gaun to meet Johnnie—he's young and he's
    bonny ;
He's been at Meg's bridal, fu' trig and fu' braw [2] :
Oh, nane dances sae lightly, sae gracefu', sae tightly ;—
His cheek's like the new rose, his brow's like the
    snaw."

" Dear Marion, let that flee stick fast to the wa' [3] :
Your Jock's but a gowk [4], and has naething ava ;—
The hale o' his pack he has now on his back :
He's thretty, and I am but threescore and twa.
Be frank now and kindly : I'll busk [5] ye aye finely,—
To kirk or to market they'll few gang sae braw :—
A bein [6] house to bide in, a chaise for to ride in,
And flunkies to 'tend ye as aft as ye ca'."

" My father's aye tauld me, my mither and a',
Ye'd make a gude husband, and keep me aye braw :
It's true I lo'e Johnnie—he's gude and he's bonnie,—
But, wae's me ! ye ken he has naething ava.
I hae little tocher [7] : you've made a good offer :
I'm now mair than twenty—my time is but sma' ;
Sae, gie me your plaidie, I'll creep in beside ye,—
I thocht ye'd been aulder than threescore and twa."

[1] grandsire. [2] so smart and well-attired. [3] dismiss that foolish
idea. [4] a duffer : *lit.* cuckoo. [5] attire. [6] cosy. [7] marriage-
portion.

She crap in ayont him, aside the stane wa',
Where Johnnie was list'ning, and heard her tell a' :
The day was appointed,—his proud heart it dunted [1],
And strack 'gainst his side as if bursting in twa.
He wander'd hame weary : the night it was dreary ;
And, thowless [2], he tint his gate [3] 'mang the deep
   snaw :
The owlet was screamin' ; while Johnnie cried,
   " Women
Wad marry Auld Nick if he'd keep them aye braw ! "

---

[1] thumped.　[2] downhearted.　[3] lost his direction.

SUSANNA BLAMIRE

1747–1794

156   *And Ye shall Walk in Silk Attire*

AND ye shall walk in silk attire,
    And siller [1] hae to spare,
Gin ye'll consent to be his bride,
    Nor think o' Donald mair.
—Oh, wha wad buy a silken gown
    Wi' a puir broken heart?
Or what's to me a siller crown,
    Gin frae my love I part?

The mind wha's every wish is pure
    Far dearer is to me ;
And ere I'm forced to break my faith,
    I'll lay me doun and dee ;
For I hae pledged my virgin troth
    Brave Donald's fate to share ;
And he has gi'en to me his heart,
    Wi' a' its virtues rare.

His gentle manners wan my heart,—
    He gratefu' took the gift ;
Could I but think to tak' it back,
    It would be waur [2] than theft.
For langest life can ne'er repay
    The love he bears to me ;
And ere I'm forced to break my troth
    I'll lay me doun and dee !

[1] money.   [2] worse.

426

LADY ANNE LINDSAY

1750–1825

Auld Robin Gray

WHEN the sheep are in the fauld, and the kye
    at hame,
And a' the warld to rest are gane,
The waes o' my heart fa' in showers frae my e'e,
Unkent [1] by my gudeman, wha sleeps sound by me.

Young Jamie lo'ed me weel, and sought me for his
    bride ;
But saving a crown he had naething else beside :
To make the crown a pund, young Jamie gaed to
    sea,—
And the crown and the pund were baith for me.

He hadna been awa' a week but only twa,
When my faither brak' his airm, and the coo was
    stown [2] awa' ;
My mither she fell sick,—and my Jamie at the sea ;
And auld Robin Gray cam' a-courtin' me.

My faither couldna wark, and my mither couldna
    spin :
I toil'd day and nicht, but their bread I couldna
    win :
Auld Rob maintain'd them baith, and wi' tears in
    his e'e
Said "Jeanie, for their sakes, will ye no marry me ? "

[1] unknown. [2] stolen.

My heart it said nay—I look'd for Jamie back ;
But the wind it blew high, and the ship it was a
    wrack ;
His ship it was a wrack—why didna Jamie dee ?
Or why do I live to cry, Wae's me ?

My faither urged me sair : my mither didna speak ;
But she look'd in my face till my heart was like to
    break.
They gi'ed him my hand,—my heart was at the sea ;
Sae auld Robin Gray he was gudeman to me.

I hadna been a wife a week but only four,
When, mournfu' as I sat on the stane at the door,
I saw my Jamie's wraith,—for I couldna think it he,
Till he said, " I'm come hame to marry thee."

O sair did we greet [1], and muckle did we say :
We took but ae kiss, and I bade him gang away.
I wish that I were dead, but I'm no like to dee,—
And why was I born to say, Wae's me ?

I gang like a ghaist, and I carena to spin :
I daurna think on Jamie, for that wad be a sin ;
But I'll do my best a gude wife to be,
For auld Robin Gray is kind to me.

[1] weep.

ROBERT GRAHAM OF GARTMORE

1750-1797

IF doughty deeds my lady please,
  Right soon I'll mount my steed ;
And strong his arm and fast his seat,
  That bears frae me the meed.
I'll wear thy colours in my cap,
  Thy picture in my heart ;
And he that bends not to thine eye
  Shall rue it to his smart !
      Then tell me how to woo thee, love ;
        O tell me how to woo thee !
      For thy dear sake nae care I'll take,
        Tho' ne'er another trow me.

If gay attire delight thine eye,
  I'll dight me in array ;
I'll tend thy chamber door all night,
  And squire thee all the day.
If sweetest sounds can win thine ear,
  These sounds I'll strive to catch,—
Thy voice I'll steal to woo thysel'—
  That voice that nane can match.
      Then tell me how to woo thee, love ;
        O tell me how to woo thee !
      For thy dear sake nae care I'll take,
        Tho' ne'er another trow me.

But if fond love thy heart can gain,
    I never broke a vow ;—
Nae maiden lays her skaith to me ;
    I never loved but you.
For you alone I ride the ring,
    For you I wear the blue ;
For you alone I strive to sing,
    O tell me how to woo !
        Then tell me how to woo thee, love ;
            O tell me how to woo thee !
        For thy dear sake nae care I'll take,
            Tho' ne'er another trow me.

ROBERT FERGUSSON

1750–1774

159 *The Farmer's Ingle*

WHAN gloamin' grey out owre the welkin keeks[1]
    Whan Bawtie[2] ca's his owsen to the byre ;
Whan Thrasher John, sair dung[3], his barn-door
    steeks[4],
    And histy[5] lasses at the dightin'[6] tire ;
What bangs[7] fu' leal the e'ening's comin' cauld,
    And gars snaw-tappit Winter freeze in vain ;
Gars dowie[8] mortals look baith blithe and bauld,
    Nor fley'd[9] wi' a' the poortith o' the plain ;
    Begin, my Muse ! and chant in hamely strain.

Frae the big stack, weel winnow't on the hill,
    Wi' divots theekit[10] frae the weet and drift,
Sods, peats, and heathery turfs the chimley fill,
    And gar their thick'ning smeek salute the lift.
The gudeman, new come hame, is blithe to find,
    Whan he out owre the hallan[11] flings his een,
That ilka turn is handled to his mind,
    That a' his housie looks sae cosh[12] and clean !
    For cleanly house lo'es he, though e'er sae mean.

[1] peeps. [2] the dog. [3] much wearied. [4] fastens. [5] dry, dusty.
[6] winnowing. [7] overcomes. [8] woeful. [9] scared. [10] thatched
with turf. [11] partition. [12] snug.

431

Weel kens the gudewife that the pleughs require
  A heartsome meltith [1], and refreshin' synd [2]
O' nappy liquor, owre a bleezin' fire :
  Sair wark and poortith downa weel be joined.
Wi' buttered bannocks now the girdle reeks,
  I' the far nook the bowie [3] briskly reams [4] ;
The redded kail [5] stand by the chimley cheeks,
  And haud the riggin' [6] het wi' welcome streams ;
  Whilk than the daintiest kitchen [7] nicer seems.

Frae this lat gentler gabs [8] a lesson lear' ;
  Wad they to labouring lend an eident [9] hand,
They'd rax fell strang [10] upon the simplest fare,
  Nor find their stamacks ever at a stand.
Fu' hale and healthy wad they pass the day ;
  At night, in calmest slumbers dose fu' sound ;
Nor doctor need their weary life to spae [11],
  Nor drogs their noddle and their sense confound,
  Till death slip sleely on, and gi'e the hindmost
    wound.

On siccan [12] food has mony a doughty deed
  By Caledonia's ancestors been done ;
By this did mony wight fu' weirlike [13] bleed
  In bruilzies [14] frae the dawn to set o' sun.
'Twas this that braced their gardies [15] stiff and
    strang ;
  That bent the deadly yew in ancient days ;
Laid Denmark's daring sons on yird [16] alang ;
  Gar'd Scottish thristles bang the Roman bays ;
  For near our crest their heads they doughtna [17]
    raise.

[1] meal. [2] wash down. [3] milk-pail. [4] foams. [5] soup made
ready. [6] roof-trees. [7] cookery. [8] mouths. [9] diligent. [10] wax
mighty strong. [11] diagnose. [12] suchlike. [13] warlike. [14] broils.
[15] arms. [16] earth. [17] durst not.

The couthy cracks[1] begin whan supper's owre ;
  The cheering bicker gars them glibly gash[2]
O' Simmer's showery blinks, and Winter's sour,
  Whase floods did erst their mailin's[3] produce hash.
'Bout kirk and market eke their tales gae on ;
  How Jock wooed Jenny here to be his bride ;
And there, how Marion, for a bastard son,
  Upo' the cutty-stool[4] was forced to ride,
   The waefu' scauld o' our Mess John to bide.

The fient a cheep's[5] amang the bairnies now ;
  For a' their anger's wi' their hunger gane ;
Aye maun the childer, wi' a fastin' mou',
  Grumble, and greet, and mak' an unco maen.
In rangles[6] round before the ingle's lowe[7],
  Frae gude-dame's mouth auld-warld tales they hear,
O' warlocks loupin' round the wirrikow[8] ;
  O' ghaists that win in glen and kirkyard drear,
  Whilk touzles a' their tap[9] and gars them shake
    wi' fear !

For weel she trows that fiends and fairies be
  Sent frae the de'il to fleetch[10] us to our ill ;
That kye ha'e tint[11] their milk wi' evil e'e ;
  And corn been scowdered[12] on the glowin' kiln.
Oh, mock na this, my friends ! but rather mourn,
  Ye in life's brawest spring wi' reason clear ;
Wi' eild[13] our idle fancies a' return,
  And dim our dolefu' days wi' bairnly[14] fear ;
  The mind's aye cradled whan the grave is near.

---

[1] familiar talk.   [2] talk on.   [3] farm's.   [4] stool of repentance.
[5] never a chirp's.   [6] heaps.   [7] flame.   [8] devil.   [9] makes their hair
stand on end.   [10] cajole.   [11] lost.   [12] scorched.   [13] age.
[14] childish.

Yet thrift, industrious, bides her latest days ;
   Though age her sair-dow'd [1] front wi' runcles [2] wave,
Yet frae the russet lap the spindle plays,
   Her e'enin' stent [3] reels she as weel's the lave.
On some feast-day the wee things, buskit braw,
   Shall heeze [4] her heart up wi' a silent joy,
Fu' cadgie [5] that her head was up, and saw
   Her ain spun cleedin' [6] on a darlin' oy [7] ;
   Careless though death should mak' the feast her
      foy [8].

In its auld lerroch [9] yet the deas [10] remains,
   Whare the gudeman aft streiks him at his ease ;
A warm and canny lean for weary banes
   O' lab'rers doiled [11] upon the wintry leas.
Round him will baudrins [12] and the colley come,
   To wag their tail, and cast a thankfu' e'e
To him wha kindly flings them mony a crumb
   O' kebbuck whang'd [13], and dainty fadge to prie [14] ;
   This a' the boon they crave, and a' the fee.

Frae him the lads their mornin' counsel tak' ;
   What stacks he wants to thrash, what rigs to till ;
How big a birn [15] maun lie on Bassie's [16] back,
   For meal and mu'ter [17] to the thirlin' mill [18].
Niest, the gudewife her hirelin' damsels bids
   Glower through the byre, and see the hawkies [19]
      bound ;
Tak' tent, 'case Crummy tak' her wonted tids [20],
   And ca' the leglin's [21] treasure on the ground,
   Whilk spills a kebbuck nice, or yellow pound.

[1] sorely faded.   [2] wrinkles.   [3] task.   [4] lift.   [5] cheerful.
[6] clothing.   [7] grandson.   [8] parting treat.   [9] place.   [10] settle.
[11] stupefied with fatigue.   [12] pussy.   [13] cheese cut in lumps.
[14] bannock to taste.   [15] burden.   [16] old horse.   [17] grinding fee.
[18] estate mill.   [19] cows.   [20] humours.   [21] milking-pail.

Then a' the house for sleep begin to grien¹,
　　Their joints to slack frae industry a while ;
The leaden god fa's heavy on their een,
　　And haflins steeks² them frae their daily toil ;
The cruizie³ too can only blink and bleer ;
　　The restit ingle's⁴ done the maist it dow⁵ ;
Tacksman⁶ and cotter eke to bed maun steer,
　　Upo' the cod⁷ to clear their drumly pow⁸,
　　Till waukened by the dawnin's ruddy glow.

Peace to the husbandman and a' his tribe,
　　Whase care fells a' our wants frae year to year !
Lang may his sack and cou'ter turn the glybe,
　　And bauks⁹ o' corn bend down wi' laded ear !
May Scotia's simmers ay look gay and green ;
　　Her yellow har'sts frae scowry¹⁰ blasts decreed !
May a' her tenants sit fu' snug and bien¹¹,
　　Frae the hard grip o' ails and poortith freed ;
　　And a lang lasting strain o' peacefu' hours succeed !

160　　　　　*Braid Claith*

　　Y E wha are fain to hae your name
　　　　Wrote i' the bonnie book o' Fame,
Let Merit nae pretension claim
　　　　　　To laurell'd wreath ;
But hap¹² ye weel, baith back and wame¹³
　　　　　　In gude Braid Claith.

　　He that some ells o' this may fa'¹⁴,
　　And slae-black hat on pow¹⁵ like snaw,

---

¹ yearn.　² partly shuts.　³ lamp.　⁴ the smoke-dried fire-side's.
⁵ can.　⁶ farmer.　⁷ pillow.　⁸ hazy head.　⁹ ridges.　¹⁰ showery.
¹¹ comfortable.　¹² wrap.　¹³ belly.　¹⁴ claim as his portion.
¹⁵ poll.

Bids bauld to bear the gree [1] awa'
　　　Wi a' this graith [2],
When beinly [3] clad wi' shell fu' braw
　　　O' gude Braid Claith.

Waesucks [4] for him wha has nae feck [5] o't !
For he's a gowk [6] they're sure to geck at [7]—
A chiel that ne'er will be respeckit,
　　　While he draws breath,
Till his four quarters are bedeckit
　　　Wi' gude Braid Claith.

On Sabbath-days the barber spark,
Whan he has done wi' scrapin' wark,
Wi' siller broachie in his sark,
　　　Gangs trigly [8], faith !
Or to the meadows, or the Park,
　　　In gude Braid Claith.

Weel might ye trow, to see him there,
That he to shave your haffits [9] bare,
Or curl and sleek a pickle hair,
　　　Wad be right laith—
When pacing wi' a gawsy [10] air
　　　In gude Braid Claith.

If ony mettled stirrah [11] grene
For favour frae a lady's een,
He maunna care for bein' seen
　　　Before he sheath
His body in a scabbard clean
　　　O' gude Braid Claith.

---

[1] prize.　[2] gear.　[3] comfortably.　[4] alas !　[5] portion.　[6] fool.
[7] deride.　[8] in dandy fashion.　[9] side-locks.　[10] stately.　[11] lad of
spirit.

For, gin he come wi' coat threadbare,
A feg [1] for him she winna care,
But crook her bonnie mou' fu' sair,
      And scauld him baith :
Wooers should aye their travel spare
      Without Braid Claith.

Braid Claith lends folk an unco heeze [2]
Maks mony kail-worms [3] butterflees,
Gies mony a doctor his degrees,
      For little skaith [4] :—
In short, you may be what you please
      Wi' gude Braid Claith.

For, tho' ye had as wise a snout on
As Shakespeare, or Sir Isaac Newton,
Your judgment folk wad hae a doubt on,
      I'll tak my aith,
Till they could see ye wi' a suit on
      O' gude Braid Claith.

161   *An Eclogue*

WILLIE AND SANDY

'TWAS e'enin' when the spreckled gowdspink [5] sang ;
    When new-fa'en dew in blobs o' crystal hang ;
Then Will and Sandy thought they'd wrought
    eneugh,
And lows'd their sair-toil'd owsen frae the pleugh.
Before they ca'd [6] their cattle to the town,
The lads, to draw their breath, e'en sat them down ;
To the stiff sturdy aik they lean'd their backs,
While honest Sandy thus began the cracks [7].

[1] fig.   [2] rise.   caterpillars.   [4] damage.   [5] goldfinch.   [6] drove.
[7] conversation.

SANDY

Ance I could hear the lavrock's[1] shrill-tuned throat,
And listen to the clatterin' gowdspink's note :
Ance I could whistle cantily[2] as they,
To owsen, as they till'd my raggit[3] clay :
But now, I would as lieve maist bend my lugs
To tuneless puddocks[4] croakin' i' the bogs.
I sigh at hame ; a-field I'm dowie[5] too ;
To sowf[6] a tune I'll never crook my mou.

WILLIE

Foul fa'[7] me ! gif your bridal hadna been
Nae langer bygane than sin' Hallowe'en,
I could hae tell't you, but a warlock's[8] art,
That some daft lightlyin[9] quean had stown your
    heart :
Our beasties here will take their e'enin' pluck ;
And now, sin' Jock's gane hame the byres[10] to muck,
Fain would I houp my friend will be inclined
To gie me a' the secrets o' his mind :
Heh, Sandy, lad ! what dool's come owre ye now,
That you to whistle ne'er will crook your mou ?

SANDY

Ah, Willie, Willie ! I may date my wae
Frae what betid me on my bridal day ;
Sair may I rue the hour in which our hands
Were knit thegither in the haly bands :
Sin' that I thrave sae ill, in troth, I fancy,
Some fiend or fairy, nae sae very chancy[11],
Has driven me, by pawky[12] wiles uncommon,
To wed this flytin'[13] fury o' a woman.

[1] lark's. [2] cheerily. [3] poor. [4] frogs. [5] mournful. [6] hum.
[7] ill betide. [8] without a wizard's. [9] wild, slighting. [10] cattle-sheds. [11] auspicious. [12] cunning. [13] scolding.

WILLIE

Oh, Sandy! aften hae I heard you tell,
Amang the lasses a' she bure the bell;
And say, the modest glances o' her een
Far dang[1] she brightest beauties o' the green:
You ca'd her aye sae innocent, sae young,
I thought she kenn'd na how to use her tongue.

SANDY

Before I married her, I'll tak my aith,
Her tongue was never louder than her breath;
But now it's turn'd sae souple and sae bauld,
That Job himsel could scarcely thole[2] the scauld.

WILLIE

Let her yelp on; be you as calm 's a mouse,
Nor let your whist[3] be heard into the house:
Do what she can, or be as loud's she please,
Ne'er mind her flytes, but set your heart at ease:
Sit down and blaw your pipe, nor fash your thumb[4],
And there's my hand, she'll tire and soon sing dumb.
Sooner should winter's cauld confine the sea,
And let the sma'est o' our burns rin free;
Sooner at Yule-day shall the birk[5] be drest,
Or birds in sapless busses big[6] their nest,
Before a tonguey woman's noisy plea
Should ever be a cause to daunton me.

SANDY

Weel could I this abide; but oh! I fear
I'll soon be twin'd[7] o' a' my warldly gear.
My kirnstaff[8] now stand gizzen'd[9] at the door;

[1] surpassed.   [2] endure.   [3] hush!   [4] distress yourself.   [5] birch-tree.   [6] build.   [7] deprived.   [8] churn-stick.   [9] drought-cracked.

My cheese-rack toom [1], that ne'er was toom before;
My kye may now rin rowtin' [2] to the hill,
And on the naked yird [3] their milkness spill :
She seenil [4] lays her hand upon a turn ;
Neglects the kebbuck [5], and forgets the kirn.
I vow, my hair-mould [6] milk would poison dogs,
As it stands lapper'd [7] i' the dirty cogs [8].

Before the seed, I sell'd my ferra [9] cow,
And with the profit coft [10] a stane o' woo' ;
I thought, by priggin' [11], that she might hae spun
A plaidie, light, to screen me frae the sun ;
But though the siller's scant, the cleedin' dear,
She hasna ca'd about a wheel the year.
Last ouk [12] but ane I was frae hame a day,
Buying a threave [13] or twa o' beddin' strae :
O' ilka thing the woman had her will ;
Had fouth [14] o' meal to bake, and hens to kill ;
But hyne [15] awa' to Edinburgh scour'd she
To get a makin' o' her fav'rite tea ;
And 'cause I leftna her the weary clink,
She sell't the very trunchers frae my bink [16].

WILLIE

Her tea ! ah, wae betide sic costly gear,
Or them that ever wad the price o't spier [17] !
Sin' my auld gutcher [18] first the warld knew,
Fouk hadna fund the Indies, whare it grew.
I mind mysel', it's nae sae lang sin' syne,
When auntie Marion did her stamack tyne [19],
That Davs, our gard'ner, cam frae Applebog,
And gae her tea to tak by way o' drog.

[1] empty. [2] bellowing. [3] soil. [4] seldom. [5] cheese.
[6] moulded. [7] clotted. [8] bowls. [9] farrow. [10] bought.
[11] begging. [12] week. [13] a measure. [14] abundance. [15] hence.
[16] trunchers from my dresser. [17] ask. [18] grandsire. [19] lose her
appetite.

SANDY

When ilka herd for cauld his fingers rubs,
And cakes o' ice are seen upo' the dubs [1] ;
At mornin', when frae pleugh or fauld I come,
I'll see a braw reek [2] rising frae my lum [3],
And aiblins [4] think to get a rantin' blaze,
To fley [5] the frost awa', and toast my taes ;
But when I shoot my nose in, ten to ane
If I weelfar'dly [6] see my ain hearthstane.
She round the ingle wi' her gimmers [7] sits,
Crammin' their gebbies [8] wi' her nicest bits ;
While the gudeman out-by maun fill his crap
Frae the milk coggie or the parritch cap [9].

WILLIE

Sandy, gif this were ony common plea,
I should the lealest o' my counsel gie ;
But mak or meddle betwixt man and wife
Is what I never did in a' my life.
It's wearin' on now to the tail o' May,
And just between the bear-seed [10] and the hay ;
As lang's an orra [11] mornin' may be spared,
Stap your wa's east the haugh [12], and tell the laird ;
For he's a man weel versed in a' the laws,
Kens baith their outs and ins, their cracks and flaws ;
And aye right gleg [13], when things are out o' joint,
At settlin' o' a nice or kittle [14] point.
But yonder's Jock ; he'll ca' your owsen hame,
And tak thir tidings to your thrawart [15] dame,
That ye're awa' ae peacefu' meal to prie [16],
And tak your supper, kail or sowens [17], wi' me.

[1] pools.   [2] smoke.   [3] chimney.   [4] perhaps.   [5] scare.
[6] properly.   [7] contemptuous term for women.   [8] crops.   [9] bowl.
[10] barley seed-time.   [11] odd.   [12] step eastward of the river
meadow.   [13] quick.   [14] ticklish.   [15] perverse.   [16] taste.   [17] broth
or oatcake.

162   *Mutual Complaint of Plainstanes and*
Causey [1]

IN THEIR MOTHER-TONGUE

SINCE Merlin laid Auld Reekie's causey,
  And made her o' his wark right saucy,
The spacious street and gude plainstanes
Were never kenn'd to crack [2] but ance ;
Whilk happen'd on the hinder night,
When Fraser's ulie [3] tint its light.
O' Highland sentries nane were waukin'
To hear their cronies glibly taukin' ;
For them this wonder might hae rotten,
And, like night robbery, been forgotten,
Hadna a caddie [4], wi' his lantern,
Been gleg [5] enough to hear them bant'rin',
Wha cam to me neist mornin' early
To gie me tidings o' this ferly [6].
  Ye tauntin' louns, trow this nae joke,
For ance the ass of Balaam spoke,
Better than lawyers do, forsooth,
For it spak naething but the truth !
Whether they follow its example,
You'll ken best when you hear the sample.

PLAINSTANES

My friend ! thir hunder years, and mair,
We've been forfoughen [7] late and ear' [8] ;
In sunshine and in weety weather,
Our thrawart [9] lot we bure thegither.

---

[1] side-walk and roadway.   [2] converse.   [3] oil.   [4] street-runner,
or corner-boy.   [5] smart.   [6] marvel.   [7] overworked.   [8] early.
[9] untoward.

I never growl'd, but was content
When ilk ane had an equal stent [1];
But now to flyte [2] I'se e'en be bauld,
When I'm wi' sic a grievance thrall'd.
How haps it, say, that mealy bakers,
Hair-kaimers, creishy gizzy-makers [3],
Should a' get leave to waste their pouthers
Upon my beaux' and ladies' shouthers?
My travellers are fley'd to dead [4]
Wi' creels wanchancy [5], heap'd wi' bread,
Frae whilk hing down uncanny nicksticks [6],
That aften gie the maidens sic licks
As mak them blythe to screen their faces
Wi' hats and muckle maun bon-graces [7],
And cheat the lads that fain would see
The glances o' a pawky [8] e'e,
Or gie their loves a wily wink,
That erst might lend their hearts a clink [9]!
Speak, was I made to dree the ladin'
O' Gallic chairman heavy treadin',
Wha in my tender buke [10] bore holes
Wi' waefu' tackets [11] i' the soles
O' brogs [12], whilk on my body tramp,
And wound like death at ilka clamp?

Causey

Weel crackit, friend!—It aft hauds true,
Wi' naething fouk mak maist ado.
Weel ken ye, though ye doughtna [13] tell,
I pay the sairest kain [14] mysel'.
Owre me, ilk day, big waggons rumble,
And a' my fabric birze [15] and jumble.

[1] allowance.   [2] objurgate.   [3] greasy periwig-makers.
[4] frightened to death.   [5] unlucky baskets.   [6] notched sticks (for keeping scores).   [7] very large bonnets.   [8] cunning.   [9] blow.
[10] bulk.   [11] nails.   [12] shoes.   [13] would not.   [14] tribute.   [15] bruise.

Owre me the muckle horses gallop,
Eneugh to rug [1] my very saul up ;
And coachmen never trow they're sinnin'
While down the street their wheels are spinnin'.
Like thee, do I not bide the brunt,
O' Highland chairman's heavy dunt [2] ?
Yet I hae never thought o' breathing
Complaint, or makin' din for naething.

PLAINSTANES

Haud sae, and let me get a word in.
Your back's best fitted for the burden :
And I can eithly [3] tell you why—
Ye're doughtier [4] by far than I :
For whinstanes houkit [5] frae the Craigs
May thole [6] the prancin' feet o' naigs,
Nor ever fear uncanny hotches [7]
Frae clumsy carts or hackney coaches ;
While I, a weak and feckless creature,
Am moulded by a safter nature.
Wi' mason's chisel dighted neat [8],
To gar me look baith clean and feat,
I scarce can bear a sairer thump
Than comes frae soul of shoe or pump.
I grant, indeed, that now and then
Yield to a patten's pith I maun ;
But pattens, though they're aften plenty,
Are aye laid douu wi' feet fu' tenty [9] ;
And strokes frae ladies, though they're teazin',
I freely maun avow, are pleasin'.
  For what use was I made, I wonder ?
It wasna tamely to chap [10] under

---

[1] drag.   [2] stroke.   [3] easily.   [4] sturdier.   [5] dug.   [6] bear.
jolts.   [8] deftly prepared.   [9] careful.   [10] sound.

The weight o' ilka codroch [1] chiel,
That does my skin to targets [2] peel,
But, if I guess aright, my trade is
To fend frae skaith [3] the bonny ladies ;
To keep the bairnies free frae harms
When airin' i' their nurses' arms ;
To be a safe and canny bield [4]
For growin' youth and droopin' eild [5].

Tak, then, frae me the heavy load
O' burden-bearers heavy shod ;
Or, by my troth, the gude auld town sall
Hae this affair before the Council.

CAUSEY

I dinna care a single jot,
Though summon'd by a shelly-coat [6] ;
Sae leally I'll propone defences,
As get ye flung for my expenses.
Your libel I'll impugn *verbatim*,
And hae a *magnum damnum datum :*
For though frae Arthur's-Seat I sprang
And am in constitution strang,
Would it no fret the hardest stane
Beneath the Luckenbooths [7] to grane ?
Though magistrates the Cross discard,
It maksna [8] when they leave the Guard—
A lumbersome and stinkin' biggin' [9]
That rides the sairest on my riggin' [10].
Poor me ower meikle do ye blame
For tradesmen trampin' on your wame [11] ;
Yet a' your advocates and braw fouk
Come still to me 'twixt ane and twa o'clock,

[1] rustic   [2] tatters.   [3] protect from injury.   [4] shelter.   [5] age.
[6] bum-bailiff.   [7] certain tenements neighbouring St. Giles's.
[8] matters not.   [9] building.   [10] ridge, the "crown of the cause-way."   [11] belly.

And never yet were ken'd to range
At Charlie's statue or Exchange[1] :
Then tak your beaux and macaronies ;
Gie me trades-fouk and country Johnnies ;
The deil's in't gin ye dinna sign
Your sentiments conjunct wi' mine.

PLAINSTANES

Gin we twa could be as auldfarrant[2]
As gar the Council gie a warrant,
Ilk loun[3] rebellious to tak
Wha walks not in the proper track,
And o' three shillin's Scottish souk him,
Or in a water-hole sair douk him ;
This might assist the poor's collection,
And gie baith parties satisfaction.

CAUSEY

But first, I think, it will be good
To bring it to the Robinhood[4],
Where we sall hae the question stated,
And keen and crabbitly debated—
Whether the provost and the bailies,
For the town's gude whase daily toil is,
Should listen to our joint petitions,
And see obtemper'd[5] the conditions.

PLAINSTANES

Content am I. But east the gate is
The sun, wha taks his leave of Thetis,
And comes to wauken honest fouk,
That gang to wark at sax o'clock.
It sets[6] us to be dumb a while,
And let our words gie place to toil.

[1] two spots which had been paved for the express convenience of merchants, who declined to frequent them. [2] wise. [3] fellow. [4] an Edinburgh Debating Society. [5] obeyed. [6] becomes.

My Last Will

WHILE sober folks, in humble prose,
    Estate, and goods, and gear dispose,
A poet surely may disperse
His moveables in doggerel verse ;
And fearing death my blood will fast chill,
I hereby constitute my last Will.

Then, wit ye me to have made o'er
To Nature my poetic lore ;
To her I give and grant the freedom
Of paying to the bards who need 'em
As many talents as she gave,
When I became the Muse's slave.

Thanks to the gods, who made me poor,
No lukewarm friends molest my door,
Who always show a busy care
For being legatee or heir.
Of this stamp none will ever follow
The youth that's favour'd by Apollo.

But to those few who know my case,
Nor thought a poet's friend disgrace,
The following trifles I bequeath,
And leave them with my kindest breath ;
Nor will I burden them with payment
Of debts incurr'd, or coffin raiment.
As yet 'twas never my intent
To pass an Irish compliment.

To Jamie Rae, who oft *jocosus*
With me partook of cheering doses,
I leave my snuff-box, to regale
His senses after drowsy meal,

And wake remembrance of a friend
Who loved him to his latter end :
But if this pledge should make him sorry,
And argue like *memento mori*,
He may bequeath't 'mong stubborn fellows
To all the finer feelings callous,
Who think that parting breath's a sneeze
To set sensations all at ease.

To Oliphant, my friend, I legate
Those scrolls poetic which he may get,
With ample freedom to correct
Those writs I ne'er could retrospect ;
With power to him and his succession
To print and sell a new impression :
And here I fix on Ossian's head
A domicile for Doric reed,
With as much power *ad musæ bona*
As I in *propria persona*.

To Hamilton I give the task
Outstanding debts to crave and ask ;
And that my Muse e may not dub ill,
For loading him with so much trouble,
My debts I leave him *singulatim*,
As they are mostly *desperatim*.

To Woods whose genius can provoke
His passions to the bowl or sock ;
For love to thee, and to the Nine,
Be my immortal Shakespeare thine.
Here may you through the alleys turn,
Where Falstaff laughs, where heroes mourn,
And boldly catch the glowing fire
That dwells in raptures on his lyre.

Now, at my dirge (if dirge there be),
Due to the Muse and poetry,
Let Hutchison attend ; for none is
More fit to guide the ceremonies :
As I, in health, with him would often
This clay-built mansion wash and soften,
So let my friends with him partake
The gen'rous wine at dirge or wake.

And I consent to registration
Of this my Will for preservation,
That patent it may be, and seen,
In Walter's Weekly Magazine.
Witness whereof, these presents wrote are
By William Blair, the public notar,
And, for the tremor of my hand,
Are sign'd by him at my command.

R. F. + HIS MARK.

JOHN DUNLOP

1755–1820

164   *Oh! Dinna ask Me gin I Lo'e Thee*

OH! dinna ask me gin I lo'e thee,—
    Troth, I dar'na tell :
Dinna ask me gin I lo'e ye—
    Ask it o' yersel'.

Oh! dinna look sae sair at me,
    For weel ye ken me true :
Oh, gin ye look sae sair at me,
    I dar'na look at you!

When ye gang to yon braw, braw toun,
    And bonnier lassies see,
Oh, dinna, Jamie, look at them,
    Lest you should mind na me.

For I could never bide the lass
    That ye'd lo'e mair than me ;
And oh, I'm sure my heart would break
    Gin ye'd prove false to me!

ANDREW SCOTT

1757–1839

165 *Symon and Janet* [1]

SURROUNDED wi' bent and wi' heather,
  Where muircocks and plivers [2] are rife,
For mony a lang towmont [3] thegither
  There lived an auld man and his wife.

About the affairs o' the nation
  The twasome [4] they seldom were mute;
Bonaparte, the French, and invasion,
  Did saur [5] in their wizens like soot.

In winter, when deep are the gutters,
  And night's gloomy canopy spread,
Auld Symon sat luntin' his cuttie [6],
  And lowsin' his buttons for bed:

Auld Janet, his wife, out a-gazin'
  (To lock in the door was her care),
She, seeing our signals a-blazin',
  Cam' running in rivin' her hair.

"O Symon, the Frenchmen are landit!
  Gae look, man, and slip on your shoon;
Our signals I see them extendit,
  Like the red rising blaze o' the moon!"

[1] Suggested by the False Alarm (of Bonaparte's landing) in the year 1804, when the beacons in the Border Country were lighted by mistake.
[2] plover.   [3] twelvemonth.   [4] two.   [5] savour, smack.
[6] smoking his short pipe.

" What plague, the French landit ! " quo' Symon,
   And clash ! gaed his pipe to the wa' :
" Faith, then there's be loadin' and primin',"
   Quo' he, " if they're landit ava' !

" Our youngest son's in the militia ;
   Our eldest grandson's volunteer ;
And the French to be fu' o' the flesh o',
   I too in the ranks will appear."

His waistcoat-pouch fill'd he wi' pouther,
   And bang'd down his rusty auld gun ;
His bullets he put in the other,
   That he for the purpose had run.

Then humpled [1] he out in a hurry,
   While Janet his courage bewails,
And cries out, " Dear Symon, be wary ; "
   Whilst teughly [2] she hung by his tails.

" Let be wi' your kindness," quo' Symon,
   " Nor vex me wi' tears and your cares ;
If now I be ruled by a woman,
   Nae laurels shall crown my grey hairs."

Quo' Janet, " O keep frae the riot !
   Last night, man, I dreamt ye was dead ;—
This aught days I've tentit a pyot [3]
   Sit chatterin' upon the house-head.

" And yesterday, workin' my stockin',
   And you wi' your sheep on the hill,
A muckle black corbie [4] sat croakin',—
   I kenn'd it foreboded some ill."

---

[1] shuffled.   [2] stoutly.   [3] observed a magpie.   [4] raven.

ANDREW SCOTT

453

"Hout¹, cheer up, dear Janet, be hearty;
 For, ere the next sun may gae doun,
Wha kens but I'll shoot Bonaparte,
 And end my auld days in renown?"

"Then, hear me," quo' Janet, "I pray thee:
 I'll tend thee, love, livin' or dead;
And if thou should fa' I'll die wi' thee,
 Or tie up thy wounds if thou bleed."

Syne aff in a hurry he stumpled²,
 Wi' bullets, and pouther, and gun;
At's curpin³ auld Janet too humpled,—
 Awa' to the neighbouring toon.

There footmen and yeomen, paradin',
 To scour aff in dirdum⁴ were seen—
Auld wives and young lassies a-sheddin
 The briny saut tears frae their een.

Then aff wi' his bonnet gat Symon,
 And to the commander he gaes;
Quo' he, "Sir, I mean to go wi' ye, man,
 And help ye to lounder⁵ our faes.

"I'm auld, yet I'm teugh as the wire;
 Sae we'll at the rogues have a dash—
And, fegs⁶, if my gun winna fire,
 I'll turn her butt-end and I'll thrash!"

"Well spoken, my hearty auld hero!"
 The Captain did smiling reply;
But begg'd he would stay till to-morrow,
 Till daylight should glent in the sky.

¹ pshaw!   ² stamped.   ³ buttocks.   ⁴ tumult.   ⁵ thrash.
⁶ faith!

What reck[1]? a' the stour cam' to naething ;
　Sae Symon and Janet, his dame,
Hale-skart[2] frae the wars, without skaithing,
　Gaed bannin' the French again hame.

[1] what odds ?　[2] without a scratch.

JEAN GLOVER

1758–1801

166   *O'er the Moor amang the Heather*

COMING through the craigs[1] o' Kyle,
   Amang the bonnie bloomin' heather—
There I met a bonnie lassie,
   Keeping a' her ewes thegither.

      O'er the moor amang the heather,
      O'er the moor amang the heather—
      There I met a bonnie lassie,
      Keeping a' her ewes thegither.

Says I, My dear, where is the hame,—
   In moor or dale, pray tell me whether?
Says she, I tent[2] the fleecy flocks
   That feed amang the bloomin' heather.

We laid us down upon a bank,
   Sae warm and sunny was the weather:
She left her flocks at large to rove,
   Amang the bonnie bloomin' heather.

While thus we lay, she sang a song—
   Till echo rang a mile and farther;
And aye the burden o' the song
   Was—o'er the moor amang the heather.

<hr>

[1] crags.   [2] tend.

She charm'd my heart, and aye sinsyne[1]
I couldna think on ony ither :
By sea and sky she shall be mine—
The bonnie lass amang the heather !

O'er the moor amang the heather,
Down amang the bloomin' heather,—
By sea and sky she shall be mine,
The bonnie lass amang the heather.

[1] ever since.

ROBERT BURNS

1759–1796

167   *The Cotter's Saturday Night*

> " Let not Ambition mock their useful toil,
>   Their homely joys, and destiny obscure ;
> Nor Grandeur hear, with a disdainful smile,
>   The short and simple annals of the poor."—GRAY.

MY loved, my honoured, much-respected friend!
    No mercenary bard his homage pays ;
With honest pride I scorn each selfish end—
    My dearest meed a friend's esteem and praise :
To you I sing, in simple Scottish lays,
    The lowly train in life's sequestered scene ;
The native feelings strong, the guileless ways ;
    What Aiken in a cottage would have been ;
Ah ! though his worth unknown, far happier there, I
    ween.

November chill blaws loud wi' angry sugh [1] ;
    The shortening winter day is near a close ;
The miry beasts retreating frae the pleugh,
    The blackening trains o' craws to their repose ;
The toil-worn cotter frae his labour goes—
    This night his weekly moil is at an end—
Collects his spades, his mattocks, and his hoes,
    Hoping the morn in ease and rest to spend,
And weary, o'er the moor his course does hameward
    bend.

[1] blast.

457

At length his lonely cot appears in view,
  Beneath the shelter of an agèd tree ;
The expectant wee things, toddlin', stacher [1] through
  To meet their dad, wi' flichterin' [2] noise an' glee.
His wee bit ingle, blinking bonnily,
  His clean hearthstane, his thriftie wifie's smile,
The lisping infant prattling on his knee,
  Does a' his weary carking cares beguile,
An' makes him quite forget his labour an' his toil.

Belyve [3] the elder bairns come drapping in,
  At service out amang the farmers roun' ;
Some ca' the pleugh, some herd, some tentie [4] rin
  A cannie errand to a neebor town :
Their eldest hope, their Jenny, woman grown,
  In youthfu' bloom, love sparkling in her ee,
Comes hame, perhaps, to show a braw new gown,
  Or deposite her sair-won penny-fee,
To help her parents dear, if they in hardship be.

Wi' joy unfeigned brothers and sisters meet,
  An' each for other's weelfare kindly spiers [5] :
The social hours, swift-winged, unnoticed fleet ;
  Each tells the uncos [6] that he sees or hears ;
The parents, partial, eye their hopeful years ;
  Anticipation forward points the view.
The mother, wi' her needle an' her shears,
  Gars auld claes look amaist as weel's the new ;
The father mixes a' wi' admonition due.

Their masters' an' their mistresses' command
  The younkers a' are warnèd to obey,
An' mind their labours wi' an eydent [7] hand,
  An' ne'er, though out o' sight, to jauk [8] or play :

[1] move unsteadily.   [2] eagerly welcoming.   [3] anon.   [4] carefully.
[5] inquires.   [6] things extraordinary.   [7] diligent.   [8] trifle.

"An' oh! be sure to fear the Lord alway,
  An' mind your duty duly morn an' night!
Lest in temptation's path ye gang astray,
  Implore His counsel and assisting might;
They never sought in vain that sought the Lord
    aright!"

But hark! a rap comes gently to the door:
  Jenny, wha kens the meaning o' the same,
Tells how a neebor lad cam' o'er the moor,
  To do some errands and convoy her hame.
The wily mother sees the conscious flame
  Sparkle in Jenny's e'e and flush her cheek;
With heart-struck, anxious care inquires his name,
  While Jenny hafflins is afraid [1] to speak;
Weel pleased the mother hears it's nae wild, worth-
    less rake.

Wi' kindly welcome Jenny brings him ben [2]—
  A strappin' youth, he taks the mother's eye.
Blithe Jenny sees the visit's no ill ta'en;
  The father cracks [3] of horses, pleughs, and kye;
The youngster's artless heart o'erflows wi' joy,
  But blate [4] and laithfu', scarce can weel behave;
The mother, wi' a woman's wiles, can spy
  What makes the youth sae bashfu' an' sae grave—
Weel pleased to think her bairn's respected like the
    lave [5].

O happy love, where love like this is found!
  O heartfelt raptures, bliss beyond compare!
I've pacèd much this weary mortal round,
  And sage experience bids me this declare:

[1] is half afraid. [2] within. [3] chats. [4] bashful. [5] rest.

" If Heaven a draught of heavenly pleasure spare,
    One cordial in this melancholy vale,
'Tis when a youthful, loving, modest pair,
    In other's arms breathe out the tender tale
Beneath the milk-white thorn that scents the evening
      gale."

Is there in human form, that bears a heart,
    A wretch, a villain ! lost to love and truth !
That can, with studied sly, ensnaring art,
    Betray sweet Jenny's unsuspecting youth ?
Curse on his perjured arts ! dissembling smooth !
    Are honour, virtue, conscience, all exiled ?
Is there no pity, no relenting ruth,
    Points to the parents fondling o'er their child ?
Then paints the ruined maid, and their distraction
      wild ?

But now the supper crowns their simple board—
    The halesome parritch, chief o' Scotia's food,
The soupe their only hawkie [1] does afford,
    That 'yont the hallan [2] snugly chows her cood ;
The dame brings forth in complimental mood,
    To grace the lad, her weel-hained kebbuck fell [3],
An' aft he's prest, an' aft he ca's it guid ;
    The frugal wifie, garrulous, will tell
How 'twas a towmond [4] auld, sin' lint was i' the bell.

The cheerfu' supper done, wi' serious face
    They round the ingle form a circle wide ;
The sire turns o'er, wi' patriarchal grace,
    The big ha' Bible, ance his father's pride :

[1] cow.   [2] partition.   [3] well-saved pungent cheese.   [4] twelve-month.

His bonnet reverently is laid aside,
 His lyart haffets [1] wearing thin an' bare ;
Those strains that once did sweet in Zion glide,
 He wales [2] a portion with judicious care ;
And "Let us worship God!" he says, with solemn
  air.

They chant their artless notes in simple guise ;
 They tune their hearts, by far the noblest aim :
Perhaps "Dundee's" wild warbling measures rise,
 Or plaintive "Martyrs," worthy of the name ;
Or noble "Elgin" beets [3] the heavenward flame,
 The sweetest far of Scotia's holy lays.
Compared with these, Italian trills are tame ;
 The tickled ears no heartfelt raptures raise ;
Nae unison hae they with our Creator's praise.

The priest-like father reads the sacred page,
 How Abraham was the friend of God on high ;
Or Moses bade eternal warfare wage
 With Amalek's ungracious progeny ;
Or how the royal bard did groaning lie
 Beneath the stroke of Heaven's avenging ire ;
Or Job's pathetic plaint and wailing cry ;
 Or rapt Isaiah's wild, seraphic fire ;
Or other holy seers that tune the sacred lyre.

Perhaps the Christian volume is the theme—
 How guiltless blood for guilty man was shed ;
How He who bore in heaven the second name
 Had not on earth whereon to lay His head ;

---

[1] grizzled side-locks. [2] selects. [3] supplies.

How His first followers and servants sped,
   The precepts sage they wrote to many a land;
How he, who lone in Patmos banishèd,
   Saw in the sun a mighty angel stand,
And heard great Babylon's doom pronounced by
    Heaven's command.

Then kneeling down, to heaven's eternal King
   The saint, the father, and the husband prays:
Hope "springs exulting on triumphant wing," [1]
   That thus they all shall meet in future days;
There ever bask in uncreated rays,
   No more to sigh, or shed the bitter tear,
Together hymning their Creator's praise,
   In such society, yet still more dear;
While circling time moves round in an eternal sphere.

Compared with this, how poor Religion's pride,
   In all the pomp of method and of art,
When men display to congregations wide
   Devotion's every grace, except the heart!
The Power, incensed, the pageant will desert,
   The pompous strain, the sacerdotal stole;
But haply, in some cottage far apart,
   May hear, well pleased, the language of the soul,
And in His book of life the inmates poor enrol.

Then homeward all take off their several way:
   The youngling cottagers retire to rest;
The parent pair their secret homage pay,
   And proffer up to Heaven the warm request

---

[1] Pope's "Windsor Forest."

That He who stills the raven's clamorous nest,
  And decks the lily fair in flowery pride,
Would, in the way His wisdom sees the best,
  For them and for their little ones provide ;
But chiefly in their hearts with grace divine preside.

From scenes like these old Scotia's grandeur springs,
  That makes her loved at home, revered abroad ;
Princes and lords are but the breath of kings,
  "An honest man's the noblest work of God : "[1]
And certes, in fair virtue's heavenly road,
  The cottage leaves the palace far behind ;
What is a lordling's pomp ?—a cumbrous load,
  Disguising oft the wretch of human kind,
Studied in arts of hell, in wickedness refined !

O Scotia, my dear, my native soil,
  For whom my warmest wish to Heaven is sent !
Long may thy hardy sons of rustic toil
  Be blest with health, and peace, and sweet content !
And oh, may Heaven their simple lives prevent
  From Luxury's contagion, weak and vile !
Then, howe'er crowns and coronets be rent,
  A virtuous populace may rise the while,
And stand a wall of fire around their much-loved isle.

O Thou who poured the patriotic tide
  That streamed through Wallace's undaunted heart ;
Who dared to nobly stem tyrannic pride,
  Or nobly die, the second glorious part

[1] Pope's " Essay on Man."

(The patriot's God peculiarly Thou art,
　　His friend, inspirer, guardian, and reward),—
O never, never Scotia's realm desert ;
　　But still the patriot, and the patriot bard,
In bright succession raise, her ornament and guard !

168   *Halloween*[1]

[*Kilmarnock Ed.*, 1786.]

The following poem will, by many readers, be well enough
understood ; but for the sake of those who are unacquainted with
the manners and traditions of the country where the scene is
cast, notes are added, to give some account of the principal charms
and spells of that night, so big with prophecy to the peasantry
in the west of Scotland. The passion of prying into futurity makes
a striking part of the history of human nature in its rude state, in
all ages and nations ; and it may be some entertainment to a
philosophic mind, if any such honour the author with a perusal, to
see the remains of it among the more enlightened in our own.

　　" Yes ! let the rich deride, the proud disdain,
　　The simple pleasures of the lowly train ;
　　To me more dear, congenial to my heart,
　　One native charm, than all the gloss of art."
　　　　　　　　　　　　　　　　　　GOLDSMITH.

U PON that night, when fairies light
　　　On Cassilis Downans[2] dance,
Or owre the lays[3], in splendid blaze,
　　On sprightly coursers prance ;

[1] Is thought to be a night when witches, devils, and other
mischief-making beings are all abroad on their baneful, midnight
errands ; particularly those aerial people, the fairies, are said, on
that night, to hold a grand anniversary.—*R. B.*
[2] Certain little romantic, rocky, green hills in the neighbourhood of the ancient seat of the Earls of Cassilis.—*R. B.*
[3] leas, or sloping fields.

Or for Colean the rout is ta'en,
  Beneath the moon's pale beams;
There, up the Cove[1], to stray an' rove,
  Amang the rocks and streams
        To sport that night:

Amang the bonie winding banks,
  Where Doon rins, wimplin[2], clear;
Where Bruce[3] ance ruled the martial ranks,
  An' shook his Carrick spear;
Some merry, friendly, country-folks
  Together did convene,
To burn their nits, an' pou their stocks,
  An' haud their Halloween
        Fu' blythe that night.

The lasses feat[4], an' cleanly neat,
  Mair braw than when they're fine;
Their faces blythe, fu' sweetly kythe[5],
  Hearts leal[6], an' warm, an' kin':
The lads sae trig, wi' wooer-babs[7]
  Weel-knotted on their garten;
Some unco blate[8], an' some wi' gabs[9]
  Gar lasses' hearts gang startin
        Whyles fast at night.

Then, first an' foremost, thro' the kail[10],
  Their "stocks[11]" maun a' be sought ance;

---

[1] A noted cavern near Colean House, called the Cove of Colean; which, as well as Cassilis Downans, is famed, in the country, for being a favourite haunt of the fairies.—*R. B.*   [2] meandering.

[3] The famous family of that name, the ancestors of ROBERT, the great deliverer of his country, were Earls of Carrick.—*R. B.*

[4] trim.   [5] show.   [6] loyal.   [7] love-knots.   [8] shy.   [9] chatter.
[10] cabbage.

[11] The first ceremony of Halloween is, pulling each a "stock," or plant of kail. They must go out, hand in hand, with eyes shut, and pull the first they meet with: its being big or little, straight or

They steak their een, an' grape [1] an' wale [2]
 For muckle anes, an' straught anes.
Poor hav'rel [3] Will fell aff the drift,
 An' wandered thro' the " bow-kail,"
An' pou't, for want o' better shift,
  A runt, was like a sow-tail
     Sae bow't [4] that night.

Then, straught or crooked, yird or nane,
 They roar an' cry a' throw'ther ;
The vera wee-things, toddlin [5], rin,
 Wi' stocks out owre their shouther :
An' gif the custok's sweet or sour,
 Wi' joctelegs [6] they taste them ;
Syne coziely [7], aboon the door,
 Wi' cannie care, they've plac'd them
    To lie that night.

The lasses staw [8] frae 'mang them a',
 To pou their stalks o' corn [9] ;
But Rab slips out, an' jinks about,
 Behint the muckle thorn :

crooked, is prophetic of the size and shape of the grand object of all their spells—the husband or wife. If any " yird," or earth, stick to the root, that is " tocher," or fortune ; and the taste of the " custoc," that is, the heart of the stem, is indicative of the natural temper and disposition. Lastly, the stems, or, to give them their proper appellation, the " runts," are placed somewhere above the head of the door ; and the Christian names of people whom chance brings into the house are, according to the priority of placing the " runts," the names in question.—R. B.

[1] grope. [2] select. [3] half-witted. [4] crooked. [5] tottering.
[6] pocket-knives. [7] snugly. [8] stole away,
[9] They go to the barnyard, and pull each, at three several times, a stalk of oats. If the third stalk wants the " top-pickle," that is, the grain at the top of the stalk, the party in question will come to the marriage-bed anything but a maid.—R. B.

He grippet Nelley hard an' fast :
  Loud skirl'd [1] a' the lasses ;
But her tap-pickle maist was lost,
  Whan kiutlin in the, " fause-house [2] "
        Wi' him that night.

The auld guid-wife's weel-hoordet nits [3]
  Are round an' round divided,
An' mony lads' an' lasses' fates
  Are there that night decided :
Some kindle couthie [4], side by side,
  An' burn thegither trimly ;
Some start awa wi' saucy pride,
  An' jump out owre the chimlie
        Fu' high that night.

Jean slips in twa, wi' tentie e'e ;
  Wha 'twas, she wadna tell ;
But this is *Jock*, an' this is *me*,
  She says in to hersel :
He bleez'd owre her, an' she owre him,
  As they wad never màir part ;
Till fuff ! he started up the lum,
  And Jean had e'en a sàir heart.
        To see't that night.

Poor Willie, wi' his bow-kail runt,
  Was brunt wi' primsie [5] Mallie ;

[1] screamed.
[2] When the corn is in a doubtful state, by being too green or wet,
the stack-builder, by means of old timber, &c., makes a large apart-
ment in his stack, with an opening in the side which is fairest ex-
posed to the wind : this he calls a "faust-house."—*R. B.*
[3] Burning the nuts is a favourite charm. They name the lad
and lass to each particular nut, as they lay them in the fire ; and
according as they burn quietly together, or start from beside one
another, the course and issue of the courtship will be.—*R. B.*
[4] agreeable. [5] prudish.

An' Mary, nae doubt, took the drunt[1],
  To be compar'd to Willie :
Mall's nit lap out, wi' pridefu' fling,
  An' her ain fit, it burnt it ;
While Willie lap, an' swoor by " jing,"
  'Twas just the way he wanted
              To be that night.

Nell had the " fause-house " in her min',
  She pits hersel an' Rob in ;
In loving bleeze they sweetly join,
  Till white in ase they're sobbin :
Nell's heart was dancin at the view ;
  She whisper'd Rob to leuk for't :
Rob, stownins[2], prie'd[3] her bonie mou,
  Fu' cozie in the neuk for't,
              Unseen that night.

But Merran sat behint their backs,
  Her thoughts on Andrew Bell ;
She lea'es them gashin[4] at their cracks[5],
  An' slips out-by hersel :
She thro' the yard the nearest taks,
  An' for the kiln she goes then,
An' darklins grapet for the " bauks[6],"
  And in the " blue-clue "[7] throws then,
              Right fear't that night.

---

[1] pet.   [2] stealthily.   [3] tasted.   [4] talking volubly.   [5] conversation.   [6] cross-beams.

[7] Whoever would, with success, try this spell, must strictly observe these directions : Steal out, all alone, to the kiln, and, darkling, throw into the "pot" a clue of blue yarn ; wind it in a new clue off the old one ; and, towards the latter end, something will hold the thread : demand, " Wha hauds ? " i.e., who holds ? and answer will be returned from the kiln-pot, by naming the christian and surname of your future spouse.—R. B.

An' ay she win't [1], an' ay she swat—
    I wat she made nae jaukin [2];
Till something held within the pat,
    Guid L—d ! but she was quaukin !
But whether 'twas the deil himsel,
    Or whether 'twas a bauk-en',
Or whether it was Andrew Bell,
    She did na wait on talkin
              To spier that night.

Wee Jenny to her graunie says,
    "Will ye go wi' me, graunie ?
I'll eat the apple at the glass [3],
    I gat frae uncle Johnie " :
She fuff't her pipe wi' sic a lunt [4],
    In wrath she was sae vap'rin [5],
She notic't na an aizle [6] brunt
    Her braw, new, worset apron
              Out thro' that night.

"Ye little skelpie-limmer's-face [7] !
    I daur you try sic sportin,
As seek the foul thief ony place,
    For him to spae [8] your fortune :
Nae doubt but ye may get a sight !
    Great cause ye hae to fear it ;
For mony a ane has gotten a fright,
    An' liv'd an' died deleeret,
              On sic a night.

---

[1] winded.   [2] delay.
[3] Take a candle and go alone to a looking-glass ; eat an apple
before it, and some traditions say, you should comb your hair all
the time ; the face of your conjugal companion, *to be*, will be seen
in the glass, as if peeping over your shoulder.—*R. B.*
[4] quantity of smoke.   [5] agitated.   [6] cinder.
[7] A technical term in female scolding.—*R. B.*   [8] foretell.

"Ae hairst afore the Sherra-moor,
    I mind't as weel's yestreen—
I was a gilpey [1] then, I'm sure
    I was na past fyfteen :
The simmer had been cauld an' wat,
    An' stuff was unco green ;
An' ay a rantin kirn [2] we gat,
    An' just on Halloween
              It fell that night.

"Our 'stibble-rig,' [3] was Rab M'Graen,
    A clever, sturdy fallow ;
His sin gat Eppie Sim wi' wean,
    That liv'd in Achmacalla :
He gat hemp-seed [4], I mind it weel,
    An' he made unco light o't ;
But mony a day was by himsel,
    He was sae sairly frighted
              That vera night."

Then up gat fechtin Jamie Fleck,
    An' he swoor by his conscience,
That he could saw hemp-seed a peck ;
    For it was a' but nonsense :

[1] young romp.   [2] harvest-home.   [3] leaders of the reapers.
[4] Steal out, unperceived, and sow a handful of hemp-seed, harrowing it with anything you can conveniently draw after you. Repeat, now and then—"Hemp-seed I saw thee, hemp-seed I saw thee ; and him (or her) that is to be my true love, come after me and pou thee." Look over your left shoulder, and you will see the appearance of the person invoked, in the attitude of pulling hemp. Some traditions say, "Come after me and shaw thee," that is, show thyself ; in which case, it simply appears. Others omit the harrowing, and say, "Come after me and harrow thee."—R. B.

The auld guidman raught [1] down the pock,
  An' out a handfu' gied him;
Syne bad him slip frae 'mang the folk,
  Sometime when nae ane see'd him,
         An' try't that night.

He marches thro' amang the stacks,
  Tho' he was something sturtin [2];
The graip he for a harrow taks,
  An' haurls [3] at his curpin [4]:
And ev'ry now an' then, he says,
  " Hemp-seed I saw thee,
An' her that is to be my lass
  Come after me, an' draw thee
         As fast this night."

He whistl'd up " Lord Lenox' March,"
  To keep his courage cheery;
Altho' his hair began to arch,
  He was sae fley'd [5] an' eerie [6]:
Till presently he hears a squeak,
  An' then a grane an' gruntle;
He by his shouther gae a keek,
  An' tumbled wi' a wintle [7]
         Out-owre that night.

He roar'd a horrid murder-shout,
  In dreadfu' desperation !
An' young an' auld come rinnin' out,
  An' hear the said narration :

[1] reached.   [2] staggered.   [3] drags.   [4] rear.   [5] timorous.
[6] possessed by a sense of the supernatural.   [7] somersault.

He swoor 'twas hilchin [1] Jean M'Craw,
  Or croucie [2] Merran Humphie—
Till stop ! she trotted thro' them a' ;
  An' wha was it but grumphie [3]
              Asteer that night ?

Meg fain wad to the barn gaen,
  To winn three wechts o' naething [4] ;
But for to meet the deil her lane,
  She pat but little faith in :
She gies the herd a pickle [5] nits,
  An' twa red cheekit apples,
To watch, while for the barn she sets,
  In hopes to see Tam Kipples
              That vera night.

She turns the key wi' cannie thraw,
  An' owre the threshold ventures ;
But first on Sawnie gies a ca',
  Syne bauldly in she enters :
A ratton rattl'd up the wa',
  An' she cry'd, L—d preserve her !
An' ran thro' midden-hole an' a',
  An' pray'd wi' zeal and fervour,
              Fu' fast that night.

---

[1] halting.   [2] crook-backed.   [3] the pig.

[4] This charm must likewise be performed unperceived and alone. You go to the barn, and open both doors, taking them off the hinges, if possible ; for there is danger that the being about to appear, may shut the doors, and do you some mischief.   Then take that instrument used in winnowing the corn, which in our country dialect we call a " wecht," and go through all the attitudes of letting down corn against the wind.   Repeat it three times, and the third time, an apparition will pass through the barn, in at the windy door, and out at the other, having both the figure in question, and the appearance or retinue, marking the employment or station in life.—R. B.   [5] few.

They hoy't[1] out Will, wi' sair advice ;
   They hecht[2] him some fine braw ane ;
It chanc'd the stack he faddom't thrice,[3]
   Was timmer-propt for thrawin :
He taks a swirlie[4] auld moss-oak
   For some black, grousome carlin ;
An' loot a winze[5], an' drew a stroke,
   Till skin in blypes[6] cam haurlin
              Aff's nieves[7] that night.

A wanton widow Leezie was,
   As cantie as a kittlen ;
But och ! that night, amang the shaws[8],
   She gat a fearfu' settlin !
She thro' the wins, an' by the cairn,
   An' owre the hill gaed scrievin[9] ;
Whare three lairds' lan's met at a burn[10],
   To dip her left sark-sleeve in,
              Was bent that night.

Whyles owre a linn the burnie plays,
   As thro' the glen it wimpl't[11];
Whyles round a rocky scaur[12] it strays,
   Whyles in a wiel[13] it dimpl't;

[1] inveigled.   [2] promised.

[3] Take an opportunity of going unnoticed to a "bear-stack," and fathom it three times round. The last fathom of the last time, you will catch in your arms the appearance of your future conjugal yoke-fellow.—*R. B.*

[4] crooked.   [5] an oath.   [6] shreds.   [7] off his fists.   [8] woods. [9] careering.

[10] You go out, one or more (for this is a social spell), to a south running spring, or rivulet, where "three lairds' lands meet," and dip your left shirt sleeve. Go to bed in sight of a fire, and hang your wet sleeve before it to dry. Lie awake, and, some time near midnight, an apparition, having the exact figure of the grand object in question, will come and turn the sleeve, as if to dry the other side of it.—*R. B.*

[11] flowed.   [12] precipitous bank.   [13] pool.

Whyles glitter'd to the nightly rays,
  Wi' bickerin, dancin dazzle ;
Whyles cookit [1] underneath the braes,
  Below the spreading hazel
              Unseen that night.

Amang the brackens [2], on the brae,
  Between her an' the moon,
The deil, or else an outler quey [3],
  Gat up an' ga'e a croon :
Poor Leezie's heart maist lap the hool [4] ;
  Near lav'rock [5]-height she jumpet,
But mist a fit, an' in the pool
  Out-owre the lugs she plumpet,
              Wi' a plunge that night.

In order, on the clean hearth-stane,
  The " luggies " [6] three are ranged ;
An' ev'ry time great care is ta'en
  To see them duly changed :
Auld uncle John, wha wedlock's joys
  Sin' " Mar's-year " [7] did desire,
Because he gat the toom dish thrice,
  He heav'd them on the fire,
              In wrath that night.

---

[1] appeared and disappeared alternately.   [2] ferns.   [3] strayed heifer. [4] sheath. [5] lark.

[6] Take three dishes, put clean water in one, foul water in another, and leave the third empty ; blindfold a person, and lead him to the hearth where the dishes are ranged ; he (or she) dips the left hand : if by chance in the clean water, the future (husband or) wife will come to the bar of matrimony a maid ; if in the foul, a widow ; if in the empty dish, it fortells, with equal certainty, no marriage at all. It is repeated three times, and every time the arrangement of the dishes is altered.—R. B.

[7] 1715, when the Earl of Mar headed an insurrection.

Wi' merry sangs, an' friendly cracks,
  I wat they did na weary ;
And unco tales, an' funnie jokes—
  Their sports were cheap an' cheery :
Till butter'd sow'ns [1], wi' fragrant lunt [2],
  Set a' their gabs a-steerin' [3] ;
Syne, wi' a social glass o' strunt [4],
  They parted aff careerin
            Fu' blythe that night.

169   *Tam o' Shanter :*

A Tale.

"Of Brownyis and of Bogillis full is this Buke."
                       GAWIN DOUGLAS.

WHEN chapman billies [5] leave the street,
    And drouthy neibors, neibors meet ;
As market days are wearing late,
An' folk begin to tak the gate [6] ;
While we sit bowsing at the nappy [7],
An' getting fou [8] and unco happy,
We think na on the lang Scots miles,
The mosses, waters, slaps [9], and styles,
That lie between us and our hame,
Where sits our sulky, sullen dame,
Gathering her brows like gathering storm,
Nursing her wrath to keep it warm.

This truth fand honest TAM O' SHANTER,
As he frae Ayr ae night did canter :
(Auld Ayr, whom ne'er a town surpasses,
For honest men and bonie lasses).

[1] Sowens, with butter instead of milk to them, is always the Halloween supper.—*R. B.*
[2] steam.   [3] mouths to work.   [4] whisky.   [5] pedlar fellows.
[6] road.   [7] ale.   [8] tipsy.   [9] gaps.

O Tam ! had'st thou but been sae wise,
As taen thy ain wife Kate's advice !
She tauld thee weel thou was a skellum [1],
A bletherin, blustering, drunken blellum [2] ;
That frae November till October,
Ae market-day thou was na sober ;
That ilka melder [3] wi' the Miller,
Thou sat as lang as thou had siller ;
That ev'ry naig was ca'd a shoe on
The Smith and thee gat roarin fou on ;
That at the L—d's house, ev'n on Sunday,
Thou drank wi Kirkton Jean till Monday.
She prophesied, that, late or soon,
Thou wad be found, deep drown'd in Doon,
Or catch'd wi' warlocks in the mirk,
By Aloway's auld, haunted kirk.

Ah, gentle dames ! it gars me greet [4],
To think how mony counsels sweet,
How mony lengthen'd, sage advices,
The husband frae the wife despises !

But to our tale :—Ae market night,
Tam had got planted unco right,
Fast by an ingle, bleezing finely,
Wi' reaming swats [5], that drank divinely ;
And at his elbow, Souter Johnie,
His ancient, trusty, drouthy crony [6] :
Tam lo'ed him like a very brither ;
They had been fou for weeks thegither.
The night drave on wi' sangs an' clatter ;
And ay the ale was growing better :

---

[1] ne'er-do-weel.   [2] waster.   [3] grinding.   [4] makes me weep.
[5] frothing ale.   [6] associate.

The Landlady and Tam grew gracious,
Wi' secret favours, sweet and precious :
The Souter tauld his queerest stories ;
The Landlord's laugh was ready chorus :
The storm without might rair and rustle,
Tam did na mind the storm a whistle.

Care, mad to see a man sae happy,
E'en drown'd himsel amang the nappy.
As bees flee hame wi' lades o' treasure,
The minutes wing'd their way wi' pleasure :
Kings may be blest but Tam was glorious,
O'er a' the ills o' life victorious !

But pleasures are like poppies spread,
You seize the flow'r, its bloom is shed ;
Or like the snow falls in the river,
A moment white—then melts for ever ;
Or like the Borealis race,
That flit ere you can point their place ;
Or like the Rainbow's lovely form
Evanishing amid the storm.
Nae man can tether Time nor Tide,
The hour approaches Tam maun ride—
That hour, o' night's black arch the key-stane,
That dreary hour Tam mounts his beast in ;
And sic a night he took the road in,
As ne'er poor sinner was abroad in.

The wind blew as 'twad blawn its last ;
The rattling showers rose on the blast ;
The speedy gleams the darkness swallow'd
Loud, deep, and lang the thunder bellow'd :
That night, a child might understand,
The deil had business on his hand.

Weel mounted on his gray meare Meg,
A better never lifted leg,
Tam skelpit [1] on thro' dub [2] and mire,
Despising wind, and rain, and fire;
Whiles holding fast his gude blue bonnet,
Whiles crooning [3] o'er an auld Scots sonnet,
Whiles glow'ring [4] round wi' prudent cares,
Lest bogles catch him unawares;
Kirk-Aloway was drawing nigh,
Where ghaists and houlets [5] nightly cry.

By this time he was cross the ford,
Where in the snaw the chapman smoor'd [6];
And past the birks and meikle stane,
Where drunken Charlie brak 's neck-bane;
And thro' the whins [7], and by the cairn [8],
Where hunters fand the murder'd bairn;
And near the thorn, aboon the well,
Where Mungo's mither hang'd hersel.
Before him Doon pours all his floods,
The doubling storm roars thro' the woods,
The lightnings flash frae pole to pole,
Near and more near the thunders roll,
When, glimmering thro' the groaning trees,
Kirk-Aloway seem'd in a bleeze,
Thro' ilka bore [9] the beams were glancing,
And loud resounded mirth and dancing.

Inspiring bold John Barleycorn!
What dangers thou canst make us scorn!
Wi' tippenny, we fear nae evil;
Wi' usquabae [10], we'll face the devil!

---

[1] pounded.   [2] puddle.   [3] humming.   [4] staring.   [5] owls.
[6] smothered.   [7] furze.   [8] pile of stones.   [9] chink.   [10] whisky.

The swats [1] sae ream'd [2], in Tammie's noddle,
Fair play, he car'd na deils a boddle [3],
But Maggie stood, right sair astonish'd,
Till, by the heel and hand admonish'd,
She ventur'd forward on the light ;
And, wow ! Tam saw an unco sight !

Warlocks and witches in a dance :
Nae cotillon, brent new [4] frae France,
But hornpipes, jigs, strathspeys, and reels,
Put life and mettle in their heels.
A winnock-bunker [5] in the east,
There sat auld Nick, in shape o' beast ;
A towzie tyke [6], black, grim, and large,
To gie them music was his charge :
He screw'd the pipes and gart them skirl [7],
Till roof and rafters a' did dirl [8].—
Coffins stood round, like open presses,
That shaw'd the Dead in their last dresses ;
And (by some devilish cantraip [9] sleight)
Each in its cauld hand held a light,
By which heroic Tam was able
To note upon the haly table,
A murderer's banes, in gibbet-airns ;
Twa span-lang, wee, unchristen'd bairns ;
A thief, new-cutted frae a rape,
Wi' his last gasp his gab did gape ;
Five tomahawks, wi' blude red-rusted :
Five scymitars, wi' murder crusted ;
A garter, which a babe had strangled :
A knife a father's throat had mangled,

---

[1] new ale.   [2] mantled.   [3] copper coin.   [4] brand-new.
[5] window-seat. [6] shaggy dog. [7] scream. [8] vibrate. [9] magic.

Whom his ain son of life bereft,
The grey-hairs yet stack to the heft ;
Wi' mair of horrible and awefu',
Which even to name wad be unlawfu'.

As Tammie glowr'd, amaz'd, and curious,
The mirth and fun grew fast and furious ;
The Piper loud and louder blew,
The dancers quick and quicker flew,
They reel'd, they set, they cross'd, they cleekit [1],
Till ilka carlin swat and reekit [2],
And coost her duddies [3] on the wark,
And linket at it [4] in her sark !

Now Tam, O Tam ! had thae been queans,
A' plump and strapping in their teens !
Their sarks, instead o' creeshie [5] flainen,
Been snaw-white seventeen hunder linen [6] !—
Thir breeks o' mine, my only pair,
That ance were plush, o' guid blue hair,
I wad hae gi'en them off my hurdies,
For ae blink o' the bonie burdies !
But wither'd beldams, auld and droll,
Rigwoodie [7] hags wad spean [8] a foal,
Louping an' flinging on a crummock [9],
I wonder did na turn thy stomach.

But Tam kent what was what fu' brawlie :
There was ae winsome wench and waulie [10],
That night enlisted in the core,
Lang after kenn'd on Carrick shore ;

---

[1] took each other's arms.   [2] perspired and steamed.   [3] cast off
her rags.   [4] set to it.   [5] greasy.
[6] The manufacturer's term for very fine linen, woven in a reed of
1700 divisions.   [7] gallows-worthy.   [8] wean.   [9] staff.   [10] nimble.

(For mony a beast to dead she shot,
And perish'd mony a bonie boat,
And shook baith meikle corn and bear [1],
And held the country-side in fear)
Her cutty [2] sark, o' Paisley harn [3],
That while a lassie she had worn,
In longitude tho' sorely scanty,
It was her best, and she was vauntie.
Ah ! little kent thy reverend grannie,
That sark she coft for her wee Nannie,
Wi' twa pund Scots ('twas a' her riches),
Wad ever grac'd a dance of witches !

But here my Muse her wing maun cour,
Sic flights are far beyond her power ;
To sing how Nannie lap and flang
(A souple jade she was and strang),
And how Tam stood, like ane bewitch'd,
And thought his very een enrich'd ;
Even Satan glowr'd, and fidg'd [4] fu' fain,
And hotch'd [5] and blew wi' might and main :
Till first ae caper, syne anither,
Tam tint his reason a' thegither,
And roars out, " Weel done, Cutty-sark ! "
And in an instant all was dark :
And scarcely had he Maggie rallied,
When out the hellish legion sallied.

As bees bizz out wi' angry fyke [6],
When plundering herds assail their byke [7] ;
As open pussie's [8] mortal foes,
When, pop ! she starts before their nose ;

[1] barley.   [2] short cut.   [3] coarse cloth.   [4] fidgeted.   [5] jerked.
[6] fret.   [7] nest.   [8] the hare.

31

As eager runs the market-crowd,
When " Catch the thief ! " resounds aloud ;
So Maggie runs, the witches follow,
Wi' mony an eldritch skriech [1] and hollow.

Ah, Tam ! Ah, Tam ! thou'll get thy fairin !
In hell they'll roast thee like a herrin !
In vain thy Kate awaits thy coming !
Kate soon will be a woefu' woman !
Now, do thy speedy utmost, Meg,
And win the key-stane o' the brig [2] ;
There, at them thou thy tail may toss,
A running stream they dare na cross.
But ere the key-stane she could make,
The fient a tail she had to shake !
For Nannie, far before the rest,
Hard upon noble Maggie prest,
And flew at Tam wi' furious ettle [3] ;
But little wist she Maggie's mettle !
Ae spring brought off her master hale,
But left behind her ain grey tail :
The carlin claught [4] her by the rump,
And left poor Maggie scarce a stump.

Now, wha this tale o' truth shall read,
Each man, and mother's son, take heed :
Whene'er to Drink you are inclin'd,
Or Cutty-sarks rin in your mind,
Think ! ye may buy the joys o'er dear,
Remember Tam o' Shanter's meare.

[1] unearthly screech.
[2] It is a well-known fact that witches, or any evil spirits, have
no power to follow a poor wight any farther than the middle of
the next running stream.   It may be proper likewise to mention to
the benighted traveller, that when he falls in with *bogles*, whatever
danger may be in going forward, there is much more hazard in
turning back.—*R. B.*   [3] attempt.   [4] clutched.

170   *Auld Lang Syne*

S HOULD auld acquaintance be forgot,
   And never brought to mind ?
Should auld acquaintance be forgot,
  And auld lang syne !
     For auld lang syne, my dear,
      For auld lang syne,
     We'll tak a cup o' kindness yet
      For auld lang syne,

And surely ye'll be your pint stowp !
  And surely I'll be mine !
And we'll tak a cup o' kindness yet
  For auld lang syne.

We twa hae run about the braes,
  And pou'd the gowans fine ;
But we've wander'ed mony a weary fitt
  Sin' auld lang syne.

We twa hae paidl'd in the burn,
  Frae morning sun till dine ;
But seas between us braid hae roar'd
  Sin' auld lang syne.

And there's a hand, my trusty fiere [1] !
  And gie's a hand o' thine !
And we'll tak a right gude willie waught [2],
  For auld lang syne.

     [1] mate. [2] copious draught.

171   *To a Mouse*

On turning her up in her nest with the plough, November, 1787.

WEE, sleekit, cow'rin', tim'rous beastie,
    O what a panic's in thy breastie !
Thou need na start awa' sae hasty,
        Wi' bickering brattle [1] !
I wad be laith to rin and chase thee,
        Wi' murd'ring pattle [2] !

I'm truly sorry man's dominion
Has broken Nature's social union,
And justifies that ill opinion,
        Which mak's thee startle
At me, thy poor, earth-born companion,
        And fellow-mortal !

I doubt na, whyles, but thou may thieve.
What then ? poor beastie, thou maun live !
A diamen-icker in a thrave [3]
        'S a sma' request,
I'll get a blessin' wi' the lave [4],
        And never miss't !

Thy wee bit housie, too, in ruin !
It's silly [5] wa's the win's are strewin' !
And naething, now, to big [6] a new ane,
        O' foggage [7] green !
And bleak December's winds ensuin',
        Baith snell [8] and keen !

[1] at racing speed.   [2] plough-stick.   [3] an occasional ear of corn
in a pair of stooks.   [4] rest.   [5] frail.   [6] build.   [7] vegetation.
[8] biting.

Thou saw the fields laid bare and waste,
And weary winter comin' fast,
And cozie here, beneath the blast,
   Thou thought to dwell,
Till crash ! the cruel coulter passed
   Out through thy cell.

That wee bit heap o' leaves and stibble
Has cost thee mony a weary nibble !
Now thou's turned out, for a' thy trouble,
   But house or hald,
To thole the winter's sleety dribble,
   And cranreuch [1] cauld !

But, Mousie, thou art no thy lane,
In proving foresight may be vain :
The best laid schemes o' mice and men,
   Gang aft a-gley [2],
And lea'e us nought but grief and pain,
   For promised joy.

Still thou art blest, compared wi' me !
The present only toucheth thee ;
But Och ! I backward cast my e'e
   On prospects drear ;
And forward, though I canna see,
   I guess and fear.

172   *For a' That, and a' That*

IS there, for honest poverty,
 That hangs his head, and a' that ?
The coward slave, we pass him by,
 We dare be poor for a' that !

    [1] hoar-frost. [2] askew.

For a' that, and a' that ;
  Our toils obscure, and a' that !
The rank is but the guinea's stamp,
  The man's the gowd for a' that.

What though on hamely fare we dine,
  Wear hodden grey [1], and a' that ;
Gi'e fools their silks, and knaves their wine,
  A man's a man for a' that !
For a' that, and a' that,
  Their tinsel show, and a' that,
The honest man, though e'er sae poor ;
  Is king o' men for a' that !

You see yon birkie [2], ca'd a lord,
  Wha struts, and stares, and a' that,
Though hundreds worship at his word,
  He's but a coof [3] for a' that ;
For a' that, and a' that,
  His riband, star, and a' that ;
The man of independent mind,
  He looks and laughs at a' that.

A prince can mak' a belted knight,
  A marquis, duke and a' that ;
But an honest man's aboon his might,
  Guid faith, he maunna fa' [4] that !
For a' that, and a' that,
  Their dignities, and a' that,
The pith o' sense, and pride o' worth,
  Are higher ranks than a' that !

[1] coarse woollen cloth.   [2] forward fellow. [3] ninny. [4] must not claim that.

Then let us pray that come it may—
    As come it will for a' that—
That sense and worth, o'er a' the earth,
    May bear the gree [1], and a' that!
For a' that, and a' that,
    Its comin' yet, for a' that,
That man to man, the warld o'er,
    Shall brothers be for a' that.

173 *Bruce's Address to his Army at Bannockburn*

SCOTS, wha ha'e wi' Wallace bled ;
    Scots, wham Bruce has aften led ;
Welcome to your gory bed,
      Or to victory.

Now's the day, and now's the hour ;
See the front o' battle lour ;
See approach proud Edward's power—
      Chains and slavery !

Wha will be a traitor knave ?
Wha can fill a coward's grave ?
Wha sae base as be a slave ?
      Let him turn and flee !

Wha for Scotland's king and law
Freedom's sword will strongly draw,
Freeman stand, or freeman fa',
      Let him follow me !

By oppression's woes and pains !
By your sons in servile chains !
We will drain our dearest veins,
      But they shall be free !

[1] bear off the palm.

Lay the proud usurpers low !
Tyrants fall in every foe !
Liberty's in every blow !
    Let us do, or die !

174   *Mary Morison*

SONG

O MARY, at thy window be,
    It is the wish'd, the trysted hour !
Those smiles and glances let me see,
    That make the miser's treasure poor :
How blythely wad I bide the stoure [1],
    A weary slave frae sun to sun,
Could I the rich reward secure,
    The lovely Mary Morison.

Yestreen, when to the trembling string
    The dance gaed thro' the lighted ha',
To thee my fancy took its wing,
    I sat, but neither heard nor saw :
Tho' this was fair and that was braw [2],
    And yon the toast of a' the town,
I sigh'd, and said amang them a',
    " Ye are na Mary Morison."

Oh, Mary, canst thou wreck his peace,
    Wha for thy sake wad gladly die ?
Or canst thou break that heart of his,
    Whase only faut is loving thee ?
If love for love thou wilt na gie,
    At least be pity to me shown ;
A thought ungentle canna be
    The thought o' Mary Morison.

[1] turmoil.   [2] gaily dressed.

175   *The Rigs o' Barley*

SONG

I T was upon a Lammas night,
     When corn rigs are bonie,
Beneath the moon's unclouded light,
     I held awa to Annie ;
The time flew by, wi' tentless heed ;
     Till, 'tween the late and early,
Wi' sma' persuasion she agreed
     To see me thro' the barley.
          Corn rigs, an' barley rigs,
               An' corn rigs are bonie :
          I'll ne'er forget that happy night,
               Amang the rigs wi' Annie.

The sky was blue, the wind was still,
     The moon was shining clearly ;
I set her down, wi' right good will,
     Amang the rigs o' barley :
I ken't her heart was a' my ain ;
     I loved her most sincerely ;
I kiss'd her owre and owre again,
     Amang the rigs o' barley.

I lock'd her in my fond embrace ;
     Her heart was beating rarely :
My blessings on that happy place,
     Amang the rigs o' barley !
But by the moon and stars so bright,
     That shone that hour so clearly !
She ay shall bless that happy night
     Amang the rigs o' barley.

I hae been blythe wi' comrades dear ;
  I hae been merry drinking :
I hae been joyfu' gath'rin gear ;
  I hae been happy thinking :
But a' the pleasures e'er I saw,
  Tho' three times doubl'd fairly—
That happy night was worth them a',
  Amang the rigs o' barley.

176   *My Nanie, O*

SONG

BEHIND the hills where Lugar flows,
    'Mang moors an' mosses [1] many, O,
The wintry sun the day has clos'd,
  And I'll awa to Nanie, O.

The westlin wind blaws loud an' shrill ;
  The night's baith mirk and rainy, O ;
But I'll get my plaid an' out I'll steal,
  An' owre the hill to Nanie, O.

My Nanie's charming, sweet, an' young ;
  Nae artfu' wiles to win ye, O :
May ill befa' the flattering tongue
  That wad beguile my Nanie, O.

Her face is fair, her heart is true ;
  As spotless as she's bonnie, O ;
The op'ning gowan [2], wat wi' dew,
  Nae purer is than Nanie, O.

[1] bogs.   [2] daisy.

A country lad is my degree,
  An' few there be that ken me, O ;
But what care I how few they be,
  I'm welcome ay to Nanie, O.

My riches a's my penny-fee,
  An' I maun guide it cannie, O ;
But warl's gear ne'er troubles me,
  My thoughts are a'—my Nanie, O.

Our auld guidman delights to view
  His sheep an' kye thrive bonie O ;
But I'm as blythe that hauds his pleugh,
  An' has nae care but Nanie, O.

Come weel, come woe, I care na by ;
  I'll tak what Heav'n will sen' me, O :
Nae ither care in life have I,
  But live, an' love my Nanie, O.

177   *Green Grow the Rashes*

SONG

THERE'S nought but care on ev'ry han',
  In every hour that passes, O :
What signifies the life o' man,
  An' 'twere na for the lasses, O.

Chor.—Green grow the rashes, O ;
  Green grow the rashes, O ;
  The sweetest hours that e'er I spend,
  Are spent among the lasses, O.

The war'ly race may riches chase,
 An' riches still may fly them, O ;
An' tho' at last they catch them fast,
 Their hearts can ne'er enjoy them, O.

But gie me a cannie [1] hour at e'en,
 My arms about my dearie, O ;
An' war'ly cares, an' war'ly men,
 May a' gae tapsalteerie [2], O !

For you sae douce [3], ye sneer at this ;
 Ye're nought but senseless asses, O :
The wisest man the warl' e'er saw,
 He dearly lov'd the lasses, O.

Auld Nature swears, the lovely dears
 Her noblest work she classes, O :
Her prentice han' she try'd on man,
 An' then she made the lasses, O.

178   *For a' That*

SONG

THO' women's minds, like winter winds,
 May shift, and turn, an' a' that,
The noblest breast adores them maist—
A consequence I draw that.

 Chor.—For a' that an' a' that,
   And twice as meikle's a' that ;
   The bonie lass that I loe best
   Shall be my ain for a' that.

---

[1] quiet. [2] topsy-turvy. [3] grave.

Great love I bear to a' the fair,
  Their humble slave, an' a' that ;
But lordly will, I hold it still
  A mortal sin to thraw [1] that.

But there is ane aboon the lave [2],
  Has wit, and sense, an' a' that ;
A bonie lass, I like her best,
  And wha a crime dare ca' that ?

In rapture sweet this hour we meet,
  Wi' mutual love an' a' that,
But for how lang the fly may stang [3],
  Let inclination law that.

Their tricks an' craft hae put me daft [4],
  They've taen me in an' a' that ;
But clear your decks, and—here's " The sex ! "
  I like the jads for a' that.

179   *Theniel Menzies' Bonie Mary*

IN comin by the brig o' Dye,
  At Darlet we a blink [5] did tarry ;
As day was dawin [6] in the sky,
  We drank a health to bonie Mary.

Chor.—Theniel Menzies' bonie Mary,
      Theniel Menzies' bonie Mary,
    Charlie Grigor tint [7] his plaidie,
      Kissin' Theniel's bonie Mary.

---

[1] oppose.   [2] above the rest.   [3] " fit may last."   [4] beside myself.
[5] a moment.   [6] dawning.   [7] lost.

Her een sae bright, her brow sae white,
    Her haffet locks [1] as brown's a berry ;
And ay they dimpl't wi' a smile,
    The rosy cheeks o' bonie Mary.

We lap an' danc'd the lee-lang [2] day,
    Till piper lads were wae and weary ;
But Charlie gat the spring [3] to pay,
    For kissin Theniel's bonie Mary.

180   *Blythe was She*

BY Oughtertyre grows the aik,
    On Yarrow banks the birken shaw [4] ;
But Phemie was a bonier lass
    Than braes o' Yarrow ever saw.

Chor.—Blythe, blythe and merry was she,
        Blythe was she but and ben [5];
        Blythe by the banks o' Earn,
        And blythe in Glenturit glen.

Her looks were like a flow'r in May,
    Her smile was like a simmer morn :
She trippèd by the banks o' Earn,
    As light's a bird upon a thorn.

Her bonie face it was as meek
    As ony lamb upon a lea ;
The evening sun was ne'er sae sweet,
    As was the blink o' Phemie's e'e.

[1] sidelocks.   [2] live-long.   [3] "the piper."   [4] birchen copse.
[5] about the house.

The Highland hills I've wander'd wide,
  As o'er the Lawlands I hae been ;
But Phemie was the blythest lass
  That ever trode the dewy green.

181   *To the Weaver's Gin Ye Go*

M Y heart was ance as blythe and free
        As simmer days were lang ;
But a bonie, westlin [1] weaver lad
  Has gart me change my sang.

Chor.—To the weaver's gin ye go, fair maids,
      To the weaver's gin ye go ;
    I rede you right, gang ne'er at night,
      To the weaver's gin ye go.

My mither sent me to the town,
  To warp a plaiden [2] wab ;
But the weary, weary warpin o't
  Has gart me sigh and sab.

A bonie, westlin weaver lad
  Sat working at his loom ;
He took my heart as wi' a net,
  In every knot and thrum.

I sat beside my warpin-wheel,
  And ay I ca'd it roun' ;
But every shot and every knock,
  My heart it gae a stoun [3].

[1] from the west.   [2] coarse woollen cloth.   [3] ache.

The moon was sinking in the west,
  Wi' visage pale and wan,
As my bonie, westlin weaver lad
  Convoy'd me thro' the glen.

But what was said, or what was done,
  Shame fa' me gin I tell ;
But Oh ! I fear the kintra [1] soon
  Will ken as weel's mysel !

182   *How Long and Dreary is the Night*

HOW long and dreary is the night,
    When I am frae my dearie !
I sleepless lye frae e'en to morn,
  Tho' I were ne'er so weary !

When I think on the happy days
  I spent wi' you, my dearie :
And now what lands between us lie,
  How can I be but eerie !

How slow ye move, ye heavy hours,
  As ye were wae and weary !
It was na sae—ye glinted by,
  When I was wi' my dearie !

183   *Jumpin John*

HER daddie forbad, her minnie [2] forbad,
    Forbidden she wadna be :
She wadna trow't [3], the browst [4] she brew'd,
  Wad taste sae bitterlie.

---

[1] neighbourhood. [2] mammy. [3] believe it. [4] brew.

Chor.—The lang lad they ca' Jumpin John
   Beguil'd the bonie lassie,
  The lang lad they ca' Jumpin John
   Beguil'd the bonie lassie.

A cow and a cauf, a yowe [1] and a hauf,
 And thretty gude shillins and three ;
A vera gude tocher, a cotter-man's dochter,
 The lass wi' the bonie black e'e.

184   *To Daunton Me*

THE blude-red rose at Yule may blaw,
 The simmer lilies bloom in snaw,
The frost may freeze the deepest sea ;
But an auld man shall never daunton me.

Refrain.—To daunton me, to daunton me,
   An auld man shall never daunton me.

To daunton me, and me sae young,
Wi' his fause heart and flatt'ring tongue,
That is the thing you shall never see,
For an auld man shall never daunton me.

For a' his meal and a' his maut,
For a' his fresh beef and his saut,
For a' his gold and white monie,
An auld man shall never daunton me.

His gear may buy him kye and yowes,
His gear may buy him glens and knowes ;
Bur me he shall not buy nor fee,
For an auld man shall never daunton me.

[1] sheep.

32

He hirples twa-fauld as he dow,[1]
Wi' his teethless gab and his auld beld pow,
And the rain rains down frae his red blear'd e'e ;
That auld man shall never daunton me.

185　　*The Bonie Lad that's Far Awa.*

O HOW can I be blythe and glad,
　　Or how can I gang brisk and braw,
When the bonie lad that I lo'e best
　　Is o'er the hills and far awa !

It's no the frosty winter wind,
　　It's no the driving drift and snaw ;
But ay the tear comes in my e'e,
　　To think on him that's far awa.

My father pat me frae his door,
　　My friends they hae disown'd me a' ;
But I hae ane will tak my part,
　　The bonie lad that's far awa.

A pair o' glooves he bought to me,
　　And silken snoods[2] he gae me twa ;
And I will wear them for his sake,
　　The bonie lad that's far awa.

O weary Winter soon will pass,
　　And Spring will cleed[3] the birken shaw ;
And my young babie will be born,
　　And he'll be hame that's far awa.

---

[1] shuffles along, bent double, as best he can.　[2] ribands for the hair.　[3] clothe.

186   *Of a' the Airts[1] the Wind can Blaw*

OF a' the airts the wind can blaw,
    I dearly like the west,
For there the bonie lassie lives,
    The lassie I lo'e best :
There's wild-woods grow, and rivers row[2],
    And mony a hill between :
But day and night my fancy's flight
    Is ever wi' my Jean.

I see her in the dewy flowers,
    I see her sweet and fair :
I hear her in the tunefu' birds,
    I hear her charm the air :
There's not a bonie flower that springs
    By fountain, shaw, or green ;
There's not a bonie bird that sings,
    But minds me o' my Jean.

187   *O were I on Parnassus Hill*

SONG

O WERE I on Parnassus hill,
    Or had o' Helicon my fill,
That I might catch poetic skill,
    To sing how dear I love thee !
But Nith maun be my Muse's well,
My Muse maun be thy bonie sel',
On Corsincon I'll glowr[3] and spell,
    And write how dear I love thee.

          [1] ways.   [2] roll.   [3] gaze.

Then come, sweet Muse, inspire my lay!
For a' the lee-lang simmer's day
I couldna sing, I couldna say,
  How much, how dear, I love thee,
I see thee dancing o'er the green,
Thy waist sae jimp[1], thy limbs sae clean,
Thy tempting lips, thy roguish een—
  By Heaven and Earth I love thee!

By night, by day, a-field, at hame,
The thoughts o' thee my breast inflame;
And ay I muse and sing thy name—
  I only live to love thee.
Tho' I were doom'd to wander on,
Beyond the sea, beyond the sun,
Till my last weary sand was run;
  Till then—and then I love thee!

188 *My Bonie Mary*

GO, fetch to me a pint o' wine,
 And fill it in a silver tassie[2];
That I may drink before I go,
 A service to my bonie lassie.
The boat rocks at the pier o' Leith;
 Fu' loud the wind blaws frae the Ferry,
The ship rides by the Berwick-law,
 And I maun leave my bonie Mary.

The trumpets sound, the banners fly,
 The glittering spears are rankèd ready;
The shouts o' war are heard afar,
 The battle closes deep and bloody;

[1] slim. [2] cup.

It's not the roar o' sea or shore,
  Wad mak me langer wish to tarry ;
Nor shouts o' war that's heard afar—
  It's leaving thee, my bonie Mary !

189   *Young Jockie was the Blythest Lad*

YOUNG Jockie was the blythest lad,
  In a' our town [1] or here awa ;
Fu' blythe he whistled at the gaud [2],
  Fu' lightly danc'd he in the ha' :

He roos'd [3] my een sae bonie blue,
  He roos'd my waist sae genty sma' ;
An' ay my heart cam to my mou,
  When ne'er a body heard or saw.

My Jockie toils upon the plain,
  Thro' wind and weet, thro' frost and snaw;
And o'er the lea I leuk fu' fain,
  When Jockie's owsen hameward ca'.

An' ay the night comes round again,
  When in his arms he taks me a' ;
An' ay he vows he'll be my ain,
  As lang as he hath breath to draw.

190   *Jamie, Come Try Me*

IF thou should ask my love,
    Could I deny thee ?
If thou would win my love,
    Jamie, come try me !

[1] farm.   [2] plough.   [3] praised.

Chor.—Jamie, come try me,
　　Jamie, come try me,
　If thou would win my love,
　　Jamie, come try me.

　If thou should kiss me, love,
　　Wha could espy thee ?
　If thou wad be my love,
　　Jamie, come try me !

191　　　*I Love my Love in Secret*

M Y Sandy gied to me a ring,
　　Was a' beset wi' diamonds fine ;
But I gied him a far better thing,
I gied my heart in pledge o' his ring.

Chor.—My Sandy O, my Sandy O,
　　My bonie, bonie Sandy O ;
　　Tho' the love that I owe
　　To thee I dare na show,
　Yet I love my love in secret, my Sandy O.

My Sandy brak a piece o' gowd,
While down his cheeks the saut tears row'd ;
He took a hauf, and gied it to me,
And I'll keep it till the hour I die.

192　　　*Ay Waukin O*

S IMMER'S a pleasant time,
　　Flowers of ev'ry colour ;
The water rins owre the heugh [1],
　And I long for my true lover !

[1] fall.

Ay waukin O,
  Waukin still and weary :
Sleep I can get nane,
  For thinking on my dearie.

When I sleep I dream,
  When I wauk I'm eerie ;
Sleep I can get nane,
  For thinking on my dearie.
Lanely night comes on,
  A' the lave [1] are sleepin' :
I think on my bonie lad,
  And I bleer my een wi' greetin' [2].

193   *Laddie, Lie Near Me*

LANG hae we parted been,
    Laddie, my dearie ;
Now we are met again,
  Laddie, lie near me.
    Near me, near me,
      Laddie, lie near me ;
    Lang hae I lain my lane [3],
      Laddie, lie near me.

A' that I hae endured,
  Laddie, my dearie,
Here in thy arms is cured,—
  Laddie, lie near me.

194   *John Anderson, my Jo*

JOHN ANDERSON, my jo, John,
    When we were first acquent ,
  Your locks were like the raven,
  Your bonnie brow was brent [4] ;

[1] all the rest.   [2] weeping.   [3] alone.   [4] smooth.

But now your brow is beld, John,
  Your locks are like the snaw ;
But blessings on your frosty pow [1],
  John Anderson, my jo.

John Anderson, my jo, John,
  We clamb the hill thegither ;
And mony a cantie [2] day, John,
  We've had wi' ane anither :
Now we maun totter down, John,
  And hand in hand we'll go,
And sleep thegither at the foot,
  John Anderson, my jo.

195   *My Love, She's But a Lassie Yet*

MY love, she's but a lassie yet,
  My love, she's but a lassie yet ;
We'll let her stand a year or twa,
  She'll no be hauf sae saucy yet :
I rue the day I sought her O !
I rue the day I sought her O !
Wha gets her need na say he's woo'd,
  But he may say he has bought her O.

Come draw a drap o' the best o't yet,
  Come draw a drap o' the best o't yet ;
Gae seek for pleasure whare ye will,
  But here I never miss'd it yet :
We're a' dry wi' drinkin o't,
We're a' dry wi' drinkin o't ;
The minister kiss't the fiddler's wife ;
  He could na preach for thinkin o't.

[1] head.   [2] merry.

196 *Tam Glen*

SONG

M Y heart is a breaking, dear Tittie [1],
  Some counsel unto me come len',
To anger them a' is a pity,
  But what will I do wi' Tam Glen?

I'm thinking, wi' sic a braw fellow,
  In poortith I might mak a fen' [2];
What care I in riches to wallow,
  If I mauna marry Tam Glen!

There's Lowrie the laird o' Dumeller—
  "Gude day to you"—brute! he comes ben:
He brags and he blaws o' his siller,
  But when will he dance like Tam Glen!

My Minnie does constantly deave [3] me,
  And bids me beware o' young men;
They flatter, she says, to deceive me,
  But wha can think sae o' Tam Glen!

My daddie says, gin I'll forsake him,
  He'd gie me gude hunder marks ten;
But, if its ordain'd I maun take him,
  O wha will I get but Tam Glen!

Yestreen at the Valentine's dealing,
  My heart to my mou gied a sten [4];
For thrice I drew ane without failing,
  And thrice it was written "Tam Glen"!

[1] sister.   [2] shift.   [3] deafen, overwhelm (with admonitions).
[4] jump.

The last Halloween I was waukin [1]
　　My droukit sark-sleeve [2], as ye ken,
His likeness came up the house staukin,
　　And the very grey breeks o' Tam Glen!

Come, counsel, dear Tittie, don't tarry;
　　I'll gie ye my bonie black hen,
Gif ye will advise me to marry
　　The lad I lo'e dearly, Tam Glen.

197　　　　　*The Laddie's Dear Sel'*

THERE'S a youth in this city, it were a great pity
　　That he from our lasses should wander awa';
For he's bonie and braw, weel-favor'd witha',
　　An' his hair has a natural buckle [3] an' a'.

His coat is the hue o' his bonnet sae blue,
　　His fecket [4] is white as the new-driven snaw;
His hose they are blae [5], and his shoon like the slae,
　　And his clear siller buckles, they dazzle us a'.

For beauty and fortune the laddie's been courtin;
　　Weel-featur'd, weel-tocher'd [6], weel-mounted an'
　　　　braw;
But chiefly the siller that gars him gang till her,
　　The penny's the jewel that beautifies a'.

There's Meg wi' the mailen [7] that fain wad a haen
　　　　him,
　　And Susie, wha's daddie was laird o' the Ha';
There's lang-tocher'd Nancy maist fetters his fancy,
　　But the laddie's dear sel', he lo'es dearest of a'.

---

[1] watching.　　[2] wet shirt-sleeve.　　[3] curl.　　[4] an under-vest.
[5] purple.　[6] dowered.　[7] farm.

198   *Whistle o'er the Lave o't*

FIRST when Maggie was my care,
    Heav'n, I thought, was in her air,
Now we're married—speir [1] nae mair,
    But whistle o'er the lave [2] o't !
Meg was meek, and Meg was mild,
Sweet and harmless as a child—
Wiser men than me's beguil'd ;
    Whistle o'er the lave o't !

How we live, my Meg and me,
How we love, and how we gree,
I care na by how few may see—
    Whistle o'er the lave o't !
Wha I wish were maggot's meat,
Dish'd up in her winding-sheet,
I could write—but Meg may see't—
    Whistle o'er the lave o't !

199   *I Gaed a Waefu' Gate Yestreen*

I GAED a waefu' gate yestreen,
    A gate I fear I'll dearly rue ;
I gat my death frae twa sweet een,
    Twa lovely een o' bonie blue.
'Twas not her golden ringlets bright,
    Her lips, like roses wat wi' dew,
Her heaving bosom, lily-white—
    It was her een sae bonie blue.

She talk'd, she smil'd, my heart she wyl'd ;
    She charm'd my soul I wist na how ;
And ay the stound [3], the deadly wound,
    Cam frae her een sae bonie blue.

        [1] ask.   [2] rest.   [3] pain.

But "spare to speak, and spare to speed;"
    She'll aiblins[1] listen to my vow:
Should she refuse, I'll lay my dead
    To her twa een sae bonie blue.

200   *To Mary in Heaven*

THOU ling'ring star, with less'ning ray,
    That lov'st to greet the early morn,
Again thou usher'st in the day
    My Mary from my soul was torn.
O Mary! dear departed shade!
    Where is thy place of blissful rest?
See'st thou thy lover lowly laid?
    Hear'st thou the groans that rend his breast?

That sacred hour can I forget,
    Can I forget the hallow'd grove,
Where, by the winding Ayr, we met,
    To live one day of parting love!
Eternity can not efface
    Those records dear of transports past,
Thy image at our last embrace,
    Ah! little thought we 'twas our last!

Ayr, gurgling, kiss'd his pebbled shore,
    O'erhung with wild-woods, thickening green,
The fragrant birch and hawthorn hoar
    'Twin'd amorous round the raptur'd scene:
The flowers sprang wanton to be prest,
    The birds sang love on every spray;
Till, too, too soon, the glowing west,
    Proclaim'd the speed of wingèd day.

[1] maybe.

Still o'er these scenes my mem'ry wakes,
   And fondly broods with miser-care;
Time but th' impression stronger makes,
   As streams their channels deeper wear.
My Mary! dear departed shade!
   Where is thy place of blissful rest?
See'st thou thy lover lowly laid?
   Hear'st thou the groans that rend his breast?

201   *Out over the Forth*

SONG

OUT over the Forth, I look to the north;
   But what is the north and its Highlands to me?
The south nor the east gie ease to my breast,
   The far foreign land, or the wide rolling sea.

But I look to the west when I gae to rest,
   That happy my dreams and my slumbers may be;
For far in the west lives he I loe best,
   The man that is dear to my babie and me.

202   *The Banks o' Doon*

YE banks and braes o' bonie Doon,
   How can ye bloom sae fresh and fair?
How can ye chant, ye little birds,
   And I sae weary fu' o' care!
Thou'll break my heart, thou warbling bird,
   That wantons thro' the flowering thorn:
Thou minds me o' departed joys,
    Departed never to return.

Aft hae I rov'd by bonie Doon,
　　To see the rose and woodbine twine ;
And ilka bird sang o' its Luve,
　　Ane fondly sae did I o' mine ;
Wi' lightsome heart I pu'd a rose,
　　Fu' sweet upon its thorny tree !
And my fause Luver staw my rose,
　　But ah ! he left the thorn wi' me.

203　*What can a Young Lassie do wi' an
Auld Man*

WHAT can a young lassie, what shall a young
　　　lassie,
　　What can a young lassie do wi' an auld man ?
Bad luck on the penny that tempted my minnie
　　To sell her puir Jenny for siller an' lan' !

He's always compleenin frae mornin to eenin,
　　He hoasts[1] and he hirples[2] the weary day lang ;
He's doylt[3] and he's dozin[4], his blude it is frozen,—
　　O dreary's the night wi' a crazy auld man !

He hums and he hankers, he frets and he cankers,
　　I never can please him do a' that I can ;
He's peevish and jealous o' a' the young fellows,—
　　O dool[5] on the day I met wi' an auld man !

My auld auntie Katie upon me taks pity,
　　I'll do my endeavour to follow her plan ;
I'll cross him an' wrack him, until I heartbreak him,
　　And then his auld brass 'ill buy me a new pan.

　　　[1] coughs.　[2] halts.　[3] confused.　[4] stupid.　[5] woe.

204   *O for Ane an' Twenty, Tam*

THEY snool[1] me sair, and haud[2] me down,
    An' gar[3] me look like bluntie[4], Tam ;
But three short years will soon wheel roun',
    An' then comes ane an' twenty, Tam.

Chor.—An' O for ane an' twenty, Tam !
       And hey, sweet ane an' twenty, Tam
       I'll learn my kin a rattlin sang,
       An' I saw ane an' twenty, Tam.

A glieb[5] o' lan', a claut[6] o' gear,
    Was left me by my Auntie, Tam ;
At kith or kin I need na spier[7],
    An' I saw ane an' twenty, Tam.

They'll hae me wed a wealthy coof[8],
    Tho' I mysel' hae plenty, Tam ;
But, hear'st thou, laddie ! there's my loof[9],
    I'm thine at ane an' twenty, Tam.

205   *Sweet Afton*

FLOW gently, sweet Afton ! among thy green
      braes,
Flow gently, I'll sing thee a song in thy praise ;
My Mary's asleep by thy murmuring stream,
Flow gently, sweet Afton, disturb not her dream.

Thou stock dove whose echo resounds thro' the glen,
Ye wild whistling blackbirds, in yon thorny den,
Thou green crested lapwing thy screaming forbear,
I charge you, disturb not my slumbering Fair.

[1] snub.   [2] hold.   [3] make.   [4] a cowed person.   [5] a portion.
[6] hoard.   [7] consult.   [8] blockhead.   [9] palm of the hand.

How lofty, sweet Afton, thy neighbouring hills,
Far mark'd with the courses of clear winding rills;
There daily I wander as noon rises high,
My flocks and my Mary's sweet cot in my eye.

How pleasant thy banks and green vallies below,
Where, wild in the woodlands, the primroses blow;
There oft, as mild Ev'ning weeps over the lea,
The sweet-scented birk shades my Mary and me.

Thy crystal stream, Afton, how lovely it glides,
And winds by the cot where my Mary resides;
How wanton thy waters her snowy feet lave,
As, gathering sweet flowerets, she stems thy clear
    wave.

Flow gently, sweet Afton, amang thy green braes,
Flow gently, sweet river, the theme of my lays;
My Mary's asleep by thy murmuring stream,
Flow gently, sweet Afton, disturb not her dream.

206   *The Dearest o' the Quorum*

O MAY, thy morn was ne'er sae sweet
        As the mirk night o' December!
For sparkling was the rosy wine,
    And private was the chamber:
And dear was she I dare na name,
    But I will ay remember:
And dear was she I dare na name,
    But I will ay remember.

And here's to them that, like oursel,
    Can push about the jorum!
And here's to them that wish us weel,
    May a' that's gude watch o'er 'em!

And here's to them we dare na tell,
  The dearest o' the quorum!
And here's to them we dare na tell,
  The dearest o' the quorum!

207 *Parting Song to Clarinda*

AE fond kiss, and then we sever;
  Ae farewell, and then forever!
Deep in heart-wrung tears I'll pledge thee,
Warring sighs and groans I'll wage thee.
Who shall say that Fortune grieves him,
While the star of hope she leaves him?
Me, nae cheerful twinkle lights me;
Dark despair around benights me.

I'll ne'er blame my partial fancy,
Naething could resist my Nancy;
But to see her was to love her;
Love but her, and her for ever.
Had we never lov'd sae kindly,
Had we never lov'd sae blindly,
Never met—or never parted,
We had ne'er been broken-hearted.

Fare-thee-weel, thou first and fairest!
Fare-thee-weel, thou best and dearest!
Thine be ilka joy and treasure,
Peace, Enjoyment, Love and Pleasure!
Ae fond kiss, and then we sever!
Ae farewell, alas, for ever!
Deep in heart-wrung tears I'll pledge thee,
Warring sighs and groans I'll wage thee.

208   *The Country Lass*

IN simmer, when the hay was mawn,
   And corn waved green in ilka field,
While claver [1] blooms white o'er the lea
   And roses blaw in ilka bield [2],
Blythe Bessie in the milking shiel [3],
   Says—I'll be wed, come o't what will:
Out spake a dame in wrinkled eild [4]—
   O' gude advisement comes nae ill.

It's ye hae wooers mony ane,
   And lassie, ye're but young ye ken;
Then wait a wee, and cannie wale [5]
   A routhie butt, a routhie ben [6];
There's Johnie o' the Buskie-glen,
   Fu' is his barn, fu' is his byre;
Tak this frae me, my bonie hen,
   It's plenty beets [7] the luver's fire.

For Johnie o' the Buskie-glen,
   I dinna care a single flie;
He lo'es sae weel his craps and kye,
   He has nae love to spare for me;
But blythe's the blink o' Robie's e'e,
   And weel I wat he lo'es me dear:
Ae blink o' him I wad na gie
   For Buskie-glen and a' his gear.

O thoughtless lassie, life's a faught;
   The canniest gate, the strife is sair;
By ay fu'-han't is fechtin best [8],
   A hungry care's an unco care:

[1] clover.   [2] sheltered spot.   [3] shed.   [4] age.   [5] choose.   [6] a house well provided both outside and in.   [7] sustains.   [8] he fights best who fights full-handed.

But some will spend and some will spare,
  An' wilfu' folk maun hae their will ;
Syne as ye brew, my maiden fair,
  Keep mind that ye maun drink the yill [1].

O gear will buy me rigs o' land,
  And gear will buy me sheep and kye ;
But the tender heart o' leesome [2] loove,
  The gowd and siller canna buy ;
We may be poor—Robie and I—
  Light is the burden luve lays on ;
Content and loove brings peace and joy—
  What mair hae Queens upon a throne ?

209   *Bonie Lesley*

O SAW ye bonie Lesley,
    As she gaed o'er the Border ?
She's gane, like Alexander,
    To spread her conquests farther.

To see her is to love her,
  And love but her for ever ;
For Nature made her what she is,
  And never made anither !

Thou art a queen, fair Lesley,
  Thy subjects, we before thee ;
Thou art divine, fair Lesley,
  The hearts o' men adore thee.

        [1] ale. [2] pleasant.

The deil he could na scaith thee,
  Or aught that wad belang thee;
He'd look into thy bonie face,
  And say—"I canna wrang thee!"

The Powers aboon will tent[1] thee,
  Misfortune sha'na steer[2] thee;
Thou'rt like themsel' sae lovely,
  That ill they'll ne'er let near thee.

Return again, fair Lesley,
  Return to Caledonie!
That we may brag we hae a lass
  There's nane again sae bonie.

210   *I'll meet Thee on the Lea-rig*[3]

WHEN o'er the hill the e'ening star
  Tells bughtin[4] time is near, my jo,
And owsen[5] frae the furrow'd field
  Return sae dowf[6] and weary O;
Down by the burn, where birken buds
  Wi' dew are hangin' clear, my jo,
I'll meet thee on the lea-rig,
  My ain kind Dearie O.

At midnight hour, in mirkest glen,
  I'd rove, and ne'er be eerie O,
If thro' that glen I gaed to thee,
  My ain kind Dearie O;
Altho' the night were ne'er sae wild,
  And I were ne'er sae weary O,
I'll meet thee on the lea-rig,
  My ain kind Dearie O.

[1] watch over.   [2] injure.   [3] pasture ground.   [4] folding.   [5] oxen.
[6] dull.

The hunter lo'es the morning sun,
  To rouse the mountain deer, my jo :
At noon the fisher takes the glen
  Adown the burn to steer, my jo :
Gie me the hour o' gloamin grey,
  It maks my heart sae cheery O,
To meet thee on the lea-rig,
  My ain kind Dearie O.

211   *My Wife's a Winsome Wee Thing*

I NEVER saw a fairer,
  I never lo'ed a dearer,
And neist [1] my heart I'll wear her,
  For fear my jewel tine [2].

Chor.—She is a winsome wee thing,
    She is a handsome wee thing,
    She is a lo'esome wee thing,
      This dear wee wife o' mine.

The warld's wrack we share o't ;
The warstle [3] and the care o't,
Wi' her I'll blythely bear it,
  And think my lot divine.

212   *Highland Mary*

YE banks and braes and streams around
    The castle o' Montgomery !
Green be your woods, and fair your flowers,
  Your waters never drumlie [4] :

[1] next. [2] be lost. [3] struggle. [4] troubled.

There Simmer first unfald her robes,
  And there the langest tarry ;
For there I took the last Fareweel
  O' my sweet Highland Mary.

How sweetly bloom'd the gay, green birk,
  How rich the hawthorn's blossom,
As underneath their fragrant shade,
  I clasp'd her to my bosom !
The golden Hours on angel wings,
  Flew o'er me and my Dearie ;
For dear to me, as light and life,
  Was my sweet Highland Mary.

Wi' mony a vow, and lock'd embrace,
  Our parting was fu' tender ;
And, pledging aft to meet again,
  We tore oursels asunder ;
But oh ! fell Death's untimely frost,
  That nipt my Flower sae early !
Now green's the sod, and cauld's the clay,
  That wraps my Highland Mary !

O pale, pale now, those rosy lips,
  I aft hae kiss'd sae fondly !
And clos'd for ay the sparkling glance,
  That dwalt on me sae kindly !
And mouldering now in silent dust,
  That heart that lo'ed me dearly !
But still within my bosom's core
  Shall live my Highland Mary.

213   *Duncan Gray*

DUNCAN GRAY cam' here to woo,
    Ha, ha, the wooing o't,
On blythe Yule-night when we were fou [1],
    Ha, ha, the wooing o't.
Maggie coost [2] her head fu' high,
Look'd asklent [3] and unco skeigh [4],
Gart poor Duncan stand abeigh [5] ;
    Ha, ha, the wooing o't.

Duncan fleech'd [6] and Duncan pray'd ;
    Ha, ha, the wooing o't ;
Meg was deaf as Ailsa craig,
    Ha, ha, the wooing o't :
Duncan sigh'd baith out and in,
Grat [7] his e'en baith bleer't [8] an' blin',
Spak o' lowpin' o'er a linn [9] ;
    Ha, ha, the wooing o't.

Time and Chance are but a tide,
    Ha, ha, the wooing o't :
Slighted love is sair to bide,
    Ha, ha, the wooing o't :
Shall I like a fool quoth he,
For a haughty hizzie [10] die ?
She may gae to—France for me !
    Ha, ha, the wooing o't.

How it comes, let doctor's tell,
    Ha, ha, the wooing o't ;
Meg grew sick, as he grew hale,
    Ha, ha, the wooing o't :

---

[1] tipsy.   [2] cast.   [3] sideways.   [4] proud.   [5] aside.   [6] flattered.
[7] cried.   [8] red and inflamed.   [9] waterfall.   [10] jade.

Something in her bosom wrings,
For relief a sigh she brings :
And ho ! her een they spak sic things !
 Ha, ha, the wooing o't.

Duncan was a lad o' grace,
 Ha, ha, the wooing o't ;
Maggie's was a piteous case,
 Ha, ha, the wooing o't :
Duncan could na be her death,
Swelling pity smoor'd[1] his wrath ;
Now they're crouse[2] and canty[3] baith,
 Ha, ha, the wooing o't.

214 *O Poortith Cauld*

O POORTITH[4] cauld, and restless love,
 Ye wrack my peace between ye ;
Yet poortith a' I could forgive,
 An' twere na for my Jeanie.

Chor.—O why should Fate sic pleasure have,
 Life's dearest bands untwining ?
 Or why sae sweet a flower as love
 Depend on Fortune's shining ?

The warld's wealth, when I think on,
 It's pride and a' the lave o't[5] ;
O fie on silly coward man,
 That he should be the slave o't !

Her e'en, sae bonie blue, betray
 How she repays my passion ;
But prudence is her o'erword[6] ay,
 She talks o' rank and fashion.

---

[1] quenched. [2] brisk. [3] merry. [4] poverty. [5] rest of it. [6] the burden of her talk.

O wha can prudence think upon,
  And sic a lassie by him?
O wha can prudence think upon,
  And sae in love as I am?

How blest the simple cotter's fate!
  He woo's his artless dearie;
The silly bogles[1], wealth and state,
  Can never make him eerie.

215   *Galla Water*

BRAW, braw lads on Yarrow-braes,
  They rove amang the blooming heather;
But Yarrow braes, nor Ettrick shaws
  Can match the lads o' Galla Water.

But there is ane, a secret ane,
  Aboon them a' I loe him better;
And I'll be his, and he'll be mine,
  The bonie lad o' Galla Water.

Altho' his daddie was nae laird,
  And tho' I hae na meikle tocher[2],
Yet rich in kindest, truest love,
  We'll tent[3] our flocks by Galla Water.

It ne'er was wealth, it ne'er was wealth,
  That coft[4] contentment, peace, or pleasure:
The bands and bliss o' mutual love,
  O that's the chiefest warld's treasure.

  [1] bugbears. [2] dower. [3] watch. [4] purchased.

216　*Open the Door to Me, Oh*

OH, open the door, some pity to show,
　　Oh, open the door to me, oh,
Tho' thou hast been false, I'll ever prove true,
　　Oh, open the door to me, oh.

Cauld is the blast upon my pale cheek,
　　But caulder thy love for me, oh :
The frost that freezes the life at my heart
　　Is nought to my pains frae thee, oh.

The wan Moon is setting behind the white wave,
　　And Time is setting with me, oh :
False friends, false love, farewell ! for mair
　　I'll ne'er trouble them, nor thee, oh.

She has open'd the door, she has open'd it wide,
　　She sees the pale corse on the plain, oh :
" My true love ! " she cried, and sank down by his
　　　side,
　　Never to rise again, oh.

217　*Meg o' the Mill*

O KEN ye what Meg o' the Mill has gotten,
　　An' ken ye what Meg o' the Mill has gotten ?
She's gotten a coof[1] wi' a claute[2] o' siller,
And broken the heart o' the barley Miller.

The Miller was strappin, the Miller was ruddy ;
A heart like a lord, and a hue like a lady ;
The laird was a widdifu'[3], bleerit knurl[4] ;
She's left the gude fellow, and taen the churl.

[1] blockhead.　[2] hoard.　[3] twisted.　[4] dwarf.

The Miller he hecht¹ her a heart leal and loving,
The laird did address her wi' matter mair moving,
A fine pacing horse wi' a clear chained bridle,
A whip by her side, and a bonie side-saddle.

O wae on the siller, it is sae prevailin',
And wae on the love that is fixed on a mailen²!
A tocher's nae word in a true lover's parl,
But gie me my love, and a fig for the warl!

218   *O were my Love yon Lilac Fair*

O WERE my love yon Lilac fair,
    Wi' purple blossoms to the Spring,
And I, a bird to shelter there,
    When wearied on my little wing!
How I wad mourn when it was torn
    By Autumn wild, and Winter rude!
But I wad sing on wanton wing,
    When youthfu' May its bloom renew'd.

O gin my love were yon red rose,
    That grows upon the castle wa';
And I mysel a drap o' dew,
    Into her bonie breast to fa'!
O there, beyond expression blest,
    I'd feast on beauty a' the night;
Seal'd on her silk-saft faulds to rest,
    Till fley'd³ awa by Phœbus' light!

---

¹ promised.   ² farm.   ³ frighted.

219   *Whistle an' I'll come to You, my Lad*

Chor.—O whistle an' I'll come to ye, my lad,
        O whistle an' I'll come to ye, my lad,
        Tho' father an' mother an' a' should gae mad,
        O whistle an' I'll come to ye, my lad.

BUT warily tent[1] when ye come to court me,
    And come nae unless the back-yett be a-jee[2];
Syne up the back-style[3], and let naebody see,
And come as ye were na comin to me.

At kirk, or at market, whene'er ye meet me,
Gang by me as tho' that ye car'd na' a flie;
But steal me a blink o' your bonie black e'e,
Yet look as ye were na lookin to me.

Ay vow and protest that ye care na for me,
And whyles ye may lightly[4] my beauty a wee;
But court na anither tho' jokin ye be,
For fear that she wyle your fancy frae me.

220   *Dainty Davie*

NOW rosy May comes in wi' flowers,
    To deck her gay, green-spreading bowers;
And now comes in the happy hours,
    To wander wi' my Davie.

Chor.—Meet me on the warlock knowe[5],
        Dainty Davie, Dainty Davie;
        There I'll spend the day wi' you,
        My ain dear Dainty Davie.

    [1] take heed.   [2] ajar.   [3] back approach.   [4] disparage.
    [5] wizard's knoll.

The crystal waters round us fa',
The merrie birds are lovers a',
The scented breezes round us blaw,
    A wandering wi' my Davie.

As purple morning starts the hare,
To steal upon her early fare,
Then thro' the dews I will repair,
    To meet my faithfu' Davie.

When day, expiring in the west,
The curtain draws o' Nature's rest,
I'll flee to his arms I loe the best,
    And that's my ain dear Davie.

221   *A Red, Red Rose*

MY Luve is like a red, red rose,
    That's newly sprung in June:
My Luve is like the melodie,
    That's sweetly play'd in tune.

As fair art thou, my bonie lass,
    So deep in luve am I;
And I will luve thee still, my Dear,
    Till a' the seas gang dry.

Till a' the seas gang dry, my Dear,
    And the rock melt wi' the sun;
And I will luve thee still, my Dear,
    While the sands o' life shall run.

And fare-thee-well, my only Luve !
And fare-thee-well, a while !
And I will come again, my Luve,
Tho' 'twere ten thousand mile !

222   *It was a' for our Rightfu' King*

IT was a' for our rightfu' King
    We left fair Scotland's strand ;
It was a' for our rightfu' King
    We e'er saw Irish land, my dear,
    We e'er saw Irish land.

Now a' is done that men can do,
    And a' is done in vain ;
My Love and Native Land fareweel,
    For I maun cross the main, my dear,
    For I maun cross the main.

He turn'd him right and round about,
    Upon the Irish shore !
And gae his bridle reins a shake,
    With adieu for evermore, my dear,
    And adieu for evermore.

The soger frae the wars returns,
    The sailor frae the main ;
But I hae parted frae my love,
    Never to meet again, my dear,
    Never to meet again.

When day is gane, and night is come,
  And a' folk bound to sleep;
I think on him that's far awa,
  The lee-lang [1] night and weep, my dear,
  The lee-lang night and weep.

223   *Ca' [2] the Yowes [3] to the Knowes [4]*

HARK the mavis' [5] e'ening sang,
    Sounding Clouden's wood's amang;
Then a-faulding let us gang,
    My bonie Dearie.

Chor.—Ca' the yowes to the knowes,
        Ca' them where the heather grows,
        Ca' them where the burnie rowes [6],
            My bonie Dearie.

We'll gae down by Clouden side,
Thro' the hazels, spreading wide
O'er the waves that sweetly glide
    To the moon sae clearly.

Yonder Clouden's silent towers,
Where, at moonshine's midnight hours,
O'er the dewy bending flowers,
    Fairies dance sae cheery.

Ghaist nor bogle shalt thou fear,
Thou'rt to Love and Heav'n sae dear
Nocht of ill may come thee near,
    My bonie Dearie.

[1] live-long.   [2] drive.   [3] ewes.   [4] green hillocks.   [5] thrush.
[6] flows.

Fair and lovely as thou art,
Thou hast stown[1] my very heart ;
I can die—but canna part,
    My bonie Dearie.

224   *Lassie wi' the Lint-white[2] Locks*

NOW Nature cleeds[3] the flowery lea,
    And a' is young and sweet like thee,
O wilt thou share it's joys wi' me,
    And say thou'lt be my Dearie, O.

Chor.—Lassie wi' the lint-white locks,
        Bonie lassie, artless lassie,
    Wilt thou wi' me tend the flocks,
        Wilt thou be my Dearie, O.

The primrose bank, the wimpling[4] burn,
The cuckoo on the milk-white thorn,
The wanton lambs at early morn,
    Shall welcome thee, my Dearie, O.

And when the welcome simmer shower
Has cheer'd ilk drooping little flower,
We'll to the breathing woodbine-bower,
    At sultry noon, my Dearie, O.

When Cynthia lights wi' silvery ray,
The weary shearer's[5] hameward way,
Thro' yellow waving fields we'll stray,
    And talk o' love, my Dearie, O.

---

[1] stolen.   [2] flaxen.   [3] clothes.   [4] softly flowing.   [5] reaper.

And when the howling wintry blast
Disturbs my Lassie's midnight rest,
Enclaspèd to my faithfu' breast,
   I'll comfort thee, my Dearie, O.

225   *My Nanie's Awa*

NOW in her green mantle blythe Nature arrays,
   And listens the lambkins that bleat o'er her
   braes,
While birds warble welcomes in ilka green shaw [1];
But to me it's delightless—my Nanie's awa.

The snawdrap and primrose our woodlands adorn,
And violets bathe in the weet o' the morn;
They pain my sad bosom, sae sweetly they
   blaw,
They mind me o' Nanie,—and Nanie's awa.

Thou lav'rock that springs frae the dews of the
   lawn,
The shepherd to warn o' the grey-breaking
   dawn,
And thou mellow mavis that hails the night-fa',
Give over for pity—my Nanie's awa.

Come Autumn, sae pensive, in yellow and grey,
And soothe me wi' tidings o' Nature's decay:
The dark, dreary Winter, and wild-driving snaw
Alane can delight me—now Nanie's awa.

[1] grove.

226   *For the Sake o' Somebody*

MY heart is sair—I dare na tell,
    My heart is sair for Somebody;
I could wake a winter night
    For the sake o' Somebody.
        O-hon! for Somebody!
        O-hey! for Somebody!
I could range the warld around,
    For the sake o' Somebody.

Ye Powers that smile on virtuous love,
    O, sweetly smile on Somebody!
Frae ilka danger keep him free,
    And send me safe my Somebody!
        O-hon! for Somebody!
        O-hey! for Somebody!
I wad do—what wad I not?
    For the sake o' Somebody.

227   *The Lass o' Ecclefechan*

GAT ye me, O gat ye me,
    O gat ye me wi' naething?
Rock[1] an reel, and spinning wheel,
    A mickle quarter bason:
Bye attour[2], my Gutcher[3] has
    A heich house and a laich ane,
A' for bye my bonie sel,
    The toss[4] o' Ecclefechan.

[1] distaff. [2] more than that. [3] grandsire. [4] toast.

O haud your tongue now, Lucky Lang,
  O haud your tongue and jauner [1];
I held the gate [2] till you I met,
  Syne I began to wander:
I tint my whistle and my sang,
  I tint my peace and pleasure;
But your green graff [3], now Lucky Lang,
  Wad airt [4] me to my treasure.

228   *O Let Me in this Ae Night*

O LASSIE, are ye sleepin yet,
  Or are ye waukin, I wad wit?
For Love has bound me hand an' fit,
  And I would fain be in, jo.

    Chor.—O let me in this ae night,
      This ae, ae, ae night;
      O let me in this ae night,
      I'll no come back again, jo!

O hearst thou not the wind an' weet?
Nae star blinks thro' the driving sleet;
Tak pity on my weary feet,
  And shield me frae the rain, jo.

The bitter blast that round me blaws,
Unheeded howls, unheeded fa's;
The cauldness o' thy heart's the cause
  Of a' my care and pine, jo.

[1] idle talk. [2] kept the straight road. [3] grave. [4] guide.

229   *Her Answer*

O TELL me na o' wind an' rain,
    Upbraid na me wi' cauld disdain,
Gae back the gate ye cam again,
    I winna let ye in, jo.

    Chor.—I tell you now this ae night,
       This ae, ae, ae night,
       And ance for a' this ae night,
       I winna let ye in, jo.

The snellest [1] blast, at mirkest hours,
That round the pathless wand'rer pours
Is nocht to what poor she endures,
    That's trusted faithless man, jo.

The sweetest flower that deck'd the mead,
Now trodden like the vilest weed—
Let simple maid the lesson read
    The weird [2] may be her ain, jo.

The bird that charm'd his summer day
Is now the cruel Fowler's prey ;
Let witless, trusting, Woman say
    How aft her fate's the same, jo !

230   *I'll ay ca' in by Yon Town*

THERE'S nane shall ken, there's nane can guess
    What brings me back the gate again,
But she, my fairest faithfu' lass,
    And stow'nlins [3] we sall meet again.

         [1] keenest.   [2] fate.   [3] by stealth.

Chor.—I'll ay ca' in by yon town [1],
    And by yon garden-green again ;
    I'll ay ca' in by yon town,
    And see my bonie Jean again.

She'll wander by the aiken tree,
    When trystin time draws near again ;
And when her lovely form I see,
    O haith ! she's doubly dear again.

231   *The Cardin o't, the Spinnin o't*

I COFT a stane o' haslock woo [2],
    To mak a wab [3] to Johnie, o't ;
For Johnie is my only jo,
    I loe him best of onie yet.

    Chor.—The cardin o't, the spinnin o't,
        The warpin o't, the winnin o't ;
        When ilka ell cost me a groat,
        The tailor staw the lynin o't.

For tho' his locks be lyart grey [4],
    And tho' his brow he beld [5] abune,
Yet I hae seen him on a day
    The pride of a' the parishen.

232   *The Braw Wooer*

LAST May, a braw wooer cam doun the lang glen,
    And sair wi' his love he did deave [6] me ;
I said, there was naething I hated like men—
    The deuce gae wi'm, to believe me, believe me ;
    The deuce gae wi'm to believe me.

[1] house, hamlet, or steading.   [2] soft wool from the throat of the
sheep.   [3] web.   [4] grizzled.   [5] bald.   [6] pester.

He spak o' the darts in my bonie black e'en,
  And vow'd for my love he was diein,
I said, he might die when he liket for Jean —
  The Lord forgie me for liein, for liein ;
  The Lord forgie me for liein !

A weel-stocket mailen [1], himsel for the laird,
  And marriage off-hand, were his proffers ;
I never loot on [2] that I kenn'd it, or car'd ;
  But thought I might hae waur offers, waur offers ;
  But thought I might hae waur offers.

But what wad ye think ?—in a fortnight or less—
  The deil tak his taste to gae near her !
He up the *Gate-slack* to my black cousin, Bess—
  Guess ye how, the jad ! I could bear her, could
    bear her ;
  Guess ye how, the jad ! I could bear her.

But a' the niest week, as I petted [3] wi' care,
  I gaed to the tryste o' Dalgarnock ;
And wha but my fine fickle wooer was there,
  I glowr'd as I'd seen a warlock, a warlock,
  I glowr'd as I'd seen a warlock.

But owre my left shouther I gae him a blink,
  Lest neibours might say I was saucy ;
My wooer he caper'd as he'd been in drink,
  And vow'd I was his dear lassie, dear lassie,
  And vow'd I was his dear lassie.

---

[1] a well-stocked farm.   [2] allowed it to be suspected.   [3] fretted.

I spier'd[1] for my cousin fu' couthy[2] and sweet,
  Gin she had recover'd her hearin,
And how her new shoon fit her auld shachl't[3] feet,
  But heavens ! how he fell a swearin, a swearin,
  But heavens ! how he fell a swearin.

He beggèd, for gudesake, I wad be his wife,
  Or else I wad kill him wi' sorrow ;
So e'en to preserve the poor body in life,
  I think I maun wed him to-morrow, to-morrow ;
  I think I maun wed him to-morrow.

233   *This is no my ain Lassie*

I SEE a form, I see a face,
  Ye weel may wi' the fairest place ;
It wants, to me, the witching grace,
  The kind love that's in her e'e.

   Chor.—This is no my ain lassie,
      Fair tho' the lassie be ;
      Weel ken I my ain lassie,
      Kind love is in her e'e.

She's bonie, blooming, straight, and tall,
And lang has had my heart in thrall ;
And ay it charms my very saul,
  The kind love that's in her e'e.

A thief sae pawkie[4] is my Jean,
To steal a blink, by a' unseen ;
But gleg[5] as light are lover's een,
  When kind love is in the e'e.

  [1] inquired. [2] kindly. [3] twisted. [4] sly. [5] quick.

It may escape the courtly sparks,
It may escape the learnèd clerks ;
But well the watching lover marks
The kind love that's in her e'e.

234   *A Lass wi' a Tocher* [1]

AWA wi' your witchcraft o' Beauty's alarms,
     The slender bit Beauty you grasp in your arms
O, gie me the lass that has acres o' charms,
O, gie me the lass wi' the weel-stockit farms.

  Chor.—Then hey, for a lass wi' a tocher,
      Then hey, for a lass wi' a tocher,
      Then hey, for a lass wi' a tocher ;
        Then nice yellow guineas for me.

Your Beauty's a flower, in the morning that blows,
And withers the faster, the faster it grows :
But the rapturous charm o' the bonie green knowes,
Ilk spring they're new deckit wi' bonie white yowes.

And e'en when this Beauty your bosom hath blest,
The brightest o' Beauty may cloy when possess'd ;
But the sweet yellow darlings wi' Geordie impress'd,
The langer ye hae them, the mair they're carest.

235   *O wert Thou in the Cauld Blast*

OWERT thou in the cauld blast,
     On yonder lea, on yonder lea,
My plaidie to the angry airt [2],
     I'd shelter thee, I'd shelter thee ;

            [1] a marriage-portion.   [2] quarter.

Or did Misfortune's bitter storms
  Around thee blaw, around the blaw,
Thy bield [1] should be my bosom,
  To share it a', to share it a'.

Or were I in the wildest waste,
  Sae black and bare, sae black and bare,
The desert were a Paradise,
  If thou wert there, if thou wert there ;
Or were I Monarch o' the globe,
  Wi' thee to reign, wi' thee to reign,
The brightest jewel in my crown
  Wad be my Queen, wad be my Queen.

[1] refuge.

LADY NAIRNE, *born* CAROLINA OLIPHANT

1766–1845

236   *The Land o' the Leal*

I'M wearin' awa', John,
    Like snaw-wreaths in thaw, John—
I'm wearin' awa'
    To the land o' the leal.
There is nae sorrow there, John ;
There's neither cauld nor care, John,—
The day is aye fair
    In the land o' the leal.

Our bonnie bairn's there, John ;
She was baith guid and fair, John ;
And, oh! we grudged her sair
    To the land o' the leal.
But sorrow's sel' wears past, John,
And joy is coming fast, John—
The joy that's aye to last
    In the land o' the leal.

Ye were aye leal and true, John ;
Your task's ended now, John,
And I'll welcome you
    To the land o' the leal.
Now fare-ye-weel, my ain John :
This warld's cares are vain, John ;—
We'll meet and we'll be fain
    In the land o' the leal.

237 *Caller Herrin'*

WHA'LL buy my caller [1] herrin'?
  They're bonnie fish and halesome farin';
Wha'll buy my caller herrin',
New drawn frae the Forth?

When ye were sleepin' on your pillows,
Dream'd ye aught o' our puir fellows—
Darkling as they faced the billows,
A' to fill our woven willows?

Wha'll buy my caller herrin'?
They're no brought here without brave daring:
Buy my caller herrin',
Haul'd thro' wind and rain.

Wha'll buy my caller herrin'?
Oh, ye may ca' them vulgar farin',—
Wives and mithers, 'maist despairin',
Ca' them lives o' men.

When the creel [2] o' herrin' passes,
Ladies clad in silks and laces
Gather in their braw pelisses,
Cast their necks and screw their faces.

Caller herrin' 's no got lightly:
Ye can trip the spring fu' tightly;
Spite o' tauntin', flauntin', flingin',
Gow [3] has set you a' a-singin'.

----

[1] fresh. [2] fish-basket. [3] This song was written for Nathaniel
Gow, a musical composer, son of the more celebrated Neil Gow.

Neebour wives, now tent [1] my tellin' :
When the bonnie fish ye're sellin',
At ae word be in your dealin',—
Truth will stand when a' thing's failin'.

238   *The Lass o' Gowrie*

'TWAS on a simmer's afternoon,
    A wee afore the sun gaed doun,
A lassie wi' a braw new goun
    Cam' owre the hills to Gowrie.
The rosebud wash'd in simmer's shower
Bloom'd fresh within the sunny bower;
But Kitty was the fairest flower
    That e'er was seen in Gowrie.

To see her cousin she cam' there ;
An' oh ! the scene was passing fair,
For what in Scotland can compare
    Wi' the Carse o' Gowrie ?
The sun was setting on the Tay,
The blue hills melting into grey,
The mavis and the blackbird's lay
    Were sweetly heard in Gowrie.

O lang the lassie I had woo'd,
And truth and constancy had vow'd,
But cam' nae speed wi' her I lo'ed
    Until she saw fair Gowrie.
I pointed to my faither's ha'—
Yon bonnie bield ayont the shaw [2],
Sae lown [3] that there nae blast could blaw :—
    Wad she no bide in Gowrie ?

    [1] heed.   [2] building beyond the wood.   [3] sheltered.

Her faither was baith glad and wae ;
Her mither she wad naething say ;
The bairnies thocht they wad get play
    If Kittie gaed to Gowrie.
She whiles did smile, she whiles did greet ;
The blush and tear were on her cheek ;
She naething said, and hung her head ;—
    But now she's Leddy Gowrie.

239   *The Laird o' Cockpen*

THE Laird o' Cockpen, he's proud an' he's great,
    His mind is ta'en up wi' things o' the State :
He wanted a wife, his braw house to keep ;
But favour wi' wooin' was fashous [1] to seek.

Down by the dyke-side a lady did dwell ;
At his table-head he thought she'd look well—
McClish's ae daughter o' Claverse-ha' Lee,
A penniless lass wi' a lang pedigree.

His wig was weel pouther'd and as gude as new ;
His waistcoat was white, his coat it was blue :
He put on a ring, a sword, and cock'd hat,—
And wha could refuse the Laird wi' a' that ?

He took the grey mare, and rade cannily,
An' rapp'd at the yett o' Claverse-ha' Lee :
"Gae tell Mistress Jean to come speedily ben,—
She's wanted to speak to the Laird o' Cockpen."

Mistress Jean was makin' the elder-flower wine :
"And what brings the Laird at sic a like time ? "
She put aff her apron and on her silk goun,
Her mutch [2] wi' red ribbons, and gaed awa doun.

         [1] irksome.   [2] cap.

An' when she cam' ben he bow'd fu' low ;
An' what was his errand he soon let her know.
Amazed was the Laird when the lady said " Na " ;—
And wi' a light curtsey she turn'd awa.

Dumbfounder'd was he ; nae sigh did he gie,
He mounted his mare, he rade cannily ;
And aften he thought as he gaed thro' the glen,
"She's daft to refuse the Laird o' Cockpen !"

And, now that the Laird his exit had made,
Mistress Jean she reflected on what she had said :
"Oh, for ane I'll get better, it's waur I'll get ten !
I was daft to refuse the Laird o' Cockpen."

Next time that the Laird and the lady were seen
They were gaun arm-in-arm to the kirk on the green :
Now she sits in the ha', like a weel-tappit [1] hen ;
But as yet there's nae chickens appear'd at Cockpen. [2]

240   *The Pleughman*

THERE'S high and low, there's rich and poor,
     There's trades and crafts eneuch, man ;
But, east and west, his trade's the best
     That kens to guide the pleugh, man.
         Then, come weel speed my pleughman lad,
         And hey my merry pleughman :
         Of a' the trades that I do ken,
         Commend me to the pleughman !

His dreams are sweet upon his bed,
     His cares are light and few, man ;
His mother's blessing's on his head,
     That tents [3] her weel—the pleughman.

[1] crested.   [2] The two last verses are by the novelist, Miss Ferrier, and are quite in her style.   [3] cares for.

The lark sae sweet, that starts to meet
   The morning fresh and new, man—
Blithe tho' she be, as blithe is he,
   That sings as sweet—the pleughman.

All fresh and gay, at dawn of day,
   Their labours they renew, man :
Heaven bless the seed, and bless the soil,
   And Heaven bless the pleughman !

241   *The Auld House*

OH, the auld house, the auld house !
   What tho' the rooms were wee ?
Oh, kind hearts were dwelling there,
   And bairnies fu' o' glee !
The wild rose and the jessamine
   Still hang upon the wa' :
How mony cherish'd memories
   Do they sweet flowers reca' !

Oh, the auld laird, the auld laird,
   Sae canty [1], kind, and crouse [2] !
How mony did he welcome to
   His ain wee dear auld house !
And the leddy too, sae genty [3],
   That shelter'd Scotland's heir ;
And clipt a lock wi' her ain hand
   Frae his lang yellow hair.

The mavis still doth sweetly sing,
   The blue-bells sweetly blaw ;
The bonnie Earn's clear winding still,
   But the auld house is awa'.

[1] cheerful.   [2] lively.   [3] graceful.

The auld house, the auld house !
  Deserted tho' ye be,
There ne'er can be a new house
  Will seem sae fair to me.

242   *Will Ye No Come Back Again ?*

BONNIE CHARLIE'S now awa',
    Safely ower the friendly main ;
Mony a heart will break in twa
  Should he ne'er come back again.
        Will ye no come back again ?
        Will ye no come back again ?
        Better lo'ed ye canna be—
        Will ye no come back again ?

Ye trusted in your Hieland men ;
  They trusted you, dear Charlie !
They kent you hiding in the glen,—
  Your cleading was but barely.

English bribes were a' in vain ;—
  Tho' puir and puirer we maun be,
Siller canna buy the heart
  That beats aye for thine and thee.

We watch'd thee in the gloamin' hour,
  We watch'd thee in the mornin' grey ;—
Tho' thirty thousand pounds they'd gi'e,
  Oh, there was nane that wad betray !

Sweet's the laverock's note and lang,
 Lilting wildly up the glen ;
But aye to me he sings ae sang,—
 Will ye no come back again ?

  Will ye no come back again ?
  Will ye no come back again ?
  Better lo'ed ye canna be—
  Will ye no come back again ?

JAMES HOGG ("THE ETTRICK SHEPHERD")

1770–1835

243   *When the Kye* [1] *Comes Hame*

COME, all ye jolly shepherds
    That whistle through the glen,
I'll tell ye of a secret
    That courtiers dinna ken:
What is the greatest bless
    That the tongue o' man can name?
'Tis to woo a bonnie lassie
    When the kye comes hame,
      When the kye comes hame,
      When the kye comes hame,
    'Tween the gloaming and the mirk,
    When the kye comes hame.

'Tis not beneath the coronet,
    Nor canopy of state,
'Tis not on couch of velvet,
    Nor arbour of the great—
'Tis beneath the spreading birk,
    In the glen without the name,
Wi' a bonnie, bonnie lassie,
    When the kye comes hame.

There the blackbird bigs his nest
    For the mate he lo'es to see,
And on the topmost bough,
    Oh, a happy bird is he;

[1] cows.

Where he pours his melting ditty,
   And love is a' the theme,
And he'll woo his bonnie lassie
   When the kye comes hame.

When the blewart[1] bears a pearl,
   And the daisy turns a pea,
And the bonnie lucken gowan[2]
   Has fauldit up her e'e,
Then the laverock frae the blue lift
   Drops down, an' thinks nae shame
To woo his bonnie lassie
   When the kye comes hame.

See yonder pawkie[3] shepherd,
   That lingers on the hill,
His ewes are in the fauld,
   An' his lambs are lying still ;
Yet he downa[4] gang to bed,
   For his heart is in a flame
To meet his bonnie lassie
   When the kye comes hame.

When the little wee bit heart
   Rises high in the breast,
An' the little wee bit starn
   Rises red in the east,
Oh there's a joy sae dear,
   That the heart can hardly frame,
Wi' a bonnie, bonnie lassie,
   When the key comes hame !

[1] bilberry-flower.   [2] globe-flower.   [3] sly.   [4] cannot.

Then since all nature joins
  In this love without alloy,
Oh, wha wad prove a traitor
  To Nature's dearest joy?
Or wha wad choose a crown,
  Wi' its perils and its fame,
And *miss* his bonnie lassie
  When the kye comes hame,
    When the kye comes hame,
    When the kye comes hame,
  'Tween the gloaming and the mirk,
    When the kye comes hame!

244   *The Skylark*

BIRD of the wilderness,
  Blithesome and cumberless,
Sweet be thy matin o'er moorland and lea!
  Emblem of happiness,
  Blest is thy dwelling-place—
Oh, to abide in the desert with thee!

  Wild is thy lay and loud,
  Far in the downy cloud,
Love gives its energy, love gave it birth.
  Where, on thy dewy wing,
  Where art thou journeying?
Thy lay is in heaven, thy love is on earth.

  O'er fell and fountain sheen,
  O'er moor and mountain green,
O'er the red streamer that heralds the day,
  Over the cloudlet dim,
  Over the rainbow's rim,
Musical cherub, soar, singing, away!

Then when the gloaming comes,
     Low in the heather blooms
Sweet will thy welcome and bed of love be !
     Emblem of happiness,
     Blest is thy dwelling-place—
Oh, to abide in the desert with thee !

245   *Bonnie Prince Charlie*

CAM' ye by Athol, lad wi' the philabeg[1],
     Down by the Tummel, or banks o' the Garry ;
Saw ye our lads, wi' their bonnets and white cockades,
Leaving their mountains to follow Prince Charlie ?
     Follow thee ! follow thee ! wha wadna follow thee ?
     Lang has thou loved and trusted us fairly :
     Charlie, Charlie, wha wadna follow thee,
     King o' the Highland hearts, bonnie Prince Charlie ?

I hae but ae son, my gallant young Donald ;
But if I had ten, they should follow Glengarry.
Health to M'Donnel, and gallant Clan-Ronald,
For these are the men that will die for their Charlie.
I'll to Lochiel and Appin, and kneel to them,
Down by Lord Murray, and Roy of Kildarlie ;
Brave M'Intosh he shall fly to the field with them ;
These are the lads I can trust wi' my Charlie !

Down through the Lowlands, down wi' the Whiga-
     more !
Loyal true Highlanders, down wi' them rarely !
Ronald and Donald, drive on wi' the broad clay-
     more,
Over the necks of the foes of Prince Charlie !

[1] kilt.

Follow thee ! follow thee ! wha wadna follow thee ?
Lang hast thou loved and trusted us fairly :
Charlie, Charlie, wha wadna follow thee,
King o' the Highland hearts, bonnie Prince Charlie ?

246   *Flora Macdonala's Farewell*

FAR over yon hills of the heather sae green,
    An' down by the correi [1] that sings to the sea,
The bonnie young Flora sat sighing her lane,
    The dew on her plaid, and the tear in her e'e.
She look'd at a boat wi' the breezes that swung
    Away, on the wave, like a bird of the main,
An' aye as it lessen'd, she sighed an' she sung,
    Fareweel to the lad I shall ne'er see again !
Fareweel to my hero, the gallant an' young,
    Farweel to the lad I shall ne'er see again.

The muircock that craws on the brows of Ben-Connal,
    He kens of his bed in a sweet mossy hame ;
The eagle that soars o'er the cliffs of Clan-Ronald,
    Unawed and unhunted, his eyry can claim ;
The solan can sleep on the shelve of the shore,
    The cormorant roost on his rock of the sea,
But ah ! there is one whose sad fate I deplore,
    Nor house, ha', nor hame, in this country has he—
The conflict is past, and our name is no more—
    There's nought left but sorrow for Scotland and me !

The target is torn from the arm of the just,
    The helmet is cleft on the brow of the brave,
The claymore for ever in darkness must rust,
    But red is the sword of the stranger and slave ;

---

[1] a glen containing a stream.

The hoof of the horse, and the foot of the proud,
  Have trod o'er the plumes on the bonnet of blue :
Why slept the red bolt in the breast of the cloud
  When tyranny revell'd in blood of the true?
Fareweel, my young hero, the gallant and good ;
  The crown of thy fathers is torn from thy brow !

247   *M'Lean's Welcome*

COME o'er the stream, Charlie
    Dear Charlie, brave Charlie ;
Come o'er the stream, Charlie,
  And dine with M'Lean ;
And though you be weary,
We'll make your heart cheery,
And welcome our Charlie,
  And his loyal train.
We'll bring down the track deer,
We'll bring down the black steer [1],
The lamb from the bracken,
  And doe from the glen ;
The salt sea we'll harry,
And bring to our Charlie
The cream from the bothy [2],
  And curd from the pen.

Come o'er the stream, Charlie,
Dear Charlie, brave Charlie ;
Come o'er the sea, Charlie,
  And dine with M'Lean ;
And you shall drink freely
The dews of Glen-sheerly,

[1] ox.   [2] hut.

That stream in the starlight
　　When kings do not ken.
And deep be your meed
Of the wine that is red,
To drink to your sire,
　　And his friend the M'Lean.

Come o'er the stream, Charlie,
Dear Charlie, brave Charlie ;
Come o'er the stream, Charlie,
　　And dine with M'Lean ;
If aught will invite you,
Or more will delight you,
　　'Tis ready, a troop of our bold Highland-
　　　　men,
All ranged on the heather,
With bonnet and feather,
Strong arms and broad claymores,
　　Three hundred and ten !

248　　　　　　*Lock the door, Lariston*

" LOCK the door, Lariston, lion of Liddesdale ;
　　Lock the door, Lariston, Lowther comes on ;
The Armstrongs are flying,
The widows are crying,
The Castletown's burning, and Oliver's gone !

" Lock the door, Lariston—high on the weather-gleam
See how the Saxon plumes bob on the sky—
　　Yeomen and carbineer,
　　Billman and halberdier,
Fierce is the foray, and far is the cry !

" Bewcastle brandishes high his broad scimitar ;
Ridley is riding his fleet-footed grey ;
    Hedley and Howard there,
    Wandale and Windermere ;
Lock the door, Lariston ; hold them at bay.

" Why dost thou smile, noble Elliot of Lariston ?
Why dost the joy-candle gleam in thine eye?
    Thou bold Border ranger,
    Beware of thy danger ;
Thy foes are relentless, determined, and nigh."

Jack Elliot raised up his steel bonnet and lookit,
His hand grasp'd the sword with a nervous embrace ;
    " Ah, welcome, brave foemen,
    On earth there are no men
More gallant to meet in the foray or chase !

" Little know you of the hearts I have hidden here ;
Little know you of our moss-troopers' might—
    Linhope and Sorbie true,
    Sundhope and Milburn too,
Gentle in manner, but lions in fight !

" I have Mangerton, Ogilvie, Raeburn, and Netherbie,
Old Sim of Whitram, and all his array ;
    Come all Northumberland,
    Teesdale and Cumberland,
Here at the Breaken tower end shall the fray !"

Scowled the broad sun o'er the links[1] of green Lid-
    desdale,
Red as the beacon-light tipped he the wold ;

[1] windings.

Many a bold martial eye
Mirror'd that morning sky,
Never more oped on his orbit of gold.

Shrill was the bugle's note, dreadful the warrior's shout,
Lances and halberds in splinters were borne ;
Helmet and hauberk then
Braved the claymore in vain,
Buckler and armlet in shivers were shorn.

See how they wane—the proud files of the Winder-
mere !
Howard ! ah, woe to thy hopes of the day !
Here the wide welkin rend,
While the Scot's shouts ascend—
" Elliot of Lariston, Elliot for aye ! "

249   *The Witch of Fife*

QUHARE haif ye been, ye ill womyne,
These three lang nightis fra hame ?
Quhat garris [1] the sweit drap fra yer brow,
Like clotis of the saut sea faem ?

" It fearis me muckil ye haif seen
Quhat good man never knew ;
It fearis me muckil ye haif been
Quhare the gray cock never crew.

" But the spell may crack, and the brydel breck,
Then sherpe yer werde [2] will be ;
Ye had better sleipe in yer bed at hame,
Wi yer deire littil bairnis and me."—

[1] causes. [2] destiny.

"Sit dune, sit dune, my leile auld man,
   Sit dune, and listin to me ;
I'll gar the hayre stand on yer crown,
   And the cauld sweit blind yer e'e.

"But tell nae wordis, my gude auld man,
   Tell never a word again ;
Or deire shall be yer courtisye,
   And driche[1] and sair yer pain.

"The first leet-night[2], quhan the new moon set,
   Quhan all was douffe[3] and mirk,
We saddled ouir naigis wi the moon-fern leif,
   And rode fra Kilmerrin kirk.

"Some horses ware of the brume-cow[4] framit,
   And some of the greine bay tree ;
But mine was made of ane humloke schaw[5],
   And a stout stallion was he.

"We raide the tod[6] doune on the hill,
   The martin on the law ;
And we huntyd the hoolet out of brethe,
   And forcit him doune to fa."—

"Quhat guid was that, ye ill womyn ?
   Quhat guid was that to thee ?
Ye wald better haif bein in yer bed at hame,
   Wi yer deire littil bairnis and me."—

"And ay we raide, and se merrily we raide,
   Throw the merkist gloffis[7] of the night ;
And we swam the floode, and we darnit[8] the woode,
   Till we cam to the Lommond height.

---

[1] dreary.   [2] nomination.   [3] dull.   [4] sprig of broom.   [5] hemlock-stalk.   [6] fox.   [7] of varying degrees of darkness.   [8] threaded.

"And quhen we cam to the Lommond height,
    Se lythlye we lychted doune ;
And we drank fra the hornis that never grew,
    The beer that was never browin.

" Than up there rase ane wee wee man,
    Franethe¹ the moss-gray stane ;
His fece was wan like the collifloure,
    For he nouthir had blude nor bane.

" He set ane reid-pipe till his muthe,
    And he playit se bonnilye,
Till the grey curlew, and the black-cock, flew
    To listen his melodye.

" It rang se sweet through the green Lommond,
    That the nycht-winde lowner² blew ;
And it soupit³ alang the Loch Leven,
    And wakinit the white sea-mew.

" It rang se sweet through the grein Lommond,
    Se sweitly butt and se shill⁴,
That the wezilis laup out of their mouldy holis,
    And dancit on the mydnycht hill.

" The corby craw cam gledgin⁵ near,
    The ern⁶ gede veeryng bye ;
And the troutis laup out of the Leven Louch,
    Charmit with the melodye.

"And ay we dancit on the green Lommond,
    Till the dawn on the ocean grew :
Ne wonder I was a weary wycht
    Quhan I cam hame to you."—

¹ from under.   ² more suavely.   ³ swept.   ⁴ and likewise so
shill.   ⁵ peering.   ⁶ eagle.

"Quhat guid, quhat guid, my weird weird wyfe,
    Quhat guid was that to thee ?
Ye wald better haif bein in yer bed at hame,
    Wi yer deire littil bairnis and me."—

"The second nychte, quhan the new moon set,
    O'er the roaryng sea we flew ;
The cockle-shell our trusty bark,
    Our sailis of the grein sea-rue.

"And the bauld windis blew, and the fire-flauchtis[1] flew,
    And the sea ran to the skie ;
And the thunner it growlit, and the sea dogs howlit,
    As we gaed scouryng bye.

"And ay we mountit the sea green hillis,
    Quhill we brushit thro' the cludis of the hevin ;
Than sousit dounright like the stern-shot[2] light,
    Fra the liftis[3] blue casement driven.

"But our taickil stood, and our bark was good,
    And se pang[4] was our pearily prowe ;
Quhan we culdna speil the brow of the wavis,
    We needilit them throu belowe.

"As fast as the hail, as fast as the gale,
    As fast as the midnycht leme[5],
We borit the breiste of the burstyng swale[6],
    Or fluffit i' the flotyng faem.

"And quhan to the Norraway shore we wan,
    We muntyd our steedis of the wynd,
And we splashit the floode, and we darnit the woode,
    And we left the shouir behynde.

[1] lightning.   [2] star-shot.   [3] sky's.   [4] pressed.   [5] gleam.
[6] swell.

"Fleet is the roe on the green Lommond,
  And swift is the couryng grew [1];
The rein-deir dun can eithly run,
  Quhan the houndis and the hornis pursue.

"But nowther the roe, nor the rein-deir dun,
  The hinde nor the couryng grew,
Culde fly owr muntaine, muir, and dale,
  As owr braw steedis they flew.

"The dales war deep, and the Doffrinis steep,
  And we rase to the skyis ee-bree;
Quhite, quhite was ouir rode, that was never trode,
  Owr the snawis of eternity!

"And quhan we cam to the Lapland lone
  The fairies war all in array,
For all the genii of the north
  War keepyng their holeday.

"The warlock [2] men and the weerd wemyng,
  And the fays of the wood and the steep,
And the phantom hunteris all war there,
  And the mermaidis of the deep.

"And they washit us all with the witch-water,
  Distillit fra the moorland dew,
Quhill our beauty blumit like the Lapland rose,
  That wylde in the foreste grew."—

"Ye lee, ye lee, ye ill womyne,
  Se loud as I heir ye lee!
For the warst-faurd [3] wyfe on the shoris of Fyfe
  Is cumlye comparet wi thee."—

[1] greyhound. [2] wizard. [3] worst-favoured.

"Then the mermaidis sang and the woodlandis rang,
  Se sweetly swellit the quire;
On every cliff a herpe they hang,
  On every tree a lyre.

"And ay they sang, and the woodlandis rang,
  And we drank, and we drank se deep;
Then soft in the armis of the warlock men,
  We laid us dune to sleep."—

"Away, away, ye ill womyne,
  An ill deide met ye dee!
Quhan ye hae pruvit se false to yer God,
  Ye can never pruve trew to me."—

"And there we lernit fra the fairy foke,
  And fra our master true,
The wordis that can beire us throu the air,
  And lokkis and baris undo.

"Last nycht we met at Maisry's cot;
  Richt weil the wordis we knew;.
And we set a foot on the black cruik-shell,
  And out at the lum [1] we flew.

"And we flew owr hill, and we flew owr dale,
  And we flew owr firth and sea,
Until we cam to merry Carlisle,
  Quhar we lightit on the lea.

"We gaed to the vault beyound the towir,
  Quhar we enterit free as ayr;
And we drank, and we drank of the bishopis wine
  Quhill we culde drynk ne mair."—

[1] chimney.

"Gin that be trew, my gude auld wyfe,
    Whilk thou hast tauld to me,
Betide my death, betide my lyfe,
    I'll beire thee companye.

"Neist tyme ye gaung to merry Carlisle
    To drynk of the blude-reid wine,
Beshrew my heart, I'll fly with thee,
    If the diel shulde fly behynde."—

"Ah ! little do ye ken, my silly auld man,
    The daingeris we maun dree [1] ;
Last nichte we drank of the bishopis wyne,
    Quhill near near taen war we.

"Afore we wan to the sandy ford,
    The gor-cockis [2] nichering [3] flew ;
The lofty crest of Ettrick Pen
    Was wavit about with blew,
And, flichtering throu the air, we fand
    The chill chill mornyng dew.

"As we flew owr the hillis of Braid,
    The sun rase fair and clear ;
There gurly [4] James, and his baronis braw,
    War out to hunt the deere.

"Their bowis they drew, their arrowis flew,
    And peircit the ayr with speede,
Quhill purpil fell the mornyng dew
    With witch-blude rank and reide.

"Littil do ye ken, my silly auld man,
    The dangeris we maun dree ;
Ne wonder I am a weary wycht
    Quhan I come hame to thee."—

[1] endure.   [2] moorcock, grouse.   [3] "bicker."   [4] surly.

" But tell me the word, my gude auld wyfe,
   Come tell it me speedilye ;
For I lang to drink of the gude reide wyne,
   And to wyng the ayr with thee.

"Yer hellish horse I wilna ryde,
   Nor sail the seas in the wynd ;
But I can flee as well as thee,
   And I'll drynk quhill ye be blynd."—

"O fy ! O fy ! My leil auld man,
   That word I darena tell ;
It wald turn this warld all upside down,
   And make it warse than hell.

"For all the lasses in the land
   Wald munt the wynd and fly ;
And the men wald doff their doublets syde,
   And after them wald ply."—

But the auld gudeman was ane cunnyng auld man,
   And ane cunnyng auld man was he ;
And he watchit, and he watchit for mony a night,
   The witches' flychte to see.

Ane nychte he darnit [1] in Maisry's cot ;
   The fearless haggs came in ;
And he heard the word of awsome weird,
   And he saw their deedis of synn.

Then ane by ane, they said that word,
   As fast to the fire they drew ;
Then set a foot on the black cruik-shell,
   And out at the lum they flew.

[1] hid.

The auld gude-man cam fra his hole
  With feire and muckil dreide,
But yet he couldna think to rue,
  For the wyne came in his head.

He set his foot in the black cruik-shell,
  With ane fixit and ane wawlyng[1] ee ;
And he said the word that I darena say,
  And out at the lum flew he.

The witches skalit the moon-beam pale ;
  Deep groanit the trembling wynde ;
But they never wist till our auld gude-man
  Was hoveryng them behynde.

They flew to the vaultis of merry Carlisle,
  Quhair they enterit free as ayr ;
And they drank and they drank of the byshopis wyne
  Quhill they culde drynk ne mair.

The auld gude-man he grew se crouse[2],
  He dancit on the mouldy ground,
And he sang the bonniest sangis of Fife,
  And he tuzzlit the kerlyngs[3] round.

And ay he percit the tither butt,
  And he suckit, and he suckit se lang,
Quhill his een they closit, and his voice grew low ;
  And his tongue wold hardly gang,

The kerlyngs drank of the bishopis wyne
  Quhill they scentit the mornyng wynde ;
Then clove again the yeilding ayr,
  And left the auld man behynde.

        [1] wild-looking.   [2] bold.   [3] old women.

And ay he slepit on the damp damp floor,
   He slepit and he snorit amain ;
He never dremit he was far fra hame,
   Or that the auld wyvis war gane.

And ay he slepit on the damp damp floor
   Quhill past the mid-day highte,
Quhan wakenit by five rough Englishmen,
   That trailit him to the lychte.

" Now quha are ye, ye silly auld man,
   That sleepis se sound and se weil ?
Or how gat ye into the bishopis vault
   Throu lokkis and barris of steel ? "—

The auld gude-man he tryit to speak,
   But ane word he culdna fynde ;
He tryit to think, but his head whirlit round,
   And ane thing he culdna mynde :—
" I cam fra Fyfe," the auld man cryit,
   "And I cam on the midnycht wynde."

They nickit the auld man, and they prickit the auld
     man,
   And they yerkit [1] his limbis with twine,
Quhill the reid blude ran in his hose and shoon,
   But some cryit it was wyne.

They lickit the auld man, and they prickit the auld
     man,
   And they tyit him till ane stone ;
And they set ane bele-fire him about,
   And they burnit him skin and bone.

[1] bound tightly.

Now wae be to the puir auld man
 That ever he saw the day !
And wae be to all the ill wemyng,
 That lead puir men astray !

Let never ane auld man after this
 To lawless greide inclyne ;
Let never an auld man after this
 Rin post to the diel for wyne.

250   *Kilmeny*

BONNYE Kilmeny gede up the glen ;
 But it walsna to meite Duneira's men,
Nor the rozy munke of the isle to see,
For Kilmeny was pure as pure culde be.
It was only to heire the yorline [1] syng,
And pu the blew kress-flour runde the spryng ;
To pu the hyp and the hyndberrye [2],
And the nytt that hang fra the hesil tree ;
For Kilmeny was pure as pure culde be.
But lang may her minny [3] luke ouir the wa,
And lang may scho seike in the greinwood schaw ;
Lang the lairde of Duneira bleme,
And lang, lang greite [4] or Kilmeny come heme.

Quhan mony lang day had comit and fledde,
Quhan grief grew caulm, and hope was deade,
Quhan mes for Kilmeny's soul had beine sung,
Quhan the bedis-man had prayit, and the deide-
 bell rung ;
Lete, lete in ane glomyn, quhan all was still,
Quhan the freenge was reid on the wastlin hill,

---

[1] yellow-hammer. [2] raspberry, or bramble-berry. [3] mother.
[4] weep.

The wud was sere, the moon i' the wene,
The reike of the cot hang ouir the playne,
Like ane littil wee cludde in the worild its lene ;
Quhan the ingil lowit with ane eiry leme [1],
Lete, lete in the glomyn, Kilmeny came heme !

"Kilmeny, Kilmeny, quhair haif ye beine ?
Lang haif we socht beth holt and deine ;
By lynn [2], by furde, and greinwudde tree,
Yet ye ir helsome and fayir to see.
Quhair gat ye that joup [3] of the lille scheine ?
That bonny snoode [4] of the byrk so greine ?
And these rosis, the fayrist that ever war seine ?
Kilmeny, Kilmeny, quhair haif ye beine ! "—

Kilmeny luckit up with ane lovelye grace,
But ne smyle was seine on Kilmeny's face ;
Als still was her luke, and als still was her ee,
Als the stilnesse that lay on the emerant lee,
Or the myst that sleips on ane waveless sea.
For Kilmeny had beine scho kend nocht quhair,
And Kilmeny had seine quhat scho culde not
    declayre ;
Kilmeny had beine quhair the cocke nevir crew,
Quhair the rayne nevir fell, and the wynd nevir
    blue.
But it seemit as the herpe of the skye had rung,
And the ayries of heauin playit runde her tung,
Quhan scho spak of the luvlye formis scho had
    seine,
And ane land quhair synn had nevir beine ;
Ane land of love, and ane land of lychte,
Withoutten sonne, or mone, or nychte :

---

[1] gleam.   [2] waterfall.   [3] petticoat.   [4] fillet.

Where the ryver swait ane lyving streime,
And the lychte ane pure and cludlesse beime :
The land of veizion it wald seime,
And still ane everlestyng dreime.
In yond grein wudde there is a waike,
And in that waike there is a wene [1],
And in that wene there is a maike [2],
That nouther hes flesch, blude, nor bene ;
And dune in yond greinwudde he walkis his lene.

In that greine wene Kilmeny lay,
Her bosom happit with flouris gay ;
But the ayre was soft, and the silens deipe,
And bonny Kilmeny fell sunde asleipe.
Scho kend ne mair, nor openit her ee,
Till wekit by the hymis of ane farr cuntrye.

Scho wekit on ane cuche of the sylk se slim,
All stryppit with the barris of the raynbowis rim ;
And luvlye beingis runde war ryfe,
Quha erst had travellit mortyl lyfe ;
And ay they smilet, and gan to speire [3],
" What spyrit hes brochte this mortyl heire ? "

" Lang haif I raikit the worild wide,"
Ane meike and reverent fere [4] replyit ;
" Beth nycht and day I haif watchit the fayre,
Eident [5] a thousande eiris and mayre,
Yes, I haif watchit ouir ilk degree,
Quhairevir blumis femenitye ;
And sinless virgin, free of stain
In mind and body, faund I nane.

___

[1] cave.   [2] mate.   [3] ask.   [4] companion.   [5] diligent.

Nevir, sen the banquhet of tyme,
Fand I vyrgin in her pryme,
Quhill anis this bonny maydin I saw
As spotless as the mornyng snaw:
Full twentye eiris scho has levit as fre
As the spirits that sojurn this countrye.
I haif brochte her away fra the snairis of men,
That synn or dethe scho nevir may ken."

They claspit her weste and handis fair,
They kissit her cheik, and they kembit her hayir
And runde cam ilka blumyng fere,
Sayn, " Bonny Kilmeny, yer welcome here !
Wemyng are freit [1] of the littand scorne :
O, blest be the day Kilmeny was born !
Now shall the land of the spiritis see,
Now shall it ken what ane womyn may be !
Mony long eir, in sorrow and pain,
Mony long eir thro' the worild we haif gane,
Comyshonit to watch fayir womynkinde,
For its they quha nurice the imortyl minde.
We haif watchit their stepis as the dawnyng shone,
And deipe in the greinwud walkis alone,
By lille bouir, and silken bedde,
The vewless teiris haif ouir them shedde ;
Haif suthit their ardent myndis to sleep,
Or left the cuche of luife to weip.
We haif sein ! we haif sein ! but the tyme mene come,
And the angelis will blush at the day of doom !

O, wald the fayrest of mortyl kynde
Ay keipe thilke holye troths in mynde,
That kyndred spyritis ilk motion see,
Quha watch their wayis with ankshes ee,

[1] freed.

And griefe for the guilt of humainitye!
Och, sweit to hevin the maydenis prayer,
And the siche that hevis ane bosom se fayir!
And deire to hevin the wordis of truthe,
And the prayze of vertu fra beautyis muthe!
And deire to the viewles formis of ayir,
The mynde that kythis[1] as the body fayir!

O, bonnye Kilmeny! fre fra stayne,
Gin evir ye seike the worild agayne,
That worild of synn, of sorrow, and feire,
O, tell of the joyis that are wayting heire!
And tell of the sygnis ye shall shortlye see;
Of the tymes that are now, and the tymes that
　　shall be."

They liftit Kilmeny, they ledde her away,
And scho walkit in the lychte of ane sonles day:
The skye was ane dome of kristel brichte,
The fountyn of veezion, and fountyn of lichte:
The emerant feildes war of dazzling glow,
And the flouris of everlestyng blow.
Than deipe in the streime her body they layde,
That her yudith[2] and beautye mocht nevir fede;
And they smylit on hevin, quhan they saw her lye
In the streime of lyfe that wanderit bye.
And scho herde ane songe, scho herde it sung,
Scho kend nochte quhair; but se sweitlye it rung,
It fell on her eare lyke ane dreime of the morne:
"O! blist be the daye Kilmeny was born!
Now shall the land of the spyritis see,
Now shall it ken quhat ane womyn may be!
The sun that shynis on the worild se brychte,
Ane borrowit gleide[3] fra the fountaine of lychte;

---

[1] reveals itself.　　[2] youth.　　[3] spark.

And the moone that sleikis the skye se dun,
Lyke ane gouden bow, or ane beimles sun,
Shall skulk awaye, and be seine ne mayir,
And the angelis shall miss them travelling the ayr.
But lang, lang aftir bethe nychte and day,
Quhan the sun and the worild haif elyit [1] awaye ;
Quhan the synnir hes gene to his wesum doome,
Kilmeny shall smyle in eternal bloome ! "

They soofit [2] her awaye to ane mountyn greine,
To see quhat mortyl nevir had seine ;
And they seted her hiche on ane purpil swerde,
And bade her heide quhat scho saw and herde ;
And note the chaingis the spyritis wrochte,
For now scho leevit in the land of thochte.
Scho lukit, and scho saw ne sone nor skyis,
But ane kristel dome of a thusend dyis.
Scho luckit, and scho saw ne land arychte,
But ane endles whirle of glory and lychte.
And radiant beingis went and came
Far swifter than wynde, or the lynkit flame.
Scho haide her ene fra the daiziling view ;
Scho lukit agayn, and the schene was new.

Scho saw ane sun on a simmer skye,
And cludis of amber sailing bye ;
Ane lovlye land anethe her laye.
And that land had lekis and mountaynis graye ;
And that land had vallies and horye pylis,
And merlit [3] seas, and a thusande ylis.
Scho saw the korne waif on the vaile ;
Scho saw the deire rin down the daile ;
And mony a mortyl toyling sore,
And scho thochte scho had seine the land before.

[1] vanished.   [2] wafted.   [3] speckled.

Scho saw ane ledy sit on a throne,
The fayrest that evir the sun shone on !
Ane lyon lickit her hand of mylke,
And scho held him in ane leish of sylk ;
And ane leifu [1] mayden stude at her knee,
With ane sylver wand, and meltyng ee.
But ther cam ane leman out of the west,
To woo the ledy that he luvit best ;
And he sent ane boy her herte to prove,
And scho took him in, and scho callit him love ;
But quhan to her breist he gan to cling,
Scho dreit [2] the payne of the serpentis sting.

Than ane gruff untowyrd gysart [3] came,
And he hundit the lyon on his dame ;
And the leifu mayde with the meltyng eye,
Scho droppit ane tear, and passit bye ;
And scho sew quhill the queen fra the lyon fled,
Quhill the bonniest flouir in the worild lay deide.
Ane koffin was set on a distant playne,
And scho saw the reide blude fall like rayne :
Then bonny Kilmeny's heart grew saire,
And scho turnit away, and dochte [4] luke ne maire.

Then the gruff grim keryl girnit [5] amain,
And they trampit him downe, but he rase againe ;
And he baitit the lyon to diedis of weir,
Quhill he lepit the blude to the kyngdome deire.
But the lyon grew straung, and dainger-prief,
Quhan crownit with the rose and the claiver leife ;
Then he lauchit at the keryl, and chesit him away
To feide with the deire on the mountayn gray :

---

[1] discreet.   [2] endured.   [3] a person who is disfigured or disguised.   [4] could.   [5] grinned.

He goulit [1] at the keryl, and he geckit [2] at hevin,
But his merk was set, and his erilis [3] given.
Kilmeny a while her ene withdrewe ;
Scho lukit agene, and the schene was new.

Scho saw arunde her, fayir wanfurlit,
Ane haf of all the glowing worild,
Quhair oceanis rowit [4], and ryveris ran,
To bunde the aymis of sinful man.
Scho saw ane pepil, ferse and fell,
Burst fra their bundis like feindis of hell ;
The lille grew, and the egil flew,
And scho herkit [5] on her revining crew.
The wedos wailit, and the reid blude ran,
And scho thretinit ane end to the race of man :
Scho nevir lenit [6], nor stoode in awe,
Quhill claught by the lyonis deadly paw.
Och ! then the egil swinkit [7] for lyfe,
And brainzelit [8] up ane mortyl stryfe ;
But flew scho north, or flew scho suthe,
Scho met with the goul of the lyonis muthe.

With ane mootit [9] wing, and wefu mene,
The egil sochte her eiry agene ;
But lang may scho cour in her bloodye este [10],
And lang, lang sleik her oundit breste,
Afore scho sey [11] ane other flychte,
To play with the norlan lyonis mychte.

To sing of the sychtis Kilmeny saw,
Se far surpassing naturis law,
The syngeris voyse wald synk away,
And the stryng of his herpe wald cese to play.

---

[1] howled. [2] mocked. [3] pledge. [4] rolled. [5] incited. [6] ceased.
[7] toiled. [8] raised. [9] moulted. [10] nest. [11] essay.

But scho saw quhill the sorrouis of man war bye,
And all was lufe and hermonye ;
Quhill the sternis of hevin fell lownly [1] away,
Lyke the flekis of snaw on a winter day.

Then Kilmeny beggit agene to see
The freindis scho had left in her ayn countrye,
To tell of the plesse quhair scho had been,
And the wonderis that lay in the land unseen ;
To warn the living maydenis fayir,
The luvit of hevin, the spiritis care,
That all quhase myndis unmelit [2] remaine
Shall blume in beauty quhan tyme is gene.

With distant museke, soft and deipe,
They lullit Kilmeny sunde asleepe ;
And quhan scho wekinit, scho lay her lene,
All happit with flouris, in the greinwud wene.
Quhan sevin lang yeiris had cumit and fledde ;
Quhan grief was calm and hope was dede ;
Quhan scairse was rememberit Kilmeny's neme,
Lete, lete in a gloamyn Kilmeny cam heme !

And O, her beauty was fayir to see,
But still and steedfast was her ee !
Her seymar [3] was the lille flouir,
And her cheik the moss-rose in the shouir ;
And her voyse lyke the distant melodye,
That floatis alang the silver sea.
But scho luvit to raike [4] the lenely glen,
And keepit away fra the hauntis of men ;
Her holy hymis unherde to syng,
To suke the flouris, and drynk the spryng.

[1] quietly.   [2] unmingled.   [3] garment.   [4] roam.

But quhairevir her pecefu form appeirit,
The wylde besties of the hill war cheirit ;
The ouf [1] playit lythely runde the feilde,
The lordlye byson lowit and kneilit ;
The dun deire wooit with manyr bland,
And courit aneath her lille hand.
And quhan at evin the woodlandis rung,
Quhan hymis of other worildis scho sung,
In extacye of sweite devotion,
Och, then the glen was all in motion.
The wylde bestis of the foreste came,
Brak fra their buchtis [2] and faldis the tame,
And govit [3] by, charmit and amaizit ;
Even the dull cattil crunit [4] and gazit,
And waulit about in ankshuse payne
For some the misterye to explayne.
The bizerd cam with the thrystle-coke [5] ;
The korbye left hir houf [6] in the roke ;
The black-burd alang with the egil flew ;
The hynde cam trippyng ouir the dew ;
The ouf and the kydd their raike [7] began,
And the tod [8], and the lam, and the leurit [9] ran ;
The hauke and the herne attour [10] them hung,
And the merl and the mavies forehooit [11] their yung ;
And all in ane pecefu ryng war hurlit :
It was lyke ane eve in a sinlesse worild !

Quhan a munthe and a day had comit and gene,
Kilmeny sochte the greinwud wene ;
There layde her doune on the levis se greine,
But Kilmeny on yirth was nevir mayre seine.
But och, the wordis that fell fra her muthe,
War wordis of wonder, and wordis of truthe !

[1] wolf.   [2] pen.   [3] gazed.   [4] whined.   [5] missel-thrush.   [6] haunt.
[7] wandering.   [8] fox.   [9] leveret.   [10] over.   [11] forsook.

But all the land was in fiere and dreide,
For they kendna whether scho was lyving or deide.
It walsna her heme, and scho culdna remayne ;
Scho left this worlld of sorrow and paine,
And returnit to the land of thocthe againe.

SIR WALTER SCOTT

1771–1832

The Convent

(*From "Marmion"*)

WHILE round the fire such legends go,
      Far different was the scene of woe,
Where, in a secret aisle beneath,
Council was held of life and death.
  It was more dark and lone, that vault,
      Than the worst dungeon cell;
  Old Colwulf built it, for his fault,
      In penitence to dwell,
When he, for cowl and beads, laid down
The Saxon battle-axe and crown.
This den, which, chilling every sense
  Of feeling, hearing, sight,
Was called the Vault of Penitence,
  Excluding air and light,
Was, by the prelate Sexhelm, made
A place of burial, for such dead
As, having died in mortal sin,
Might not be laid the church within.
'Twas now a place of punishment;

Where, if so loud a shriek were sent,
  As reached the upper air,
The hearers blessed themselves, and said,
The spirits of the sinful dead
  Bemoaned their torments there.

But though, in the monastic pile,
Did of this penitential aisle
  Some vague tradition go,
Few only, save the Abbot, knew
Where the place lay; and still more few
Were those, who had from him the clew
  To that dread vault to go.
Victim and executioner
Were blind-fold when transported there.
In low dark rounds the arches hung,
From the rude rock the side-walls sprung;
The grave-stones, rudely sculptured o'er,
Half sunk in earth, by time half wore,
Were all the pavement of the floor;
The mildew drops fell one by one,
With tinkling plash, upon the stone.
A cresset, in an iron chain,
Which served to light this drear domain,
With damp and darkness seemed to strive,
As if it scarce might keep alive;
And yet it dimly served to shew
The awful conclave met below.

There, met to doom in secrecy,
Were placed the heads of convents three:
All servants of Saint Benedict,
The statutes of whose order strict
  On iron table lay;

In long black dress, on seats of stone,
Behind were these three judges shewn,
   By the pale cresset's ray:
The Abbess of Saint Hilda's, there,
Sate for a space with visage bare,
Until, to hide her bosom's swell,
And tear-drops that for pity fell,
   She closely drew her veil:
Yon shrouded figure, as I guess,
By her proud mien and flowing dress,
Is Tynemouth's haughty Prioress,
   And she with awe looks pale:
And he, that Ancient Man, whose sight
Has long been quenched by age's night,
Upon whose wrinkled brow alone,
Nor ruth, nor mercy's trace is shown,
   Whose look is hard and stern,—
Saint Cuthbert's Abbot is his stile;
For sanctity called, through the isle,
   The Saint of Lindisfarn.

Before them stood a guilty pair;
But, though an equal fate they share,
Yet one alone deserves our care.
Her sex a page's dress belied;
The cloak and doublet, loosely tied,
Obscured her charms, but could not hide.
   Her cap down o'er her face she drew;
      And, on her doublet breast,
   She tried to hide the badge of blue,
      Lord Marmion's falcon crest.
But, at the Prioress' command,
A Monk undid the silken band,
   That tied her tresses fair,

37

And raised the bonnet from her head,
And down her slender form they spread,
   In ringlets rich and rare.
Constance de Beverley they know,
Sister professed of Fontevraud,
Whom the church numbered with the dead,
For broken vows, and convent fled.

When thus her face was given to view,
(Although so pallid was her hue,
It did a ghastly contrast bear,
To those bright ringlets glistering fair,)
Her look composed, and steady eye,
Bespoke a matchless constancy ;
And there she stood so calm and pale,
That, but her breathing did not fail,
And motion slight of eye and head,
And of her bosom, warranted,
That neither sense nor pulse she lacks,
You might have thought a form of wax,
Wrought to the very life, was there ;
So still she was, so pale, so fair.

Her comrade was a sordid soul,
   Such as does murther for a meed ;
Who, but of fear, knows no controul,
Because his conscience, seared and foul,
   Feels not the import of his deed ;
One, whose brute-feeling ne'er aspires
Beyond his own more brute desires.
Such tools the tempter ever needs,
To do the savagest of deeds ;
For them, no visioned terrors daunt,
Their nights no fancied spectres haunt ;

One fear with them, of all most base,
The fear of death,—alone finds place.
This wretch was clad in frock and cowl,
And shamed not loud to moan and howl,
His body on the floor to dash,
And crouch, like hound beneath the lash ;
While his mute partner, standing near,
Waited her doom without a tear.

Yet well the luckless wretch might shriek,
Well might her paleness terror speak !
For there were seen, in that dark wall,
Two niches, narrow, deep and tall.
Who enters at such griesly door,
Shall ne'er, I ween, find exit more.
In each a slender meal was laid,
Of roots, of water, and of bread :
By each, in Benedictine dress,
Two haggard monks stood motionless ;
Who, holding high a blazing torch,
Shewed the grim entrance of the porch :
Reflecting back the smoky beam,
The dark-red walls and arches gleam.
Hewn stones and cement were displayed,
And building tools in order laid.

These executioners were chose,
As men who were with mankind foes,
And, with despite and envy fired,
Into the cloister had retired ;
  Or who, in desperate doubt of grace,
  Strove, by deep penance, to efface
    Of some foul crime the stain ;

For, as the vassals of her will,
Such men the church selected still,
As either joyed in doing ill,
    Or thought more grace to gain,
If, in her cause, they wrestled down
Feelings their nature strove to own.
By strange device were they brought there,
They knew not how, and knew not where.

And now that blind old Abbot rose,
    To speak the Chapter's doom,
On those the wall was to inclose,
    Alive, within the tomb;
But stopped, because that woeful maid,
Gathering her powers, to speak essayed;
Twice she essayed, and twice, in vain;
Her accents might no utterance gain;
Nought but imperfect murmurs slip
From her convulsed and quivering lip;
    'Twixt each attempt all was so still,
    You seemed to hear a distant rill—
    'Twas ocean's swells and falls;
For though this vault of sin and fear
Was to the sounding surge so near,
A tempest there you scarce could hear,
    So massive were the walls.

At length, an effort sent apart
The blood that curdled to her heart,
    And light came to her eye,
And colour dawned upon her cheek,
A hectic and a fluttered streak,
Like that left on the Cheviot peak,
    By Autumn's stormy sky;

And when her silence broke at length,
Still as she spoke, she gathered strength,
  And arm'd herself to bear.
It was a fearful sight to see
Such high resolve and constancy,
  In form so soft and fair.

" I speak not to implore your grace ;
Well know I for one minute's space
  Successless might I sue :
Nor do I speak your prayers to gain ;
For if a death of lingering pain,
To cleanse my sins, be penance vain,
  Vain are your masses too.—
I listened to a traitor's tale,
I left a convent and the veil,
For three long years I bowed my pride,
A horse-boy in his train to ride ;
And well my folly's meed he gave,
Who forfeited, to be his slave,
All here, and all beyond the grave.—
He saw young Clara's face more fair,
He knew her of broad lands the heir,
Forgot his vows, his faith forswore,
And Constance was beloved no more.—
  'Tis an old tale, and often told ;
    But, did my fate and wish agree,
  Ne'er had been read, in story old,
  Of maiden true betrayed for gold,
    That loved, or was avenged, like me.

" The king approved his favourite's aim ;
In vain a rival barred his claim,

Whose faith with Clare's was plight,
For he attaints that rival's fame
With treason's charge—and on they came,
    In mortal lists to fight.
        Their oaths are said,
        Their prayers are prayed,
        Their lances in the rest are laid,
    They meet in mortal shock;
And hark! the throng, with thundering cry,
Shout 'Marmion, Marmion, to the sky!
    De Wilton to the block!'
Say ye, who preach heaven shall decide,
When in the lists two champions ride,
    Say, was heaven's justice here?
When, loyal in his love and faith,
Wilton found overthrow or death,
    Beneath a traitor's spear.
How false the charge, how true he fell,
This guilty packet best can tell"—
Then drew a packet from her breast,
Paused, gathered voice, and spoke the rest.

"Still was false Marmion's bridal staid;
To Whitby's convent fled the maid,
    The hated match to shun.
'Ho! shifts she thus?' king Henry cried,
'Sir Marmion, she shall be thy bride,
    If she were sworn a nun.'
One way remained—the king's command
Sent Marmion to the Scottish land:
I lingered here, and rescue plann'd
    For Clara and for me:
This caitiff monk, for gold, did swear,
He would to Whitby's shrine repair,

And, by his drugs, my rival fair
  A saint in heaven should be.
But ill the dastard kept his oath,
Whose cowardice hath undone us both.

" And now my tongue the secret tells,
Not that remorse my bosom swells,
But to assure my soul, that none
Shall ever wed with Marmion.
Had fortune my last hope betrayed,
This packet, to the king conveyed,
Had given him to the headsman's stroke,
Although my heart that instant broke.—
Now, men of death, work forth your will,
For I can suffer, and be still ;
And come he slow, or come he fast,
It is but Death who comes at last.

" Yet dread me, from my living tomb,
Ye vassal slaves of bloody Rome,
If Marmion's late remorse should wake,
Full soon such vengeance will he take,
That you will wish the fiery Dane
Had rather been your guest again.
Behind, a darker hour ascends !
The altars quake, the crosier bends,
The ire of a despotic king
Rides forth upon destruction's wing ;
Then shall these vaults, so strong and deep,
Burst open to the sea-wind's sweep ;
Some traveller then shall find my bones,
Whitening amid disjointed stones,

And, ignorant of priests' cruelty,
Marvel such relics here should be."—

Fixed was her look, and stern her air ;
Back from her shoulders streamed her hair ;
The locks, that wont her brow to shade,
Stared up erectly from her head ;
Her figure seemed to rise more high ;
Her voice, despair's wild energy
Had given a tone of prophecy.
Appalled the astonished conclave sate ;
With stupid eyes, the men of fate
Gazed on the light inspired form,
And listened for the avenging storm ;
The judges felt the victim's dread,
No hand was moved, no word was said,
Till thus the Abbot's doom was given,
Raising his sightless balls to heaven :—
" Sister, let thy sorrows cease ;
Sinful brother part in peace ! "
　　From that dire dungeon, place of doom,
　　Of execution too, and tomb,
　　　Paced forth the judges three ;
　　Sorrow it were, and shame, to tell
　　The butcher-work that there befell,
　　When they had glided from the cell
　　　Of sin and misery.

An hundred winding steps convey
That conclave to the upper day ;
But, ere they breathed the fresher air,
They heard the shriekings of despair,
　　And many a stifled groan :
With speed their upward way they take,
(Such speed as age and fear can make,)

And crossed themselves for terror's sake,
  As hurrying, tottering on.
Even in the vesper's heavenly tone,
They seemed to hear a dying groan,
And bade the passing knell to toll
For welfare of a parting soul.
Slow o'er the midnight wave it swung,
Northumbrian rocks in answer rung ;
To Warkworth cell the echoes rolled,
His beads the wakeful hermit told ;
The Bamborough peasant raised his head,
But slept ere half a prayer he said ;
So far was heard the mighty knell,
The stag sprung up on Cheviot Fell,
Spread his broad nostrils to the wind,
Listed before, aside, behind ;
Then couched him down beside the hind,
And quaked among the mountain fern,
To hear that sound so dull and stern.

252   *The Battle of Flodden*
              (*From " Marmion"*)

NEXT morn the Baron climbed the tower,
    To view afar the Scottish power,
  Encamped on Flodden edge :
The white pavilions made a show,
Like remnants of the winter snow
  Along the dusky ridge.
Long Marmion looked :—at length his eye
Unusual movements might descry,
  Amid the shifting lines :

The Scottish host drawn out appears,
For, flashing on the hedge of spears
   The eastern sunbeam shines.
Their front now deepening, now extending;
Their flank inclining, wheeling, bending,
Now drawing back, and now descending,
The skilful Marmion well could know,
They watched the motions of some foe,
Who traversed on the plain below.

Even so it was ;—from Flodden ridge
   The Scots beheld the English host
   Leave Barmore-wood, their evening post,
   And heedful watched them as they crossed
The Till by Twisel Bridge.
   High sight it is, and haughty, while
   They dive into the deep defile ;
   Beneath the caverned cliff they fall,
   Beneath the castle's airy wall.
     By rock, by oak, by hawthorn tree,
   Troop after troop is disappearing ;
   Troop after troop their banners rearing,
     Upon the eastern bank you see.
   Still pouring down the rocky den,
     Where flows the sullen Till,
   And rising from the dim-wood glen,
   Standards on standards, men on men,
     In slow succession still,
And bending o'er the Gothic arch,
And pressing on, in ceaseless march,
   To gain the opposing hill.
That morn, to many a trumpet-clang,
Twisel ! thy rock's deep echo rang ;
And many a chief of birth and rank,
Saint Helen ! at thy fountain drank.

Thy hawthorn glade, which now we see
In spring-tide bloom so lavishly,
Had then from many an axe its doom,
To give the marching columns room.

And why stands Scotland idly now,
Dark Flodden! on thy airy brow,
Since England gains the pass the while,
And struggles through the deep defile?
What checks the fiery soul of James?
Why sits that champion of the dames
  Inactive on his steed,
And sees, between him and his land,
Between him and Tweed's southern strand,
  His host Lord Surrey lead?
What vails the vain knight-errant's brand?—
O, Douglas, for thy leading wand!
  Fierce Randolf, for thy speed!
O for one hour of Wallace might,
Or well-skilled Bruce, to rule the fight,
And cry—"Saint Andrew and our right!"
Another sight had seen that morn,
From Fate's dark book a leaf been torn,
And Flodden had been Bannock-bourne!—
The precious hour has passed in vain,
And England's host has gained the plain;
Wheeling their march, and circling still,
Around the base of Flodden-hill.

Ere yet the bands met Marmion's eye,
Fitz-Eustace shouted loud and high,—
  "Hark! hark! my lord, an English drum!
  And see ascending squadrons come
  Between Tweed's river and the hill,

Foot, horse, and cannon :—hap what hap,
My basnet to a prentice cap,
    Lord Surrey's o'er the Till !—
Yet more ! yet more !—how fair arrayed
They file from out the hawthorn shade,
    And sweep so gallant by !
With all their banners bravely spread,
    And all their armour flashing high,
Saint George might waken from the dead,
    To see fair England's banners fly."—
    " Stint in thy prate," quoth Blount ; " Thou'dst
        best,
And listen to our lord's behest."—
With kindling brow Lord Marmion said,—
    " This instant be our band arrayed ;
The river must be quickly crossed,
That we may join Lord Surrey's host.
If fight King James,—as well I trust,
That fight he will, and fight he must,—
The Lady Clare behind our lines
Shall tarry, while the battle joins."—

Himself he swift on horseback threw,
Scarce to the Abbot bade adieu ;

    *   *   *   *   *
Then on that dangerous ford, and deep,
Where to the Tweed Leat's eddies creep,
    He ventured desperately ;
And not a moment will he bide,
Till squire, or groom, before him ride ;
Headmost of all he stems the tide,
    And stems it gallantly.
Eustace held Clare upon her horse,
    Old Hubert led her rein,

Stoutly they braved the current's course,
And, though far downward driven per force,
  The southern bank they gain ;
Behind them, struggling, came to shore,
  As best they might, the train :
Each o'er his head his yew-bow bore,
  A caution not in vain ;
Deep need that day that every string,
By wet unharmed, should sharply ring.
A moment then Lord Marmion staid,
And breathed his steed, his men arrayed,
  Then forward moved his band,
Until, Lord Surrey's rear-guard won,
He halted by a cross of stone,
That, on a hillock standing lone,
  Did all the field command.

Hence might they see the full array
Of either host, for deadly fray ;
Their marshalled lines stretched east and west,
  And fronted north and south,
And distant salutation past
From the loud cannon mouth ;
Not in the close successive rattle,
That breathes the voice of modern battle,
  But slow and far between.—
The hillock gained, Lord Marmion staid :
  " Here, by this cross," he gently said,
  " You well may view the scene.
Here shalt thou tarry, lovely Clare :
O ! think of Marmion in thy prayer !—
Thou wilt not ?—well,—no less my care
Shall, watchful, for thy weal prepare.—

You, Blount and Eustace, are her guard,
  With ten picked archers of my train ;
With England if the day go hard,
  To Berwick speed amain.—
But, if we conquer, cruel maid !
My spoils shall at your feet be laid,
  When here we meet again."—
He waited not for answer there,
And would not mark the maid's despair,
  Nor heed the discontented look
From either squire ; but spurred amain,
And, dashing through the battle-plain,
  His way to Surrey took.

"——The good Lord Marmion, by my life !
  Welcome to danger's hour !—
Short greeting serves in time of strife :—
  Thus have I ranged my power :
Myself will rule this central host,
  Stout Stanley has the right,
My sons command the vaward post,
  With Brian Tunstall, stainless knight ;
  Lord Dacre, with his horsemen light,
  Shall be in rear-ward of the fight,
And succour those that need it most.
  Now, gallant Marmion, well I know,
  Would gladly to the vanguard go ;
Edmund, the Admiral, Tunstal there,
With thee their charge will blithely share ;
There fight thine own retainers too,
Beneath De Burg, thy steward true."—
  " Thanks, noble Surrey ! " Marmion said,
  Nor further greeting there he paid ;

But, parting like a thunder-bolt,
First in the vanguard made a halt,
  Where such a shout there rose
Of "Marmion! Marmion!" that the cry
Up Flodden mountain shrilling high,
  Startled the Scottish foes.

Blount and Fitz-Eustace rested still
With Lady Clare upon the hill;
On which, (for far the day was spent,)
The western sunbeams now were bent.
The cry they heard, its meaning knew,
Could plain their distant comrades view:
Sadly to Blount did Eustace say,
  "Unworthy office here to stay!
No hope of gilded spurs to-day.—
But, see! look up—on Flodden bent,
The Scottish foe has fired his tent."
  And sudden, as he spoke,
From the sharp ridges of the hill,
All downward to the banks of Till,
  Was wreathed in sable smoke;
Volumed and vast, and rolling far,
The cloud enveloped Scotland's war,
  As down the hill they broke;
Nor martial shout, nor minstrel tone,
Announced their march; their tread alone,
At times one warning trumpet blown,
  At times a stifled hum,
Told England, from his mountain-throne
  King James did rushing come.—
Scarce could they hear, or see their foes,
Until at weapon-point they close.—

They close, in clouds of smoke and dust,
With sword-sway, and with lance's thrust ;
  And such a yell was there,
Of sudden and portentous birth,
As if men fought upon the earth,
  And fiends in upper air.
Long looked the anxious squires ; their eye
Could in the darkness nought descry.

At length the freshening western blast
Aside the shroud of battle cast ;
And, first, the ridge of mingled spears
Above the brightening cloud appears ;
And in the smoke the pennons flew,
As in the storm the white sea-mew.
Then marked they dashing broad and far,
The broken billows of the war,
And plumed crests of chieftains brave,
Floating like foam upon the wave ;
  But nought distinct they see :
Wide raged the battle on the plain ;
Spears shook, and faulchions flashed amain ;
Fell England's arrow-flight like rain ;
Crests rose, and stooped, and rose again,
  Wild and disorderly.
Amid the scene of tumult, high
They saw Lord Marmion's falcon fly :
And stainless Tunstall's banner white,
And Edmund Howard's lion bright,
Still bear them bravely in the fight ;
  Although against them come,
Of gallant Gordons many a one,
And many a stubborn Highlandman,
And many a rugged Border clan,
  With Huntley, and with Home.

Far on the left, unseen the while,
Stanley broke Lennox and Argyle :
Though there the western mountaineer
Rushed with bare bosom on the spear,
And flung the feeble targe aside,
And with both hands the broad-sword plied :
'Twas vain.—But Fortune, on the right,
With fickle smile, cheered Scotland's fight.
Then fell that spotless banner white,
    The Howard's lion fell ;
Yet still Lord Marmion's falcon flew
With wavering flight, while fiercer grew
    Around the battle yell.
The border slogan rent the sky :
A Home ! a Gordon ! was the cry ;
    Loud were the clanging blows ;
Advanced,—forced back,—now low, now high,
    The pennon sunk and rose ;
As bends the bark's mast in the gale,
When rent are rigging, shrouds, and sail,
    It wavered 'mid the foes.
No longer Blount the view could bear :—
" By heaven, and all its saints ! I swear,
    I will not see it lost !
Fitz-Eustace, you with Lady Clare
May bid your beads, and patter prayer,—
    I gallop to the host."
And to the fray he rode amain,
Followed by all the archer train.
The fiery youth, with desperate charge,
Made, for a space, an opening large,—
    The rescued banner rose,—
But darkly closed the war around,
Like pine-tree, rooted from the ground
    It sunk among the foes.

38

Then Eustace mounted too ;—yet staid,
As loth to leave the helpless maid,
  When, fast as shaft can fly,
Blood-shot his eyes, his nostrils spread,
The loose rein dangling from his head,
Housing and saddle bloody red,
  Lord Marmion's steed rushed by ;
And Eustace, maddening at the sight,
  A look and sign to Clara cast,
  To mark he would return in haste,
Then plunged into the fight.

Ask me not what the maiden feels,
  Left in that dreadful hour alone :
Perchance her reason stoops, or reels ;
  Perchance a courage, not her own,
  Braces her mind to desperate tone.—
The scattered van of England wheels ;—
  She only said, as loud in air
  The tumult roared, " Is Wilton there ? "—
  They fly, or, maddened by despair,
  Fight but to die.—" Is Wilton there ? "—
With that, straight up the hill there rode
  Two horsemen drenched with gore,
And in their arms, a helpless load,
  A wounded knight they bore.
His hand still strained the broken brand ;
His arms were smeared with blood, and
  sand.
Dragged from among the horses' feet,
With dinted shield, and helmet beat,
The falcon-crest and plumage gone,
Can that be haughty Marmion ! . . .

Young Blount his armour did unlace,
And, gazing on his ghastly face,
  Said—"By Saint George, he's gone !
That spear-wound has our master sped ;
And see the deep cut on his head !
  Good-night to Marmion."—
  "Unnurtured Blount ! thy brawling cease :
He opes his eyes," said Eustace ; "peace !"—

When, doffed his casque, he felt free air,
Around gan Marmion wildly stare ;—
"Where's Harry Blount ? Fitz-Eustace where ?
Linger ye here, ye hearts of hare !
Redeem my pennon,—charge again !
Cry—'Marmion to the rescue !' Vain !
Last of my race, on battle-plain
That shout shall ne'er be heard again !—
Yet my last thought is England's :—fly,
  To Dacre bear my signet-ring ;
  Tell him his squadrons up to bring.—
Fitz-Eustace, to Lord Surrey hie :
  Tunstall lies dead upon the field ;
  His life-blood stains the spotless shield :
  Edmund is down ;—my life is reft ;—
  The Admiral alone is left.
  Let Stanley charge with spur of fire,—
  With Chester charge, and Lancashire,
  Full upon Scotland's central host,
  Or victory and England's lost.—
  Must I bid twice ?—hence, varlets ! fly !
  Leave Marmion here alone—to die."—
  They parted, and alone he lay ;
Clare drew her from the sight away,

Till pain wrung forth a lowly moan,
And half he murmured,—" Is there none,
  Of all my halls have nurst,
Page, squire, or groom, one cup to bring
Of blessed water, from the spring,
  To slake my dying thirst ! "—

O, Woman ! in our hours of ease,
Uncertain, coy, and hard to please,
And variable as the shade
By the light quivering aspen made ;
When pain and anguish wring the brow,
A ministering angel thou !—
Scarce were the piteous accents said,
When, with the Baron's casque, the maid
  To the nigh streamlet ran :
Forgot were hatred, wrongs, and fears ;
The plaintive voice alone she hears,
  Sees but the dying man.
She stooped her by the runnel's side,
  But in abhorrence backward drew,
For, oozing from the mountain's side,
Where raged the war, a dark red tide
  Was curdling in the streamlet blue.
Where shall she turn ?—behold her mark
  A little fountain-cell,
Where water, clear as diamond-spark,
  In a stone basin fell.
Above, some half-worn letters say,

" Drink . weary . pilgrim . drink . and . pray .
For . the . kind . soul . of . Sybil . Grey .
Who . built . this . cross . and . well."

She filled the helm, and back she hied,
And with surprise and joy espied

A Monk supporting Marmion's head ;
A pious man, whom duty brought
To dubious verge of battle fought,
 To shrieve the dying, bless the dead.

Deep drank Lord Marmion of the wave,
And, as she stooped his brow to lave—
"Is it the hand of Clare," he said,
"Or injured Constance, bathes my head ?"
 Then, as remembrance rose—
"Speak not to me of shrift or prayer !
 I must redress her woes.
Short space, few words, are mine to spare ;
Forgive and listen, gentle Clare !"—
 "Alas !" she said, "the while,—
O think of your immortal weal !
In vain for Constance is your zeal ;
 She died at Holy Isle."—
Lord Marmion started from the ground,
As light as if he felt no wound ;
Though in the action burst the tide,
In torrents, from his wounded side.
"Then it was truth !"—he said—"I knew
That the dark presage must be true—
 I would the Fiend, to whom belongs
 The vengeance due to all her wrongs,
  Would spare me but a day !
 For wasting fire, and dying groan,
 And priests slain on the altar-stone,
  Might bribe him for delay.
It may not be !—this dizzy trance—
Curse on yon base marauder's lance,
And doubly cursed my failing brand !
A sinful heart makes feeble hand."—

Then, fainting, down on earth he sunk,
Supported by the trembling Monk.

With fruitless labour, Clara bound,
And strove to staunch, the gushing wound :
The Monk, with unavailing cares,
Exhausted all the Church's prayers ;
Ever, he said, that, close and near,
A lady's voice was in his ear,
And that the priest he could not hear,
    For that she ever sung,
"*In the lost battle, borne down by the flying,
Where mingles war's rattle with groans of the
        dying !*"
        So the notes rung ;
    "Avoid thee, Fiend !—with cruel hand,
Shake not the dying sinner's sand !—
O look, my son, upon yon sign
Of the Redeemer's grace divine ;
    O think on faith and bliss !—
By many a death-bed I have been,
And many a sinner's parting seen,
    But never aught like this."—
The war, that for a space did fail,
Now trebly thundering swelled the gale,
    And—STANLEY ! was the cry ;—
A light on Marmion's visage spread,
    And fired his glazing eye :
With dying hand, above his head
He shook the fragment of his blade,
    And shouted " Victory !—
Charge, Chester, charge ! On, Stanley, on ! ". .
Were the last words of Marmion.

By this, though deep the evening fell,
Still rose the battle's deadly swell,
For still the Scots, around their king,
Unbroken, fought in desperate ring.
Where's now their victor vaward wing,
　　Where Huntley, and where Home ?—
O for a blast of that dread horn,
On Fontarabian echoes borne,
　　That to King Charles did come,
When Rowland brave, and Olivier,
And every paladin and peer,
　　On Roncesvalles died !
Such blast might warn them, not in vain,
To quit the plunder of the slain,
And turn the doubtful day again,
　　While yet on Flodden side,
Afar, the Royal Standard flies,
And round it toils and bleeds and dies,
　　Our Caledonian pride !
In vain the wish—for far away,
While spoil and havoc mark their way,
Near Sybil's Cross the plunderers stray.—
　　"O Lady," cried the Monk, "away !"—
　　And placed her on her steed ;
And led her to the chapel fair,
　　Of Tilmouth upon Tweed.
There all the night they spent in prayer,
And, at the dawn of morning, there
She met her kinsman, Lord Fitz-Clare.

But as they left the dark'ning heath,
More desperate grew the strife of death.
The English shafts in vollies hailed,
In headlong charge their horse assailed ;

Front, flank, and rear, the squadrons sweep,
To break the Scottish circle deep,
   That fought around their king.
But yet, though thick the shafts as snow,
Though charging knights like whirlwinds go,
Though bill-men deal the ghastly blow,
   Unbroken was the ring ;
The stubborn spear-men still made good
Their dark impenetrable wood,
Each stepping where his comrade stood,
   The instant that he fell.
No thought was there of dastard flight ;—
Linked in the serried phalanx tight,
Groom fought like noble, squire like knight,
   As fearlessly and well,
Till utter darkness closed her wing
O'er their thin host and wounded king.
Then skilful Surrey's sage commands
Led back from strife his shatter'd bands ;
   And from the charge they drew,
As mountain-waves, from wasted lands,
   Sweep back to ocean blue.
Then did their loss his foemen know ;
Their king, their lords, their mightiest low,
They melted from the field as snow,
When streams are swoln, and south winds
    blow,
   Dissolves in silent dew.
Tweed's echoes heard the ceaseless plash,
   While many a broken band,
Disordered, through her currents dash,
   To gain the Scottish land ;
To town and tower, to down and dale,
To tell red Flodden's dismal tale,
And raise the universal wail.

Tradition, legend, tune, and song,
Shall many an age that wail prolong:
Still from the sire the son shall hear
Of the stern strife, and carnage drear,
　　Of Flodden's fatal field,
Where shivered was fair Scotland's spear,
　　And broken was her shield!

Day dawns upon the mountain's side :—
There, Scotland! lay thy bravest pride,
Chiefs, knights, and nobles, many a one ;
The sad survivors all are gone.—
View not that corpse mistrustfully,
Defaced and mangled though it be ;
Nor to yon Border castle high
Look northward with upbraiding eye ;
　　Nor cherish hope in vain,
That, journeying far on foreign strand,
The Royal Pilgrim to his land
　　May yet return again.
He saw the wreck his rashness wrought ;
Reckless of life, he desperate fought,
　　And fell on Flodden plain :
And well in death his trusty brand,
Firm clenched within his manly hand,
　　Beseemed the monarch slain.

253　　　　　*The Outlaw*

O BRIGNALL banks are wild and fair,
　　　And Greta woods are green,
And you may gather garlands there
　　Would grace a summer-queen.

And as I rode by Dalton-Hall
    Beneath the turrets high,
A Maiden on the castle-wall
    Was singing merrily :
"O Brignall Banks are fresh and fair,
    And Greta woods are green ;
I'd rather rove with Edmund there
    Than reign our English queen."

" If, Maiden, thou wouldst wend with me,
    To leave both tower and town,
Thou first must guess what life lead we
    That dwell by dale and down.
And if thou canst that riddle read,
    As read full well you may,
Then to the greenwood shalt thou speed
    As blithe as Queen of May."
Yet sung she " Brignall banks are fair,
    And Greta woods are green ;
I'd rather rove with Edmund there
    Than reign our English queen.

" I read you by your bugle-horn
    And by your palfrey good,
I read you for a ranger sworn
    To keep the king's greenwood."
" A Ranger, lady, winds his horn,
    And 'tis at peep of light ;
His blast is heard at merry morn,
    And mine at dead of night."
Yet sung she " Brignall banks are fair,
    And Greta woods are gay ;
I would I were with Edmund there
    To reign his Queen of May !

"With burnish'd brand and musketoon
  So gallantly you come,
I read you for a bold Dragoon
  That lists the tuck of drum."
"I list no more the tuck of drum,
  No more the trumpet hear ;
But when the beetle sounds his hum
  My comrades take the spear.
And O ! though Brignall banks be fair
  And Greta woods be gay,
Yet mickle must the maiden dare
  Would reign my Queen of May !

"Maiden ! a nameless life I lead,
  A nameless death I'll die !
The fiend whose lantern lights the mead
  Were better mate than I !
And when I'm with my comrades met
  Beneath the greenwood bough,
What once we were we all forget,
  Nor think what we are now."

CHORUS.

Yet Brignall banks are fresh and fair,
  And Greta woods are green,
And you may gather garlands there
  Would grace a summer queen.

254   *Jock o' Hazeldean*

"WHY weep ye by the tide, ladie ?
    Why weep ye by the tide ?
I'll wed ye to my youngest son,
  And ye sall be his bride :

And ye sall be his bride, ladie,
　　Sae comely to be seen "—
But aye she loot the tears down fa'
　　For Jock of Hazeldean.

" Now let this wilfu' grief be done,
　　And dry that cheek so pale ;
Young Frank is chief of Errington
　　And lord of Langley-dale ;
His step is first in peaceful ha,'
　　His sword in battle keen "—
But aye she loot the tears down fa'
　　For Jock of Hazeldean.

"A chain of gold ye sall not lack,
　　Nor braid to bind your hair,
Nor mettled hound, nor managed hawk,
　　Nor palfrey fresh and fair ;
And you the foremost o' them a'
　　Shall ride our forest-queen "—
But aye she loot the tears down fa'
　　For Jock of Hazeldean.

The kirk was deck'd at morning-tide,
　　The tapers glimmer'd fair ;
The priest and bridegroom wait the bride,
　　And dame and knight are there :
They sought her baith by bower and ha' ;
　　The ladie was not seen !
She's o'er the Border, and awa'
　　Wi' Jock of Hazeldean.

255   *From " Marmion "*

WHERE shall the lover rest
    Whom the fates sever
From his true maiden's breast
    Parted for ever?
Where, through groves deep and high
    Sounds the far billow,
Where early violets die
    Under the willow.
      Eleu loro
    Soft shall be his pillow.

There, through the summer day
    Cool streams are laving :
There, while the tempests sway,
    Scarce are boughs waving ;
There thy rest shalt thou take,
    Parted for ever,
Never again to wake
    Never, O never !
      Eleu loro
    Never, O never !

Where shall the traitor rest,
    He, the deceiver,
Who could win maiden's breast,
    Ruin, and leave her ?
In the lost battle,
    Bore down by the flying,
Where mingles war's rattle
    With groans of the dying ;
      Eleu loro
    There shall he be lying.

Her wing shall the eagle flap
 O'er the falsehearted ;
His warm blood the wolf shall lap
 Ere life be parted :
Shame and dishonour sit
 By his grave ever ;
Blessing shall hallow it
 Never, O never !
  Eleu loro
Never, O never !

256   *The Rover*

(*From " Rokeby "*)

" A WEARY lot is thine, fair maid,
  A weary lot is thine !
To pull the thorn thy brow to braid,
 And press the rue for wine.
A lightsome eye, a soldier's mien,
 A feather of the blue,
A doublet of the Lincoln green—
 No more of me you knew
  My Love !
No more of me you know.

"The morn is merry June, I trow,
 The rose is budding fain ;
But she shall bloom in winter snow
 Ere we two meet again."
He turn'd his charger as he spake
 Upon the river shore,
He gave the bridle-reins a shake,
 Said " Adieu for evermore
  My Love !
And adieu for evermore."

257   *Pibroch of Donald Dhu*

PIBROCH of Donuil Dhu,
    Pibroch of Donuil,
Wake thy wild voice anew,
    Summon Clan Conuil.
Come away, come away,
    Hark to the summons !
Come in your war-array,
    Gentles and commons.

Come from deep glen, and
    From mountain so rocky ;
The war-pipe and pennon
    Are at Inverlochy.
Come every hill-plaid, and
    True heart that wears one,
Come every steel blade, and
    Strong hand that bears one.

Leave untended the herd,
    The flock without shelter ;
Leave the corpse uninterr'd,
    The bride at the altar ;
Leave the deer, leave the steer,
    Leave nets and barges ;
Come with your fighting gear,
    Broadswords and targes.

Come as the winds come, when
    Forests are rended,
Come as the waves come, when
    Navies are stranded :

Faster come, faster come,
    Faster and faster,
Chief, vassal, page and groom,
    Tenant and master.

Fast they come, fast they come ;
    See how they gather !
Wide waves the eagle plume,
    Blended with heather.
Cast your plaids, draw your blades,
    Forward each man set !
Pibroch of Donuil Dhu
    Knell for the onset !

258   *Proud Maisie*

PROUD Maisie is in the wood,
    Walking so early ;
Sweet Robin sits on the bush
    Singing so rarely.

" Tell me, thou bonny bird,
    When shall I marry me ? "
—" When six braw gentlemen
    Kirkward shall carry ye."

" Who makes the bridal bed,
    Birdie, say truly ! "
—" The gray-headed sexton
    That delves the grave duly.

" The glowworm o'er grave and stone
    Shall light thee steady ;
The owl from the steeple sing,
    Welcome, proud lady."

259   *Coronach*

H E is gone on the mountain,
      He is lost to the forest,
Like a summer-dried fountain,
   When our need was the sorest.
The fount reappearing
   From the raindrops shall borrow,
But to us comes no cheering,
   To Duncan no morrow !

The hand of the reaper
   Takes the ears that are hoary,
But the voice of the weeper
   Wails manhood in glory.
The autumn winds rushing
   Waft the leaves that are serest,
But our flower was in flushing
   When blighting was nearest.

Fleet foot on the correi [1],
   Sage counsel in cumber,
Red hand in the foray,
   How sound is thy slumber !
Like the dew on the mountain,
   Like the foam on the river,
Like the bubble on the fountain,
   Thou art gone ; and for ever !

[1] a hollow in a hill.

39

260   .   *Rosabelle*

O LISTEN, listen, ladies gay !
    No haughty feat of arms I tell;
Soft is the note, and sad the lay
    That mourns the lovely Rosabelle.

" Moor, moor the barge, ye gallant crew,
    And, gentle lady, deign to stay !
Rest thee in Castle Ravensheuch,
    Nor tempt the stormy firth to-day.

" The blackening wave is edged with white ;
    To inch [1] and rock the sea-mews fly ;
The fishers have heard the Water-Sprite,
    Whose screams forebode that wreck is nigh.

" Last night the gifted Seer did view
    A wet shroud swathed round lady gay ;
Then stay thee Fair, in Ravensheuch :
    Why cross the gloomy firth to-day ? "

" 'Tis not because Lord Lindesay's heir
    To-night at Roslin leads the ball,
But that my lady-mother there
    Sits lonely in her castle-hall.

" 'Tis not because the ring they ride,
    And Lindesay at the ring rides well,
But that my sire the wine will chide
    If 'tis not fill'd by Rosabelle."

[1] islet.

—O'er Roslin all that dreary night,
 A wondrous blaze was seen to gleam ;
'Twas broader than the watch-fire's light,
 And redder than the bright moonbeam.

It glared on Roslin's castled rock,
 It ruddied all the copse-wood glen ;
'Twas seen from Dryden's groves of oak,
 And seen from cavern'd Hathornden.

Seem'd all on fire that chapel proud
 Where Roslin's chiefs uncoffin'd lie,
Each Baron, for a sable shroud,
 Sheath'd in his iron panoply.

Seem'd all on fire within, around,
 Deep sacristy and altar's pale ;
Shone every pillar foliage-bound,
 And glimmer'd all the dead men's mail.

Blazed battlement and pinnet high,
 Blazed every rose-carved buttress fair—
So still they blaze, when fate is nigh
 The lordly line of high Saint Clair.

There are twenty of Roslin's barons bold
 Lie buried within that proud chapelle ;
Each one the holy vault doth hold,
 But the sea holds lovely Rosabelle !

And each Saint Clair was buried there
 With candle, with book, and with knell ;
But the sea-caves rung, and the wild winds sung
 The dirge of lovely Rosabelle.

261   *Song from the " Doom of Devorgoil "*

THE sun upon the lake is low,
    The wild birds hush their song,
The hills have evening's deepest glow,
    Yet Leonard tarries long.
Now all whom varied toil and care
    From home and love divide,
In the calm sunset may repair
    Each to the loved one's side.

The noble dame on turret high,
    Who waits her gallant knight,
Looks to the western beam to spy
    The flash of armour bright.
The village maid, with hand on brow
    The level ray to shade,
Upon the footpath watches now
    For Colin's darkening plaid.

Now to their mates the wild swans row,
    By day they swam apart,
And to the thicket wanders slow
    The hind beside the hart.
The woodlark at his partner's side
    Twitters his closing song—
All meet whom day and care divide,
    But Leonard tarries long !

262   *Hunting Song*

WAKEN, lords and ladies gay,
    On the mountain dawns the day ;
All the jolly chase is here
With hawk and horse and hunting-spear ;

Hounds are in their couples yelling,
Hawks are whistling, horns are knelling,
Merrily merrily mingle they,
Waken, lords and ladies gay.

Waken, lords and ladies gay,
The mist has left the mountain gray,
Springlets in the dawn are steaming,
Diamonds on the brake are gleaming,
And foresters have busy been
To track the buck in thicket green ;
Now we come to chant our lay
Waken, lords and ladies gay.

Waken, lords and ladies gay,
To the greenwood haste away ;
We can show you where he lies,
Fleet of foot and tall of size ;
We can show the marks he made
When 'gainst the oak his antler's fray'd ;
You shall see him brought to bay ;
Waken, lords and ladies gay.

Louder, louder chant the lay,
Waken, lords and ladies gay !
Tell them youth and mirth and glee
Run a course as well as we ;
Time, stern huntsman ! who can baulk,
Staunch as hound and fleet as hawk ;
Think of this, and rise with day,
Gentle lords and ladies gay !

ROBERT TANNAHILL

1774–1810

263   *Jessie, the Flower o' Dunblane*

THE sun has gane down o'er the lofty Benlomond,
    And left the red clouds to preside o'er the
      scene,
While lanely I stray, in the calm simmer gloamin',
    To muse on sweet Jessie, the flower o' Dunblane.
How sweet is the brier wi' its saft faulding blossom,
    And sweet is the birk wi' its mantle o' green ;
Yet sweeter and fairer, and dear to this bosom,
    Is lovely young Jessie, the flower o' Dunblane.

She's modest as ony, and blithe as she's bonny,
    For guileless simplicity marks her its ain ;
And far be the villain, divested of feeling,
    Wha'd blight in its bloom the sweet flower o'
      Dunblane.
Sing on, thou sweet mavis, thy hymn to the e'ening,—
    Thou'rt dear to the echoes of Calderwood glen :
Sae dear to this bosom, sae artless and winning,
    Is charming young Jessie, the flower o' Dunblane.

264   *Gloomy Winter's Now Awa'*

GLOOMY winter's now awa',
    Saft the westlan' breezes blaw,
'Mang the birks o' Stanley shaw
    The mavis sings fu' cheery, O !

Sweet the crawflower's early bell
Decks Gleniffer's dewy dell,
Blooming like thy bonnie sel',
     My young, my artless dearie, O !
Come, my lassie, let us stray
O'er Glenkilloch's sunny brae—
Blithely spend the gowden day
     'Midst joys that never weary, O !

Towering o'er the Newton woods,
Lav'rocks fan the snaw-white clouds ;
Siller saughs [1], wi' downy buds,
     Adorn the banks sae briery, O !
Round the sylvan fairy nooks
Feathery brackens fringe the rocks ;
'Neath the brae the burnie jouks [2],
     And ilka thing is cheery, O !
Trees may bud and birds may sing,
Flowers may bloom and verdure spring,
Joy to me they canna' bring
     Unless wi' thee, my dearie, O !

265   *The Braes o' Balquhither*

L   ET us go, lassie, go
         To the braes o' Balquhither,
Where the blaeberries grow
     'Mang the bonnie Highland heather ;
Where the deer and the rae,
     Lightly bounding together,
Sport the lang simmer day
     On the braes o' Balquhither.

          [1] willows.   [2] streamlet plays.

I will twine thee a bower
  By the clear siller fountain,
And I'll cover it o'er
  Wi' the flowers o' the mountain :
I will range thro' the wilds
  And the deep glens sae dreary,
And return wi' their spoils
  To the bower o' my dearie.

When the rude wintry win'
  Idly raves round our dwelling,
And the roar of the linn [1]
  On the night breeze is swelling,
So merrily we'll sing,
  As the storm rattles o'er us,
Till the dear shieling ring
  Wi' the light lilting chorus.

Now the simmer's in prime,
  Wi' the flowers richly blooming,
And the wild mountain thyme
  A' the moorlands perfuming ;—
To our dear native scenes
  Let us journey together,
Where glad innocence reigns
  'Mang the braes o' Balquhither.

266   *The Braes o' Gleniffer*

KEEN blaws the wind o'er the braes o' Gleniffer,
  The auld castle's turrets are cover'd wi' snaw ;
How changed frae the time when I met wi' my lover
  Amang the broom bushes by Stanley-green shaw ! [2]

---

[1] waterfall. [2] copse.

The wild flowers o' summer were spread a' sae bonnie,
   The mavis sang sweet frae the green birken tree ;—
But far to the camp they hae march'd my dear Johnnie,
   And now it is winter wi' nature and me.

Then ilk thing around us was blithesome and cheery,
   Then ilk thing around us was bonnie and braw ;
Now naething is heard but the wind whistling dreary,
   And naething is seen but the wide-spreading snaw :
The trees are a' bare, and the birds mute and dowie [1]—
   They shake the cauld drift frae their wings as they
      flee,
And chirp out their plaints, seeming wae for my
      Johnnie,—
   'Tis winter wi' them and 'tis winter wi' me.

Yon cauld sleety cloud skiffs alang the bleak mountain,
   And shakes the dark firs on the stey [2] rocky brae ;
While down the deep glen bawls the snaw-flooded
      fountain,
   That murmur'd sae sweet to my laddie and me.
'Tis no its loud roar on the wintry wind swellin',
   'Tis no the cauld blast brings the tears i' my e'e ;
For, O, gin I saw but my bonnie Scotch callan',
   The dark days o' winter were summer to me !

267   *O ! Are Ye Sleeping, Maggie ?*

"O ! ARE ye sleeping, Maggie ?
      O ! are ye sleeping, Maggie ?
Let me in, for loud the linn
Is roaring o'er the warlock craigie [3] !

---

[1] dreary.   [2] steep.   [3] wizard crag.

" Mirk and rainy is the night,—
    No a starn in 'a the carry [1];
Lightnings gleam athwart the lift [2],
    And winds drive wi' winter's fury.

" Fearful soughs the bour-tree bank [3],
    The rifted wood roars wild and dreary ;
Loud the iron yett [4] does clank ;
    The cry of howlets makes me eerie.

" Aboon my breath I daurna speak,
    For fear I raise your waukrife [5] daddy :
Cauld's the blast upon my cheek,—
    O rise, rise, my bonnie lady ! "

She oped the door, she let him in :
    He cuist aside his dreepin' plaidie :—
" Blaw your warst, ye rain and win' !
    Since, Maggie, now I'm in beside ye.

" Now, since ye're waking, Maggie,
    Now, since ye're waking, Maggie,
What care I for howlet's cry,
    For bour-tree bank, or warlock craigie ? "

[1] The " carry " commonly signifies the direction in which the clouds are being carried by the wind, but it stands here for the sky. [2] sky. [3] sighs the elder-tree bank. [4] gate. [5] easily roused.

SIR ALEXANDER BOSWELL

1775–1822

Jenny's Bawbee

I MET four chaps yon birks amang,
    Wi' hanging lugs [1] and faces lang ;
I speir'd at neighbour Bauldy Strang,
    Wha's they I see ?
Quo' he, Ilk cream-faced, pawky chiel' [2]
Thinks himsel' cunnin' as the de'il ;
And here they cam' awa' to steal
    Jenny's bawbee.

The first, a Captain to his trade,
Wi' skull ill-lined and back weel clad,
March'd round the barn and by the shed,
    And papp'd on's knee :
Quo' he, My goddess, nymph, and queen,
Your beauty's dazzled baith my een !—
But de'il a beauty he had seen
    But Jenny's bawbee.

A Lawyer neist,—wi' bleth'rin' gab [3],
Wha speeches wove like ony wab,
In ilk ane's corn aye took a dab,
    And a' for a fee :

[1] ears.   [2] artful fellow.   [3] fulsome tongue.

Accounts he owed thro' a' the toun,
And tradesmen's tongues nae mair could droun :
Haith ! now he thought to clout [1] his goun
    Wi' Jenny's bawbee.

A Norland Laird neist trotted up,
Wi' bawsint naig [2] and siller whup,—
Cried, There's my beast, lad—haud the grup,
    Or tie it till a tree.
What's gowd to me ? I've wealth o' lan' !
Bestow on ane o' worth your han'.
(He thought to pay what he was awn [3]
    Wi' Jenny's bawbee.)

A' spruce frae band-boxes and tubs,
A fool came neist. But life has rubs ;—
Foul were the roads, and fu' the dubs [4],
    And jaupit [5] a' was he.
He danced up, squintin' through a glass,
And girn'd [6], I' faith, a bonnie lass !—
He thought to win wi' front o' brass
    Jenny's bawbee.

She bade the laird gae kaim his wig,
The sodger no to strut sae big,
The lawyer no to be a prig :
    The fool he cried, Te-hee !
I kent that I could never fail !—
But she pinn'd the dish-clout to his tail,
And soused him frae the water-pail,
    And kept her bawbee.

[1] patch. [2] brindled nag. [3] owing. [4] puddles. [5] bespattered.
[6] grinned.

Then Johnnie came—a lad o' sense
Although he hadna mony pence—
And took young Jenny to the spence [1],
    Wi' her to crack a wee [2].
Now Johnnie was a clever chiel';
And here his suit he press'd sae weel
That Jenny's heart grew saft as jeel [3],
    And she birl'd [4] her bawbee.

[1] an inner room.   [2] chat a while.   [3] jelly.   [4] set her coin spinning.

RICHARD GALL

1776–1801

Cradle Song

BALOO, baloo [1], my wee wee thing,
  O saftly close thy blinkin' e'e !
Baloo, baloo, my wee wee thing,
  For thou art doubly dear to me.
Thy daddie now is far awa'—
  A sailor laddie o'er the sea !
But hope aye hechts [2] his safe return
  To you, my bonnie lamb, an' me.

Baloo, baloo, my wee wee thing,
  O saftly close thy blinkin' e'e !
Baloo, baloo, my wee wee thing,
  For thou art doubly dear to me.
Thy face is simple, sweet, an' mild,
  Like ony simmer e'ening fa' ;
Thy sparkling e'e is bonnie black,
  Thy neck is like the mountain snaw.

Baloo, baloo, my wee wee thing,
  O saftly close thy blinkin' e'e !
Baloo, baloo, my wee wee thing,
  For thou art doubly dear to me.
O, but thy daddie's absence lang
  Might break my dowie heart in twa,
Wert thou not left, a dautit [3] pledge,
  To steal the eerie hours awa' !

[1] hush thee.   [2] promises.   [3] cherished.

THOMAS CAMPBELL

1777–1844

Ye Mariners of England

A NAVAL ODE

I

YE Mariners of England
   That guard our native seas,
Whose flag has braved, a thousand years,
The battle and the breeze—
Your glorious standard launch again
To match another foe !
And sweep through the deep,
While the stormy winds do blow,—
While the battle rages loud and long,
And the stormy winds do blow.

II

The spirits of your fathers
Shall start from every wave !
For the deck it was their field of fame,
And Ocean was their grave.
Where Blake and mighty Nelson fell
Your manly hearts shall glow,
As ye sweep through the deep
While the stormy winds do blow,—
While the battle rages loud and long,
And the stormy winds do blow.

III

Britannia needs no bulwarks,
No towers along the steep;
Her march is o'er the mountain waves,
Her home is on the deep.
With thunders from her native oak
She quells the floods below,
As they roar on the shore
When the stormy winds do blow,—
When the battle rages loud and long
And the stormy winds do blow.

IV

The meteor flag of England
Shall yet terrific burn,
Till danger's troubled night depart
And the star of peace return.
Then, then, ye ocean warriors!
Our song and feast shall flow
To the fame of your name,
When the storm has ceased to blow,—
When the fiery fight is heard no more,
And the storm has ceased to blow.

271 *Battle of the Baltic*

I

OF Nelson and the North
Sing the glorious day's renown,
When to battle fierce came forth
All the might of Denmark's crown,

And her arms along the deep proudly shone,—
By each gun the lighted brand
In a bold determined hand;
And the Prince of all the land
Led them on.

II

Like leviathans afloat
Lay their bulwarks on the brine,
While the sign of battle flew
On the lofty British line:
It was ten of April morn by the chime:
As they drifted on their path
There was silence deep as death,
And the boldest held his breath
For a time.

III

But the might of England flushed
To anticipate the scene;
And her van the fleeter rushed
O'er the deadly space between.
"Hearts of oak!" our captain cried; when each
    gun
From its adamantine lips
Spread a death-shade round the ships,
Like the hurricane eclipse
Of the sun.

IV

Again! again! again!
And the havoc did not slack,
Till a feeble cheer the Dane
To our cheering sent us back:

40

Their shots along the deep slowly boom;
Then ceased—and all is wail
As they strike the shattered sail,
Or in conflagration pale
Light the gloom.

V

Out spoke the victor then
As he hailed them o'er the wave,
" Ye are brothers ! ye are men !
And we conquer but to save ;
So peace instead of death let us bring :
But yield, proud foe, thy fleet
With the crews at England's feet,
And make submission meet
To our King."

VI

Then Denmark blessed our chief
That he gave her wounds repose ;
And the sounds of joy and grief
From her people wildly rose,
As death withdrew his shades from the day ;
While the sun looked smiling bright
O'er a wide and woeful sight,
Where the fires of funeral light
Died away.

VII

Now joy, Old England, raise
For the tidings of thy might
By the festal cities blaze,
While the wine-cup shines in light ;

And yet, amidst that joy and uproar,
Let us think of them that sleep,
Full many a fathom deep,
By thy wild and stormy steep,
Elsinore !

VIII

Brave hearts ! to Britain's pride
Once so faithful and so true,
On the deck of fame that died
With the gallant good Riou—
Soft sigh the winds of Heaven o'er their grave !
While the billow mournful rolls
And the mermaid's song condoles,
Singing glory to the souls
Of the brave !

272   *Hohenlinden*

ON Linden, when the sun was low,
    All bloodless lay the untrodden snow,
And dark as winter was the flow
    Of Iser, rolling rapidly.

But Linden saw another sight
When the drum beat at dead of night,
Commanding fires of death to light
    The darkness of her scenery.

By torch and trumpet fast arrayed,
Each horseman drew his battle blade,
And furious every charger neighed
    To join the dreadful revelry.

Then shook the hills with thunder riven,
Then rushed the steed to battle driven,
And louder than the bolts of heaven
    Far flashed the red artillery.

But redder yet that light shall glow
On Linden's hills of stainèd snow,
And bloodier yet the torrent flow
    Of Iser, rolling rapidly.

'Tis morn, but scarce yon level sun
Can pierce the war-clouds, rolling dun,
Where furious Frank and fiery Hun
    Shout in their sulphurous canopy.

The combat deepens. On, ye brave,
Who rush to glory, or the grave!
Wave, Munich! all thy banners wave,
    And charge with all thy chivalry!

Few, few shall part where many meet!
The snow shall be their winding-sheet,
And every turf beneath their feet
    Shall be a soldier's sepulchre.

273   *The Soldier's Dream*

OUR bugles sang truce—for the night-cloud had
    lowered,
And the sentinel stars set their watch in the sky;
And thousands had sunk on the ground overpowered,
    The weary to sleep, and the wounded to die.

When reposing that night on my pallet of straw,
  By the wolf-scaring faggot that guarded the
    slain,
At the dead of the night a sweet vision I saw,
  And thrice ere the morning I dreamt it again.

Methought from the battle-field's dreadful array
  Far, far I had roamed on a desolate track:
'Twas autumn,—and sunshine arose on the way
  To the home of my fathers, that welcomed me
    back.

I flew to the pleasant fields, traversed so oft
  In life's morning march when my bosom was
    young;
I heard my own mountain-goats bleating aloft,
  And knew the sweet strain that the corn-reapers
    sung.

Then pledged we the wine-cup, and fondly I swore
  From my home and my weeping friends never to
    part;
My little ones kissed me a thousand times o'er,
  And my wife sobbed aloud in her fulness of heart.

"Stay, stay with us,—rest, thou art weary and
    worn!"
  And fain was their war-broken soldier to stay;
But sorrow returned with the dawning of morn,
  And the voice in my dreaming ear melted away.

274 *Lochiel's Warning*

WIZARD—LOCHIEL

WIZARD

LOCHIEL, Lochiel! beware of the day
　　When the Lowlands shall meet thee in battle
　　　array!
For a field of the dead rushes red on my sight,
And the clans of Culloden are scattered in fight.
They rally, they bleed for their kingdom and crown;
Woe, woe to the riders that trample them down!
Proud Cumberland prances, insulting the slain,
And their hoof-beaten bosoms are trod to the plain.
But hark! through the fast-flashing lightning of war
What steed to the desert flies frantic and far?
'Tis thine, oh Glenullin! whose bride shall await,
Like a love-lighted watch-fire, all night at the gate.
A steed comes at morning: no rider is there;
But its bridle is red with the sign of despair.
Weep, Albin! to death and captivity led!
Oh weep! but thy tears cannot number the dead;
For a merciless sword on Culloden shall wave,
Culloden! that reeks with the blood of the brave.

LOCHIEL

Go, preach to the coward, thou death-telling seer!
Or, if gory Culloden so dreadful appear,
Draw, dotard, around thy old wavering sight
This mantle to cover the phantoms of fright.

WIZARD

Ha ! laugh'st thou, Lochiel, my vision to scorn ?
Proud bird of the mountain, thy plume shall be torn !
Say, rushed the bold eagle exultingly forth
From his home in the dark-rolling clouds of the north ?
Lo ! the death-shot of foemen outspeeding, he rode
Companionless, bearing destruction abroad ;
But down let him stoop from his havoc on high !
Ah ! home let him speed,—for the spoiler is nigh !
Why flames the far summit ? Why shoot to the blast
Those embers, like stars from the firmament cast ?
'Tis the fire-shower of ruin, all dreadfully driven
From his eyrie, that beacons the darkness of heaven !
Oh, crested Lochiel ! the peerless in might,
Whose banners arise on the battlements' height,
Heaven's fire is around thee to blast and to burn ;
Return to thy dwelling ! all lonely return !
For the blackness of ashes shall mark where it stood,
And a wild mother scream o'er her famishing brood.

LOCHIEL

False Wizard, avaunt ! I have marshalled my clan—
Their swords are a thousand, their bosoms are one !
They are true to the last of their blood and their
    breath,
And like reapers descend to the harvest of death.
Then welcome be Cumberland's steed to the shock !
Let him dash his proud foam like a wave on the rock !
But woe to his kindred, and woe to his cause,
When Albin her claymore indignantly draws !
When her bonneted chieftains to victory crowd,
Clanranald the dauntless and Moray the proud,
All plaided and plumed in their tartan array——

Wizard

Lochiel, Lochiel! beware of the day;
For, dark and despairing, my sight I may seal,
But man cannot cover what God would reveal.
'Tis the sunset of life gives me mystical lore,
And coming events cast their shadows before.
I tell thee Culloden's dread echoes shall ring
With the bloodhounds that bark for thy fugitive king.
Lo! anointed by Heaven with the vials of wrath,
Behold where he flies on his desolate path!
Now, in darkness and billows he sweeps from my
    sight:
Rise, rise! ye wild tempests, and cover his flight!
'Tis finished. Their thunders are hushed on the
    moors:
Culloden is lost, and my country deplores.
But where is the iron-bound prisoner? Where?
For the red eye of battle is shut in despair.
Say, mounts he the ocean-wave, banished, forlorn,
Like a limb from his country cast bleeding and torn?
Ah no! for a darker departure is near;
The war-drum is muffled, and black is the bier;
His death-bell is tolling: oh! mercy dispel
Yon sight that it freezes my spirit to tell!
Life flutters convulsed in his quivering limbs,
And his blood-streaming nostril in agony swims;
Accursed be the faggots that blaze at his feet,
Where his heart shall be thrown ere it ceases to beat,
With the smoke of its ashes to poison the gale——

Lochiel

Down, soothless insulter! I trust not the tale:
For never shall Albin a destiny meet
So black with dishonour, so foul with retreat.

Though my perishing ranks should be strewed in their
    gore,
Like ocean-weeds heaped on the surf-beaten shore,
Lochiel, untainted by flight or by chains,
While the kindling of life in his bosom remains,
Shall victor exult, or in death be laid low
With his back to the field, and his feet to the
    foe !
And, leaving in battle no blot on his name,
Look proudly to Heaven from the death-bed of fame

275   *Lord Ullin's Daughter*

A CHIEFTAIN to the Highlands bound
    Cries " Boatman, do not tarry !
And I'll give thee a silver pound
    To row us o'er the ferry."

" Now who be ye would cross Lochgyle,
    This dark and stormy water ? "
" O, I'm the chief of Ulva's isle,
    And this Lord Ullin's daughter.

" And fast before her father's men
    Three days we've fled together,
For, should he find us in the glen,
    My blood would stain the heather.

" His horsemen hard behind us ride ;
    Should they our steps discover,
Then who will cheer my bonny bride
    When they have slain her lover ? "

Outspoke the hardy Highland wight,
  " I'll go, my chief ! I'm ready ;
It is not for your silver bright,
  But for your winsome lady.

"And, by my word ! the bonny bird
  In danger shall not tarry ;
So, though the waves are raging white
  I'll row you o'er the ferry."

By this the storm grew loud apace,
  The water-wraith [1] was shrieking ;
And in the scowl of heaven each face
  Grew dark as they were speaking.

But still, as wilder blew the wind,
  And as the night grew drearer,
Adown the glen rode armèd men—
  Their trampling sounded nearer.

"O haste thee, haste !" the lady cries,
  "Though tempests round us gather ;
I'll meet the raging of the skies,
  But not an angry father."

The boat has left a stormy land,
  A stormy sea before her,—
When, oh ! too strong for human hand,
  The tempest gathered o'er her.

And still they rowed amidst the roar
  Of waters fast prevailing :
Lord Ullin reached that fatal shore,—
  His wrath was changed to wailing.

       [1] the evil spirit of the waters.

For sore dismayed, through storm and shade,
  His child he did discover :
One lovely hand she stretched for aid,
  And one was round her lover.

"Come back ! come back !" he cried in grief
  Across the stormy water :
"And I'll forgive your Highland chief,
  My daughter ! oh my daughter !"

'Twas vain : the loud waves lashed the shore,
  Return or aid preventing ;
The waters wild went o'er his child,
  And he was left lamenting.

276   *Napoleon and the British Sailor*

I LOVE contemplating, apart
  From all his homicidal glory,
The traits that soften to our heart
  Napoleon's story.

'Twas when his banners at Boulogne
  Arm'd in our island every freeman
His navy chanced to capture one
  Poor British seaman.

They suffer'd him, I know not how,
  Unprisoned on the shore to roam ;
And aye was bent his longing brow
  On England's home.

His eye, methinks, pursued the flight
  Of birds to Britain half-way over
With envy ; they could reach the white
  Dear cliffs of Dover.

A stormy midnight watch, he thought,
  Than this sojourn would have been dearer,
If but the storm his vessel brought
  To England nearer.

At last, when care had banished sleep,
  He saw one morning, dreaming, doting,
An empty hogshead from the deep
  Come shoreward floating.

He hid it in a cave, and wrought
  The live-long day laborious, lurking,
Until he launched a tiny boat
  By mighty working.

Heaven help us ! 'twas a thing beyond
  Description wretched : such a wherry
Perhaps ne'er ventured on a pond,
  Or crossed a ferry.

For ploughing in the salt-sea field
  It would have made the boldest shudder—
Untarr'd, uncompass'd, and unkeel'd,
  No sail, no rudder.

From neighbouring woods he interlaced
  His sorry skiff with wattled willows ;
And thus equipp'd he would have passed
  The foaming billows.

But Frenchmen caught him on the beach,—
  His little Argo sorely jeering
Till tidings of him chanced to reach
  Napoleon's hearing.

With folded arms Napoleon stood,
  Serene alike in peace and danger;
And, in his wonted attitude,
  Address'd the stranger:

"Rash man, that wouldst yon Channel pass
  On twigs and staves so rudely fashioned!
Thy heart with some sweet British lass
  Must be impassioned."

"I have no sweetheart," said the lad;
  "But, absent long from one another,
Great was the longing that I had
  To see my mother."

"And so thou shalt," Napoleon said,
  "Ye've both my favour fairly won;
A noble mother must have bred
  So brave a son."

He gave the tar a piece of gold,
  And, with a flag of truce, commanded
He should be shipp'd to England Old,
  And safely landed.

Our sailor oft could scantly shift
  To find a dinner, plain and hearty;
But never changed the coin and gift
  Of Bonaparté.

277 *Song*

EARL MARCH looked on his dying child,
  And, smit with grief to view her—
"This youth," he cried, "whom I exiled,
  Shall be restored to woo her."

She's at the window many an hour
  His coming to discover;
And her love looked up to Ellen's bower,
  And she looked on her lover—

But ah! so pale, he knew her not,
  Though her smile on him was dwelling.
"And am I then forgot—forgot?"—
  It broke the heart of Ellen.

In vain he weeps, in vain he sighs;
  Her cheek is cold as ashes;
Nor love's own kiss shall wake those eyes
  To lift their silken lashes.

ROBERT JAMIESON

1780–1844

278

My Wife's a Winsome Wee Thing

MY wife's a winsome wee thing,
    A bonnie, blythesome wee thing,
My dear, my constant wee thing,
    And evermair sall be :
It warms my heart to view her ;
I canna choose but lo'e her,
And oh, weel may I trow her
    How dearly she lo'es me !

For—though her face sae fair be
As nane could ever mair be,
And though her wit sae rare be
    As seenil [1] do we see—
Her beauty ne'er had gain'd me,
Her wit had ne'er enchain'd me,
Nor baith sae lang retain'd me,
    But for her love to me.

When wealth and pride disown'd me,
A' views were dark around me ;
And sad and laigh she found me
    As friendless worth could be :

[1] seldom.

When ither hope gaed frae me
Her pity kind did stay me,
And love for love she ga'e me ;
    And that's the love for me.

And, till this heart is cauld, I
That charm of life will hald by ;
And, though my wife grow auld, my
    Leal love aye young will be ;
For she's my winsome wee thing,
My canty[1], blythesome wee thing,
My tender, constant wee thing,
    And evermair sall be.

[1] cheery.

WILLIAM LAIDLAW

1780–1845

279

Lucy's Flittin'

'TWAS when the wan leaf frae the birk-tree [1] was
 fa'in',
And Martinmas dowie [2] had wound up the year,
That Lucy row'd up her wee kist [3] wi' her a' in',
 And left her auld maister and neebours sae dear.
For Lucy had served in the Glen a' the simmer,—
 She cam' there afore the flower bloom'd on the pea :
An orphan was she, and they had been gude till
 her,—
Sure that was the thing brocht the tear to her e'e.

She gaed by the stable where Jamie was stan'in' ;
 Richt sair was his kind heart the flittin' to see.
" Fare-ye-weel, Lucy ! " quo' Jamie, and ran in,—
 The gatherin' tears trickled fast frae his e'e.
As down the burn-side she gaed slaw wi' the flittin',
 Fare-ye-weel, Lucy ! was ilka bird's sang ;
She heard the craw sayin't, high on the tree sittin',
 And robin was chirpin't the brown leaves amang.

" Oh, what is't that pits my puir heart in a flutter ?
 And what gars the tears come sae fast to my e'e ?
If I wasna ettled [4] to be ony better,
 Then what gars me wish ony better to be ?

---

[1] birch-tree. [2] dreary. [3] packed up her wee chest. [4] intended.
destined.

I'm just like a lammie that loses its mither,—
   Nae mither or friend the puir lammie can see ;
I fear I hae tint [1] my puir heart a'thegither,—
   Nae wonder the tear fa's sae fast frae my e'e.

" Wi' the rest o' my claes I hae row'd up the ribbon—
   The bonnie blue ribbon that Jamie gae me :
Yestreen, when he gae me't, and saw I was sabbin',
   I'll never forget the wae blink o' his e'e.
Though now he said naething but, ' Fare-ye-weel,
   Lucy ! '
It made me I neither could speak, hear, nor see :
He couldna say mair, but just ' Fare-ye-weel, Lucy ! '—
   Yet that I will mind till the day that I dee.

" The lamb likes the gowan wi' dew when it's
   drookit [2] ;
  The hare likes the brake, and the braird [3] on the
   lea ;
But Lucy likes Jamie,"—she turn'd and she lookit—
   She thocht the dear place she wad never mair see.
—Ah, weel may young Jamie gang dowie and cheer-
   less !
  And weel may he greet on the bank o' the burn !
For bonnie sweet Lucy, sae gentle and peerless,
   Lies cauld in her grave, and will never return.

[1] lost. [2] drenched. [3] first sprouting of grain.

WILLIAM NICHOLSON

1782–1842

The Brownie of Blednoch

THERE cam' a strange wight to our town-en';
  And the fient a body did him ken:
He tirl'd[1] na lang; but he glided ben,
      Wi' a weary dreary hum.

His face did glow,—like the glow o' the west
When the drumly cloud has it half o'ercast,
Or the strugglin' moon when she's sair distrest,
      O, sirs! 'twas Aiken-drum.

I trow the bauldest stood aback—
Wi' a gape an' a glower till their lugs[2] did crack—
As the shapeless phantom mumblin' spak',
      "Hae ye wark for Aiken-drum?"

O! had ye seen the bairns' fright
As they stared at this wild and unyirthly wight,
As he stauket in, 'tween the dark and the light,
      And graned out, "Aiken-drum!"

"Sauf us!" quoth Jock, "d'ye see sic een?"
Cries Kate, "There's a hole where a nose should
    ha' been;
And the mouth's like a gash that a horn has ri'en[3].
      Wow! keep's frae Aiken-drum!"

[1] sought admittance. [2] ears. [3] riven.

The black dog, growling, cower'd his tail;
The lassie, swarf'd [1], loot fa' the pail;
Rob's lingle [2] brak, as he men't the flail,
    At the sight o' Aiken-drum.

His matted head on his breast did rest;
A lang blue beard wan'er'd down like a vest;—
But the glare o' his e'e hath nae bard exprest,
    Nor the skimes [3] o' Aiken-drum.

Roun' his hairy form there was naething seen
But a philabeg [4] o' the rashes green;
An' his knotted knees play'd aye knoit between [5]:—
    What a sight was Aiken-drum!

On his wauchie [6] arms three claws did meet,
As they trail'd on the grun' by his taeless feet:
E'en the auld gudeman himsel' did sweat
    To look at Aiken-drum.

But he drew a score [7], himsel' did sain [8]:
The auld wife tried, but her tongue was gane;
While the young ane closer clasp'd her wean [9]
    And turn'd frae Aiken-drum.

But the canny auld wife cam' till her breath;
And she deem'd the Bible might ward off scaith—
Be it benshee, bogle, ghaist, or wraith;—
    But it fear'd na Aiken-drum.

---

[1] swooning.　[2] twine.　[3] lurid glare.　[4] kilt.　[5] kept striking together.　[6] sallow, greasy.　[7] a charm against the powers of evil.
[8] crossed himself.　[9] infant.

" His presence protect us !" quoth the auld gude-
          man,
" What wad ye ; where won [1] ye—by sea or by lan' ?
I conjure ye—speak—by the beuk in my han' ! "—
          What a grane ga'e Aiken-drum !

" I lived in a lan' where we saw nae sky ;
I dwalt in a spot where a burn rins na by ;
But I'se dwall now wi' you, if ye like to try :—
          Hae ye wark for Aiken-drum ?

" I'll shiel' a' your sheep i' the mornin' sune ;
I'll berry [2] your crap by the light o' the moon ;
And baa [3] the bairns wi' an unkenn'd tune,—
          If ye'll keep puir Aiken-drum.

" I'll loup the linn when ye canna wade ;
I'll kirn [4] the kirn, and I'll turn the bread ;
And the wildest filly that ever ran rede [5]
          I'se tame't," quoth Aiken-drum.

" To wear the tod [6] frae the flock on the fell—
To gather the dew frae the heather-bell—
And to look at my face in your clear crystal well,
          Might gi'e pleasure to Aiken-drum.

"I'se seek nae guids, gear, bond, nor mark :
I use nae beddin', shoon, nor sark ;
But a cogfu' o' brose[7] 'tween the light an' the dark
          Is the wage o' Aiken-drum."

[1] dwell.   [2] thresh.   [3] hush.   [4] churn.   [5] ran wild.   [6] fox.
[7] bowlful of porridge.

Quoth the wylie auld wife, " The thing speaks weel :
Our workers are scant ;—we hae routh ¹ o' meal :
Gif he'll do as he says—be he man, be he de'il—
　　　Wow ! we'll try this Aiken-drum."

But the wenches skirl'd ², " He'se no be here !
His eldritch ³ look gars us swarf wi' fear ;
An' the fient a ane will the hoose come near
　　　If they think but o' Aiken-drum :

" For a foul and a stalwart ghaist is he ;
Despair sits brooding aboon his e'e-brae ;
And unchancie ⁴ to light on a maiden's e'e
　　　Is the glower o' Aiken-drum."

" Puir slipmalabors ⁵, ye hae little wit !
Is'tna Hallowmas now, an' the crap out yet ? "
Sae she silenced them a' wi' a stamp o' her fit :
　　　" Sit yer wa's down, Aiken-drum."

Roun' a' that side what wark was dune,
By the streamers' ⁶ gleam, or the glance o' the moon !
A word or a wish, and the brownie cam' sune,—
　　　Sae helpfu' was Aiken-drum.

But he slade aye awa' or the sun was up ;
He ne'er could look straught on Macmillan's cup⁷ :
They watch'd ;—but nane saw him his brose ever sup ;
　　　Nor a spune sought Aiken-drum.

---

¹ abundance.　　² shrieked.　　³ eerie.　　⁴ unlucky.　　⁵ lazy sluts.
⁶ Northern Lights.　　⁷ a local communion cup, used as a test in
cases of suspected heresy.

On Blednoch banks, and on crystal Cree,
For mony a day a toil'd wight was he ;
And the bairns play'd harmless roun' his knee—
    Sae social was Aiken-drum.

But a new-made wife, fu' o' frippish freaks [1],
Fond o' a' things feat for the first five weeks,
Laid a mouldy pair o' her ain man's breeks
    By the brose o' Aiken-drum.

Let the learned decide, when they convene,
What spell was him and the breeks between ;
For, frae that day forth, he was nae mair seen ;—
    And sair miss'd was Aiken-drum

He was heard by a herd gaun by the Thrieve,
Crying, " Lang, lang now may I greet and grieve ;
For, alas ! I hae gotten baith fee and leave—
    O, luckless Aiken-drum ! "

Awa', ye wrangling sceptic tribe !
Wi' your pros and your cons wad ye decide
'Gain the 'sponsible voice o' a hale country-side
    On the facts 'bout Aiken-drum ?

Though the Brownie o' Blednoch lang be gane,
The mark o' his feet's left on mony a stane ;
And mony a wife and mony a wean
    Tell the feats o' Aiken-drum.

[1] fancies affecting costume.

E'en now light loons, that gibe and sneer
At spiritual guests and a' sic gear,
At the Glashnoch mill hae swat wi' fear,
    An look'd roun' for Aiken-drum ;

And guidly folks hae gotten a fright,
When the moon was set and the stars gied nae light,
At the roarin' linn, in the howe o' the night [1],
    Wi' sughs [2] like Aiken-drum.

[1] dead of the night. [2] moans.

CAPTAIN CHARLES GRAY

1782–1851

281

The Social Cup

BLYTHE, blythe, and merry are we!
   Blythe are we, ane and a'!
Aften ha'e we canty [1] been,
   But sic a night we never saw.

The gloamin' saw us a' sit down,
   And meikle mirth has been our fa';—
Then let the sang and toast gae roun'
   Till chanticleer begins to craw.
Blythe, blythe, and merry are we—
   Pick and wale [2] o' merry men:
What care we though the cock may craw?
   We're masters o' the tappit-hen [3]!

The auld kirk bell has chappit [4] twal,—
   Wha cares though she had chappit twa?
We're licht o' heart, and winna part,
   Though time and tide may rin awa'.
Blythe, blythe, and merry are we—
   Hearts that care can never ding [5]:
Then let time pass,—we'll steal his glass,
   And pu' a feather frae his wing!

[1] cheery.   [2] choice.   [3] crested hen : name applied to a quart
vessel.   [4] struck.   [5] overcome.

Now is the witching time of nicht,
   When ghaists, they say, are to be seen ;
And fays dance to the glow-worm's licht,
   Wi' fairies in their gowns of green.
Blythe, blythe, and merry are we !—
   Ghaists may tak' their midnicht stroll,
Witches ride, on brooms astride,
   While we sit by the witchin' bowl !

Tut ! never speer [1] how wears the morn,—
   The moon's still blinkin' i' the sky ;
And gif, like her, we fill our horn,
   I dinna doubt we'll drink it dry.
Blythe, blythe, and merry are we—
   Blythe out-owre the barley bree [2] ;
And, let me tell, the moon hersel'
   Aft dips her toom [3] horn i' the sea !

Then fill us up a social cup,
   And never mind the dapple-dawn :
Just sit awhile—the sun may smile,
   And licht us a' across the lawn.
Blythe, blythe, and merry are we ;—
   See ! the sun is keekin' ben [4] !
Gi'e time his glass,—for months may pass
   Ere we ha'e sic a nicht again !

[1] ask.   [2] over the barley brew.   [3] empty.   [4] peeping in.

ALLAN CUNNINGHAM
1784-1842

282

A WET sheet and a flowing sea,
　A wind that follows fast,
And fills the white and rustling sail,
　And bends the gallant mast—
And bends the gallant mast, my boys,
　While, like the eagle, free,
Away the good ship flies, and leaves
　Old England on the lee.

O for a soft and gentle wind !
　I heard a fair one cry ;
But give to me the snoring breeze
　And white waves heaving high—
And white waves heaving high, my boys,
　The good ship tight and free,—
The world of waters is our home,
　And merry men are we.

There's tempest in yon hornéd moon,
　And lightning in yon cloud ;
But hark the music, mariners !
　The wind is piping loud—
The wind is piping loud, my boys,
　The lightning flashes free ;
While the hollow oak our palace is,
　Our heritage the sea.

283 *It's Hame, and it's Hame*

IT'S hame, and it's hame, hame fain wad I be,
   An' it's hame, hame, hame, to my ain countree!
When the flower is i' the bud and the leaf is on
   the tree,
The lark shall sing me hame in my ain countree ;
It's hame, and it's hame, hame fain wad I be,
An' it's hame, hame, hame, to my ain countree !

The green leaf o' loyaltie's beginning for to fa',
The bonnie white rose it is withering an' a' ;
But I'll water 't wi' the blude of usurping tyrannie
An' green it will grow in my ain countree.
It's hame, and it's hame, hame fain wad I be,
An' it's hame, hame, hame, to my ain countree !

There's naught now frae ruin my country can save,
But the keys o' kind heaven to open the grave,
That a' the noble martyrs who died for loyaltie
May rise again and fight for their ain countree.
It's hame, and it's hame, hame fain wad I be,
An' it's hame, hame, hame, to my ain countree !

The great now are gane—a' who ventured to save ;
The new grass is springing on the tap o' their
   grave ;
But the sun thro' the mirk blinks blythe in my ee :
" I'll shine on ye yet in your ain countree."
It's hame, and it's hame, hame fain wad I be,
An' it's hame, hame, hame, to my ain countree !

The Bonnie Bairns

(Notwithstanding a foundation in antiquity, this ballad, says
Mr. S. C. Hall[1], "must be considered as, in reality, the composi-
tion of Cunningham.")

THE lady she walk'd in yon wild wood,
    Aneath the hollin tree ;
And she was aware of two bonnie bairns
    Were running at her knee.

The tane[2] it pull'd a red, red rose,
    With a hand as soft as silk ;
The other, it pull'd the lily pale,
    Wi' a hand mair white than milk.

"Now, why pull ye the red rose, fair bairns ?
    And why the white lily ?"
"O we sue wi' them at the seat of grace
    For the soul of thee, ladie !"

"O bide wi' me, my twa bonnie bairns !
    I'll cleid[3] ye rich and fine ;
And all for the blaeberries of the wood,
    Ye se hae white bread and wine."

She heard a voice, a sweet low voice,
    Say, "Weans[4], ye tarry lang ;"
She stretch'd her hand to the youngest bairn :
    "Kiss me before ye gang."

[1] "Book of British Ballads," p. 235.   [2] the one.   [3] clothe.
[4] children.

She sought to take a lily hand,
    And kiss a rosie chin :—
"O, nought sae pure can bide the touch
    Of a hand red-wet wi' sin !"

The stars were shooting to and fro,
    And wild-fire fill'd the air,
As that lady follow'd thae bonnie bairns
    For three lang hours and mair.

"O ! where dwell ye, my ain sweet bairns ?
    I'm wae and weary grown !"
"O ! lady, we live where woe never is,
    In a land to sin unknown."

There came a shape which seem'd to her
    As a rainbow 'mang the rain ;
And sair these sweet babes pled for her,
    And they pled and pled in vain.

"And O ! and O !" said the youngest babe,
    "My mother maun come in :"
"And O ! and O !" said the eldest babe,
    "Wash her twa hands frae sin."

"And O ! and O !" said the youngest babe,
    "She nursed me on her knee :"
"And O ! and O !" said the eldest babe,
    "She's a mither yet to me."

"And O ! and O !" said the babes baith,
    "Take her where waters rin,
And white as the milk o' her white breast
    Wash her twa hands frae sin."

285   *The Poet's Bridal-day Song*

O! MY love's like the steadfast sun,
    Or streams that deepen as they run ;
Nor hoary hairs, nor forty years,
Nor moments between sighs and tears,
Nor nights of thought, nor days of pain,
Nor dreams of glory dream'd in vain ;
Nor mirth, nor sweetest song that flows
To sober joys and soften woes,
Can make my heart or fancy flee
One moment, my sweet wife, from thee.

Even while I muse I see thee sit
In maiden bloom and matron wit,—
Fair, gentle, as when first I sued
Ye seem, but of sedater mood :
Yet my heart leaps as fond for thee
As when, beneath Arbigland tree,
We stay'd and woo'd, and thought the moon
Set on the sea an hour too soon ;
Or linger'd 'mid the falling dew,
When looks were fond and words were few.

Though I see, smiling at thy feet,
Five sons and ae fair daughter sweet ;
And time, and care, and birth-time woes,
Have dimm'd thine eye and touch'd thy rose ;
To thee and thoughts of thee belong
Whate'er charms me in tale or song :
When words descend, like dews, unsought,
With gleams of deep enthusiast thought,
And Fancy in her heaven flies free,—
They come, my love, they come from thee.

O, when more thought we gave of old
To silver than some give to gold,
'Twas sweet to sit and ponder o'er
How we should deck our humble bower !
'Twas sweet to pull, in hope, with thee,
The golden fruit of Fortune's tree ;
And sweeter still to choose and twine
A garland for these locks of thine—
A song-wreath which may grace my Jean,
While rivers flow and woods are green.

At times there come, as come there ought,
Grave moments of sedater thought,
When Fortune frowns, nor lends our night
One gleam of her inconstant light ;
And Hope, that decks the peasant's bower,
Shines like the rainbow through the shower :—
O then I see, while seated nigh,
A mother's heart shine in thine eye,
And proud resolve, and purpose meek,
Speak of thee more than words can speak ;
I think this wedded wife of mine
The best of all things not divine !

286 *The Lord's Marie* [1]

THE lord's Marie has kepp'd [2] her locks
Up wi' a gowden kame ;
An' she has put on her net-silk hose,
An' awa' to the tryste has gane.

[1] This poem in the manner of an old ballad is founded on a traditional story told of the daughter of a Lord Maxwell of Nithsdale, who is said to have been present, in disguise, at a rustic dancing tryst.   [2] caught.

O saft, saft fell the dew on her locks,
    An' saft, saft on her brow ;—
Ae sweet drap fell on her strawberry lip,
    An' I kiss'd it aff I trow.

" O where gat ye that leal maiden
    Sae jimpy[1] laced an' sma' ?
An' where gat ye that young damsel
    Wha dings[2] our lasses a' ?
O where gat ye that bonny, bonny lass
    Wi' heaven in her e'e ?
O here's ae drap o' the damask wine ;—
    Sweet maiden, will ye pree[3] ? "

Fu' white, white was her taper neck,
    Twist wi' the satin twine ;
But ruddy, ruddy grew her hawse[4]
    While she supp'd the blude-red wine.
"Come, here's thy health, young stranger doo[5],
    Wha wears the gowden kame !
This night will mony drink thy health,
    An' ken na wha to name."

" Play me up *Sweet Marie*," I cried,
    An' loud the piper blew ;
But the fiddler played aye *Struntum strum*,—
    An' down his bow he threw :
" Now here's thy health i' the red, red wine,
    Fair dame o' the stranger land !
For never a pair of een before
    Could mar my gude bow-hand."

[1] slenderly.   [2] surpasses.   [3] sip.   [4] throat.   [5] dove.

Her lips were a cloven hinny-cherry,
  Ripe tempting to the sight ;
Her locks o'er alabaster brows
  Fell like the morning light ;
An' O ! her hinny breath raised her locks,
  As thro' the dance she flew ;
While love laugh'd out o' her bright blue e'e,
  An' dwalt on her rosy mou'.

"Loose hings yere broider'd gowd garter,
  Fair lady,—daur I speak ? "—
She, trembling, raised her snowy hand
  To her red, red flushing cheek.
" Ye've drapt yere broach o' the beaten gowd,
  Thou lord's daughter sae gay."—
The tears swam bright in her bonny blue e'e :
  " O come, O come away !

" O haste—unbar the siller bolt—
  To my chamber let me win !
An' take this kiss, thou peasant youth,—
  For I daurna let ye in.
An' take," quo' she, " this kame o' gowd,
  Wi' this tress o' yellow hair ;
For mickle my beating heart forbodes
  I never maun meet ye mair ! "

ALEXANDER RODGER
1784-1846

My Auld Breeks [1]

MY mither men't my auld breeks,—
    An' wow but they were duddy [2]!
And sent me to get Mally shod
    At Robin Tamson's smiddy.
The smiddy stands beside the burn
    That wimples through the clachan [3];—
I never yet gae by the door
    But aye I fa' a-laughin'.

For Robin was a walthy carle,
    And had ae bonnie dochter;
Yet ne'er wad let her tak' a man,
    Tho' mony lads had sought her:
But what think ye o' my exploit?—
    The time our mare was shoeing,
I slippit up beside the lass
    And briskly fell a-wooing!

An' aye she e'ed my auld breeks,
    The time that we sat crackin' [4].
Quo' I, "My lass, ne'er mind the clouts,—
    I've new anes for the makin';—
But gin ye'll just come hame wi' me,
    An' lea' the carle, your father,
Ye'se get my breeks to keep in trim,
    Mysel', an' a' thegither."

[1] breeches.   [2] ragged.   [3] winds through the hamlet.   [4] chatting.

" 'Deed, lad," quo' she, " your offer's fair,—
   I really think I'll tak' it ;
Sae gang awa', get out the mare,—
   We'll baith slip on the back o't :
For gin I wait my father's time,
   I'll wait till I be fifty.
But na !—I'll marry in my prime,
   An' mak' a wife most thrifty."

Wow ! Robin was an angry man
   At tyning[1] o' his dochter :
Thro' a' the kintra-side he ran,
   An' far an' near he sought her.
But when he cam' to our fire-end
   An' fand us baith thegither,
Quo' I, " Gudeman, I've ta'en your bairn,
   An' ye may tak' my mither ! "

Auld Robin girn'd an' sheuk his pow[2] :
   " Guid sooth," quo' he, " you're merry !
But I'll just tak' ye at your word,
   An' end this hurry-burry."—
So Robin an' our auld wife
   Agreed to creep thegither :—
Now I hae Robin Tamson's pet,
   An' Robin has my mither !

---

[1] losing.   [2] scowled and shook his head.

JOHN WILSON ("CHRISTOPHER NORTH")
1785–1854

288 *The Evening Cloud*

A CLOUD lay cradled near the setting sun :—
  A gleam of crimson tinged its braided snow :
Long had I watch'd the glory moving on
  O'er the still radiance of the lake below.
Tranquil its spirit seem'd, and floated slow !
  Even in its very motion there was rest;
While every breath of eve that chance to blow
  Wafted the traveller to the beauteous west.
Emblem, methought, of the departed soul,—
  To whose white robe the gleam of bliss is given,
And by the breath of mercy made to roll
  Right onwards to the golden gates of heaven ;—
Where, to the eye of faith, it peaceful lies,
And tells to man his glorious destinies !

DAVID WEBSTER

1787–183

289   *Tak' it, Man, Tak' it*

WHEN I was a miller in Fife,
    Losh! I thought that the sound o' the happer
Said, Tak' hame a wee flow[1] to your wife,
    To help to be brose[2] to your supper.
Then my conscience was narrow and pure :
    But, someway, by random it rackit[3] ;
For I lifted twa nievefu'[4] or mair,—
    While the happer said, Tak' it, man, tak' it.

      Then hey for the mill and the kill[5],
        The garland and gear for my cogie[6]!
      And hey for the whisky and yill[7],
        That washes the dust frae my craigie[8]!

Although it's been lang in repute
    For rogues to make rich by deceiving,
Yet I see that it doesna weel suit
    Honest men to begin to the thieving ;
For my heart it gaed dunt upon dunt[9],—
    Od, I thought ilka dunt it wad crackit !
Sae I flang frae my nieve what was in't :—
    Still the happer said, Tak' it, man, tak' it.

A man that's been bred to the plough
    Might be deaved[10] wi' its clamorous clapper ;
Yet there's few but would suffer the sough
    After kenning what's said by the happer.

[1] portion.   [2] a sort of porridge.   [3] stretched.   [4] fistful.   [5] kiln.
[6] bowl.   [7] ale.   [8] throat.   [9] stroke.   [10] deafened.

I whiles thought it scoff'd me to scorn,
    Saying, Shame! is your conscience no chackit?
But when I grew dry for a horn,
    It changed aye to, Tak' it, man, tak' it.

The smugglers whiles cam' wi' their packs,
    'Cause they kent that I likit a bicker [1];
Sae I barter'd whiles wi' the gowks—
    Gied them grain for a soup o' their liquor.
I had lang been accustom'd to drink;
    And aye when I purposed to quat it,
The thing wi' its clapperty-clink
    Said aye to me, Tak' it, man, tak' it.

But the warst thing I did in my life,
    (Nae doubt but ye'll think I was wrong o't),
Od, I tauld a bit body in Fife
    A' my tale, and he made a bit sang o't.
I have aye had a voice a' my days,
    But for singin' I ne'er got the knack o't;
Yet I try whiles,—just thinking to please
    My frien's here wi', Tak' it, man, tak' it.

Now, miller and a' as I am,
    This far I can see thro' the matter:
There's men mair notorious to fame
    Mair greedy than me o' the mutter [2].
For 'twad seem that the hale race o' men,
    (Or wi' safety the half we may mak' it),
Hae some speaking happer within
    That says aye to them, Tak' it, man, tak' it!

        [1] bowl.   [2] the miller's due.

WILLIAM KNOX

1789–1825

The Wooer's Visit

MY native Scotland! how the youth is blest
　　To mark thy first star in the evening sky,
When the far curfew bids the weary rest,
　　And in his ear the milk-maid's wood-notes die !
　　Oh then, unseen by every human eye,
Soon as the lingering daylight hath decay'd,
　　Dear, dear to him o'er distant vales to hie—
While every head in midnight rest is laid—
To that endearing cot where dwells his favourite
　　maid !

Though he has labour'd, from the dawn of morn,
　　Beneath the summer sun's unclouded ray,
Till evening's dewdrops glisten'd on the thorn,
　　And wild-flowers closed their petals with the day, —
　　And though the cottage home be far away
Where all the treasure of his bosom lies,—
　　Oh, he must see her (though his raptured stay
Be short,—like every joy beneath the skies),
And yet be at his task by morning's earliest rise !

Behold him wandering o'er the moonlit dales,
　　The only living thing that stirs abroad,—
Tripping as lightly as the breathing gales
　　That fan his cheek upon the lonesome road,
　　Seldom by any other footstep trod !

Even though no moon shed her conducting ray
  And light his night-path to that sweet abode,
Angels will guide the lover's dreariest way,
If but for her dear sake whose heart is pure as they.

And see him now, upon the very hill
  From which, in breathless transport, he doth hail
(At such an hour—so exquisitely still)
  To him the sweetest, far the sweetest, vale
  That e'er was visited by mountain gale !
And oh, how fondly shall be hail'd by him
  The guiding lamp that never yet did fail—
That very lamp which her dear hand doth trim,
To light his midnight way when moon and stars are
    dim !

But who shall tell what her fond thoughts may
    be—
  The lovely damsel's sitting all alone,
When every inmate of the house but she
  To sweet oblivion of his cares hath gone ?
  By harmless stealth, unnoticed and unknown,
Behold her seated by her midnight fire,
  And turning many an anxious look upon
The lingering clock,—as if she would require
The steady foot of Time to haste at her desire.

But, though the appointed hour is fondly sought,
  At every sound her little heart will beat ;
And she will blush even at the very thought
  Of meeting him whom she delights to meet.

Be't as it may, her ear would gladly greet
The house-dog's bark that watch'd the whole night
 o'er;
 And oh, how gently shall she leave her seat,
And gently step across the sanded floor,
With trembling heart and hand to ope the creaking
 door!

The hour is past; and still her eager ear
 Hears but the tinkle of the neighbouring rill;—
No human footstep yet, approaching near,
 Disturbs the night calm so serene and still,
 That broods, like slumber, over dale and hill.
Ah! who may tell what phantoms of dismay
 The anxious feelings of her bosom chill—
The wiles that lead a lover's heart astray—
The darkness of the night—the dangers of the way?

But, lo! he comes;—and soon shall she forget
 Her griefs in sunshine of this hour of bliss.
Their hands in love's endearing clasp have met,
 And met their lips in loves' delicious kiss:—
 Oh, what is all the wealth of worlds to this!
Go,—thou mayst cross each foreign land, each sea,
 In search of honours, yet for ever miss
The sweetest boon vouchsafed by Heaven's decree—
The heart that loves thee well, the heart that's dear
 to thee!

And may I paint their pleasures yet to come,—
 When, like their hearts, their willing hands are
 join'd,
The loving inmates of a wedded home,
 For ever happy and for ever kind?

And may I paint their various charms combined
In the sweet offspring that around them plays ;
  Who, tho' on mountains with the bounding hind
Nursed rudely, yet may claim a nation's praise,
And on their native hills some proud memorial raise ?

My native Scotland ! Oh, thy northern hills,
  Thy dark brown hills, are fondly dear to me ;
And aye a warmth my swelling bosom fills
  For all the filial souls that cling to thee !
  Pure be their loves as human love can be ;
And still be worthy of their native land
  The little beings nursed beside their knee,—
What may at length their country's guardians stand,
And own the undaunted heart, and lift the uncon-
    quer'd hand !

THOMAS PRINGLE

1789–1834

291   *O the Ewe-Buchting's*[1] *Bonny*[2]

O THE ewe-buchting's bonny, both e'ening and
   morn,
When our blithe shepherds play on the bog-reed
   and horn ;
While we're milking they're lilting sae jocund and
   clear ;
But my heart's like to break when I think o' my
   dear.
O the shepherds take pleasure to blow on the horn,
To raise up their flocks i' the fresh simmer morn :
On the steep ferny banks they feed pleasant and
   free—
But alas ! my dear heart, all my sighing's for thee !

O the sheep-herding's lightsome amang the green
   braes,
Where Kale wimples clear 'neath the white-blossom'd
   slaes—
Where the wild-thyme and meadow-queen scent the
   saft gale,
And the cushat croods leesomely[3] down in the dale.

---

[1] the folding of the ewes.
[2] The first verse of this song is old. It was transcribed by
Pringle from a fragment in the handwriting of the celebrated Lady
Grisell Baillie.   [3] joyously.

There the lintwhite and mavis[1] sing sweet frae the
    thorn,
And blithe lilts the laverock[2] aboon the green corn,
And a' things rejoice in the simmer's glad prime—
But my heart's wi' my love in the far foreign clime!

O the haymaking's pleasant, in bright, sunny June—
The hay-time is cheery when hearts are in tune—
But while others are joking and laughing sae free,
There's a pain at my heart and a tear i' my e'e.
At e'en i' the gloaming, adown by the burn,
Fu' dowie and wae[3] 'aft I daunder[4] and mourn;
Amang the lang broom I sit greeting alane,
And sigh for my dear and the days that are gane.

O the days o' our youtheid were heartsome and gay,
When we herded thegither by sweet Gateshaw brae,
When we plaited the rushes and pu'd the witch-bells
By the Kale's ferny howms[5] and on Hownam's
    green fells.
But young Sandy bood[6] gang to the wars wi' the
    laird,
To win honour and gowd—(gif his life it be spared!).
Ah! little care I for walth, favour, or fame,
Gin I had my dear shepherd but safely at hame!

Then, round our wee cot though gruff winter s'ould
    roar,
And poortith glower in like a wolf at the door;
Though our toom purse had barely twa boddles[7] to
    clink,
And a barley-meal scone were the best on our bink[8];

---

[1] linnet and thrush.   [2] lark.   [3] dreary and sorrowful.   [4] wander.
[5] riverside meadows.   [6] must.   [7] coppers.   [8] dresser.

Yet, he wi' his hirsel[1], and I wi' my wheel,
Through the howe o' the year[2] we wad fend unco
    weel—
Till the lintwhite and laverock, and lambs bleating
    fain,
Brought back the blithe time o' ewe-buchting again.

292   *The Nameless Stream*

I FOUND a Nameless Stream among the hills,
    And traced its course through many a changeful
      scene ;—
  Now gliding free through grassy uplands green
And stately forests—fed by limpid rills ;
Now dashing through dark grottoes, where distils
  The poison dew ; then issuing all serene
   'Mong flowery meads, where snow-white lilies screen
The wild swan's whiter breast. At length it fills
Its deepening channels—flowing calmly on
  To join the Ocean on his billowy beach.
  —But that bright bourne its current ne'er shall
    reach :
It meets the thirsty Desert—and is gone
  To waste oblivion ! Let its story teach
The fate of one who sinks, like it, unknown.

293   *A Farewell to the Borderland*

OUR native Land—our native Vale—
    A long and last adieu !
Farewell to bonny Teviotdale,
    And Cheviot's mountains blue !

---

[1] flock. [2] dead of winter.

Farewell, ye hills of glorious deeds,
   And streams renown'd in song;
Farewell, ye blithesome braes and meads
   Our hearts have loved so long.

Farewell, ye broomy elfin knowes,
   Where thyme and harebells grow;
Farewell, ye hoary haunted howes[1],
   O'erhung with birk and sloe.

The battle-mound, the Border tower,
   That Scotland's annals tell;
The martyr's grave, the lover's bower—
   To each—to all—farewell!

Home of our hearts! our father's home!
   Land of the brave and free!
The keel is flashing through the foam
   That bears us far from thee:

We seek a wild and distant shore
   Beyond the Atlantic main;
We leave thee to return no more,
   Nor view thy cliffs again:

But may dishonour blight our fame,
   And quench our household fires,
When we, or ours, forget thy name,
   Green Island of our sires!

Our native Land—our native Vale—
   A long, a last adieu!
Farewell to bonny Teviotdale,
   And Cheviot's mountains blue.

[1] hollows.

JOHN GIBSON LOCKHART

1794–1854

294   *Captain Paton's Lament*

TOUCH once more a sober measure,
   And let punch and tears be shed
For a prince of good old fellows
   That, alack-o-day! is dead,—
For a prince of worthy fellows,
   And a pretty man also,
That has left the Saltmarket
   In sorrow, grief, and woe.
Oh! we ne'er shall see the like of Captain Paton
no mo'e!

His waistcoat, coat, and breeches
   Were all cut off the same web,
Of a beautiful snuff-colour,
   Or a modest genty[1] drab:
The blue stripe in his stocking
   Round his neat slim leg did go,
And his ruffles of the cambric fine
   They were whiter than the snow.
Oh! we ne'er shall see the like of Captain Paton
no mo'e!

[1] elegant.

His hair was curled in order,
 At the rising of the sun,
In comely rows and buckles smart
 That about his ears did run ;
And, before, there was a toupee
 That some inches up did grow,
And behind there was a long queue
 That did o'er his shoulders flow.
Oh ! we ne'er shall see the like of Captain Paton
 no mo'e !

And whenever we foregather'd
 He took off his wee " three-cockit,"
And he proffer'd you his snuff-box,
 Which he drew from his side-pocket ;
And on Burdett or Bonaparte
 He would make a remark or so ;
And then along the plainstones
 Like a provost he would go.
Oh ! we ne'er shall see the like of Captain Paton
 no mo'e !

In dirty days he pick'd well
 His footsteps with his rattan ;—
Oh ! you ne'er could see the least speck
 On the shoes of Captain Paton.
And on entering the coffee-room,
 About two, all men did know
They would see him with his *Courier*
 In the middle of the row.
Oh ! we ne'er shall see the like of Captain Paton
 no mo'e !

Now and then, upon a Sunday,
    He invited me to dine
On a herring and a mutton chop,
    Which his maid dress'd very fine :
There was also a little Malmsey
    And a bottle of Bordeaux,
Which between me and the Captain
    Pass'd nimbly to and fro.
Oh ! I ne'er shall take pot-luck with Captain Paton
    no mo'e !

Or, if a bowl was mention'd,
    The Captain he would ring
And bid Nelly run to the West Port
    And a stoup of water bring :
Then would he mix the genuine stuff,
    As they made it long ago,
With limes that on his property
    In Trinidad did grow.
Oh ! we ne'er shall taste the like of Captain Paton's
    punch no mo'e !

And then all the time he would discourse
    So sensible and courteous,—
Perhaps talking of last sermon
    He had heard from Dr. Porteous,—
Of some little bit of scandal
    About Mrs. So-and-so,
Which he scarce could credit—having heard
    The *con.* but not the *pro.*
Oh ! we ne'er shall see the like of Captain Paton
    no mo'e !

Or, when the candles were brought forth
  And the night was fairly setting in,
He would tell some fine old stories
  About Minden field or Dettingen,—
How he fought with a French major
  And dispatch'd him at a blow,
While his blood ran out like water
  On the soft grass below.
Oh! we ne'er shall hear the like from Captain Paton
  no mo'e!

But at the last the Captain sicken'd,
  And grew worse from day to day;
And all miss'd him in the coffee-room
  From which now he stay'd away:
On Sabbaths, too, the Wynd Kirk
  Made a melancholy show,
All for wanting of the presence
  Of our venerable beau.
Oh! we ne'er shall see the like of Captain Paton
  no mo'e!

And, in spite of all that Cleghorn
  And Corkindale could do,
It was plain from twenty symptoms
  That death was in his view;
So the Captain made his test'ment,
  And submitted to his foe;
And we laid him by the Ram's-horn Kirk,—
  'Tis the way we all must go!
Oh! we ne'er shall see the like of Captain Paton
  no mo'e!

Join all in chorus, jolly boys!
  And let punch and tears be shed
For this prince of good old fellows,
  That, alack-a day! is dead,—
For this prince of worthy fellows,
  And a pretty man also,
That has left the Saltmarket
  In sorrow, grief, and woe!
For we ne'er shall see the like of Captain Paton
  no mo'e!

295   *Beyond*

WHEN youthful faith hath fled,
  Of loving take thy leave;
Be constant to the dead,—
  The dead cannot deceive.

Sweet, modest flowers of spring,
  How fleet your balmy day!
And man's brief year can bring
  No secondary May,—

No earthly burst again
  Of gladness out of gloom:
Fond hope and vision wane,
  Ungrateful to the tomb.

But 'tis an old belief
  That on some solemn shore,
Beyond the sphere of grief,
  Dear friends shall meet once more,—

Beyond the sphere of time
  And sin and fate's control,
Serene in endless prime
  Of body and of soul.

That creed I fain would keep;
  That hope I'll not forego:
Eternal be the sleep,
  Unless to waken so!

WILLIAM MOTHERWELL

1797–1835

296   *Jeanie Morrison*

I 'VE wander'd east, I've wander'd west,
　　Thro' mony a weary way,
But never, never can forget
　　The luve o' life's young day!
The fire that's blawn on Beltane[1] e'en
　　May weel be black gin Yule;
But blacker fa'[2] awaits the heart
　　Where first fond luve grows cule.

O, dear, dear Jeanie Morrison,
　　The thochts o' bygane years
Shall fling their shadows ower my path,
　　And blind my een wi' tears:
They blind my een wi' saut, saut tears,
　　And sair and sick I pine,
As memory idly summons up
　　The blithe blinks o' langsyne[3].

'Twas then we luvit ilk ither weel;
　　'Twas then we twa did part:
Sweet time—sad time! twa bairns at scule—
　　Twa bairns and but ae heart!
'Twas then we sat on ae laigh bink[4]
　　To leir ilk ither lear[5];
And tones and looks and smiles were shed,
　　Remember'd evermair.

[1] May Day.　[2] fate.　[3] long ago.　[4] low bench.　[5] teach each other lessons.

I wonder, Jeanie, aften yet,
    When sitting on that bink,
Cheek touchin' cheek, loof lock'd in loof [1],
    What our wee heads could think?
When baith bent down ower ae braid page,
    Wi' ae buik on our knee,
Thy lips were on thy lesson, but
    My lesson was in thee.

Oh, mind ye how we hung our heads,
    How cheeks brent red wi' shame,
Whene'er the scule-weans [2], laughin', said
    We cleek'd [3] thegither hame?
And mind ye o' the Saturdays,
    (The scule then skail't [4] at noon,)
When we ran aff to speel [5] the braes—
    The broomy braes o' June?

My head rins round and round about,
    My heart flows like a sea,
As, ane by ane, the thochts rush back
    O' scule-time and o' thee.
O mornin' life! O mornin' luve!
    O lichtsome days and lang,
When hinnied hopes around our hearts
    Like simmer blossoms sprang!

Oh, mind ye, luve, how aft we left
    The deavin' [6] dinsome toun,
To wander by the green burn-side,
    And hear its waters croon?

[1] palm.   [2] school-children.   [3] went arm in arm.   [4] broke up.
[5] climb. [6] deafening.

The simmer leaves hung ower our heads,
  The flowers burst round our feet,
And, in the gloamin' o' the wood,
  The throssil whusslit sweet ;—

The throssil whusslit in the wood,
  The burn sang to the trees,
And we, with Nature's heart in tune,
  Concerted harmonies ;
And on the knowe [1] abune the burn
  For hours thegither sat,
In the silentness o' joy, till baith
  Wi' very gladness grat [2].

Ay, ay, dear Jeanie Morrison,
  Tears trinkled doun your cheek,
Like dew-beads on a rose, yet nane
  Had ony power to speak !
That was a time, a blessed time,
  When hearts were fresh and young,
When freely gush'd all feelings forth,
  Unsyllabled—unsung !

I marvel, Jeanie Morrison,
  Gin I hae been to thee
As closely twined wi' earliest thochts
  As ye hae been to me ?
Oh, tell me gin their music fills
  Thine ear as it does mine ?
Oh, say gin e'er your heart grows grit
  Wi' dreamings o' langsyne ?

[1] hillock.　[2] wept.

I've wander'd east, I've wander'd west,
  I've borne a weary lot ;
But in my wanderings, far or near,
  Ye never were forgot.
The fount that first burst frae this heart
  Still travels on its way,
And channels deeper as it rins
  The luve o' life's young day.

O, dear, dear Jeanie Morrison,
  Since we were sinder'd young,
I've never seen your face, nor heard
  The music o' your tongue ;
But I could hug all wretchedness,
  And happy could I dee,
Did I but ken your heart still dream'd
  O' bygane days and me !

297   *The Ettin [1] o' Sillarwood*

"O SILLARWOOD, sweet Sillarwood !
    Gin Sillarwood were mine,
I'd big a bouir in Sillarwood
  And theik it ower wi' thyme :
At ilka door and ilka bore [2]
  The red, red rose wud shine !"

It's up and sang the bonnie bird
  Upon her milk-white hand :
" I wudna lig [3] in Sillarwood
  For all a gude Earl's land ;
I wudna sing in Sillarwood,
  Tho' gowden glist [4] ilk wand !

[1] giant, evil spirit.   [2] hole, window.   [3] lie.   [4] shone.

"The wild boar rakes [1] in Sillarwood,
   The buck drives thro' the shaw [2],
And simmer woo's the Southern wind
   Thro' Sillarwood to blaw:
Thro' Sillarwood, sweet Sillarwood,
   The deer-hounds run so free;
But the hunter stark of Sillarwood
   An Ettin lang is he!"

"O, Sillarwood, sweet Sillarwood,"
   Fair Marjorie did sing,
"On the tallest tree in Sillarwood
   That Ettin lang will hing!"

The Southern wind it blaws fu' saft,
   And Sillarwood is near;
Fair Marjorie's sang in Sillarwood
   The stark hunter did hear.

He band his deer-hounds in their leash,
   Set his bow against a tree,
And three blasts on his horn has brocht
   The wood-elf to his knee.

"Gae bring to me a shapely weed
   Of silver and of gold,
Gae bring to me as stark a steed
   As ever stept on mold;
For I maun ride frae Sillarwood
   This fair maid to behold!"

[1] ranges.   [2] wood.

The wood-elf twisted sunbeams red
  Into a shapely weed ;
And the tallest birk in Sillarwood
  He hew'd into a steed,—
And shod it wi' the burning gold
  To glance like ony glede [1].

The Ettin shook his bridle-reins
  And merrily they rung,
For four-and-twenty sillar bells
  On ilka side were hung.

The Ettin rade, and better rade,
  Some thretty miles and three ;
A bugle-horn hung at his breast,
  A lang sword at his knee :
"I wud I met," said the Ettin lang,
  "The maiden Marjorie !"

The Ettin rade and better rade
  Till he has reach'd her bouir ;
And there he saw fair Marjorie
  As bricht as lily flouir.

"O Sillarwood ! Sweet Sillarwood !
  Gin Sillarwood were mine,
The sleuthest [2] hawk o' Sillarwood
  On dainty flesh wud dine !"

"Weel met, weel met !" the Ettin said,
  "For ae kiss o' thy chin,
I'll welcome thee to Sillarwood
  And a' that grows therein !"

[1] spark.   [2] most slothful.

"If ye may leese [1] me Sillarwood,
  Wi' a' that grows therein,
Ye're free to kiss my cheek," she said,
  "Ye're free to kiss my chin :
The Knicht that hechts [2] me Sillarwood
  My maiden thocht sal win !

"My luve I've laid on Sillarwood,
  Its bonnie aiken [3] tree ;
And gin that I hae Sillarwood
  I'll link alang wi' thee [4] !"

Then on she put her green mantel
  Weel furr'd wi' minivere ;
Then on she put her velvet shoon,
  The silver shining clear :

She proudly vaulted on the black,
  He bounded on the bay—
The stateliest pair that ever took
  To Sillarwood their way.

It's up and sang the gentil bird
  On Marjorie's fair hand,
"I wudna wend to Sillarwood
  For a' its timber'd land ;
Nor wud I lig in Sillarwood
  Tho' gowden glist ilk wand !

"The Hunters chace thro' Sillarwood
  The playfu' herte and rae :
Nae maiden that socht Sillarwood
  Ere back was seen to gae !"

[1] let me enjoy.   [2] promises.   [3] oaken.   [4] go arm in arm with thee, join my lot to thine.

The Ettin leuch[1], the Ettin sang,
  He whistled merrilie :
" If sic a bird," he said, " were mine,
  I'd hing it on a tree."

"Were I the Lady Marjorie,
  Thou hunter fair but free,
My horse's head I'd turn about
  And think nae mair o' thee ! "

It's on they rade, and better rade—
  They shimmer'd in the sun ;
'Twas sick and sair grew Marjorie
  Lang ere that ride was done !

Yet on they rade and better rade—
  They near'd the Cross o' stane ;
The tall Knicht when he pass'd it by
  Felt cauld in every bane.

But on they rade and better rade :—
  It evir grew mair mirk :
O loud, loud nicher'd[2] the bay steed
  As they pass'd Mary's Kirk !

" I'm wearie o' this eerie road,"
  Maid Marjorie did say,
" We canna weel get Sillarwood
  Afore the set o' day ! "

" It's no the sinkin' o' the sun
  That gloamin's sae the ground ;
The heicht it is o' Sillarwood
  That shadows a' around."

[1] laughed.   [2] whinnied.

"Methocht, Sir Knicht, broad Sillarwood
  A pleasant bield [1] wud be,
Wi' nuts on ilka hazel bush,
  And birds on ilka tree ;
But oh! the dimness o' this wood
  Is terrible to me!"

"The trees ye see seem wondrous big,
  The branches wondrous braid ;
Then marvel nae if sad suld be
  The path we hae to tread."

Thick grew the air, thick grew the trees,
  Thick hung the leaves around ;
And deeper did the Ettin's voice
  In the dread dimness sound.
"I think," said Maiden Marjorie,
  "I hear a horn and hound."

"Ye weel may hear the hound," he said,
  "Ye weel may hear the horn ;
For I can hear the wild halloo
  That freichts the face o' Morn!

"The Hunters fell o' Sillarwood
  Hae packs full fifty-three :
They hunt all day, they hunt all nicht—
  They never bow [2] an ee :

"The Hunters fell o' Sillarwood,
  Hae steeds but [3] blude or bane :
They bear fiert [4] maidens to a weird
  Where mercy there is nane!

[1] shelter   [2] close.   [3] without.   [4] proud.

"And I, the Laird o' Sillarwood
　Hae beds baith deep and wide,
(Of clay-cauld earth) whereon to streik [1]
　A proud and dainty bride!

"Ho! look beside yon bonny birk,—
　The latest blink o' day
Is gleamin' on a comely heap
　Of freshly dug red clay.

"Richt cunning hands they were that digg'd
　Forenent [2] the birken tree,
Where every leaf that draps, frore maid,
　Will piece a shroud for thee:
It's they can lie on lily breast
　As they can lie on lea.

"And they will hap thy lily breist
　Till flesh fa's aff the bane,
Nor tell thy feres how Marjorie
　To Sillarwood hath gane.

"Thy bed is strew'd, Maid Marjorie,
　Wi' bracken and wi' brier;
And ne'er will grey cock clarion wind
　For ane that slumbers here:
Ye wedded hae the Ettin stark,—
　He rules the Realms of Fear!"

[1] lay out.　[2] before.

JAMES HYSLOP

1798–1827

298   *The Cameronian's Dream* [1]

IN a dream of the night I was wafted away
    To the muirland of mist where the martyrs lay,—
Where Cameron's sword and his Bible are seen
Engraved on the stone where the heather grows
    green.

'Twas a dream of those ages of darkness and blood,
When the minister's home was the mountain and
    wood,—
When in Wellwood's dark valley the standard of
    Zion,
All bloody and torn, 'mong the heather was lying.

'Twas morning; and summer's young sun from the
    east
Lay in lovely repose on the green mountain's breast:
On Wardlaw and Cairntable the clear shining dew
Glisten'd sheen 'mong the heath-bells and mountain
    flowers blue;

And far up in heaven, near a white sunny cloud,
The song of the lark was melodious and loud;
And in Glenmuir's wild solitudes, lengthen'd and deep,
Were the whistling of plovers and bleating of sheep.

[1] The incident referred to is the fight of Airs Moss, in Ayrshire,
in which Richard Cameron, the Covenanting leader, and eight of
his followers met their death, July 22nd, 1680.

And Wellwood's sweet valley breathed music and
    gladness ;
The fresh meadow blooms hung in beauty and red-
    ness ;
Its daughters were happy to hail the returning,
And drink the delights, of July's sweet morning.

But, ah ! there were hearts cherish'd far other feel-
    ings
(Illumed by the light of prophetic revealings),
And drank from the scenery of beauty but sorrow ;
For they knew that their blood would bedew it to-
    morrow.

'Twas the few faithful ones who with Cameron were
    lying,
Conceal'd 'mong the mist, where the heath-fowl were
    crying ;
For the horsemen of Earlshall around them were
    hovering,
And their bridle-reins rung thro' the thin misty cover-
    ing.

Their faces grew pale, and their swords were
    unsheath'd ;
But the vengeance that darken'd their brow was un-
    breath'd ;—
With eyes raised to heaven in calm resignation,
They sung their last song to the God of Salvation.

The hills with the sweet mournful music were
    ringing,
The curlew and plover in concert were singing ;
But the melody died 'mid derision and laughter
As the host of ungodly rush'd on to the slaughter.

44

Though in mist and in darkness and fire they were
    shrouded,
Yet the souls of the righteous were calm and
    unclouded :
Their dark eyes flash'd lightning as, firm and un-
    bending,
They stood like the rock which the thunder is rending.

The muskets were flashing, the blue swords were
    gleaming,
The helmets were cleft, and the red blood was
    streaming :
The heavens grew black, and the thunder was rolling,
When in Wellwood's dark muirlands the mighty were
    falling.

When the righteous had fallen, and the combat was
    ended,
A chariot of fire through the dark cloud descended :
Its drivers were angels on horses of whiteness,
And its burning wheels turn'd upon axles of bright-
    ness.

A seraph unfolded its door bright and shining—
All dazzling like gold of the seventh refining ;
And the souls that came forth out of great tribulation
Have mounted the chariot and steeds of salvation.

On the arch of the rainbow the chariot is gliding ;
Through the path of the thunder the horsemen are
    riding :
Glide swiftly, bright spirits ! the prize is before ye—
A crown never fading, a kingdom of glory !

HENRY SCOTT RIDDELL

1798–1870

299

Scotland Yet

GAE bring my guid auld harp ance mair,—
    Gae bring it free and fast,—
For I maun sing anither sang,
    Ere a' my glee be past;
And trow ye as I sing, my lads,
    The burden o't shall be
Auld Scotland's howes and Scotland's knowes
    And Scotland's hills for me;—
We'll drink a cup to Scotland yet,
    Wi' a' the honours three.

The heath waves wild upon her hills,
    And, foaming frae the fells,
Her fountains sing o' freedom still,
    As they dance down the dells;
And weel I loo the land, my lads,
    That's girded by the sea;—
Then Scotland's vales and Scotland's dales
    And Scotland's hills for me;—
We'll drink a cup to Scotland yet,
    Wi' a' the honours three.

The thistle wags upon the fields
    Where Wallace bore his blade—
That gave her foeman's dearest bluid
    To dye her auld grey plaid;

When looking to the lift[1], my lads,
  He sang this doughty glee—
Auld Scotland's right and Scotland's might,
  And Scotland's hills for me ;—
We'll drink a cup to Scotland yet,
  Wi' a' the honours three.

They tell o' lands wi' brighter skies,
  Where freedom's voice ne'er rang—
Gie me the hills where Ossian lies,
  And Coila's minstrel sang ;
For I've nae skill o' lands, my lads,
  That ken na to be free ;—
Then Scotland's right and Scotland's might,
  And Scotland's hills for me ;—
We'll drink a cup to Scotland yet,
  Wi' a' the honours three.

[1] heavens.

JAMES STEWART

1801–1843

300

The Tailor o' Monzie [1]

OUR gudeman's breeks were riven sair ;
   The tailor cam' to mak' a pair ;
When gloamin' fell assembled were
   O's a' 'bout thretty-three, man :
On stools an' auld tree-roots we sat,
An' O, sae muckle fun's we gat
Frae funny Patie Whip-the-cat,
   The tailor o' Monzie, man !
     O, he's a curiosity,
     A curious curiosity,
     A perfect curiosity,
       The Tailor o' Monzie, man !

The lasses' spindles hadna space
To whirl an' bob their circlin' race,
For, head an' thrawart [2], back an' face,
   We sat promiscouslie, man,

[1] *Author's Note* to the " Tailor o' Monzie."—The genuine old
travelling tailor, or *whip-the-cat*, as he was generally termed
throughout Scotland, is now extinct. To our forefathers the arrival
of the tailor in the way of his *calling* was an advent long remembered. He very often united in his person the talent of wit with
an accurate knowledge of mankind ; and being likewise a
chronicle of all the gossip in his rounds, few people received such
a hearty welcome within the *hallan* as the tailor. The author of
the sketch has seen in his younger days something akin to what he
attempts to describe.   [2] higgledy-piggledy.

"Like midges i' the motty sun,
Or corbie craws on tattie grun',"—
Sae thick were we to hear the fun
      Frae Patie o' Monzie, man.

A lang dispute anent the State
Gley'd [1] Andro Toshack held wi' Pate,
Wha, drawin' a steek wi' nettled heat,
      Drobb'd [2] Andro's ringle ee [3], man.
Andro roar'd, grew pale and faint:
"My feth," quo' the gudeman, "I kent
He'd gie ye piercing argument,
      Our Tailor o' Monzie, man!"

Wee Gibbie Bryce was greetin', vext
That he had made the Kirk his text;
For Patie gat him jamm'd an' fixt
      In Patronage's plea, man:
He rave poor Gibbie's sense to rags,
Made him a lauchin'-stock to wags:—
The hale house waved their arms like flags:
      "Hurrah for Patie Monzie, man!"

Wi' canty tale an' funny joke,
Wi' lauchin' when the tailor spoke,
The nicht wore on till twal' o'clock
      In loud guffaw an' glee, man:
The gudewife reavilt a' her yarn;
She tint [4] the thread-end o' her pirn [5],
Lauchin' like her youngest bairn
      At Patie o' Monzie, man.

[1] squinting. [2] pricked. [3] wall eye. [4] lost. [5] reel.

'Twad tak' a tale as lang's an ell,
'Twad tak' an hour that tale to tell
O' what I heard an' saw mysel'
  That nicht o' nichts to me, man.
If there's a man that we should dawt [1],
Whom nature made without a faut,
He's surely Patie Whip-the-ca ,
   The Tailor o' Monzie, man !

  [1] make much of.

301 *Young Randal*

YOUNG RANDAL was a bonnie lad when he
gaed awa',
Young Randal was a bonnie lad when he gaed awa' :
'Twas in the sixteen hundred year o' grace and
thritty-twa
That Randal, the laird's youngest son, gaed awa'.

It was to seek his fortune in the High Germanie—
To fecht the foreign loons in the High Germanie,
That he left his father's tower o' sweet Willanslee
And mony mae friends in the North Countrie.

He left his mother in her bower, his father in
the ha',
His brother at the outer yett [1] but and his sisters
twa,
And his bonnie cousin Jean, that look'd owre the
castle wa',
And, mair than a' the lave [2], loot the tears down fa'.

" Oh, whan will ye come back ? " sae kindly did she
speir [3],
" Oh, whan will ye come back, my hinny and my
dear ? "
"Whenever I can win eneuch o' Spanish gear
To dress ye out in pearlins [4] and silks, my dear."

[1] gate.　[2] the rest.　[3] ask.　[4] laces.

Oh, Randal's hair was coal-black when he gaed awa';
Oh, Randal's cheeks were roses red when he gaed
    awa';
And in his bonnie e'e a spark glintit high,
Like the merrie, merrie look in the morning sky.

Oh, Randal was an altert man when he came hame—
A sair altert man was he whan he came hame ;—
Wi' a ribbon at his breast, and a Sir at his name,
And grey, grey cheeks did Randal come hame.

He lichtit at the outer yett and rispit wi' the ring [1],
And down came a ladye to see him come in ;
And after the ladye came bairns feifteen :
" Can this muckle wife be my true love Jean ? "

" Whatna stoure carle [2] is this," quo' the dame,
" Sae gruff and sae grand, and sae feckless and sae
    lame ? "
" Oh, tell me, fair madame, are ye bonnie Jeanie
    Graham ? "
" In troth," quo' the ladye, " sweet sir, the very
    same."

He turn'd him about wi' a waefu' e'e,
And a heart as sair as sair could be ;
He lap on his horse, and awa' did wildly flee,
And never mair came back to sweet Willanslee.

Oh, dule [3] on the poortith o' this countrie,
And dule on the wars o' the High Germanie,
And dule on the love that forgetfu' can be ;
For they've wreck'd the bravest heart in this hale
    countrie !

[1] an old-world means of seeking admittance.   [4] what rough
fellow.   [3] sorrow.

HENRY GLASSFORD BELL

1805–1874

302   *Mary Queen of Scots*

I LOOK'D far back into the past ; and lo ! in bright
    array,
I saw, as in a dream, the forms of ages pass'd
    away.

It was a stately convent, with its old and lofty walls,
And gardens with their broad green walks, where
    soft the footstep falls ;
And o'er the antique dial-stone the creeping shadow
    crept,
And all around the noonday light in drowsy radiance
    slept.
No sound of busy life was heard, save, from the
    cloister dim,
The tinkling of the silver bell, or the sisters' holy
    hymn.
And there five noble maidens sat beneath the orchard
    trees,
In that first budding spring of youth when all its
    prospects please ;
And little reck'd they, when they sang, or knelt
    at vesper prayers,
That Scotland knew no prouder names—held none
    more dear than theirs ;

And little even the loveliest thought, before the
    Virgin's shrine,
Of royal blood and high descent from the ancient
    Stuart line :
Calmly her happy days flew on, uncounted in their
    flight ;
And, as they flew, they left behind a long continuing light.

The scene was changed.—It was the court—the gay
    court of Bourbon,
Where, 'neath a thousand silver lamps, a thousand
    courtiers throng ;
And proudly kindles Henry's eye, well pleased, I
    ween, to see
The land assemble all its wealth of grace and
    chivalry :—
Grey Montmorency, o'er whose head has pass'd a
    storm of years,
Strong in himself and children, stands the first among
    his peers :
Next him the Guises, who had so well Fame's
    steepest heights assail'd,
And walk'd Ambition's diamond ridge where bravest
    hearts have fail'd ;
(And higher yet their path shall be, and stronger
    wax their might,
For before them Montmorency's star shall pale its
    waning light.)
There, too, the Prince of Condé wears his all-uncon-
    quer'd sword,
With great Coligni by his side,—each name a house-
    hold word :
And there walks she of Medici, that proud Italian line,
The mother of a race of kings — the haughty
    Catherine.

The forms that follow in her train a glorious sunshine make—
A Milky Way of stars that grace a comet's glittering
wake ;
But fairer far than all the crowd who bask on
fortune's tide,
Effulgent in the light of youth, is she—the new-made
bride !
The homage of a thousand heart's, the fond deep
love of one,
The hopes that dance around a life whose charms
are but begun—
They lighten up her chestnut eye, they mantle o'er
her cheek,
They sparkle on her open brow, and high-soul'd joy
bespeak.
Ah, who shall blame if scarce that day—through all
its brilliant hours—
She thought of that quiet convent's calm, its sunshine
and its flowers ?

The scene was changed.—It was a bark that slowly
held its way ;
And o'er its lee the coast of France in the light of
evening lay ;
And on its deck a lady sat, who gazed with tearful eyes
Upon the fast-receding hills that dim and distant rise.
No marvel that the lady wept :—there was no land
on earth
She loved like that dear land, although she owed it
not her birth :
It was her mother's land,—the land of childhood and
of friends ;
It was the land where she had found for all her
griefs amends,—

The land where her dead husband slept; the land
   where she had known
The tranquil convent's hush'd repose and the splen-
   dours of a throne :
No marvel that the lady wept,—it was the land of
   France,
The chosen home of chivalry, the garden of romance!
The past was bright, like those dear hills so far
   behind her bark ;
The future, like the gathering night, was ominous
   and dark.
One gaze again—one long last gaze: "Adieu, fair
   France, to thee !"
The breeze comes forth,—she is alone on the uncon-
   scious sea.

The scene was changed.—It was an eve of raw and
   surly mood ;
And, in a turret-chamber high of ancient Holyrood,
Sat Mary—listening to the rain, and sighing with the
   winds,
That seem'd to suit the stormy state of men's uncertain minds.
The touch of care had blanch'd her cheek, her smile
   was sadder now,—
The weight of royalty had press'd too heavy on her
   brow ;
And traitors to her councils came, and rebels to the
   field :
The Stuart *sceptre* well she sway'd, but the *sword* she
   could not wield.
She thought of all her blighted hopes—the dreams
   of youth's brief day,
And summon'd Rizzio with his lute, and bade the
   minstrel play

The songs she loved in other years—the songs of gay
    Navarre—
The songs, perchance, that erst were sung by gallant
    Chastelard :
They half beguiled her of her cares, they sooth'd her
    into smiles,
They won her thoughts from bigot zeal and fierce
    domestic broils.
But hark !—the tramp of armed men ! the Douglas'
    battle-cry !
They come, they come ! and lo ! the scowl of Ruthven's
    hollow eye.
Stern swords are drawn, and daggers gleam—her
    words, her prayers are vain ;
The ruffian steel is in his heart—the faithful Rizzio's
    slain !
Then Mary Stuart brush'd aside the tears that
    trickling fell :
" Now for my father's arm," she said ; " my woman's
    heart, farewell ! "

The scene was changed.—It was a lake, with one
    small lonely isle ;
And there, within the prison walls of its baronial pile,
Stern men stood menacing their queen, till she
    should stoop to sign
The traitorous scroll that snatch'd the crown from
    her ancestral line.
" My lords, my lords ! " the captive cried, " were I
    but once more free,
With ten good knights, on yonder shore, to aid
    my cause and me,
That parchment would I scatter wide to every
    breeze that blows,
And reign once more, a Stuart queen, o'er my
    remorseless foes ! "

A red spot burn'd upon her cheek ; stream'd her
    rich tresses down :
She wrote the words—she stood erect, a queen
    without a crown !

The scene was changed.—A royal host a royal
    banner bore ;—
The faithful of the land stood round their smiling
    queen once more :
She stay'd her steed upon a hill, she saw them
    marching by,
She heard their shouts, she read success in every
    flashing eye.
The tumult of the strife begins—it roars—it dies
    away ;
And Mary's troops and banners now, and courtiers—
    where are they ?
Scatter'd and strewn, and flying far, defenceless
    and undone :
O God ! to see what she has lost, and think what
    guilt has won !
Away ! away !—thy gallant steed must act no
    laggard's part ;
Yet vain his speed, for thou dost bear the arrow
    in thy heart.

The scene was changed.—Beside the block a sullen
    headsman stood ;
And gleam'd the broad axe in his hand, that soon
    must drip with blood.
With slow and steady step there came a lady
    through the hall,
And breathless silence chain'd the lips, and touch'd
    the hearts of all.

Rich were the sable robes she wore, her white
veil round her fell,
And from her neck there hung the cross—that
cross she loved so well !
I knew that queenly form again, though blighted
was its bloom ;
I saw that grief had deck'd it out—an offering for
the tomb !
I knew the eye, though faint its light, that once so
brightly shone ;
I knew the voice, though feeble now, that thrill'd
with every tone ;
I knew the ringlets, almost grey, once threads of
living gold ;
I knew that bounding grace of step, that symmetry
of mould.
Even now I see her far away, in that calm convent
aisle,
I hear her chant her vesper-hymn, I mark her
holy smile :
Even now I see her bursting forth, upon her bridal
morn—
A new star in the firmament to light and glory born !
Alas, the change ! she placed her foot upon a triple
throne ;
And on the scaffold now she stands, beside the
block, alone !—
The little dog that licks her hand, the last of all
the crowd
Who sunn'd themselves beneath her glance and
round her footsteps bow'd !
Her neck is bared,—the blow is struck,—the soul
has pass'd away !—
The bright, the beautiful, is now a bleeding piece
of clay.

A solemn text! Go, think of it, in silence and
    alone ;
Then weigh against a grain of sand the glories of
    a throne !

303   *The End*

I KNOW at length the truth, my friend :—
    Some ten or fifteen seasons more,
And then for me there comes the end—
    My joys and sorrows will be o'er !

Nor deem I the remaining years—
    Which soon must come and soon must go,
Which wake no hopes, excite no fears—
    Will teach me more than now I know.

They'll bring the same unfruitful round—
    The nightly rest, the daily toil,
The smiles that soothe, the slights that wound,
    The little gain, the feverish moil.

As manhood's fires burn less and less,
    The languid heart grows cold and dull—
Alike indifferent to success,
    And careless of the beautiful :

Nought but the past awakes a throb,
    And even the past begins to die ;—
The burning tear, the anguish'd sob,
    Give place to listless apathy.

And when at last death turns the key
    And throws the earth and green turf on,
Whate'er it was that made up *me*,
    Is it, my friend, for ever gone ?

45

Dear friend, is all we see a dream?
  Does this brief glimpse of time and space
Exhaust the aims, fulfil the scheme,
  Intended for the human race?

Shall even the star-exploring mind
  Which thrills with spiritual desire
Be, like a breath of summer wind,
  Absorb'd in sunshine and expire?

Or will what men call death restore
  The living myriads of the past?—
Is dying but to go before
  The myriads who will come at last?

If not, whence sprung the thought? and whence
  Perception of a power divine
Who symbols forth omnipotence
  In flowers that bloom, in suns that shine?

'Tis not these fleshly limbs that think,
  'Tis not these filmy eyes that see:
Tho' mind and matter break the link,
  Mind does not therefore cease to be.

Such end is but an end in part,
  Such death is but the body's goal:
Blood makes the pulses of the heart,
  But not the emotions of the soul!

JAMES BALLANTINE

1808–1877

304   *Castles in the Air*

THE bonnie, bonnie bairn who sits poking in the
     ase [1],
Glowering in the fire wi' his wee round face,
Laughing at the fuffin' lowe [2]—what sees he there?
Ha! the young dreamer's bigging [3] castles in the air.

His wee chubby face and his touzie curly pow [4]
Are laughing and nodding to the dancing lowe;
He'll brown his rosy cheeks, and singe his sunny hair,
Glowering at the imps wi' their castles in the air.

He sees muckle castles towering to the moon;
He sees little sodgers pu'ing them a' doun;
Warlds whommlin up and doun [5], bleezing wi' a flare,—
See how he loups [6] as they glimmer in the air!

For a' sae sage he looks, what can the laddie ken?
He's thinking upon naething, like mony mighty men:
A wee thing mak's us think, a sma' thing mak's us
     stare,—
There are mair folk than him bigging castles in the air.

Sic a night in winter may weel mak' him cauld:
His chin upon his buffy [7] hand will soon mak' him auld;
His brow is brent sae braid—O pray that daddy Care
Would let the wean alane wi' his castles in the air!

[1] cinders.   [2] blowing flame.   [3] building.   [4] head.   [5] being
overturned.   [6] leaps.   [7] chubby.

He'll glower at the fire, and he'll keek¹ at the light ;
But mony sparkling stars are swallow'd up by Night :
Aulder e en than his are glamour'd by a glare,—
Hearts are broken, heads are turn'd, wi' castles in the
    air.

305   *Naebody's Bairn*

SHE was Naebody's Bairn, she was Naebody's
    Bairn :
She had mickle to thole², she had mickle to learn,
Afore a kind word or kind look she could earn ;
For naebody cared about Naebody's Bairn.

Though father or mither ne'er own'd her ava,
Though rear'd by the fremmit³, for fee unco sma',
She grew in the shade like a young lady-fern ;
For Nature was bounteous to Naebody's Bairn.

Though toited⁴ by some, and though lightlied⁵ by mair,
She never compleen'd, though her young heart was
    sair,
And warm virgin tears that might melted cauld airn⁶
Whiles glist in the blue e'e o' Naebody's Bairn.

Though nane cheer'd her childhood, an' nane hail'd
    her birth,
Heaven sent her, an angel, to gladden the earth ;
And when the earth doom'd her in laigh nook to dern⁷
Heaven couldna but tak' again Naebody's Bairn.

She cam' smiling sweetly as young mornin' daw⁸ ;—
Like lown⁹ simmer gloamin' she faded awa' :
And lo ! how serenely that lone e'ening starn
Shines on the green sward that haps¹⁰ Naebody's Bairn

---

¹ peep.   ² endure.   ³ strangers.   ⁴ vexed.   ⁵ slighted.   ⁶ iron
⁷ be hidden.   ⁸ dawn.   ⁹ still.   ¹⁰ enfolds.

JOHN USHER

1809–1896

The Channel-Stane [1]

(Inscribed wi' britherly love to a' keen curlers)

UP! curlers, up! oor freen' John Frost
    Has closed his grip on loch an' lea :
Up! time's ower precious to be lost—
    An' rally roun' the rink an' tee [2] ;
Wi' steady han', an' nerve, an' e'e—
    Noo cannie, noo wi' micht an' main,
To test by "wick" [3], an' "guard" [4], an' "draw" [5],
    Oor prowess wi' the Channel-Stane.
        O the roarin' Channel-Stane !
        The cannie, creepin' Channel-Stane !
        What music to the curler's ear
            Like music o' the Channel-Stane !

It's bliss to curlers' eye an' ear
    When "crack an egg" [6], or "chap an' lie" [7]
Is greeted wi' responsive cheer,
    And waving besoms raised on high ;
Or—when nocht else is left to try—
    Wi' rapid glance, an' easy swing,
The "ootring" [8] o' a stane is chipp'd,
    And twirl'd within the inner ring.

---

[1] the stone used in the game of curling.   [2] the mark on the ice aimed at in the game.   [3] an indirect shot.   [4] guard upon a stone which has been well aimed.   [5] a straight shot.   [6] touch very gently.   [7] strike and lie.   [8] that edge of a stone which happens to lie outward from the tee.

O the roarin' Channel-Stane !
The toddlin', twinklin' Channel-Stane !
What music to the curler's ear
    Like music o' the Channel-Stane !

The time is call'd—the match a tie ;
  The game contestit close an' keen
Seems seal'd, for guards like bulwarks lie—
  Nae vestige o' the winner seen :
Anon the skip [1], wi' dauntless mien,
  Puts doon his broom—" Creep till't," cries he ;—
The stone's sent hirplin' through the " port " [2],
  And soopit deftly to the tee.
        O the roarin' Channel-Stane !
        The hirplin', wimplin' Channel-Stane !
        What music to the curler's ear
            Like music o' the Channel-Stane !

It boots not whence the curler hails,
  If curler keen an' staunch he be—
Frae Scotland, England, Ireland, Wales,
  Or colonies ayont the sea ;—
A social brotherhood are we,
  And, after we are deid and gane,
We'll live in literature an' lair—
  In annals o' the Channel-Stane !
        O the roarin' Channel-Stane !
        The witchin', winsome Channel-Stane !
        What music to the curler's ear
            Like music o' the Channel-Stane !

---

[1] the captain of a side.   [2] a narrow passage between other stones.

LADY JOHN SCOTT
(*née* ALICIA ANNE SPOTTISWOODE)

1810–1900

307   *Durisdeer*

WE'LL meet nae mair at sunset, when the weary
    day is dune,
Nor wander hame thegither, by the lee licht o' the
    mune !
I'll hear your step nae longer amang the dewy corn,
For we'll meet nae mair, my bonniest, either at eve or
    morn.

The yellow broom is waving, abune the sunny brae,
And the rowan berries dancing, where the sparkling
    waters play,
Tho' a' is bright and bonnie, it's an eerie place to me,
For we'll meet nae mair, my dearest, either by burn
    or tree.

Far up into the wild hills, there's a kirkyard auld and
    still,
Where the frosts lie ilka morning, and the mists hang
    low and chill,
And there ye sleep in silence, while I wander here my
    lane,
Till we meet ance mair in Heaven, never to part
    again !

308   *O Murmuring Waters*

O MURMURING waters !
    Have ye no message for me ?
Ye come from the hills of the west,
    Where his steps wander free.

Did he not whisper my name ?
   Did he not utter one word ?
And trust that its sound o'er the rush
   Of thy streams might be heard.

O murmuring waters !
   The sounds of the moorlands I hear,
The scream of the hern and the eagle,
   The bell of the deer.
The rustling of heather and fern,
   The shiver of grass on the lea,
The sigh of the wind from the hill,
   Have ye no voice for me ?

O murmuring waters !
   Flow on, ye have no voice for me—
Bear the wild songs of the hills
   To the depths of the sea.
Bright stream from the founts of the west,
   Rush on, with thy music and glee.
O to be borne to my rest
   In the cold waves with thee !

309   *The Bounds o' Cheviot*

SHALL I never see the bonnie banks o' Kale again ?
   Nor the dark craigs o' Hownam Law ?
Nor the green dens o' Chatto, nor Twaeford's mossy
    stane,
   Nor the birks upon Philogar Shaw ?
     Nae mair ! nae mair !
  I shall never see the bounds o' Cheviot mair !

Shall I never watch the breakin' o' the simmer day
 Ower the shouther o' the Deer Buss height,
When the Stainchel, and the Mote, and the flowery
     Bughtrigg brae
  Redden slowly wi' the mornin' light?
       Nae mair! nae mair!
  I shall never see the bounds o' Cheviot mair!

Shall I never wander lanely, when the gloamin' fa's
 And the wild birds flutter to their rest,
Ower the lang heathery muir, to the bonnie Brunden
     laws
  Standin' dark against the glitter o' the West?
       Nae mair! nae mair!
  I shall never see the bounds o' Cheviot mair!

Shall I never ride the mossy braes o' Heatherhope
     mair?
  Shall I never see the Fairlone burn?
Nor the wild heights o' Hindhope, wi' its corries green
     and fair
  And the waters trinklin' down amang the fern?
       Nae mair! nae mair!
  I shall never see the bounds o' Cheviot mair!

Shall I never win the marches at the Coquet head,
 Thro' the mists and the driftin' snaw?
Nor the dark doors o' Cottenshope, nor the quiet
     springs o' Rede,
  Glintin' bright across the Border, far awa?
       Nae mair! nae mair!
  I shall never see the bounds o' Cheviot mair!

THOMAS TOD STODDART

1810–1880

The Taking of the Salmon

A BIRR! a whirr! a salmon's on,
　　A goodly fish! a thumper!
Bring up, bring up the ready gaff,
And if we land him we shall quaff
　　Another glorious bumper!
　　　Hark! 'tis the music of the reel,
　　　　The strong, the quick, the steady;
　　　The line darts from the active wheel,
　　　　Have all things right and ready.

A birr! a whirr! the salmon's out,
　　Far on the rushing river;
Onward he holds with sudden leap,
Or plunges through the whirlpool deep,
　　A desperate endeavour!
　　　Hark to the music of the reel!
　　　　The fitful and the grating;
　　　It pants along the breathless wheel,
　　　　Now hurried—now abating.

A birr! a whirr! the salmon's off!—
　　No, no, we still have got him;
The wily fish is sullen grown,
And, like a bright imbedded stone,
　　Lies gleaming at the bottom.

Hark to the music of the reel!
'Tis hush'd, it hath forsaken;
With care we'll guard the magic wheel,
Until its notes rewaken.

A birr! a whirr! the salmon's up,
Give line, give line and measure;
But now he turns! keep down ahead,
And lead him as a child is led,
And land him at your leisure.
Hark to the music of the reel!
'Tis welcome, it is glorious;
It wanders thro' the winding wheel,
Returning and victorious.

A birr! a whirr! the salmon's in,
Upon the bank extended;
The princely fish is gasping slow,
His brilliant colours come and go,
All beautifully blended.
Hark to the music of the reel!
It murmurs and it closes;
Silence is on the conquering wheel,
Its wearied line reposes.

No birr! no whirr! the salmon's ours,
The noble fish—the thumper:
Strike through his gill the ready gaff,
And bending homewards, we shall quaff
Another glorious bumper!
Hark to the music of the reel!
We listen with devotion;
There's something in that circling wheel
That wakes the heart's emotion!

311 *The Angler's Grave*

SORROW, sorrow, bring it green !
   True tears make the grass to grow ;
And the grief of the good, I ween,
   Is grateful to him that sleeps below.
Strew sweet flowers, free of blight—
   Blossoms gather'd in the dew :
Should they wither before night,
   Flowers and blossoms bring anew.

Sorrow, sorrow, speed away
   To our angler's quiet mound,
With the old pilgrim, twilight grey,
   Enter thou on the holy ground ;
There he sleeps, whose heart was twined
   With wild stream and wandering burn,
Wooer of the western wind !
   Watcher of the April morn !

Sorrow at the poor man's hearth !
   Sorrow in the hall of pride !
Honour waits at the grave of worth,
   And high and low stand side by side.
Brother angler ! slumber on ;
   Haply thou shalt wave the wand,
When the tide of time is gone,
   In some far and happy land.

WILLIAM MILLER

1810–1872

312   *Willie Winkie*

WEE Willie Winkie rins through the town,
  Upstairs and doonstairs, in his nicht-gown,—
Tirling [1] at the window, crying at the lock,
"Are the weans [2] in their bed, for it's now ten
  o'clock?"

Hey, Willie Winkie, are ye coming ben [3]?
The cat's singing grey thrums [4] to the sleeping hen;
The dog's spelder'd [5] on the floor, and disna gi'e a
  cheep [6];
But here's a waukrife [7] laddie that winna fa' asleep!

Onything but sleep, you rogue! glow'ring like the
  moon,
Rattling in an airn [8] jug wi' an airn spoon,
Rumbling, tumbling, round about, crawing like a cock,
Skirling like a kenna-what [9], wauk'ning sleeping fock.

Hey, Willie Winkie—the wean's in a creel [10]!
Wambling [11] aff a body's knee like a very eel,
Rugging [12] at the cat's lug and raveling a' her thrums—
Hey, Willie Winkie—see, there he comes!

[1] tapping.   [2] children.   [3] in.   [4] purring.   [5] outstretched.
[6] sound.   [7] wakeful.   [8] iron.   [9] crying out like I know not what.
[10] basket.   [11] wriggling.   [12] tugging.

Wearied is the mither that has a stoorie [1] wean—
A wee stumpie stoussie [2] that canna rin his lane,
That has a battle aye wi' sleep before he'll close an
    e'e ;—
But ae kiss frae aff his rosy lips gi'es strength anew
    to me.

313   *The Sleepy Laddie*

ARE ye no gaun to wauken the-day, ye rogue ?
    Your parritch is ready, and cool in the cog [3] ;
Auld baudrons [4] sae gaucy [5], and Tam o' that ilk,
Would fain hae a drap o' the wee laddie's milk.

There's a wee birdie singing—get up, get up !
And listen ! it says, tak' a whup, tak' a whup !
But I'll kittle his bosie [6]—a far better plan,
And pouther his pow wi' a watering-can.

There's a house redd up [7] like a palace—I'm sure
That a pony might dance a jig on the floor ;
And father is coming, so wauken and meet
And welcome him hame wi' your kisses sae sweet.

It's far in the day now, and brawly ye ken
Your father has scarcely a minute to spen' ;
But ae blink o' his wifie and bairn on her knee
He says lightens his toil, tho' sair it may be.

So, up to your parritch, and on wi' your claes !—
There's a fire that might warm the cauld Norlan'
    braes ;
For a coggie weel fill'd and a clean fire-en'
Should mak' ye jump up and gae skelping ben [8] !

---

[1] obstreperous. [2] chubby fellow. [3] bowl. [4] pussy. [5] plump.
[6] tickle his breast. [7] set in order. [8] racing into the next room.

WM. EDMONDSTOUNE AYTOUN

1813–1865

314

The Execution of Montrose [1]

COME hither, Evan Cameron!
  Come, stand beside my knee—
I hear the river roaring down
  Towards the wintry sea.
There's shouting on the mountain side,
  There's war within the blast—
Old faces look upon me,
  Old forms go trooping past.
I hear the pibroch wailing
  Amidst the din of fight,
And my dim spirit wakes again
  Upon the verge of night!

'Twas I that led the Highland host
  Through wild Lochaber's snows,
What time the plaided clans came down
  To battle with Montrose.
I've told thee how the Southrons fell
  Beneath the broad claymore,
And how we smote the Campbell clan
  By Inverlochy's shore :
I've told thee how we swept Dundee,
  And tamed the Lindsay's pride ;
But never have I told thee yet
  How the Great Marquis died !

[1] James Graham, Marquis of Montrose, the champion of the
Royalist cause in Scotland, was executed in Edinburgh, May 21st,
1650.

A traitor sold him to his foes ;—
  O deed of deathless shame !
I charge thee, boy, if e'er thou meet
  With one of Assynt's name—
Be it upon the mountain's side,
  Or yet within the glen,
Stand he in martial gear alone,
  Or back'd by armèd men—
Face him, as thou would'st face the man
  Who wrong'd thy sire's renown ;
Remember of what blood thou art,
  And strike the caitiff down !

They brought him to the Watergate,
  Hard bound with hempen span,
As though they held a lion there,
  And not a 'fenceless man.
They set him high upon a cart—
  The hangman rode below—
They drew his hands behind his back,
  And bared his noble brow.
And then a mournful shudder
  Through all the people crept,
And some that came to scoff at him,
  Now turn'd aside and wept.

But onwards—always onwards,
  In silence and in gloom,
The dreary pageant labour'd,
  Till it reach'd the house of doom :
Then first a woman's voice was heard
  In jeer and laughter loud,
And an angry cry and a hiss arose
  From the heart of the tossing crowd :

Then, as the Græme look'd upwards,
  He saw the ugly smile
Of him who sold his King for gold,—
  The master-fiend Argyle !

The Marquis gazed a moment,
  And nothing did he say,
But the cheek of Argyle grew ghastly pale,
  And he turn'd his eyes away.
The painted harlot by his side,
  She shook through every limb,
For a roar like thunder swept the street,
  And hands were clench'd at him ;
And a Saxon soldier cried aloud,
  " Back, coward, from thy place !
For seven long years thou hast not dared
  To look him in the face."

Had I been there with sword in hand,
  And fifty Camerons by,
That day through high Dunedin's streets,
  Had peal'd the slogan-cry [1].
Not all their troops of trampling horse,
  Nor might of mailèd men—
Not all the rebels in the South
  Had borne us backwards then !
Once more his foot on Highland heath
  Had trod as free as air,
Or I, and all who bore my name,
  Been laid around him there !

It might not be. They placed him next
  Within the solemn hall,
Where once the Scottish kings were throned
  Amidst their nobles all.

[1] war-cry of a clan.

46

But there was dust of vulgar feet
  On that polluted floor,
And perjured traitors fill'd the place
  Where good men sate before.
Then, as a hound is slipp'd from leash,
  They cheer'd the common throng,
And blew the note with yell and shout,
  And bade him pass along.

It would have made a brave man's heart
  Grow sad and sick that day,
To watch the keen malignant eyes
  Bent down on that array.
There stood the Whig west-country lords
  In balcony and bow,
There sat their gaunt and wither'd dames,
  And their daughters all a-row ;
And every open window
  Was full as full might be
With black-robed Covenanting carles,
  That goodly sport to see !

But when he came, though pale and wan,
  He look'd so great and high,
So noble was his manly front,
  So calm his steadfast eye :—
The rabble rout forebore to shout,
  And each man held his breath,
For well they knew the hero's soul
  Was face to face with death.
With savage glee came Warristoun [1]
  To read the murderous doom ;
And then uprose the great Montrose
  In the middle of the room.

[1] Johnstone of Warristoun, an eminent Covenanter.

"Now, by my faith as belted knight,
    And by the name I bear,
And by the bright Saint Andrew's cross
    That waves above us there—
Yea, by a greater, mightier oath—
    And oh, that such should be!—
By that dark stream of royal blood
    That lies 'twixt you and me—
I have not sought in battle-field
    A wreath of such renown,
Nor dared I hope, on my dying day,
    To win the martyr's crown!

"There is a chamber far away
    Where sleep the good and brave,
But a better place ye have named for me
    Than by my fathers' grave.
For truth and right, 'gainst treason's might,
    This hand hath always striven,
And ye raise it up for a witness still
    In the eye of earth and heaven.
Then nail my head on yonder tower—
    Give every town a limb—
And God who made shall gather them:
    I go from you to Him!"

The morning dawn'd full darkly,
    The rain came flashing down,
And the jagged streak of the levin-bolt
    Lit up the gloomy town:
The thunder crash'd across the heaven,
    The fatal hour was come;
Yet aye broke in, with muffled beat,
    The 'larum of the drum.

There was madness on the earth below,
    And anger in the sky,
And young and old, and rich and poor,
    Came forth to see him die.

Ah, God ! that ghastly gibbet !
    How dismal 'tis to see
The great tall spectral skeleton,
    The ladder and the tree !
Hark ! hark ! it is the clash of arms—
    The bells begin to toll—
He is coming ! he is coming !
    God's mercy on his soul !
One last long peal of thunder—
    The clouds are clear'd away,
And the glorious sun once more looks down
    Amidst the dazzling day.

He is coming ! he is coming !—
    Like a bridegroom from his room,
Came the hero from his prison
    To the scaffold and the doom.
There was glory on his forehead,
    There was lustre in his eye,
And he never walk'd to battle
    More proudly than to die :
There was colour in his visage,
    Though the cheeks of all were wan,
And they marvell'd as they saw him pass,
    That great and goodly man !

He mounted up the scaffold,
    And he turn'd him to the crowd ;
But they dared not trust the people,
    So he might not speak aloud.

But he look'd upon the heavens,
   And they were clear and blue,
And in the liquid ether
   The eye of God shone through ;
Yet a black and murky battlement
   Lay resting on the hill,
As though the thunder slept within—
   All else was calm and still.

The grim Geneva ministers
   With anxious scowl drew near,
As you have seen the ravens flock
   Around the dying deer.
He would not deign them word nor sign,
   But alone he bent the knee ;
And veil'd his face for Christ's dear grace
   Beneath the gallows-tree.
Then radiant and serene he rose,
   And cast his cloak away :
For he had ta'en his latest look
   Of earth, and sun, and day.

A beam of light fell o'er him,
   Like a glory round the shriven,
And he climb'd the lofty ladder
   As it were the path to heaven.
Then came a flash from out the cloud,
   And a stunning thunder-roll ;
And no man dared to look aloft,
   For fear was on every soul.
There was another heavy sound,
   A hush, and then a groan ;
And darkness swept across the sky—
   The work of death was done !

ROBERT NICOLL

1814–1837

315

Life's Pilgrimage

INFANT! I envy thee
    Thy seraph smile, thy soul without a stain :
Angels around thee hover in thy glee,
    A look of love to gain.

Thy paradise is made
Upon thy mother's bosom ; and her voice
Is music rich as that by spirits shed
    When blessèd things rejoice.

Bright are the opening flowers :
Ay, bright as thee, sweet babe, and innocent
They bud and bloom ;—and straight their infant
        hours,
    Like thine, are done and spent !

Boy ! infancy is o'er :
Go with thy playmates to the grassy lea,
Let thy bright eye with yon far lavercock soar,
    And blithe and happy be !

Go, crow thy cuckoo notes
Till all the greenwood alleys loud are ringing !
Go, listen to the thousand tuneful throats
    That 'mong the leaves are singing !

I would not sadden thee ;
Nor wash the rose upon thy cheek with tears :
Go, while thine eye is bright—unbent thy knee,
    Forget all cares and fears !

    YOUTH ! is thy boyhood gone ?—
The fever-hour of life at length has come,
And passion sits in reason's golden throne,
    While sorrow's voice is dumb.

    Be glad ! it is thy hour
Of love ungrudging, faith without reserve ;
And, from the right, ill hath not yet the power
    To make thy footsteps swerve.

    Now is thy time to know
How much of trusting goodness lives on earth ;
And, rich in pure sincerity, to go
    Rejoicing in thy birth.

    Youth's sunshine unto thee—
Love, first and dearest—has unveil'd her face ;
And thou hast sat beneath the trysting-tree
    In love's first fond embrace.

    Enjoy thy happy dream ;
For life hath not another such to give :
The stream is flowing—love's enchanted stream ;
    Live, happy dreamer, live !

    Though sorrow dwelleth here,
And falsehood, and impurity, and sin,
The light of love, the gloom of earth to cheer,
    Comes sweetly, sweetly in.

'Tis o'er—thou art a man !—
The struggle and the tempest both begin,
Where he who faints must fail—he fight who can,
A victory to win.

Say, toilest thou for gold ?
Will all that earth can give of drossy hues
Compensate for that land of love foretold,
Which mammon makes thee lose ?

Or, waitest thou for power ?
A proud ambition, trifler, doth thee raise !—
To be the gilded bauble of the hour,
That fools may, wondering, gaze !

But would'st thou be a man—
A lofty, noble, uncorrupted thing,
Beneath whose eye the false might tremble wan,
The good with gladness sing ?

Go, cleanse thy heart, and fill
Thy soul with love and goodness ;—let it be
Like yonder lake, so holy, calm, and still,
And full of purity !

This is thy task on earth—
This is thy eager manhood's proudest goal :
To cast all meanness and world-worship forth,
And thus exalt the soul !

'Tis manhood makes the man
A high-soul'd freeman or a fetter'd slave,
The mind a temple fit for God to span,
Or a dark dungeon-grave.

God doth not man despise,—
He gives him soul—mind—heart—that living flame :
Nurse it, and upwards let it brightly rise
 To heaven, from whence it came !

Go hence, go hence, and make
Thy spirit pure as morning-light and free !
The pilgrim shrine is won, and I awake—
 Come to the woods with me !

316   *Death*

THE dew is on the Summer's greenest grass,
 Through which the modest daisy blushing
  peeps ;
The gentle wind, that like a ghost doth pass,
 A waving shadow on the corn-field keeps ;
But I, who love them all, shall never be
Again among the woods, or on the moorland lea !

The sun shines sweetly—sweeter may it shine !—
 Bless'd is the brightness of a summer day :
It cheers lone hearts ; and why should I repine,
 Although among green fields I cannot stray ?
Woods ! I have grown, since last I heard you wave,
Familiar with death, and neighbour to the grave !

These words have shaken mighty human souls :
 Like a sepúlchre's echo drear they sound—
E'en as the owl's wild whoop at midnight rolls
 The ivied remnants of old ruins round.
Yet wherefore tremble ? Can the soul decay ?—
Or that which thinks and feels in aught e'er fade
 away ?

Are there not aspirations in each heart
   After a better, brighter world than this?—
Longings for beings nobler in each part—
   Things more exalted—steep'd in deeper bliss?
Who gave us these? What are they? Soul! in thee
The bud is budding now for immortality.

Death comes to take me where I long to be :
   One pang—and bright blooms the immortal flower.
Death comes to lead me, from mortality,
   To lands which know not one unhappy hour.
I have a hope—a faith ;—from sorrow here
I'm led by Death away :—why should I start and
      fear ?

If I have loved the forest and the field,
   Can I not love them deeper, better, there?
If all that Power hath made to *me* doth yield
   Something of good and beauty—something fair,—
Freed from the grossness of mortality,
May I not love them all, and better all enjoy ?

A change from woe to joy—from earth to heaven,
   Death gives me this : it leads me calmly where
The souls that long ago from mine were riven
   May meet again! Death answers many a prayer.
Bright day ! shine on—be glad :—days brighter far
Are stretch'd before my eyes than those of mortals
      are !

I would be laid among the wildest flowers,
   I would be laid where happy hearts can come :—
The worthless clay I heed not ; but in hours
   Of gushing noontide joy, it may be some
Will dwell upon my name, and I will be
A happy spirit there, Affection's look to see.

Death is upon me, yet I fear not now.
  Open my chamber window,—let me look
Upon the silent vales—the sunny glow
  That fills each alley, close, and copse-wood nook.
I know them—love them—mourn not them to leave:
Existence and its change my spirit cannot grieve!

317   *A Dirge*

  SLEEP on, sleep on, ye resting dead!
      The grass is o'er ye growing
In dewy greenness. Ever fled
From you hath Care; and, in its stead,
Peace hath with you its dwelling made,
      Where tears do cease from flowing.
              Sleep on!

Sleep on, sleep on! Ye do not feel
      Life's ever-burning fever;
Nor scorn that sears, nor pains that steel
And blanch the loving heart, until
'Tis like the bed of mountain-rill
      Which waves have left for ever.
              Sleep on!

Sleep on, sleep on! Your couch is made
      Upon your mother's bosom:
Yea, and your peaceful, lonely bed
Is all with sweet wild-flowers inlaid;
And over each earth-pillow'd head
      The hand of Nature strews them
              Sleep on!

Sleep on, sleep on ! I would I were
   At rest within your dwelling,—
No more to feel, no more to bear
The World's falsehood and its care,
The arrows it doth never spare
   On him whose feet are failing.
                    Sleep on !

THOMAS CARSTAIRS LATTO

Born 1818

When We Were at the Schule

THE laddies plague me for a sang,—
  I e'en maun play the fule :
I'll sing them ane about the days
  When we were at the schule ;—
Though now the frosty pow is seen
  Whaur ance waved gowden hair ;
An' mony a blythesome heart is cauld
  Sin' first we sported there.

    When we were at the schule, my frien',
      When we were at the schule !
    An' O sae merry pranks we play'd
      When we were at the schule !

Yet muckle Jock is to the fore,
  That used our lugs [1] to pu' ;
An' Rob, the pest, an' Sugar Pouch,
  An' canny Davie Dow :
An' raggit Willie is the laird
  O' twa-three land'art [2] farms ;
An' Katie Spens, the pridefu' thing,
  Now cuddles in his arms.

O, do ye mind the maister's hat,
  Sae auld, sae bare an' brown,
We carried to the burnie's side
  An' sent it soomin' down ?

    [1] ears. [2] outlying.

We thocht how clever a' was plann'd,
    When—whatna voice was that?
A head is raised aboon the hedge:
    "I'll thank ye for my hat!"

O weel I mind our hingin' lugs,
    Our het an' tinglin' paws;
O weel I mind his solemn look,
    An' weel I mind the tawse [1]!
What awfu' snuffs that day he took,
    An' pang'd [2] them up his nose,
An' rapp'd the box as if to strike
    A terror to his foes.

An' do ye mind, at countin' time,
    How watchfu' he has lain,
To catch us steal frae ithers' slates
    An' jot it on our ain?
An' how we fear'd, at writin' hour,
    His glunches [3] and his glooms:
How many times a day he said
    Our fingers a' were thooms?

I'll ne'er forget the day ye stood—
    'Twas manfu', like yersel'—
An' took the pawmies [4] an' the shame
    To save wee Johnnie Bell.
The maister found it out belyve [5]:
    He took ye on his knee;
And, as he look'd into your face,
    The tear was in his e'e.

---

[1] instrument of correction.   [2] crammed.   [3] cross looks.   [4] strokes.
[5] anon.

But mind ye, lad, yon afternoon,
  How fleet ye skipp'd awa';
For ye had crack'd auld Jenny's pane,
  When playin' at the ba'?
Nae pennies had we: Jenny grat[1];—
  It cut us to the core:
Ye took your mither's hen at nicht
  An' left it at her door.

An' sic a steer[2] his granny made
  When tale-py't[3] Jamie Rae
We dookit[4], roarin', at the pump,
  Syne row'd[5] him down the brae!
But how the very maister leuch[6]
  When leein' saddler Wat
Cam' in an' threept[7] that cripple Tam
  Had chased an' kill'd his cat!

Ay, laddies, ye may wink awa'!
  Truth maunna aye be tauld:
I fear the schules o' modern days
  Are just siclike's the auld.
An' arena we but laddies yet
  Wha get the name o' men?
How sweet at ane's fireside to live
  The happy days again—

    When we were at the schule, my frien',
      When we were at the schule;
    An' fling the snawba's ower again
      We flang when at the schule!

[1] wept. [2] fuss. [3] sneakish. [4] ducked. [5] rolled. [6] laughed.
[7] insisted.

SIR WILLIAM STIRLING MAXWELL

1818–1878

319   *The Abdication of Charles V.*

IN Bruxelles Emperor Charles abode—fifth Cæsar
    of the name :
Weary with life's long toil was he ; and rack'd with
    gout his frame ;
His cheek was pale, his step was frail, seldom he
    crossed the door ;—
He could not rule as he had ruled in the good days
    of yore,
Nor meet the French in field and trench as he was
    wont to do,
When o'er the Flemish border the lilied banner flew.
Wherefore he had devised and dealt to lay the
    burden down
Of pomp, and power, and majesty,—of sceptre, orb,
    and crown ;
And all his world-wide heritage, and all his sword
    had won,
To give unto Don Philip now, his dear and only
    son—
Don Philip, King of England, who that noble realm
    had brought
Back to Christ's faith from heresy by rebel Luther
    taught.

So Cæsar and the English King in Bruxelles town
  were met ;
And paction was between them made, and time of
  signing set :
The year of grace one thousand was, five hundred
  fifty-five—
The famous year that saw the morn of this great
  deed arrive ;
Friday, October twenty-five, three afternoon, the day
And hour when Cæsar sign'd and seal'd his diadems
  away.

At Bruxelles, in the ancient hall within the castle gate,
Where valiant Dukes of Burgundy erst kept their
  royal state,
Upon the dais richly dight, beneath the canopy,
The throne was set, and all a-row stood chairs of
  honour three.
Fair Flanders' looms had spread the walls with
  storied hangings o'er ;
And Cæsar and Don Philip came, with trumpet
  blown before,
With Mary, Queen of Hungary, high lady wise and
  wight,
And Savoy's Duke of iron mould, and many a lord
  and knight
Of broad Brabant and proud Castille—great chiefs of
  war and peace,
Grave magistrates of towns and states, knights of the
  Golden Fleece.

Then Cæsar sat upon his throne with calm and
  gracious mien ;
And right and left—on either hand—bade sit the
  King and Queen :

47

And near the Queen the Duke was set ; and down
  below, the floor
Scarce held the folk that throng'd to see—a thousand
  souls and more.
So, when the heralds silence call'd, the whispering
  hum was still,
And rose the Chancellor of the Fleece to speak the
  Emperor's will :
In weighty, well-graced words he said how Cæsar's
  Majesty
Would pass the evening of his days from broil and
  battle free,—
And, giving to Don Philip now his royal place and
  state,
Will'd that his loving people's will the gift should
  consecrate.

Then slowly, when the Chancellor ceased, the
  Emperor arose ;
And told of all his toils at home, and wars with
  foreign foes,—
How twice to heathen Barbary his Christian flag he
  bore,
And now eleven times had pass'd the stormy ocean
  o'er ;
And how one passage more—the twelfth—for him
  did yet remain,
If God should grant his sole desire—to end his days
  in Spain.
From his first hour of royal power, it had been his
  endeavour
Justice to mete, and right to do, with equal balance ever ;
But if, in absence, or by chance or frailty led astray,
Wrong he had done, he pray'd them all to pardon
  him that day.

And so he bade them all farewell, and left them to
    his son,
Their lord, whose rule in other realms the people's
    hearts had won :—
This witting, he, for such a son, could joyfully lay
    down
The sacred trust he else had kept of sceptre, sword,
    and crown.
And, last of all, in earnest wise three things he did
    commend
Unto their care, and bid them hold in honour to the
    end :
Their holy faith, their country's peace, their duty to
    their lord,
Who loved them, and would win their love :—this
    was his parting word.

Then rose the King unbonneted, and stood before
    the throne,
And for his father's gracious words, and grace and
    favour done,
Gave thanks : and, humbly kneeling down, he sought
    to kiss his hand ;
But Cæsar threw his arms about his neck and bade
    him stand :
And many a tear was shed the while by loving sire
    and son,
And by the Queen, and Duke, and Knights and nobles
    every one.

Next, for the Cities and Estates a learned jurist spake,
And told the Emperor how well they were content
    to take

His hopeful son their lord to be. Whereon Don
 Philip bade
The reverend Lord of Arras speak ; who courteous
 answer made.

Then last the good Queen Mary rose, of her long
 reign to tell,
And bid, in fair and gentle speech, her people all
 farewell:
Foremost of lands to make their land—for this she
 still had striven ;
And now for faults and errors past she sued to be
 forgiven.

In courtly words th' Estates replied, they mourn'd
 to see her go ;
But with them still was law her will, — and she
 would have it so.
Wherewith the goodly company arose and went their
 way,
As evening fell :—and so the King became our Lord
 that day.

JOHN CAMPBELL SHAIRP

1819–1885

320   *The Bush Aboon Traquair*

WILL ye gang wi' me and fare
    To the bush aboon Traquair?
Ower the high Minchmuir we'll up and awa',
    This bonnie simmer noon,
    While the sun shines fair aboon [1],
And the licht sklents [2] saftly doun on holm and
    ha'.

    And what wad ye do there,
    At the bush aboon Traquair?
A long dreich [3] road, ye had better let it be;
    Save some auld skrunts [4] o' birk
    I' the hill-side lirk [5],
There's nocht i' the warld for man to see.

    But the blithe lift o' that air,
    "The Bush aboon Traquair"—
I need nae mair, it's eneuch for me:
    Ower my cradle its sweet chime
    Cam' sughin' frae auld time—
Sae tide what may I'll awa' and see.

    And what saw ye there,
    At the bush aboon Traquair?

[1] above.   [2] slants.   [3] dreary.   [4] stumps.   [5] hollow, bosom.

Or what did ye hear that was worth your heed?
    I heard the cushies croon [1]
    Thro' the gowden afternoon,
And the Quair burn singing doun to the vale o'
    Tweed.

    And birks saw I three or four,
    Wi' grey moss bearded ower—
The last that are left o' the birken shaw [2] ;
    Whar mony a simmer e'en
    Fond lovers did convene,
Thae bonny, bonny gloamins that are lang awa'.

    Frae mony a but and ben [3],
    By muirland, holm, and glen,
They cam' ane hour to spen' on the greenwood
    swaird ;
    But lang ha'e lad an' lass
    Been lying 'neath the grass—
The green, green grass o' Traquair kirkyaird.

    They were blest beyond compare
    When they held their trysting there—
Amang thae greenest hills shone on by the sun ;
    And then they wan a rest,
    The lownest [4] and the best,
I' Traquair kirkyaird when a' was dune.

    Now the birks to dust may rot,
    Names o' luvers be forgot,
Nae lads and lasses there ony mair convene ;
    But the blythe lilt o' yon air
    Keeps the bush aboon Traquair
And the luve that ance was there aye fresh and green.

---

[1] ring-doves coo.   [2] copse.   [3] cottage interior.   [4] stillest.

JAMES THOMSON, OF HAWICK

1827–1888

Hogmanay [1]

UP frae their cosie beds
    Afore the peep o' day,
Skippin' round the corner,
    Brattlin' [2] down the brae—
Hearts a' sae happy,
    Faces blithe and gay,
A merry band o' bairnies
    Seek their Hogmanay.

Careless o' the blast sae bleak,
    Snawy drift or shower,
Though the roses on their cheek
    Turn like the blaewart flower [3],—
Frae ilka door they're jinkin' [4]
    To hail the happy day ;
And they a' gang a-linkin' [5]
    To seek their Hogmanay.

[1] Children in Scotland go on the morning of the last day of the year to the neighbours' houses and sing—

> "We are children come out to play,
> Gie's our cakes and let's away."

On receiving a cake of oatmeal, they sing—

> "We joyful wish ye a good day,
> And thank ye for your Hogmanay !"

[2] clattering.   [3] bilberry.   [4] slipping out.   [5] arm-in-arm.

Bonnie bairnies, come awa'!
   It's little I've to gi'e,
But ye shall ha'e my blessing a',
   An' ae bawbee.
When manhood's care comes o'er ye,
   Ye'll mind the merry day
When, happy-hearted bairnies,
   Ye sought your Hogmanay.

322   *Hairst* [1]

THE yellow corn waves in the field,
   The merry hairst's begun ;
And steel-plate sickles, sharp and keen,
   Are glintin' in the sun,
While strappin' lads, and lassies braw,
   A' kiltit to the knee,
Bring to my mind a hairst langsyne,
   When Robin shuire [2] wi' me.

Light lie the mools [3] upon his breast;
   He was a strappin' chield,—
A better shearer ne'er drew huik
   Upon a harvest field.
And didna joy loup in my heart,
   And sparkle frae my e'e,
Sae proud was I, when Robin said
   He'd shear alang wi' me.

That was a lightsome hairst to me,—
   For love mak's light o' toil,—
The kindly blink o' Robin's e'e
   Could a' my care beguile.

[1] harvest.   [2] reaped   [3] sods.

A   restin' time amang the stooks[1]
  I sat upon his knee,
And wonder'd if the warld could haud
  A blither lass than me.

Lang Sandy and his sister Jean
  Thocht nane wi' them could shear,
And a' the hairst at Rab an' me
  Threw mony a taunt an' jeer.
Rab ga'e them aye as guid's they brought,
  And took it a' in fun :
But inly vowed to heat their skin
  Afore the hairst was done.

The kirn-day[2] cam', a kemp[3] began,
  And hard and fast it grew ;
Across the rig wi' lightnin' speed
  The glintin' sickles flew.
Lang Sandy wam'let[4] like an eel,
  But soon fell in the rear ;
For no a pair in a' the boon[5]
  Wi' Rab an' me could shear.

We clear'd our rig baith tight and clean,
  And thought the day our ain,
When wae's my heart ! I brak' my huik
  Upon a meikle stane.
"Mak' bands," quo' Robin—while the sweat
  Like rain-drops trickled doon ;—
But Robin reach'd the land-end first
  And foremost o' the boon.

[1] shocks of corn.   [2] harvest home.   [3] contest.   [4] staggered.
[5] band of reapers.

I thought that I wad swoon wi' joy
   When dightin'[1] Robin's brow,
He says, " Meg, gin ye'll buckle to[2],
   I'll shear through life wi' you."
What could I do but buckle to—
   He was sae frank an' free?
And often did I bless the day
   That Robin shuire wi' me.

323   *The Auld Smiddy End*

OH, the Auld Smiddy end, where in youth's
   happy day
A merry band o' bairnies wad gather at their play!
I mind the happy faces, and the hours we wad
   spend
Wi' the bools and the peeries[3] at the Auld Smiddy
   end.

Against the batter'd gable were mony orra[4] things—
Auld pleughs that wanted couters[5], new wheels that
   wanted rings,
A pair o' broken harrows that for years had lain to
   mend :—
There was meikle claithin' riven at the Auld Smiddy
   end.

O the fun and frolic, and the mischief that we
   wrought,—
There was lums to set alow[6], and battles to be fought,
And jury courts to haud when some coward laddie
   henn'd[7],
And gat his buttons scartit at the Auld Smiddy end.

---

[1] wiping.   [2] marry me.   [3] marbles and spinning-tops.   [4] ill-assorted.   [5] coulters.   [6] chimneys to set afire.   [7] showed the white feather.

We never thought o' parting at the hour o' gloamin'
    grey,—
The fun was aye beginnin' when the daylight was
    away :
When beddin' time cam' round ilka mither brawly
    kenn'd
She wad find her truant laddie at the Auld Smiddy
    end.

And in winter we wad gather round the bleezin'
    smiddy hearth,
While block and stithy rang wi' our daffin'[1] an' our
    mirth :
The independent blacksmith—to kings he wadna
    bend—
Was kind to the laddies at the Auld Smiddy end.

But youthfu' pleasures winna last, and youthfu' scenes
    will change ;
The smiddy and the smith are gane, and ilka thing
    is strange :
'Mang a' the happy faces that in ither days I kenn'd
There's nane to meet me noo at the Auld Smiddy
    end.

But in the quiet gloamin' hour I sit and muse alane,
Till Fancy wi' her fairy wand brings vanish'd scenes
    again ;
The Memory, like a bird, to its ain hame will wend,
And familiar faces gather round the Auld Smiddy
    end.

[1] sport.

EARL OF SOUTHESK

1827–1905

324   *Pigworm and Dixie*

[Joey Peggram, or " Pigworm," laments over the bygone
bachelor days of Ben Dixie, his former boon companion.—ED.]

WELL! if ever a man is in want of a wife
    To poison his pleasure and pester his life,
First place let him go to Ben Dixie's, you know,
And see what that awful example will show.

Oh, such a good fellow was rollicking Ben,
Beloved by the girls and the right sort of men!
You may call me a lie, but—'pon honour 'tis said—
For a twelvemonth he never went sober to bed.

Yes; rollicking Ben was a fellow of sense,
Who hated all stick-me-up, humbug pretence;
As to that I can swear, for no hogs in the sty
Were more thick with each other than Dixie and I.

What a jolly old crib was his house in the dale,
A Garden of Eden of 'baccy and ale:
Any hour of the day you could eat at your ease,
There were always some ends of cold bacon or
    cheese.

Lawk! now if you enter his prig of a house,
Not a scrap can you find that would serve for a
    mouse;
And you wait and you wait till the dinner comes in,
Though perhaps you're as hungry and thirsty as sin.

But at last there's a row,—jingle-jing goes a bell,
And you sit yourself down, and you feed like a
    swell.
Oh, that shiny new tablecloth !—give me the cheer
Of the old one, all gravy and mustard and beer !

Ah yes, Mrs. Dixie, you're awfully neat,
With your fat little hands and your smart little feet ;
And you trot up and down, and you perk up your
    head,
And you smell like a rose in a lavender bed.

And you smirk and you smile, and you puff out
    your breast
Like a pigeon a-pouting and walking its best ;
And so mighty polite—why, a fellow can't dare
To chaff when he wants to, and swagger and swear !

Lawk ! I'd like to yell out, like a throttle-choked
    hen,
When I think of the days of good *bachelor* Ben ;
No wife to torment one, dressed up like a doll,—
But that jolly kind creature, young housekeeper Moll.

She was something to see, as you smoked in your
    chair,
With her rolling black eyes and the kink in her
    hair ;
With her shoes down at heel, and her cheeks pink
    as paint,
And holes in her stockings—no beastly constraint !

And her ringlets they smelt like a hairdresser's
    shop :
And her dress was green stuff, spattered over with
    slop :
And her hands were good large ones, her ankles
    were thick,
And her nails they were bitten clean down to the
    quick.

She'd a taste of a temper, but nothing like vice—
It is downright unchristian to be too precise ;
For a shy with a bottle I don't know her match ;
But good lawk ! what is that when a fellow can
    catch ?

Oh, wasn't it prime ! you could drink, you could
    smoke,
You could chuck out a curse, you could sing, you
    could joke ;
Things are changed now, alas !—all is bother and
    bore,—
Why, the Missus looks wild if you spit on the floor !

Faugh ! to hear how they jaw, it quite gives one a
    turn,—
As if words were hot mealy potatoes that burn ;
" A little more beef, please,"—then faces they
    pull ;
Can't he say,—" Shove us over some more of the
    bull " ?

Yes, I hate the whole set with their finikin ways.
It was " live and let live " in the jolly old days,
The hens in the kitchen took all that they chose,
And the pups in the parlour rolled over your toes.

But now (set us up!) they've a precious fine lot
Of young-uns who gobble the pick of the pot;
And they sit up so pert, each small brat in its
    place,
And when stuffed nigh to bursting they squeak out a
    grace!

Well, perhaps I'm not perfect, though fairly so-so;
But thank Heav'n, I'm no hypocrite—hang it all, no!
Before I'd go in for that sanctified bosh—
I'd as soon send a red flannel shirt to the wash!

Jolly Ben, bless his soul! when he used to begin
He would swear till you thought the old Deuce had
    come in:
Now see him with Missus, as prim as a pea,
Trudging slowly to church, with the brats in their
    lee.

Mrs. Dixie got up in her lavender dress;
And poor Ben such a swell as no words can express,
With white pants, and a rose, and a tile with a
    twist,
And a pair of small girls hanging on to his fist.

So they toddle along to the jole of the bell,
And they go to a pew, and get blest with a spell
Of singing and preaching and things in that style—
Ben sleeps, I'll be bound, for the most of the while!

But humbug for ever! hypocrisy pays,
Like the bills on the walls about pickles and plays;
Yes, it's worth heaps of cash to be called "honest
    Ben,"
And be toadied and praised by all manner of men.

Who but he! they can't meet to be jolly and dine,
After judging the horses and cattle and swine,
But up starts Squire Blount—"Fill a bumper," says he,
"For a toast in which no one can fail to agree,—

"The health of that pattern to farmers and all,
Mr. Benjamin Dixie of Rosemary Hall!"
Then they clap their fat paws, and they roar, and they swill—
Euch! bring me a basin, I'm going to be ill.

If there's one thing I hate it's that bumptious conceit—
To set up to be tidy and pretty and neat:
It's as much as to say to a fellow, you see,
"What does nicely for you is not fit for big me!"

Instead of the grass and the puddles of muck,
And the sow with her piggies, and goosey and duck,
And a midden, and plenty old kettles and tubs,
They've got gardens and roses, and things they call shrubs.

Just you walk through the garden and tear off a flow'r
For a shy at the hens—don't the Missus look sour!
Or go near those cantankerous buffers of bees—
After you, sir, is manners; you first, if you please!

Why those brutes won't abide me I really can't say,
For whenever they see me they hunt me away:
They object to bad smells,—but that isn't my case,
Few days but I souse both my hands and my face.

Now Ben Dixie he scrubs in a terrible way,
Till he shines like a sixpence and smells of new
    hay ;
I liked him far better all mire, muck, and grease,
When the man and his midden were quite of a
    piece.

What nonsense they talk about scrubbing off dirt—
As if things that come natural ever could hurt !
But Ben, the big booby, has grown like the eels,
The more he is skinned, the more lively he feels.

If you stay for the night at that Rosemary Hall,
You're a mighty queer chap if you like it at all.
" Fresh air," quoth the blockhead ! I say it's a chouse
To hang out in a windmill and call it a house.

And there's lots of oak panels as bright as the stars,
And the place stinks of roses and blue-and-white
    jars ;
And your bed's got white curtains that can't be
    drawn round,
And you tumble and grunt like a pig in a pound.

And you're nearly sent mad with the peppery smell
Of dead flow'rs dry in bowls, and of live ones as
    well ;
And the nightingales sing till you wish 'em in Spain,
And at dawn you've the thrushes and blackbirds
    again.

And your nice morning sleep is disturbed by the
    noise
Of dear Ben's blessêd darlings, his girls and his boys,
A-feeding the turkeys with stuff from a pail,
And screechy pea-devils with eyes in the tail.

And there's booing of oxen and mooing of cows ;
And the hogs and the horses—confound 'em for rows !
And the sheep, and the cur-dog bow-wowing the
    flock :
Oh, of course ! Master Dixie keeps excellent stock.

Poor wretch ! I don't fancy that anything pays
For toiling and moiling—I live all *my* days :
A sort of a god, with my 'baccy and bowl,
As jolly and snug as a toad in a hole.

No, it ain't mighty grand, but it suits to a T,
It's a capital den for a fellow like me.
No draughts and dry roses to keep you a-snort,
But a sensible place looking into a court.

On the ground-floor of course,—I object to a stair,
For the higher you go you get more of the air ;
The grate's pretty big, but the window's quite small—
Such a fit, sir ! in fact it won't open at all.

There ain't neither shutter nor bothersome blind,
But there's dust on the glass, and the sun keeps
    behind ;
And I snooze on my bed for the most of the day,
And the best of the night I am up and away.

Oh, it's jolly to lie on your back half a-doze,
And to kick off the quilt with your lazy old toes ;
And you stare at your stockings as long as you
    please,
And you wriggle your trousers right over your knees.

Then you stretch, and get hold of your pipe for a
    whiff,
And make matters serene with a drop of the "stiff";
If you're peckish inclined, there is nothing to do
More easy than fry a red herring or two.

As Bill Shakespeare remarks, "There is no place like
    home,"
I'm as proud of my crib as a cock of his comb;
Life's sweet there—though once, I must really confess,
I had nearly dropped in for a bit of a mess.

A young cove he came canting with tracts on the
    sly,
"Converting" he called it: "Now, Mister," said I,
"Unless your name's 'Walker' this instant, d'ye see,
We'll 'convert' you to sausage, will Towzer and me."

So he turned—did this cove—pretty white in the gill:
"Good-day, sir," says he; "as you like me so ill,
I'll never come in to annoy you no more,—
Though I'm bound to be sometimes a-passing your
    door."

Well, before it got dark on that very same day,
I was taken all no-how, a queer kind of way:
All my bones and my gizzards were aching like fun,
And my brains were like boots hanging out in the
    sun.

Oh, I felt monstrous bad, and I soon got so weak
I could scarce raise my head, and I hardly could
    speak;
And no creature came near me, I thought I should
    die,—
When at length sounds the step of a man passing by.

And old Towzer he kicks up a deuce of a din,
And the door opens slow, and a fellow peeps in—
Nick Chousem, my partner ;—says he, " Here's a go !
Bye-bye, Joey Pigworm,—it's small-pox, you know."

And I lay and I blubbered. The rest I forget.
When I opened my peepers, the first thing I met
Was the mission-cove, watching me anxious and fond,
Like a hen whose small ducks are a-swim in a pond.

Well, of course I recovered—that's middling clear,
For if I'd skedaddled I shouldn't be here :
That good cove pulled me out of Old Gooseberry's
　　　gripe,—
And his tracts came quite useful for lighting one's
　　　pipe.

Not ungrateful, sir, no ! he declined my advice,
But I showed him neat things with the cards and
　　　the dice ;
And my dog runs to meet him a-wagging its tail,
And it grins, " How d'ye do " like a shark in a gale.

No, it don't pay a bit to be seedy, you see,—
Not, at least, for mere common-sense snobbies like
　　　me :
But Ben !—let his thumb ache, they rush to in-
　　　quire,—
Town, village, and country, lord, parson, and squire.

Lawk, when Ben comes to die ! bless their heads and
　　　their eyes,
How the crape and the white pocket-wipers will rise!
And the funeral cards will be scattered like peas,
And the folks will come swarming like mites on a
　　　cheese.

And they'll drive up a gimcracky hypocrite hearse;
And they'll shove him inside, like a pig in a purse;
And they'll carry him off to the burial crib;
And the parson will come, like a rook in a bib.

Then they'll earth up his corpse in a daisy-bank
    hole;
And the boom of the organ will sweep off his soul,
As you blow off the froth from a buzzy brown
    bowl:
And the bloodhound bell will jole—jole—jole.

O lawk! can't I see it? and afterwards too,
The Missus and children all making boohoo;
And creeping like blackbirds down Sweetbriar Lane,
A-weeping, and wishing him with them again.

And the little pale girls in their bombazine stuff,
With their hair running loose like a parcel of fluff,
And nice flow'rs in their hands for the grave of
    " Papa "—
Such a comfort to Ben in his coffin, ha ha!

Rum business is life! but it ends all a-piece
For the easy good chaps and the hard-working
    geese:
And why should they grudge a poor beast of a man
To be happy and jolly the best way he can?

Says the mission-cove once,—" You've no sort of excuse
For to cumber the earth, if you're no sort of use."
" How," says I, " could the beggarsome planet be filled,
If the coves that do nothing were taken and killed? "

Some fine day, by and by, I shall likely expire—
They'll not take up Joe Pigworm in char'ots of fire ;—
Well ! when Gooseberry wants me I'll meet him quite
  brave :
I wonder what folk will strew over *my* grave !

Nick Chousem, I daresay, will miss me a bit,
And he'll sit on my grave, and he'll smoke there and
  spit ;
And perhaps I'll be missed by my brute of a dog,
For I lick him and kick him, and give him his prog.

Lawk, what do I care ! My blest body will rot,
My blest soul (if I've got one) will toddle to pot,
And I'll treat the poor worms to a famous repast—
Oh yes, I'll be useful to something at last !

325   *The Flitch of Dunmow*

COME Micky and Molly and dainty Dolly,
    Come Betty and blithesome Bill ;
Ye gossips and neighbours, away with your labours !
  Come to the top of the hill.
For there are Jenny and jovial Joe ;
Jolly and jolly, jolly they go,
    Jogging over the hill.

By apple and berry, 'tis twelve months merry
  Since Jenny and Joe were wed !
And never a bother or quarrelsome pother
  To trouble the board or bed.
So Joe and Jenny are off to Dunmow :
Happy and happy, happy they go,
    Young and rosy and red.

Oh, Jenny's as pretty as doves in a ditty;
  And Jenny, her eyes are black;
And Joey's a fellow as merry and mellow
  As ever shouldered a sack.
So quick, good people, and come to the show!
Merry and merry, merry they go,
    Bumping on Dobbin's back.

They've prankt up old Dobbin with ribands and bobbin,
  And tethered his tail in a string:
That fat flitch of bacon is not to be taken
  By many that wear the ring!
Good luck, good luck, to Jenny and Joe!
Jolly and jolly, jolly they go.
    Hark! they merrily sing.

"O merry, merry, merry are we,
Happy as birds that sing in a tree!
All of the neighbours are happy to-day,
Merry are we and merry are they.
O merry are we! for love, you see,
Fetters a heart and sets it free.

"O happy, happy, happy is life
For Joe (that's me) and Jenny my wife!
All of the neighbours are happy, and say—
'Never were folk so happy as they!'
O happy are we! for love, you see,
Fetters a heart and sets it free.

"O jolly, jolly, jolly we go,
I and my Jenny, and she and her Joe.
All of the neighbours are jolly, and sing—
'She is a queen, and he is a king!'
O jolly are we! for love, you see,
Fetters a heart and sets it free."

UNKNOWN

326   *Canadian Boat-song*

(From the Gaelic)

First published in the "Noctes Ambrosianæ," No. XLVI., in *Black-wood's Magazine* for September, 1829. The authorship is unknown. (See an article in the *Cornhill Magazine* for December, 1909; also "The Lone Shieling," by G. M. Fraser, Smith, Aberdeen, 1908.)

I

LISTEN to me, as when ye heard our father
    Sing long ago the song of other shores—
Listen to me, and then in chorus gather
    All your deep voices, as ye pull your oars:

CHORUS

Fair these broad meads—these hoary woods are
    grand;
But we are exiles from our fathers' land.

II

From the lone shieling of the misty island
    Mountains divide us, and the waste of seas—
Yet still the blood is strong, the heart is Highland,
    And we in dreams behold the Hebrides.

III

We ne'er shall tread the fancy-haunted valley,
   Where 'tween the dark hills creeps the small clear
     stream,
In arms around the patriarch banner rally,
   Nor see the moon on royal tombstones gleam.

IV

When the bold kindred, in the time long vanish'd,
   Conquer'd the soil and fortified the keep,—
No seer foretold the children would be banish'd,
   That a degenerate lord might boast his sheep.

V

Come foreign rage—let Discord burst in slaughter!
   O then for clansman true and stern claymore—
The hearts that would have given their blood like
     water,
   Beat heavily beyond the Atlantic roar:

     Fair these broad meads—these hoary woods are
       grand;
     But we are exiles from our fathers' land.

ALEXANDER SMITH

1830–1867

327   *Squire Maurice*

I THREW from off me yesterday
    The dull life I am doomed to wear—
A worn-out garment dim and bare,
And left it in my chambers grey:
The salt breeze wanders in my hair
Beside the splendour of the main:
Ere on the deep three sunsets burn,
To the old chambers I return,
And put it on again.
An old coat, worn for many a year,
No wonder it is something dear!

Ah, year by year life's fire burns out,
And year by year life's stream runs dry:
The wild deer dies within the blood,
The falcon in the eye.
And Hope, who sang miraculous songs
Of what should be, like one inspired,
How she should right the ancient wrongs,
(The generous fool!) grows hoarse and tired;
And turns from visions of a world renewed,
To dream of tripled rents, fair miles of stream and
     wood.
The savage horse, that leads

His tameless herd across the endless plain,
Is taught at last, with sullen heart, to strain
Beneath his load, nor quiver when he bleeds.
We cheat ourselves with our own lying eyes,
We chase a fleeting mirage o'er the sand,
Across a grave the smiling phantom flies,
O'er which we fall with a vain-clutching hand.
What matter—if we heave laborious breath,
And crack our hearts and sinews, groan and weep,
The pain of life but sweetens death,
The hardest labour brings the soundest sleep.

On bank and brae how thick they grow,
The self-same clumps, the self-same dyes,
The primroses of long ago—
But ah! the altered eyes!
I dream they are the very flowers,
Warm with the sun, wet with the showers,
Which, years ago, I used to pull
Returning from the murmuring school.
Sweet Nature is a mother ever more;
A thousand tribes are breathing on the shore;
The pansy blows beside the rock,
The globe-flower, where the eddy swirls;
And on this withered human stock
Burst rosy boys and girls.
Sets Nature little store
On that which once she bore?
Does she forget the old, in rapture bear the new?
Are ye the flowers that grew
In other seasons? Do they e'er return,
The men who built the cities on the plain?—
Or must my tearless eyeballs burn
For ever o'er that early urn,
Ne'er to be cooled by a delicious dew?

Let me take back my pain
Unto my heart again ;
Before I can recover that I lack
The world must be rolled back.

Inland I wander slow,
Mute with the power the earth and heaven wield :
A black spot sails across the golden field,
And through the air a crow.
Before me wavers springs's first butterfly ;
From out the sunny noon there starts the cuckoo's
   cry ;
The daisied meads are musical with lambs ;
Some play, some feed, some, white as snow-flakes, lie
In the deep sunshine, by their silent dams.
The road grows white and level to the feet ;
The wandering woodbine through the hedge is drawn,
Unblown its streaky bugles dim and sweet ;
Knee-deep in fern stand startled doe and fawn,
And lo ! there gleams upon a spacious lawn
An Earl's marine retreat.
A little foot-path quivers up the height,
And what a vision for a townsman's sight !
A village, peeping from its orchard bloom,
With lowly roofs of thatch, blue threads of smoke,
O'erlooking all, a parsonage of white.
I hear the smithy's hammer, stroke on stroke ;
A steed is at the door ; the rustics talk,
Proud of the notice of the gaitered groom ;
A shallow river breaks o'er shallow falls.
Beside the ancient sluice that turns the mill
The lusty miller bawls ;
The parson listens in his garden-walk,
The red-cloaked woman pauses on the hill.
This is a place, you say, exempt from ill,

A paradise, where, all the loitering day,
Enamoured pigeons coo upon the roof,
Where children ever play.—
Alas! Time's webs are rotten, warp and woof;
Rotten his cloth of gold, his coarsest wear:
Here, black-eyed Richard ruins red-cheeked Moll,
Indifferent as a lord to her despair.
The broken barrow hates the prosperous dray;
And, for a padded pew in which to pray,
The grocer sells his soul.

This cosy hostelrie a visit craves;
Here will I sit awhile,
And watch the heavenly sunshine smile
Upon the village graves.
Strange is this little room in which I wait,
With its old table, rough with rustic names.
'Tis summer now; instead of blinking flames,
Sweet-smelling ferns are hanging o'er the grate.
With curious eyes I pore
Upon the mantel-piece, its precious wares,
Glazed Scripture prints in black lugubrious frames,
Filled with old Bible lore:
The whale is casting Jonah on the shore;
Pharaoh is drowning in the curly wave;
And to Elijah sitting at his cave,
The hospitable ravens fly in pairs,
Celestial food within their horny beaks;
On a slim David, with great pinky cheeks,
A towered Goliath stares.
Here will I sit at peace:
While, piercing through the window's ivy-veil,
A slip of sunshine smites the amber ale;
And as the wreaths of fragrant smoke increase,
I'll read the letter which came down to-day.

Ah, happy Maurice! while in chambers dun,
I pore o'er deeds and parchments growing gray,
Each glowing realm that spreads beneath the
    sun
Is but a paradise where you may play.
I am a bonded workman, you are free;
In your blood's hey-day—mine is early cold.
Life is rude furze at best; the sea-breeze wrings
And eats my branches on the bitter lea;
But you have root in dingle fat and old,
Fat with decayings of a hundred springs,
And blaze all splendid in your points of gold,
And in your heart a linnet sits and sings.

"Unstable as the wind, infirm as foam,
I envy, Charles, your calmness and your peace;
The eye that marks its quarry from afar,
The heart that stoops on it and smites it down.
I, struggling in a dim and obscure net,
Am but enmeshed the more. When you were here,
My spirit often burned to tell you all;
I urged the horse up to the leap, it shied
At something in the hedge. This must not last;
In shame and sorrow, ere I sleep to-night,
I'll shrive my inmost soul.

               I have knelt, and sworn
By the sweet heavens—I have madly prayed
To be by them forsaken, when I forsake
A girl whose lot should be to sleep content
Upon a peasant's breast, and toil all day
'Mong flaxen-headed children. She sits to-night,
When all the little town is lost in dream,
Her lax hands sunk in her neglected work,
Thinking of me. Smile not, my man of law,
Who, with a peering candle, walkest through

Black places in men's hearts, which only hear
The foot of conscience at the dead of night!
Her name might slip into my holiest prayer;
Her breath has come and gone upon my cheek,
Yet I dare stand before my mother's face,
Dare look into the heavenly eyes that yearn
For ever through a mist of golden hair,
With no shame on my brow. 'Tis not that way
My trouble looks. Yet, friend, in simple truth,
Could this thing be obliterated quite,
Expunged for ever, like a useless cloak
I'd fling off my possessions, and go forth,
My roof the weeping heaven.
                              Though I would die
Rather than give her pain, I grimly smile
To think, were I assured this horrid dream
Which poisons day to me, would only prove
A breath upon the mirror of her mind—
A moment dim, then gone (an issue which,
Could *I* have blotted out all memory,
Would let me freely breathe)—this love would
    turn
To bitterest gall of hate. O Vanity,
Thou god, who on the altar thou hast built
Pilest myrrh and frankincense, appliest the flame,
Then snuff'st the smoky incense, high and calm!
Thou nimble Proteus of all human shapes!
Malvolio, cross-gartered in the sun,
The dying martyr, gazing from his fire
Upon the opened heavens, filled with crowds
Of glorious angel-faces:—thou art all
We smile at, all we hymn! For thee we blush,
For thee shed noble tears! The glowing coal,
O'er which the frozen beggar spreads his hands,
Is of one essence with the diamond,

That on the haughty forehead of a queen
Trembles with dewy light. Could *I*, through pain,
Give back the peace I stole, my heart would leap ;
Could *she* forget me and regain content—
How deeply I am wronged !

"Is it the ancient trouble of my house
That makes the hours so terrible ? Other men
Live to more purpose than those monstrous weeds
That drink a breath of sunshine, and give back
Nor hue nor fragrance ; but my spirit droops,
A dead and idle banner from its staff,
Unstirred by any wind. Within a cell,
Without a straw to play with, or a nail
To carve my sorrow on the gloomy stone,
I sit and watch, from stagnant day to day,
The bloated spider hanging on its thread,
The dull fly on the wall. The blessed sleep
For which none are too poor ; the sleep that comes
So sweetly to the weary labouring man,
The march-worn soldier on the naked ground,
The martyr in the pauses of the rack,
Drives me through forests full of dreadful eyes,
Flings me o'er precipices, makes me kneel,
A sentenced man, before the dark platoon,
Or lays me helpless in the dim embrace
Of formless horror. Long ago, two foes
Lay in the yellow evening in their gore :
Like a malignant fury, that wild hour
Threw madness in the river of our blood :
Though it has run for thrice a century,
Been sweetened all the way by mothers' tears,
'Tis poisoned until now.

                        See how I stand

Delaying on the brink, like one who fears
And yet would meet the chill! When you were
    here
You saw a smoking-cap among my books;
A fond and fluttering letter badly spelt,
Each sentence headed with a little *i*,
Came with it, read with a blush, tossed in the
    fire,
Nor answered yet. Can you not now detect
The snail's slime on the rose?
                  This miserable thing
Grew round me like the ivy round the oak;
Sweet were its early creeping rings, though now
I choke, from knotted root to highest bough.
In those too happy days I could not name
This strange new thing which came upon my youth,
But yielded to its sweetness. Fling it off?
Trample it down? Bid me pluck out the eye
In which the sweet world dwells!—One night she
    wept;
It seemed so strange that *I* could make her weep:
Kisses may lie, but tears are surely true.
Then unbelief came back in solitude,
And love grew cruel; and to be assured
Cried out for tears, and with a shaking hand
And a wild heart that could have almost burst
With utter tenderness, yet would not spare,
He clutched her heart, and at the starting tears
Grew soft with all remorse. For those mad hours
Remembrance frets my heart in solitude,
As the lone mouse when all the house is still
Gnaws at the wainscot.
              'Tis a haunting face,
Yet oftentimes I think I love her not;
Love's white hand flutters o'er my spirit's keys

49

Unkissed by grateful music. Oft I think
The Lady Florence at the county ball,
Quenching the beauties as the lightning dims
The candles in a room, scarce smiles so sweet.
The one oppresses like a crown of gold,
The other gladdens like a beam in spring,
Stealing across a dim field, making blithe
Its daisies one by one.—I deemed that I
Had broke my house of bondage, when one night
The memory of her face came back so sweet,
And stood between me and the printed page ;
And phantoms of a thousand happy looks
Smiled from the dark. It was the old weak tale
Which time has told from Adam to this hour :
The slave comes back, takes up his broken chain.
I rode through storm toward the little town ;
The minster, gleamed on by the flying moon,
Tolled midnight as I passed. I only sought
To see the line of light beneath her door,
The knowledge of her nearness was so sweet.
Hid in the darkness of the church, I watched
Her window like a shrine: a light came in,
And a soft shadow broke along the roof ;
She raised the window and leaned forth awhile.
I could have fallen down and kissed her feet ;
The poor dear heart, I knew it could not rest ;
I stood between her and the light—my shade
Fell 'cross her silver sphere. The window closed.
When morn with cold bleak crimson laced the
    east,
Against a stream of raw and rainy wind
I rode back to the Hall.
                    The play-book tells
How Fortune's slippery wheel in Syracuse
Flung prosperous lordship to the chilly shades,

Heaved serfdom to the sun : in precious silks
Charwomen flounced, and scullions sat and laughed
In golden chairs, to see their fellows play
At football with a crown. Within my heart
In this old house, when all the fiends are here,
The story is renewed. Peace only comes
With a wild ride across the barren downs,
One look upon her face. She ne'er complains
Of my long absences, my hasty speech,—
"Crumbs from thy table are enough for me."
She only asks to be allowed to lean
Her head against my breast a little while,
And she is paid for all. I choke with tears,
And think myself a devil from the pit
Loved by an angel. O that she would change
This tenderness and drooping-lily look,
The flutter when I come, the unblaming voice,
Wet eyes held up to kiss—one flash of fire,
A moment's start of keen and crimson scorn,
Would make me hers for ever !
                    I draw my birth
From a long line of gallant gentlemen,
Who only feared a lie—but what is this ?
I dare not slight the daughter of a peer ;
Her kindred could avenge. Yet I dare play
And palter with the pure soul of a girl
Without a friend, who, smitten, speaks no word,
But with a helpless face sinks in the grave
And takes her wrongs to God. Thou dark Sir
    Ralph,
Who lay with broken brand on Marston Moor,
What think you of this son ?

"This prison that I dwell in hath two doors,
Desertion, marriage ; both are shut by shame,

And barred by cowardice. A stronger man
Would screw his heart up to the bitter wrench,
And break through either and regain the air.
I cannot give myself or others pain.
I wear a conscience nice and scrupulous,
Which, while it hesitates to draw a tear,
Lets a heart break. Conscience should be clear-eyed,
And look through years : conscience is tenderest oft
When clad in sternness, when it smites to-day,
To stay the ruin which it hears afar
Upon the wind. Pure womanhood is meek—
But which is nobler, the hysterical girl
Weeping o'er flies huddling in slips of sun
On autumn sills, who has not heart enough
To crush a wounded grasshopper and end
Torture at once ; or she, with flashing eyes,
Among the cannon, a heroic foot
Upon a fallen breast ? My nerveless will
Is like a traitorous second, and deserts
My purpose in the very gap of need.
I groan beneath this cowardice of heart,
Which rolls the evil to be borne to-day
Upon to-morrow, loading it with gloom.
The man who clothes the stony moor with green,
In virtue of the beauty he creates,
Has there a right to dwell. And he who stands
Firm in this shifting sand and drift of things,
And rears from out the wasteful elements
An ordered home, in which the awful Gods,
The lighter Graces, serene Muses, dwell,
Holds in that masterdom the chartered right
To his demesne of Time. But I hold none ;
I live by sufferance, am weak and vain
As a shed leaf upon a turbid stream,
Or an abandoned boat which can but drift

Whither the currents draw—to maelstrom, or
To green delicious shores. I should have had
My pendent cradle rocked by laughing winds
Within some innocent and idle isle
Where the sweet bread-fruit ripens and falls down,
Where the swollen pumpkin lolls upon the ground,
The lithe and slippery savage, drenched with oil,
Sleeps in the sun, and life is lazy ease.
But lamentation and complaint are vain :
The skies are stern and serious as doom ;
The avalanche is loosened by a laugh ;
And he who throws the dice of destiny,
Though with a sportive and unthinking hand,
Must bide the issue, be it life or death.
One path is clear before me. It may lead
O'er perilous rock, 'cross sands without a well,
Through deep and difficult chasms, but therein
The whiteness of the soul is kept, and that,
Not joy nor happiness, is victory.

"Ah, she is not the creature who I dreamed
Should one day walk beside me dearly loved :
No fair majestic woman, void of fear,
And unabashed from purity of heart ;
No girl with liquid eyes and shadowy hair,
To sing at twilight like a nightingale,
Or fill the silence with her glimmering smiles,
Deeper than speech or song. She has no birth,
No dowry, graces ; no accomplishments,
Save a pure cheek, a fearless innocent brow,
And a true-beating heart. She is no bank
Of rare exotics which o'ercome the sense
With perfumes—only fresh uncultured soil
With a wild-violet grace and sweetness born
Of Nature's teeming foison. Is this not

Enough to sweeten life ?   Could one not live
On brown bread, clearest water ?   Is this love
(What idle poets feign in fabling songs)
An unseen god, whose voice is heard but once
In youth's green valleys, ever dead and mute
'Mong manhood's iron hills ?   A power that comes
On the instant, whelming, like the light that smote
Saul from his horse ; never a thing that draws
Its exquisite being from the light of smiles
And low sweet tones and fond companionship ?
Brothers and sisters grow up by our sides,
Unfelt and silently are knit to us,
And one flesh with our hearts ; would love not grow
In the communion of long-wedded years,
Sweet as the dawning light, the greening spring ?
Would not an infant be the marriage priest,
To stand between us and unite our hands,
And bid us love and be obeyed ? its life,
A fountain, with a cooling fringe of green
Amid the arid sands, by which we twain
Could dwell in deep content ?   My sunshine drew
This odorous blossom from the bough ; why then
With frosty fingers wither it, and seal up
Sun-ripened fruit within its barren rind,
Killing all sweet delights ?   I drew it forth :
If there is suffering, let me bear it all.

"A very little goodness goes for much.
Walk 'mong my peasants—every urchin's face
Lights at my coming ; girls at cottage-doors
Rise from their work and curtsey as I pass,
And old men bless me with their silent tears !
What have I done for this ?   I'm kind, they say,
Give coals in winter, cordials for the sick,
And once a fortnight stroke a curly head

Which hides half-frightened in a russet gown.
'Tis easy for the sun to shine. My alms
Are to my riches like a beam to him.
They love me, these poor hinds, though I have ne'er
Resigned a pleasure, let a whim be crossed,
Pinched for an hour the stomach of desire
For one of them. Good Heaven! what am I
To be thus servitored? Am I to range
Like the discourseless creatures of the wood,
Without the common dignity of pain,
Without a pale or limit? To take up love
For its strange sweetness, and when'er it tires,
Fling it aside as careless as I brush
A gnat from off my arm, and go my way
Untwinged with keen remorse? All this must end.
Firm land at last begins to peer above
The ebbing waves of hesitance and doubt.
Throughout this deepening spring my purpose grows
To flee with her to those young morning lands—
Australia, where the earth is gold, or where
The prairies roll toward the setting sun.
Not Lady Florence with her coronet,
Flinging white arms around me, murmuring
"Husband" upon my breast—not even that
Could make me happy, if I left a grave
On which the shadow of the village spire
Should rest at eve. The pain, if pain there be,
I'll keep locked up within my secret heart,
And wear what joy I have upon my face ;
And she shall live and laugh, and never know.

"Come, Brother, at your earliest, down to me.
To-morrow night I sleep at Ferny-Chase :
There, shadowed by the memory of the dead,
We'll talk of this. My thought, mayhap, will take

A different hue, seen in your purer light,
Free from all stain of passion. Ere you come,
Break that false mirror of your ridicule,
Looking in which, the holiest saint beholds
A grinning Jackanapes, and hates himself.
More men hath Laughter driven from the right
Than Terror clad with fire. You have been young,
And know the mystery, that when we love,
We love the thing, not only for itself
But somewhat also for the love we give.
Think of the genial season of your youth
When you dwelt here, and come with serious heart."

So, in that bitter quarter sits the wind:
The village fool could tell, unless it shifts
'Twill bring the rain in fiercest flaws and drifts!
How wise we are, yet blind,
Judging the wood's grain from the outer rind;
Wrapt in the twilight of this prison dim,
He envies me, I envy him!

The stream of my existence boils and leaps
Through broken rainbows 'mong the purple fells,
And breaks its heart 'mid rocks, close-jammed, con-
    fined,
And plunges in a chasm black and blind,
To rage in hollow gulfs and iron hells,
And thence escaping, tamed and broken, creeps
Away in a wild sweat of beads and bells.
Though *his* slides lazy through the milky meads,
And once a week the sleepy slow-trailed barge
Rocks the broad water-lilies on its marge,
A dead face wavers from the oozy weeds.
It is but little matter where we dwell,
In fortune's centre, on her utter verge;

Whether to death our weary steps we urge,
Or ride with ringing bridle, golden selle.
Life is one pattern wrought in different hues,
And there is nought to choose
Between its sad and gay—'tis but to groan
Upon a rainy common or a throne,
Bleed 'neath the purple or the peasants' serge.

  At his call I will go,
Though it is very little love can do;
In spite of all affection tried and true,
Each man alone must struggle with his woe.
He pities her, for he has done her wrong,
And would repair the evil—noble deed,
To flash and tingle in a minstrel's song,
To move the laughter of our modern breed!
And yet the world is wise; each curve and round
Of custom's road is no result of chance;
It curves but to avoid some treacherous ground,
Some quagmire in the wilds of circumstance;
Nor safely left. The long-drawn caravan
Wavers through heat, then files o'er Mecca's stones;
Far in the blinding desert lie the bones
Of the proud-hearted solitary man.
He marries her, but ere the year has died,—
'Tis an old tale,—they wander to the grave
With hot revolting hearts, yet lashed and tied
Like galley-slave to slave.
Love should not stoop to Love, like prince to lord:
While o'er their heads proud Cupid claps his wings,
Love should meet Love upon the marriage sward,
And kiss, like crownèd kings.
If both are hurt, then let them bear the pain
Upon their separate paths; 't will die at last:
The deed of one rash moment may remain

To darken all the future with the past.
And yet I cannot tell,—the beam that kills
The gipsy's fire, kindles the desert flower;
Where he plucks blessings I may gather ills,
And in his sweetest sweet find sourest sour.
If what of wisdom and experience
My years have brought, be either guide or aid,
They shall be his, though to my mournful sense
The lights will steal away from wood and glade;
The garden will be sad with all its glows,
And I shall hear the glistening laurels talk
Of her, as I pass under in the walk,
And my light step will thrill each conscious rose.

The lark hangs high o'er Ferny-Chase
In slant of sun, twinkle of rain;
Though loud and clear, the song I hear
Is half of joy, and half of pain.
I know by heart the dear old place,
The place where Spring and Summer meet—
By heart, like those old ballad rhymes,
O'er which I brood a million times,
And sink from sweet to deeper sweet.
I know the changes of the idle skies,
The idle shapes in which the clouds are blown;
The dear old place is now before my eyes,
Yea, to the daisy's shadow on the stone.
When through the golden furnace of the heat
The far-off landscape seems to shake and beat,
Within the lake I see old Hodge's cows
Stand in their shadows in a tranquil drowse,
While o'er them hangs a restless steam of flies.
I see the clustered chimneys of the Hall
Stretch o'er the lawn toward the blazing lake;

And in the dewy even-fall
I hear the mellow thrushes call
From tree to tree, from brake to brake.
Ah ! when I thither go
I know that my joy-emptied eyes shall see
A white Ghost wandering where the lilies blow,
A Sorrow sitting by the trysting tree.
I kiss this soft curl of her living hair,
'Tis full of light as when she did unbind
Her sudden ringlets, making bright the wind :
'Tis here, but she is—where ?
Why do I, like a child impatient, weep ?
Delight dies like a wreath of frosted breath ;
Though here I toil upon the barren deep,
I see the sunshine yonder lie asleep,
Upon the calm and beauteous shores of Death.
Ah, Maurice, let thy human heart decide,
The first best pilot through distracting jars.
The lowliest roof of love at least will hide
The desolation of the lonely stars.
Stretched on the painful rack of forty years,
I've learned at last the sad philosophy
Of the unhoping heart, unshrinking eye—
God knows ; my icy wisdom and my sneers
Are frozen tears !

    The day wears, and I go.
Farewell, Elijah ! may you heartily dine !
I cannot, David, see your fingers twine
In the long hair of your foe.
Housewife, adieu, Heaven keep your ample form,
May custom never fail ;
And may your heart, as sound as your own ale,
Be soured by never a storm !

Though I have travelled now for twice an hour,
I have not heard a bird or seen a flower.
This wild road has a little mountain rill
To sing to it, ah ! happier than I.
How desolate the region, and how still
The idle earth looks on the idle sky !
I trace the river by its wandering green ;
The vale contracts to a steep pass of fear,
And through the midnight of the pines I hear
The torrent raging down the long ravine.
At last I've reached the summit high and bare ;
I fling myself on heather dry and brown :
As silent as a picture lies the town,
Its peaceful smokes are curling in the air ;
The bay is one delicious sheet of rose,
And round the far point of the tinted cliffs
I see the long strings of the fishing skiffs
Come home to roost like lines of evening crows.
I can be idle only one day more
As the nets drying on the sunny shore ;
Thereafter, chambers, still 'mid thronged resorts,
Strewn books and littered parchments, nought to see,
Save a charwoman's face, a dingy tree,
A fountain plashing in the empty courts.

But let me hasten down this shepherd's track,
The Night is at my back.

328 *Glasgow*

SING, Poet, 'tis a merry world ;
  That cottage smoke is rolled and curled
    In sport, that every moss
Is happy, every inch of soil ;—

Before *me* runs a road of toil
    With my grave cut across.
Sing, trailing showers and breezy downs—
I know the tragic hearts of towns.

City! I am true son of thine;
Ne'er dwelt I where great mornings shine
    Around the bleating pens;
Ne'er by the rivulets I strayed,
And ne'er upon my childhood weighed
    The silence of the glens.
Instead of shores where ocean beats,
I hear the ebb and flow of streets.

Black Labour draws his weary waves,
Into their secret-moaning caves;
    But with the morning light,
That sea again will overflow
With a long weary sound of woe,
    Again to faint in night.
Wave am I in that sea of woes,
Which, night and morning, ebbs and flows.

I dwelt within a gloomy court,
Wherein did never sunbeam sport;
    Yet there my heart was stirr'd—
My very blood did dance and thrill,
When on my narrow window-sill,
    Spring lighted like a bird.
Poor flowers—I watched them pine for weeks,
With leaves as pale as human cheeks.

Afar, one summer, I was borne ;
Through golden vapours of the morn,
    I heard the hills of sheep :
I trod with a wild ecstasy
The bright fringe of the living sea :
    And on a ruined keep
I sat, and watched an endless plain
Blacken beneath the gloom of rain.

O fair the lightly sprinkled waste,
O'er which a laughing shower has raced !
    O fair the April shoots !
O fair the woods on summer days,
While a blue hyacinthine haze
    Is dreaming round the roots !
In thee, O City ! I discern
Another beauty, sad and stern.

Draw thy fierce streams of blinding ore,
Smite on a thousand anvils, roar
    Down to the harbour-bars ;
Smoulder in smoky sunsets, flare
On rainy nights, with street and square
    Lie empty to the stars.
From terrace proud to alley base
I know thee as my mother's face.

When sunset bathes thee in his gold,
In wreaths of bronze thy sides are rolled,
    Thy smoke is dusky fire ;
And, from the glory round thee poured,
A sunbeam like an angel's sword
    Shivers upon a spire.
Thus have I watched thee Terror ! Dream !
While the blue Night crept up the stream.

The wild Train plunges in the hills,
He shrieks across the midnight rills;
    Streams through the shifting glare,
The roar and flap of foundry fires,
That shake with light the sleeping shires;
    And on the moorlands bare,
He sees afar a crown of light
Hang o'er thee in the hollow night.

At midnight, when thy suburbs lie
As silent as a noonday sky,
    When larks with heat are mute,
I love to linger on thy bridge,
All lonely as a mountain ridge,
    Disturbed but by my foot;
While the black lazy stream beneath,
Steals from its far-off wilds of heath.

And through thy heart, as through a dream,
Flows on that black disdainful stream;
    All scornfully it flows,
Between the huddled gloom of masts,
Silent as pines unvexed by blasts—
    'Tween lamps in streaming rows.
O wondrous sight! O stream of dread!
O long dark river of the dead!

Afar, the banner of the year
Unfurls: but dimly prisoned here,
    'Tis only when I greet
A dropt rose lying in my way,
A butterfly that flutters gay
    Athwart the noisy street,
I know the happy Summer smiles
Around thy suburbs, miles on miles.

'Twere neither pæan now, nor dirge,
The flash and thunder of the surge
    On flat sands wide and bare ;
No haunting joy or anguish dwells
In the green light of sunny dells,
    Or in the starry air.
Alike to me the desert flower,
The rainbow laughing o'er the shower.

While o'er thy walls the darkness sails,
I lean against the churchyard rails ;
    Up in the midnight towers
The belfried spire, the street is dead,
I hear in silence over head
    The clang of iron hours :
It moves me not—I know her tomb
Is yonder in the shapeless gloom.

All raptures of this mortal breath,
Solemnities of life and death,
    Dwell in thy noise alone :
Of me thou hast become a part—
Some kindred with my human heart
    Lives in thy streets of stone ;
For we have been familiar more
Than galley-slave and weary oar.

The beech is dipped in wine ; the shower
Is burnished ; on the swinging flower
    The latest bee doth sit.
The low sun stares through dust of gold,
And o'er the darkening heath and wold
    The large ghost-moth doth flit.
In every orchard Autumn stands,
With apples in his golden hands.

But all these sights and sounds are strange ;
Then wherefore from thee should I range ?
    Thou hast my kith and kin :
My childhood, youth, and manhood brave ;
Thou hast that unforgotten grave
    Within thy central din.
A sacredness of love and death
Dwells in thy noise and smoky breath.

JAMES THOMSON

1834–1882

329   *From "The City of Dreadful Night"*

THE mansion stood apart in its own ground;
  In front thereof a fragrant garden-lawn,
High trees about it, and the whole walled round;
  The massy iron gates were both withdrawn;
And every window of its front shed light,
Portentous in that City of the Night.

But though thus lighted it was deadly still
  As all the countless bulks of solid gloom:
Perchance a congregation to fulfil
  Solemnities of silence in this doom,
Mysterious rites of dolour and despair
Permitting not a breath of chant or prayer?

Broad steps ascended to a terrace broad
  Whereon lay still light from the open door;
The hall was noble, and its aspect awed,
  Hung round with heavy black from dome to floor;
And ample stairways rose to left and right
Whose balustrades were also draped with night.

I paced from room to room, from hall to hall,
  Nor any life throughout the maze discerned;
But each was hung with its funereal pall,
  And held a shrine, around which tapers burned,
With picture or with statue or with bust,
All copied from the same fair form of dust:

A woman very young and very fair ;
  Beloved by bounteous life and joy and youth,
And loving these sweet lovers, so that care
  And age and death seemed not for her in sooth :
Alike as stars, all beautiful and bright,
These shapes lit up that mausoléan night.

At length I heard a murmur as of lips,
  And reached an open oratory hung
With heaviest blackness of the whole eclipse ;
  Beneath the dome a fuming censer swung ;
And one lay there upon a low white bed,
With tapers burning at the foot and head :

The Lady of the images : supine,
  Deathstill, lifesweet, with folded palms she lay :
And kneeling there as at a sacred shrine
  A young man wan and worn who seemed to pray :
A crucifix of dim and ghostly white
Surmounted the large altar left in night :—

The chambers of the mansion of my heart,
  In every one whereof thine image dwells,
Are black with grief eternal for thy sake.

The inmost oratory of my soul,
  Wherein thou ever dwellest quick or dead,
Is black with grief eternal for thy sake.

I kneel beside thee and I clasp the cross,
  With eyes for ever fixed upon that face,
So beautiful and dreadful in its calm.

I kneel here patient as thou liest there ;
  As patient as a statue carved in stone,
Of adoration and eternal grief.

While thou dost not awake I cannot move ;
And something tells me thou wilt never wake,
And I alive feel turning into stone.

Most beautiful were Death to end my grief,
Most hateful to destroy the sight of thee,
Dear vision better than all death or life.

But I renounce all choice of life or death,
For either shall be ever at thy side,
And thus in bliss or woe be ever well.—

He murmured thus and thus in monotone,
  Intent upon that uncorrupted face,
Entranced except his moving lips alone :
  I glided with hushed footsteps from the place.
This was the festival that filled with light
That palace in the City of the Night.

         *   *   *   *   *

I sat me weary on a pillar's base,
  And leaned against the shaft ; for broad moon-
      light
O'erflowed the peacefulness of cloistered space,
  A shore of shadow slanting from the right :
The great cathedral's western front stood there,
A wave-worn rock in that calm sea of air.

Before it, opposite my place of rest,
  Two figures faced each other, large, austere ;
A couchant sphinx in shadow to the breast,
  An angel standing in the moonlight clear ;
So mighty by magnificence of form,
They were not dwarfed beneath that mass enorm.

Upon the cross-hilt of a naked sword
   The angel's hands, as prompt to smite, were held ;
His vigilant, intense regard was poured
   Upon the creature placidly unquelled,
Whose front was set at level gaze which took
No heed of aught, a solemn trance-like look.

And as I pondered these opposèd shapes
   My eyelids sank in stupor, that dull swoon
Which drugs and with a leaden mantle drapes
   The outworn to worse weariness. But soon
A sharp and clashing noise the stillness broke,
And from the evil lethargy I woke.

The angel's wings had fallen, stone on stone,
   And lay there shattered ; hence the sudden sound ;
A warrior leaning on his sword alone
   Now watched the sphinx with that regard profound ;
The sphinx unchanged looked forthright, as aware
Of nothing in the vast abyss of air.

Again I sank in that repose unsweet,
   Again a clashing noise my slumber rent ;
The warrior's sword lay broken at his feet :
   An unarmed man with raised hands impotent
Now stood before the sphinx, which ever kept
Such mien as if with open eyes it slept.

My eyelids sank in spite of wonder grown ;
   A louder crash upstartled me in dread :
The man had fallen forward, stone on stone,
   And lay there shattered, with his trunkless head
Between the monster's large quiescent paws,
Between its grand front changeless as life's laws.

The moon had circled westward full and bright,
  And made the temple-front a mystic dream,
And bathed the whole enclosure with its light,
  The sworded angel's wrecks, the sphinx supreme :
I pondered long that cold majestic face
Whose vision seemed of infinite void space.

330   *In the Room*

I

THE sun was down, and twilight grey
    Filled half the air ; but in the room,
Whose curtain had been drawn all day,
    The twilight was a dusky gloom :
Which seemed at first as still as death,
    And void ; but was indeed all rife
With subtle thrills, the pulse and breath
    Of multitudinous lower life.

II

In their abrupt and headlong way
    Bewildered flies for light had dashed
Against the curtain all the day,
    And now slept wintrily abashed
And nimble mice slept, wearied out
    With such a double night's uproar ;
But solid beetles crawled about
    The chilly hearth and naked floor.

III

And so throughout the twilight hour
    That vaguely murmurous hush and rest
There brooded ; and beneath its power
    Life throbbing held its throbs supprest :

Until the thin-voiced mirror sighed,
   I am all blurred with dust and damp,
So long ago the clear day died,
   So long has gleamed nor fire nor lamp.

IV

Whereon the curtain murmured back,
   Some change is on us, good or ill;
Behind me and before is black
   As when those human things lie still:
But I have seen the darkness grow
   As grows the daylight every morn;
Have felt out there long shine and glow,
   In here long chilly dusk forlorn.

V

The cupboard grumbled with a groan,
   Each new day worse starvation brings;
Since he came here I have not known
   Or sweets or cates or wholesome things:
But now! a pinch of meal, a crust,
   Throughout the week is all I get.
I am so empty; it is just
   As when they said we were to let.

VI

What is become, then, of our Man?
   The petulant old glass exclaimed;
If all this time he slumber can,
   He really ought to be ashamed.
I wish we had our Girl again,
   So gay and busy, bright and fair:
The girls are better than these men,
   Who only for their dull selves care.

VII

It is so many hours ago—
  The lamp and fire were both alight—
I saw him pacing to and fro,
  Perturbing restlessly the night.
His face was pale to give one fear,
  His eyes when lifted looked too bright;
He muttered; what, I could not hear:
  Bad words though; something was not right.

VIII

The table said, He wrote so long
  That I grew weary of his weight;
The pen kept up a cricket song,
  It ran and ran at such a rate:
And in the longer pauses he
  With both his folded arms downpressed,
And stared as one who does not see,
  Or sank his head upon his breast.

IX

The fire-grate said, I am as cold
  As if I never had a blaze;
The few dead cinders here I hold,
  I held unburned for days and days.
Last night he made them flare; but still
  What good did all his writing do?
Among my ashes curl and thrill
  Thin ghosts of all those papers too.

X

The table answered, Not quite all;
  He saved and folded up one sheet,
And sealed it fast, and let it fall;
  And here it lies now white and neat.

Whereon the letter's whisper came,
  My writing is closed up too well ;
Outside there's not a single name,
  And who should read me I can't tell.

XI

The mirror sneered with scornful spite,
  (That ancient crack which spoiled her looks
Had marred her temper), Write and write !
  And read those stupid worn-out books !
That's all he does, read, write, and read,
  And smoke that nasty pipe which stinks :
He never takes the slightest heed
  How any of us feels or thinks.

XII

But Lucy fifty times a day
  Would come and smile here in my face,
Adjust a tress that curled astray,
  Or tie a ribbon with more grace :
She looked so young and fresh and fair,
  She blushed with such a charming bloom,
It did one good to see her there,
  And brightened all things in the room.

XIII

She did not sit hours stark and dumb
  As pale as moonshine by the lamp ;
To lie in bed when day was come,
  And leave us curtained chill and damp.
She slept away the dreary dark,
  And rose to greet the pleasant morn ;
And sang as gaily as a lark
  While busy as the flies sun-born.

XIV

And how she loved us every one ;
 And dusted this and mended that,
With trills and laughs and freaks of fun,
 And tender scoldings in her chat!
And then her bird, that sang as shrill
 As she sang sweet ; her darling flowers
That grew there in the window-sill,
 Where she would sit at work for hours.

XV

It was not much she ever wrote ;
 Her fingers had good work to do ;
Say, once a week a pretty note ;
 And very long it took her too.
And little more she read, I wis ;
 Just now and then a pictured sheet,
Besides those letters she would kiss
 And croon for hours, they were so sweet.

XVI

She had her friends too, blithe young girls,
 Who whispered, babbled, laughed, caressed,
And romped and danced with dancing curls,
 And gave our life a joyous zest.
But with this dullard, glum and sour,
 Not one of all his fellow-men
Has ever passed a social hour ;
 We might be in some wild beast's den.

XVII

This long tirade aroused the bed,
 Who spoke in deep and ponderous bass,
Befitting that calm life he led,
 As if firm-rooted in his place :

In broad majestic bulk alone,
　　As in thrice venerable age,
He stood at once the royal throne,
　　The monarch, the experienced sage :

XVIII

I know what is and what has been ;
　　Not anything to me comes strange,
Who in so many years have seen
　　And lived through every kind of change.
I know when men are good or bad,
　　When well or ill, he slowly said ;
When sad or glad, when sane or mad,
　　And when they sleep alive or dead.

XIX

At this last word of solemn lore
　　A tremor circled through the gloom,
As if a crash upon the floor
　　Had jarred and shaken all the room :
For nearly all the listening things
　　Were old and worn, and knew what curse
Of violent change death often brings,
　　From good to bad, from bad to worse ;

XX

They get to know each other well,
　　To feel at home and settled down ;
Death bursts upon them like a shell,
　　And strews them over all the town.
The bed went on, This man who lies
　　Upon me now is stark and cold ;
He will not any more arise,
　　And do the things he did of old.

XXI

But we shall have short peace or rest ;
　For soon up here will come a rout,
And nail him in a queer long chest,
　And carry him like luggage out.
They will be muffled all in black,
　And whisper much, and sigh and weep ;
But he will never more come back,
　And some one else in me must sleep.

XXII

Thereon a little phial shrilled,
　Here empty on the chair I lie :
I heard one say, as I was filled,
　With half of this a man would die.
The man there drank me with slow breath,
　And murmured, Thus ends barren strife :
O sweeter, thou cold wine of death,
　Than ever sweet warm wine of life.

XXIII

One of my cousins long ago,
　A little thing, the mirror said,
Was carried to a couch to show,
　Whether a man was really dead.
Two great improvements marked the case :
　He did not blur her with his breath,
His many-wrinkled, twitching face
　Was smooth old ivory : verdict, Death.—

XXIV

It lay, the lowest thing there, lulled
　Sweet-sleep-like in corruption's truce ;
The form whose purpose was annulled,
　While all the other shapes meant use.

It lay, the *he* become now *it*,
  Unconscious of the deep disgrace,
Unanxious how its parts might flit
  Through what new forms in time and space.

XXV

It lay and preached, as dumb things do,
  More powerfully than tongues can prate ;
Though life be torture through and through,
  Man is but weak to plain of fate :
The drear path crawls on drearier still
  To wounded feet and hopeless breast ?
Well, he can lie down where he will,
  And straight all ends in endless rest.

XXVI

And while the black night nothing saw,
  And till the cold morn came at last,
That old bed held the room in awe
  With tales of its experience vast.
It thrilled the gloom ; it told such tales
  Of human sorrows and delights,
Of fever moans and infants wails,
  Of births and deaths and bridal nights.

JAMES THOMSON   797

THOMAS DAVIDSON
1838–1870

331   *The Auld Ash Tree*

THERE grows an ash by my bour door,
    And a' its boughs are buskit braw,[1]
In fairest weeds o' simmer green ;
    And birds sit singing on them a'.
But cease your sangs, ye blithesome birds ;
    An' o' your liltin' let me be :
Ye bring deid simmers frae their graves,
    To weary me—to weary me !

There grows an ash by my bour door,
    And a' its boughs are clad in snaw ;
The ice-drap hings at ilka twig,
    And sad the nor' wind soughs thro' a'.
Oh, cease thy mane, thou norlan' wind ;
    And o' thy wailin' let me be :
Thou brings deid winters frae their graves,
    To weary me—to weary me !

Oh, I wad fain forget them a' ;
    Remember'd guid but deepens ill—
As gleids[2] o' licht far seen by nicht
    Mak' the near mirk but mirker still.
Then silent be, thou dear auld tree—
    O' a' thy voices let me be ;
They bring the deid years frae their graves,
    To weary me—to weary me !

[1] bravely adorned. [2] sparks.

332

On the Cheviots:

A Reverie at the end of Summer.

ONCE more, once more upon the hills!
    No more the splendour, quivering bright—
Which laid, at summer's height,
A finger on the lips of half the rills—
    Pours on them; but the year's most mellow light.
    Far through yon opening of the vale,
    Upon the slopes of Teviotdale,
The green has ta'en a fainter tinge:
    It is the time when flowers grow old,
And Summer trims her mantle fringe
    With stray threads of autumnal gold.

The west wind blows from Liddesdale [1];
    And, as I sit—between the springs
Of Bowmont [2] and of Kale [2]—
    To my half-listening ear it brings
All floating voices of the hill—
    The hum of bees in heather bells,
    And bleatings from the distant fells,
The curlew's whistle far and shrill,
And babblings from the restless rill
    That hastes to leave its lone hill-side,
And hurries on to sleep in Till,
    Or join the tremulous flow of Teviot's sunny tide.

It has not changed—the old hill tune!
    And marks that years in me have wrought
Fade as its low familiar croon
    Wakens by turns full many a thought,
    And many an olden fancy brought

[1] a hill district of Roxburghshire. [2] streams having their sources
in the Cheviot hills.

From glooms of long oblivion,—
Forlornest fragments, torn and strewn,
Of dreams which I have dream'd at noon,
Long since, when Summer led a fairer June,
And wealthier autumns spread the slopes,
And younger hearts nursed larger hopes
  Of bounties that the years should bring,
  Nor dream'd of all the care and all the war-
    faring.

Oh, western wind, so soft and low,
  Long-lingering by furze and fern,
Rise ! From thy wing the languor throw,
  And by the marge of mountain tarn,
  By rushy brook, and lonely cairn,
Thy thousand bugles take, and blow
  A wilder music up the fells !
  Thy whisper'd spells—
About my heart I feel them twined ;
  And all the landscape far around
  'Neath their still strength lies thrall'd and bound :
The sluggard clouds, the loitering streams,
And all the hills are dreaming dreams,
And I, too, dream with them, O western wind !

This morn, I thought to linger here
  Till fall of evening and the dew—
To think some fresher thought perchance, or rear
  Old hopes in forms and colours new ;
Then homeward by the burn-side wend,
  When over Cheviot, keen and clear,
The moon look'd down upon the land.
But sad sweet spots hath each lost year—

As ruins have their crevice-flowers
    That sprinkle beauty o'er decay;
And I've been sitting hours on hours,
While those old seasons, hovering near,
    Beguiled me of to-day!

I said that they were faded out,
The lines that years in me have wrought.
    Alas! there is no hand to smooth
Life's graven record from our brows;
    Fate drives us from the fields of Youth,
And no returning step allows.
Let me no more, then, with reverted eyes—
Let me no more with covetous sighs
Gaze at the light that on them lies.
    But come, assail me without ruth,
    Pains of the life that's still my own!
    Crowd out of sight the time that's gone:
Come, living cares; and come, the hour's anxieties.

333   *Love's Last Suit*

LOVE, forget me when I'm gone!
    When the tree is overthrown,
Let its place be digg'd and sown
O'er with grass;—when that is grown,
The very place shall be unknown!
So court I oblivion.
So I charge thee, by our love,
Love, forget me when I'm gone!

Love of him that lies in clay
    Only maketh life forlorn—
Clouding o'er the new-born day
    With regrets of yester morn.

And what is love of him that's low,
Or sunshine on his grave that floats?
Love nor sunshine reacheth now
Deeper than the daisy roots!

So, when he that nigh me hovers—
Death—that spares not happy lovers—
Comes to claim his little due,
Love—as thou art good and true—
Proudly give the churl his own
And forget me when I'm gone!

DAVID GRAY

1838–1861

From " The Luggie "

BENEATH an ash in beauty tender leaved,
 And thro' whose boughs the glimmering sun-
 shine flow'd
In rare ethereal jasper, making cool
A chequered shadow in the dark-green grass,
I lay enchanted. At my head there bloomed
A hedge of sweet-brier, fragrant as the breath
Of maid belovèd when her cheek is laid
To yours in downy pressure, soft as sleep.
A bank of harebells, flowers unspeakable
For half-transparent azure, nodding, gleamed
As a faint zephyr, laden with perfume,
Kissed them to motion, gently, with no will.
Before me streams most dear unto my heart,
Sweet Luggie, sylvan Bothlin—fairer twain
Than ever sung themselves into the sea,
Lucid Ægean, gemmed with sacred isles—
Were rolled together in an emerald vale ;
And into the severe bright noon, the smoke
In airy circles o'er the sycamores
Upcurled—a lonely little cloud of blue
Above the happy hamlet. Far away,
A gently-rising hill with umbrage clad,
Hazel and glossy birch and silver fir,
Met the keen sky. Oh, in that wood, I know,
The woodruff and the hyacinth are fair

In their own season ; with the bilberry
Of dim and misty blue, to childhood dear.
Here, on a sunny August afternoon,
A vision stirred my spirit half-awake
To fling a purer lustre on those fields
That knew my boyish footsteps ; and to sing
Thy pastoral beauty, Luggie, into fame.
Now, while the nights are long, by the dear hearth
Of home I write ; and ere the mavis trills
His smooth notes from the budding boughs of March,
While the red windy morning o'er the east
Widens, or while the lowly sky of eve
Burns like a topaz ;—all the dear design
May reach completion, married to my song
As far as words can syllable desire.

May yet the inspiration and delight
That proved my soul on that Autumnal day,
Be with me now, while o'er the naked earth
Hushfully falls the soft, white, windless snow !

Once more, O God, once more before I die,
Before blind darkness and the wormy grave
Contain me, and my memory fades away
Like a sweet-coloured evening, slowly sad—
Once more, O God, thy wonders take my soul.
A winter day ! the feather-silent snow
Thickens the air with strange delight, and lays
A fairy carpet on the barren lea.
No sun, yet all around that inward light
Which is in purity,—a soft moonshine,
The silvery dimness of a happy dream.
How beautiful ! afar on moorland ways,
Bosomed by mountains, darkened by huge glens,

(Where the lone altar raised by Druid hands
Stands like a mournful phantom,) hidden clouds
Let fall soft beauty, till each green fir branch
Is plumed and tassel'd, till each heather stalk
Is delicately fringed. The sycamores,
Thro' all their mystical entanglement
Of boughs, are draped with silver. All the green
Of sweet leaves playing with the subtle air
In dainty murmuring ; the obstinate drone
Of limber bees that in the monkshood bells
House diligent ; the imperishable glow
Of summer sunshine never more confessed
The harmony of Nature, the divine
Diffusive spirit of the Beautiful.
Out in the snowy dimness, half revealed
Like ghosts in glimpsing moonshine, wildly run
The children in bewildering delight.
There is a living glory in the air—
A glory in the hush'd air, in the soul
A palpitating wonder hush'd in awe.

Softly—with delicate softness—as the light
Quickens in the undawned east ; and silently—
With definite silence—as the stealing dawn
Dapples the floating clouds, slow fall, slow fall,
With indecisive motion eddying down,
The white-winged flakes—calm as the sleep of sound,
Dim as a dream. The silver-misted air
Shines with mild radiance, as when thro' a cloud
Of semi-lucent vapour shines the moon.
I saw last evening (when the ruddy sun,
Enlarged and strange, sank low and visibly,
Spreading fierce orange o'er the west,) a scene
Of winter in his milder mood. Green fields,
Which no kine cropped, lay damp ; and naked trees

Threw skeleton shadows. Hedges thickly grown,
Twined into compact firmness with no leaves,
Trembled in jewelled fretwork as the sun
To lustre touched the tremulous waterdrops.
Alone, nor whistling as his fellows do
In fabling poem and provincial song,
The ploughboy shouted to his reeking team ;
And at the clamour, from a neighbouring field
Arose, with whirr of wings, a flock of rooks
More clamorous ; and thro' the frosted air,
Blown wildly here and there without a law,
They flew, low-grumbling out loquacious croaks.
Red sunset brightened all things ; streams ran red
Yet coldly ; and before the unwholesome east,
Searching the bones and breathing ice, blew down
The hill with a dry whistle, by the fire
In chamber twilight rested I at home.

335   *From the Same*

OH, let the bard describe
      The sacred spot where, underneath the round
Green odoriferous sycamore, he lay
Sleepless, yet half-asleep, in that one mood
When the quick sense is duped, and angel wings
Make spiritual music. Sweet and dim
The sacred spot, belovëd not alone
For its own beauty : but the memories,
The pictures of the past which in the mind
Arise in fair profusion, each distinct
With the soft hue of some peculiar mood,
Enchant to living lustre what before
Was to the untaught vision simply fair,
In a fair valley, carpeted with turf
Elastic, sloping upwards from the stream,

A rounded sycamore in honied leaves
Most plenteous, murmurous with humming bees,
Shadows a well. Darkly the crystal wave
Gleams cold, secluded ; on its polished breast
Imaging twining boughs. No pitcher breaks
Its natural sleep, except at morn and eve
When my good mother thro' the dewy grass
Walks patient with her vessels, bringing home
The clear refreshment. Every blowing Spring,
A snowdrop, with pure streaks of delicate green
Upon its inmost leaves, from withered grass
Springs whitely, and within its limpid breast
Is mirror'd whitely. Not a finger plucks
This hidden beauty ; but it blooms and dies,
In lonely lustre blooms and lonely dies—
Unknown, unloved, save by one simple heart
Poetic, the creator of this song.
And after this frail luxury hath given
Its little life in keeping to the soul
Of all the worlds, a robin builds its nest
In lowly cleft, a foot or so above
The water. His dried leaves, and moss, and grass
He hither carries, lining all with hair
For softness. I have laid the hand that writes
These rhymes belovëd, on the crimson breast,
Sleek-soft, that panted o'er the five unborn ;
While, leaf-hid, o'er me sang the watchful mate
Plaintive, and with a sorrow in the song,
In silvan nook where anchoret might dwell
Contented. Often on September days,
When woods were efflorescent, and the fields
Refulgent with the bounty of the corn,
And warming sunshine filled the breathless air
With a pale steam,—in heart-confusëd mood
Have I worn holidays enraptured there ;

For, O dear God ! there is a pure delight
In dreaming : in those mental-weary times,
When the vext spirit finds a false content
In fashioning delusions. Oh, to lie
Supinely stretched upon the shaded turf,
Beholding thro' the openings of green leaves
White clouds in silence navigating slow
Cerulean seas illimitable ! Hushed
The drowsy noon, and, with a stilly sound
Like harmony of thought, the Luggie frets—
Its bubbling mellowed to a musical hum
By distance. Then the influences faint,
Those visionary impulses that swell
The soul to inspiration, crowding come
Mysterious : and phantom memory
(Ghost of dead feeling) haunts the undissolved,
The unsubvertive temple of the soul !

ROBERT BUCHANAN

1841–1901

The Wake of O'Hara

(SEVEN DIALS)

TO the Wake of O'Hara
    Came company ;
All St. Patrick's Alley
    Was there to see,
With the friends and kinsmen
    Of the family.
On the long deal table lay Tim in white,
And at his pillow the burning light.
Pale as himself, with the tears on her cheek
The mother received us, too full to speak ;
But she heaped the fire, and on the board
Set the black bottle with never a word,
While the company gather'd, one and all,
Men and women, big and small—
Not one in the alley but felt a call
    To the Wake of Tim O'Hara.

At the face of O'Hara,
    All white with sleep,
Not one of the women
    But took a peep,
And the wives new-wedded
    Began to weep.

The mothers gather'd round about,
And praised the linen and laying out,—
For white as snow was his winding-sheet,
And all was peaceful, and clean, and sweet ;
And the old wives, praising the blessèd dead,
Were thronging around the old press-bed,
Where O'Hara's widow, tatter'd and torn,
Held to her bosom the babe new-born,
And stared all around her, with eyes forlorn,
    At the Wake of Tim O'Hara.

        For the heart of O'Hara
            Was good as gold,
        And the life of O'Hara
            Was bright and bold,
        And his smile was precious
            To young and old !
Gay as a guinea, wet or dry,
With a smiling mouth, and a twinkling eye !
Had ever an answer for chaff and fun ;
Would fight like a lion, with any one !
Not a neighbour of any trade
But knew some joke that the boy had made ;
Not a neighbour, dull or bright,
But minded *something*—frolic or fight,
And whisper'd it round the fire that night,
    At the Wake of Tim O'Hara !

        " To God be glory
            In death and life,
        He's taken O'Hara
            From trouble and strife ! "
        Said one-eyed Biddy,
            The apple-wife.

" God bless old Ireland ! " said Mistress Hart,
Mother to Mike of the donkey-cart ;
" God bless old Ireland till all be done,
She never made wake for a better son ! "
And all join'd chorus, and each one said
Something kind of the boy that was dead ;
And the bottle went round from lip to lip,
And the weeping widow, for fellowship,
Took the glass of old Biddy and had a sip,
  At the Wake of Tim O'Hara.

   Then we drank to O'Hara,
    With drams to the brim,
   While the face of O'Hara
    Look'd on so grim,
   In the corpse-light shining
    Yellow and dim.
The cup of liquor went round again,
And the talk grew louder at every drain ;
Louder the tongues of the women grew !—
The lips of the boys were loosening too !
The widow her weary eyelids closed,
And, soothed by the drop o' drink, she dozed ;
The mother brighten'd and laugh'd to hear
Of O'Hara's fight with the grenadier,
And the hearts of all took better cheer,
  At the Wake of Tim O'Hara.

   Tho' the face of O'Hara
    Lookt on so wan,
   In the chimney-corner
    The row began—
   Lame Tony was in it,
    The oyster-man ;

For a dirty low thief from the North came near,
And whistled " Boyne Water " in his ear,
And Tony, with never a word of grace,
Flung out his fist in the blackguard's face ;
And the girls and women scream'd out for fright,
And the men that were drunkest began to fight,—
Over the tables and chairs they threw,—
The corpse-light tumbled,—the trouble grew,—
The new-born join'd in the hullabaloo,—
        At the Wake of Tim O'Hara.

            " Be still ! be silent !
                Ye do a sin !
            Shame be his portion
                Who dares begin ! "
            'Twas Father O'Connor
                Just enter'd in !—
All look'd down, and the row was done—
And shamed and sorry was every one ;
But the Priest just smiled quite easy and free—
" Would ye wake the poor boy from his sleep ? "
        said he :
And he said a prayer, with a shining face,
Till a kind of brightness fill'd the place ;
The women lit up the dim corpse-light,
The men were quieter at the sight,
And the peace of the Lord fell on all that night
        At the Wake of Tim O'Hara !

337   *The Ballad of Judas Iscariot*

'TWAS the body of Judas Iscariot
        Lay in the Field of Blood ;
'Twas the soul of Judas Iscariot
    Beside the body stood.

Black was the earth by night,
    And black was the sky ;
Black, black were the broken clouds,
    Tho' the red Moon went by.

'Twas the body of Judas Iscariot
    Strangled and dead lay there ;
'Twas the soul of Judas Iscariot
    Look'd on it in despair.

The breath of the World came and went
    Like a sick man's in rest ;
Drop by drop on the World's eyes
    The dews fell cool and blest.

Then the soul of Judas Iscariot
    Did make a gentle moan—
" I will bury underneath the ground
    My flesh and blood and bone.

" I will bury deep beneath the soil,
    Lest mortals look thereon,
And when the wolf and raven come
    The body will be gone !

" The stones of the field are sharp as steel,
    And hard and cold, God wot ;
And I must bear my body hence
    Until I find a spot !"

'Twas the soul of Judas Iscariot
    So grim, and gaunt, and grey,
Raised the body of Judas Iscariot,
    And carried it away.

And as he bare it from the field
   Its touch was cold as ice,
And the ivory teeth within the jaw
   Rattled aloud, like dice.

As the soul of Judas Iscariot
   Carried its load with pain,
The Eye of Heaven, like a lanthorn's eye,
   Open'd and shut again.

Half he walk'd, and half he seem'd
   Lifted on the cold wind ;
He did not turn, for chilly hands
   Were pushing from behind.

The first place that he came unto
   It was the open wold,
And underneath were prickly whins,
   And a wind that blew so cold.

The next place that he came unto
   It was a stagnant pool,
And when he threw the body in
   It floated light as wool.

He drew the body on his back,
   And it was dripping chill,
And the next place he came unto
   Was a Cross upon a hill.

A Cross upon the windy hill,
   And a Cross on either side,
Three skeletons that swing thereon,
   Who had been crucified.

And on the middle cross-bar sat
  A white Dove slumbering ;
Dim it sat in the dim light,
  With its head beneath its wing.

And underneath the middle Cross
  A grave yawn'd wide and vast,
But the soul of Judas Iscariot
  Shiver'd, and glided past.

The fourth place that he came unto
  It was the Brig of Dread,
And the great torrents rushing down
  Were deep, and swift, and red.

He dared not fling the body in
  For fear of faces dim,
And arms were waved in the wild water
  To thrust it back to him.

'Twas the soul of Judas Iscariot
  Turn'd from the Brig of Dread,
And the dreadful foam of the wild water
  Had splash'd the body red.

For days and nights he wander'd on
  Upon an open plain,
And the days went by like blinding mist,
  And the nights like rushing rain.

For days and nights he wander'd on,
  All thro' the Wood of Woe ;
And the nights went by like moaning wind,
  And the days like drifting snow.

'Twas the soul of Judas Iscariot
  Came with a weary face—
Alone, alone, and all alone,
  Alone in a lonely place !

He wander'd east, he wander'd west,
  And heard no human sound ;
For months and years, in grief and tears,
  He wander'd round and round.

For months and years, in grief and tears,
  He walk'd the silent night ;
Then the soul of Judas Iscariot
  Perceived a far-off light.

A far-off light across the waste,
  As dim as dim might be,
That came and went like the lighthouse gleam
  On a black night at sea.

'Twas the soul of Judas Iscariot
  Crawl'd to the distant gleam ;
And the rain came down, and the rain was blown
  Against him with a scream.

For days and nights he wander'd on,
  Push'd on by hands behind ;
And the days went by like black, black rain,
  And the nights like rushing wind.

'Twas the soul of Judas Iscariot,
  Strange, and sad, and tall,
Stood all alone at dead of night
  Before a lighted hall

And the wold was white with snow,
  And his foot-marks black and damp,
And the ghost of the silver Moon arose,
  Holding her yellow lamp.

And the icicles were on the eaves,
  And the walls were deep with white,
And the shadows of the guests within
  Pass'd on the window light.

The shadows of the wedding guests
  Did strangely come and go,
And the body of Judas Iscariot
  Lay stretch'd along the snow.

The body of Judas Iscariot
  Lay stretch'd along the snow;
'Twas the soul of Judas Iscariot
  Ran swiftly to and fro.

To and fro, and up and down,
  He ran so swiftly there,
As round and round the frozen Pole
  Glideth the lean white bear.

'Twas the Bridegroom sat at the table-head,
  And the lights burnt bright and clear—
"Oh, who is that," the Bridegroom said,
  "Whose weary feet I hear?"

'Twas one look'd from the lighted hall,
  And answer'd soft and slow,
"It is a wolf runs up and down
  With a black track in the snow."

52

The Bridegroom in His robe of white
   Sat at the table head—
"Oh, who is that who moans without?"
   The blessèd Bridegroom said.

'Twas one look'd from the lighted hall,
   And answer'd fierce and low,
"'Tis the soul of Judas Iscariot
   Gliding to and fro."

'Twas the soul of Judas Iscariot
   Did hush itself and stand,
And saw the bridegroom at the door
   With a light in His hand.

The Bridegroom stood in the open door,
   And He was clad in white,
And far within the Lord's Supper
   Was spread so broad and bright.

The Bridegroom shaded His eyes and look'd,
   And His face was bright to see—
"What dost thou here at the Lord's Supper
   With thy body's sins?" said He.

'Twas the soul of Judas Iscariot
   Stood black, and sad, and bare—
"I have wander'd many nights and days;
   There is no light elsewhere."

'Twas the wedding guests cried out within
   And their eyes were fierce and bright—
"Scourge the soul of Judas Iscariot
   Away into the night!"

The Bridegroom stood in the open door,
  And He waved hands still and slow,
And the third time that He waved His hands
  The air was thick with snow.

And of every flake of falling snow,
  Before it touched the ground,
There came a dove, and a thousand doves
  Made sweet sound.

'Twas the body of Judas Iscariot
  Floated away full fleet,
And the wings of the doves that bare it off
  Were like its winding-sheet.

'Twas the Bridegroom stood at the open door,
  And beckon'd, smiling sweet ;
'Twas the soul of Judas Iscariot
  Stole in, and fell at His feet.

" The Holy Supper is spread within,
  And the many candles shine,
And I have waited long for thee
  Before I pour'd the wine ! "

The supper wine is pour'd at last,
  The lights burn bright and fair,
Iscariot washes the Bridegroom's feet,
  And dries them with his hair.

ANDREW LANG

Born 1844

Almæ Matres

(*St. Andrews*, 1862.   *Oxford*, 1865)

ST. *Andrews by the Northern Sea,*
    A haunted town it is to me!
A little city, worn and grey,
    The grey North Ocean girds it round :
And o'er the rocks, and up the bay,
    The long sea-rollers surge and sound :
And still the thin and biting spray
    Drives down the melancholy street,
And still endure, and still decay,
    Towers that the salt winds vainly beat.
Ghost-like and shadowy they stand
Dim mirrored in the wet sea-sand.

St. Leonard's Chapel, long ago
    We loitered idly where the tall
Fresh-budded mountain ashes blow
    Within thy desecrated wall :
The tough roots rent the tomb below,
    And April birds sang clamorous,
We did not dream, we could not know
    How hardly Fate would deal with us !

820

O, broken minster, looking forth
    Beyond the bay, above the town,
O, winter of the kindly North,
    O, college of the scarlet gown,
And shining sands beside the sea,
    And stretch of links beyond the sand,
Once more I watch you, and to me
    It is as if I touched his hand !

And therefore art thou yet more dear,
    O, little city, grey and sere,
Though shrunken from thine ancient pride
    And lonely by thy lonely sea,
Than these fair halls on Isis' side,
    Where Youth an hour came back to me !

A land of waters green and clear,
    Of willows and of poplars tall,
And, in the spring-time of the year,
    The white may breaking over all,
And Pleasure quick to come at call,
    And Summer rides by marsh and wold,
And Autumn with her crimson pall
    About the towers of Magdalen rolled ;
And strange enchantments from the past,
    And memories of the friends of old,
And strong Tradition, binding fast
    The " flying terms " with bands of gold,—

All these hath Oxford : all are dear,
    But dearer far the little town,
The drifting surf, the wintry year,
    The college of the scarlet gown,
        St. Andrews by the Northern Sea,
        That is a haunted town to me !

339 *Martial in Town*

LAST night, within the stifling train,
  Lit by the foggy lamp o'erhead,
Sick of the sad Last News, I read
Verse of that joyous child of Spain,

Who dwelt when Rome was waxing cold
  Within the Roman din and smoke.
  And like my heart to me they spoke,
These accents of his heart of old :—

  Brother, had we but time to live,
    And fleet the careless hours together,
  With all that leisure has to give
    Of perfect life and peaceful weather,

  The Rich Man's halls, the anxious faces,
  The weary Forum, courts, and cases
    Should know us not ; but quiet nooks,
  But summer shade by field and well,
    But country rides, and talk of books,
  At home, with these, we fain would dwell !

  Now neither lives, but day by day
    Sees the suns wasting in the west,
  And feels their flight, and doth delay
    To lead the life he loveth best.

So from thy city prison broke,
  Martial, thy wail for life misspent,
And so, through London's noise and smoke
  My heart replies to the lament.

For dear as Tagus with his gold,
  And swifter Salo, were to thee,
So dear to me the woods that fold
  The streams that circle Fernielea!

340   *Twilight on Tweed*

THREE crests against the saffron sky,
    Beyond the purple plain,
The kind remembered melody
  Of Tweed once more again.

Wan water from the border hills,
  Dear voice from the old years,
Thy distant music lulls and stills,
  And moves to quiet tears.

Like a loved ghost thy fabled flood
  Fleets through the dusky land;
Where Scott, come home to die, has stood
  My feet returning stand.

A mist of memory broods and floats,
  The Border waters flow;
The air is full of ballad notes
  Borne out of long ago.

Old songs that sung themselves to me,
  Sweet through a boy's day-dream,
While trout below the blossom'd tree
  Plashed in the golden stream.
        *   *   *   *   *

Twilight, and Tweed, and Eildon Hill,
  Fair and too fair you be;
You tell me that the voice is still
  That should have welcomed me.

ALEXANDER ANDERSON ("SURFACEMAN")

1845-1909

341 · *Cuddle Doon*

THE bairnies cuddle doon at nicht
    Wi' muckle faught an' din ;
" Oh try and sleep, ye waukrife [1] rogues,
    Your faither's comin' in. "
They never heed a word I speak ;
    I try to gie a froon,
But aye I hap them up an' cry,
    " Oh, bairnies, cuddle doon."

Wee Jamie wi' the curly heid—
    He aye sleeps next the wa',
Bangs up an' cries, " I want a piece "—
    The rascal starts them a'.
I rin an' fetch them pieces, drinks,
    They stop awee the soun',
Then draw the blankets up an' cry,
    " Noo, weanies, cuddle doon."

But ere five minutes gang, wee Rab
    Cries out, frae 'neath the claes,
" Mither, mak' Tam gie ower at ance,
    He's kittlin' [2] wi' his taes."
The mischief's in that Tam for tricks,
    He'd bother half the toon ;
But aye I hap them up and cry,
    " Oh, bairnies, cuddle doon."

[1] wakeful.   [2] tickling.

At length they hear their faither's fit,
   An', as he steeks [1] the door,
They turn their faces to the wa',
   While Tam pretends to snore.
" Hae a' the weans been gude ? " he asks,
   As he pits aff his shoon ;
" The bairnies, John, are in their beds,
   An' lang since cuddled doon."

An' just afore we bed oorsel's,
   We look at our wee lambs,
Tam has his airm roun' wee Rab's neck,
   And Rab his airm round Tam's.
I lift wee Jamie up the bed,
   An' as I straik each croon,
I whisper till my heart fills up,
   " Oh, bairnies, cuddle doon."

The bairnies cuddle doon at nicht
   Wi' mirth that's dear to me ;
But soon the big warl's cark an' care
   Will quaten doon their glee.
Yet, come what will to ilka ane,
   May He who rules aboon
Aye whisper, though their pows be bald,
   " Oh, bairnies, cuddle doon."

[1] fastens.

JAMES LOGIE ROBERTSON ("HUGH HALIBURTON")

Born circ. 1847

342 *Hughie's Advice to his Brother John*

(From "Horace in Homespun")

"Omnes eodem cogimur."—CAR II. 3.

DEAR Jock, ye're higher up the brae
 Than me, your aulder brither—
Keep mind the higher up ye gae
 The mair ye're in the weather.
I'm no' misdootin' that ye're wice [1],
 An', for your ploo-share, speed it !
But I may better gi'e advice,
 An' ye may better need it.

The higher up the brae ye speel [2]
 The farrer it's below ye,—
Tak' tent [3] ye dinna gi'e the deil
 Occasion to dounthrow ye.
Be douce an' ceevil wi' success,
 For Fortune's no' to trust aye ;
Then if your head should tak' the gress
 Ye're whaur ye were at first aye.

An honest fa', wi' conscience clear,
 It never brak' a bane yet ;
There's aye the honest course to steer
 For a' that's come an' gane yet.

[1] sensible. [2] climb. [3] heed.

But letna lucre be your aim,
　　Pursued thro' thick an' thin aye ;
The honour o' an honest name,
　　That's what you first should win aye.

For happiness (to God be thanks !)
　　Is no' the gift o' Fortun' ;
Wi' place the limmer [1] plays her pranks,
　　Wi' men like puppets sportin'—
Rich folk lookin' idly on
　　At puir folk busy dargin' [2]—
But happiness, my brither John,
　　It wasna in the bargain.

The ups an' douns o' human life
　　Are like a fairy revel ;
But a' the warld, an' his wife,
　　Maun lie at ae great level.
An' that's a thocht for me an' you
　　When Fate's awards perplex us ;
In calm eternity's wide view
　　There's little that should vex us.

Fate's like the waves aneth the mune,
　　An' we are vessels ridin' ;
It's doon an' up, an' up an' doon,
　　An' here there's nae abidin' ;
But on the far horizon's edge,
　　To which we're ever driftin',
The changes on oor pilgrimage
　　Are but a paltry shiftin'.

[1] jade.　[2] working for a day's wage.

343 *Hughie's Indignation at the Conduct of the Absconding Elder*

"*Mala soluta navis exit alite.*"—CAR. V. 10.

HE'S aff the kintra at a spang[1]!
  He's on the sea—they've tint[2] him!
The warst o' weather wi' him gang!
  Gude weather bide ahint him!
O for a rattlin' bauld Scots blast
  To follow an' owretak' him—
To screed[3] his sails, an' brak' his mast,
  An' grup his ship, an' shak' him.

Yet wha was less possessed wi' guile,
  Or prayed wi' readier unction?
He brocht the sweetness o' a smile
  To every public function.
There wasna ane had half the grace
  Or graciousness o' Peter;
There wasna ane in a' the place
  For the millennium meeter.

He's fairly aff, he's stown[4] awa',
  A wolf that wore a fleece, man!
He's cheated justice, jinkit[5] law,
  An' lauch'd at the policeman.
The mission fund, the parish rate,
  He had the haill control o't;
The very pennies i' the plate—
  He's skirtit[6] wi' the whole o't!

[1] bound. [2] lost. [3] rend. [4] stolen. [5] dodged. [6] made off.

It's juist a year—it's no' a year,
  I'm no' a hair the belder,
Since in the Session Chaumer here
  We made him rulin' elder.
An' juist a month as Feursday fell
  He gat the gold repeater,
That in a speech I made mysel
  We handit owre to Peter.

A bonnie lever, capp'd an' jew'ld,
  Perth never saw the mak' [1] o't,
An' wi' his character in goold
  Engraven on the back o't.
He's aff ! He's aff wi' a' the spoil,
  Baith law and justice jinkit !
O for a wind o' winds the wale [2]
  To chase his ship and sink it !

To lift the watter like a fleece
  An' gie him sic a drookin' [3],
Whaur on his growf [4] he groans for grace
  But canna pray for pukin'.
Then wash'd owre seas upon a spar,
  Wi' seaweeds roun' the head o'm,
Let neither licht o' sun nor star
  Shine down upon the greed o'm !

But let a shark fra oonderneath,
  It's jaws wi' hunger tichtenin',
Soom round him, shawin' izzet [5] teeth
  At every flash o' lichtnin' !

[1] equal. [2] pick. [3] drenching. [4] belly. [5] jagged.

Till in the end the angry waves
Transport him to a distance
To herd wi' wolves an' sterve in caves
An' fecht for an existence !

344   *Hughie Refuses to Emigrate*

"*Ibi tu calentem*
Debita sparges lacrima favillam
Vatis amici."—CAR II. 6.

MATTHIE, nae mair ! ye'se gang your lane !
    Tak' my best wishes wi' ye,
An' may guid fortun' ower the main
    An' snugly settled see ye !
I wuss ye weel ! the kintra's lairge,
    An' ye're but twa wi' Mary ;
Ye'll shortly hae the owner's chairge
    Nae doot o' half a prairie.
There's ample room in sic a park
    To foond a score a' nations,
An' flourish like a patriarch
    Amon' your generations.

But me may Scotland's bonnie hills
    Maintain to utmost auld age,
Leadin' my flocks by quiet rills,
    An' lingerin' thro' the gold age ;
Untemptit wi' a foreign gain
    That mak's ye merely laird o't,
An' thinkin' Scotland a' min' ain
    Tho' ownin' ne'er a yaird o't !

What hills are like the Ochil hills?
  There's nane sae green, tho' grander;
What rills are like the Ochil rills?
  Nane, nane on earth that wander!
There Spring returns amon' the sleet,
  Ere Winter's tack[1] be near thro';
There Spring an' Simmer fain wad meet
  To tarry a' the year thro'!

An' there in green Glendevon's shade
  A grave at last be found me,
Wi' daisies growin' at my head
  An' Devon lingerin' round me!
Nae stane disfigurement o' grief
  Wi' lang narration rise there;
A line wad brawly serve, if brief,
  To tell the lave wha lies there.
But ony sculptur'd wecht o' stane
  Wad only overpow'r me;
A shepherd, musin' there his lane,
  Were meeter bendin' owre me.

345   *Hughie takes His Ease in His Inn*

> "*Vates quid orat de patera novum*
>   *Fundens liquorem.*"—CAR. I. 31.

NOO, by my croon, the sun sends doun
    Uncommon drouthy[2] weather,
But here's an inn—if it were sin
    We'll spill a dram thegither!
An' while we sit an' rest oor fit,
    Surveyin' man's dominion,
We'll tak' a glance at things that chance,
    An' freely pass opinion.

                [1] term.   thirsty.

Yon stookit grain [1] that dots the plain—
　　We canna ca' a lead [2] o't ;
The herd that strays on yonder braes—
　　We canna claim a head o't.
It's no' in beeves an' baundit sheaves
　　That we can coont oor wealth, Tam ;
Yet, nane the less, there's happiness
　　To puir folk wi' their health, Tam.

There needs but sma' estate to ca'
　　Awa' the wants that fear folk,
While mony wares bring mony cares
　　That never trouble puir folk.
An' for the yield o' hill or field—
　　It's little that we're spar'd o't,
But to the ee it's juist as free
　　To hiz as him that's laird o't.

Gie knaves their wine—this drink be mine,
　　Auld Scotland's native brewin' !
O' this bereft, there's watter left,
　　Wi' that we'll e'en be doin' !
Gie fules their braws [3]—they've aiblins [4] cause
　　To be sae finely wrappit ;
The man that's in a healthy skin
　　He's brawly if he's happit.

Gie him a horse wha wants the force
　　To drive his ain shanks' naigie [5] ;
What can he ken o' wud or glen,
　　Or mountain wild an' craigie ?

[1] grain in shocks.　　[2] drive a load.　　[3] adornments.　　[4] maybe.
[5] " shanks's mare."

Wad Fortun' grant me what I want
    I'd pray for health o' body,
A healthy mind to sang inclin'd,
    An' nae distaste for toddy·!

346 *Hughie's Reply to the Laird's Intimation*
               of a Visit

          "*Mea nec Falernæ*
    Temperant viles neque Formiani
        Pocula colles."—Hor., Car. I. 20.

DEAR Laird, ye're comin' up the brae
        As lang's gude weather haulds?
Ye're surely welcome to a day
    Amang your ain sheep-faulds.

If caller [1] air, an' caperin' lamb,
    An' knowes o' noddin' green,
Wi' noo an' then a social dram
    Or twa-haund crack [2] atween;

The food whar'on your fathers fared
    A girdle scone an' cheese—
Ye'er freely welcome to them, laird,
    If thae hae power to please;

But if your craig [3] maun hae its waucht [4]
    O' wines I canna name,—
They're no' within a shepherd's aucht [5]:
    Ye'd better bide at hame.

[1] fresh.   [2] conversation *à deux*.   [3] throat.   [4] draught.
[5] owning.
                        53

347 *Hughie's Delight in the Return of Spring*

" *Audire et videor pios*
Errare per lucos, amœnœ
Quos et aquœ subeunt et aurœ."
HOR., Car. III. 4.

I

FRA whaur in fragrant wuds ye bide
Secure fra winter care,
Come, gentle Spring, to Ochilside
And Ochil valleys fair.
For sweet as any pagan spring
Are Devon's watters clear ;
And life wad be a lovely thing
Gif ye were only here.

II

She comes ! the waffin' [1] o' her wings
Wi' music fills the air ;
An' wintry thochts o' men an' things
Vex human hearts nae mair.
On Devon banks wi' me she strays,
Her poet for the while,
And Ochil brooks and Ochil braes
Grow classic in her smile !

348 *A Winter View*

I

THE rime lies cauld on ferm an' fauld,
The lift's a drumlie [2] grey ;
The hill-taps a' are white wi' snaw,
An' dull an' dour's [3] the day.

[1] waving.   [2] troubled.   [3] sullen.

The canny sheep thegither creep,
  The govin'[1] cattle glower ;
The plooman staunds to chap[2] his haunds
  An' wuss the storm were ower.

II

But ance the snaw's begoud to fa'
  The cauld's no' near sae sair :
'Neth stingin' drift oor herts we lift
  The winter's warst to dare.
Wi' frost an' cauld we battle bauld,
  Nor fear a passin' fa',
But warstle up wi' warmer grup
  O' life, an' hope, an' a'.

III

An' sae, my frien', when to oor een
  Oor warldly ills appear
In prospect mair than we can bear,
  An outlook cauld and drear ;
Let's bear in mind—an' this, ye'll find
  Has heartened not a few—
When ance we're in the battle's din
  We'll find we're half gate thro'.

349   *Hughie's Friend, the Farmer of
          Westerha'*

  "*In reducta valle mugientium
  Prospectat errantes greges.*"—EPOD. 2.

ABUNE the braes I see him stand,
    The tapmost corner o' his land,
An' scan wi' care, owre hill an' plain,
A prospect he may ca' his ain.

[1] staring. [2] clap.

His yowes ayont the hillocks feed,
Weel herdit in by wakefu' Tweed ;
An' canny thro' the bent his kye
Gang creepin' to the byre doun-by.

His hayfields lie fu' smoothly shorn,
An' ripenin' rise his rigs o' corn ;
A simmer's evenin' glory fa's
Upon his hamestead's sober wa's.

A stately figure there he stands
An' rests upon his staff his hands :
Maist like some patriarch of eld,
In sic an evenin's calm beheld.

A farmer he of Ochilside,
For worth respectit far an' wide ;
A friend of justice and of truth,
A favourite wi' age an' youth.

There's no' a bairn but kens him weel,
And ilka collie's at his heel ;
Nor beast nor body e'er had ocht
To wyte[1] him wi', in deed or thocht.

Fu' mony a gloamin' may he stand
Abune the brae to bless the land !
Fu' mony a simmer rise an' fa'
In beauty owre his couthie[2] ha' !

For peacefu' aye, as simmer's air,
The kindly hearts that kindle there ;
Whase friendship, sure an' aye the same,
For me mak's Ochilside a hame.

[1] blame.   [2] cosy.

350   *Dave (sc. Daphnis)*

"Ton Mosais philon andra, ton ou Numphaisin apechthe."

WITH the smell of the meads in his plaiden
     dress,
He comes from the broomy wilderness.

The dewdrop burns in his bushy hair,
His forehead shines, and is free from care.

He looks round-orb'd thro' the blue of his eyes,
With the fearless fulness of summer skies.

The red that breaks on the brown of his cheek,
Is the russet apple's ripen'd streak.

White as the milk of nuts are his teeth,
And crisp and black is his beard beneath.

What can he show to the strife of towns ?
A vision of peace on the distant downs.

Green hollows and hillocks, and skies of blue,
And white sheep feeding the long day thro'.

The apples are ruddy, the nuts are ripe,
By every pool there grows a pipe.

How can he touch the world's dull'd ear ?
What can he play that the world will hear ?

His pipe is slender, and softly blown,
The music sinks ever in undertone.

Yet sweet to hear of an autumn night,
When the sheaves on the shorn rigs glimmer white,

It sounds in the dusk like the joy of a star,
When the lattice of heaven is left ajar,

To clasping lovers that thread the threaves
Like a shadow moving among the sheaves.

351   *Hughie moralizes on the Value of Life*

> *"Eheu, fugaces, Postame, Postume,*
> *Labuntur anni ! "*—CAR. II. 14.

ALAS ! alas ! my fellow feres,
    We may no more deny
The pressure of the speeding years ;
    Oor days are driving by.

Already on the downward track
    The posting furies fare ;
For virtuous life they will not slack,
    For purpose will not spare.

This is the ill beneath the sun
    That vexes ageing men—
Oor lease of life is half-gate run
    Before of lease we ken.

We waste or ware [1] oor strength of youth
    On idols of the ee,
Infidel of the wholesome truth
    Of our mortalitie.

Ye callants [2], what avails the strife
    That twyns [3] ye o' your prime ?
The dearest gift of life is life,
    The dearest enemy time.

[1] spend.   [2] lads.   [3] deprives.

O ne'er can rank or wealth enhance
   The gift that ne'er was awn,
The lovely gift, the glorious chance,
   Ance offer'd, sune withdrawn!

To them that on the shaded slope
   Are faring down, like me,
With ever daily dwining[1] hope,
   How fair it tak's the ee!

What had been oors from hour of birth
   We learn to value then;
Sweet grow the common joys of earth,
   And dear the face of men.

352   *Hughie's Monument*

"*Non omnis moriar.*"—CAR. III. 30.

IN vain the future snaps his fangs,
   The tyke[2] may rage—he canna wrang's,
I put my haund upon my sangs
      Withoot a swither[3];
To me this monument belangs,
      I need nae ither.

It's no' in granite to endoor,
Sandstane comes ripplin' doon like stoor[4],
Marble—it canna stand the shoo'r,
      It lasts nae time;
There's naething yet has hauf the poo'r
      O' silly rhyme.

   [1] dwindling.   [2] dog.   [3] hesitation.   [4] dust.

The pyramids hae tint their tale [1],
It's lang sin' they begoud to fail,
They're either murlin' [2] doun to meal
    Or fog-enwrappit,
While Homer at this hoor's as hale
    As e'er he stappit.

Sae I may say't withoot a lee,
I dinna a'thegither dee !
Therefore forbear to greet [3] for me
    When I'm awa',
An' keep a dry, a drouthie [4] ee,
    I chairge ye a'.

When at my door the hearse draws up
An' Kate haunds roun' the dirgy-cup [5],
Nae friend o' mine will tak' a sup
    For that the less,
But calmly wi' a steady grup
    Cowp [6] owre his gless.

The better pairt o' me remains !
Whaur Allan Watter weets the plains,
An' Devon, crystal but for rains,
    Gangs wanderin' wide,
Lang after me ye'll hear my strains
    On Ochilside.

---

[1] forgotten their history.   [2] crumbling.   [3] weep.   [4] thirsty.
[5] drink for the funeral guests.   [6] spill.

ROBERT LOUIS STEVENSON

1850–1894

353   *Requiem*

UNDER the wide and starry sky,
    Dig the grave and let me lie.
Glad did I live and gladly die,
    And I laid me down with a will.
This be the verse you grave for me :
Here he lies where he longed to be ;
Home is the sailor, home from sea,
    And the hunter home from the hill.

354   *The Death-child*

S HE sits beneath the elder-tree
   And sings her song so sweet,
And dreams o'er the burn that darksomely
Runs by her moonwhite feet.

Her hair is dark as starless night,
Her flower-crown'd face is pale,
But O her eyes are lit with light
Of dread ancestral bale.

She sings an eerie song, so wild
With immemorial dule—
Though young and fair Death's mortal child
That sits by that dark pool.

And oft she cries an eldritch scream
When red with human blood
The burn becomes a crimson stream,
A wild, red, surging flood:

Or shrinks, when some swift tide of tears—
The weeping of the world—
Dark eddying 'neath man's phantom-fears
Is o'er the red stream hurl'd.

For hours beneath the elder-tree
She broods beside the stream ;
Her dark eyes filled with mystery,
Her dark soul rapt in dream.

The lapsing flow she heedeth not
Through deepest depths she scans :
Life is the shade that clouds her thought,
As Death's the eclipse of man's.

Time seems but as a bitter thing
Remember'd from of yore :
Yet ah (she thinks) her song she'll sing
When Time's long reign is o'er.

Erstwhiles she bends alow to hear
What the swift water sings,
The torrent running darkly clear
With secrets of all things.

And then she smiles a strange sad smile
And lets her harp lie long ;
The death-waves oft may rise the while,
She greets them with no song.

Few ever cross that dreary moor,
Few see that flower-crown'd head ;
But whoso knows that wild song's lure
Knoweth that he is dead.

355 *High Noon at Midsummer on the Campagna*

(*From "Sospiri di Roma"*)

HIGH noon,
　　And from the purple-veilèd hills
To where Rome lies in azure mist,
Scarce any breath of wind
Upon this vast and solitary waste,
These leagues of sunscorch'd grass
Where i' the dawn the scrambling goats maintain
A hardy feast,
And where, when the warm yellow moonlight floods
　　the flats,
Gaunt laggard sheep browse spectrally for hours,
While not less gaunt and spectral shepherds stand
Brooding, or with hollow vacant eyes
Stare down the long perspectives of the dusk.
Now not a breath :
No sound ;
No living thing,
Save where the beetle jars his bristling shards,
Or where the hoarse cicala fills
The heavy heated hour with palpitant whirr.
Yet hark !
Comes not a low deep whisper from the ground,
A sigh as though the immemorial past
Breathed here a long, slow, breath ?
Lost nations sleep below ; an empire here
Is dust ; and deeper, deeper still,
Dim shadowy peoples are the mould that warms
The roots of every flower that blooms and blows :
Even as we, too, bloom and fade,

Frail human flowers, who are so bitter fain
To be as the wind that bloweth evermore,
To be as this dread waste that shroudeth all
In garments green of grass and wilding sprays,
To be as the Night that dies not, but forever
Weaves her immortal web of starry fires ;
To be as Time itself,
Time, whose vast holocausts
Lie here, deep buried from the ken of men,
Here, where no breath of wind
Ruffles the brooding heat,
The breathless blazing heat
Of Noon.

356   *Red Poppies*

(In the Sabine valleys near Rome)

THROUGH the seeding grass,
　　And the tall corn,
The wind goes :
With nimble feet,
And blithe voice,
Calling, calling.
The wind goes
Through the seeding grass,
And the tall corn.

What calleth the wind,
Passing by—
The shepherd-wind ?
Far and near
He laugheth low,
And the red poppies
Lift their heads
And toss i' the sun.

A thousand thousand blooms
Tost i' the air,
Banners of joy,
For 'tis the shepherd-wind
Passing by,
Singing and laughing low
Through the seeding grass
And the tall corn.

357   *The Wild Mare*

(*In Maremma*)

LIKE a breath that comes and goes
    O'er the waveless waste
Of sleeping Ocean,
So sweeps across the plain
The herd of wild horses.
Like banners in the wind
Their flying tails,
Their streaming manes :
And like spume of the sea
Fang'd by breakers,
The white froth tossed from their blood-red nostrils.
Out from the midst of them
Dasheth a white mare,
White as a swan in the pride of her beauty :
And, like the whirlwind,
Following after,
A snorting stallion,
Swart as an Indian
Diver of coral !
Wild the gyrations,
The rush and the whirl ;

Loud the hot panting
Of the snow-white mare,
As swift upon her
The stallion gaineth :
Fierce the proud snorting
Of him, victorious :
And loud, swelling loud on the wind from the
    mountains,
The hoarse savage tumult of neighing and stamping
Where, wheeling, the herd of wild horses awaiteth—
Ears thrown back, tails thrashing their flanks or
    swept under—
The challenging scream of the conqueror-stallion.

358   *The White Peacock*

H ERE where the sunlight
    Floodeth the garden,
Where the pomegranate
Reareth its glory
Of gorgeous blossom ;
Where the oleanders
Dream through the noontides ;
And like surf o' the sea
Round cliffs of basalt,
The thick magnolias
In billowy masses
Front the sombre green of the ilexes :
Here where the heat lies
Pale blue in the hollows,
Where blue are the shadows
On the fronds of the cactus,
Where pale blue the gleaming
Of fir and cypress,

With the cones upon them
Amber or glowing
With virgin gold :
Here where the honey-flower
Makes the heat fragrant,
As though from the gardens
Of Gulistân,
Where the bulbul singeth
Through a mist of roses,
A breath were borne :
Here where the dream-flowers,
The cream-white poppies
Silently waver,
And where the Scirocco,
Faint in the hollows,
Foldeth his soft white wings in the sunlight,
And lieth sleeping
Deep in the heart of
A sea of white violets :
Here, as the breath, as the soul of this beauty
Moveth in silence, and dreamlike, and slowly,
White as a snow-drift in mountain valleys
When softly upon it the gold light lingers :
White as the foam o' the sea that is driven
O'er billows of azure agleam with sun-yellow :
Cream-white and soft as the breasts of a girl,
Moves the White Peacock, as though through the
    noontide
A dream of the moonlight were real for a moment.
Dim on the beautiful fan that he spreadeth,
Foldeth and spreadeth abroad in the sunlight,
Dim on the cream-white are blue adumbrations,
Shadows so pale in their delicate blueness
That visions they seem as of vanishing violets,
The fragrant white violets veinèd with azure,

Pale, pale as the breath of blue smoke in far wood-
    lands.
Here, as the breath, as the soul of this beauty,
White as a cloud through the heats of the noontide
Moves the White Peacock.

359   *The Swimmer of Nemi*

            (*The Lake of Nemi : September*)

WHITE through the azure,
        The purple blueness,
Of Nemi's waters
The swimmer goeth.
Ivory-white, or wan white as roses
Yellowed and tanned by the suns of the Orient,
His strong limbs sever the violet hollows ;
A shimmer of white fantastic motions
Wavering deep through the lake as he swimmeth.
Like gorse in the sunlight the gold of his yellow hair,
Yellow with sunshine and bright as with dew-drops,
Spray of the waters flung back as he tosseth
His head i' the sunlight in the midst of his laughter :
Red o'er his body, blossom-white mid the blueness,
And trailing behind him in glory of scarlet,
A branch of the red-berried ash of the mountains.
White as a moon-beam
Drifting athwart
The purple twilight,
The swimmer goeth—
Joyously laughing,
With o'er his shoulders,
Agleam in the sunshine
The trailing branch
With the scarlet berries.

                        54

Green are the leaves, and scarlet the berries,
White are the limbs of the swimmer beyond them,
Blue the deep heart of the still, brooding lakelet,
Pale-blue the hills in the haze of September,
The high Alban hills in their silence and beauty,
Purple the depths of the windless heaven
Curv'd like a flower o'er the waters of Nemi.

360   *The Naked Rider*

        (*In the Volscians*)

THROUGH the dark gorge
    With its cliffs of basalt,
The rider comes.
The sunlight floodeth
The breast of the hill,
And all the mouth
Of the sullen pass
Is light with the foam of
A thousand blooms
Of the white narcissi,
With a waving sea
Of asphodels.
On a white horse,
A cream-white stallion
With blood-red nostrils
And wild dark eyes,
The naked rider
Laughs as he cometh,
And hails the sunlight breaking upon him.
Full breaks the flood
Of the yellow light
On the naked youth,

Glowing, as ivory
In the amber of moonrise
In the violet eves
Of August-tides.
Dark as the heart of a hill-lake his tresses,
Scarlet the crown of the poppies inwoven
I' the thick wavy hair that crowneth his
    whiteness,
Strong the white arms,
The broad heaving breast,
The tent thighs guiding
The mighty stallion.

Out from the gloom
Of the mountain valley,
Where cliffs of basalt
Make noontide twilight,
And where the grey bat
Swingeth his heavy wings,
And echo reverberates
The screams of the falcons:
Where nought else soundeth
Save the surge or the moaning
Of mountain-winds,
Or the long crash and rattle
Of falling stones
Spurned by the hill fox
Seeking his hollow lair:
Out from the gorge
Into the sunlight,
To the glowing world,
To the flowers and the birds
And the west wind laden
With the breaths of rosemary, basil, and thyme—
Comes the white rider,

The naked youth,
Glowing like ivory
In the yellow sunshine.
Beautiful, beautiful, this youth of the mountain,
Laughing low as he rideth
Forth to the sunlight,
The scarlet poppies agleam in his tresses
Dark as the thick-cluster'd grapes of the ivy;
While over the foam
Of the sea of narcissi,
And high through the surf
Of the asphodels,
Trampleth, and snorteth
From his blood-red nostrils,
The cream-white stallion.

PUBLISHED AS BY "FIONA MACLEOD"

361   *Hushing Song*

EILIDH, Eilidh,[1]
    My bonnie wee lass:
The winds blow,
    And the hours pass.

But never a wind
    Can do thee wrong,
Brown Birdeen, singing
    Thy bird-heart song.

And never an hour
    But has for thee
Blue of the heaven
    And green of the sea:

[1] The name Eilidh is pronounced "Eily."

Blue for the hope of thee,
  Eilidh, Eilidh ;
Green for the joy of thee,
  Eilidh, Eilidh.

Swing in thy nest, then,
  Here on my heart,
Birdeen, Birdeen,
  Here on my heart,
  Here on my heart !

362   *Lullaby*

LENNAVAN-MO,
    Lennavan-mo,
Who is it swinging you to and fro,
With a long low swing and a sweet low croon,
And the loving words of the mother's rune ?

Lennavan-mo,
Lennavan-mo,
Who is it swinging you to and fro ?
I am thinking it is an angel fair,
The Angel that looks on the gulf from the lowest
    stair
And swings the green world upward by its leagues
    of sunshine hair.

Lennavan-mo,
Lennavan-mo,
Who swingeth you and the Angel to and fro ?
It is He whose faintest thought is a world afar,
It is He whose wish is a leaping seven-moon'd star,
It is He, Lennavan-mo,
To whom you and I and all things flow.

Lennavan-mo,
Lennavan-mo,
It is only a little wee lass you are, Eilidh-mo-chree,
But as this wee blossom has roots in the depths of
    the sky,
So you are at one with the Lord of Eternity—
Bonnie wee lass that you are,
My morning-star,
Eilidh-mo-chree, Lennavan-mo,
        Lennavan-mo.

363   *Mo-Lennav-a-Chree*

EILIDH, Eilidh, Eilidh, dear to me, dear and
    sweet,
In dreams I am hearing the noise of your little running
    feet—
The noise of your running feet that like the sea-hoofs
    beat
A music by day and night, Eilidh, on the sands of
    my heart, my Sweet !

Eilidh, blue i' the eyes, as all babe-children are,
And white as the canna that blows with the hill-breast
    wind afar,
Whose is the light in thine eyes—the light of a star ?—
    a star
That sitteth supreme where the starry lights of heaven
    a glory are !

Eilidh, Eilidh, Eilidh, put off your wee hands from
    the heart o' me,
It is pain they are making there, where no more pain
    should be :

For little running feet, an' wee white hands, an'
 croodlin' as of the sea,
Bring tears to my eyes, Eilidh, tears, tears, out of the
 heart o' me—

Mo-lennav-a-chree,
Mo-lennav-a-chree !

364   *The Lonely Hunter*

GREEN branches, green branches, I see you
 beckon ; I follow !
Sweet is the place you guard, there in the rowan-tree
 hollow.
There he lies in the darkness, under the frail white
 flowers,
Heedless at last, in the silence, of these sweet midsummer hours.

But sweeter, it may be, the moss whereon he is sleeping now,
And sweeter the fragrant flowers that may crown his
 moon-white brow :
And sweeter the shady place deep in an Eden hollow
Wherein he dreams I am with him—and, dreaming,
 whispers, " Follow ! "

Green wind from the green-gold branches, what is the
 song you bring ?
What are all songs for me, now, who no more care to
 sing ?
Deep in the heart of Summer, sweet is life to me
 still,
But my heart is a lonely hunter that hunts on a lonely
 hill.

Green is that hill and lonely, set far in a shadowy
place ;
White is the hunter's quarry, a lost-loved human face :
O hunting heart, shall you find it, with arrow of failing
breath,
Led o'er a green hill lonely by the shadowy hound
of Death ?

Green branches, green branches, you sing of a sorrow
olden,
But now it is midsummer weather, earth-young, sun-
ripe, golden :
Here I stand and I wait, here in the rowan-tree
hollow,
But never a green leaf whispers, " Follow, oh, Follow,
Follow ! "

O never a green leaf whispers, where the green-gold
branches swing :
O never a song I hear now, where one was wont to
sing.
Here in the heart of Summer, sweet is life to me still,
But my heart is a lonely hunter that hunts on a
lonely hill.

365   *Invocation*

(*From " The Hour of Beauty "*)

PLAY me a lulling tune, O Flute-Player of Sleep,
Across the twilight bloom of thy purple havens.
Far off a phantom stag on the moonyellow high-
lands
Ceases ; and, as a shadow, wavers ; and passes :
So let Silence seal me and Darkness gather, Piper of
Sleep.

Play me a lulling chant, O anthem-maker,
Out of the fall of lonely seas, and the wind's sorrow :
Behind are the burning glens of the sunset sky
Where like blown ghosts the seamews wail their
    desolate sea-dirges:
Make me of these a lulling chant, O anthem-maker.

No—no—from nets of silence weave me, O Sigher
    of Sleep,
A dusky veil ash-grey as the moonpale moth's grey
    wing ;
Of thicket-stillness woven, and sleep of grass, and thin
    evanishing air
Where the tall reed spires breathless—for I am tired,
    O Sigher of Sleep,
And long for thy muffled song as of bells on the wind,
    and the wind's cry
        Falling, and the dim wastes that lie
        Beyond the last, low, long, oblivious sigh.

366   *Deirdrê is Dead*

            (*From "Foam of the Past"*)

      Deirdrê the beautiful is dead . . . . is dead !
                    THE HOUSE OF USNA.

THE *grey wind weeps, the grey wind weeps, the grey
    wind weeps :*
*Dust on her breast, dust on her eyes, the grey wind
    weeps !*

Cold, cold it is under the brown sod, and cold under
    the grey grass ;
Here only the wet wind and the flittermice and
    the plovers pass :

I wonder if the wailing birds, and the soft hair-covered
    things
Of the air, and the grey wind hear what sighing song
    she sings

Down in the quiet hollow where the coiled twilights of
    hair
Are gathered into the darkness that broods on her
    bosom bare ?

It is said that the dead sing, though we have no ears
    to hear,
And that whoso lists is lickt up of the Shadow too,
    because of fear—

But this would give me no fear, that I heard a sighing
    song from her lips :
No, but as the green heart of an upthrust towering
    billow slips

Down into the green hollow of the ingathering wave,
So would I slip, and sink, and drown, in her grassy
    grave.

For is not my desire there, hidden away under the
    cloudy night
Of her long hair that was my valley of whispers and
    delight—

And in her two white hands, like still swans on a
    frozen lake,
Hath she not my heart that I have hidden there for
    dear love's sake ?

Alas, there is no sighing song, no breath in the silence
  there :
Not even the white moth that loves death flits through
  her hair

As the bird of Brigid, made of foam and the pale
  moonwhite wine
Of dreams, flits under the sombre windless plumes of
  the pine.

I hear a voice crying, crying, crying : is it the wind
I hear, crying its old weary cry time out of mind ?

The grey wind weeps, the grey wind weeps, the grey wind
  weeps :
Dust on her breast, dust on her eyes, the grey wind
  weeps !

SIR GEORGE DOUGLAS

Born 1856

367   *A Vignette in June*

I

THE rich clusters wreathing
   This redthorn are breathing
  A perfume too heady—it mounts to the brain:
As, once, for a bay-tree,
So now for the May-tree
  The fervours of Phœbus prove ill to sustain!

II

In the trim-shaven pleasaunce,
His worshipful presence
  With fan of faint silver the white peacock screens:
His bearing is stately,
He ponders sedately—
  His breed is Olympian, his service a queen's.

III

Around, on the brightness,
Now firm, now with lightness,
  In shade as in pigment of China is traced,
Like veins in fair marble,
A sketch the winds garble
  Of leaf-laden branches and boughs interlaced.

368   *The Twelfth of August*

I

GRASS-heads, drooping on their stems,
    Wear a thousand spherèd gems ;
And from the foxglove's freckled lip
Distillations drip and drip ;
Beaded bluebells, frail and fine,
Have ta'en a fill of rainy wine :
    So all those blooms in thriftless beauty blowing
        Which of the waste are claim'd,
    With milfoil, meadow-sweet and kingcups growing—
        Nameless or never named.

II

The world looms darkly, as thro' glass,
Between the tepid showers that pass ;
Mid-mountain-high the mist-wreaths form—
To melt with each successive storm ;
The loch's still waters dully gleam,
Fill'd as with shadows of a dream :
    But in the bracken-depths the heather-bleater
        Sings his small song alone ;
    The shrill sandpiper answers—skimming fleeter,
        The stone-chat from its stone.

369   *The Border Breed*

I

BOB ROBSON o' the Windy Door,
    A ticht chap and a trim—
What wrestler bold at Pennymuir
    Could long stand up to him ?

II

Wi' "hipe," "cross-buttock" or "back heel,"
    Wi' science or main strength,
He gars ilk ane his mettle feel,
    An' measures ilk his length:

III

Against all comers so he stood
    Thro' half a summer's day—
So stood, and so his richt made good
    To bear the belt away.

IV

Bob Robieson o' Windy Door
    Neat fi' foot ten he stands,
And many a time has proved himsel'
    A rare man o' his hands:

V

In fair fight when the blood is up,
    The back again' the wa',
The mildest man does what he can—
    But Bob fights aye for twa.

VI

At mercat, tryst, or hiring-fair,
    At Jethart at the sports,
At Common-ridings or whaur-e'er
    Good Border blood resorts—

VII

Wi' bonnet cock'd abune his broo',
    A twinkle in his e'e,
To gie the chiel his nakit due,
    Richt kenspeckle [1] is he:

[1] noticeable.

VIII

That Bobby is 'a' body's man'
    Fu' easy 'twere to tell
By, "Hech, man! hoo're ye lastin'?" an'
    "Hulloa, man! hoo's yersel'?"

IX

At Yetholm, at the ba'-playing,
    It's whiles a kittle[1] job
The ba' frae Bowmont's bed to bring—
    So here's a ploy for Bob:

X

The "gaugies"[2] birl,[3] the gude-wives skirl,[4]
    The cry goes up, "She's haled!"[5]
And "doonies" sulk, for over bulk
    His prowess has prevail'd!

XI

But maist of a' things, for his sins,
    Bob loves a munelicht splore,[6]
Where Kale or where lone Owsenam rins
    By green or grave'ly shore;

XII

Where deep beneath the alder shade,
    By darksome dub or linn,
The saumon, by the streamlet sway'd,
    Shows scarce a moving fin.

XIII

Bob's e'e is as the kestrel's keen,
    Or howlet's in the dark;
And trust him, aince his prey he's seen,
    To make the shortest wark:

[1] ticklish.   [2] a word current in the Gipsy village of Kirk-Yetholm, probably corrupted from the Romany.   [3] spin round.
[4] shriek.   [5] equivalent to "A goal!"   [6] frolic.

XIV

His airm strikes true, without ado,
  And lo! wi' glimmering flank,
Full seventeen pound (and scarce a sound!)
  Is tumblin' on the bank!

XV

The watter-bailies, still and on,
  Their luck hae cause to rue—
A wat skin for the orra¹ man,
The fear o' deith for ane who ran,
  And broken heids for two!

XVI

A plain chap is Bob Robison,
  A trapper to his trade—
His tongue is rough, and like enough
  He calls a spade a spade:

XVII

In Politics a Radical—
  Belike a rank ane too!
He'll ding² the Lords, an' ding the Crown,
An' ding the Constitution down,
  And big³ it up anew.

XVIII

He comes o' stock who many a flock
  By many a stream have fed—
Where, hard by Hen's Hole, College springs;
Or self-involved, in endless rings,
  Flows idly infant Jed:

¹ odd. ² smash. ³ build.

XIX

Who thro' long generations still
  Held fast by Cheviot slopes ;
Whose thoughts were centred on the hill,
  And fix'd on Heaven whose hopes :

XX

Who oft their weary hirsels [1] drove
  Frae busy marts afar,
When skies were foul, by Windy Gowl
  Or by the Carter Bar :

XXI

Who now in scatter'd kirkyards sleep,
  Beneath green hillocks sma'—
Good shepherds, faithful to their sheep,
  And kindly hairts witha'.

XXII

A rough chap is Bob Robieson,
  His fauts I scorn to shirk—
A rough chap, but an eident one,
  And one wha knows his work :

XXIII

A careless and convivial blade,
  His failings not to blink—
He haunts the pub, but—here's the rub !
  For comp'ny mair as drink :

XXIV

Of conscience maybe no owre nice,
  To break an irksome law,
When so it suits ; but free from vice,
  Or deep and ingrain'd flaw.

[1] flocks.

55

XXV

In natur' as in body sound,
  Nor wantin' for good sense—
His schulin' 's sma', but I'll stand bound
  For his intelligence.

XXVI

Ye Ministers and Dominies!
  Fill fu' the land wi' saints,
Wi' scholar-lads wha hold degrees,
  And all your fancy paints!

XXVII

Ye bude to [1] own that, mair as once,
  (So your ain Histories tell)
A mis-ca'd wastrel or a dunce
  Has served his country well!

XXVIII

Such men as *he* oft, silently,
  In wakeful Scrope's despite,
Drave English kye, in days gone by,
  Thro' Krissop fords by night:

XXIX

What reck'd they then o' mailèd men,
  What of the Warden they?
Theirs was to reive, to ride was theirs—
To live the life he lives who dares,
  And none shall say him nay!

XXX

Such were bold Johnie Armstrong's men,
  The Laird's Jock, good at need,
Such Hobbie Ha', and such they a'
  Wha Kinmont Willie freed:

---

[1] needs must.

XXXI

And such again shall be the men,
   Should Britain's foes attack,
From fold and glen who rising then
   Shall hurl the invader back ;

XXXII

For ill were it frae Cheviot heicht
   Thro' Tweed and Teviot dale,
If from the old Border Land outright,
   The old Border breed should fail !

370   *The Old Border Town*

ERECT in spite of Churchmen's broils,
   Set squarely o'er the town,
With lancets pierced and quatre-foils
   King David's tower looks down ;
And, since kind Nature still abhors
   A lifeless solitude,
There, in aërial corridors,
   The pigeons haunt and brood ;
And there—from David's lantern-tower—
   A hooded cenobite,
The owl, night's watchman, cries the hour
   And revels in the night.

Beneath the piled and huddled walls
   Of vennel, wynd, and close,
Murmuring its tuneful intervals,
   A lordly river flows—
Beneath the spanning arches five
   Where anglers congregate,

To mark the salmon upward strive,
 Or watch the raging spate,—
Then, turning from its onward course
 To one whom dear it holds,
The town, as if with soft remorse,
 It lovingly enfolds.

By flower-plot, lawn and garden-ground,
 With greenery interspersed,
There old wall-fruit-trees much abound,
 From monkish seedlings nursed ;
Around, the richly-wooded heights
 Of manor and demesne—
Fair scenes of ever new delights—
 Embosom and sustain ;
Whilst, stretching to the utmost bounds
 Of heaven-aspiring hill,
A rural paradise surrounds,
 To bless the old burgh still.

But phantom, wraith and wandering ghost
 People the streets and square ;
And still I seek the friend I lost,
 The friend I injured there :
At noontide in the market-place,
 Dreaming, alone I stand—
See no face but an absent face,
 Grasp but an absent hand :
So is it with all men who live—
 To this we come at last,
Seek what the Present *cannot* give,
 Spoils of a deathless Past.

371   *On Flodden Edge*

I

WHAT generous error shaped his course,
    What scruple false withheld
That Monarch whom a mightier force
    Than monarch's will impell'd ;

II

When from his kingdom forth he pass'd
    (By what vain dream possess'd !)
And on broad Scotland look'd his last
    From this lone mountain-crest ?

III

When on, as to his sport, he sped—
    His stake a life, a Crown ;
And radiant, hence to ruin led
    The world's best manhood down ?

IV

The skies, they say with portents fill'd—
    Heaven's self had fain deterr'd
A king who was *too* kingly-will'd,
    And faithful to his word.

V

What powers obscure against him wrought—
    The brave but brave in vain ;
And now, in toils of darkness caught,
    Turn'd honour to his bane ?

VI

Thus, fruitlessly inquisitive,
    We ask !—The hour was nigh
When he, who but as man did live,
    Should as a hero die.

VII

Loud woke the clamour, loud turmoil,
    Where late yon harvest stood ;
Deep drank the thirsting English soil
    Of Scotland's noblest blood.

VIII

And, as a regal oak o'erthrown,
    That in dense woodland grew,
Goes crashing earthward not alone,
    But drags less giants too :

IX

So in his dark hour, Royal James,
    Hurl'd graveward off his throne,
Whelm'd in his fall a thousand names
    Less only than his own.

JOHN DAVIDSON

1857–1909

A Ballad of a Nun

FROM Eastertide to Eastertide
   For ten long years her patient knees
Engraved the stones—the fittest bride
   Of Christ in all the diocese.

She conquered every earthly lust ;
   The abbess loved her more and more ;
And, as a mark of perfect trust,
   Made her the keeper of the door.

High on a hill the convent hung,
   Across a duchy looking down,
Where everlasting mountains flung
   Their shadows over tower and town.

The jewels of their lofty snows,
   In constellations flashed at night ;
Above their crests the moon arose ;
   The deep earth shuddered with delight.

Long ere she left her cloudy bed,
   Still dreaming in the orient land,
On many a mountain's happy head
   Dawn lightly laid her rosy hand.

The adventurous sun took Heaven by storm ;
    Clouds scattered largesses of rain ;
The sounding cities, rich and warm,
    Smouldered and glittered in the plain.

Sometimes it was a wandering wind,
    Sometimes the fragrance of the pine,
Sometimes the thought how others sinned,
    That turned her sweet blood into wine.

Sometimes she heard a serenade
    Complaining sweetly far away :
She said, " A young man woos a maid " ;
    And dreamt of love till break of day.

Then would she ply her knotted scourge
    Until she swooned ; but evermore
She had the same red sin to purge,
    Poor, passionate keeper of the door !

For still nights' starry scroll unfurled,
    And still the day came like a flood :
It was the greatness of the world
    That made her long to use her blood.

In winter-time when Lent drew nigh,
    And hill and plain were wrapped in snow,
She watched beneath the frosty sky
    The nearest city nightly glow.

Like peals of airy bells outworn
    Faint laughter died above her head
In gusts of broken music borne :
    " They keep the Carnival," she said.

Her hungry heart devoured the town :
   " Heaven save me by a miracle !
Unless God sends an angel down,
   Thither I go though it were Hell."

She dug her nails deep in her breast,
   Sobbed, shrieked, and straight withdrew the
      bar :
A fledgling flying from the nest,
   A pale moth rushing to a star.

Fillet and veil in strips she tore ;
   Her golden tresses floated wide ;
The ring and bracelet that she wore
   As Christ's betrothed, she cast aside.

" Life's dearest meaning I shall probe ;
   Lo ! I shall taste of love at last !
Away ! " She doffed her outer robe,
   And sent it sailing down the blast.

Her body seemed to warm the wind ;
   With bleeding feet o'er ice she ran :
" I leave the righteous God behind ;
   I go to worship sinful man."

She reached the sounding city's gate ;
   No question did the warder ask :
He passed her in : " Welcome, wild mate ! "
   He thought her some fantastic mask.

Half-naked through the town she went ;
   Each footstep left a bloody mark ;
Crowds followed her with looks intent ;
   Her bright eyes made the torches dark.

Alone and watching in the street
　　There stood a grave youth nobly dressed ;
To him she knelt and kissed his feet ;
　　Her face her great desire confessed.

Straight to his house the nun he led :
　　"Strange lady, what would you with me ? "
" Your love, your love, sweet lord," she said ;
　　" I bring you my virginity."

He healed her bosom with a kiss ;
　　She gave him all her passion's hoard ;
And sobbed and murmured ever, "This
　　Is life's great meaning, dear, my lord.

" I care not for my broken vow ;
　　Though God should come in thunder soon,
I am sister to the mountains now,
　　And sister to the sun and moon."

Through all the towns of Belmarie
　　She made a progress like a queen.
" She is," they said, "whate'er she be,
　　The strangest woman ever seen.

" From fairyland she must have come,
　　Or else she is a mermaiden."
Some said she was a ghoul, and some
　　A heathen goddess born again.

But soon her fire to ashes burned ;
　　Her beauty changed to haggardness ;
Her golden hair to silver turned ;
　　The hour came of her last caress.

At midnight from her lonely bed
    She rose, and said, "I have had my will."
The old ragged robe she donned, and fled
    Back to the convent on the hill.

Half-naked as she went before,
    She hurried to the city wall,
Unnoticed in the rush and roar
    And splendour of the carnival.

No question did the warder ask :
    Her ragged robe, her shrunken limb,
Her dreadful eyes ! " It is no mask ;
    It is a she-wolf, gaunt and grim ! "

She ran across the icy plain ;
    Her worn blood curdled in the blast ;
Each footstep left a crimson stain ;
    The white-faced moon looked on aghast.

She said between her chattering jaws,
    " Deep peace is mine, I cease to strive ;
Oh, comfortable convent laws,
    That bury foolish nuns alive !

" A trowel for my passing-bell,
    A little bed within the wall,
A coverlet of stones ; how well
    I there shall keep the Carnival ! "

Like tired bells chiming in their sleep,
    The wind faint peals of laughter bore ;
She stopped her ears and climbed the steep,
    And thundered at the convent door.

It opened straight : she entered in,
  And at the wardress' feet fell prone :
" I come to purge away my sin ;
  Bury me, close me up in stone."

The wardress raised her tenderly ;
  She touched her wet and fast-shut eyes :
" Look, sister ; sister, look at me ;
  Look ; can you see through my disguise ? "

She looked and saw her own sad face,
  And trembled, wondering, " Who art thou ? "
" God sent me down to fill your place :
  I am the Virgin Mary now."

And with the word, God's mother shone :
  The wanderer whispered, " Mary, hail ! "
The vision helped her to put on
  Bracelet and fillet, ring and veil.

" You are sister to the mountains now,
  And sister to the day and night ;
Sister to God." And on the brow
  She kissed her thrice, and left her sight.

While dreaming in her cloudy bed,
  Far in the crimson orient land,
On many a mountain's happy head
  Dawn lightly laid her rosy hand.

373   *Thirty Bob a Week*

I COULDN'T touch a stop and turn a screw,
   And set the blooming world a-work for me,
Like such as cut their teeth—I hope, like you—
   On the handle of a skeleton gold key ;
I cut mine on a leek, which I eat it every week :
   I'm a clerk at thirty bob as you can see.

But I don't allow it's luck and all a toss ;
   There's no such thing as being starred and crossed ;
It's just the power of some to be a boss,
   And the bally power of others to be bossed :
I face the music, sir ; you bet I ain't a cur ;
   Strike me lucky if I don't believe I'm lost !

For like a mole I journey in the dark,
   A-travelling along the Underground
From my Pillar'd Halls and broad Suburbean Park,
   To come the daily dull official round ;
And home again at night with my pipe all alight,
   A-scheming how to count ten bob a pound.

And it's often very cold and very wet,
   And my missis stitches towels for a hunks ;
And the Pillar'd Halls is half of it to let—
   Three rooms about the size of travelling trunks.
And we cough, my wife and I, to dislocate a sigh,
   When the noisy little kids are in their bunks.

But you never hear her do a growl or whine,
   For she's made of flint and roses, very odd ;
And I've got to cut my meaning rather fine,
   Or I'd blubber, for I'm made of greens and sod :
So p'r'aps we are in Hell for all that I can tell,
   And lost and damn'd and served up hot to God.

I ain't blaspheming, Mr. Silver-tongue ;
  I'm saying things a bit beyond your art :
Of all the rummy starts you ever sprung,
  Thirty bob a week's the rummiest start !
With your science and your books and your the'ries
    about spooks,
  Did you ever hear of looking in your heart ?

I didn't mean your pocket, Mr., no :
  I mean that having children and a wife,
With thirty bob on which to come and go,
  Isn't dancing to the tabor and the fife :
When it doesn't make you drink, by Heaven ! it makes
    you think,
  And notice curious items about life.

I step into my heart and there I meet
  A god-almighty devil singing small,
Who would like to shout and whistle in the street,
  And squelch the passers flat against the wall ;
If the whole world was a cake he had the power
    to take,
  He would take it, ask for more, and eat them all.

And I meet a sort of simpleton beside,
  The kind that life is always giving beans ;
With thirty bob a week to keep a bride
  He fell in love and married in his teens :
At thirty bob he stuck ; but he knows it isn't
    luck :
  He knows the seas are deeper than tureens.

And the god-almighty devil and the fool
  That meet me in the High Street on the strike,
When I walk about my heart a-gathering wool,
  Are my good and evil angels if you like.
And both of them together in every kind of weather
  Ride me like a double-seated bike.

That's rough a bit and needs its meaning curled.
  But I have a high old hot un in my mind—
A most engrugious notion of the world,
  That leaves your lightning 'rithmetic behind :
I give it at a glance when I say "There ain't no chance,
  Nor nothing of the lucky-lottery kind."

And it's this way that I make it out to be :
  No fathers, mothers, countries, climates—none ;
Not Adam was responsible for me,
  Nor society, nor systems, nary one :
A little sleeping seed, I woke—I did, indeed—
  A million years before the blooming sun.

I woke because I thought the time had come ;
  Beyond my will there was no other cause ;
And everywhere I found myself at home,
  Because I chose to be the thing I was ;
And in whatever shape of mollusc or of ape
  I always went according to the laws.

I was the love that chose my mother out ;
  I joined two lives and from the union burst ;
My weakness and my strength without a doubt
  Are mine alone for ever from the first :
It's just the very same with a difference in the name
  As " Thy will be done." You say it if you durst !

They say it daily up and down the land
　　As easy as you take a drink, it's true ;
But the difficultest go to understand,
　　And the difficultest job a man can do,
Is to come it brave and meek with thirty bob a week,
　　And feel that that's the proper thing for you.

It's a naked child against a hungry wolf ;
　　It's playing bowls upon a splitting wreck ;
It's walking on a string across a gulf
　　With millstones fore-and-aft about your neck ;
But the thing is daily done by many and many a one ;
　　And we fall, face forward, fighting, on the deck.

374　　　　　　　*From Grub Street*

RONDEAU

MY love, my wife, three months ago
　　I joined the fight in London town.
I haven't conquered yet, you know,
And friends are few, and hope is low ;
　　Far off I see the shining crown.

I'm daunted, dear ; but blow on blow
With ebbing force I strike, and so
I am not felled and trodden down,
　　　　My love, my wife !

I wonder when the tide will flow,
Sir Oracle cease saying, " No,"
　　And Fortune smile away her frown.
　　Well, while I swim I cannot drown ;
And while we sleep the harvests grow,
　　　　My love, my wife.

ROUNDEL

My darling boys, heaven help you both !
  Now in your happy time of toys
Am I to die ? How I am loth,
  My darling boys !

  My heart is strong for woes or joys ;
My soul and body keep their troth,
  One in a love no clasping cloys.

Why with me is the world so wroth ?
  What fiend at night my work destroys ?
Has fate against me sworn an oath,
  My darling boys ?

VILLANELLE

On her hand she leans her head,
  By the banks of the busy Clyde ;
Our two little boys are in bed.

The pitiful tears are shed ;
  She has nobody by her side ;
On her hand she leans her head.

I should be working ; instead
  I dream of my sorrowful bride,
And our two little boys in bed.

Were it well if we four were dead ?
  The grave at least is wide.
On her hand she leans her head.

She stares at the embers red ;
　　She dashes the tears aside,
And kisses our boys in bed.

" God, give us our daily bread ;
　　Nothing we ask beside."
On her hand she leans her head ;
Our two little boys are in bed.

CHARLES MURRAY

375   *The Whistle*

HE cut a sappy sucker from the muckle rodden-
    tree [1],
He trimmed it, an' he wet it, an' he thumped it on
    his knee ;
He never heard the teuchat [2] when the harrow broke
    her eggs,
He missed the craggit heron nabbin' puddocks [3] in
    the seggs [4],
He forgot to hound the collie at the cattle when
    they strayed,
But you should hae seen the whistle that the wee
    herd made !

He wheepled on't at mornin' an' he tweetled on't
    at nicht,
He puffed his freckled cheeks until his nose sank
    oot o' sicht,
The kye were late for milkin' when he piped them
    up the closs,
The kiltlins [5] got his supper syne, an' he was beddit
    boss [6] ;
But he cared na doit nor docken what they did or
    thocht or said,
There was comfort in the whistle that the wee herd
    made.

  [1] mountain ash.   [2] lapwing.   [3] frogs.   [4] sedge.   [5] kittens.
[6] hollow, fasting.

For lyin' lang o' mornin's he had clawed the caup [1]
    for weeks,
But noo he had his bonnet on afore the lave had
    breeks ;
He was whistlin' to the porridge that were hott'rin' [2]
    on the fire,
He was whistlin' ower the travise [3] to the baillie in
    the byre [4] ;
Nae a blackbird nor a mavis, that hae pipin' for
    their trade,
Was a marrow [5] for the whistle that the wee herd
    made.

He played a march to battle, it cam' dirlin' [6] through
    the mist,
Till the halflin' [7] squared his shou'ders an' made up
    his mind to 'list ;
He tried a spring for wooers, though he wistna what
    it meant,
But the kitchen-lass was lauchin' an' he thocht she
    maybe kent ;
He got ream [8] an' buttered bannocks for the lovin'
    lilt he played.
Wasna that a cheery whistle that the wee herd
    made ?

He blew them rants sae lively, schottisches, reels,
    an' jigs,
The foalie flang his muckle legs an' capered ower
    the rigs,

---

[1] cleaned the dish (a punishment for late rising).   [2] simmering.
[3] partition.   [4] cattleman in the cow-shed.   [5] match.   [6] thrilling
[7] half-grown lad, hobbledehoy.   [8] cream.

The grey-tailed futt'rat [1] bobbit oot to hear his ain
strathspey,
The bawd [2] cam' loupin' through the corn to " Clean
Pease Strae " ;
The feet o' ilka man an' beast gat youkie [3] when he
played—
Hae ye ever heard o' whistle like the wee herd
made ?

But the snaw it stopped the herdin' an' the winter
brocht him dool,
When in spite o' hacks [4] and chilblains he was shod
again for school ;
He couldna' sough [5] the catechis nor pipe the rule
o' three,
He was keepit in an' lickit when the ither loons
got free ;
But he aften played the truant—'twas the only thing
he played,
For the maister brunt the whistle that the wee herd
made !

[1] weasel. [2] hare. [3] itched. [4] chaps. [5] hum.

DOUGLAS AINSLIE

Born 1865

376   *Battle of Largs*

(*From* " *The Song of the Stewarts* ")

A T midsummer from Herlover
⠀⠀⠀Sails for the Orcades
The Norsemen's fleet and everywhere
⠀⠀⠀The sun vies with the breeze,
As though together they conspire
⠀⠀⠀To bless them on their way ;
Not the Isles alone, but the land entire,
⠀⠀⠀They offer them for a prey ;
For the sun glints on their coats of mail
⠀⠀⠀And the western breeze makes light
The oars of the galleys that they sail
⠀⠀⠀As by enchanter's might.
In the first where the golden dragons hiss,
⠀⠀⠀Stands Haco at the prow,
And the spray flies up as though 'twould kiss
⠀⠀⠀The King o' Norroway's brow.
Haco the king, no youth is he,
⠀⠀⠀But his een shine blue and clear
And stout his arm for mastery
⠀⠀⠀That hath ruled full many a year.
An hundred and fifty sail they glide,
⠀⠀⠀Like a serpent of old ocean,
Risen from the depths where he doth bide,
⠀⠀⠀But now in awful motion ;

An hundred and fifty sail they glide
    O'er the waves with sunlight paven,
And now at even, see them ride
    Safe in Orcadian haven.
The morning dawns on Ronaldsvoe,
    And the sun climbs up the sky ;
But lo ! But lo ! what weird of woe
    Blinds us his golden eye ?
 For a curtain covereth up his face,
    Till only a ring is bright :
The Norsemen kneel and pray for grace
    At midday in midnight.
Perchance their prayers are heard, perchance
    'Twere better for most to die
With a stainless sword and a couchant lance,
    And their hands clasped to the sky !

Sunlight again ! and the king makes mirth
    With Magnus the dutiful,
As they sail to the Lewes by the Pentland Firth,
    Then hold for the Sound of Mull.
Magnus of Man and Dugal Sire
    Of the foam-kissed Hebrides,
He bids them reive the Mull of Kintire :
    This makes them muckle ease.

   *   *   *   *   *

Now as Haco the king in Gigha lay.
    John of the Isles drew near,
Bowed to the King of Norroway,
    Would whisper in his ear.
"Speak loud," cried Haco, "lest the waves
    That break upon this isle
Bury thy whispers in their graves :
    Here is nor fear nor guile."

Then John spake forth : " Thy man was I
    Faithful and leal and true,
For the King of Scots I did defy,
    Till the old king was the new.
But now I yield thee back those lands
    Thou gavest me of yore
And crave a pardon at thy hands
    Whom I dare not follow more.
For of the Young King lands I hold,
    Oxen and sheep in fee,
But more than a thousand sheep in fold
    Is one dear head to me ;
My son lies in Dunfermline town
    An hostage to the Scot
And the sword once drawn for thee cuts
    down
    What cut can be garnered not."

Then Haco mused and his Viking Lords
    Half-circle stood around ;
Their mail-clad hands did grip their swords,
    But the wind their locks unwound.
Haco made answer : " John o' the Isles
    Thou art my liegeman, born,
But I have known a wee bairn's smiles,
    Like the face of the rosy morn ;
And for I wot thy son must die,
    Thy sword once drawn for me,
Behold ! Thy king no more am I :
    John o' the Isles is free !
And the armoured Norsemen stood amazed
    When the royal speech they heard,
But thinking on their sons they praised
    The royal heart-strings stirred.

Down on his knees fell John o' the Isles,
 Would kiss King Haco's hand,
But he raised him up with gracious smiles,
 Bade him "God speed" from the strand.

  *   *   *   *   *

Now when Magnus and Dugal backward wound
 From the reiving of Kintire ;
By the Firth of Clyde to Kilbrennan's sound
 They bare the sword and the fire.
Carrick and Kyle and Wigtown quailed
 As the Norsemen's fleet went by,
And the Barefoot Friars to Haco sailed,
 For peaceful pact to try.
But the Norseman claimed the Cumrays twain,
 Arran and Bute and Clyde,
With the Hebrides—such terms were vain—
 And the battle must decide.

  *   *   *   *   *

Well are Loch Lomond's waters met,
 Clipt in the lands embrace !
Welcome the islands jewel-set
 Upon her crystal face !
Hither from fenceless shores of Clyde
 Fled the Scot with wife and child,
By the waves land-bound on every side
 To a Paradise beguiled.
The sun had dropped into the west,
 His conqueror's ruddy shield,
Those breathing islets were at rest,
 At rest the mainland field ;
When of a sudden voices brake
 The silence of the shore ;
An unknown, outland tongue they spake,
 They gathered more and more.

In sixty boats those voices crept
    Forth on Loch Lomond's water,
While still serene the Scotsmen slept,
    Like sheep foredoomed to slaughter.

Whispers no more, but fearsome yells,
    Pierce the silence of the night,
And the twenty isles are as twenty hells,
    Where a thousand demons fight.
Woman and bairn the Norseman slew,
    From gentle slumbers riven,
But many a tiny bairn ne'er knew
    Why it woke with wings in heaven.
How came the Norseman's craft to sail
    Over the Tarbet lands ?
With the breath of a thousand lungs for gale,
    With the oars of a thousand hands.
Thus was their goblet of success
    Filled full of blood for wine,
But the fates from their vats of sorrow press
    Thy woe as well as mine.
For as those Norsemen backward passed
    To their ships in the Loch of Long,
The hail and the rain and the furious blast
    Wreaked vengeance on the strong :
Ten mighty galleys, ten score men
    Whelmed in the ravenous waves !
Then the ocean rested, but to gain
    Fresh food for its floating graves.
Dire powers that wait upon the wand
    Of the enchanter's will,
These hurled the Norsemen on the strand,
    And the tempest ragèd still,
And heathen Haco, when he felt
    That this enchantment was

Passed to the Cumrays, prayed and knelt
    Before the Christian Cross ;
As though the Christ our Lord would fight
    For the heathen reivers' sake !
Lo ! as he knelt, within his sight
    His seven anchors brake,
And the royal galley slid away
    And others were hurled ashore,
And the lave they drave right furiously
    Towards Largs 'mid the tempests' roar.
Beacons and eyes from cliff and bent
    Down glared as the fleet surged by,
At strife with the raging element,
    And the Scots blest their ally.
But when they saw those galleys hurled
    On the spumy rocks of Clyde
Down like the tempest's self they whirled :
    Death grapples in the tide !
Night fell, but on the morrow morn
    Through the surf grim warriors waded
And the Norsemen's valour was reborn,
    Came Haco's self to aid it.

Upsprings the sun, the day's begun,
    And the flashing of his rays
Makes joy the Norsemen every one ;
    Less joyous as it plays
On the steel of Scotland's main array
    That like the sun obscured
Bursts through the cloud-racks of delay,
    With the king and his Lord High Stewart,
And fifteen hundred men at arms,
    All mail-clad cap-a-pie,
Gathered from peels and burgs and farms,
    A lusty company.

Mounted upon their mail-clad steeds,
 See them gallop to the charge,
Each king his foremost battle leads,
 But we force them to the marge.
The Lord High Stewart on the right,
 On the left his brother Walter,
Both hurl them back and then unite
 When they see the Norsemen falter.
Vainly they signal to their ships,
 No succour can come ashore,
For again the storm its leashes slips,
 As the hounds of hell its roar.
They battle on the banks of Clyde,
 Scot, storm, and gallant Norsemen ;
Forth from our vanguard see him ride
 Yon golden armoured horseman.
Sir Piers de Curry is he hight,
 Bravest of Scotland's scions,
Forward he pricks to single fight :
 Defiance meets defiance ;
For a mighty Norseman turns about
 And a twin-edged sword he swings,
And each crieth out his battle shout,
 As Norse upon Scots steel rings.
Parry and stroke and stroke again,
 And the battle stays to see
Which side of the strenuous clashing twain
 Will fall the victory.
Half-circle back, like the lightning flash,
 The Norseman swings his sword,
Then forward with an awful crash ;
 He breaks the Scotsman's ward,
Cleaveth the steely cuisse and bone
 As these were empty air,
Down from his steed the Scotsman thrown
 Must bite the wet sand there.

On his curious armour, gold-inwrought,
    Swoop down the ravenous Norse,
And the battle joins and the battle's fought
    Around the hero's corse.
Perdie ! the Norsemen payed right dear
    Sir Piers his cloven thigh,
And methinks his spirit made good cheer,
    So be it floated nigh :
Five yarls that led the Norsemen on,
    King Haco's brother's bairn,
And ten score more piled high upon
    Sir Piers to build his cairn !
Battle upon the beach till night,
    Upon the blood-red hill,
On Clyde the wave and the tempest smite
    The foes of Scotland still.
Driven from their anchors hurled ashore,
    One on the other dashing,
Nightlong amid the tempest's roar
    We heard their galleys crashing.
At dawn the rocks of Clyde are fed
    With corpses, masts and ropes,
And for the burial of their dead,
    For the burial of their hopes
A truce the stormy Norsemen crave,
    And one by one another
They range stone sentries for their brave,
    Whom time nor tide can smother,
For ye shall see them standing yet,
    Ye shall hear them tell their tale
Of the brave whom all but they forget
    With the voice of the northern gale.
Their duty done unto the dead
    Northward the Norsemen passed,
Bowed was King Haco's sovran head,
    As he leaned upon the mast.

Arran and Bute and Skye he saw
    Frown through their mist and rain ;
Of the Western Isles where he was law
    Harbour he sought in vain.
Onward unto the Orcades.
    He sought for friendly earth,
But the wrath unappeased of the winds and the
    seas
    Oped the jaws of the Pentland Firth.
One galley and three score souls gulped down,
    By a miracle saved the king,
Now ashore he may rest his storm-struck crown
    And his fleet of weary wing.
(An hundred and fifty sail they passed
    O'er the waves with sunlight paven ;
Now the Scot and the sea and the ravenous blast
    Spare ten for Orcadian haven.)
Heavy on hill and valley shed
    Lay drear December snows,
And heavy upon King Haco's head
    The winter of his woes.
Now some would pass to Norroway
    Back o'er the heaving billow :
To these King Haco bowed his, " Yea,"
    With weary head on pillow.
But most they stood around his couch,
    For to them he was full dear,
And gallantly they did avouch
    To make their monarch cheer,
That with the coming of the spring
    Over the seas again
A mightier fleet its way should wing
    Free of enchantment's chain.
Well spoken ! warrior hearts so true,
    Blessed be your loyal lie ;

What matter though you and he well knew
    That the end of all was nigh ?
Then to the royal chamber came
    Full many a monk and priest,
And they promised much in Jesus' name
    Once the soul from the flesh released.
But Haco wearied of their prayers,
    Wearied of all they told
Of the Christ and His Virgin Mother's cares,
    And the saints in their crowns of gold.
For the days of his youth came back again
    And he called for the history
Of the Pirate Kings that swept the main,
    His royal ancestry.
And as they read his een shone bright
    As he rose on his couch as though
He would brace himself to one last fight,
    With death itself for foe.
Full soon his head fell back once more
    And his spirit passed away,
And with it passed for evermore
    The peril of Norroway.

LAUCHLAN MACLEAN WATT

Born 1867

377 *Ode on the Coronation of King Edward
the Seventh*

HERE, all alone in the dark,
    While the stars are dying,
My soul grows still, and I hark
    To the voice of the sea-winds crying
From far away, where, low on the long-ridged
    sands,
The tired grey sea beats out his time-old song with
    weary hands.
And, as I listen, up from the ghostly street,
I hear the throb of a thousand marching feet,
    And ever, as they come,
The faint, dull, guiding pulse of a distant drum.

The windows are silent all, and darkened, the
    lights are gone :
And the dying starlight flickers, dimly wan,
But I know that the town is full of the shadows of
    marching men,
Though never a trace of their passing shall wait
    the dawn,
And never on earth, except in dream, shall their
    faces gleam again.

896

And my soul is caught from its stillness,
    And the stars awake in the night,
And the winds, from the waste and the
      waters,
    Cry, half in joy and in fright :
" Who are ye, ghostly marchers,
    And whence do your squadrons come,
And your companies pressing onward
    To the beat of a phantom drum ? "

" We are the dead of England :
    Our dust is under the leas.
They buried us deep, in our battle-sleep,
    They plunged us down in the seas.
We are the brave of England,
    We fought for the bristling breach,
And died that our brothers might climb on
      our bones,
    And carry the flag where we could not
      reach. . . .
We went down in the waste of waters :
    We grappled the foe on ships . . .
In mist and smoke, where battle broke,—
    And her name was on our lips,
      Living or dying,
      Our flag still flying,
    Where our hands had nailed it fast,
We fell for the might of England,
    And we were not her last.

" Never a cannon's booming,
    Never a battle's roar,
Never the marching of armies
    Thundrous, along the shore,

57

But it stirred us in our sleeping,
    And we turned in our nameless bed,
For we knew there were wars for England,
    And we were England's dead . . .
We   have   heard . . . we   have   burst   our
        prison,
    For a king's to be hailed, and crowned.
We have waked for a while and risen
    To gather, and guard him round.
For a king's to be crowned in the Minster,
    And the bravest should be there. . . .
The living and dead of England
    Her sorrows and joys must share."

Beat, O phantom drums of the dead—O bravely,
    proudly beat.
        There's never a sea
        But set you free,
O dead with the marching feet!
    For the north and the south
    Had sealed your mouth,
        And the sundered east and west
    Had all looked down
    From their starry crown,
        Above you, in your rest.
Ye girdled the globe for England,
    Ye fought for her and God.
Dust of the old, grey, wave-worn isles,
    Ye blew her name abroad.
Come back, and stand for England,
    Ye that were true and tried:
We need the brave from the field and the
        wave
    To teach us how ye died! . . .

Ah, 'tis no crown of a witling,
    This crown of ours :
Iron and gold the meed of it,
Blood of the best the seed of it :
    No path of flowers
Men walked in till they won it. Alfred wight
Wrested it back, with blade of peerless might
        From the invaders' hand,
        And set his land
Fair by the waters, Godwards, seeking light.

Long was the hammering at it, early and late,
        Until it grew
The treasure of our islands, with the blue
    Engirdling waters round it for its guard :
        And hot and hard
The anvil of its shaping. Many a day,
    The smiths who toiled till evening, in the
        breaking
Of grey dawns out of darkness, silent lay,
    For ever weary with the toil of making.

Never a morning's dawn but wakeful eyes
    Saw the day rise
        Out of the shimmering sea . . .
Never night darkened, but an anxious gaze
Looked through the deepening haze,
        Wondering of days to be.
Heavy the burden of it on the brows
    Of kings, and on the hearts of weary folk,
Till, out of troubled ages,
        Gladness broke.

Ah, 'tis no empty fluttering of a dream,
    Our flag's proud gleam :
Many and tired the fingers that have sewn it,
    Seam by seam,
Staining it with life's crimson, and the blue
    Of northern skies and seas, till winds
      have blown it
      Wider than all their wonder and
      their dream.

Thin red lines of pulsing lives were the thread
    of it,
Pulsing lives that bled away for its sake beneath
    the spread of it,
    Till the wide seas knew it,
    And the winds of the wide world blew it,
And the host of England followed the flag till
earth trembled under the tread of it.

Up with it into the sky,
Let it blow abroad, let its message fly
    Like the grey gull, over the deep,
    As glad and free.
There are names of pride emblazoned on
    every fold,
But deeper, more dear than ever was script
    in gold,
  . .Names that can never sleep,
Though only the heart of love and the eye
    of God can see . . .

Sad, ah sad was the heart of us, when
    the word
We feared to hear, came fluttering like a
    bird

Blown,   out   of   the   dark,   against   our
        faces,
How she, to us and all the nations dear,
Mother and queen, to all her children near,
    Lowly, and crowned with love and tenderest
            graces,
        Lay at the gate of peace,
        Beating with feeble fingers for release,
    To seek her dead, afar in heavenly places :
            Till the great passing-bell
            Rang through the night to tell
        O'er waking shore and sea,
The soul of England's greatest queen from earth
    was free.

Sad was the spell that stole across the waves
        As her spirit passed . . .
        The red flag drooped from the mast,
        And thunders throbbed their sorrows o'er
            the tide :
Far through the bush it sped,
Like a swift-footed Sorrow, with silent tread,
Waking the sleepers to tell them, "She is dead."
        And the dawn bore it wide
            Over the waters,
Till, with a weary wail it reached the shores,
Crying its message in at the seaward-opening
        doors,
        Where England's sons and daughters,
Borne far in ships, had built them homes and graves.

Now who is the king for the crown that fell from
    her hand,
            The crown of our land,

And our Empire wide-world wide,
Where the circling stars, unsetting, ever behold
   The gleam of our sails on the tide :
And the glittering day, from the shadows un-
   rolled,
   Each dawning, somewhere, kisses our flag to gold?

Son of the mother we loved, we look to thee,—
Our king by thy mother's name, our king to be,
   Lifting the crown she left thee, to thy lips,
To win with her name a glory from Time which
      time shall never eclipse.

Now who is the king whose glory shall not die—
Whose coronet, crushed and shattered shall not lie
   In dust of shame, out in the trampling street,
   Scorned by the heedless feet
That spurn and pass it by?

Earth has her hour for kingship still, and the day
For crowning of truth can fade not ever away.
   Still do her multitudes wait
   For the knock of the hand of her king on her
      palace gate.

He is the king whose power shall be
Upheld by angels three,
   Beside his throne—
      Strength, pity, and love,
      Lifting his life above
   The mighty mockeries making misery moan,

The little dreams that hold the world in
    fee . . .
      Strength, to whose brave right hand 'tis
      given
To bring to stillness all earth's din and the clang
that would silence heaven ;
      And, cleaving clash and noise,
Fetch once again to weary hearts the music of
    God's voice. . . .
      Pity, too, clothed in strength more strong
      than steel,
        Stretching her gaze,
    Like the smile of dawn, through darkness
      and dismal haze,
    To wake the heartless and those who know
      no hope,
        Making them feel
    Old impulses half-forgotten, and ways of
      boundless scope,
      Where their tired feet, from time-long
      shackles free,
May move where music meets them, stirring new
   dreams by shore and sea. . . .
      Love, too, greatest of angels born of
      God,
      Leaving the throne, to walk where shadow
      lies,
      Kissing to joy the tears of darkened eyes,
      And gathering into song all saddening cries,
And making a triumphing gladness grow where sorrow
  in darkness trod :
      Till peace springs near and far,
      Star merging into star,
      Till a day like Christ's steals over the mid-
      night bar,

And the tide of a people's contented joy breaks sing-
ing around the throne,
> Where, in oblivion swathed, as in a shroud,
> Dead and forgotten shall sink the cruel and
> proud,
>> And tyranny have no name,
>> And the shaming be crushed with shame,
>> And be unknown :
But the loving and lovely in dream and
deed
> Have love shook into their days,
And angels of peace their feet shall lead
> By blossoming ways
>> No more to bleed.
Great shall that monarch be,
Great on the shore, and the sea ;
> And the nations near and far,
> Shall see his star,
>> And know that the day of darkness
>> now is done,
>> And wait for the rising sun,
'That bringeth the days to be.
> Great, God-giftedly great ;
> On him shall wait
> The ragged and poor, the spangled and
> proud in state,
>> The nameless, the lost, the lone,—
The noble, the true, the renowned,
Alike with the lorn, the unpitied, forgotten, new-
named, new-found,
Lifted by pity and strength and love to the shade
and the shield of his throne.
Bravest and best girdling him round,
By hands out of darkness, and hands out of
brightness crowned,

True is that king in his power,
      To him no hell comes crying,
      Hate for him has no hour,
And no calendar holds the star of his dynasty's
      dying . . .

      O king, thine is the gift and glory
      Of all our island story,—
Heaven help thee, guard it well,
That still in dawns unborn, mothers to babes shall
      tell,
      Of thee, and kingship true,
      Of the love men bore thee at home, and
      far o'er the waters blue,
And in ships, and in desert places, where the sons
of the grey land roam,
      Bearing afar
The name of the land their mother, up under
the lone north star,
      The land that men call home,
      Telling thy fame with pride,
Son of a hundred kings, yet most the son of
      her who died.

      And the love of the living and dead
      Puts the crown of grace on the head
      Of the lady who stands by thee,—
      The lily, who, over the sea,
      Out of old gardens of heroes her loveliness
      bore,
      Here, to our island-shore,
      From the sea-king's city set by the
      distant tide,
      To shine by thy side,—
Mother of kings and queens in the days to be.

Still, though the song of the years,
Has brought to her laughter and sorrow and
    tears,
The lips of her people praise,
    And the hearts of the nations love her,
And prayers, like wings, upraise
    A shadow of peace above her. . . .

Lone isles, isles belov'd, crowned with the prayers
    of the free,
Throned on the waters, backed by the mountains,
    gazing over the sea—
            Ye, for whose sake,
            Brave spirits brake,
        For whom our fathers fell,
            In stranger climes,
            In danger times,
        Or where deep-sea billows swell . . .
            Lone rocks at whose feet
            The wan tides meet,
        And the surges break and sing,
            Stand firm, as of yore,
            For the race ye bore,
        And the man ye have crowned as king.
            The shades of the dead are round
                you . . .
            The prayers of the dead have bound
                you,
        And wherever the lone seas beat and cry,
            From the shores of the world your sons
                are ready,
            To come at your call, and, calm and
                steady,
        If need be, die. . . .

Gather them in, O mother of men, gather them close
    to your feet.
               They are blown far and wide,
               O'er the broad sea's tide,
        But the name of their mother is sweet . . .
               And, when the pale day breaks,
               And the earth, affrighted, shakes,
   With thunder, and cries of war, and battle-drums,
               And, through the distant hills,
               Rumbling, shall growl the voice of coming
                  ills,
Shout, when you see how the long brave line of your
    wandering children comes.

378   *The Grey Mother*

L O, how they come to me,
    Long through the night I call them,—
Ah, how they turn to me.

East and South my children scatter,
North and West the world they wander,

Yet they come back to me,
   Come, with their brave hearts beating,
Longing to die for me,

Me, the grey, old, weary mother,
Throned amid the Northern waters,

Where they have died for me,
   Died with their songs around me,
Girding my shores for me.

Narrow was my dwelling for them,
Homes they builded o'er the ocean,

Yet they leave all for me,
  Hearing their mother calling,
Bringing their lives for me.

Up from South seas swiftly sailing,
Out from under stars I know not,

Come they to fight for me,
  Sons of the sons I nurtured ;
God keep them safe for me !

Long ago their fathers saved me,
Died for me among the heather,

Now they come back to me,
  Come, in their children's children—
Brave of the brave for me.

In the wilds and waves they slumber,
Deep they slumber in the deserts,

Rise they from graves for me,
  Graves where they lay forgotten,
Shades of the brave for me. . . .

Yet my soul is veiled in sadness,
For I see them fall and perish,

Strewing the hills for me,
  Claiming the world in dying,
Bought with their blood for me,

Hear the grey, old, Northern mother,
Blessing now her dying children,—

God keep you safe for me,
    Christ watch you in your sleeping,
Where ye have died for me,

And when God's own slogan soundeth,
All the dead world's dust awaking,

Ah, will ye look for me?
    Bravely we'll stand together—
I and my sons with me.

WILL H. OGILVIE

Born 1869

Kirkhope Tower

GREY to the grey of the hill, fronting the quiet
    places,
  Where under their plaid of the purple the red
    grouse cower,
Alone with the wind of the wold and the feeding
    blackfaces
  Stands, like a king on the Marches, old Kirkhope
    Tower.

Its stones are riven apart 'neath the weight of the
    weather,
  In its cold and crumbling chimneys the corbies
    nest,
A heron flaps from the burn, and out of the heather
  A blackcock sails as my step breaks in on his
    rest.

Under the walls four-square, weird and lichened and
    hoary,
  I stand at the open port in a dream and gaze
At the worn old stones that have borne swift feet
    to the foray,
  And light feet down to the burn in forgotten
    days.

I climb by the broken stairway ; the great grey wall
  Runs fair and free to the roof, uncrossed of beam ;
And that that was lady's bower, and this that was
    hall
    Where the strong men feasted, are one ; and again
      I dream,

And I see the board with its English sirloin laden,
  I hear the spurred heels clink as the benches fill,
I see the goblet snatched aloft from the hand of a
    maiden,
    And I hear the raiders' toast as it rings to the hill.

A fair dame sits at her bower-window and spins,
  Looking forth to the Ettrick, whose blossoms of
    foam
Leap not so light and white down the shadowy
    linns
  As the white hand here in the shadow above the
    comb.

High on the rampart crest, where the wind blows
    free
  On his sunburnt cheek and his rough hilt-hardened
    hand,
One looks southward and east over tide and tree
  Searching the moor for foes as a sailor searches
    for land.

Below me, huddled and dumb, in the darkened floor
    of the keep,
  I can hear a reined horse stamp, clicking his
    snaffle-bar ;
I can hear the sudden rustle of startled sheep
  As a spurred foot treads the silence and hinges jar.

West wind, wailing so sadly over the buttress stone,
  You that have lifted the beard of the watcher on
    the tower,
You that have stirred the arras where the dame
    sits spinning alone,
  Stay, and whisper to me the secrets of board and
    bower !

You that have stooped and sung to this old grey
    silent warden,
  You that have carried the tidings of hoofs on the
    plain,
When home with their plunder came riding the
    vassals of Harden
  With mud of the moss of the Carter on rowel
    and rein !

The west wind rides past me unheeding. The shadows
    that lower
  On the hillside have darkened the purple ; depart-
    ing, I turn,
For a white hand is waving farewell to me out of
    the tower
  And a brown hand is pointing my path as I climb
    by the burn.

Grey to the grey of the hill, lichen-covered and
    hoary,
  I leave you alone in the silent dusk of the hour ;
What I have guessed I have guessed, but you keep
    your own story
  Held safe in your heart and for ever, O Kirkhope
    Tower !

380   *The Harp of Ettrick*

IN a green kirkyard where the silent hills
   Are a guard to the clamour that Ettrick keeps,
Rocked by the music of rain-fed rills
  The shepherd friend of the fairies sleeps.
Nought nameth his grave the rest among,
  Save the simple slab as a headstone set,
With the deep-cut date when he lived and sung,
  And a carven harp—lest the world forget !
Round him the sheep and the moorfowl feed,
  Close to his shoulder the heathbells blow,
And the sun may shine and he does not heed,
   And the flowers may bloom and he does not
     know.

But at night, when the arras of cloud is torn
  And tossed by the Solway winds aside,
When the moon comes sailing above Delorne
  And sets in her silver the Ettrick tide,
When the magic wing of the midnight hour
  Stoops low to the worn old Gamescleuch walls,
And a lonely owl on the Thirlestane Tower
  With a querulous note to the silence calls,
Then a murmur wakes in the heath and fern,
  And the fairies gather, unseeen of men,
Riding up from the Rankleburn
  And trooping down from the Tima Glen.

So soft is the fall of their feet in the grass,
  So light is the lift of each gossamer wing,
You might think it the murmur of breezes that pass
  Leaving whispers of love on the lips of the ling.

They cross the low Ettrick by light of the moon
　　That has robed in her lilies the foam on its wave,
They climb the dark dyke where the shadows are
　　　　strewn,
　　And stand with bowed heads on the marge of his
　　　　grave.
However so soft be their step, he has heard,
　　And he moves to their midst like a king to his
　　　　throne,
Not a leaf, not a blade in the grasses is stirred
　　As he lifts the grey harp from its place on the stone.

The dead strings waken beneath his hand,
　　And the echoes ring through the cleuch and ford,
As he sings of a new Kilmeny's land
　　And a new Earl Walter's matchless sword ;
'Tis a song that is never for mortal ear,
　　And the grave to the world is unstirred and still,
And he who might pass by the kirk would hear
　　No sound but the wind as it crossed on the hill ;
Yet those golden words to the vale belong,
　　And the tale is a tale that the fairies know,
And the wail of that harp is the deathless song
　　That the dreamer hears in the Ettrick's flow.

381　　　　　　*The Gipsies*

LOITERING in the sunlight, O ye lotus-loving
　　people,
　　Dawdling through the daisies with your slow, slow
　　　　feet,
Every lane's an aisle for you and every tree's a
　　　　steeple,
　　And the wind your organ-music as it murmurs in
　　　　the wheat !

You that know the splendour of the rosy risen
    morning,
  You that hold the secrets of the calm un-numbered
    stars,
You that steal the brownness of the berries for
    adorning,
  You to whom the wide earth is a roadway for
    your cars !

You that wrap the white dust round your naked feet
    for ever
  As you travel through wild roses to your goal of
    dim desires,
You that chase the South wind and the raindrops
    down the river,
  You that seek contentment with a heart that never
    tires !

When my thoughts are carried over from your camp
    fires to the city,
  When I follow in my fancy where the feet of
    fashion play,
Then my scorn is for the scornful and my heart goes
    forth in pity
  To the people that would wean you from your royal,
    reckless way !

Live and loiter in the sunlight, O ye lotus-loving
    people,
  In your azure-domed cathedral ye shall worship as is
    meet,
Where every lane's an aisle for you and every stem's
    a steeple,
  And the wind is organ-music as it murmurs through
    the wheat !

382   *Kings in Exile*

WE were serfs ; there were roads to us for-
bidden,
There were barriers they would not let us pass,
Till the fairies brought the purple they had hidden
And the palfreys they had tethered in the grass.

Then we rode out past the wonder of the world,
Past desire and disenchantment that it brings,
Till on battlements we saw the flags unfurled
Of faëry, and knew that we were kings !

We were kings and our playmates were princesses,
We were rulers and our empire lay afar
Beyond things proved, beyond the gate of guesses,
And a thousand miles beyond the furthest star.

We were kings !—Now around us fall the shadows
Of our serfdom like a raven's dropping wings.
Not a footstep of a fairy in the meadows—
Not a comrade who remembers we were kings !

LORD ALFRED DOUGLAS

Born 1870

383   *To Olive*

WHEN in dim dreams I trace the tangled maze
      Of the old years that held and fashioned me,
And to the sad assize of Memory
From the wan roads and misty time-trod ways,
The timid ghosts of dead forgotten days
Gather to hold their piteous colloquy,
Chiefly my soul bemoans the lack of thee
And those lost seasons empty of thy praise.

Yet surely thou wast there when life was sweet,
(We walked knee-deep in flowers) and thou wast
      there,
When in dismay and sorrow and unrest,
With weak bruised hands and wounded bleeding
      feet,
I fought with beasts and wrestled with despair
And slept (how else?) upon thine unseen breast.

JOHN HOGBEN

384 *The Sorrow of the Sea*

IT is nor storm nor calm, but yesterday
    The wild winds leapt in sudden thunder down ;
Shook the dark waters into starry spray,
    And thrilled the soul of many a seaside town.
      Ah, cruel are the hungry tides that drown !
They kill, yet cast ashore their tender prey ;
    Tossing it carelessly as seaweed brown,—
Heedless of lovers young and parents grey.

But now remorse is here ! The ponderous wave
    Upcoils full wearily its snowy crest,—
Of after-brooding, not of Passion, slave !—
    Lit by the low slant yellow of the West.
Unquiet grave ! Thyself without a grave,
    Till there be no more sea,—in foam,—at rest !

385   *Enchanted*

A NEW-WORLD on my vision broke
  When once I saw the Fairy-folk.
Since unto them I gave my heart
I find my joy in things apart.

My Mother chides me that I will
Not wed with any neighbour. Still
Could I, who so the Fairies love,
Content with mortal man e'er prove ?

My Father sighs out day by day,
My harp I will no longer play.
He knows not I my music find
In Fairy-voices on the wind.

My sisters with their lovers talk :
They mock me that alone I walk.
They know not when alone I see
The Fairies come to talk with me.

Me to my spinning-wheel they set :
I spin awhile—then I forget
And let my wool in tangles fall,
Thinking I hear the Fairies call.

They let me to the herding go ;
I like it well because I know
I may, in these long summer days,
Learn something of my Fairies' ways.

So is it that I have lost touch
With all the world : for over-much
The Fairies have been with me.   I
With them would live, with them would die!

386   *Une Nuit Blanche*

TO-NIGHT the nightingale sings to the rose ;
   And, as he sings, the all-entrancing strain
(So sweet its sweetness is anigh to pain)
Awakes some echo in my restless brain,
That keeps me from my much-desired repose.

Ah! had I slept, as I had thought to do,
I should have dreamed of you the whole night long.
Therefore I hate the rose and hate the song
That holding sleep from me, does me such wrong
By keeping me apart, in dreams, from you.

For had I dreamed of you I might have had
Your well-belovéd face before mine eyes,
Your hands to hold, or felt in rapt surprise,
Your lips touch mine, or heard your dear replies
To words of love, such as make lovers glad.

O bird, be silent!   Yet in vain I plead.
He sings enraptured ; and, in liquid flight—
Telling of love and infinite delight—
The silver voice sounds through the silent night,
And has no pity on me, in my need!

INDEX OF FIRST LINES

UNWIN BROTHERS, LIMITED, THE GRESHAM PRESS, WOKING AND LONDON.